GLASSMAKERS OF STOURBRIDGE AND DUDLEY 1612-2002

Glassmakers of Stourbridge and Dudley 1612-2002

A Biographical History of a Once Great Industry

Jason Ellis

First Edition 2002

Copyright © Jason Ellis

Published by Jason Ellis
3 Green Way, Harrogate, England HG2 9LR

Library of Congress Number: 2002093707
ISBN :   Hardcover   1-4010-6799-9
               Softcover   1-4010-6798-0

All rights reserved. No part of this book may be reproduced or transmitted in any form or by any means, electronic or mechanical, including photocopying, recording, or by any information storage and retrieval system, without permission in writing from the copyright owner.

This book was printed in the United States of America.

To order additional copies of this book, contact:
Xlibris Corporation
1-888-795-4274
www.Xlibris.com
Orders@Xlibris.com

15996-ELLI

CONTENTS

Author's Introduction 11
Physical and Parochial Geography of Stourbridge 17
Archaeology and Cartography 25
Norman and Lorraine Origins 28
The Weald 32
Migration of Glassmakers in England 40
The Search for Fuel 53
Colemans Glasshouse, Lye 58
Ridgrave Glasshouse, Hungary Hill 66
Holloway End Glasshouse, Amblecote 72
Henzey's Brettell Lane Glasshouse 98
Bague's Glasshouses, Brettell Lane 106
Withymoor Glasshouse, Amblecote 119
Hawbush Glasshouse, Brettell Lane 124
Hagley Glasshouse 128
Jacob's Well Glasshouse, Audnam 130
Heath Glassworks, Stourbridge 133
Fimbrell Glasshouse, Amblecote 148
Harlestones Glasshouse, Coalbournbrook 158
Worcester City Glasshouse, Claines 170
Dial Glasshouse, Brettell Lane 172
Platts Glassworks, Amblecote 177
Waterford Glassworks 187
Coalbournhill Glassworks, Amblecote 194
Audnam Glassworks 217
Dob Hill Glassworks, Wordsley 240
Moor Lane Glassworks, Brierley Hill 243
Springsmire Glasshouse, Dudley 255
Holly Hall Glassworks, Dudley 258

Dudley Flint Glassworks, Dudley 267
Dixon's Green Glassworks, Dudley 285
Phoenix Glassworks, Dudley 299
Moor Lane Bottleworks, Brierley Hill 312
Wordsley Flint Glassworks 317
Castle Foot Glassworks, Dudley 353
White House Glassworks, Wordsley 360
Red House Glassworks, Wordsley 377
Dial Glasshouses, Audnam 397
Grazebrook's Canalside Glassworks, Audnam 416
Wheeley's Brettell Lane Glasshouses 421
Grafton's Brierley Glasshouse, Brettell Lane 430
Novelty Glassworks, Wollaston 434
Parkfield Glassworks, Amblecote 437
Albert Glassworks, Wordsley 440
Dennis Glassworks, Amblecote 458
North Street Glassworks, Brierley Hill 477
Kinver Street Glassworks, Wordsley 492
Eve Hill Glassworks, Dudley 493
Delph Bottleworks, Brierley Hill 496
Harts Hill Glassworks, Brierley Hill 498
Wallows Street Glassworks, Brierley Hill 501
Round Oak Glassworks, Brierley Hill 502
Premier Glassworks, Brettell Lane 504
Brewery Street Glassworks, Wordsley 505
Stour Glassworks, Audnam 507
Dennis Hall Co-operative Crystal, Brockmoor 511
Chronology of Styles 513
Bibliography 551

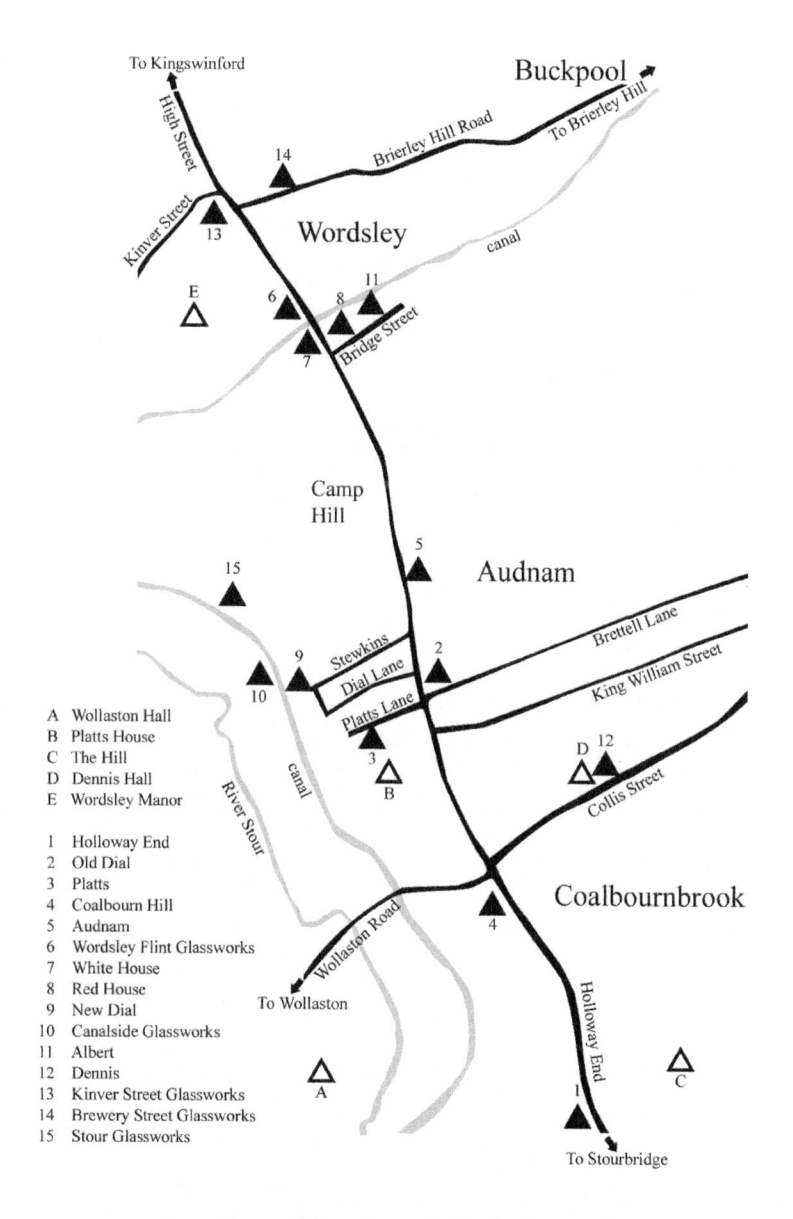

Locations of the 'Stourbridge' glassworks

A Wollaston Hall
B Platts House
C The Hill
D Dennis Hall
E Wordsley Manor

1   Holloway End
2   Old Dial
3   Platts
4   Coalbourn Hill
5   Audnam
6   Wordsley Flint Glassworks
7   White House
8   Red House
9   New Dial
10 Canalside Glassworks
11 Albert
12 Dennis
13 Kinver Street Glassworks
14 Brewery Street Glassworks
15 Stour Glassworks

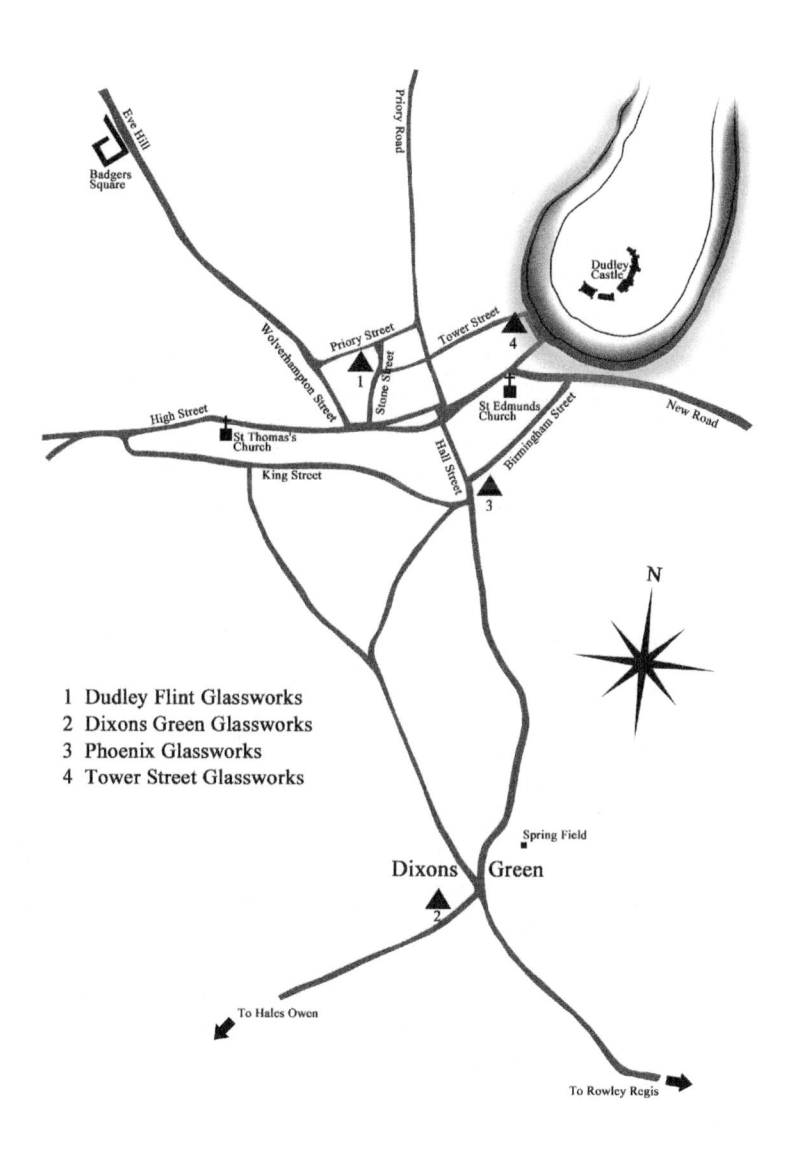

1 Dudley Flint Glassworks
2 Dixons Green Glassworks
3 Phoenix Glassworks
4 Tower Street Glassworks

Locations of the Dudley glassworks

CHAPTER 1

Author's Introduction

The sorrows include murder, suicide, deceit, fraud and many cases of bankruptcy. The joys include close family bonds, love, artistry, wealth and altruism. The glassmakers endured and enjoyed it all.

The development of the Stourbridge glass industry is a microcosm of the industrial revolution, commencing at the end of the sixteenth century and reaching maturity at the end of Victorian times. It is a chronicle of great charm, with many oft-repeated pieces of folklore involving eccentric characters, foreign intrigues, tales of subterfuge and great endeavours. Its subject matter, the glass itself, is one of great mystery and great beauty.

Being descended from several generations of Stourbridge glassmakers, my interest is with the people who developed this great industry. Entrepreneurs who built profitable concerns from humble beginnings—glassmakers who surmounted the problems of an unexplained chemistry to make glass of dazzling clarity or colour—businessmen who sustained, indeed developed an industry in spite of punitive and iniquitous taxation—designers who developed a seemingly endless variety of products to titillate the public's taste; and the workmen who refined their craftsmanship to take the accolade of 'finest in the world'.

I hope this will be the reference book I always wanted, but could not find. Reading other books on this subject always left me hungry for more information. Mark Pattison wrote 'In research the horizon recedes as we advance, and is no nearer at sixty than it was at twenty. As the power of endurance weakens with age, the urgency of the pursuit grows more intense . . . And research is always incomplete.' I make no apologies for quoting from other authors' works as a considerable amount of excellent research has already been performed, although I have taken great care to verify dubious or incomplete assertions against their original sources. It is through a fascination with the characters concerned, that I hope to add to the accumulated knowledge of this subject. I also hope my approach—of treating each glassworks individually—will benefit the researcher of this subject in a way not catered for by previous writers.

Throughout this text I have retained original spellings in any quotations. When an entire document is quoted in its archaic form this will be obvious. However, I have retained individuals' names in their contemporary form, in the context of the event. This often leads to individuals having variant spellings of their name, even within the same paragraph. This is deliberate on my part and results from the crude standards of literacy in the sixteenth to nineteenth centuries. Imagine the difficulty for an English country parson when confronted at the font with French or Italian parents. He would inevitably record the baptism in the parish register phonetically. More often than not, little would be gained by asking parents to spell their names—they were frequently unable to do so.

I would like to acknowledge my indebtedness to the many scholars and authors who by their previous works helped to make this book possible.

The first significant work to shed light on the history of glassmakers in this country was *Collections for a Genealogy of the Noble Families of Henzey, Tyttery and Tyzack* by H. Sydney Grazebrook, FRHS, published in 1877. It is a phenomenal piece of research by an ardent genealogist on the aforementioned families and their descendants. Mr D. Tyzack has recently developed our knowledge of his Tyzack ancestors and their Lorrainer kin with his wonderful book, *Glass Tools & Tyzacks*. I would like to thank Mr Tyzack for freely sharing with me his research as we both prepared publication of our books.

The first authoritative study of glassware was *Old English*

Glasses by Albert Hartshorne FSA. Published in 1897, it is a masterpiece of scholarly research, although some of Hartshorne's conclusions have been disproved by facts discovered subsequently. When it was written, Hartshorne could not have been aware that although the heyday of Stourbridge glass as an industry had passed, many craftsmen, whose work we admire today, had yet to reach the pinnacle of their trade.

An invaluable reference to the life and times of the people of Dudley between 1800 and 1860 is found in *The Curiosities of Dudley and the Black Country* compiled and edited by C.F.G. Clark and published in 1881. This book also includes a print of Dud Dudley's *Mettallum Martis*.

Aspects of glassmaking in the Weald are described by George Hugh Kenyon, FSA in his book *The Glass Industry of the Weald* published in 1967. A fuller analysis of the early history of the industry followed in *Development of English Glassmaking 1560-1640* published in 1975 by Eleanor S. Godfrey.

From 1912 onwards, Francis Buckley published many works, as the result of extensive research into trade directory and newspaper sources. These publications have been invaluable as mileposts around which to assemble further detail.

In 1934, Roland Wakefield published *The Old Glasshouses of Stourbridge and Dudley*. This little book of thirty-seven pages provides the first reliable summary of the glasshouses of the district. Wakefield wrote from memory about many glasshouses demolished in his lifetime and his well-written commentary is completely reliable. The late D.R. Guttery produced the first detailed study of the Stourbridge manufacturers in *From Broad-glass to Cut Crystal* published in 1956. Guttery built upon the genealogical work performed by Grazebrook, but added much original research, particularly from the Palfrey Collection in Worcester Record Office. His main source was the previously untapped seventeenth century manor rolls. Despite the archaic nature of this source material, the book is delightfully written and adds greatly to our knowledge of the subject. The only disappointment is that Guttery rarely acknowledged his sources.

Mr H.J. Haden has written—and continues to write—extensively on the subject. His *Notes on the Stourbridge Glass Trade*, originally published in 1949, is particularly rich in references to the district. He humbly wrote, 'I am convinced many sources remain virtually untapped, and until the numerous documents in public and private possession have been sifted and such records as wills and parish registers thoroughly examined, much will remain uncertain and obscure.' In similar fashion, I would like to suggest I have carried Jack Haden's torch for the last nineteen years while taking his advice and researching wills and parish registers. I now look forward to passing the same torch to future researchers.

The history of the glass trade in Ireland is covered extensively in *Irish Glass* published by M.S. Dudley Westropp in 1920. Westropp's work has been usefully supplemented by Phelps Warren in his book, also called *Irish Glass*, published in 1970.

The history of the Red House Glassworks was thoroughly researched by Mr M. Buckridge during study for a diploma in industrial archaeology. His findings were published in 1985 and his incisive analysis helped to form the backbone of the chapter on the Red House Glassworks in this text.

The history of the firm of Thomas Webb & Sons is well recorded by the late Herbert W. Woodward in his book *Art Feat and Mystery*. During his time as the librarian in charge of Brierley Hill library, Mr Woodward played a critical role in gathering documents and books on the subject of glass, as well as starting the first permanent collection of locally made glass. His knowledge and experience of the subject and friendships with many local characters—past and present—made him one of the foremost experts on the subject. I would like to record my gratitude to Herbert Woodward for graciously entertaining me and freely sharing the results of a lifetime interest in glass.

Most recently, Charles R. Hajdamach, the senior museums keeper for Dudley Metropolitan Borough, published a beautiful book, *British Glass 1800-1914*. This book is rich in historical fact and illustrations of the superb collection of glass at Broadfield House

Glass Museum, Kingswinford. I would like to record my thanks to Charles Hajdamach for being so helpful and encouraging.

I have also been fortunate to receive help from Mr Peter Boland, the archaeologist of Dudley Metropolitan Borough. Peter was an enthusiastic supporter of my project and very kindly shared with me his research on the location of glasshouse sites.

Genealogical research was greatly assisted by the indices produced by the Birmingham and Midland Society for Genealogy and Heraldry. These marvellous publications are all the work of the society's volunteer workers to whom great thanks are due.

Several individuals were kind enough to share their research with me. Mr B.J.M. Hardyman, who is compiling an index of glassmakers, provided much valuable information over many years. Mr F. Ensell gave up hours of his time to enlighten me on the genealogy of the Ensell and Bradley families, from whom he is descended. Mrs G. Kingsley, a former employee of Stevens and Williams and now a professional researcher, provided much useful information. Mr C.R. Coogan supplied information on the Staffordshire Yeomanry. Mrs C. Golledge, the former curator of the Red House museum, helped me with the history of the Red House Glassworks and provided great encouragement. Mr R. Kilburn, who is researching the Glass Sellers Company, provided valuable information concerning trade with London and Bristol. Lawrence and Honor Conklin, in America, have shared their research on their Conckclaine ancestors.

Mr G. P. Kernan of Sheffield assisted greatly in the latter stages of my research, especially on the Mills and Green families. His indefatigable research into the unindexed Harward & Evers papers resolved many previously unanswered questions. Mr P. Luter of Telford provided information on the glasshouses of Shropshire and unending encouragement. I am indebted to both of these gentlemen who have been extraordinary in their co-operation and friendship.

I would also like to thank Mr R. Dodsworth, the curator of Broadfield House Glass Museum at Kingswinford, who diligently, professionally and patiently answered many questions I posed to him.

Many other authors' works were consulted in the preparation of this text and references are given at appropriate places in the document and in the bibliography.

CHAPTER 2

Physical and Parochial Geography of Stourbridge

Often referred to as a 'Black Country' town, technically Stourbridge lies just beyond the coalfield that delimits the 'Black Country'. However, most of what is described as 'Stourbridge Glass' was not made in the town of Stourbridge, but in the Black Country hamlets of Wordsley, Amblecote and Brierley Hill, on the coalfield just north of Stourbridge town. Stourbridge was in Worcestershire and the greater part of these three hamlets was in Staffordshire.

Stourbridge is an ancient market town that developed on a crossing of the River Stour and derived its name from its bridge. A bridge over the Stour must have existed by 1255 when early references to Stourbridge indicate its increasing prominence.[1] Stourbridge was thriving by the medieval period due to its early development of a cloth and clothing trade. Stourbridge was in, and remains in, the parish of Oldswinford.

The glassmakers traded, banked and revelled in gentlemen's clubs in Stourbridge. Phil Drabble states, 'The myth that Stourbridge is still the headquarters, they say, continued because of the Talbot there. It was the only decent pub in the district and the local glassmakers used it as a headquarters, from which strangers misconstrued the significance of the address.'[2] Despite Drabble's self-confessed predilection for old-fashioned Black Country public houses, there is probably more than an element of truth in this. For example The Friendly Association of the Gentlemen of the County of Worcester dined at the Talbot in 1767 and again in 1772.[3] In 1776 the commissioners of the Ashwood Hay and Wall Heath Enclosure Act chose to base themselves across the parish border at the Talbot Inn rather than in any of Kingswinford's forty inns. The commissioners of the Pensnett Chase Enclosure Act repeated this in 1784_4. Perhaps the main reason for the importance of the Talbot to the early glassmakers, apart from its ambience, is because their mail was addressed there, before the establishment of the modern-day postal system in Victorian times$_5$.

Talbot Hotel, Stourbridge

Dudley is one of the oldest settlements in the west midlands. Its castle was built and occupied during Saxon times when, during the reign of Edward the Confessor, Earl Edwin held it. Following the Norman Conquest, ownership passed to the powerful William Fitz Ansculf. The castle passed to the de Somerys and later, to the de Suttons. In the sixteenth century John Dudley, the Duke of Northumberland, built a Tudor mansion within the old castle where Queen Elizabeth stayed in 1575. In 1621, following the end of the de Sutton family line, the castle passed to the Ward family who became Earls of Dudley. Dudley Castle was a royalist stronghold during the Civil War until it was captured by Cromwell's troops in 1646. The castle suffered substantial damage during the conflict although much of the Tudor mansion remained intact. However, a fire in 1750 destroyed the fabric of the building and so the Wards moved to Himley Hall. The town of Dudley developed at the foot of the castle and along the ridge that now forms the High Street.

Dudley is anomalous in that its ancient parish formed an island of Worcestershire in Staffordshire, measuring eleven miles in circumference. Ecclesiastically it was part of the Diocese of Worcestershire. An Act of 1844 ordered all such detached portions of counties to be amalgamated, but somehow Dudley was ignored. After 1888 the enclave was the only land remaining in England detached from its county. The enclave was briefly incorporated into Staffordshire in 1966 but only remained there until it was merged into the artificially created West Midlands Metropolitan County in 1974.

Dudley's medieval town had two churches, St. Edmund's (bottom church) and St. Thomas's (top church). St. Edmund's twelfth-century church suffered being dismantled by the Royalist defenders of Dudley Castle in May 1646 to avoid it being used as a besieging position during the Civil War. It was not rebuilt until 1724. St. Thomas's was rebuilt and enlarged, largely funded by glass masters, in 1816_6. As a hotbed of non-conformism, Dudley had an extensive number of dissenting chapels.

The relative importance of these towns in the early eighteenth century is portrayed on early maps, such as Herman Moll's 1724 map of Staffordshire. This particular map is chosen as an example because it dates shortly before the first Turnpike Act in the Black Country was passed in May 1727. On the map, Dudley is a town of importance, being on a major east-west road, between Birmingham and Bridgnorth, the most northerly navigable port on the River

Severn. Stourbridge is indicated as a town of equal importance, but devoid of any road links. Before the establishment of turnpikes in 1727 and the later canals, Stourbridge's importance was primarily as a crossing of the River Stour. In the region, the other towns portrayed of similar importance are Bewdley[7], Birmingham[8], Coleshill[9], Wolverhampton[10], Tamworth[11] and of greater importance still, Lichfield, the medieval cathedral city.

Oldswinford is an ancient parish in the county and diocese of Worcester granted by King Eadred to his minister Burhelm in 951 AD[12] surrounded by Kingswinford to the north, Kinver to the west, Pedmore to the south and Halesowen to the east. Oldswinford relied on agriculture for centuries but was at the forefront of the industrial revolution as the parish was rich in coal, clay and other minerals. The River Stour and its fast-flowing tributary, the Smestow Brook provided the power for many of England's earliest ironworks and forges. The parish church of Oldswinford, St. Mary's, is situated to the south of Stourbridge town.

Kingswinford is an ancient parish at the southern edge of Staffordshire in the diocese of Lichfield. It takes its name from Sweyn, the Danish king who was crowned king of England about the year 1000 and remained a possession of the crown until King John gave it to Baron Dudley. A trap for the unwary concerns the records of the parish church of Kingswinford, St. Mary's. The church still stands today, with part of its tower dating back to the 11th century; and was Kingswinford's parish church until 1831. By 1826 St. Mary's Church Committee recognised the building was hopelessly inadequate for the 'vast and extensive population' of the parish[13]. A new parish church for Kingswinford was duly built at Wordsley. It was named Holy Trinity Church and opened in 1831. It became Kingswinford parish church and remains so today, with the incumbent holding the position of Vicar of Kingswinford. St. Mary's church was closed at the same time because of fears of mining subsidence and remained in that state for fifteen years. In 1846 it was realised the likelihood of collapse was remote and after further investigations it was reopened and has been in use ever since. The problem this causes for researchers is that in 1831 the

Kingswinford parish registers were transferred to Holy Trinity, Wordsley and continued there. In 1846 when St. Mary's Kingswinford was considered safe and reopened, the original registers remained at Wordsley and a new set was begun at St. Mary's Kingswinford, catering for the smaller parish, no longer including Wordsley.

Amblecote has always been a great anomaly, being parochially in Oldswinford and Worcestershire, but territorially in the county of Stafford. It appears in Domesday Book and was historically a hamlet in Oldswinford parish until it became a separate ecclesiastical parish, in the diocese of Worcester, in 1845[14]. The building of Amblecote Church began in August 1841 at Holloway End[15]. It was opened in 1842 and consecrated in November 1844[16]. This new parish of Amblecote incorporated the township of Wollaston until 1860 when St. James' Church was built and Wollaston became a separate parish. Administratively, Amblecote converted from a parish council to an urban district council in 1894 when it was the smallest urban district council in the country with an area of just 665 acres. It remained as an administrative area until 1966 when it was divided between Stourbridge and Brierley Hill.

Wordsley was formerly a liberty in the ancient parish of Kingswinford, in the county of Stafford and the diocese of Lichfield and Coventry[17]. It became a separate ecclesiastical parish when its church, Holy Trinity was consecrated in 1831. Holy Trinity Church, Wordsley was built between 1829 and 1831 at a cost of £10,000 and consecrated on 9th December 1831.

There always was a Brierley Hill, a prominence on Pensnett Chase, in Kingswinford ancient parish, covered in brier, broom and bramble. However, it is first named as a place of human habitation in the Court Rolls of Kingswinford Manor in 1619[18]. It grew into a small village in the seventeenth century as a settlement of squatters, where the lane from Dudley to Stourbridge crossed over common land of the Pensnett Chase. Here the ordinary villager had inalienable rights of ancient origin, to dig turf, gather dead wood and to graze his sheep and cattle. However, the ordinary villagers of the Pensnett Chase were among the first to move from an agrarian existence to an industrial one. Thick coal seams lay at shallow depths on the Chase and in many places cropped out at the surface. Increasingly, Brierley Hill became a community of colliers, smiths, nailers, sythesmiths and glassmakers.

As colliers disembowelled the earth, hammers rang, sparks flew and spoil heaps grew, Brierley Hill gained notoriety:

> When Satan stood on Brierley Hill
> And far around it gazed
> He said, 'I never more shall feel
> At Hell's fierce flames amazed.'

Although its church St. Michael and All Angels was built in 1765 as a chapel of ease, Brierley Hill did not become a separate ecclesiastical parish until 1842.

Lye was formerly part of Oldswinford ancient parish until Christ Church in Lye was built in 1813 and consecrated in 1843[19].

Wills and administrations are a rich source of information, but they also are subject to some vagaries worthy of explanation. Before the Court of Probate Act of 1857, the proving of wills and the granting of administrations lay with the ecclesiastical courts and some manorial courts. There was an elaborate network of probate courts. The factors that decided in which court a grant should be made were the place of death and the size and distribution of the estate in question. The estate of a person of small means was usually dealt with in the lowest permissible court, that of the archdeacon. The will of a person with goods in more than one archdeaconry was proved in the diocesan court. There were also various peculiar jurisdictions, such as those exercised by the deans and chapters of cathedrals. Those leaving goods in more than one diocese or peculiar to the value of £5[20] or more were deemed to be in possession of *bona notabilia*. As such, their estates came under the cognisance of one of the provincial courts, the Prerogative Court of Canterbury or the Prerogative Court of York. The use of the PCC in preference to the diocesan courts became fashionable, probably because it gave an elevated sense of status to the deceased's beneficiaries. Then, in the early nineteenth century, the Bank of England ruled that—for their purposes—only PCC grants of probate were valid. This meant a considerable increase in business for the PCC and consequently many smaller courts were moribund by 1858.

This means the will of a glassmaker who died with property in Kingswinford was proved at the probate court in Lichfield. These records are now kept at the Staffordshire County Council Joint Record Office, The Friary, Lichfield. The will of a glassmaker who died with property in Oldswinford—including Amblecote—or Dudley was proved at the probate court in Worcester. (Original) records are kept at Worcestershire County Record Office, Spetchley Road, Worcester WR5 2NP. However, if the deceased owned property in both dioceses the will was proved in the Prerogative Court of Canterbury. These records are now kept in the Family Record Centre, 1 Myddelton Street, Islington, London, EC1R 1UW. Finally, civil jurisdiction took over from ecclesiastical. From 12th January 1858, all wills proved were registered with the Principal Registry of the Family Division and these records are now kept at The Probate Searchroom, First Avenue House, 42-49 High Holborn, London, WC1V 6NP.

With the glassworks of the Stourbridge district straddling the county, parish and diocesan borders it will be appreciated why it is often difficult to predict, with any certainty, in which court wills were proven.

---

1 G.B. Grundy, *Saxon Charters of Worcestershire* (1928); A. Mawer & F. Stenton, *The Place-names of Worcestershire* (1927), p311; R.L. Chambers, *Oldswinford, Bedcote and Stourbridge Manors and Boundaries*, p27.

2 P. Drabble, *Black Country* (1952), p211.

3 H.E. Palfrey, *Gentlemen at the Talbot Stourbridge* (1952), p18.

4 Samuel Wyatt, gentleman of Burton-on-Trent, Edward Palmer Esquire of Coleshill and John Broome. Broome died before the work was complete and was replaced by Harry Court of Stourbridge. Court was one of the two professional surveyors employed – the other being Thomas Hanson of Birmingham.

5 Daniel Clarke, formerly of Newport, Shropshire, had been the landlord from 1695 until his death in 1707. His widow Mary took on the lease and purchased the freehold from Revd. Samuel Foley in 1710. She had previously

kept the local post office handling five to eight hundred letters a month and now combined both activities.

6 The last service was held in the old building on Sunday 15th Oct 1815. The foundation stone of the new building was laid on Friday 25th Oct 1816. The Bishop of Worcester consecrated the rebuilt church, which cost £24,0000, on St. Thomas's day, 21st Dec 1819.

7 Port on the River Severn.

8 Junction of three major roads.

9 On the River Blyth.

10 Birmingham to Stafford road.

11 Ancient fortress on the River Tame.

12 Della Hooke, *Worcestershire Anglo-Saxon Charter-Bounds* (1990), p162.

13 Minutes of Kingswinford Church Committee.

14 Revd. George Miller, *The Parishes of the Diocese of Worcester v 2* (1889).

15 It is built with local yellow firebricks supplied at cost by William King of Amblecote Hall from his Withymoor works.

16 Revd. S. Pritt, *Holy Trinity Church Amblecote 1842-1942* (1942), pp6-7.

17 After 1836, the Archdeaconry of Coventry was transferred to the Diocese of Worcester. In recent years, the Deanery of Himley, which includes Wordsley, has been transferred from the Diocese of Lichfield to the Diocese of Worcester.

18 *venellam ducentm vsus brireley hill* – the lane leading towards Brierley Hill.

19 The church had many rich benefactors, one of who was Thomas Hill (1736-1824), glass manufacturer of Dennis House; a fact commemorated in the east window of the church. Hill family members were involved with the people of Lye for several generations. Thomas Hill's uncle, also Thomas Hill (1711-1782) made possible the first school at Lye. In his will, dated March 1782, he left £130 for 'educating and teaching to read 20 poor children of The Waste and The Lye, whose parents are not able to pay for such learning...' Thomas Hill's grandson, Reverend Henry Thomas Hill (1814-1882), was perpetual curate of Lye from 1839-1843 when he became the first incumbent of Christ Church.

20 £10 in London.

CHAPTER 3

Archaeology and Cartography

Apart from genealogical evidence, there is clearly a need to identify the physical sites of the old glasshouses, most of which have disappeared. Seventeenth century map evidence for glassworks sites is almost non-existent. 'Canal-mania' in the following century provides the researcher with two useful, but unreliable, maps detailing glasshouse sites.

The Stourbridge and Dudley canals were part of a single scheme initiated in 1775[1] to bring coal from the mines around Dudley to works near Stourbridge and also to the Severn towns by way of the Staffs & Worcs canal, and to carry ironstone and limestone for local use. The scheme was so well supported—particularly by glass manufacturers[2]—that Parliament passed the Stourbridge Canal Act[3] the following year; on 2nd April 1776, the same day as the Dudley Canal Act[4]. The first general assembly of the Stourbridge Navigation Company was held at the Talbot Hotel in Stourbridge on 1st June 1776 where many glassmakers signed the minutes of the proceedings[5]. The first meeting of the Dudley Canal Company was held on 6th June 1776 at the Swan Inn in Dudley. This was similarly well supported by glassmakers and Abiathar Hawkes[6] was appointed treasurer. The Dudley section was finished about 24th June 1779. The Stourbridge section took a little longer. The entire canal was fully opened to traffic in December 1779[7] and was an immediate success.

The first map resulting from the scheme is *A Plan for a Navigable Canal from Stourbridge to the canal from the Trent to the Severn*. This was surveyed by Robert Whitworth in 1774 and published in 1775[8]. The second is *A plan of the Intended Extension of the Dudley Canal into the Birmingham Canal.* This was published by John Snape in 1785[9].

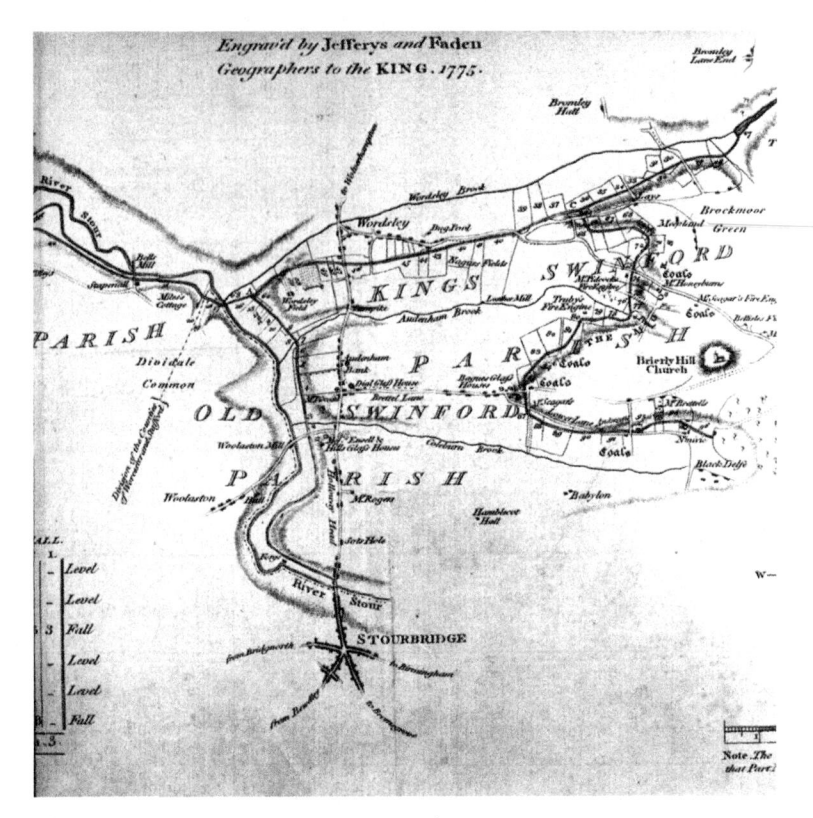

1775 Canal Map

By the end of the nineteenth century, ordnance surveys provide extensive information. However, for many of the earlier glasshouses, this is too late as they had disappeared by then. Fortunately, there are some useful maps from the early nineteenth century. The first is the *Plan of the Mines of Lord Dudley and others, situate in the Parishes of Wolverhampton, Bilston, Wednesbury, Tipton, Sedgley, Kingswinford and Rowley, in the County of Stafford, Dudley and Old Swinford in the County of Worcester; and Halesowen in the County of Salop* published in 1812 by James

Sherriff[10]. For Dudley glasshouses, the researcher can refer to J. Treasure's 1835 *Plan of the Town of Dudley*, which shows four of the five Dudley glasshouses in existence at that time.

The most detailed evidence can be found on two plans of the vicinity surveyed by the Birmingham-based firm of surveyors, Richard & William Fowler & Son. The first is William Fowler's 1822 *Map of the Parish of Kingswinford in the County of Stafford*—scale 7.9" to 1 mile. The second is a plan of the same name surveyed in 1839 by William Fowler & Son.—scale 5.6" to 50 chains. In 1824, W. Hodgetts of 16 Spiceal Street, Birmingham published a *Reference to a Plan of the Parish of Kingswinford*. This lists all the reference numbers of properties with names of occupiers, proprietors, descriptions of premises and their areas with additional remarks where appropriate.

---

1 Gloucester Journal, 20th Feb 1775.
2 This was 'notwithstanding the most effectual opposition possible' by the Birmingham Canal Company. Birmingham Canal Minute Book, 29th Mar 1776.
3 16 Geo III c.28.
4 16 Geo III c.66.
5 PRO, RAIL, 874.1.
6 Infra, Dudley Flint Glassworks.
7 Aris's Birmingham Gazette, 6th Dec 1779.
8 BRL, 436711.
9 BRL, 340683.
10 DA.

CHAPTER 4

Norman and Lorraine Origins

The story of the early glassmakers of the Stourbridge district can now begin and it starts where they did—in France.

In medieval times, both in England and on the continent, many trades and businesses were carried out only by royal permission and the granting of letters patent or monopolies[1]. Sometime after 1330, the glassmaking families of de Cacqeray, de Bongard, de Brossard and le Vaillant received monopoly privileges for producing crown glass in Normandy, and were granted the noble rank of ecuyer[2]. Their method of producing window glass was to fashion a disc of glass which when rotated on a blowing iron at the furnace mouth would spin out to a considerable size. When cool, the crown of glass was cut into panes, the piece attached to the iron was the bulls-eye as is often reproduced in pseudo-antique fashion today. Their crowns, which were known throughout Europe as Normandy glass, achieved great prestige and a wide international market.

Towards the end of the fourteenth century four other families of glassmakers, the de Hennezells, de Thiètrys, du Thysacs and de Bisvals come to prominence in the forest of Darney. It is suggested, but not proven, that they migrated there from Bohemia and Saxony[3]. The forest of Darney is situated in the southwestern foothills of *la Vôge*. It consists today of about a hundred square miles of rolling green country, richly covered with oak and beech—the most calorific of trees—and interspersed with pools and meres. Fine sand and bracken for flux abound. Added to this ideal combination of natural riches is the fact that from the earliest times the area has been much traversed. Some Roman roads and several recent ones meet there and the road system gave access to the Saône, one of Europe's main waterways. The method employed by these families to fashion window glass was to blow a cylinder, slit it, and flatten it. Glass in the Lorraine tradition, like Normandy glass, achieved a high reputation. These four families petitioned John of Calabria, acting as regent in the absence of his father, René of Anjou, the Duke of Lorraine for an Act of Incorporation. This was granted to the four Lorrainer families in a charter entitled *La Charte des Verriers* on 21st June 1448[4]. John of Calabria succeeded to the Dukedom of Lorraine in 1453 and confirmed the charter on 15th September 1469. The privileges granted were because of their craft, and like those granted to the Norman families, were substantial. It gave them the rank of noblemen, to be recognised as chevaliers, esquires and noble persons of the Duchy of Lorraine, with exemption from tallage and other taxation. However, this was more by way of a reaffirmation of their position because the charter refers to their rights and privileges having been held from time immemorial[5]. To support their petition, letters patent confirming their prerogatives from earlier Dukes of Lorraine were produced[6].

It is difficult for us today to realise these noble gentlemen were the craftsmen who laboured at the furnace and produced the glass. The term *gentilhomme verrier* or 'gentleman glassmaker' has caused much puzzlement in modern times. It has often been asked 'Were these people of noble families who became glassmakers, or were they ennobled as a result of choosing glassmaking as their trade, and if so why?' The French poet François Maynard[7] wrote an epigram against the poet Saint Armand. In the form of an extended metaphor, he cleverly compared the glassmakers' dubious claim to nobility with the fragility of glass:

> Votre noblesse est mince,
> Car ce n'est pas d'un prince,
> Daphnis, que vous sortez;
> Gentilhomme de verre,
> Si vous tombez a terre,
> Adieu vos qualités;[8]

Bernard Palissy[9], the celebrated Huguenot potter expressed a

contrary view:
> 'L'art de la verrerie est noble et ceux qui y besognent sont nobles.'[10]

To understand the subject fully requires a certain knowledge of French medieval social structure. True nobles were strictly prohibited from indulging in commerce. Their wealth and titles came from land ownership and their primary role was to be subservient to their monarch and to provide him with armies from among their vassals when the many frequent occasions dictated. For this, they were rewarded by the monarch with glory, but rarely with money. Conversely, the monarch adopted a policy to encourage commerce, particularly when the absence of a native industry was causing imports, which were always regarded as injurious to the realm. Artisans and ecuyers were given the incentive that if their trade or craft were perfected, they would be ennobled and exempted from the myriad forms of taxation as a way of easing their course. This was the claim to *noblesse* known as *par chevalerie* and was one of the seven different claims to nobility under the *ancien régime*. In English terms, it most resembles a knighthood. Although more normally conferred on the field of battle, it could also be granted for services rendered in the field of civil affairs.

The nobility of the early glassmakers was therefore originally a lesser nobility. As time passed, the monarch ceased the incentive as the craft reached maturity. However, it was conveniently overlooked by the glassmakers how they gained their position. They were nobles and conceitedly acted as such. They despised the plebeians, but as true nobles treated them disdainfully, so they intermarried. This ensured they kept their processes secret and it was therefore unnecessary for them to be organised in guilds. They were not subject to the authority of corporate towns as were most artisans, but despite their rank and privileges they were not accepted by the true land-owning nobility. Their social shortcomings were a source of amusement and derision on the infrequent occasions when the two came into contact. Norman and Lorrainer alike, they were fiercely independent in spirit, proud, clannish, hot-headed and secretive. In common with many artisans, soon after the reformation most of them became staunch Protestants. A typical example is Charles de Hennezel of Belrupt glasshouse, cousin of Georges de Hennezel of Houdrichapelle glasshouse. They left *la Vôge* together, arriving in Montbéliard in 1574 and after many wanderings eventually led their families to England as will be described subsequently[11].

---

1 E.W. Hulme, *The Early History of the English Patent System* (1909).

2 J. Barrelet, *Le Verrerie en France de l'époque gallo-romaine à nos jours* (1953), pp46, 9.

3 E. Graham Clark, *Glass-making in Lorraine*, TSGT v 15, No 58 (1931), p107; Anita Engle Berkoff, *A study of the names of the early glass-making families as a source of glass history*, a paper in *Studies in Glass History and Design* (1968), pp62-65.

4 Bibliothèque Nationale, Paris, *Charte octroyée par Jehan, Duc de Lorraine en faveur des gentilshommes verriers de la Foret de Darney (Vosges)*, Juin 21 1448. Printed in full in J.N. Beaupré, *Recherches sur l'industrie verrière et les privilèges des verriers de l'ancienne Lorraines* (1841).

5 'tenuz de tous temps passez.'

6 Ibid, J.N. Beaupré; E. Graham Clark; J. Barrelet, p55; W.C. Scoville, *Capitalism and French Glassmaking 1640-1789* (1950), p84.

7 1582-1646.

8 Your nobility is puny, for you are not descended from a Prince, Daphnis, gentleman of glass, should you fall to the ground, then farewell to your dignity.

9 1510-1559.

10 'Glassmaking is a noble art, and those engaged in it are noble.' Palissy wrote an often quoted autobiography, but for a precis of his life's work see Walter Gandy, *The romance of Glass-Making* (1898) pp114-115 or Noel Currer-Briggs & Royston Gambier, *Huguenot Ancestry* (1985), pp5-6. See also *Memoir of Bernard de Palissy with some Account of Coloured Glass and Enamel*, 8th May 1847, E.O. Sharpe's London Magazine, No 80 and Henry Morley, *Palissy the Potter* (1852).

11 Bibliothèque Nationale, Collection de Lorraine, 60, folio 222, sale in 1575 to Guilliaume du Houx on behalf of Charles de Hennezel of the Belrupt glasshouse 'adis demeurant et ouvrant de son art de gros verre et à présent absent des pais de notre souverain seigneur, pour la faict de la religion.'

CHAPTER 5

The Weald

The earliest reference to glassmaking in the Weald dates from 1226, when Laurence Vitrarius de Dunkshurstlonde acquired twenty acres of land at Dyer's Cross, Pickhurst, near Chiddingfold. On this land he almost certainly established a glasshouse, for in 1270 the records of Westminster Abbey[1] show that Laurence supplied both clear and coloured glass for King Henry III's Chapel then nearing completion at its east end. There are further references to glassmaking in the area although its prominence appears to decline. For example, the glass for glazing St. Stephen's Chapel, Westminster (1349-1356) was obtained from no less than twenty-seven counties throughout England.

The credit for re-establishing the making of window-glass in England is due to a foreigner, Jean Carré, who eventually secured the English monopoly with Anthony Becku. Other authors state that neither Carré nor Becku had any practical knowledge of glassmaking, that they were speculators from Antwerp, who saw the opportunity to make their fortunes. This may be true of Becku, but Carré, a native of Arras, was engaged in the glass trade in Antwerp as a maker of vessel glass[2]. The *Returns of Aliens*[3] notes that he 'came hither for religion'. Carré and his family were devout Calvinists and his move to England followed closely after the religious riots in Antwerp in 1566 that provoked King Philip II of Spain to set up the dreaded Council of Blood. Carré came to the attention of the *Conseil des Troubles* and fled Antwerp in 1567. The rebellion and civil disorder had disrupted trade and so Carré, apart from religious reasons, would have anticipated economic advantage in a move to England.

Carré arrived in London early in the spring of 1567[4] intent upon establishing glassworks. He was armed with considerable technical knowledge, a sizeable amount of capital and extensive contacts with glassmakers of several traditions.

Upon his arrival, Carré wasted no time in setting about his project. By July 1567 he secured a licence from Queen Elizabeth and established two furnaces in the Weald, on leased land in Fernfold Wood, near the village of Alfold on the Surrey-Sussex border[5]. Glass had been made in this area since about 1226 and it would be an obvious location for Carré to choose[6]. Thomas Charnock's *Breviary of Naturall Philosophy* published in 1557[7] remarked:

>As to glassmakers they be scant in this land
>Yet one there is as I doe understand,
>And in Sussex is now his habitacion,
>At Chiddingfold he works by his occupacion.
>To go to him is necessary and meete,
>Or send a servant who is discreet:
>And desire him, in most humble wise,
>To blow thee a glasse after thy devise:
>It were worth many an Arme or a Legg.
>He could shape it like to an egge;
>To open and to close as close as a haire,
>If thou have such a one, thou needst not feare.
>Yet if thou hadst a number in to' store,
>It is the better, for store is no sore.

To avoid the threat of competition Carré began to petition for a monopoly patent[8]. Queen Elizabeth eventually granted a monopoly on 8th September 1567. Jean Carré and Anthony Becku undertook to exercise and practise:

>'the arte feate, or Mysterie of makinge of glas for glasinge such as is made in ffraunce, Lorayne, and Burgondy . . . Anthony Becku and John Carr have promysed and vndertaken to make within oure said realme of England as

much of the saide glasse for glasinge . . . and to sell the same
glasse to oure sobjectes as cheape or better cheape than the
like glass made in foren partes . . . And also to teatche Englishe
men . . . the same scyence or arte of glas makinge perfectlie
and effectuallie, so as the same scyence or arte after the end
of xxj yeares maye be perfectually and substancyally used
and practysed by englishe men.'[9]

The first glassmakers Carré invited to England were Lorrainers[10]. Although Normans and Italians were to follow, Carré knew the Lorrainers to be available and susceptible to the inducement of profitable employment and religious freedom. Carré made a contract with John Chevalier[11]; the cousins Thomas[12] and Balthazar de Hennezel[13] and four other 'gentleman glassmakers' including a Thisac and a Thiétry:

'We Thomas and Balthazar de Hennezel esquires, dwelling
at the glasshouses of Vosges in the countrie of Lorrayne,
John Chevalier, Chastelain and receyvor of fontenay le
Chastell. I the said Chevalier aswell in myn owne name as of
John Quarre of Andwerp at this present dwelling in London . . .' The contract continues 'we the said Thomas and
Balthazar de Hennezel esquiers shalbe bounden to transporte
our selues as sone as possible maye be to the said countrie of
England, and there to cause to be builded and edified two
Ovens to make greate glas.'[14]

During the summer of 1568 the de Hennezels arrived and began to work at one of Carré's two furnaces at Alfold. They were closely followed by Pierre and John de Bungard from Normandy. By October the Bungars were engaged in making crown glass at the other of Carré's Alfold furnaces. Carré left the Lorrainers and the Normans to their labours and continued to live in London. To complete his plan he set about creating a glasshouse for the third glassmaking tradition. He established a furnace for the Venetian style *crystallo* within the walls of the Crutched Friars, an abandoned monastery, near the Tower of London. The development of this venture, although fascinating, is outside the context of this text and has been admirably covered by others.

The contract between Carré and Becku was one forced out of necessity and their relationship was always stormy. Trouble soon developed at the two furnaces at Alfold. The main cause of antagonism concerned the provision for the mandatory training of native English glassmakers. Problems came to a head when Becku discovered Carré had signed the agreement with the de Hennezells naming John Chevalier instead of himself as co-partner. Instead of confronting Carré, Becku sent his partner Peter Briet to the Weald to mediate with the Lorrainers. Briet arrived and informed the de Hennezells that Becku, rather than their kinsman, held half the interest in the monopoly. He also insisted, as part of their agreement, they were obliged to train Englishmen in the mysteries of glassmaking. The de Hennezells made their total disapproval clear by quitting the glassworks and leaving the country. It is recorded that they:

> 'departed owt of the realme and made no further meadle in the sayd works.'[15]

The Norman Bungars were still at work and Becku attempted to enforce his rights upon them also. Since Briet failed him, Becku sent first his son, Anthony and then, in July 1568, his son-in-law James Arnold as his deputies. The Bungars were even more truculent than the de Hennezells. Peter Bungar attacked young Anthony Becku and later both Peter and John Bungar set upon Arnold seriously wounding him. The glassmakers used their working tools as weapons:

> 'First it appeared unto us by the testimony of many and sufficient witnesses that Peter Bongar and John Bongar his brother being the glass makers without any just occasion ministered to them did the 19th July last make an assault the one with a great staff, the other with a hot iron having hot glass metal upon it upon James Arnold, son-in-law to Anthony Beku and his deputy there and did so strike wound and burn to the great peril of his life whereof he is now recovered. Also that the said Peter Bongar did at one time before without any just cause make affray upon Anthony Beku and strike him on the head with a staff'[16].

Not unreasonably, in July 1569 the elder Becku appealed to the Privy Council. After an investigation, which dragged on for six years, the Bungars were forced to pay compensation to Arnold and promised to behave themselves in future[17]. They vehemently declared they would never instruct Englishmen and were not bound to do so by the terms of their contract. The Privy Council reluctantly accepted that the foreigners could continue to produce glass despite this violation of the terms of the patent. Becku complained to Sir William Cecil, Queen Elizabeth's principal secretary:

> 'I understand that ther is some lack found that the making of the glass dothe not better proceade . . . Firste, John Carré my copartener did procure out of Loraine workemen for to make that kind of glass, and agreed with some of them in his owne proper name, for the one half, and in the name of one John Chevalier for the other half, who hathe no privilege in the glass making, which being so done gave me suspicion of double dealing, considering that we were in company together, and did not nominate me in the said contracte.' He continued 'since the ending of this present I have received newes from the glass house that the workemen have missused my sonne in lawe, which was ther to see unto my busines and to preserve my right, and he is in such sorte handeled that he is at the pointe of death throwe the woundes he hathe receyved of the said workemen, which workemen have heretofore missused my owne sonne without cause.'[18]

After this disruption, Carré sent to Lorraine for new glassmakers to work for him and his fellowship alone, although we do not know if this occurred. Balthazar de Hennezel returned to his château at Lichecourt in Lorraine in 1570 and eventually died there[19]. It is doubtful if others replaced the first group in Carré's lifetime. Lorrainers are not mentioned in Carré's will and few Frenchmen appear in the Wisborough Green parish records between 1567 and 1581. Carré eventually died at his house in Fernfold Wood in 1572[20] and was buried in Alfold churchyard.

Alfold Church

The Bungars continued to make their crown glass at Alfold and flourished there. Isaac Bungar inherited the arrogance and fiery disposition of his father. Born in England, he was the son of Peter Bungar$_{21}$ who Carré brought from Normandy to Alfold. After the death of his father, Isaac Bungar carried on the production of crown glass at a furnace near Wisborough Green. He was astute in securing a supply of fuel by a policy of buying up woodlands. By careful selection of allies in the city, combined with his natural aggression, he effectively cornered the London market for window glass$_{22}$.

---

1 Professor W.R. Lethaby, *L'Eglise abbatiale de Westminster et ses tombeaux* (1913).

2 PRO, PCC will of Johis Carr, 11 May 1572, Daper 39.

3 R.E.G. Kirk & E.F. Kirk, *Returns of Aliens Dwellings in the City and Suburbs of London from the Reign of Henry VIII to that of James I* (1887), pt ii, pp 39-40.

4 Ibid, R.E.G. Kirk & E.F. Kirk, pp39-40.

5 State Papers, Domestic, v 13, no. 89, Jul 1567, Jean Carré to the Secretary.

6 Brenda C. Halahan, *Chiddingfold Glass and its Makers in the Middle Ages*, TNS, (1925), pp77-85.

7 Elias Ashmole, *Theatrum Chemicum Britannicum* (1652).
8 State Papers, Domestic, v XLIII, no.44, 9th Aug 1567, Jean Carré to Cecil.
9 Patent Roll of Elizabeth, 8th Sep 1567, quoted in full by A. Hartshorne, *Old English Glasses* (1897), pp393-6.
10 Marnef, *Antwerpen in Reformatietijd*, Appendix V No. 132, 137.
11 Jehan Chevalier was not a glassmaker but was married to Anthoinette de Hennezel of Hasterel. He was the Duke's collector of taxes on glass, well known by the glassmakers and the merchants of Antwerp. Intelligent, diplomatic and entrepreneurial, it was quite possibly his idea, proposed to Carré, to set up glassworks in England.
12 Thomas de Hennezel d'Ormois of Grandmont Glasshouse near Vioménil.
13 Balthazar de Hennezel, son of Nicolas de Hennezel and his wife Nicole, nee Tisac. Balthazar de Hennezel of Grandmont had been Master Glassmaker of Lichecourt which had ceased production in 1560. It is therefore not surprising he was willing to immigrate to England.
14 Lansdowne MSS 59, No. 76 dated 22nd Apr 1568, letter from Anthony Becku alias Dolin to Cecil. A full transcript appears in R.H. Tawney & Eileen Power, *Tudor Economic Documents*, v 1, (1924), pp 302-304.
15 Loseley House, Loseley MSS, unnumbered letters, Moore and Onslow to the Council, 18th Aug 1569, Fol. 3.
16 Loseley House, Loseley MSS, Moore and Onslow to the Council, 18th Aug 1569, Fol. 1.
17 Loseley Correspondence, v 12, No 34 & v 12, No 39; Molyneux MSS 11 Aug. 1569, Hist. MSS Comm., Rep. VII, p621.
18 Lansdowne MSS. 59, No.76. A full transcription appears in R.H. Tawney & Eileen Power, *Tudor Economic Documents*, v 1, (1924), p305-7.
19 He was killed during a quarrel by his cousin Christophe Thysac at a feast at Senonges on 1st Oct 1579. Christophe Thysac fled to England abandoning his wife and children at Lichecourt. Although he begged pardon from Duke Charles II of Lorraine, Thysac never returned to Lorraine and died in England in 1595.
20 Wisborough Green PR, 23rd May 1572, 'Joh Carry, Mr. of ye Glasshouse was bur: at Awfolde.'
21 State Papers, Domestic, v 14, p162, no 231.
22 G.H. Kenyon, *The Glass Industry of the Weald* (1967), p131-136; G.D.

Bungard, 'MEN OF GLASS' A Personal View of the De Bongar Family in the 16th and 17th Centuries, JGC, v 3 (1979), pp79-86.

CHAPTER 6

Migration of Glassmakers in England

Although glass had been made in the Weald for centuries, its quality had declined from its heyday in 1226. Before the arrival of Carré's men, there was already a steady output of vessel glass. The particular skill of the glassmakers of Normandy and Lorraine was of making glass for glazing. During the sixteenth century, more commodious houses were being built and there was a growing demand for window glass. Hardwick Hall in Derbyshire is a good example. It was built between 1591 and 1597 by Elizabeth, Countess of Shrewsbury, who is popularly known as Bess of Hardwick. She lived to the age of ninety, married four times and became richer and more powerful with each marriage. She built Hardwick Hall with its lofty towers and enormous windows that increase in height from the ground floor upwards$_1$. This reflects the interior arrangement of the hall, with servants quarters on the ground floor, family apartments on the second and staterooms on the third. It was these windows that gave rise to an old saying:

'Hardwick Hall

more glass than wall.'

When Carré applied for his patent in August 1567 he stated that the materials used were *fougère*, *ronces*, and *cailloux*$_2$, stressing that they were of little value. He wrote to Queen Elizabeth's principal councillor, Lord Burghley$_3$ that no English glassmaker would be displaced, because:

'on his enquiry at Chiddingfold of one of the masters of the furnaces at that place he found that they could make only such little works as orinaux, bottles and other small things.'$_4$

Native Englishmen showed great animosity to the foreigners in their midst. Foreigners who would not share the knowledge or benefit of their art and whose furnaces consumed prodigious swathes of English woodland in the making of their product. Protests reached the highest levels. In 1574 the Bishop of Chichester wrote to Lord Burghley concerning a plot at Petworth:

> 'of very late, aboute Petworth, certayne had conference to robbe the Frenchmen that make glasse and to burne there houses, but they be apprehended and punished.'[5]

Complaints came in from all quarters. Lord Montague brought one before the Privy Council that he had received from Hastings:

> 'whereas in the laste Session of Parliament there was a Statute made for the prohibiting of iron mylles to be erected within some myles of certen townes uppon the sea coastes for the preservacion and maintenaunce of woodes and tymber to be employed for buylding of shippes, in which Statute there was a speciall regard had unto the towne of Hastings in that countie of Sussex, the inhabitauntes whereof have now latelie exhibited this inclosed compaintcte unto their Lordships, shewing that to defrawde the said Statute there is founded within a myle of the said towne a glasse howse by one Gerard Ansye, a Frenche man, and others his co-parteners, Frenchemen, to the great hinderance of that towne, and therefore fitte to be removed forthwith . . . .'[6]

Later, on 8th December 1584, a Mr Newkener, a member of parliament from Sussex, brought in a bill that attempted to suppress all the glasshouses operated by foreigners. His bill refers to the glasshouses operated by 'dyvers and sundry frenchmen and other straungers.' The 'preservacion of tymber and woodes spoyled by glasshouses' was given as sufficient justification. A revised form of the bill was drafted in 1585 'against the making of glass by strangers and outlandish men'. It provided that 'no one should carry on the trade of glassmaking unless he employed one Englishman for every two foreigners, or should cut timber within 22 miles of London, 7 of Guildford, 4 of Winchelsea, Rye and Pevenset, and the foot of the hills called the Downs of Sussex.' The bill received the assent of both Houses, but the Queen refused her signature.[7]

From 1576 until at least 1579 there were two glasshouses operated at Buckholt in Hampshire, manned by three Lorrainers, four Normans and a Flemming. Hartshorne[8] suggested these included Balthazar de Hennezel, having worked out his nine-year agreement with Carré. It is now known the Lorrainers did not complete the term of their agreement after their argument with Becku's agents. However, others, led by Pierre du Houx, arrived either during or just before 1576 and established a glass furnace at Buckholt Wood[9]. This was then a vast beechwood forest on the line of the Roman road, about two-thirds of the way between Winchester and Salisbury. The site of this early furnace has been identified and excavated. At the time this occurred—from 1860 onwards—the archaeologists were confounded because remnants of the sixteenth century glass were mixed with much earlier remnants of Roman glass[10]. The puzzle was solved and the presence of the Lorrainers at Buckholt confirmed, some thirty years later, when the registers of *L'Eglise Wallonne de Southampton* were published by the Huguenot Society[11]. Huguenot immigrants were obliged to show evidence of their genuine Protestant beliefs before being admitted to communion. Phrases such as: *Avec attestation, Témoinage par écrit* or simply *Témoinage* often appear against the names of the attesters. In a list of those who professed their faith and were admitted to the Lord's Supper, are the following:

> 1576, 7 October. Jean du Tisac, Pierre Vaillant, Claude Potier, ouvriers de Verre a la Verriere de boute haut.
>
> 1577, 6 October. Monsieur de Henneze et s.f., Louis de Hennezee, Arnoul Bisson and Jean Berne, tous de bocquehaut.
>
> 1577, 7 October. Jean Buré JF [ie bachelor]
>
> 1579, 4 Janry. Monsr, du Houx. Verrierer, a bouque haut

Both *boute haut* and *boc-quehaut* can clearly be seen as a record of the place of Buckholt, spoken with a French accent. The date of cessation of the Buckholt glasshouse can only tentatively be assessed as c1579. The last admission to the Lord's supper was Monsieur du Houx in 1579. He may be the same Jean du Houx who was still living in Buckholt in September 1580. He may also be the same John de Hooe 'a Frenchman at the glasshouse' who was buried at Cheswardine 10th May 1613. Jean du Tisac appear to move to Ewhurst, Surrey—if he is the same as the John Tysac who appears there a few years later. Pierre Vaillant may be the same person as the Valyan who appears at Knole, Kent in 1587[12]. The glassmakers had definitely departed Buckholt by 1586, as they do not appear in the lay subsidy roll of that year[13]. It must surely be more than a co-incidence that 1579 was the year that William Overton was elevated to the Bishopric of Lichfield and moved from Buriton, Hampshire to Eccleshall Castle, Staffordshire[14].

From 1579 onwards, glassmakers originally from Lorraine and Normandy began a steady migration to other parts of England. Other kinsmen followed them and it is possible that apart from the opportunity to practice their craft in new markets, some of them were fleeing religious persecution. The trickle of emigrants from mainland Europe to England turned into a flood after the massacre of Huguenot leaders in Paris on St. Bartholomew's Day in 1572[15] and the Spanish Fury in Antwerp in 1576[16]. However, it is important not to give too much emphasis to this aspect. The civil wars and massacres that ravaged France at this time did not spread to the Duchy of Lorraine. Until 1587 Charles III[17], the Duke of Lorraine took a practical stance towards Protestantism[18]. There had been brutal repression under his predecessor, the Duke Antoine[19], but this did not touch the glassmakers hidden away in their forest enclaves. Overproduction and increasingly oppressive taxation were the main incentives causing the Lorrainers to migrate, repression of their religion was just an additional irritant. Clearly, Balthazar de Hennezel travelled to and from Lorraine just as he wished, both before and after 1572.

The parish register of Wisborough Green, between 1581 and 1600, includes the names: Tyzack, Henzey, Tittery, Bongar and Cockery. These being the anglicised forms of: du Thisac, de

Hennezel, de Thiètry, de Bongar and de Caquery. Glassmaking developed in the whole area of the Weald: at Chiddingfold, Kirdford, Wisborough Green, Loxwood, Petworth, Horsham and Alfold.

An early glassworks was little more than a crude furnace in a forest clearing. As the surrounding woodland was stripped for fuel, the glasshouse would simply move on elsewhere in search of a fresh source of fuel. It is estimated a forest furnace would have consumed four acres of fifteen-year old coppice every month[20]. In 1589 George Longe wrote to the Lord Treasurer Burghley referring to:

> 'Dollyne[21] and Carye, being merchants and having themselves no skill in the misterye, were driven to lease out the benefit of their Patent, to the Frenchmen, who by no means would teach Englishmen, nor at any time paid one penny custom . . . For non performance of covenants, their patent being then voide, about VI yeares after their Grant, other men erected and set on worke divers glass-houses in sundry parts of the Realm, and having spent the woods in one place, doe dayly so continue erecting newe Workes in another place without checke or controule.'[22]

The glassmakers inevitably began to move further afield in search of fuel for their furnaces. About 1580 one of the earliest groups[23] to leave the Weald settled at Bishop's Wood, between Eccleshall and Market Drayton, on land belonging to the Bishopric of Lichfield. The incumbent was the newly-elevated William Overton, formerly Rector of Buriton, Hampshire. The parish register of Eccleshall, Staffordshire, records the baptism of Peregrinus Hensie on 28th October 1586[24]. Several other clear references to glassmakers appear in the parish register. The majority refer to the location of the glassworks as Blower P'ke[25]. Blore is a medieval village situated about four miles from Eccleshall Parish Church and the adjoining castle where the Bishops of Lichfield resided[26]. Blore Heath is famous as the battlefield that saw the disastrous defeat of Lord Audley's Lancastrian army in 1459[27]. Blore appears again in the annals of history when the Duke of Buckingham and other fugitives from the Battle of Worcester escaped:

'into Bloore Park, near Cheswardine, about five miles from Newport, where they received some refreshments at a little obscure house of Mr George Barlow's.'[28]

T. Pape excavated the furnace at Bishop's Wood in 1931 and found a large variety of glass fragments[29]. It was the window-glass makers, the Henzeys and Tyzacks, who arrived first in Eccleshall. They were followed by the Bigos and du Houx, makers of vessel glass.

The du Houx left no significant mark at Eccleshall and by about 1605[30], certainly by 1616, they were living in Stockport, Cheshire, although their glasshouse was across the border formed by the River Tame at Haughton Green in Lancashire[31]. The Haughton Green Glasshouse, at Denton near Manchester was established by Isaac du Houx, under lease to Sir Robert Mansell and functioned from about 1615 to 1653. The rectors of Stockport were almost continuously Puritan in sympathy. This may have influenced Isaac du Houx's choice of location, rather than the heavily Roman Catholic areas of southwest Lancashire where high-grade coal and vast quantities of sand were located[32].

This migration northwards was at the instigation of William Overton, the Bishop of Lichfield. Before Overton[33] became Bishop of Lichfield in 1580, he held many clerical positions in the Weald. In 1553 he became Rector of Balcombe, Sussex and vicar of Eccleshall, when, through this unusual juxtaposition of plurality he probably first became aware of the long tradition of forest glassmaking in the Weald and on the Bagot estates in Stafford-shire. In 1567 he became Treasurer of Chichester Cathedral and married Margaret, the daughter of the Bishop, William Barlow. The furnaces set up by Jean Carré under royal licence in 1567-8 at Alfold and Wisborough Green were within the diocese of Chichester where Overton, through his position as treasurer, would have taken a close interest in the developing industry. As a canon of Salisbury in 1573 he may possibly have sponsored or supported the Buckholt venture of 1576-79.

The first evidence suggesting Overton's involvement in glassmaking dates from the period of his twelve-year rectorship of the parish of Buriton, Hampshire from 1567 to 1579. A glasshouse at Ditcham Woods, in the parish of Buriton was discovered in 1970 and subsequently excavated[34]. The remains of the furnace suggest a rectangular type, probably of French origin, and particularly favoured in the Weald. The finds include fragments of Lorrainer style window glass and vessels resembling those found at Brooklands Farm, Wisborough Green and Bagot's Park. Such is the circumstantial evidence that this was a Lorrainer site, as sadly the parish records provide no evidence of Lorrainer names. However, the chronology does suggest that the Buriton glasshouse occupied Lorrainers during Overton's rectorship (1567-79), contemporaneously with Buckholt (1576-79) and ceasing with Overton's elevation to the Bishopric in 1579[35]. While holding the canonry of Salisbury, he became Rector of Hanbury and Stoke-on-Trent, and in 1579 he became Bishop of Coventry and Lichfield, living at Eccleshall Castle for the rest of his life. Once settled and with influence in Staffordshire his involvement in glassmaking became direct and is documented.

After three years at Bishop's Wood, members of the Henzey family were tempted by Sir Richard Bagot to a new location on his estate at Blithfield, less than twenty miles away. On 5th June 1585 Ambrose Henzey made an agreement with Bagot to make glass in Bagot's Park, providing his own clay and ash. Bagot's heavily wooded estate was about three miles north of Abbots Bromley, and he was to supply the wood[36]. Since glassmaking was practised there earlier in the century[37] Bagot, like the Bishop, was familiar with glassmaking and eager to profit from the sale of his wood. Ambrose Henzey was joined three weeks later by his brother Edward, leaving behind their brother George as Edward did not get on with him[38]. George married Jeanne and they baptised four children at Eccleshall. George died and was buried at Eccleshall, just before his fourth child, Thomas, was born. The latest reference to the glassworks at Blore Park is 11th October 1639, when Constance Williams 'of the glasshouse' was buried at Cheswardine.

Edward Henzey's move to Blithfield is recorded in a testimonial dated 26th June 1585 given by Thomas Playfer from Eccleshall Castle:

'Sir whereas this bearer Edward Henzey gent glasse maker, beinge one of my Lord Bishopppe workemen at his Lordshippe glasshouse and is now lisensed to depart and att libertie to worke else where att his pleasure and hath desired mee to testifie unto you the same these and to sygnifie unto you that hee hath demeaned him self very honosly and hath delt nisly with all men to my knowledge since his coming to his Lordshippe workes and so well as for my part I would very willingly have keept him still but that his brother and hee could not agree so that hee would rather depart than live in continuall trouble thus with my hasty commendation to your self I take my leave from Eccleshall Castle the 26 of this present June 1585. Your friend ever assured in Christ Thomas Playfer.'[39]

Fourteen months after making his contract Ambrose Henzey died on 22nd August 1586[40]. His brother Edward stayed for a while at Blithfield, but returned to Wisborough Green sometime before 1602. He married Sara Tetrye of Eccleshall, at Eccleshall[41], but their son Izhac was born in Wisborough Green the following year[42]. Edward lived as part of the protestant community in the Wisborough Green area[43]. Isaac Bungar was the largest producer in the region[44] and Edward Henzey of North Chapel, Sussex was the second largest[45]. The two co-operated closely. He was one of six Sussex Henzeys and two Tisacks named in an order to the Privy Council in 1614 for infringing Zouch's patent and represented his fellow glassmakers as their spokesman[46]. Edward's peripatetic nature is abundantly displayed, for when he died in 1621 his will[47] described him as 'of Amblecoate, in the parish of Old Swinford, in the County of Stafford, Glassmaker.'

Glassmaking continued at Bagot's Park for several more years and John Conckclaine was there in 1609[48]. Bagot's glasshouse was one of those forced to close following King James' prohibition of the burning of timber as fuel. This caused great indignation to Sir Walter Bagot[49], who wrote to Sir Robert Mansell.

'Worthie Knight, I have long been silent but now enforced thereto, must challenge, a loosers' privilage to speake.'

Bagot complained that he had wood to the value of £300 cut,

corded and waiting at the glasshouse door, which he was now unable either to use or sell. He suggested that, although Mansell could not give permission for the wood to be used, as this would be contrary to the King's proclamation, if he would promise to take no action upon it, he for his part would take the risk of using the wood in his furnace. He further complained[50] that Mansell had caused his chief workman, Jacob Henzey[51], to be arrested and sent to work for Mansell at his glasshouse at Wollaton[52]. In a further letter of 1617 Bagot claimed that an agreement to purchase the remaining stock had not been carried out[53].

The migration continued further west to another forest outpost, as on 29th October 1599, 'Tyzack Abram sonne of a frenchman at the glasse-house' was baptised at Newent in the Forest of Dean[54]. The evidence for a gradual move westwards and northwards is convincing[55].

---

1 Longleat House, Marquess of Bath MS 114A, v E, pp 68-70; Chatsworth House, Hardwick MS 10, Fol. 25V.

2 Bracken (or fern), briars and flints.

3 William Cecil was ennobled as Lord Burghley and raised to the post of Lord Treasurer in 1572 following his adroit handling of Mary Stuart's intrigues.

4 State Papers, Domestic v 43, No. 43 [new No 104].

5 State Papers, Domestic, v XCV, No 82, 25th Apr 1574, Bishop of Chichester to the Privy Council.

6 A.P.C. 1581, p578.

7 Draft 16th Feb 1584/5 House of Lords MS and Hist. MSS Comm., Report III, p5.

8 Ibid, A. Hartshorne, pp 170-3.

9 Southampton Record Office, SC2/6/5, f.64, lease of 1578 refers to the 'great glasse house with the store house and the dwelling house' at Buckholt, which had recently been in the tenure of James Knollis, being leased to Pierre du Houx by Sir William West, Lord de la Warr, for five years at £20 per annum.

10 E. Kell, *On the Discovery of a Glass Factory at Buckholt*, Journal of British Archaeological Association, (1861), v 17, pp 55-58.

11 H. M. Godfray (ed.), *Registre des Baptesmes, Marriages & Mortz, et Jeusnes*

de L'Eglise Wallonne . . .étable à Southampton (1890), Publications of the Huguenot Society, v 4, pp 12,14.

12 T. B. Lennard, *Glass-making at Knole, Kent* (1905), ANT, v 41 pp127-9.

13 Southampton Record Office, SC2/6/5 f. 83, C.R. Davey (ed.) *The Hampshire Lay Subsidy Rolls*, 1586 (Hampshire Record Series, 4, 1981).

14 Infra.

15 Huguenot leaders had assembled in Paris for the wedding of their leader Prince Henry of Bourbon (later Henry IV) with Margaret of Valois, which took place on 18th Aug. On the morning of 24th Aug 1572, with the consent of the Queen Mother and of Charles IX, who were fearful of Huguenot power at court, the Duke of Angoulême, the Duke of Guise and other catholic lords left the Louvre and raised the Paris mob. A massacre of all the Huguenots ensued. Over a thousand were killed in Paris and in the following weeks probably twenty-five thousand were killed in the provinces.

16 The citadel of Antwerp was garrisoned in November 1576 by a body of mutinous Spanish troops under Sancho d'Avila. In a brief struggle the Spanish mutineers routed the forces of the town's governor, Champagny and for hours murdered, ravaged, destroyed and pillaged. Some seven thousand citizens of Antwerp were killed. This happened while the Calvinist leaders of the Low Countries were meeting at the Congress of Ghent to discuss the very question of the toleration of Catholicism in their provinces.

17 1552-1608.

18 For example, in 1567 the Duke allowed German Protestants to travel across the Duchy to go to the aid of their persecuted coreligionists in France. A Ducal ordnance of 14th Feb 1572 did require protestants to quit the Duchy, but allowed them one year in which to sell their goods and property before doing so.

19 Ducal Ordinances of 1523 and 1539 forbade teaching the doctrine of Luther.

20 D.W. Crossley, *Glassmaking in Bagot's Park, Staffordshire, in the Sixteenth Century*, JPMA, v 1 (1967), p63.

21 Dollyne was an alias of Anthony Becku.

22 Lansdowne MS., No 59, Art. 75 and 72.

23 This group included the brothers Edward, George, Ambrose and Peregrine Henzey, sons of Nicolas de Hennezel. Germain Rose-Villequey, in *Verre et Verriers de Lorraine* (1971), p454, suggests that Nicolas de Hennezell was

the brother of Ananias Henzey I. The author suggests this is not the case. Ananias Henzey I is known to have been born c1570. Ambrose Henzey, son of Nicolas, would have been born before 1564, which would place his father Nicolas' birth around 1543.

24 Peregrinus Henzey, son of George Henzey and his wife Jeanne.

25 Blore Park.

26 Bishop Lloyd built the present mansion in 1695 on the site of several earlier castles built since the thirteenth century by the Bishops of Lichfield, Lords of Eccleshall. Bishop Richard Sampson (1543-54) is thought to be the first bishop to make Eccleshall Castle the principal seat of the Bishops of Lichfield. The last bishop to reside at Eccleshall Castle was Bishop Lonsdale, who died in its parlour in 1867. After this the bishops lived at the Bishop's Palace in Lichfield Cathedral Close.

27 The battle of Blore Heath was fought on 23rd Sep 1459, during the War of the Roses. Lord Audley, the Lancastrian leader, allowed himself to be lured by a feint retreat of the enemy. He was killed after crossing Hemp Mill Brook and a cross in the field marks the spot where he fell.

28 Thomas Blount, *Boscobel* (1660).

29 T. Pape MA FSA, *An Elizabethan Glass Furnace*, CM, Jul-Dec 1933.

30 Stockport PR, 31st Jul 1605, An infant of one Dionise, a glassman, buryed.

31 Stockport PR, 8th Sept 1616, Katherine dau. of Isaack de Howe now of Hyde bapt.

32 This du Houx family came from the Senades Glasshouse near Clermont, Argonne in Lorraine where the family is recorded in 1582 and 1594. The du Houx are first recorded in England as members of the French Church at Rye in Sussex in 1571. Op cit Ruth Hurst Vose, *Excavations at the 17th-century glasshouse at Haughton Green, Denton, near Manchester*, JPMA, v 28, (1994).

33 Right Reverend William Overton, b. 1525, London; Admitted to Magd. Coll. Ox. 25th Jul 1539; B.A., 1550; Fellow, 1550-54; M.A., 8th Jul 1553; incorporated at Cam. Univ., 9th Jul 1562; Canon of Winchester, 20th Dec 1559; Vicar of Balcombe, Sussex, 1553; of Eccleshall, 1553; Rector of Swinnerton, 1555; of Nursling, Hampshire, 20th Feb 1559; of Upham, Hampshire, 1560, of Exton, Hampshire, 1561; of Cotton, Suffolk, 1562; B.D. Cam. Univ., 16th Feb 1565; D.D., Ox. Univ.; Treasurer of Chichester, 7th May 1567; Canon, 1563; Rector of Rotherford, Sussex, 20th Mar 1570; of Buriton, Hampshire, 1569; Bishop of Lichfield, 10th Sep 1580 to death; also held rectories of

Stoke-on-Trent and Hanbury; suspended from his bishopric by Archbishop Whitgift; married Margaret, daughter of Bishop Barlow of Winchester; d. 9th Apr 1609; bur. Eccleshall.

34 Russell Fox & Elizabeth Lewis, *William Overton & Glassmaking in Buriton* (1982).

35 The archaeological evidence for this date of cessation is a clay pipe bowl, found in the fill of the ditch, dated typologically to after 1580.

36 Bagot MS, T. Pape, *The Lorraine Glassmakers in North Staffordshire*, TNSFC, v 82 (1947), pp111-15; Hist. MSS Comm., IV, p342; W. Horridge, *Documents Relating to the Lorraine Glassmakers in North Staffordshire with some Notes Thereon* (1946), p27.

37 SRO, Photostat 623 of MS Sir Walter Bagot to Sir Robert Mansell, 1616 in which Bagot states this. On 15th Jul 1508 Lodovicus Bagot of Blithfield, in a grant to Sir John Montgomery and others, mentions a pasture called Wynsleys then in the tenure of Thomas Harve, glasier.

38 George spent the rest of his life at Blore Park where he died 7th Aug 1603. By his wife Jeanne, he had four children, Thomas, Peregrine, Marguerite and Jehuditha.

39 SRO, Bagot MS, Photostat 623, Letter from Thomas Playfer to Sir Richard Bagot.

40 Abbots Bromley PR.

41 Eccleshall PR, 24th Oct 1602, mar. Edward Henzey of the parish of Greene, Co. Sussex, glassmaker and Sara Tetrye of Eccleshall.

42 Wisborough Green PR. Izhac son of Edward Henzey bap. 6 Dec 1603.

43 Pero Bungar was licensed in 1579 to minister and serve in French at Wisborough Green church.

44 A.P.C. xx 290; Star Chamber Proc., 5 Jac I, 179/7.

45 A.P.C. xxxiii. 658, 670.

46 A.P.C. xxxiii. 643, 30th Nov 1614. Although not named in the warrant, Isaac Bungar turned up as one of their chief spokesmen. He and Edward Henzey maintained that if the new patent was to be strictly enforced, they ought in all justice to be allowed to use up their materials before shutting down their furnaces, or else the new patentee should be forced to buy their supplies.

47 PCC.

48 Abbots Bromley PR. 1609 Feb 25 Jacobus fillius John Conckclaine baptised.

49 Walter Bagot (1557-1623), son of Sir Richard Bagot, who had died in 1597.

50 SRO, Photostat 623.
51 Extrapolation of evidence suggests Jacob Henzey was born about 1578, which places him as the same generation as George, Ambrose, Edward and Peregrine, sons of Nicolas Henzey, at least two of whom are know to have worked for Bagot. However, no evidence exists to prove their relationship. Jacob Henzey baptised a son, Abraham on 30th Dec 1599 at Wisborough Green, Sussex and another, Paul, on 9th Dec 1615, at Oldswinford. This is the day after Sir Robert Mansell concluded an agreement with Sir Percival Willoughby at which time Jacob Henzey and John Squire were already resident in Wollaton, Nottinghamshire. Jacob Henzey and John Squire were employed by Sir Percival Willoughby to manage two glass furnaces at Wollaton under licence to Sir Robert Mansell. The venture was suggested by Robert Fosbrooke, a local coal factor, who often acted for Willoughby, in a letter dated 15th Jun 1615 (HMC MSS of Lord Middleton 182). Plans were drawn for the glasshouse on 30th Jul 1615 (University Library Nottingham, Middleton Collection 165/130). Willoughby made his agreement with Mansell on 8th Dec 1615 by which time Jacob Henzey and John Squire were already in residence in a dwelling house adjoining the great barn (Middleton Collection 165/131). Op cit R.S. Smith, *Glass-Making at Wollaton in the Early Seventeenth Century* (1962).
52 Jacob Henzey was seriously in debt to Bagot for wood by 1615 and may have welcomed the opportunity to work for Mansell on a salary.
53 SRO microfilm 9, L.A. 187, (original in Folger Library, Washington D.C.)
54 Gloucester Diocesan Records v 1, 164. The glassworks operated from about 1598 to 1698, when a glassworks was still in operation in Newnham, supplying the cider trade in 1698. Op cit J. Stuart Daniels, *The Woodchester Glass House* (1950), p6; Alan G. Vince, *Newent Glasshouse* (1977).
55 A glasshouse was found and excavated in 1961 at St. Weonards, Herefordshire. Glass finds are dated to 1580-1620, but unfortunately there are no extant parish registers for St. Weonards and Garway for the early 17th century. Op cit N.P. Bridgewater, *Glasshouse Farm, St. Weonards: A small Glassworking Site* (1963), pp300-315. A glasshouse was found and excavated in the early nineteen hundreds at Woodchester, near Stroud in Gloucestershire. The finds are similar to those of Newent and St. Weonards. Archaeological evidence dates it to about 1590 to 1617. Op cit, J. Stuart Daniels, *The Woodchester Glass House* (1950), p6.

CHAPTER 7

The Search for Fuel

English glassmaking moved into a new phase at the beginning of the seventeenth century. Thus far the immigrant Lorrainers had moved further afield in search of fresh woodland and to a lesser extent to escape the animosity of the indigenous English people. Under Queen Elizabeth I, the main concern was to develop a native glass industry that would leave England free from the need for imports. During the reign of King James I there was an ever-increasing concern for the amount of wood being consumed by glassmakers and ironfounders. Pressure was brought to bear on the monopolists controlling both trades to seek a new source of fuel.

The monopoly for the glass trade in England was held by Sir Jerome Bowes from 1592 until 1615 when it was transferred to Sir Robert Mansell. Mansell was an outstanding figure who pursued the rights of his monopoly with great vigour. He was another to deprecate the consumption of English timber. It is probable that as a retired Admiral, Mansell would regard this precious material as vital to the Navy. Robert Mansell was born in 1573, the fourth son of Sir Edward Mansell[1] of Margam, Glamorganshire, by his wife Lady Jane Somerset[2]. As a young naval officer he won a knighthood under Lord Howard at Cadiz in 1596. In 1603 he formed part of the escort that conducted Sir Walter Raleigh from London to his trial at Winchester. He became an Admiral and commanded the Narrow Seas Fleet from 1606 to 1610. He secured the lucrative appointment as Treasurer of the Navy in 1604 and was placed on the retired list at his own request in 1618. Upon gaining his glass patent King James 'wondered [that] Robin Mansell being a seaman, whereby he had got so much honour, should fall from water to tamper with fire, which are two contrary elements.'[3]

It is unclear when the use of coal as an alternative fuel for glassmaking was first developed or by whom. It is possible the Lorrainers heard the news of the experiments in the industrial use of pit coal being carried out on Lord Dudley's land at Kingswinford. When Sir Robert Mansell's glass patent of 1615 was being attacked in Parliament in 1621, Edward Lord Dudley was present and declared that:

> 'two yeares before this pretence of a new invention, or any Patent granted there was Glasse made with Coale upon his ground by native Glass-makers.'[4]

The claim was later repeated by his son, Dud Dudley. He stated that the manufacture of glass with pit coal was first accomplished near his house[5], Green Lodge, near Greensforge[6], in the northwest corner of Kingswinford. The Lorrainer, Tyzack, played a prominent part in this development. In the Commons debates on the glass patent it was stated he 'had the like invention' of using coal for glass-making in Lord Dudley's woods in Staffordshire[7]. We do not know if these claims were true or not. Neither Lord Dudley nor Paul Tyzack applied for a monopoly patent at the time which they would most likely have done if they were first to perfect the process. However, whether justified or not, Mansell gained the credit, for on 14th October 1635, his interminable petitions to the King were settled by a proclamation concerning the importation of foreign glass. It recited that Sir Robert Mansell, Lieutenant of the Admiralty, had perfected the manufacture of glass with sea or pit coal to the saving of wood, etc[8].

Various Lords of Dudley were involved with glassmaking and later generations were landlords to several glassmakers. An early line of the Lords of Dudley died out with the death of Edward Sutton[9], the last of the Suttons in 1645. Edward Sutton married Theodosia Harington but also took a mistress, Elizabeth Tomlinson of Tipton who bore him eleven children. He 'left that virtuous lady, his wife, in London without provision of sustenance and took to his home a lewd and infamous woman, a base collier's daughter.'[10] His wife bore him four legitimate children, but one of his eleven illegitimate children was Dud Dudley[11], who had a remarkable effect upon the industrial development of the area. Dud Dudley spent a lifetime trying to smelt iron with coal instead of charcoal. He wrote a book about it called *Mettallum Martis* in which he describes his success with 'Pitcole, Seacole, Peat and Turff.' However, most of the book is taken up by stories of his misfortunes and his persecution by rivals, who hired a mob to smash his bellows and wreck his works. The Greens Forge[12] he mentions, regarding his experiments with glass, was only one of several forges he operated in the area. The others were Cradley Forge[13], Heath Forge[14] and Swin Forge[15]. Nobody knows what process he used; his secret died with him.

The use of timber for both iron founding and glassmaking continued increasingly until 23rd May 1615, when King James I banned the use of timber as a fuel for glassmaking:

> 'understanding that of late yeers the wast of Wood and Timber, hath been exceeding great and intollerable by the Glasse-houses and Glasse-works of late in divers parts erected . . . no person or persons whatsoever, shal melt, make, or cause to be melted or made, any kind, forme or fashion of Glasse or Glasses whatsoever, with Timber or wood, or any Fewell made of Timber or wood . . . '[16]

A tremendous coal-field surrounds the Stourbridge district. The portion between Dudley and Stourbridge is divided into two irregular basins by the Netherton anticlinal that runs north-east and south-west for about three miles from Netherton to Lye. Thick coal crops around this elevation in continuous lines, with the greatest disturbance of exposed coal at Lye. The presence of pot-clay at Stourbridge was probably known to the Lorrainers as a lease had been granted for digging glasshouse pot clay there in 1566[17]. The quality of the clay was later to be praised by the ubiquitous Robert Plot:

> 'But the clay which surpasses all others of this country, is that at Amblecot, on the bank of [the] Stour, in the parish of

old Swynford, yet in Staffordshire . . . of a dark bluish colour, whereof they make the best pots for the Glasshouses of any in England . . . and so very necessary to be had, that it is sent as far as London . . . The goodness of which clay, and the cheapness of coal hereabout, no doubt has drawn the glasshouses, both for vessels and broad-glass, into these parts; there being divers set up in different forms here at Amblecote, old-Swynford, Holloways End and Cobourn [sic] brook.'[18]

As the coal and clay measures at Stourbridge are adjacent, it is therefore no surprise that on 26th April 1612 John the son of Paul and Bridgit Tyzack, was baptised at Kingswinford. Paul Tyzack was a Lorrainer who came to the area via Bishop's Wood, Eccleshall. The Tyzacks obviously arrived in the Stourbridge area at least three years before King James's proclamation of 1615. Then, just six months after the proclamation banning the use of timber as a fuel, the Henzey name first appears in the Oldswinford parish register. On 9th December 1615 'Paule the sonne of Jacob Henzie' was baptised[19] and on 16th December 1615 'Zacharias the sonne of Fowler Henzie' was baptised. Members of the Concklyn[20] and Bungar families also appear in the early Oldswinford registers. These parish register entries mark the migration of the Lorrainers to Stourbridge; the development of its glass industry had begun.

---

1 Edward Mansell (1531-1585), son of Sir Rhys Mansel; knighted 1572; Chamberlain of Chester, as was his father.

2 Lady Jane Somerset, younger daughter of Henry Somerset, second Earl of Worcester.

3 J. Howell, *Epistolae Ho Elianae* (1645), p103.

4 Cal. SP Dom. 1623-5, 215; Proc. and Debates, 11. 38-9. Commons Debates, 1621, v. 153.

5 Dud Dudley, *Mettallum Martis* (1665), pp34-5.

6 Greensforge is a tiny hamlet on the Smestow Brook 1.25 miles south of Swindon. It straddles the boundary of Kingswinford and Wombourne ancient parishes.

7 Commons Debates, 1621, vii. 632; State Papers, Domestic, James I v 162, No 64. Reasons against Sir R. Mansell's patent, 16th Apr 1624 (especially

paragraphs 11 and 12). Printed in full in A. Hartshorne, *Old English Glasses* (1897), pp423-426.

8 Mansell's first claim to the invention is documented in Mansell's Specification, dated 22nd May 1623. Quoted in full in A. Hartshorne, *Old English Glasses* (1897), pp416-423.

9 Edward Sutton, b. 1563, son of Edward, eighth Baron Dudley; Mat. Lincoln Coll., Ox., 24th Jul 1580; ninth Baron Dudley of Dudley Castle; summoned to Parliament 19th Feb 1593 - 3rd Nov 1639; married Theodosia, daughter of Sir James Harington; Knt., of Exton, Rutland; d. 23rd Jun 1645; bur. St. Edmund's, Dudley.

10 Bill of Complaint to the Court of the Star Chamber 1592 by Gilbert Lyttleton of Prestwood.

11 Dud Dudley, b. 1599, son of Edward, Lord Dudley and Elizabeth Tomlinson; of Balliol Coll., Ox. although his education was curtailed in 1619 when his father fetched him away to manage his forges; married Eleanor, daughter of Francis Heaton of Groveley Hall, Worcestershire, 12th Oct 1626, St. Helen's Worcester; Colonel in King Charles I's army; bur. 25th Oct 1684, St. Helen's, Worcester, monument on south wall of church.

12 Greens Forge stood on the Smestow Brook, south of Swindon.

13 Cradley Forge stood at the confluence of the River Stour and the Mousesweet Brook. Its location, just south of the river, is marked today by a metal plaque.

14 Heath Forge stood on the Smestow Brook, west of Wombourne.

15 Swin Forge stood on the Smestow Brook at Swindon.

16 State Papers, Domestic, James I, (Royal Proclamations, No. 42, 23rd May 1615). A full transcription appears in A. Hartshorne, *Old English Glasses* (1897), pp413-4.

17 L. Jewitt, *Ceramic Art in Gt. Brit* (1883), p156; George Harrison, *The Stourbridge Fire Clay*, a paper in *The Resources, Products and Industrial History of Birmingham and the Midland Hardware District* (1866), p133, edited by Samuel Timmins. It is significant that both writers make oblique references to the lease, neither quotes it precisely.

18 Robert Plot LLD, *The Natural History of Stafford-shire* (1686), pp121-122.

19 Supra, Migration of Glassmakers in England.

20 Bennett, son of George Conculyn, bap. 17th Dec 1616 and Judith, daughter of George Conculyn, bap. 4th Jan 1617.

CHAPTER 8

Colemans Glasshouse, Lye

Colemans Glasshouse was the first glasshouse to be established in the Stourbridge area, built sometime between 1610 and 1614 by Paul Tyzack$_1$. It was located in the Stour valley, south of the river, north of Bott Lane in Lye, about one mile east of Stourbridge town-centre$_2$. Paul Tyzack lived on the opposite bank of the Stour on land that was part of Ravensitch Coppice in the parish of Kingswinford$_3$. The glasshouse took its name from a field called Colemans that Paul Tyzack occupied.

The first reference to the Tyzacks in the Stourbridge area is the baptism of John, the son of Paul Tyzack and his wife Bridggett at Kingswinford on 26th April 1612. The Tyzacks were not the only Lorrainer glassmakers to arrive in the Stourbridge area. The earliest references in the Oldswinford parish registers are Francis Concklyn$_4$ in 1613 and Daniel Bunger in 1615. Other Lorrainers followed Paul Tyzack from Bishops Wood. First to arrive was his brother-in-law James Legré$_5$, who appears in the Kingswinford register in 1617, and then Paul's brother Zachariah Tyzack$_6$. There is every reason to suppose the first Stourbridge 'chair'; gaffer, blower and gatherer was formed by these men at Colemans Glasshouse.

Right from the start, Tyzack's enterprise was beset with problems. In 1614 the Privy Council received a complaint that Paul Tyzack had erected furnaces in Staffordshire 'in the skirts and confines of that shire' and was making glass contrary to the grant made to Sir Edward Zouche$_7$, despite orders to restrain from doing so. The council ordered his arrest and appearance before them$_8$. During 1621, the Commons pressed King James to abolish many patents previously granted. In a Royal Proclamation of 10th July he abolished eighteen and ordered that sixteen others, if abused, could be proceeded against in an ordinary court of law[9]. The glass patent however was not in either category. The Privy Council ruled Mansell's patent should remain in force until his return from sea[10]. Despite this ruling, word quickly spread that the patent was no longer in force and several glassmakers immediately set up new glassworks. Sir Robert Mansell had returned to active service on 20th July 1620 commanding an expedition against the pirates of Algiers, with Hawkins as his vice-admiral. Lady Mansell, acting in her husband's absence, appealed to the Privy Council for enforcement of their order that the patent should stand. The Privy Council agreed and on 10th July 1621, warrants went out for the arrest of the owners of the new glasshouses demanding their appearance before the Council[11]. On the same day, letters were sent to Mansell's lessees, seven in all, instructing them to make regular payments to the Council or explain their refusal[12]. Paul Tyzack was one of the seven and he complied with the order. The others who complied were John Squire[13], John Moose, Edward Percival, John de Houx and Isaac de Houx[14]. Abraham Bigo I was among the seven, but ignored the order having been continuously in dispute with Sir Robert Mansell and withholding rents in Dorset since 1618[15]. Paul Tyzack's compliance shows he was operating as Mansell's lessee and, unlike Bigo, was content with the relationship.

After his early difficulties, Paul Tyzack settled down to make glass under license to Sir Robert Mansell. At first, Colemans supplied a purely local market with window-glass at 22s 6d a case[16]. On 30th March 1636, at the Manorial Court held in the Town Hall, Stourbridge, a man was fined 2s 6d for assaulting a crate-carrier. The crate quite possibly contained window-glass purchased from Tyzack and was carried on the back. Until the seventeenth century it was common for many products to be sold in this way. Itinerant traders, known as chapmen or peddlers, would purchase products from their manufacturers and travel the countryside selling them. It must be remembered there was no established system of transport at the time and manufacturers would have welcomed this method of distributing their wares[17]. Typically, a chapman would peddle as many different products as he could; supply being a bigger problem than demand. Glass became increasingly sought after and as the supply began to increase, some peddlers began to specialise in glassware and became known as glassmen. By the end of the sixteenth century, peddlers were so numerous that an Act was passed to control them, but glassmen were excluded from its provisions. Peddlers and chapmen were adjudged rogues and vagabonds and were to be:

> 'stripped naked from the middle upwardes and shall be openly whipped untill his or her body be bloudye.' Glassmen were uniquely excluded provided they were licensed. 'this statute nor any thinge therein conteyned shall extend to any Children under the age of seaven yeares; nor to any such Glassemen as shalbe of good Behaviour, and do travaile in or through any Cuntry without begging, having lycense for their travayling under the Handes and Seales of three Justices of the peace of the same Conty where they travell.'[18]

By 1640 Paul Tyzack was sufficiently integrated into the local society to see his son, Paul II[19], marry[20] Joyce[21], the daughter of his landlord John Lyddiat[22]. John Lyddiat was a sythesmith of Wollaston Hall[23] and was a turbulent man. The pedigree of his family was recorded at the Herald's Visitation of Worcestershire in 1634 and at the Staffordshire Visitation of 1664. He was fined £18 for declining a knighthood at the coronation of Charles I. This might appear a strange thing to do, but knighthood would have brought with it onerous responsibilities. He was one of those who were to find horse in Worcestershire during the Civil War[24].

In 1655 Paul Tyzack I decided it was time to retire. He was sixty-three years old and had toiled in the glasshouse for at least forty years. He handed the business to his son, Paul II, who agreed to pay him an annuity of £40. Paul senior lived in retirement in his house in Ravensitch Coppice from where he watched over his sons' fortunes. He shared his house with his daughter Anne, her husband Paul Henzey I and their seven children[25].

In 1658, a fire destroyed Colemans Glasshouse. Paul Tyzack II was later accused by his father-in-law and landlord, John Lyddiat, of having set fire to it[26]. Although successful, the enterprise had not been particularly profitable. Presumably to raise enough capital to rebuild the glasshouse, Paul Tyzack entered into a contract with Robert Foley[27], a wealthy local ironmaster. Tyzack's partners were his cousin Zachariah[28] and his brother-in-law, Abraham Bigoe II[29]. They moved to Chelwood in Somerset where they made broad-glass, for which Foley paid them 7s 6d a case[30]. This Chelwood glasshouse appears in John Houghton's 1696 list as one of three glasshouses in Somerset making bottles and window-glass[31]. A bill of receipt dated 5th September 1660 shows Mr Robert Foley of Stourbridge paid 7s 6d per case for six hundred and forty-eight cases of glass, made at Chelwood in 'Summersettshire' by Abra Bigo, Zach Tyzacke and Paul Tyzack[32].

In 1660 the three partners returned to Colemans. John Lyddiat leased to Paul Tyzack a 'parcel of land called the Colemans with an old glasshouse at the Lye, together with colepitts and the liberty of digging and taking coal.'[33] The lease was for twelve years, and required him to rebuild the 'almost totally ruined glasshouse' at a cost of £200.

After eight happy years in retirement, Paul senior wrote his will on 8th June 1663. He still described himself as a glassmaker of Oldswinford, and as well as legacies to his children, he willed £12 to his Henzey grandchildren. He left five shillings to his son-in-law, Paul Henzey, his sole executor. Tyzack died two years later[34] and his will was proved at Worcester in 1665[35].

The Kingswinford parish registers show Italian glassmakers as well as Lorrainers were being tempted to the region. Caesar Rachetti, charmingly anglicised in the parish register as Seazer Rackett, married Meriall[36], the daughter of Paul Tyzack II, in 1665[37]. It was typical for these immigrant workers to be rapidly assimilated into the local society and by 1679 Cesar Racket, 'glazier of Oldswinford', became a churchwarden of Oldswinford.

In 1663 Paul Tyzack II secured a new contract with Robert Foley, who by now had risen to become official ironmonger to the Royal Navy[38]. The contract was arranged by Joshua Henzey II who intended to market the whole of the window glass output of the Stourbridge district. Paul Tyzack was to supply sixteen hundred cases a year. The agreement made Joshua Henzey II the 'sole Merchant' of the output of the Colemans Glasshouse and others 'called or known by the name of the Hooe Glasshouse and the glasshouse in Brettell.' The glass was to be paid for at the rate of 'twenty shillings by the case.'

However, Tyzack suffered an almost immediate setback, when Lyddiat brought an action to eject him from Colemans Glasshouse$_{39}$. Lyddiat succeeded and the partners found new premises half a mile away at Withymoor. Presumably, this characteristically turbulent act by Lyddiat spelled the end of glassmaking at Colemans Glasshouse, as there are no further references after this date.

---

1 Paul Tyzack, son of John Tyzack of Ewhurst, Surrey and his wife Mary, nee Bungard, b. c1592. Tyzack or Tyzacke is the anglicised form of the Lorrainer name du Thisac.

2 Paul Tyzack leased the land from Henry Addenbrooke's widow, Gertrude, nee Spratt.

3 D.R. Guttery, *From Broad-glass to Cut Crystal* (1956), p6.

4 Suhanna the daughter of Francis Conklyn bap. 12th Mar 1613. Francis was probably a brother or cousin of John Conckclaine who was working at Bagot's Park in 1609.

5 Eccleshall PR, mar. James Leggeeye, Frenchman of the Songles, glassmaker, and Judith Tyzack of the same place, 31st Aug 1602. Note that despite its French-sounding name, the Songles is an area of woodland near Eccleshall in Staffordshire.

6 Zachariah Tyzack, son of John Tyzack of Ewhurst, Surrey and his wife Mary, nee Bungard, b. c1596.

7 Sir Edward Zouche was appointed president of the Council in Wales by James I in 1602 and soon became one of his favourite courtiers.

8 APC, 1613-14, 634-5.

9 Proclamation of James I Touching Grievances, 10th Jul 1621. Quoted in full in W. H. Price, *The English Patents of Monopoly* (1906), pp166-8.

10 APC, xxxvll. 400-1.

11 APC, xxxviii.8.

12 APC, xxxviii (1621-23) 8; Smedmore B2/4.
13 John Squire ran a glasshouse at Wollaton, Nottinghamshire. In Dec 1615 Sir Percival Willoughby made an agreement with Sir Robert Mansell whereby Willoughby leased to Mansell a great barn at Wollaton for seven years with dwelling house and garden adjoining them in the occupation of Jacob Henzey and John Squire. He also contracted to deliver at the barn as much coal as Mansell's workmen should require to use in the two glass furnaces lately erected in the barn (University Library, Nottingham, Middleton Collection 165/131). On 23rd Jul 1617, arrangements were being made to build a further glasshouse and furnace near the coalpits at Awsworth (H.M.C., MSS. of Lord Middleton, 499-500). Ibid, R.S. Smith. The Awsworth glasshouse was run by John Conckclaine until its closure about 1634 when he emigrated to Salem, Massachusetts with his younger brother, Ananias Conckclaine, glassmaker of Kingswinford.
14 Isaac du Houx of Haughton Green glasshouse, Denton, near Manchester.
15 After working alongside the Tyzacks in Staffordshire, Abraham Bigo I (b c1591) established works in Nov 1617 to manufacture green drinking glasses at the Isle of Purbeck, in Dorset, where he rented a house and land from Sir William Clavell, a Dorsetshire squire and colliery proprietor. The venture only lasted five years. The business prospered, but Clavell refused to agree to the terms of the monopolist Mansell. After many bitter disputes Clavell was committed to the Marshalsea Prison in the summer of 1623 (APC 39 (1623-25) 34, 82; State Papers 14/151/31). When Clavell refused the Privy Council's ruling that he should sign an agreement with Mansell the order was given to demolish the glassworks. Op cit D.W. Crossley, *Sir William Clavell's Glasshouse at Kimmeridge, Dorset: The Excavations of 1980-81* (1987), pp340-382.
16 Mansell's specified price. State Papers, Domestic, James I, v 162 No. 64. Reasons against Sir R. Mansell's Patent 16th Apr 1624 para. 4. Printed in full in A. Hartshorne, *Old English Glasses* (1897), pp423-426.
17 Phillip Roles, a 'chrate carrier' was buried at Kingswinford in 1681. Adam Robinson, a 'glass carrier', was buried at Kingswinford in 1718.
18 *An Acte for Punyshment of Rogues, Vagabonds and sturdy beggars* (39 Elizabeth, c.4), 1597. Statutes of the Realm, v 4, Pt II., pp889 seq. A full transcription appears in R.H. Tawney & Eileen Power, *Tudor Economic Documents*, v 2 (1924), pp354-362.

19 Paul Tyzack, son of Paul and Bridgitt Tyzack, bap. 2nd Feb 1618, Kingswinford.
20 Mar. Paul Tyzack and Joyce Lydiate, 11th Jul 1640, Oldswinford.
21 Joyce Lyddiat, daughter of John Lyddiat and his first wife Jane, nee Rudyard.
22 John Lyddiat, son of Hugh Lyddiat and his wife Mary, nee Skrimshire.
23 Wollaston Hall stood west of the River Stour and south of the road from Amblecote to Kinver. It was a fine half-timbered building dating from 1617. It probably incorporated some of the timbers of the original Holbeche House as these were purchased by John Lyddiat following the investigation into Stephen Lyttelton's title. After suffering fire damage the hall was dismantled in 1926 and shipped to the United States.
24 H.S. Grazebrook, *The Heraldry of Worcestershire* (1873), p344.
25 DA, Earl of Dudley's Estate Records, Leases, Humble Ward to Paul Tyzacke, 24th Mar 1653; Humble Ward to Paul Henzey, 22nd May 1654.
26 PRO, 1664 Chancery Proceedings.
27 Robert Foley, son of Richard 'Fiddler' Foley and his second wife Alice, nee Brindley, bap. 19th Sep 1624, Dudley St. Thomas's. Robert Foley made his fortune during the Civil War making canons for the King at Dudley and pikes for his infantry at his mills at Kinver; the Hyde on the Stour and Gothersley on the Smestow Brook. He was granted arms on 12th Dec 1671 when he was High Sheriff of Worcester. The grant recites that he 'hath at all times been a loyal and faithful subject, and since His Majesty's happy restoration hath in regard both of his own inclination and of his great stock, and ability in managing the manufacture of iron, been chiefly intrusted to supply His Majesty's naval stores therewith, wherin he hath employed vast sums of money, and hath with singular care and industry acquitted himself therin, and still pursues the same.' K.4, College of Arms, Folio 80; d. 1676.
28 Zachariah Tyzack, son of Zachariah Tyzack and his wife Elizabeth, nee Beare, bap. 20th Jan 1621, Oldswinford.
29 Abraham Bigo II, son of Abraham Bigo I and his wife Hester, bap. 19th Apr 1612, Biddulph, Staffordshire.
30 WRO, Palfrey Collection.
31 J. Houghton, *A Collection for Improvement of Husbandry and Trade*, ix, no. 198, 15 May 1696.
32 WRO, Palfrey Collection.
33 PRO, 1664 Chancery Proceedings.

34 Paul Tyzack, bur. 28th Jun 1665, Kingswinford.
35 WRO, Will of Paul Tyzack, 5th Jul 1665.
36 Meriall Tyzack, daughter of Paul Tyzack and his wife Joyce, nee Lyddiat, bap. 15th May 1647, Kingswinford.
37 Mar. Seazer Rackett and Meriall Tyzack, 21st Sep 1665, Kingswinford.
38 Robert Foley appears in Samuel Pepys' diary. Pepys writes in 1664 of 'Folly the Ironmonger' treating Pepys and others connected with the Navy office to 'a good plain dinner' seasoned with 'right merry discourse.'
39 Ibid, D.R. Guttery, p10.

CHAPTER 9

Ridgrave Glasshouse, Hungary Hill

Ridgrave Glasshouse stood a few yards on the Lye side of what was then called Hungary Hill Lane, not far from the junction with Halfpenny Hall Lane[1], 0.7 miles east of Stourbridge town centre and 285 yards south of where now stands the Stambermill railway viaduct. It was possibly the first or second glasshouse to be built in the Stourbridge district although the only evidence to that effect is anecdotal. It is known that the Tyzacks and Henzeys arrived in the district about the same time and the Tyzacks are known to have commenced work at Colemans Glasshouse about 1612. However, the first documented evidence of a Henzey glasshouse is at Brettell Lane in 1630. It therefore seems a reasonable supposition that the Ridgrave Glasshouse was started by the Henzeys some time between 1612 and 1630.

Joshua Henzey[2] was the patriarch of the Stourbridge Henzey glassmaking dynasty. He came to the area via Wisborough Green and Eccleshall, arriving before 1618, when he married Joan Brettell[3]. His bride was of a substantial family, clear evidence that the 'art, feat and mystery' practised by the Henzeys gave them access to local society. Just six days after their marriage, Joan gave birth to their first son, Ananias[4].

Joshua was related to the brothers, Edward and Peregrine Henzey[5], who were in the area immediately after 1615. Edward Henzey had tramped through all the early glassmaking areas of England: the Weald, Eccleshall, Bagot's Park and eventually died at Amblecote in 1621[6]. In his will[7] Edward names 'Perrigrin Hennsey my brother', and 'Joshua Hensey my kinsman' as overseers. These three, Joshua, Edward and Peregrine Henzey probably formed the first Henzey 'chair' here.

The first documented record of the glasshouse is in 1699 when it was owned by John Wheeler[8]. John Wheeler was certainly not a glassmaker and presumably employed others to run it for him[9]. Wheeler was a wealthy ironmaker and sythesmith who lived at Wollaston Hall and learned his trade as the managing partner of Philip Foley's Hales[owen] forge[10]. He became a magistrate for Worcester and founded a charity school at Redhill, Oldswinford. Some time before 1700 he purchased the beautiful Wooton Lodge[11] from the third Baronet Fleetwood.

John Wheeler died in 1708[12] and in an extensive will[13] proved in PCC he bequeathed the Ridgrave Glasshouse and Wooton Lodge to his oldest son John[14]. His second son Richard[15] inherited Wollaston Hall. Wheeler's will stipulates, 'my mind and desire is that both my younger sons Richard and Edward[16] shall be brought up in and to my trade . . . to manage and carry on my own ironworks and my shares and partnerships in the ironworks wherein I have share or interest.'[17]

John junior carried out his father's wishes. In 1710, in his capacity of executor of his father's estate he purchased Lye Forge[18] and leased it to his brother Richard. He moved to Wooton Lodge in 1716.

Richard lived at Wollaston Hall and worked Lye Forge on a twenty-one year lease from his brother John. However, in 1724 the brothers sold their entire Stour business of Cradley Furnace, Cradley and Lye Forges and Cradley Rod Mill to their manager Edward Kendall who had previously been John Wheeler senior's clerk.

Richard married Mary Egerton in 1715[19] and they raised a family of six children in Wollaston Hall. The youngest, Edward[20] moved to St. Clement Danes parish, London and in 1746 sold large estates in Wollaston and Stourbridge that he apparently owned, although he was only aged twenty-four and his father Richard was still alive[21]. The land at Stourbridge included 'all that Glass house situate in Oldswinford . . commonly called Ridggrave Glasshouse.' It also included 'the parcel of land . . . commonly called the Shoulder of Mutton.' This is the field now bisected by the railway embankment south of the Stourbridge to Birmingham road and south of the Stambermill viaduct. The transfer of land was to Bertie Burgh and James Unwin of Holborn, London. The Unwins were related to the Wheelers and eventually came to live at Wooton Lodge.

John junior had only one child, a daughter Penelope$_{22}$ and upon his death she inherited the Ridgrave Glasshouse. Penelope married$_{23}$ a wealthy banker Thomas Kynnersley of nearby Loxley Hall$_{24}$. Penelope remained the owner of the glasshouse until 1761 when she sold it to John Pidcock, John Foxall and Thomas Raybould. We do not know how Pidcock, Foxall and Raybould used the works, if at all. John Pidcock was already operating the Dial Glasshouses at the time and it seems likely that his only involvement with Ridgrave Glasshouse was to supply capital.

Sometime after about 1770, but before 1776, John Hill$_{25}$ took occupation of the Ridgrave Glasshouse. He was the owner of Wordsley Flint Glassworks in May 1776, but it is difficult to discover at which of these two glassworks he first started. The most likely hypothesis is that he first rented the old Ridgrave Glasshouse until he could afford to build Wordsley Flint Glassworks. Hill was a glassmaker of Oldswinford when he married Mary Russell$_{26}$ in 1771. Their marriage was by a licence$_{27}$ in which the bondsman was Martin Paddey$_{28}$, a mercer of Oldswinford.

In 1776 John Hill worked the Ridgrave Glasshouse while it belonged to Thomas Raybould, sythesmith of Amblecote Hall$_{29}$. Both Hill and Raybould were among the seventy-two named proprietors in the Stourbridge Canal Act the following year. There are no further references to Ridgrave Glasshouse after this date. The glass excise duty had been doubled in 1777 and Hill probably decided it was no longer economic to operate the works. He then concentrated his efforts at Wordsley Flint Glassworks. The glasshouse is clearly marked, labelled Old Glafs house, standing in Glafshouse Piece on a map of Hungary Hill and the Stambermill area c1810. In 1908 W Beddoes Moore wrote:

> 'About 58 or 60 years ago my father rented off Captain
> Allin a small ironworks or forge at Clatterbach, which was

worked by a large water-wheel in the Stour. He also rented the fields under the Viaduct and the cottages on the other side of the Stour, which I have heard were at one time a cloth works; this accounts for their being so close to the water side. The Glass House, as it was always called when I was a boy, and no doubt there were people living at that time who could remember it being a glasshouse, stood on this ground, with other buildings adjoining it which were probably used in connection with it. The place was afterwards used for making clay tobacco pipes.'₃₀

---

1 Since renamed as Junction Road.

2 Joshua Henzey, son of Ananias Henzey, b. c1592. No record of Joshua's baptism in this country has been found, but he was almost certainly born in England, as his father Ananias had arrived in England c1590, aged about 20. Ananias was the son of Georges de Hennezel, originally of the Houdrichapelle Glasshouse, and his wife Moingeon de Massey. Georges moved with his cousin Charles to Montbéliard in 1574, where he became embroiled in a dispute about *droits de chasse*. After being imprisoned, Georges died sometime before 1590. In that year the Community of Granges prosecuted his widow Moingeon and her children Ananias and Israëlle de Hennezel, although minors. Moingeon promptly departed for England, taking Ananias with her. Israëlle returned to the village of Granges. Op cit Germaine Rose-Villequey, *Verre et Verriers de Lorraine* (1971), p470.

3 Mar. Joshua Henzey and Joan Brettell, 29th Sep 1618, Kingswinford.

4 Ananias Henzey, son of Joshua Henzey and his wife Joan, nee Brettell, bap. 5th Oct 1618, Kingswinford.

5 An extant purchase contract dated 17 Jun 1620 in the seigneurie of Houdrichapelle names Edouard et Peregrin de Hennezel, fils de Nicolas de Hennezel, demeurant à Amblecôte, compté de Stafford - pays d'Angleterre. Ibid, Germaine Rose Villequey, p454.

6 Edward Henzey, bur. 17th Jul 1621, Oldswinford.

7 PRO, PCC will of Edward Henzey, 18th Feb 1622.

8 John Wheeler b c1646.

9 The plot is labelled Glasshouse Piece, owned by Mr Wheeler, on J. Bach's 1699 plan of Oldswinford.

10 Hales[owen] forge was owned by Philip Foley in the 1670s and was managed by John Downing. Downing took it over himself in the 1680s but then ceased operation. In 1692 the furnace reverted to Philip Foley who went into partnership with several others including John Wheeler as managing partner. In 1705 John Wheeler bought out his partners and took sole control of Hales Furnace and Whittington Forge.

11 Wooton Lodge is an early seventeenth century house still standing one mile SW of Wooton, in the parish of Ellastone, near Eccleshall in Staffordshire. It has been described as 'the most beautiful and most beautifully situated house in Staffordshire.' It remained the home of the Wheelers and their descendants, the Unwins until the Second World War. It was the residence of Lady Diana Mosley in 1939 and her husband Sir Oswald Mosley occasionally stayed there. By 1974 it became the home of the Bamford family, famous for their manufacture of JCB excavators at Rocester.

12 John Wheeler, d. 27th Nov 1708; bur. 1st Dec 1708, Oldswinford; memorial on wall of north aisle in Oldswinford Church.

13 PRO, PROB11/508 115-121, will of John Wheeler, proved 1708.

14 John Wheeler, son of John Wheeler and his second wife Mary, nee Astley, bap. 21st Oct 1687, Oldswinford.

15 Richard Wheeler, son of John Wheeler and his second wife Mary, nee Astley, bap. 14th Aug 1694, Oldswinford.

16 Edward Wheeler, son of John Wheeler and his second wife Mary, nee Astley, bap. 22nd Nov 1696, Oldswinford.

17 The most valuable part of his estate was his share in the Foleys' ironworks in and around the Forest of Dean.

18 Lye Forge, on the River Stour was originally a corn mill owned by the Addenbrookes (1622 Perambulation of the Parish of Oldswinford). On 25th Mar 1697 John and Dorcas Addenbrooke granted a ninety-nine year lease to Zachary Downing, the son of John Downing who had managed, then owned Hales[owen] forge. Zachary converted the corn mill to a forge and ran it until his bankruptcy in 1710. His assignees sold the business to the executors of John Wheeler who were assisted in the purchase by William Rea of Monmouth who had succeeded John Wheeler as managing partner of the Foleys' ironworks.

19 Mar. Richard Wheeler and Mary, daughter of Peter Egerton of Shaw, 1st Jun 1715, Flixton, Lancashire.

20 Edward Wheeler, son of Richard Wheeler and his wife Mary, nee Egerton, bap. 4th Mar 1722, Oldswinford.
21 Deed in possession of Mrs Freda Jones of Springfield, Rowley Regis described in Black Country Bugle, 18th Oct 2001, p18.
22 Penelope Wheeler, daughter of John and his wife Penelope, bap. 7th Nov 1714, Oldswinford.
23 Mar. Thomas Kinnersly and Penelope Wheeler, 9th Oct 1739, Ellastone, Staffordshire.
24 Loxley Hall stands 2.5m southwest of Uttoxeter and has been the family home of the Kynnersleys for centuries. In the 20th century ownership passed to the Sneyd-Kinnersley's who are descended from Penelope, oldest daughter of Thomas Kynnersley and his wife Penelope, nee Wheeler.
25 John Hill, son of Waldron Hill and his second wife Elizabeth Tyzack, bap. 7th Sep 1749, Kingswinford.
26 Mar. John Hill and Mary Russell, 27th Oct 1771, Oldswinford. Mary Russell, daughter of Thomas Russell and his wife Anne, nee Haycock, bap. 27th Jun 1751, Oldswinford. Mary was the niece of Edward Russell who operated the Heath Glassworks.
27 WRO, marriage licence dated 26th Oct 1771.
28 At some stage between the years 1776 and 1782 Martin Paddey was John Hill's partner.
29 DA, Ashwood Hay and Wall Heath Enclosure Act, 16 Geo III, cap 33, 1776.
30 County Express, Apr 1908.

CHAPTER 10

Holloway End Glasshouse, Amblecote

After the Tyzacks and the Henzeys arrived, the building of a glassworks at Holloway End, Amblecote marks the establishment in the district of a third Lorrainer family, the Titterys[1]. Daniel Tittery was the founder of the Holloway End Glasshouse and is described as 'a person of piety, a refugee from Nantz [sic].'[2] The date of establishment of the Holloway End Glasshouse is open to conjecture, but a survey of 1623 contains the earliest extant reference[3]. The glassworks was certainly in existence by 1639 when it is mentioned in a deed[4]. It stood on the west side of the road, 500 yards up the Holloway into Amblecote from the bridge over the Stour. The term Holloway occurs in many parts of England and implies a well-used route, deeply rutted by the regular passage of traffic[5].

In 1639 Daniel Tittery succeeded Joshua Henzey as Overseer of the Poor; further evidence, if any is needed, of the civic duties the Lorrainers willingly undertook. Daniel died intestate in 1641[6] and administration of his estate was granted to his widow Anne, nee Tompson, otherwise Beare. In 1650 she was still living at Holloway End House and owned the nearby glasshouse[7].

Daniel and Anne had four sons who presumably all learned the trade of glassmaking from their father. Joshua[8], the youngest son, moved initially to Newcastle-upon-Tyne. In 1683 either he or his son of the same name was indentured to sail to Philadelphia and set up a glassworks. He sailed on the Pennsylvania Company's ship, the Jeffrey, arriving in August 1683, making him probably the first ever glassmaker in America. The Bristol Port book of 6th July 1683 shows that William Penn was sending '18 hhds of earth for making glass', to go on the Unicorn, Thomas Cooper, Master[9].

Daniel's daughter, Ann, married Thomas Rogers in 1652[10]. Rogers, originally from Wales[11], took over the running of the glassworks. In 1663 he entered into an agreement with Joshua Henzey that made Henzey the 'sole Merchant' of the output of the Hooe glasshouse and others 'called or known by the name of Colman's Glasshouse and the glasshouse in Brettell.' The glass was to be paid for at the rate of 'twenty shillings by the case.'[12] The glasshouse at Holloway End was known as the Hoo. Various authors suggest this name is derived from the de Houx family. Although Jacob du Houx and his wife Anne, nee Tisack had three children baptised in the area, it was more likely taken from land called Who Place. This was held in 1541 by Leonard Beare and later passed to the family of Tompson, otherwise Beare[13]. Thomas Rogers I of Amblecote died in 1680[14]. An inventory[15] was prepared by Edward Bradley and Gray Jevon valuing his goods and chattels at £214 7s 10d. His will was proved in 1681[16] in which he refers to being in a glassmaking business in co-partnership with his son Thomas Rogers[17]. He left to his widow Anne 'one halfe part of all the house glasshouses warehouses outhouses buildings lands and premises now in the possession of me the said Thomas Rogers the elder and my son Thomas Rogers the younger.' Thomas Rogers II followed the same path as many prosperous glassmakers and became a churchwarden of Oldswinford for the years 1701 and 1702.

By 1704 the glasshouse was being run by Paul Rogers[18]. That year he married Mary Haselwood[19] the only daughter of his stepmother. Their marriage was by a licence[20] and was accompanied by a letter from Paul's father, Thomas Rogers, dated 13th February 1704, to Richard Tristram. The letter confirms the relationships in what would otherwise be a most confusing arrangement:

> 'Mr Tristram, I and my wife have agreed upon a marriage between my son Paul and her daughter I defer you to assist my son Paul in taking a licence and you will oblige your servant. Tho Rogers.'

Paul's grandmother Anne, nee Tittery, had remarried Edward Jackson in 1683[21] and while she was still living Paul's father, Thomas Rogers, had to pay her an annuity of £33. Similarly, after the death of Anne Jackson, Thomas Rogers had to pay 'to his brother-in-law Henry Sanders, and to Sarah his wife' the sum of £180.

Thomas Rogers II died in 1716[22]. He had made a will on 8th August 1706[23] that shows he owned three freehold houses in Amblecote, two in Stourbridge and leases in Strankley, Worcestershire. He left one half of his glass trade and stock to his oldest son Thomas III[24]. The other half was left to his second son Paul and Paul's wife Mary. His youngest son George contested a codicil concerning two estates, claiming it to be a forgery. Joseph Bradley, glass seller of Deptford, appeared personally to confirm the handwriting was that of Thomas Rogers. The inventory[25] was appraised by John Bradley and Thomas Bolton and valued the deceased's goods and chattels at £5,464 12s 2d. It includes several interesting references to his trade and divides the contents between the 'Broad and Bottle glass House' and the 'White House', suggesting two separate furnaces were being worked. Some of his goods, particularly the heavy ones such as sand and lead, were valued 'In the Warehouse at Bewdley' confirming this once-thriving port on the River Severn to be the route to Stourbridge for raw materials. 'Two Hundred Ton of Ashes'[26] was valued at £150. 'one Ton and five hundred of Salt petre' was valued at £80. 'Half a Ton of Cullet' was valued at £14, showing what a valuable commodity it was. Most interestingly, 'five cases of Crown Glass' was valued at £15 15s. This is the earliest recorded reference to crown glass in the locality and it shows what a large premium there was for crown over broad-glass[27]. A final item of interest to the modern businessman is that his debtors, at £3,307, represented over 60% of his net worth.

A crown glasshouse exterior

A receipt issued in 1717 shows that Rogers, who had previously made bottles, broad and crown glass, had begun making tableglass. This diversification was an astute move that kept him in business when most of the broad-glass houses were going bankrupt. It reads, '19 Feb 1717 received of Mr John Foley six shillings being in full for a parsell of glass. Thos Rogers.'[28]

Thomas Rogers III did not enjoy his inheritance for very long. He never married and died in 1723[29], aged forty-seven. He made a will on 20th November 1723 in which he bequeathed his share in glasshouses with land and property to his nephew Thomas Rogers IV[30].

Paul and Thomas IV then ran the glassworks. An obscure reference to their partnership exists in the Poor Law records of Oldswinford. In 1725 a parish removal order was issued to remove a glassmaker called John Holliman from Stourbridge to Amblecote in which he is described as an apprentice to Thomas and Paul Rogers, glassmakers.

Paul Rogers was clearly a man of some worth. A Perambulation Roll of the parish of Oldswinford, dated 1733[31], refers to 'the Level Leasow which is Paul Rogers's'. He died in 1737[32], aged fifty-seven and his will was proved at Worcester[33]. The will describes him as a glassmaker of Holloway End and made his sons, Thomas Rogers IV and Paul Rogers junior, his beneficiaries. Paul junior inherited 'one half part of all my houses, glasshouses, warehouses, storehouses, lands, tenements in Amblecote which were heretofore purchased by my late father of John Newborough.' However, after his inheritance, nothing further can be found about Paul Rogers junior. Perhaps he died; perhaps he left the area? The other beneficiary, Thomas Rogers IV became a very wealthy and influential man, with interests in ironmaking as well as glass. In 1731 he married Martha[34], the daughter of Richard Knight, a wealthy ironmaster of Downton Castle[35], by whom he had twelve children. He was elected to serve as High Sheriff of Worcestershire in 1750[36] but never served in that office. Described as 'a Tory of the old school'[37], he resided at The Hill, a seven-bedroom mansion in Amblecote later developed to form the Corbett Hospital. As its name suggests, the mansion house stood on the top of the hill, on the opposite side of the road to the glassworks. It was a spacious brick mansion, 'approached by a long and lofty avenue of sycamores'[38], which was probably built by John Grove, who lived there in 1724[39]. Thomas Rogers' poet grandson, Samuel, described it fondly as:

> 'yon old Mansion frowning thro' the trees, Whose hollow turret wooes the whistling breeze.'[40]

At the end of 1753, Thomas Rogers IV—although retaining his

glassmaking business—broadened his interests by entering into partnership with Daniel Radford[41], 'a large warehouseman of Cheapside'[42].

Thomas Rogers V[43], the oldest (surviving) son of Thomas Rogers IV, left The Hill about 1756, on reaching his age of majority. He left the Tory atmosphere of the Worcestershire country house for the entirely different moral and social conditions of Stoke Newington, Middlesex[44]. Here, he won the esteem of his father's partner and married his only daughter, Mary Radford, in 1760[45]. The newlyweds moved into Daniel Radford's house at Newington Green where they lived until Radford died[46].

Thomas V clearly impressed his father-in-law who lent him £2,000 so that on 1st January 1761 he was able to buy a share in the partnership with his father and father-in-law. Thomas prospered in business and in 1765 joined George and Thomas Welch, bankers in Cornhill, to trade as Welch & Rogers[47]. In the general election of 1780 he stood as a Whig parliamentary candidate for Coventry. The campaign was subject to so much rioting that the election was postponed. When the new House of Commons assembled on 31st October, there were no members for Coventry. In December another election was held and after more disturbances Rogers and his Whig colleague, Sir Thomas Halifax, topped the poll. However, the Tories petitioned and after some disgraceful gerrymandering the seats were awarded to the defeated Tory candidates. Thomas Rogers was so disgusted he never stood again at any election.

During all of this, Thomas and Mary had a family growing up around them in Daniel Radford's house. They had five sons and five daughters, although two daughters and one son died in infancy. Their oldest son, Daniel[48], named after his grandfather, returned to the Midlands after a Cambridge education and a sojourn in Lincoln. As a magistrate for Worcestershire he lived the life of a country squire at Wassell Grove, his estate in the north west of Hagley parish[49]. Their third son, Samuel[50], achieved fame as a poet, wit and art patron and is noted as the author of *The Pleasures of Memory*.

Meanwhile, back in Stourbridge, a list of glasshouses in 1760 shows that Thomas Rogers IV was manufacturing broad-glass, bottles, phials and flint glass, best and ordinary[51]. However, in 1768 he decided to quit the glass trade due to his declining health and the glassworks was advertised to let:

> 'To be let and entered on immediately. The Glassworks belonging to Mr. Thomas Rogers near Stourbridge, with all accommodations necessary for carrying on the trade. Further particulars may be known of the said Mr. Thomas Rogers or of Mr. Edward Russell, near Stourbridge.'[52]

Presumably this was Edward Russell of the Heath Glassworks. There is no evidence of them having been in partnership, so perhaps he offered to help Thomas Rogers by answering enquiries. There was no immediate purchaser for the works and in 1769 Thomas Rogers was still in possession when there were two cones[53] shown on a map of Amblecote[54]. He placed a further advertisement in 1771, this time not naming the glassworks[55]. The advertisement was successful and the glassworks was let. Thomas Rogers IV continued to live at The Hill until his death in 1775[56]. His daughters continued to live there, still an active part of the Worcestershire 'county set' until it was sold to Thomas Homfray[57] in 1799.

The celebrated scientist James Keir[58] leased Holloway End Glasshouse from Thomas Roger IV. On 19th October 1771 fellow scientist Dr William Small[59] wrote to James Watt[60]:

> 'Mr Keir has turned glass maker at Stourbridge and has married a beauty . . . you must get Mr Keir customers, if you can, for white flint glass, tho' by and by he will make other kinds.'

On 16th December 1771 he wrote:

> 'Pray do not your Glasgow merchts send abundance of glass to America? If Mr Keir should be employed by them, altho at present he makes only flint glass, he will provide them with any kind they may want upon the best of terms. '

Keir took into partnership John Taylor[61], Samuel Skey[62] and others on 16th November 1772[63]. The following day Small again wrote to Watt:

> 'Mr Keir has just finished [making] an agreement which

gives him the management of a great glass company, & I hope it will render his situation very commodious'[64].

Keir managed the works and lived at Holloway End House[65]. Whitworth's canal map of 1774 still labelled the land at The Hill as Mr Rogers's; the outline of a cone at Holloway Head is shown, but not named. Keir was an enquiring man, typical of the scientist-entrepreneur of his period, who used the glassworks, not only as a business, but also as a laboratory in which to carry out experiments, particularly on the properties of alkalis.

A crown glasshouse interior

Keir sent a bill to Matthew Boulton[66] on 22nd October 1772, accompanied by a letter referring to his 'chemical operations in an old glass-house'[67]. Chemistry was revolutionised in the Georgian period in the same way physics had been under the Stuarts. Great progress was made partly due to improved experimental techniques, in particular quantitative analysis. Scientific research went hand in hand with entrepreneurship. This was the period when the Lunar Society[68] brought together the leading intellectuals of the time. Scientists, inventors and engineers James Watt and Matthew Boulton, poet, scientist and inspired physician Erasmus Darwin[69] and potter and scientist Josiah Wedgwood. James Keir became a member of the Lunar Society in 1767, the year after its formation. Erasmus Darwin, his lifelong friend, with whom he studied medicine at Edinburgh, had probably introduced him. Dr Darwin wrote of the Lunar Society:

> 'Lord, what invention, what wit, what rhetoric, metaphysical and mechanical, and pyrotechnical, will be on the wing, bandied like a shuttlecock from one to another of your troop of philosophers[70].'

Mary Anne Schimmelpenninck[71], the oldest daughter of the Quaker anthropologist and industrialist, Samuel Galton[72], comments on the Lunar Society in her autobiography:

> 'Mr Keir was the man of wit, and the man of the world, who maintained the accord of the Members of this Society. But Doctor Darwin was as great a necessity to its existence. Probably the secret of its origin and success may be found in the firm friendship, dating from boyhood, subsisting between these two men of independent, original, and different characters, acting in concert with each other for the accomplishment of one purpose, viz., that of drawing to a single focus the enlightenment and genius of the scientific men of the age.'[73]

Keir was the leading light of the Lunar Society. Immediately after his retirement from the army, he became a member of the London Philosophical Society that met in Old Slaughter's Coffee House in Soho. Here he met Sir Joseph Banks[74], the naturalist and explorer, John Hunter, the anatomist whom Keir had known since his Edinburgh student days, Sir Charles Blagden, Secretary of the Royal Society, Captain James Cook, Smeaton the designer of the Eddystone lighthouse, Nevil Maskelyne[75] the astronomer and many others at the forefront of invention[76]. Keir had been introduced to Josiah Wedgwood[77] by Erasmus Darwin in 1767[78]. Facing similar problems in their processes of manufacture, the two found many interests in common. In glazing his ceramics, Wedgwood frequently used a frit of ground flint glass. Keir supplied him with the recipe for making flint glass from raw materials. He sought advice from Keir on the glazing process and annealing. Wedgwood wrote to Thomas Bentley[79] on 14th February 1776:

> I have spent some Hours with Mr Keir of Stourbridge . . . & have had some good lectures upon annealing, but it will be rather difficult to put them in [pract]ice upon our Jaspers, as they must either b[e] taken out of the Kiln red hot to be put into the Ann[ealer] or the Kiln in which they are fired must be converted into an Annealer . . . '

In return for this advice, Wedgwood offered to help Keir with the problem of cords in flint glass. Although hardly noticeable in decorative glass, imperfections were a serious problem in glass to be used for lenses. Over a period of five years Keir and Wedgwood carried out many experiments and corresponded extensively[80].

Keir's knowledge of annealing, or the slow cooling of vitreous substances, was based upon these experiments and with its geological analogy constitutes one of the most significant contributions of Lunar Society members to scientific theory. Keir summarised his findings in a paper read to the Royal Society on 23rd May 1776 entitled *On the Crystallization observed on Glass*.

About 1783[81], Wedgwood consolidated his ideas in a paper entitled *An Attempt to discover the causes of cords and waviness in Flint Glass, and the most probable means of removing them. By Josiah Wedgwood, FRS and Potter to Her Majesty*[82].

In June 1776 James Keir and William Scott[83] were among the seventy-two named proprietors in the Stourbridge Canal Act[84] and about this time William Scott joined the glassmaking partnership[85]. Keir's agreement for the glassworks expired on 1st January 1778 although subsequent records suggest he retained an interest well after this date. Since the previous year he had been wooed by Matthew Boulton to take on the management of Boulton and Watt's Soho Manufactory[86]. Boulton realised that he would have to spend more time in Cornwall where his engines were at work and saw in Keir the combination of practical, entrepreneurial and scientific skills to manage the Soho works in his absence. By the beginning of

October 1778 Boulton went to Cornwall leaving Keir to manage the Soho works. Keir was never introduced into the partnership and insisted on independence to continue his chemical investigations. However, he studiously and conscientiously carried out his duties as manager. For this he was rewarded by a partnership in Watt's new business to sell his invention of the copying press. Ultimately Keir materialised his own ambitions when in 1780 he built his own works for the manufacture of alkali, with a former army colleague Captain Alexander Blair, at Bloomfield Mill, Tipton. Keir remained a partner in the Holloway End business trading as Scott, Keir, Jones and Co.[87] In 1784 Scott, Jones & Co. were running two clay mills, pot rooms and two glassworks in Amblecote[88].

The outline of two cones, on adjacent properties, is shown but not named on Snape's 1785 canal map. In the same year James Keir stated Ireland had kelp and coarse sand for bottles, and that a great quantity of the kelp used in England came from Ireland[89]. It is typical of the scientist Keir to comment on the chemistry of glass rather than its style, design or marketing.

The firm of Scott, Keir, Jones & Co. was still in occupation in 1789[90], but sometime before 1800 two Wordsley glasscutters, James[91] and Thomas[92] Parrish took over the works. Their father, Thomas Parrish, was a partner in a coal mine in the parish of Kingswinford with John Farmer 'at royalty to Messrs. Brettells and Pidcock's.'[93] He probably provided the funds for their venture. The Parrish brothers involved Thomas Hardwick as a partner and in 1800 the local furnace-builder Joseph Richardson built a seven-pot furnace for them[94]. At some point, they involved their older brother, John[95]. Nothing is known of the descent of Thomas Hardwick, nor the reason for his involvement with the Parrish brothers, although Benjamin Richardson refers to John Parrish, who had been a manufacturer at Holloway End, 'parting from Mr Hardwick.'[96] The Parrishs' venture into glass manufacture was short-lived; in 1803 they were bankrupt[97]. They returned to their previous trade and opened a cutting shop in Wordsley where workhouse women turned a large wheel to provide the motive power. Then, about 1809 they turned a barn at Wordsley into a cutting shop and installed a steam engine to power their cutting machines[98].

Their cutting shops are shown on Fowler's 1822 map fronting Brettell Lane, next door to Samuel Edge's pottery[99] and opposite William Seager Wheeley's house[100].

After a short while, the Holloway End Glasshouse was taken by Benjamin Littlewood, who had been in partnership with Thomas Wheeley at Brettell Lane Glasshouses. He moved into Holloway End House and traded in his own name as a flint glass manufacturer[101]. The glasshouse cone at Holloway End is graphically shown on Sherriff's plan of 1812.

The clay for the glasshouse pots in the Waterford Glassworks in Ireland was always obtained from Stourbridge. Several entries in their old account books show clay having been purchased from Littlewood, King and Co. of Stourbridge; another of Littlewood's ventures. In 1816 they were paid £76 12s 5d for thirty-two casks of Stourbridge clay, and in 1823, £57 5s 1d for twelve tons[102].

Benjamin Littlewood is listed as a flint glass manufacturer at Holloway End in successive trade directories of 1818, 1820, 1823 and 1825. By 1828 he was joined by his son, Benjamin II[103], when the firm traded as 'Benjamin Littlewood and Son, flint glass manufacturers'[104]. The newly constituted firm paid £419 2s 3d excise duty on flint glass on 3rd February 1829, but their arrears were £632 16s 9d[105].

Benjamin Littlewood I died sometime between 1830 and 1833 and was succeeded by his son Benjamin II and Thomas Littlewood[106]. Thomas Littlewood paid £3,645 4s excise duty for the year ending 5th January 1833[107], suggesting this was the sixth largest of the sixteen Stourbridge/Dudley glasshouses of the day. In 1833, Benjamin Littlewood II retired and Thomas Littlewood was joined in partnership by John Berry, son of William Berry, had been in partnership with glassmaker Rice H. Harris[108] of Birmingham, until their partnership was dissolved on 9th August 1832[109].

In 1834 Benjamin Richardson of Wordsley Flint Glassworks wrote in a letter to his brother that rumours in the trade were that business was so bad 'Littlewood and Berry were very likely to shut up for a time'[110], although this did not occur. Littlewood and Berry were still manufacturing plain and cut flint glass the following year[111].

Henry Causer Ensell, one of many children of Charles Ensell

II, baptised three of his children on 21st September 1838 at Kingswinford. The parish register records him as 'Clerk to Messrs. Littlewood and Berry.' Charles Ensell II had been a partner in the firm of Bradley, Ensells and Holt at the White House and Red House Glassworks.

The firm traded as Littlewood & Berry, Holloway Head Glassworks, making plain and cut flint glass. Thomas Littlewood lived at Woscot House and John Berry lived at Holloway End[112]. Benjamin Littlewood II, who had retired in 1833, died in 1844[113], aged seventy-five.

Trade up to 1843 was extremely depressed and although recovery began in 1844 Thomas Littlewood and John Berry were driven to drastic measures to stay in business. They were accused of an attempt to evade excise duty and their penalty was to be banned from participating in any trade upon which duty was payable. Inevitably, the firm collapsed and the glassworks was sold. Thomas Littlewood moved to Water Orton[114] and took up farming. John Berry took a commission from a foreign glass manufacturer to sell their goods in England[115].

On 29th September 1844 Edward Webb[116] of Wordsley and his cousin Joseph Webb[117] of Amblecote formed a partnership[118] and took over the glassworks to manufacture flint glass[119]. Edward and Joseph were cousins of Thomas Webb who operated Platts Glassworks. Edward had previously been a farmer. Joseph had worked as a packer for Webb & Richardson at the Wordsley Flint Glassworks and in 1841 worked as a clerk for his cousin Thomas at Platts Glassworks. They agreed that Joseph would make the metal and Edward would handle the commercial activities of the business[120].

The Webbs took over the works at a time when trade unions were just beginning to be established in the glass industry. Employers similarly began to combine. When the Master Flint Glass Cutters met in 1845 Edward Webb, representing E. & J. Webb, was among employers from all over the country who attended[121].

The state of antagonism between employer and employee was demonstrated when Patrick Lowe—a workman of the Webbs—

was summoned in February 1846. His crime was 'absenting himself from work and deserting his service.' This was an offence under the Masters and Workmans Act of 1823, which the unions strenuously fought to repeal. Lowe was sentenced to one-month imprisonment after stating in court he 'would rather serve time in goal than remain with his present employer.' Problems continued and by 1847 there was increasing disharmony between the employers and the workforce. A circular was issued anonymously by Benjamin Richardson of Wordsley Flint Glassworks to the flint glass manufacturers of the United Kingdom for the purpose of regulating prices and fixing wages. Of six replies still in existence, the only one from a Stourbridge firm was in support, from E. & J. Webb of 'Hollowayend Glassworks', dated 31st March 1847.

In October 1850 Joseph and Edward Webb dissolved their partnership[122]. The main reason was that Edward Webb was becoming more interested in milling than he was in glassmaking and this caused some disagreement between them. Joseph Webb therefore left to take on Coalbournhill Glassworks vacated by Joseph Stevens, leaving Edward Webb in sole control of Holloway End Glasshouse.

In 1851 Edward Webb lived with his wife and family at Wordsley and employed a hundred hands[123]. In 1853 he left Holloway End and moved to join his brother William at the White House Glassworks.

The glassworks was taken by William Richardson[124] and Elijah Smith[125]. Both Richardson and Smith had been glassmakers working for the firm of W.H., B. & J. Richardson at the Wordsley Flint Glassworks. The Richardsons' business had become insolvent in February 1852 and William Richardson[126] and Elijah Smith were among many others, such as Philip Pargeter and John Northwood, who took the opportunity to set up their own businesses.

In 1858 Elijah Smith and William Richardson were joined by Frederick James[127] the oldest son of Richard Mills of the Albert Glassworks. Frederick borrowed £950 from his father, which presumably provided his capital[128]. Little is known about his early life except that he had been an apprentice in a nail warehouse[129].

It was not an auspicious time to be investing in a glass business. Faced with an outbreak of strikes, the employers responded by holding a meeting on 1st November 1858 at the Talbot Hotel, Stourbridge, where they formed a manufacturers' organisation. Elijah Smith, William Richardson and Frederick James Mills became founder members of the Association of Flint Glass Makers. From October 1858 onwards the strike spread throughout the district and in December the Association of Flint Glass Makers enforced a national lockout that lasted for seven months. After the lockout of 1859[130], their claim from the manufacturers defence fund suggests they ran the fifth largest of the thirteen firms in the Midlands Association[131].

In 1860 the firm was making flint glass and trading as Richardson, Mills & Smith[132]. In 1861 William Richardson lived with his family at Holloway End, a glass manufacturer employing seventy men, sixteen boys and six females[133]. This implies he was the third largest employer of the six main Stourbridge glassworks in 1861. Frederick James Mills left the partnership by mutual consent on 13th August 1861 to join his second cousin William Webb Boulton at the Audnam Glassworks. Frederick received £2,000 for his share, which suggests a healthy profit for his short-lived investment.

The firm subsequently traded as Richardson & Smith[134]. William Richardson was still a glass manufacturer living at Holloway End in 1871[135]. Richardson & Smith occupied the works until 1873[136] but then abruptly ceased to trade.

In 1874 another former employee of the Richardsons of Wordsley Flint Glassworks, George Castrey took over the Holloway End Glasshouse with a partner named Gee, and traded as Castrey & Gee. George Castrey had been in business as a glasscutter in Wordsley, employing twenty-seven men, ten boys and two girls[137]. He subsequently moved to Wood Street, Wollaston[138]. The firm of Castrey & Gee traded[139] until 1894 when the works closed[140].

The glassworks stood idle, until Joseph Flemming and Co., having moved from Platts Glassworks reopened it in 1900[141]. Few references exist concerning the operation of the firm[142] and production ceased sometime in the nineteen-thirties[143].

During the nineteen-forties the Amblecote Glass Co. Ltd. used the glassworks for decorating. The original buildings, other than the cone, were pulled down about this time[144]. The old cone, long derelict, was finally demolished on Sunday 6th March 1955 as part of the scheme to extend an adjacent foundry[145].

---

1 Anglicised form of de Thiètry.
2 Revd. Henry Sanders BA, *The History and Antiquities of Shenstone, in the County of Stafford* (1794).
3 SRO, Tp 1273/11, Private collection.
4 SRO, Tp 1273/13, Private collection.
5 William Shenstone wrote to Lady Luxborough on 6th Mar 1749-50 from his home at the Leasowes, Halesowen, 'ye direct Road (betwixt me & Stourbridge) is almost one continu'd Grotto, in other terms a hollow-way; practicable for an Horse, but for no wheel-carriage.'
6 Daniel Tittery, bur. 30th Dec 1641, Oldswinford.
7 SRO, Tp 1273/13, Deed of 11th Nov 1650, Private collection.
8 Joshua Tittery, son of Daniel Tittery and his wife Anne nee Tompson alias Beare, bap. 1st Nov 1636, Oldswinford.
9 Balderson, M. (Ed), *James Claypoole's Letter Book, London and Philadelphia 1681-1684* (1967) pp123, 194.
10 Mar. Thomas Rogers and Ann Tittery, 5th Feb 1652, Sedgley.
11 Morchard Bishop (Ed.), *Recollections of the Table-Talk of Samuel Rogers* (1952), p xiii.
12 PRO Spec. Depos. Mixed Cos. 19 Cav II Easter No. 8 Exch. K.R. Depositions before a commission to enquire into a complaint brought by John Tyzack against Joshua Henzey and Henry Oseland.
13 SRO, Tp 1273/11 1623 Survey, Private collection.
14 Thomas Rogers, bur. 2nd Dec 1680, Oldswinford.
15 PRO, PROB4 7633, Inventory of the estate of Thomas Rogers, appraised 9th Jun 1681.
16 PRO, PROB 11/367 F27LH, PCC will of Thomas Rogers.
17 Thomas Rogers, son of Thomas Rogers and his wife Anne, nee Tittery, b. c1653.
18 Paul Rogers, son of Thomas Rogers and his first wife Ann, nee Jevon, bap. 11th Dec 1680, Oldswinford.
19 Mar. Paul Rogers and Mary Haselwood, 20th Feb 1704, Oldswinford.

20 WRO, marriage licence dated 15th Feb 1704. The trustees were Edward Tyzack, broad-glass manufacturer of Amblecote and John Bradley, glassmaker of Oldswinford.
21 Mar. Edward Jackson and Anne Rogers, widow, 8th Jan 1683, Oldswinford. The trustees to the marriage settlement were Edward Tyzack, who was running Colemans Glasshouse, and John Bradley who owned Fimbrell and Coalbournbrook Glassworks.
22 Thomas Rogers, bur. 30th Aug 1716, Kinver.
23 PRO, PROB11/568 sig90, will of Thomas Rogers, 14th May 1719.
24 Thomas Rogers, son of Thomas Rogers and his first wife Ann, nee Jevon, bap. 5th Aug 1676.
25 PRO, PROB3 18/101, Inventory of the estate of Thomas Rogers, appraised 10th Mar 1719.
26 Alkali used as flux.
27 The price of broad-glass had fallen two years earlier from 18s to 16s per case. London Gazette, 12th Jan 1717.
28 WRO, Palfrey collection.
29 Thomas Rogers, bur. 10th Dec 1723, Oldswinford.
30 Thomas Rogers, son of Paul Rogers and his wife Mary, nee Haselwood, bap. 27th Sep 1708, Oldswinford.
31 Ibid, R.L. Chambers, p43.
32 Paul Rogers, bur. 13th Nov 1737, Oldswinford.
33 WRO, Will of Paul Rogers, 22nd Nov 1737.
34 Martha Knight, daughter of Richard Knight (1659-1745) and his wife Elizabeth (1671-1754), daughter of Andrew Payne, Squire of Shawbury, Shropshire, bap. 20th Mar 1706, Burrington, Herefordshire.
35 Downton Castle stands five miles west of Ludlow in Herefordshire. The castellated mansion as seen today was built by Richard Knight's grandson Sir Richard Payne Knight (1750-1824) between 1774 and 1778. He was an antiquarian, philologist, numismatist, deist philosopher, expert on Greek literature, friend of Lord Byron and patron of art and learning; elected to parliament as a Whig in 1780; elected to the Society of Dilletanti in 1781. The mansion then passed to his brother Thomas Andrew Knight (1758-1838) the distinguished horticulturist, famous for his experimental work with grafting fruit trees and early observations on genetics in the breeding of peas.
36 Birmingham Gazette, 12th Nov 1750.
37 P.W. Clayden, *The Early Life of Samuel Rogers* (1887), p5.

38 H. Ridley, FLA, *A few notes on Amblecote*, County Express, 16th Jun 1917.
39 Kingswinford Court Rolls 1724 'John Grove of le Hill Amblecote.' (a John Grove of Rowley Regis owned the Bague estate between 1702 and 1706). It was subsequently the home of Daniel Grove who married Elizabeth Henzey, daughter of Paul Henzey I and his wife Anne, nee Tyzack.
40 Samuel Rogers, *The Pleasures of Memory* (1802).
41 Daniel Radford, son of Samuel Radford, linen draper of Chester and his wife Eleanor, nee Henry, third daughter of Revd. Philip Henry MA (1631-1696), a 'Bartholomew Divine'; b. 24th May 1691; d. 14th Oct 1767. Op cit A. Gordon, *Freedom after Ejection* (1917), p282. Originally from Chester, Radford settled at Newington Green after his marriage in 1731 to Mary, the only daughter of Samuel Harris, an East India merchant. For genealogy, see Sarah Lawrence, *The Descendants of Philip Henry, MA* (1844), pp48-51.
42 Ibid, H. Ridley FLA, County Express, 14th Jul 1917. Radford's original partners had died, Obadiah Wickes in 1748, and his son John Wickes in 1750.
43 Thomas Rogers, son of Thomas Rogers and his wife Martha, nee Knight, bap. 19th Sep 1735, Oldswinford.
44 Stoke Newington was a centre of religious non-conformity and political Liberalism. A regular preacher at the small Presbyterian chapel on the green was Mr (afterwards Dr) Richard Price, one of the most acute and enlightened minds the eighteenth century produced. A weekly supping club developed, meeting at the houses of Dr. Price, Thomas Rogers and Mr Burgh, the rector of Stoke Newington. It was at one of these suppers that Richard Price and Joseph Priestley first met. Richard Price, b. 23rd Feb 1723, Tynton, Glamorgan; moral philosopher; expert on insurance and finance; awarded degree of DD by Marischal College, Aberdeen in 1767; friend and correspondent of David Hume; philosophical opponent, but close personal friend of Joseph Priestley with whom he published a joint dissertation in 1778; elected Fellow of Royal Society in 1765 for work on the theory of probability, which he then turned to actuarial questions, his *Observations on Reversionary Payments*, published in 1771 laid the foundations of a scientific system for life insurance and old age pensions; friend of Benjamin Franklin and leading advocate of American Independence; granted Freedom of City of London in 1776; invited by U.S. Congress in 1778 to advise it on finance; made LL.D. together with George Washington by Yale College in 1781; d. 19th Apr 1791 at Stoke Newington.
45 Mar. Thomas Rogers V and Mary Radford, 27th Mar 1760, Islington Parish

Church.
46 Daniel Radford d. 14th Oct 1767.
47 Ibid, P.W. Clayden, pp6-7.
48 Daniel Rogers, son of Thomas Rogers V and his wife Mary, nee Radford, b. 3rd Jan 1761, Newington Green.
49 Daniel Rogers died 1st Mar 1829 and has a fine monument in Hagley parish church that commends 'a man not more distinguished for his intellectual endowment than for his goodness and singleness of heart.' His intellectual endowment included, among other things, an interest in ancient and Eastern languages. However, his chosen way of life displeased his father, who intended Daniel, as his oldest son, for the bar, for Parliament and to continue the family banking business. He was all but disinherited in his father's will and the family fortune descended upon his younger brother, the poet Samuel.
50 Samuel Rogers, son of Thomas Rogers V and his wife Mary, nee Radford, b. 30th Jul 1763, Newington Green; d. 18th Dec 1855. For biography see P.W. Clayden.
51 J.A. Langford, *Staffordshire and Warwickshire Past and Present* v 1, (1874), lxviii.
52 Birmingham Gazette, 4th Apr 1768.
53 As previously described, seventeenth century furnaces were little more than ovens, covered by a shingle roof open on all four sides. In the eighteenth century, as furnace technology developed – and capital permitted – a brick-built, bottle-shaped flue surrounded the furnace. The glassmakers continued to work around the furnace, but inside the flue. Due to their shape, these flues became known as cones.
54 SRO, Tp 1273, Private collection.
55 Birmingham Gazette, 1st Apr 1771.
56 Thomas Rogers IV, bur. 5th Apr 1775, Oldswinford.
57 Thomas Homfray, son of Francis Homfray ironmaster of the Hyde, Kinver and his second wife Catherine, nee Caswell, bap. 12th Jun 1760, Oldswinford. Thomas Homfray was a partner with Thomas Hill in his ironworks at Pennydarran and as part of the 'county set' had no doubt been entertained at The Hill.
58 James Keir, FRS, b. 20th Sep 1735; Educated at Edinburgh High School and Edinburgh University; commissioned at age of 22 in the 61st Regiment of Foot – now the Gloucestershire Regiment; left army in 1768 having just

reached rank of Captain; brief sojourn in London, then came to Wordsley in 1770; chemist; partner in Keir, Blair, and Playfair's Tividale Collieries; Colonel, Staffordshire Militia; manufacturer of soap at Tipton; d. 11th Oct 1820; bur. All Saint's, West Bromwich. For biography see Amelia Moillet, *Sketch of the life of James Keir Esq. FRS* (1868).

59 William Small (1734-1775) was a Scot who in 1758 became Professor of Natural Philosophy at the College of William and Mary, Williamsburg, Virginia, where one of his star pupils had been Thomas Jefferson. Small had been introduced to James Keir and his colleagues by Benjamin Franklin. He settled into the life of a medical practitioner in Birmingham and became doctor to Matthew Boulton. He first showed James Watt around Matthew Boulton's Soho Manufactory in Boulton's absence and so was instrumental in bringing these two great men together. In 1765 he was a founder subscriber of Birmingham General Hospital and became one of its first physicians when it opened on 20th Sep 1779.

60 James Watt, b. 19th Jan 1736, Greenock, Scotland; engineer and inventor of the modern condensing steam engine; apprenticed as instrument maker in London; patented his improvements to Newcomen's steam engine design in Jan 1769; met Matthew Boulton in 1768 who took a financial interest in his project and in 1775 obtained an Act to continue the patent for twenty-five years; elected Fellow of the Royal Society of Edinburgh in 1784; of the Royal Society of London in 1785; member of the Batavian Society in 1787; honorary degree of Doctor of Laws, University of Glasgow in 1806; elected a Member of the National Institute of France in 1808; died at his home, Heathfield House, near Birmingham, 25th Aug 1819; bur. Handsworth with monument by Chantrey. For biography see H.W. Dickinson, *James Watt, Craftsman and Engineer* (1936).

61 John Taylor (1711-1775) of Bordesley Hall, rose by his ability and good taste from being a mere artisan to become one of the leading manufacturers of Birmingham. He briefly met Dr. Johnson in 1733, which resulted in him being described in Boswell's *Life of Johnson* as one who by his ingenuity in mechanical inventions, and his success in trade, acquired an immense fortune. William Hutton called him 'the Shakespeare or the Newton of his day.' Op cit William Hutton, *An History of Birmingham* (1783), p73. After making a fortune from gilt buttons, japanned and gilt snuffboxes he founded the first Birmingham bank, Taylor & Lloyds in Jun 1765. In the same year, he was a

founder subscriber of Birmingham General Hospital. His son, John Taylor (1738-1814) married Samuel Skey's daughter, Sarah Skey at Ribbesford, Worcestershire, 30th Jun 1778.

62 Samuel Skey (1726-1800) was the third son of Thomas Skey, cider maker of Upton on Severn. Samuel became very wealthy as a grocer, drysalter and merchant in Bewdley; built chemical works in Dowles; purchased Manor of Dowles c1790; built Spring Grove, Bewdley between 1787 and 1790 (which is today, Bewdley Safari Park); married Sarah Scott (1724-1790), daughter of William Scott (1698-1766), clothier of Holloway End, Stourbridge and his wife Joanna, nee Hunt (1695-1771) 8th Nov 1752 at Halesowen; d. 27th Mar 1800; bur. 4th Apr 1800, Dowles.

63 Shrewsbury Chronicle.

64 BRL, Matthew Boulton Papers, Letters of William Small to James Watt.

65 Later called Harrington House and used as the Vicarage of Amblecote Church.

66 Matthew Boulton, b. 3rd Sep 1728, Birmingham, son of Matthew Boulton and his wife Christiana, nee Piers. Purchased lease of Soho, 1762, erected Soho Manufactory there 1765; built Soho House, 1766; introduced the steam engine commercially in partnership with James Watt, 1767; d. 17th Aug 1809 at Soho; bur. 28th Aug 1809, Handsworth.

67 BRL, Matthew Boulton Papers.

68 So called because it met monthly on the night of the full moon. The arrangement was as much practical as it was symbolic. The meetings involved a luncheon, held mainly at Erasmus Darwin's house in Lichfield, or Soho House, the Handsworth home of Matthew Boulton. The journey home in those days of poor roads was arduous. Darwin records that his carriage was well stocked with food, drink and writing materials.

69 Erasmus Darwin FRS, b. 1731, Elton, Nottinghamshire; scientist and poet regarded as the most foremost physician of his day; grandfather of the biologists Charles Darwin and Francis Galton; educated Chesterfield Grammar School, St. John's College, Cambridge; medically trained at universities of Edinburgh and Cambridge; after unsuccessful medical practice in Nottingham in 1756 moved to Lichfield; moved to Derby 1781; d. 18th Apr 1802, Derby. For biography see Anna Seward, *Memoirs of the life of Dr Darwin* (1804) and Desmond King-Hele, *Erasmus Darwin* (1963).

70 Philosopher was the eighteenth century word for scientist.

71 Mary Anne Galton, b. 25th Nov 1778 at Birmingham, daughter of Samuel

Galton and his wife Lucy, nee Barclay; lived much of her childhood at Great Barr Hall which the Galtons rented from Sir Joseph Scott, Bart.; mar. Lambert Schimmelpenninck of Berkeley Square, Bristol, 29th Sep 1806; d. 29th Aug 1856, Bristol; bur. Moravian Burial Ground, Bristol. It was Samuel Galton's butler that dubbed the members of the Lunar Society as 'Lunaticks'. There is an element of irony in this, as Great Barr Hall subsequently became St. Margaret's Hospital for the mentally handicapped.

72 Samuel Galton FRS son of Samuel Galton and his wife Mary, nee Farmer, b. 18th Jun 1753; manager and part-owner of the family gun-foundry with government contract for flintlock muskets and holster pistols, which brought him into conflict with the Society of Friends in 1795; ceased gun making in 1804 and founded a bank with his son Samuel Tertius Galton and Joseph Gibbons; of Duddeston House, Warwickshire until rented Barr Hall, purchased Warley Abbey estate in 1792; founder subscriber of Birmingham General Hospital in 1765; d. 1832.

73 *Life of Mary Anne Schimmelpenninck*. Edited by her Relation, Christiana C. Hankin. Two volumes. v 1. *Autobiography.* v 2, *Biographical Sketch and Letters* (1858).

74 Sir Joseph Banks (1744-1820); president of the Royal Society for over forty years; wealthy scientist who accompanied James Cook on his 1768-76 expedition to the Pacific, of which he financed the botanical aspects at a cost of £10,000; appointed horticultural and botanical advisor to Kew Gardens in 1771.

75 Dava Sobel, *Longitude* (1995).

76 R Bentley, *Thomas Bentley, 1730-1780, of Liverpool, Etruria, and London* (1927), p38.

77 Josiah Wedgwood, bap. 12th Jul 1730, son of Thomas Wedgwood, potter and his wife Mary, nee Stringer. After an apprenticeship as a potter and early partnerships he bought the Ridge House Estate (now Etruria) in 1766 where he built his famous works; F.S.A., 1786; FRS, 1783; mar. 25th Jan 1764 Sarah, daughter of Richard Wedgwood of Smallwood, Cheshire; d. 3rd Jan 1795; bur. Stoke Parish Church.

78 Ibid, Amelia Moilliet, p77.

79 Thomas Bentley (1731-1780), was Josiah Wedgwood's partner.

80 Wedgwood's experimental notebook for March and April 1783 records the results of 'Experiments with a view to remedy the imperfections of Flint

Glass for achromatic instruments' and discusses experiments at Mr. Knight's glasshouse in Liverpool and Mr. Holmes' in London as well as at Etruria.

81 The document can only be dated as post 1783, by its reference to Wedgwood's membership of the Royal Society.

82 Published in full, with commentary by R.E. Schofield, *Josiah Wedgwood and the Technology of Glass Manufacturing* (1962).

83 William Scott (1721-1792), son of William Scott (1698-1766) clothier of Holloway End and his wife Joanna, nee Hunt (1695-1771). William Scott was the fourth generation of the wealthy and armigerous Scott family to bear the forename William. His great-great grandfather, John Scott had moved to Stourbridge from Chaddesley Corbett in 1667 and founded a business as clothiers. Op cit John Burke, *A Genealogical and Heraldic History of the Commoners of Great Britain and Ireland*, v 3 (1838), pp 665-8. In his will dated 14th Jan 1792, William Scott left one of his shares in the Birmingham and Fazeley Canal Navigation in trust to distribute the income in money, clothes and provisions among the poor inhabitants of Stourbridge. William Scott would have been familiar with the glassmaking business all his life. When he was aged ten, his grandfather, William Scott (1666-1712) was churchwarden of Oldswinford in 1702 at the same time as Thomas Rogers, owner of the Holloway End Glasshouse and in 1703 at the same time as John Jeston, owner of the Heath Glassworks. John Scott (1763-1832), nephew of this William Scott, inherited the family's arms and lands at Stourbridge and substantial estates at Great Barr from the Addyes family. In 1816 John Scott donated land to the charity formed by his uncle William on the Wollaston Road in Stourbridge upon which was built a school. Op cit George Griffith, *The Free Schools of Worcestershire and Their Fulfilment* (1852), pp390-2.

84 PRO, RAIL 874.1.

85 William Scott was Samuel Skey's brother-in-law and as Skey's name ceases to appear in the partnership title William Scott possibly bought out his share.

86 Ibid, Amelia Moilliet, p63; R.E. Schofield, *The Lunar Society of Birmingham* (1963), pp153, 4.

87 Bailey's 1783 Western and Midland Directory.

88 SRO, Tp 1273/25, rate book, 1784, pp3,5,7.

89 M.S. Dudley Westropp, *Irish Glass* (1920), p173. Kelp, made by burning seaweed, was a raw material for both soap and glassmaking and was obtained largely from Galway and the Orkneys.

90 Tunnicliffe's 1789 Survey of Worcestershire.
91 James Parrish, son of Thomas and Joanna Parrish, bap. 28th May 1780, Brierley Hill.
92 Thomas Parrish, son of Thomas and Joanna Parrish, bap. 12th Jun 1774, Kingswinford.
93 LJRO, Will of Thomas Parrish, 18th Jun 1823.
94 Stuart Crystal, Joseph Richardson's notebook.
95 John Parrish, son of Thomas and Joanna Parrish, bap. 5th Apr 1772, Oldswinford.
96 Benjamin Richardson's notebook of 1886, p26.
97 Ibid, D.R. Guttery, p113.
98 Benjamin Richardson's notebook of 1886.
99 Infra, Bague's Glasshouses.
100 DA, William Fowler's 1822 *Map of the Parish of Kingswinford.* Plot 361 Cutting Shops – Thomas Parrish.
101 Holden's Triennial Directory for 1809, 1810 & 1811.
102 Ibid, M.S. Dudley Westropp, p173.
103 Benjamin Littlewood, son of Benjamin Littlewood and his second wife Sarah, nee Grazebrook, bap. 11th Jun 1769, Oldswinford.
104 Pigot and Co.'s 1828-9 National Commercial Directory; Pigot and Co.'s Commercial Directory of Birmingham, 1829 and 1830 editions.
105 BHGM, Receipt for payment of Excise Duty, 1829.
106 Benjamin Richardson's notebook of 1886. Richardson states these were 'two of his sons.' Thomas (b c1809) was more likely the son of Benjamin II.
107 Thirteenth Report of the Commission into the Glass Excise, 1835, Appendix 7.
108 Rice H. Harris, b. c1826, Birmingham.
109 London Gazette, 14th Aug 1832.
110 BHGM, Letter of Benjamin Richardson to William Haden Richardson.
111 Pigot and Co.'s 1835 National Commercial Directory.
112 Robson's 1839 Birmingham and Sheffield Directory; Bentley's Directory of Stourbridge, 1840 and 1841 editions; Pigot and Co.'s 1841 Directory of Birmingham.
113 Benjamin Littlewood, d. 21st Oct 1844; bur. Oldswinford family tomb. This chest tomb still exists, but is collapsing.
114 PRO HO/107/2062 Fol. 307 p4, 1851 census of Water Orton, Warwickshire.
115 Benjamin Richardson's notebook of 1886.

116 Edward Webb, son of William Webb and his wife Mary, nee Hancox, bap. 3rd Jun 1810, Kingswinford.

117 Joseph Webb, son of Richard Webb, a glass packer, and his wife Mary, nee Stamford, bap. 17th Jan 1813, Kingswinford. This is Joseph's true descent. Other sources, including the family tree that was displayed in the Dennis Hall Museum before its closure, describe Joseph as the son of William Webb and Mary Hancox and therefore the brother of Edward Webb rather than his cousin.

118 SRO 695/4/1/2. The partnership was deemed to have commenced on 29th Sep 1844, for an initial term of ten years, although it was not signed until 27th Aug 1845. Each partner subscribed £1,000, later supplemented by a £500 loan from Edward. The delay could have been while Joseph Webb raised his share of the capital. He married Jane Hammond of Enville on 10th May 1845 at Exning, Suffolk. Her family may have supplied the capital.

119 Post Office Directory of the Neighbourhood of Birmingham, 1845.

120 DA, unindexed Harward and Evers papers. Letter from Joseph Webb to his solicitors, Hunt, Price and Harwood, 25th Apr 1845.

121 Infra, Audnam Glassworks.

122 SRO 695/4/1/2. The partnership was dissolved 28th Oct 1850. Edward bought out Joseph for £3,500, which was met by an immediate payment of £1,750 followed by two instalments of £875.

123 PRO, 1851 census, 107/2036 02/040/076.

124 William Richardson, son of William and Eleanor Richardson, bap. 31st Jul 1825, Wordsley. PRO, 1851 census HO0107/2035/083 shows that William Richardson was a clerk in the glass trade, living at The Willows, Coalbournbrook.

125 Elijah Smith, son of George and Nancy Smith, b. 9th Sep 1820, Dudley; bap. 1st Oct 1820, Dudley Wesleyan Chapel. PRO, 1851 census, 107/2036 01/007/022, shows Elijah Smith as a glass manufacturer's clerk.

126 William Richardson was not directly related to the Richardsons of Wordsley Flint Glassworks.

127 Frederick James Mills, son of Richard Mills and his wife Elizabeth, nee Webb, b. Wordsley; bap. 7th Jun 1835, Kingswinford.

128 WRO, Elizabeth Mill's account book shows that Frederick James Mills borrowed £950 from his parents in 1858, which could have been the money to finance this venture. SRO, Richard Mills papers includes a cheque book

stub recording payment of £415 to Richardson, Mills and Smith on 7th Jan 1859. The executor papers also record a note of hand for £300 to the same company. The formal deed of partnership was signed on 17th May 1859.
129 PRO, 1851 Census HO 107 2036 06/102/013.
130 Infra, Coalbournhill, Audnam and North Street Glassworks.
131 £72 2s.
132 Post Office Directory of Worcestershire, 1860.
133 PRO, 1861 census, RG 9/2068 ED22 Sched 39.
134 Post Office Directory of Staffordshire, 1868.
135 PRO, 1871 census, RG10 3022 ED23 Sched 2.
136 Post Office Directory of Staffordshire, 1872 and Littlebury's 1873 Directory.
137 PRO, 1871 census, RG10 3025 ED4 Sch 11, shows George Castrey b. c1832 at Buckpool, Wordsley.
138 PRO, 1881 census of Wollaston RG11/2890/134/14.
139 Kelly's 1888 Directory of Staffordshire; Kelly's 1892 Directory of Birmingham, Staffordshire and Warwickshire.
140 R. Wakefield, *The Old Glasshouses of Stourbridge and Dudley* (1934), p11.
141 Ibid, R. Wakefield, p11.
142 Kelly's 1928 Directory of Staffordshire.
143 Ibid, R. Wakefield, p11.
144 M.W. Greenslade, *A History of Amblecote* (1984), p58.
145 County Express, 19th Mar 1955.

CHAPTER 11

Henzey's Brettell Lane Glasshouse

In 1630 Joshua Henzey I bought coal-bearing land in Brettell on which he subsequently built his glasshouse. It was positioned on the south side of Brettell Lane, about half way down its length:

'Comes to this Court Richard Nash and his wife Marjorie, and surrenders pasture land called Blakemores Meadow within the manor Aforesaid—ad opus et usum of Joshua Henzey.'[1]

Joshua consolidated his position in local society by taking up positions of civic responsibility. In 1638, he became Overseer of the Poor for Amblecote. He was a churchwarden of Oldswinford from 1643 to 1645 and in 1651 was a governor of King Edward VI Grammar School in Stourbridge.

Before he died, Joshua handed over the Brettell glasshouse to his third son Joshua II[2] and his fourth son Paul[3]. His two oldest sons were already successfully employed in the glass business—Ananias in Ireland and John[4] in Woolwich[5]. Joshua II spent much of his time marketing all the broad-glass made in the Stourbridge district[6], so Paul I was left in charge of the furnace at Brettell Lane.

Joshua senior died in 1660[7]. In his will,[8] he left practically everything to his wife Joan. Sixteen years later, on 22nd December 1676, a second administration of the will was granted at Lichfield to their oldest son, Ananias II, of Grayinfin, Kings County, Ireland, gent. The associated inventory refers to 'Severall instruments of Iron belonging to a Glasshouse in ye parish of Kingswinford in value foure pounds.'[9]

As well as four sons, Joshua senior had one daughter, Mary[10]. She married Nicholas Bradley, but after only seven years of marriage he died[11]. In 1660 Mary remarried to the Reverend Henry Oseland[12], a famous nonconformist minister and prominent 'Bartholomew Divine[13]'. Henry Oseland was born at Rock in Worcestershire[14]. After Bewdley Grammar School, he was a scholar of Trinity College, Cambridge, where he obtained his BA in 1650 and his MA in 1653. Ordained in London in 1651, he was the minister at Bewdley, Worcestershire until 1662, when he was ejected for refusing to conform to the articles of the Act of Uniformity[15]. He eventually died on 19th October 1703, aged eighty[16], when no fewer than twelve funeral sermons were preached for him.

About 1663 Joshua Henzey II entered into an agreement to be the 'sole merchant' of three glasshouses 'called or known by the names of Colman's Glass-house, the Hooe Glass-house and the Glasshouse in Brettell.' In need of a reliable assistant, he made his brother-in-law, Henry Oseland, 'his agent, bayliffe, clerk or overseer of the said three glasshouses'. His duties were to include buying material and paying the workmen. Oseland had no other source of income, being prohibited by law from practising religion[17]. Although it may seem odd for a man of the church to indulge in commerce, far stranger fates awaited other ousted priests[18].

Joshua Henzey failed to maintain payments due under his agreement, so an action was brought against him and Oseland in 1667 by John Tyzack of Withymoor Glasshouse. Shortly after this, Joshua Henzey II went to Ireland to seek out his brother Ananias[19]. It could be interpreted that he fled to Ireland, but within six months, he was dead. He died intestate and letters of administration were granted to his widow. Dorothy, his widow, returned to Oldswinford to be near her son Thomas[20]. John Tyzack continued his action against her but despite Tyzack's protestations to the contrary she pleaded poverty.

Joan, the widow of Joshua Henzey I, died in 1671[21]. Her will, which was nuncupative, was not proved until 9th January 1676[22]. In a moving testimony the testatrix left everything she had to her second son Paul: 'I give and bequeath all that I have to my son

Paull Henzey, and all that I have is too little for him, and do make him my sole executor.' The spoken testimony was witnessed by Thomas Batchelor[23] and his wife Mary.

Paul Henzey was obviously a caring family man. He had lived for many years with his father-in-law, the old Paul Tyzack I, who left half of what he had to Paul Henzey's children; his mother left him all she had; both made him their sole executor. Paul Henzey followed the tradition of service set by his father and became a churchwarden of Oldswinford in 1673. It was not a happy year for him; on 2nd August his twenty-one-year old son Joseph died and was buried there.

The oldest son of Paul Henzey and his wife Anne, nee Tyzack, was Ananias Henzey III. In 1680, Ananias married Elizabeth Jeston[24]. Elizabeth[25] was distantly related to the Jestons who were running the Heath Glassworks and was a cousin of Rose Jeston who married Edward Henzey the following year.

Paul Henzey I became wealthy as a glassmaker. In July 1685 he conveyed three cottages at Pedmore to Philip Foley[26]. On 14th April 1691, he gave a large silver communion chalice 'to be and to remain for the use and behoofe of the parishioners of Oldswinford and Stourbridge at the sacrament for ever.' Besides the Henzey arms[27] the bowl was engraved with their crest, a firebolt and fireball, and the motto, *Seigneur je te prie garde ma vie*[28].

Paul Henzey I died in 1693[29] and an inventory of his goods and chattels was performed valuing his estate at £823 14s 7d[30]. Notable among the items listed was 'The Testators Share or parte of 857 strikes of Ashes at Bewdley £23 4s 2d'. This again shows the importance of Bewdley as a route to Stourbridge for raw materials. Also listed was 'The Testators share or parte of 31 cases of Glass £11 0s 0d'[31]. When his will was proved in 1693[32], it referred to his estate including 'the Glasshouse and Glassworks with their appurtenances lying and being in Brettell in the parish of Kingswinford'. His wife, Anne, predeceased him[33] so he divided his estate between his son-in-law John Parnell[34] and his two daughters, Joane Henzey[35] and Dorothy Rainsford[36]. He left five shillings each to his sons, Ananias III and Paul II. This token gesture usually indicates those named had been well treated during the life of the deceased. In this case, both his sons had been involved in acts of fraud and so Paul Henzey probably felt no obligation to them. However, his two sons took over running the glasshouse in partnership with their cousin Edward[37]. Edward's share had descended via his father Joshua II, from his grandfather Joshua I.

Paul II died at Hawbush in 1700[38], aged fifty. In his will,[39] he left his third share in the business to his widow Elizabeth. The will refers to 'a third parte share and portion of all that glasshouse . . . situate in Brettell . . . assigned to Edward Henzey of Stourbridge Glassmaker, Ananias Henzey my brother, and my wife'. The inventory of his estate[40] valued his goods and chattels at £116 2s 4d and specifically refers to 'severall [sic] things in partnership with Mr Edward Henzey and Mr Ananias Henzey'.

Paul II had married Elizabeth Cranwell of Wolverhampton[41] but they had no children. Elizabeth, his widow, then remarried Joshua III[42] and with the marriage came her share of the Brettell Lane business. They went to live at the house attached to the glasshouse. Joshua III therefore had two working partners, Ananias III and his uncle Edward Henzey the elder, both much older than he. Edward, Ananias III and Joshua III were all party to the 1703 Perrot cartel[43].

Edward Henzey prospered in his trade. In 1704, he was assessed as a sufficiently wealthy landowner to qualify as a juror[44] and in 1706 became Overseer of the Poor for Stourbridge. He eventually retired in 1712 and Joshua III—having interests at Dial and Platts as well—handed over management of the Brettell Lane Glassworks to Ananias III. However, Joshua III was not well served by Ananias III. In 1713 shortly after Lady Day, without notice Ananias walked out and 'absented himself and work stood'. Joshua III was then 'the only sufficient man' left[45].

Elizabeth, the wife of Joshua III died in 1714[46]. Joshua III then remarried to Bridget Thompson, the sister of a Banbury doctor. He left the house by the Brettell Lane Glassworks, which he had shared with his first wife, and built a new home at the Platts. He still had his responsibilities at Dial and Platts Glassworks and had lost the management of Ananias III, so he handed over the Brettell Lane Glassworks to the three sons of Ananias III: Paul III[47], John and Joseph[48].

Faced with increasing competition, the Henzeys attempted to secure their market by cutting prices:

> 'Whereas Broad glass hath been lately sold at 18s per case at the Glass-house near Stourbridge, there is now Broad Glass to be sold at 16s per case by Paul Henzey, John Henzey and Joseph Henzey at their glasshouse in Brettell Lane near Stourbridge aforesaid. And when broad glass is raised in price, due notice shall be given in the Gazette.'[49]

Prices however continued to fall. The reason for this can quite clearly be ascribed to the public's growing preference for crown glass. The Henzeys were trying desperately to promote their sales of broad-glass, but the public was asking for crown. However, it is equally clear that demand was also suppressed by the uncertainties besetting the realm[50].

Edward, who had retired in 1712, died in 1718[51]. Ananias III died in 1720[52] at Henry Wilcox's house at Amblecote. No further references are found concerning the Brettell Lane Glassworks after this date. The broad-glass trade was in a dire state and it was quite probably abandoned.

---

1 Kingswinford Manor Rolls, 22nd May 1630.

2 Joshua Henzey, son of Joshua Henzey and his wife Joan, nee Brettell, b. c1625.

3 Paul Henzey, son of Joshua Henzey and his wife Joan, nee Brettell, bap. 27th May 1627, Kingswinford.

4 John Henzey, son of Joshua Henzey and his wife Joan, nee Brettell, bap. 17th Jun 1621, Kingswinford.

5 John Henzey made window glass at Woolwich in partnership with Robert Taynton and John Oliver. Their glasshouse was in operation in 1662 when it supplied glass to the Royal Society. It closed about 1696 and was advertised to rent in 1701.

6 Supra, Colemans.

7 Joshua Henzey, bur. 14th Apr 1660, Oldswinford.

8 PRO, PCC will of Joshua Henzey, 27th Nov 1660.

9 LJRO.
10 Mary Henzey, daughter of Joshua Henzey and his wife Joan, nee Brettell, bap. 30th May 1629, Kingswinford.
11 Nicholas Bradley, bur. 24th Dec 1654, Kingswinford.
12 Mar. Revd. Henry Oseland and Mary Bradley, widow, 24th Jul 1660, Oldswinford.
13 After the restoration of Charles II in 1660, an effort was made to secure agreement to the wording of the Book of Common Prayer at the Savoy Conference of 1661. This failed and although some concessions were made to Puritan feelings in the Prayer Book of 1662, it still contained most of the features disliked by the Puritans. As a result, over 1,600 of the 9,000 parish clergy who felt unable conscientiously to accept it were deprived of their benefices on St. Bartholomew's Day, 24th Aug 1662, and with their followers, seceded from the national church.
14 Henry Osland, son of Edward Osland and his wife Elizabeth, nee Leigh, bap. 22nd May 1625, Rock, Worcestershire.
15 J.A. Venn, *Alumini Cantabrigienses*; A.G. Matthews, *Calamy Revised* (1934); ibid, A. Gordon, p323; Robert D. Thompson, *Rock* (1981).
16 Inscription in Kingswinford church.
17 The Conventicle Act forbade meetings for worship of more than five people beyond those residing on the premises. The Five Mile Act banned all ejected ministers from living or preaching within five miles of a corporate borough or from the place where they had previously ministered.
18 The Yorkshire Dales was another stronghold of non-conformism (Dales folk were usually about fifty years behind the prevailing religious tradition). Oliver Heywood of Northowram was sheltered by Mrs Lambert of Calton Hall, near Gargrave daughter-in-law of Cromwell's General Lambert. Richard Frankland ejected from Barnard Castle returned to his family home at Rathmell near Settle and founded the first non-conformist academy. However, others found work with Philip, Lord Wharton in his lead mines in Swaledale and Arkengarthdale.
19 Rolls, Ireland, X11, 354-5 show that on 27th Aug 1667 a grant was made to Joshua Henzey of the following lands in Kings County, Curraghvenry, one moiety of Milltowne, and one moiety of Garvally. On the same day a grant of lands in the same county was made to his brother Ananias.
20 Dorothy Henzey, widow of Oldswinford, made her will 15th Mar 1681 and

was buried two days later at Oldswinford, 17th Mar 1681. Her son Thomas proved her will in PCC, 20th Oct 1682.
21 Joan Henzey, d. 19th Feb 1671; bur. Oldswinford.
22 WRO.
23 Thomas Batchelor was a glasscutter who worked for Paul Henzey. His sons were later to operate the Fimbrell Glasshouse.
24 Mar. Ananias Henzey and Elizabeth Jeston, 1st May 1680, Broom.
25 Elizabeth Jeston, daughter of John and Margaret Jeston of Hagley.
26 Philip Foley of Prestwood House, Stourton, youngest son of Thomas Foley MP of Witley Court and his wife Anne, nee Browne, b. 1653; d.1716.
27 Gules, three acorns slipped, two, and one, or.
28 Oldswinford Churchwarden's Book.
29 Paul Henzey, bur. 11th Apr 1693, Oldswinford.
30 PRO, PROB4 15743, Inventory of the estate of Paul Henzey, appraised 10th Jun 1693.
31 Presumably a third share, valuing the glass at 21s 3d per case.
32 PRO, PROB 11/415 F162LH to F162RH, PCC will of Paul Henzey, 6th Jul 1693.
33 Anne Henzey d. 1685.
34 Mar. John Parnell and Sarah Henzey, 6th Sep 1691, Pattingham.
35 Joane Henzey, daughter of Paul Henzey and his wife Anne, nee Tyzack, bap. 23rd May 1663, Kingswinford.
36 Dorothy Henzey married Thomas Rainsford.
37 Edward Henzey, son of Joshua and Dorothy Henzey, b. c1651.
38 Paul Henzey, bur. 6th May 1700, Kingswinford.
39 PRO, PROB 11/457 59LH - 59RH. PCC will of Paul Henzey, 20th Jun 1700.
40 PRO, PROB4/16868.
41 Mar. Paul Henzey and Elizabeth Cranwell, 13th Nov 1682.
42 Joshua Henzey III, son of Thomas Henzey and his wife Frances, nee Croker, b. 1572, probably in Ireland
43 Supra, Colemans.
44 H.S. Grazebrook, *The Heraldry of Worcestershire* (1873), p727.
45 Ibid, D.R. Guttery, p58.
46 Elizabeth Henzey, bur. 2nd Feb 1714, Kingswinford. She was interred with her first husband, Paul Henzey II, in a grave on the right-hand side going into the church, near the church porch.

47 Paul Henzey, son of Ananias Henzey and his wife Elizabeth, nee Jeston, b. c1680.
48 Joseph Henzey, son of Ananias Henzey and his wife Elizabeth, nee Jeston, b. c1686.
49 London Gazette, 12th Jan 1717.
50 The accession to the throne of King George I (1660-1727, r1714-1727) in 1714 had been well received by his subjects, the bulk of the country favouring the Protestant succession. However, the Jacobite rising of 1715 had led to war and an inevitable disruption in commerce. The rising was defeated with the battle of Sheriffmuir in November 1715.
51 Edward Henzey, bur. 15th Jun 1718, Oldswinford.
52 Ananias Henzey, bur. 2nd Feb 1720, Oldswinford.

CHAPTER 12

Bague's Glasshouses, Brettell Lane

The next glasshouse established in the district after the Henzeys' was also in Brettell Lane. It faced Brettell Lane on the north side, about half way along its length, just to the west of the later bridge over the Stourbridge Canal. The family who founded it was called Bague—clearly a French name. Unlike the Tyzacks, Henzeys and Titterys, the Bagues were not first generation emigrants from Lorraine. Their name does not appear in the parish registers of the Wealden villages, nor Eccleshall.

There is a Bague marriage at Alstonfield, Staffordshire as early as 1571, a baptism at Bretforton, Worcestershire in 1606 and another in 1607. However, the main influx of Bagues into the Worcestershire-Staffordshire border area occurred in the parish of Church Honeybourne from 1614 onwards. Millesenta Bagge married Johannes Blizzard there on 4th August 1614. A succession of French and Flemish names in the region suggests it was a destination for Huguenot refugees. The Bagues who interest us are three who appeared in Amblecote before 1619 and refer to each other as 'kinsmen', probably meaning cousins. That they were immediately able to establish themselves in business suggests they were skilled artisans who chose to leave France during the reign of Louis XIII[1].

In 1619 Jeremy Bague married Suzanna Henzey[2]. Jeremy was one of the three Bague kinsmen who appeared in Brettell about this time. Judging by her age, Suzanna would be a contemporary of Joshua Henzey I, possibly his sister, but her descent is unclear. By 1634 Jeremy was a churchwarden for the town of Stourbridge and parish of Oldswinford; his fellow churchwarden that year was the famous Richard 'Fiddler' Foley[3].

This was the period of Sir Robert Mansell's monopoly of the glass trade. There were constant calls from glassmakers and merchants alike to have his monopoly overturned and the opinion at large was that this was going to happen. In May 1641, after three such petitions, Mansell petitioned the House of Lords[4]. He complained several 'inconsiderable persons' were acting as though parliament had already overthrown the monopoly, though there had not been so much as a hearing. The Lords referred the matter to their own committee for petitions and ordered the offenders against the patent to appear and testify. Meanwhile they issued an order[5] that Mansell's patent should stand 'in full power and force . . . until the Parliament order the contrary'[6]. To satisfy the Lords' order, at Mansell's request, bonds for good behaviour were taken of three more men accused of violating the terms of his patent[7]. Jeremy Bague, who was running a glasshouse in Greenwich with Francis Bristowe[8], was accused of making glass without paying rent. Bague refused to put out his fires or to pay Mansell and the Lords heard the case in March 1642. The result was that Jeremy Bague was imprisoned for contempt of the Lords' order of the preceding May[9]. In April 1642 Bague and Bristowe petitioned the Privy Council that their cause against Sir Robert Mansell may be heard, or referred to the House of Commons. They also complained of his insults and injuries. In spite of several petitions, asking that the committee of the House of Commons should hear the case, they remained in jail for some time[10]. Mansell's patent was cancelled on 30th May 1642, shortly before the outbreak of the Civil War[11]. Bristowe and Bague were discharged from their bonds and allowed to resume glassmaking as free men[12].

According to Guttery, Jeremiah Bague built a glasshouse in Brettell in 1645[13]. As Guttery rarely revealed his sources of information, it is difficult to confirm or refute this assertion. Jeremy Bague had clearly been in the area since at least 1619 and had been making glass at Greenwich since at least 1641. It is also improbable that a shrewd businessman would invest capital in any venture in the year 1645, as the Civil War was raging[14]. These facts suggest the original Bague glassworks was founded at Brettell earlier than 1645, although the date may mark the building of a second glasshouse there.

In 1653 Jeremiah Bague became a churchwarden of Kingswinford, the year in which Oliver Cromwell accepted the office of Protector of the Commonwealth. That year, Bague was also one of the parishioners who appointed the Kingswinford parson, Nicholas Paston, to the new office of 'Register' as required by the Commonwealth Parliament. Kingswinford is fortunate to be a parish whose records were maintained during the Commonwealth; many churches handed over to Puritan ministers had no records kept at all during this period.

Jeremiah's wife, Susanna, died in 1655[15]. Just three months later he made another good match for himself by marrying Isabell Brettell[16], the daughter of one of the foremost families in the district. Jeremiah died in 1663[17]. The burial register refers to him as 'Jeremiah Bagge the elder, glassmaker of Brettell'. Despite his two marriages he died without issue, but the reference to him as 'the elder' was to differentiate him from one of his heirs, Jeremiah Bague II[18], the son of his kinsman George Bague. In his will[19], he left legacies to his wife Isabell and his 'kinsmen' John and George Bague. He also left £100 each to the four children of George Bague.

John Bague of Brettell survived his kinsman Jeremiah by five years and died intestate in 1668. Letters of administration were granted on 18th January 1668 to his widow Mary[20]. Although they had three young children of their own, she granted administration to 'George Bague the principal creditor of my deceased husband'. Now the interests of the three Bague kinsmen were vested in the last to survive, George Bague.

George did not long outlive his kinsmen. He made his will on 14th April 1670 and died shortly afterwards. His will was proved in PCC in November 1670[21]. He bequeathed to 'Elizabeth my wife all my glasshouse in Brettell'. Furthermore, he arranged that when his son Jeremiah should attain the age of twenty-four, they should own and run the glassworks 'equally between them in partnership'. This was however until his second son Nehemiah[22] attained the age of twenty-four at which time 'my wife shall deliver up to him the one halfe of all the tools and implements belonging to the glasshouse'. The two sons were to own and run the glassworks as partners. The testator was obviously a wealthy man, leaving land and property in Himley, Seisdon and Martly.

The whole of the first generation of the Brettell Lane Bagues died within eleven years of each other. Elizabeth[23], widow of George was the last in 1675. She made her will on the 8th December 1674 and a year later, after Jeremiah had attained the age of twenty-four, but before Nehemiah had, she died. Her will was proved in PCC in December 1675[24]. Madam Bague obviously did something to enshrine herself in the folklore of the district. Writing two hundred and eleven years later, Benjamin Richardson repeated an anecdote concerning a large flagstone in Wordsley Brook at the foot of the hill beneath the old Dob Hill Glassworks. According to legend, Madam Bague's spirit lived under the flagstone and she 'used to come again and turn the hour glass in the glass house windows.'[25]

So at the age of twenty-six Jeremiah Bague II took over the running of the glassworks from his mother. The following year he married Elizabeth Partridge[26] and by 1679 he was being afforded the title of 'Mr'. When he baptised a daughter in 1679[27], the parish register recorded him as 'Mr Jeremiah Bague, glassmaker.'

In 1692 Jeremiah II made an agreement with Ananias, Paul and Nicholas Henzey to build him a new glasshouse. The agreement was dated 27th April 1692 and the furnace was lit on 4th July 1692[28]. The Henzeys managed the whole project for Bague, based upon a plan that the glasshouse would produce forty cases of broadglass per week to be sold at 18s per case. Anticipated costs are listed in detail; 'Henzey, his brother, places the following estimate before Bague, on which he builds a glasshouse':

Wages per week	£	s	d
2 blowers	1	8	0
1 gatherer		2	0
1 cutter	1	0	0
2 teezers		16	0
1 founder		12	0
1 packer		5	0
1 pulpeece [?]		3	0
1 ash sifter		3	0
1 crate maker		13	4
1 smith		5	0
3 workmen	5	8	0
	10	15	4

Materials per week	£	s	d
Coal	3	0	0
Sand		10	0
Ashe	12	10	0
Salt		8	0
Cratewood	1	0	0
Straw		3	0
	17	11	0

Wages	10	15	4
wages omitted		7	0
	28	13	4

This business plan therefore suggested the weekly profits would be £7 6s 8d and so Bague went ahead. However, he was not at all satisfied with the outcome and in 1696/7 he sued Ananias and Paul Henzey[29]. He claimed the Henzeys were persuaded by other glassmakers around Brettell to create problems for him. The evidence given by Bague is fascinating:

> 'And the said Ananias Henzey and Paul Henzey did agree to work for your orator weekly for ye space of one whole year to commence when the fire should be put in the intended

glasshouse not being then builded'. Bague 'did build and erect a broad glasshouse . . . gave direction to one Norman to make a broad Furnace in the said new glasse house.' But the Smyth 'knew not the right art of making glass tooles.' The founder 'was careless and unexpert.' 'Such gatherers for blowers to have blowers wages.' They 'caused many of yr Orators potts which are very changeable in the making to be broken . . . some of them to be sett in the furnace before they were hott and others to be set uneasy in their seates so as to heave up part of the bottome and by suffering the potts when full of mettall and at the greatest heate to be suddenly cooled by giving air under it in the cave in so much that within the space of twenty-two weeks and one day there were eighty-four potts wasted.' He even accused the Henzeys of 'entering into yr Orators said broad glasse house at midnight and take away the said Nock yr Orators chiefe workman from his worke.'

Despite this disastrous beginning, Bague's new glasshouse eventually got underway. Apart from further entries in the Kingswinford register of baptisms there followed a period when nothing more is heard of the Bague family and their glassworks. This was probably because of a period of relative prosperity and stable conditions for commerce during the reign of Charles II[30]. This ended after his brother James II[31] succeeded him in 1685. James II's conversion to Catholicism and his attempts to reunite England to Rome ended in revolution and the flight of himself and his family. The ensuing events lead to the introduction of an excise duty on glass and brought the Bague name to the fore again.

Louis XIV of France had taken up the cause of James, the exiled pretender to the English throne and so shortly after William III's[32] accession in 1689 England joined in the war against France. The war began as much from the national dislike of France, 'Popery and Wooden Shoes' as from William's determination to break the power of Louis XIV; in its latter stages there were many new causes. By 1695, the exchequer was in need of further funds to finance the war and several industries were taxed. A rate of 20 percent on flint and one shilling per dozen on bottles was imposed. The tax became effective as an emergency measure on 29th September 1695 and was made perpetual the following year[33]. The glass industry fought this imposition strenuously for four years. John Bague and John Jeston petitioned the House of Commons in 1696[34]:

> 'A petition of John Bague, and John Jeston, on behalf of themselves, and other Glass-makers in and about Stourbridge, in the County of Worcester, was presented to the House, and read; setting forth, That the Petitioners employed many Hundred Families in the making Glass-bottles, till a Duty was laid upon Glass, which hath put a Stop to the Petitioners Trade of making Bottles; so that they have not wrought One Day since the Duty commenced; whereby they must inevitably be ruined, if the said duty be continued: And praying, That the said Duty upon Glass-wares may be taken off. Ordered, That the Consideration of the said Petition be referred to the Committee, to whom a former Petition of the Glass-makers, in and about the said Town of Stourbridge, is referred.'[35]

In response to the onslaught of complaint from the glassmakers, the House appointed a committee. After examination of evidence from all parts of the country, the tax was withdrawn as from 1st August 1699[36].

However, this was not soon enough to alleviate Jeremiah's problems. On 11th January 1698 he surrendered the glasshouse to his creditors and on 7th June he was declared bankrupt. His creditors, including Ananias Henzey, Joshua Henzey, Paul White and Oliver Dixon assigned the glasshouse to John Grove of Rowley Regis for the benefit of Bague's creditors[37]. In 1702 John Grove purchased the estate when the details of the sale show three glasshouses being worked[38]. Jeremiah Bague III[39], the oldest son of Jeremiah II, continued to work the glasshouses.

Thomas Hamond[40] became involved with the business about this time, probably initially as a partner of Jeremiah Bague III. Hamond is described as a whiteglassmaker of Oldswinford when he married[41] Mary Bradley[42] in 1702.

In 1706 John Grove and George Bague sold 'the house in which Jeremiah Bague lately lived and now Thomas Hamond with one glasshouse' to Joseph Finch. The rest of the estate passed for a time into the hands of Diana$_{43}$, Lady Dudley$_{44}$. George Bague$_{45}$ was the second son of Jeremiah Bague II. Joseph Finch was an ironmonger of Dudley and was Thomas Hamond's stepfather-in-law. The year before Mary Bradley married Thomas Hamond her father had died. Her widowed mother Anne remarried to Joseph Finch in 1702$_{46}$.

Jeremiah Bague and Thomas Hamond were the occupiers of the glasshouse in 1710$_{47}$ but it seems that Jeremiah Bague III ceased his involvement sometime shortly after this date. It is not clear what happened to the descendants of the Bague family of Brettell Lane. Their name did not persist in the area. The last Bague to be recorded in the Kingswinford parish register was George, baptised in 1701$_{48}$, the great-grandson of the original George Bague. The family left a memorial in the glassworks that continued to be known as 'Bagues' Glassworks for many years to come.

In 1717 Joseph Finch sold the glasshouse, still occupied by Thomas Hamond, to a Dudley baker who mortgaged it in the next year to William Seager of the 'Red Lion in Brettell'$_{49}$.

In 1722 Thomas Hamond's daughter Ann married Robert Honeyborne, a maltster. However, Ann died less than five years later.

Thomas Hamond died in 1743$_{50}$, aged sixty-four. An obituary describes him as the 'proprietor of a great glasshouse near Birmingham.'$_{51}$ In his will$_{52}$ —made ten years earlier—he is described as a glassmaker of Brettell. Having no surviving children, he left legacies to his son-in-law Robert Honeyborne, his nephew and sisters, but left the residue of his estate to his granddaughter, Mary Honeyborne. Robert Honeyborne and his daughter Mary moved into Thomas Hammond's former cottage adjoining the glassworks$_{53}$. Although he was no glassmaker himself, Robert Honeyborne could have continued to operate the glasshouse and may indeed have done so for a while. However, the land was leased and the cone was fifty-two years old, so Robert Honeyborne decided to build a new glasshouse on land he already owned at Moor Lane[54]. Bague's presumably ceased to operate as a glasshouse about this time.

Whitworth's canal map of 1774 clearly shows the outline of two cones, labelled 'Bague's Glass Houses', at the western end of Brettell Lane. The Stourbridge Canal Act specifically refers to the canal passing 'to or near Bague's Glass-houses in Brettell Lane.' Snape's map of 1785 shows the cone and extensive works, backing on to the canal.

The old glasshouse was finally converted into a pottery, but it is difficult to prove when. The list of glasshouses in 1796 quoted by D.N. Sandilands does not include Bague's Glasshouses; suggesting glassmaking had ceased by this date. Holden's Triennial Directory for 1809, 1810 and 1811 lists the two other Brettell Lane glassworks, but does not list Bague's Glasshouses which reinforces the suggestion. Two cones are graphically shown, but unfortunately not named, on Sherriff's plan of 1812. The change of use probably took place before 1798 when Samuel Edge was in occupation of one glasshouse and Francis Smith the other[55]. Francis Smith certainly operated the works later as a pottery and he is not known to have been a glassmaker.

By 1822 the old glassworks was occupied by Francis Smith & Sons, operating as 'Smith's Pottery'. Their pottery was the largest single concern in the district. It filled a huge complex on a site that approximates to that of the present location of the remnants of Harris and Pearson's brickyard. This can be identified by the splendid but decaying firebrick archway that been a feature on the north side of Brettell Lane for over a hundred years. The proprietor was Viscount Dudley and Ward[56]. In 1835 F. Smith & Sons was still in occupation, when the works is described as a pottery and Roman cement works. Messrs Smith and Hodnet carried on the same business between 1850 and 1865, after which the works remained closed for a long period and became very dilapidated.

In 1882 there were two cones on the site, one freestanding and the other in a group of structures described as a cement works[57].

Sometime between 1882 and 1886 one of the old cones fell down and killed a man called Bullock. It happened on a Saturday afternoon when Bullock was carrying a board of milk pans on his head into the old glasshouse to dry before being baked in the kiln. As he entered, the cone collapsed and the falling bricks hit him[58]. The glasshouse was not used again and fell into a dilapidated state[59]. It became unsafe and was demolished in the early part of this century. By 1919 the site was clear of buildings[60].

---

1 After the assassination of Henry IV on 14th May 1610, France plunged into a crisis lasting from 1610 to 1624. The period was alarmingly reminiscent of the situation in the fifteen-sixties at the outset of the religious wars. Renewed persecution led to the emigration of hundreds of Huguenot families.

2 Mar. Jeremiah Bague and Susanna Henzey, 13th Apr 1619, Oldswinford.

3 Infra.

4 House of Lords Library, House of Lords MSS., Mansell's Petition, 13 May 1641.

5 Dated 13th May 1641.

6 Journal of House of Lords iv 248.

7 House of Lords MSS, Affidavit of William Chapnell, 16 Jan 1641.

8 Bristowe, although English born, had married into the Bungar family and learned his art working at the Du Houx glasshouse at Haughton Green. After an earlier clash with Mansell (Eleanor S. Godfrey, *The Development of English Glassmaking 1560-1640* (1975), p115), Bristowe was employed by him to run Mansell's glasshouse at Wentworth in South Yorkshire. This was set up in 1631 on land provided by the Earl of Strafford, just beyond the estate wall of his mansion, Wentworth Woodhouse. It started production of window glass in April 1632, but had an unsettled existence. The Earl of Strafford fell out of favour with the King and was executed on Tower Hill in May 1641. Bristowe ceased paying Mansell the monopoly dues, which led to Mansell's petition for his imprisonment. Op cit, Denis Ashurst, *The History of South Yorkshire Glass*, pp19-21.

9 Journal of House of Lords iv 669.

10 House of Lords MSS., Petitions of Bagg and Bristow, 23 Apr 1642; 16 May 1642.

11 House of Lords MSS p569, 30 May 1642.

12 Longleat, Whitelock collection, viii, 256.

13 Ibid, D.R. Guttery, p72.

14 King Charles I was defeated at the Battle of Naseby on 14th Jun 1645. As the Royalist army fell back on Worcestershire plundering was rampant. Skirmishes took place at Willenhall and Dudley. Sir Gilbert Gerrard led a force to Stourbridge described as 'the most rude, ravenous, and ill-governed horse that I believe ever trod upon the earth.'

15 Susanna Bague, bur. 2nd Jul 1655, Kingswinford.

16 Mar. Jeremiah Bague and Isabell Brettell, 25th Oct 1655, Kingswinford.

17 Jeremiah Bague, bur. 7th Jan 1663, Kingswinford.

18 Jeremiah Bague, son of George Bague and his wife Elizabeth, nee Brettell, bap. 12th May 1649, Kingswinford.

19 PRO PROB 11/313, PCC will of Jeremiah Bague, Feb 1664.

20 LJRO.

21 PRO, PROB 11/334 RH239/RH240.

22 Nehemiah Bague, son of George Bague and his wife Elizabeth, nee Brettell, b. 31st Jan 1654, Kingswinford.

23 Mar. George Bague and Elizabeth Brettell, daughter of Richard Brettell of Amblecote, 5th Nov 1645, Kingswinford.

24 PRO, PROB 11/349 RH124/RH125.

25 Benjamin Richardson's notebook of 1886.

26 Mar. Jeremiah Bague and Elizabeth Partridge, 10th Apr 1676, Broom, Worcestershire.

27 Ann Bague, daughter of Jeremiah Bague and his wife Elizabeth, nee Partridge, bap. 11th Nov 1679, Kingswinford.

28 WSL, 45/120/56, Bague Vs Henzey.

29 Nicholas Henzey had died the previous year and was buried at Kingswinford, 4th Jul 1695. Letters of Administration for his estate were proved at Lichfield 25th Nov 1695 (LJRO) and show that working for Bague had not brought him any wealth. A letter dated 23rd Nov 1695 states 'Nicholas Henzey late of Brettell Glassmaker in July last departed this life intestate & one Mr Bague is indebted to him for wages & refuses to pay his widow unless she will take administration. She is not able of body to travell to Lichfield neither is she of purse strong enough to hire a horse. . . send a line what the charges will be that the poore woman may collect it among her friends.'

30 Charles II, 1630-1685, r1660-1685.

31 James II, b1633, r1685, ab1688.

32 William III, b1650, r1689-1702 (r alone from 1694).

33 Act for granting certain duties on glass wares, 6 & 7 William & Mary, c. 18, Statutes of the Realm, vi. 600-6.

34 John Jeston was operating the Heath Glassworks. The wording of the petition suggests John Bague was of the family running the glassworks in Brettell Lane, but no other reference to him can be found.

35 HOC Journal XI p621, 10th Dec 1696.

36 Act for removing duties on glass wares, 10 William III, c. 24, Statutes of the Realm, vii. 533-4.

37 DA, Earl of Dudley's Records, DE/T/5/287.

38 Kingswinford Court Rolls, 1702.

39 Jeremiah Bague, son of Jeremiah Bague and his wife Elizabeth, nee Partridge, bap. 29th Mar 1677.

40 Thomas Hamond of Kinlet, Shropshire, b. 1679.

41 Mar. Thomas Hamond and Mary Bradley, 4th Apr 1702, Oldswinford.

42 Mary Bradley, daughter of Edward Bradley senior, who had run the Audnam Glassworks and his wife Anne, nee Tittery, bap. 12th Aug 1682, Oldswinford.

43 Diana, nee Howard, dowager Viscountess Dudley and Ward.

44 Ibid, D.R. Guttery, p50.

45 George Bague, son of Jeremiah Bague and his wife Elizabeth, nee Partridge, bap. 24th Aug 1681, Kingswinford.

46 Mar. Joseph Finch, widower and Anne Bradley, widow, 3rd Jan 1702, Enville.

47 Kingswinford Court Rolls, 1710.

48 George Bague, son of Nehemiah and Elizabeth Bague, bap. 28th Aug 1701, Kingswinford.

49 Ibid, D.R. Guttery, p62.

50 Thomas Hamond, bur. 17th Oct 1743, Kingswinford.

51 The Craftsman, 18th Oct 1743.

52 PRO, PROB 11/735 137LH-137RH, PCC will of Thomas Hamond, 7th Sep 1744.

53 DA, Earl of Dudley's Records, DE/T/5/290.

54 Infra.

55 DA, Lord Dudley's Rent Rolls, 1798.

56 DA, William Fowler's *1822 Map of the Parish of Kingswinford.* Plot 363 Francis Smith & Sons – Pottery. The proprietor, William Ward, third Viscount Dudley and Ward was the son of John Ward, sixth Baron Ward of Birmingham and first Viscount Dudley and Ward, by his second wife Mary,

nee Carver. John Ward had been involved with Henry Bradley at his Audnam Glassworks.
57 Ordnance Survey map, 1882.
58 Benjamin Richardson's notebook of 1886.
59 The Ordnance Survey map of 1903 labelled it disused.
60 Ordnance Survey map, 1919.

CHAPTER 13

Withymoor Glasshouse, Amblecote

Glassmaking at Colemans Glasshouse ended abruptly when the partners were ejected by their landlord John Lyddiat. Zachary Tyzack II of Amblecote, Paul Tyzack II of Kingswinford and Abraham Bigo II of Amblecote took a lease in 1666 on land at Withymoor in the heart of Amblecote from Henry Grey of Enville[1] and built a new glasshouse.

Predictably, their agreement made with Joshua Henzey II in 1663 ran into problems[2]. Paul Tyzack's older brother, John[3], threatened to break the terms of the contract by building a glasshouse of his own unless he was paid an extra 10s per week. His crude attempt at blackmail worked initially and Henzey agreed to pay him the ten shillings. All the parties were to pay a share: Joshua Henzey, Paul Henzey and Paul Tyzack 2s 6d each, the contractor Foley 1s 6d, and Abraham Bigo and Zachariah Tyzack 6d each. The payments were to be made by Henzey's agent, Henry Oseland.

However, John Tyzack's antagonism led to his dismissal in June 1665 and Oseland stopped paying him the ten shillings. Tyzack immediately brought an action in the Court of Exchequer against Joshua Henzey and Henry Oseland[4]. John Tyzack had his case heard before a commission held 'at the signe of the Cocke' at Stourbridge[5]. The four magistrates heard that Henzey's agent, Henry Oseland, 'about 1664, treated with the complainant John Tyzack concerning the making of glass in the three glass-houses for three years to come.' The agreement was that Tyzack should not set up any 'glasshouse or works for the making of any manner of glass whereby to hinder the sale of glass, or impair the advantages gained [by

119

Henzey] ... Nor buy or sell any glass in the said three years.' Tyzack was to be paid ten shillings a week 'in consideration thereof whether he worked in the said glass-houses or not.' Henzey was very pleased with the agreement and promised 'of his own free will to pay the complainant twenty or thirty shillings per week over and above the said ten shillings for the better encouragement of the complainant.' In spite of these optimistic plans Henzey's weekly payments gradually dropped off although Tyzack 'ever since the agreement hath on his part ... observed the same, and that by the non-performance of the agreement by the defendant is not only impoverished but almost totally ruined.'

With relationships irreparably damaged the partnership disintegrated. John Tyzack left with his family to start his own glasshouse at Hagley[6]. Abraham Bigo II left the partnership—and indeed the Stourbridge area for good. Tired of interminable quarrels between his Tyzack and Henzey kinsmen, Abraham Bigo II facilitated his son Abraham III[7] to start a new glassworks at Snedshill Wood, near Oakengates in the parish of Shifnal, Shropshire in 1673[8]. Abraham II probably came to know the area and its rich coal deposits after Thomas Foley[9] built his iron furnace at nearby Wombridge. Abraham III ran the Snedshill glassworks for most of his life. He made window and bottle glass[10] and nearly all his workmen were imported from Stourbridge[11]. He and his wife Cicely baptised six children at St. Andrew's Church, Shifnal between 1683 and 1699. Abraham III's glassworks was out of business by 1720, but he continued to live in a cottage nearby[12]. Cicely died there in 1727[13] and Abraham III in 1729[14].

Paul Tyzack II appears to have retired and this left Zachariah Tyzack II and his family alone at Withymoor. His oldest son Zachariah III[15] died in 1678[16] and his will was proved at Worcester[17]. In the will he is described as a broad-glassmaker of Amblecote and appoints his brother Samuel Tyzack, broad-glassmaker, as one of his executors. The testator predeceased both of his parents and willed them 'the two uppermost kneelings in that seat ... in Oldswinford church.' The total value of his estate was £34 8s 2d. His brothers: Samuel[18], William[19] and Edward[20] carried on the business.

Zachary Tyzack II became a churchwarden of Oldswinford in 1684 and died in 1695[21]. Despite having outlived his son, who did leave a will, he died intestate and his estate was appraised on 23rd July 1695.

One of the earliest cartels in England was formed in the glass trade. On 1st May 1703 an agreement was made between: Samuel, William and Edward Tyzack, Thomas and John Henzey[22], Edward, Ananias and Joshua Henzey III[23], and Benjamin, Elijah and Humphrey Batchelor[24]. They agreed to deliver eight score cases of good merchantable uncut broad-glass on the River Severn, each year for eleven years. Their output was to be purchased by Benjamin Perrot and his son Benjamin, merchants of Bristol[25]. Mr R. Kilburn kindly examined the Bristol port books to determine the eventual destination of this glass, but sadly, the port books covering export shipments for the period Christmas 1702 to Christmas 1705 are missing. The 1706 book[26] records only three shipments by 'Benj Parrott', all to Jamaica. The first, on 7th February, was two tons of beer, two thousand four hundred English glass bottles and two thousand one hundred drinking glasses[27]. The second was nine hundred English made glasses on 5th March[28]. The third was two and a half tons of beer in bottles, three thousand English glass bottles and one thousand two hundred English glasses on 30th April[29]. No window glass was mentioned, which suggests Perrot was either selling it locally or shipping it to other English ports. There were a few shipments of window glass by other merchants, but not many. Evidently, the main export business was in bottles, mainly used for beer. For example, on the vessel by which Benjamin Perrot sent his first shipment, there were ten other shipments of beer and one of cider, a total of over twenty thousand bottles. If this was the cargo of one ship, the total export trade from Bristol must have been vast.

On 11th April 1717 the Stourbridge attorney Thomas Milward paid £7 5s for 'Ten cases of Broad glass to be delivered at Stourbridge by Mr Zach. Tysack[30] ' and thirty more cases to be delivered at the same rate[31]. This clearly suggests a continued fall in the price, which in 1712 had been reduced from twenty-six shillings to twenty-two shillings per case[32]. The fall in the price of broad-glass was calamitous for the local glassmakers including the Tyzacks. The bankruptcy of Samuel Tyzack glassmaker late of Kingswinford was reported in 1723_{33}. Withymoor Glasshouse probably closed about this time, as there are no further references to it.

1 Exchequer Bill filed in 1670. Henry Grey (d. 1687), of Enville Hall, son of Ambrose Grey (d. 1636) was of the same family as Lady Jane Grey (b. 1537), Queen of England for nine days in July 1553.

2 Supra, Colemans Glasshouse

3 John Tyzack, son of Paul and Bridgitt Tyzack, bap. 26th Apr 1612, Kingswinford.

4 Exchequer Bill filed in 1666 by John Tyzack, a workman, for wrongful dismissal.

5 PRO Spec. Depos. Mixed Cos. 19 Cav II Easter No. 8 Exch. K.R., Depositions before a commission to enquire into a complaint brought by John Tyzack against Joshua Henzey and Henry Oseland.

6 Infra, Hagley Glasshouse.

7 Abraham Bigo III, son of Abraham Bigo II and his wife, thought, but not proven to be Alice, nee Tyzack, bap. 9th Dec 1655, Oldswinford.

8 SRO D641/2/D/2/3 shows that Abraham Bigo II, glassmaker of Amblecote, leased land adjoining Snedshill, in Idsall Manor, containing a glasshouse and dwelling house in 1673 for twenty-one years at £10 per year; Shifnal Churchwarden's Records 1673-1726 reveals that Abraham Bigo III came to Oakengates in 1676, when he was aged 20, paying 1d to Humphrey Briggs Esquire for land.

9 Thomas Foley, son of Richard (Fiddler) Foley and his wife Alice, nee Brindley, b. 3rd Dec 1617, bap. 7th Dec 1617, Dudley St. Thomas's; purchased Witley Court in 1655; d. 1st Oct 1677; bur. Witley.

10 *Victoria County History of Shropshire*, v 10, pp295-6.

11 Poor Law and Settlement Documents of Oldswinford. His workmen included several Padgetts, a family long associated with the Tyzacks.

12 SRO D641/2/E/4/4 Survey by Richard Hill of the manor of Shifnal including Priorslee and Oakengates 1720, refers to a 'decayed glasshouse.'

13 Cicely Bigo, bur. Shifnal, St. Andrew's, 31st Mar 1727.

14 Abraham Bigo, bur. Shifnal, St. Andrew's 12th Mar 1729.

15 Zachariah Tyzack III, son of Zachariah II and Elizabeth Tyzack, bap. 14th Aug 1647, Oldswinford.
16 Zachariah Tyzack, bur. 2nd Nov 1678, Oldswinford.
17 WRO, Will of Zachariah Tyzack, 14th Feb 1679.
18 Samuel Tyzack, son of Zachariah and Elizabeth Tyzack, bap. 3rd May 1651, Oldswinford.
19 William Tyzack, son of Zachariah and Elizabeth Tyzack, b. 26th Apr 1659; bap. 8th May 1659, Oldswinford.
20 Edward Tyzack, son of Zachariah and Elizabeth Tyzack.
21 Zachariah Tyzack, bur. 26th Mar 1695, Oldswinford.
22 Of Harlestones glasshouse.
23 Of Brettell Lane glasshouse.
24 Of Fimbrell Glasshouse.
25 WRO, Palfrey collection. The historical significance of this agreement is discussed in W.H.B. Court, *The Rise of The Midland Industries 1600-1838* (1938), p126-6.
26 Bristol Port Books, E190 1160/5.
27 Ibid.
28 Ibid.
29 Ibid.
30 Zachariah Tyzack, son of William and Elizabeth Tyzack, bap. 21st May 1687, Oldswinford.
31 Society of Antiquaries, Prattinton collection, v 30, *Account Book of Thomas Milward*. Microfilm copy in WRO.
32 London Gazette, 10th Jan 1712.
33 London Gazette, 13th Aug 1723.

CHAPTER 14

Hawbush Glasshouse, Brettell Lane

The second Henzey glasshouse in Brettell Lane was founded by Ananias Henzey II[1] on land known as Hawbush, just to the west of his father's glassworks and on the south side of Brettell Lane. He bought the land in 1649[2], probably with the intention of building a glasshouse when economic conditions in England were more settled[3]. So Ananias Henzey II did not build his glassworks immediately, but spent much of his time attempting to establish himself in Ireland. He arrived in Ireland some time before 1655 and sought out his fellow Lorrainer countrymen, the Bigoes[4]. He married Philip Bigoe's daughter, Catherine Bigoe[5] and they named their first son Bigoe Henzey.

Early in 1670, when living at Graguefine, Kings County, Ananias built a glasshouse at Portarlington in Queens County but, despite his family's experience and tradition of skill, he experienced great difficulty. In November 1670 it was recorded:

> 'After some small progress in his undertaking, he is it seems at present at a stop by occasion of some disappointment in the melting of his metal.'[6]

Whether he eventually succeeded in Ireland or not is unclear, but he returned to England in 1674 and built a glasshouse at Hawbush on the land he had bought twenty-five years earlier[7]. He arranged for the glassworks to be managed by his brother, Paul Henzey I, who ran the other Henzey Brettell Lane glasshouse, inherited from their father.

Ananias's nephew, Edward Henzey[8], who had also been in Ireland, returned to England and married Rose Jeston[9] in 1681[10].

Their marriage was by a licence and although they were both stated to be of Oldswinford parish, the licence was for marriage at Astley, Shrawley or Shelsley[11]. The choice of Astley as the location for their wedding is intriguing, but is probably because of Edward's mother's connection with the parish[12]. Edward then began to work at Hawbush Glasshouse for his uncle Paul Henzey I. In 1693 Ananias Henzey II, the absentee owner, handed over the running of the Hawbush Glasshouse to his son Bigoe[13].

Economic conditions in England began to deteriorate soon after the accession of William III, leading to the imposition of an excise duty on glass[14]. In 1697 Ananias Henzey II and Elisha [sic] Batchelor presented a petition against excise duty speaking for 'the Glass Makers, and Workmen, in and about Stourbridge.'[15]

Ananias Henzey II had always been an absentee owner and in 1702 he sold the Hawbush property to Edward Finch[16]. Probably this was the Edward Finch baptised 8th September 1675 at Dudley, the brother of Joseph Finch the Dudley ironmonger who married Edward Bradley's widow, Anne, in 1702. Edward Finch must have sold the property to the Earl of Dudley, who leased the glassworks back to Bigoe Henzey.

Bigoe Henzey lived at Barnagrothy, Kings County, Ireland from about 1715 where three of his daughters married into the wealthy and respected Armstrong family. He surrendered his lease of the Hawbush Glasshouse to Burlton Compson of Burton-on-Trent on 8th January 1724. Parties to the agreement were Windsor James of Dob Hill, John Newborough of Holloway End and Henry Bradley of Audnam, all glassmakers of Wordsley. The transferred property included:

> 'all those four cottages and gardens belonging late in the several occupations, Nicholas Henzey, Thomas Batchelor, Mary ????? and Paul Henzey and all that glasshouse with the outbuildings thereto belonging and five potthouses near adjoining together with barn containing five bays of barning and meadow, late in occupation of Paul Henzey called the Blackhouse meadow coppice now is late divided into six closes or pastures containing an estimation two and twenty

acres be it more or less, all which said cottages, glasshouse buildings are situated, in Brettell within the manor of Kingswinford.'[17]

Bigoe Henzey of Barnagrothy, Kings County, Ireland died in 1733 and his will was proved in Ulster on 3rd February. There are no further references to the Hawbush Glasshouse after this time.

---

1 Ananias Henzey, son of Joshua Henzey and his wife Joan, nee Brettell, bap. 5th Oct 1618, Kingswinford.

2 Ibid, D.R. Guttery, p17.

3 These were uncertain times; King Charles I had been executed on 30th January that year.

4 Philip Bigoe ran a glasshouse at Birr, Kings County. He received denization 10th Jun 1637 and prospered. He was appointed High Sheriff of King's County in 1662. It is not proven, but Philip Bigoe was probably the brother or cousin of Abraham Bigo I who worked first with the Tyzacks on the Staffordshire / Cheshire border. Then, after Mansell's closure of his business at the Isle of Purbeck in Dorset, Abraham Bigo also came to Birr and ran a glasshouse at Clonbrone.

5 Mar. Ananias Hensey and Katherin Bego, 14th Jan 1649, St. Dunstan, Stepney, London.

6 State Papers, Ireland, op cit M.S. Dudley Westropp, p33.

7 Ibid, D.R. Guttery, p19.

8 Edward Henzey, son of Joshua and Dorothy Henzey, b. c1651.

9 Rose Jeston daughter of Edward Jeston, clothier of Stourbridge and his wife Rose, nee Hickman, bap. 23rd Aug 1662, Oldswinford. She was a cousin of Elizabeth Jeston who married Ananias Henzey III the previous year. Her branch of the Jeston family was originally from Hagley and she was distantly related to the Jestons running the Heath Glassworks.

10 Mar. Edward Henzey and Rose Jeston, 14th Dec 1681, Astley, Worcestershire.

11 WRO, marriage licence dated 10th Dec 1681.

12 H.S. Grazebrook, *Collections for a Genealogy of the Noble Families of Henzey, Tyttery and Tyzack* (1877), p39.

13 Ibid, D.R. Guttery, pp15 et seq.

14 Supra, Bagues.

15 HOC Journal XI 707.
16 Ibid, D.R. Guttery, p29, p50.
17 Manor Rolls - Court Baron Manor of Kingswinford 1724, Ref. Book (4) p319.

CHAPTER 15

Hagley Glasshouse

After the disintegration of the partnership at Withymoor Glasshouse in 1665, John Tyzack sought new premises and found them at Hagley. The date of commencement is not known other than that it was before 1678. The location is a little easier to determine. The Hagley tithe map prepared 1837-9 and its key shows a plot of land[1] between what is now the Evans-Halshaw car showroom[2] and the Lyttelton Arms Hotel, called Glass House Close.

John Tyzack died aged fifty-seven in 1670[3] and was succeeded by his only surviving son Paul III[4]. In 1677 Paul Tyzack III contributed for the good of the poor[5].

On 28th September 1678 an indenture was drawn up between Thomas Grove of Hagley, and John Pagett[6] and Paul Tyzack glassmakers of Hagley. Grove leased for ninety-nine years, at eight shillings a year rent, 'all that Glasshouse in Hagley together with all houses and buildings thereunto adjoining and now in the occupation of John Pagett and Paul Tyzack' and a further half-acre of land 'adjoining the said Glasshouse.[7] '

Paul Tyzack III died in 1685 and was succeeded by his oldest sons Paul IV[8], John[9] and William[10]. His youngest son Benjamin[11] chose the career of a sythesmith and founded the Tyzack dynasty of Sheffield, sythesmiths and edge tool manufacturers[12].

Paul Tyzack IV, glassmaker of Hagley died in 1694 and in his will, made earlier the same year, left five shillings to his cousin Robert Paget. John and William Tyzack continued to work the glasshouse. William, glassmaker of Hagley, died in 1716 and his will contains the last known reference to glassmaking in Hagley. The glasshouse probably closed about this time.

---

1 Plot Reference No 225. Area 5a. 2r. 38. p.

2 Formerly the Forge Garage.

3 John Tyzack, bur. 23rd May 1670, Oldswinford.

4 Paul Tyzack, son of John Tyzack and his second wife, name unknown, b. 24th Dec 1643. His older brother John died as an infant.

5 Society of Antiquaries, Prattinton collection, v 30, p60 *Account book of Dr Simon Ford, Rector of Oldswinford*. Microfilm copy at WRO.

6 Mar. Paul Tyzack III and Anne Patchett, Hagley, 1670.

7 BRL, 280390.

8 Paul Tyzack IV, son of Paul Tyzack III and his wife Ann, nee Patchett, bap. 6th Mar 1670, Oldswinford.

9 John Tyzack, son of Paul Tyzack III and his wife Ann, nee Patchett, bap. 1673, Hagley.

10 William Tyzack, son of Paul Tyzack III and his wife Ann, nee Patchett, bap. 1677, Hagley.

11 Benjamin Tyzack, son of Paul Tyzack III and his wife Ann, nee Patchett, bap. 1684, Hagley.

12 D. Tyzack, *Glass, Tools & Tyzacks* (1995), p113.

CHAPTER 16

Jacob's Well Glasshouse, Audnam

Jacob's Well glasshouse was built by Edward Bradley[1] and is significant as the first of the Stourbridge works to be started by a native Englishman. The name Bradley appears regularly in the early Dudley and Oldswinford parish registers as well as those of Kingswinford. The 'art, feate & mysterie' of glassmaking had to be learned and in Edward's case it presumably resulted from his marriage[2] in 1681 to Anne Tittery[3] whose grandfather Daniel—a first-generation Lorrainer immigrant—had founded the Holloway End glassworks. In 1682, already described as a white-glass maker, Edward bought land and built his glassworks at Audnam. The precise location of Jacob's Well is not known, other than it was 'near Stourbridge.'[4] In the Kingswinford Manor Rolls, Jacob's Well is described as bounded on the west by the turnpike leading from Wolverhampton to Stourbridge and near to Audnam Brook. The line of Audnam Brook marks the boundary of the pebble beds to the north and the dune sands to the south and is therefore an excellent location for a well[5].

When aged only forty Edward began to settle his affairs, probably due to illness. He made his will on 1st March 1700 being 'tired and weake in body' and died two years later. In his will[6], he is described as a whiteglassmaker of the parish of Kingswinford. He left legacies to several of his children, but as they were all aged under twenty-one, he left the bulk of his estate to his widow Anne. He made her his sole executrix and charged her with maintaining their children out of his 'store and estate and the profits thereof' until they should attain twenty-one years of age or marry[7]. An inventory of his goods and chattels was performed by Thomas Henzey and Thomas Batchelor, which includes 'in the warehouse, glassware, kelp and sand' and 'in the glasshouse, tools and implements belonging to glassmaking'. His total estate was valued at £424 12s 9d$_8$.

Edward Bradley's oldest son, Henry$_9$, came into his inheritance of 'three score pounds' when he attained the age of twenty-one in 1702 and took over running the business. In 1713 he married Mary$_{10}$, the daughter of Windsor James, of Dob Hill Glassworks. Henry now decided to build a new glassworks, probably encouraged by the success of his father-in-law. In 1715 Henry mortgaged his glasshouse and land to Joshua Henzey for £450$_{11}$. With this money, he built a new glassworks nearby at Audnam. Little did the enthusiastic Henry know that the market was at its peak. The market price for broad-glass began to fall alarmingly$_{12}$ and Henry was to become entangled in a mess of further mortgages and debts$_{13}$.

---

1 Edward Bradley, son of Thomas Bradley, yeoman of Oldswinford and his wife Frances, daughter of Richard Bradley, b. 20th Oct 1659; bap. 6th Nov 1659, Oldswinford.

2 Mar. Edward Bradley and Anne Tittery, 30th Aug 1681, Oldswinford

3 Anne Tittery, daughter of Paul Tittery, b. 18th Mar 1656, bap. 20th Mar 1656, Oldswinford.

4 It was associated with glass in 1735 by R. Wilkes. Op cit Revd, Stebbing Shaw, *The History and Antiquities of Staffordshire*, v 1(1798).

5 Stourbridge and District Water Board built a pumping station to extract water from the dune sands, which still stands today north of Wollaston Road.

6 PRO, PROB 11/460 248RH-249LH, PCC will of Edward Bradley, 30th Oct 1701.

7 The will was witnessed by Anne's cousin, Thomas Rogers II, the proprietor of the Holloway End Glasshouse. Anne quickly remarried to Joseph Finch, an ironmonger of Dudley. Mar. Joseph Finch, widower and Anne Bradley, widow, 3rd Jan 1702, Enville.

8 PRO, PROB4/25251, Inventory of the estate of Edward Bradley, appraised 22nd Apr 1701.

9 Henry Bradley, oldest son of Edward Bradley and his wife Anne, nee Tittery, b.

c1681.
10 Mar. Henry Bradley and Mary, daughter of Windsor James, 14th Feb 1713, Kingswinford.
11 DA, Earl of Dudley's Estate Records.
12 Supra, Brettell Lane.
13 Infra, Audnam Glassworks.

CHAPTER 17

Heath Glassworks, Stourbridge

The Heath Glassworks is unique among the 'Stourbridge' glasshouses as the only one of the later 'coned' glasshouses located in Stourbridge. The exact date when it was built is not known, but it was clearly a business venture of the Jeston family, upholsterers of Stourbridge. Humphrey Jeston I was their patriarch, the son of William Jeston, a blacksmith of Birmingham and later London. On 3rd June 1636 Humphrey Jeston I bought some land at the Heath in Stourbridge from Robert Wildsmith and his mother Elinor Bradley[1] and bought more in 1640[2]. During 1643 he was a churchwarden of Oldswinford, at the same time as Joshua Henzey I who ran the Brettell Lane glasshouse. It is possible that conversation with Joshua Henzey first led Humphrey Jeston I to consider a venture into the glass trade for himself or his son. However, Humphrey I died in 1645[3].

Humphrey Jeston I had lost his first son, Roger, seven days after birth; but had a second son, Humphrey II[4]. Humphrey II presumably worked with his father, as he was also an upholsterer in Stourbridge. It was a turbulent time to be in business. In 1644 Humphrey II and his brother-in-law, John Leech, both of Stourbridge, presented a petition to Parliament asking for the restitution of three horses taken from them by troopers[5]. Extensive military activity occurred in the Stourbridge area during June 1644, the second year of the Civil War[6].

Humphrey Jeston II had seven children. The oldest son Humphrey died young leaving four surviving sons. His second son was John Jeston[7], who married Mary Henzey[8]. Their marriage was by a licence[9] in which John Jeston is described as a glassmaker of Oldswinford—the first record of a Jeston as a glassmaker. This does not prove the Heath Glassworks had been built—John could have worked for his father-in-law at the Brettell Lane Glassworks—but it certainly dates the Jeston's entry into the trade of glassmaking.

In 1685 John Jeston, described as a glassmaker of Oldswinford, became Overseer of the Poor for Oldswinford. To become Overseer he must have been an independently wealthy man. It is tempting to suggest this was as the result of having built the Heath Glassworks, but again it was not necessarily so. His independence could stem from the family wealth from the upholstery trade, although this hypothesis is weak. If John were sufficiently wealthy to become Overseer, why would he bother to work as a glassmaker in somebody else's employment? The circumstances suggest John Jeston built the Heath Glassworks sometime before 1685, possibly even before 1681. Undoubtedly the capital was supplied by his father, Humphrey Jeston II.

Humphrey's youngest son, Thomas[10], was also a glassmaker. He died unmarried and intestate in 1690[11]. Letters of administration for his estate[12] were administered by his father and his brother-in-law, John Alling[13]. The fact that Thomas was also a glassmaker further reinforces the suggestion that the brothers had been running the Heath Glassworks together. It is unlikely that throughout their working lives they would have continued to live in Stourbridge and travel every day to work at the Henzey Glassworks in Brettell Lane.

The first reference to the Heath Glassworks is found the following year and involves the only son of Humphrey II not so far discussed, his oldest son and heir, William[14]. On 4th April 1691 Humphry Jeston II, upholsterer of Stourbridge and William Jeston, his oldest son and legal heir, mortgaged the Heath Glassworks to Thomas Dalton, a citizen and apothecary of London, for £200. The document refers to:

> 'the dwelling house wherin Thomas Jeston deceased (late son of the said Humfry) did lately dwell and also all that glasshouse now or late used for making drinking glasses and

whiteware ... with the stable millhouse and mill therin being for grinding mettle and materiall for making glass.'[15]

Why the Jestons mortgaged their glassworks is a mystery. However, heavy taxation and poor economic circumstances are likely causes. John Jeston petitioned Parliament about the effect of the Glass Excise in 1696[16].

Two years later, in 1698, a further petition was made to Parliament by John Jeston and Edward Houghton, a workman. They represented the proprietors of the bottle glasshouses, white glasshouses and broad glasshouses. Jeston stated 'he had not made one bottle since the commencement of the duty.'[17] Yet another petition of the glass bottlemakers and other glassmakers was presented and read on 6th March 1699[18].

On 19th March 1700 John Wheeler[19] let to Humfry Jeston, upholsterer of Oldswinford, 'two meadows or parcels of meadow and ground commonly called the Heath Meadows.'

On 19th April 1705 Humfry Jeston, upholsterer of Stourbridge, mortgaged 'a whiteware glasshouse ... situate at the Heath' to Thomas Dalton, citizen and apothecary of London. The glassworks is described as a 'glasshouse for making glass bottles'. The third member of the tripartite agreement was Edward Hallen, writingmaster of Stourbridge, an arbitrator of the 1703 Perrot cartel. In 1708 John Jeston became Overseer of the Poor for Stourbridge.

Humfry fell into arrears with interest on the mortgage and Thomas Dalton foreclosed, becoming the owner of the Heath Glassworks. So, on 5th October 1709 Dalton leased the glassworks to John Jeston. The lease refers to 'all that glasshouse near the said messuage now or late used for making drinking glasses and whiteware'. Thomas Dalton's will, dated 9th November 1714, describes him as late of Edmonton, County Middlesex, in which he leaves 'my said house and glasshouse at Stourbridge' to George Winshurestand[20].

In 1720, described as a glassbottle and white glassmaker of the Heath, John Jeston took Samuel Athersich as an apprentice for seven years. In the first year his wages were to be 2s 6d per week, rising steadily to 5s 6d in his seventh year[21].

John Jeston died in 1727[22] and his will was proved in PCC. He bequeathed his estate to his only surviving son, Humphrey III[23].

On 20th September 1727, Humfry Jeston III, glassmaker of the Heath, was forced to raise yet another mortgage, this time from William Penn[24], yeoman of Chaddesley Corbett, for £200. The indenture refers to:

> 'the dwellinghouse . . . wherin John Jeston father of the said Humfry late did inhabit and Mary Jeston, mother of the said Humfry now doth dwell . . . and also all that glasshouse called The Bottle House situate at the Heath.'[25]

Now this reference is intriguing. Had Humfry bought the glasshouse back from George Winshurestand, or were there two glasshouses on the site, only one of which was mortgaged? The latter seems likely. The mortgage on this occasion refers to 'The Bottle House', presumably the same one mortgaged previously to Dalton in 1705 described as 'glasshouse for making glass bottles'. It appears it was the 'Drinking glass and whiteware' glasshouse mortgaged in 1691 that Dalton came to own and lease back in 1709.

In 1729 Humfry Jeston III was intending to marry Elizabeth, the daughter of Anthony Ward. A tripartite agreement was signed on 23rd August 1729 that conveyed land and property, including some at the Heath, from the Ward family to Humfry Jeston, presumably by way of a dowry. His second cousin, Joshua Henzey III, glassmaker of Audnam, was a party to the agreement, which refers to 'all that estate glasshouse together with all warehouse buildings and all other utensils for the making of glass.'[26]

Despite his dowry, Humphrey Jeston III was unable to extricate himself from his financial difficulties and became bankrupt[27]. Commissioners worked the glassworks until it was offered for sale in 1736[28].

Sometime before 1745 the glassworks was taken by Edward Russell the younger[29]. This date can be extrapolated from an examination of parish of settlement that took place in 1782[30].

William Penn, who held the mortgage on the glassworks property died in 1731[31]. So a further transfer of title took place on 12th January 1749, involving his executrix and legatees[32]. Edward Russell continued to run the Heath Glassworks and in 1753 became a churchwarden of Oldswinford. In 1760 he was producing best and ordinary flint glass and phials[33]. Later, in 1762 he became Overseer of the Poor for Oldswinford. Guttery quoted from an undisclosed source that in 1769 Edward Russell the younger was the 'owner of the Heath Glassworks . . . a wealthy glass manufacturer'.[34] On 25th October 1771 Edward Russell, glassmaker of Oldswinford, took on Benjamin Bate as an apprentice. Russell and his brother-in-law, Francis Witton, are among the seventy-two people listed as proprietors in the 1776 Stourbridge Canal Act[35]. Francis Witton[36] had married[37] Edward Russell's sister, Mary[38] and was later to run the glassworks.

In 1776 Joseph Heely, passing through the district, left a record of his journey[39]. En route between Hagley and Enville, he records:

'Seeing Stourbridge before me, a town eminent for its glass manufactory I was induced having never seen the curious art of forming that delicate ware into its various uses, to breakfast there and satisfy my curiosity . . . I was really astonished to see with what facility a process was conducted, that always appeared to me so extremely mysterious—but commonly the most impenetrably one seemingly, when known appears so very simple, that we are equally astonished the other way, and blush in our ignorance at not being able to find it out without a demonstration; so in the art of glassmaking, particularly the introducing of those beautiful spiral threads of a different colour, so nicley spun within the neck of a wine glass, which appear so inexplicable, is performed, even by children. One of these glasses I desired to be made me as elegant as possible which was done almost as soon as asked for.'

The fascinated traveller then continued on his way with his 'delicate ware' in his pocket. He did not state at which glassworks this feat was performed, but it was almost certainly the Heath. The mortgage indenture of 1691 and the lease of 1709 show that 'drinking glasses' were being made at the Heath. Heely was between Stourbridge town and Kinver Edge and on leaving the glassworks he crossed 'an extensive chearful common' before arriving at the 'delicious valley at Stewponey'. It was probably while crossing the Heath that his elegant opaque-twist stem wineglass met with the fate that so many more have subsequently suffered:

> 'I put the glass into my pocket, which the half-burnt, cadaverous looking animal made me, wishing to preserve it; but the first style I came to, demolished it for ever.'

Edward Russell died in 1778[40]. His obituary describes him as 'an eminent glassmaker at Stourbridge.'[41] His will was proved in PCC in October 1778[42] and as he died without issue, he left a wide spread of legacies. He left a thousand pounds to his nephew, John Hill of Wordsley[43], and left his estate at Hawbush to John and Mary Hill's children. This was the John Hill of Audnam and Wordsley Flint Glassworks who subsequently went to Waterford. It was Edward Russell's will that 'the trade be carried on jointly by the three sons of my dear sister, namely Francis[44], Richard Russell[45] and Sarjant[46] '. These were three of the sons of his sister Mary and her husband Francis Witton of Lye. The three brothers ran the firm together for six years until Francis Witton died[47], leaving his estate to his two brothers. Then, in 1786, Richard Russell Witton conveyed his interest in the glassmaking business to the youngest brother, Serjeant Witton, for an annuity of £120 per annum. The indenture refers to the 'dwellinghouse situate at the Heath wherin the said Edward Russell lately dwelt and now in the occupation of the said Richard Russell Witton and Serjant Witton with the glasshouse thereunto adjoining.'[48]

Serjeant Witton was given his unusual name to commemorate his descent from Richard Serjeant[49], one of the 'Bartholomew Divines, who, along with Henry Oseland[50], were ejected from their livings in 1662. Serjeant Witton became Overseer of the Poor for Oldswinford in 1787 and is listed among Stourbridge traders of 1793[51]. However, he suffered financial problems and took out considerable mortgages. In 1788 he sold Heathfield House to John Witton junior, a maltster, who later bought the enclosed Short Heath opposite the house. By 1801 he was bankrupt[52]. His mansion house at the Heath and the Heath Glassworks were sold at the Talbot

Hotel[53]. Serjeant Witton died nine years later in 1810[54], aged forty-eight. The Heath estate was bought from his assignees by Francis Rufford senior[55], a banker who lived at Bank House, Stourbridge.

Francis Rufford's original business was as a carrier, running wagons from the west of England, via Hereford and on to Stourbridge[56]. Francis Rufford & Co. operated the mail coach between Stourbridge and London. He prospered and went into banking in 1797 with his youngest son Philip[57] and brother-in-law Thomas Biggs[58] as partners.

Philip Rufford took charge of running the glassworks. He moved into Heath House, next to the glassworks, and lived there for over fifty years until he retired.

Trade was buoyant throughout the Regency period, the heyday of cut glass. The only records during this period are a succession of trade directory entries showing the growing wealth and diversification of the Rufford family. Sherriff's 1812 plan shows 'Heath Glass House' with a graphically portrayed glasshouse cone.

Francis Rufford senior retired from business when he was about seventy-two years old and made his will on 14th July 1828, describing himself as a banker of Stourbridge. His son Philip continued the glassmaking business, making plain and cut glass[59]. Francis senior died in 1831[60], aged seventy-eight and his will was proved later that year[61]. He left several small legacies to his sister Sarah[62] and his nieces, but shared his extensive estate between his sons and his grandson Francis Rufford. He willed to his grandson Francis, the son of Phillip Rufford, 'that capital messuage or mansion house situate at the Heath, in the parish of Oldswinford, now in the possession of my son Philip Rufford with the glasshouse warehouse barns stables coachhouse and other offices yard garden and small close of land . . . that were purchased of and from the assignees of Mr Serjeant Witton.' He left to his son Philip 'the several newly erected tenements or dwellinghouses buildings erections and improvements built created and made by me on the said premises.' After Philip's death, they were also to pass to Francis Rufford. The testator left his banking interests in equal shares to his three sons, Francis[63], George Pierpoint[64] and Philip and his grandson Francis.

Although Heath House was bequeathed to Francis Rufford junior, known as Frank, he remained at his home, Yew Tree House, Belbroughton[65]. Philip Rufford continued to occupy Heath House, now owned by his son, rather than his father, until he retired[66].

Philip Rufford paid £2,756 10s excise duty for the year ending 5th January 1833[67], suggesting this was the ninth largest of the sixteen Stourbridge/Dudley glasshouses of the day. Shortly after the death of his father, Philip Rufford took his clerk, William Walker[68], into the business as a partner[69]. The firm traded as Rufford and Walker, manufacturers of flint glass, plain and cut[70]. Trade directories between 1839 and 1845 repeatedly list the partnership of Rufford and Walker. Philip Rufford eventually retired from business some time after 1851. He left Heath House and moved to Leamington Spa, Warwickshire where he died in 1860.

Francis Rufford appears in the 1841 Stourbridge census as a glass manufacturer living at The Heath. However, he was very ambitious and in 1847 was elected conservative member of parliament for the City of Worcester, having spent over £4,000 on his campaign. He and his bank promoted various railway schemes, an alkali works near Droitwich and other speculations. He left his partner Charles Wragge[71] to cope with the bank's affairs and became chairman of the Oxford, Worcester & Wolverhampton Railway[72]. He ran the company 'with a rod of iron' and used it to further his own personal interests. After many years of wrangling, four miles of track was opened to traffic in the Worcester area in October 1850. However, Rufford was facing mounting personal problems and in the following month he ceased to be chairman. On 26th June 1851 Rufford's bank, Messrs. Ruffords and Wragge stopped payments to the O.W.W.R.[73] The bank finally failed in July 1851. Francis Rufford was bankrupted and after becoming mentally ill, entered an asylum in Sutton Coldfield.

The failure inevitably put a great financial burden on the glassmaking business. William Walker approached Benjamin Richardson of Wordsley Flint Glassworks and asked him to take their stock to avoid it falling into the hands of their creditors at reduced prices[74]. This was arranged and Walker was able to carry on the business.

In February 1852 at the Talbot Hotel, Davies and Son auctioned the assets of the bank. Yew Tree House at Belbroughton, Heath House and Red Hill House in Stourbridge were sold. Bedcote Mill[75], collieries, public houses, banking premises, land and Heath Glassworks all came under the auctioneer's hammer. William Walker secured the glassworks and took his oldest son, James[76], into the firm.

At a meeting held in Dudley on 15th November 1858, where the name of the employer's organisation was changed to the Midland Association of Flint Glass Manufacturers, William Walker was appointed treasurer. After the lockout, in 1859[77], William Walker and Son's claim from the employers' defence fund[78] suggests the firm was the sixth largest of the thirteen in the Midlands Association.

William Walker lived at Norton House, Upper Swinford[79]. In 1861 he employed seventy-four men and twenty-four boys[80], suggesting he was the largest employer of the six main Stourbridge factories. In 1868, by which time he lived at Catherwell House, he obtained a fourteen-year extension of the lease at £200 per annum from his landlords, who also carried out some improvements to the works costing £150[81]. He died later that year[82], aged sixty-seven and his will was proved at Worcester[83], valuing his estate at less than £16,000. He left to his son, William[84], the shop he operated on the corner of Queens Square and Exchange Street, Wolverhampton, as a glass and china dealer. He left a half share in his glass business to each of his other sons, James[85] and Philip[86], with whom he had been in partnership.

The firm continued to trade under the same title until its cessation, but about 1879 James retired to Bredon House, Malvern Wells and sold his share to his younger brother, Philip[87]. James' son, James Harry Walker[88], remained employed by the firm.

In 1881 Philip Walker employed 90 workpeople[89], but the period 1882 to 1889 was one of great depression in the Stourbridge area affecting all trades, iron, mining and brick-making as well as glass. Philip Walker, was an accountant, not a glassmaker and in this difficult environment struggled with the business. He was approached by George Mills, who, having fallen out with his partner

Frederick Stuart at the Albert Glassworks was seeking a new partner. They agreed a deal that would secure a future for James' son, James Harry Walker and in 1882 he closed the Heath Glassworks putting nearly three hundred glassmakers out of work[90]. He sold the assets and goodwill to George Mills[91]. James Harry Walker joined George Mills in partnership at the Albert Glassworks. Philip Walker went to work for Thomas Webb & Sons at the Dennis Glassworks[92].

James Walker had almost certainly intended to retire. However, he became increasingly entangled in his son's business at the Albert Glassworks, providing loans and unpaid practical assistance[93]. He also remained responsible for the rental payments on the lease of the Heath Glassworks until it was surrendered in 1891[94]. It was probably these pressures that lead him to shoot himself on 2nd March 1891. The coroner recorded a 'state of temporary insanity' at an inquest held on 4th March 1891[95].

The glassworks buildings were demolished in 1895 when Edward Webb came to live at Heath House and renamed it Studley Court. The site of the glassworks is behind the Star and Garter public house, by Mary Stevens Park. It stood close to where the present high wall surrounding the park is joined to the houses standing a few yards back from the top of Norton Road. A temporary office building belonging to Dudley Metropolitan Borough covers the place where the cone stood.

---

1 WRO, 705:332 BA1943.

2 Ibid, D.R. Guttery, p48.

3 Humphrey Jeston, bur. 19th Jun 1645, Oldswinford.

4 Humphrey Jeston, son of Humphrey and Mary Jeston, bap. 12th Feb 1624, Oldswinford.

5 Hist. MSS Com Rep IV., 272.

6 John 'Tinker' Fox had established a parliamentary garrison of three hundred men at nearby Stourton Castle, an obvious strategic location. Major Hervey applied to Sir Gilbert Gerrard, the Royalist Governor of Worcester, for help to take Stourton Castle. Fox heard of this and applied on 24th March for reinforcements, but they did not arrive. Fox met Gerrard on Stourbridge

Heath and a skirmish ensued. There are conflicting accounts of which side gained the upper hand, but it certainly appears to have been a Royalist victory as Stourton Castle was surrendered. The battle involved Prince Rupert, who had spent three days the previous year at Richard 'Fiddler' Foley's house in Stourbridge (now the Talbot Hotel). At the time of the skirmish on Stourbridge Heath he was quartered at Wollescote, the home of Thomas Milward. The account of the Worcestershire historian, John Noake, states that a parliamentary trooper pursued Prince Rupert from the battlefield. He was only saved by getting through the Heath gate, leading off the common to Oldswinford, and having it slammed behind him.

7 John Jeston, son of Humphrey Jeston, b. 16th Jan 1656; bap. 7th Feb 1656, Oldswinford.

8 Mar. John Jeston and Mary, daughter of Paul Henzey I, who was running the Brettell Lane Glassworks, 14th Dec 1681, Oldswinford.

9 WRO, marriage licence, dated 4th Dec 1681.

10 Thomas Jeston, son of Humphrey Jeston, bap. 10th Feb 1662, Oldswinford.

11 Thomas Jeston, bur. 18th Jan 1690, Oldswinford.

12 WRO, Admon of Thomas Jeston, 31st Jan 1690.

13 Or Allon.

14 William Jeston, son of Humphrey Jeston II, bap. 27th Sep 1651, Oldswinford.

15 WRO, 705:332 BA1943. Thomas Dalton was a good friend of William Hickman (1668-c1705), dissenting minister, who was a nephew of Edward Jeston (1623-1679), cloth manufacturer of Stourbridge and third cousin of William Jeston, the mortgagor. When William Hickman wrote his will on 18th Mar 1692 he left to 'my friend Mr Thomas Dalton, the elder, of London, apothecary, £200.' The Hickmans were a wealthy Stourbridge family, who like the Jestons had made their fortune from the cloth-making trade. It is possible, but not proven, that as an apothecary, Dalton may have supplied materials to both the cloth-making and glass-making trades.

16 Supra, Bagues.

17 HOC Journal XII, p281, 21st May 1698.

18 HOC Journal XII, 551.

19 Supra, John Wheeler was a wealthy sythesmith of Wollaston Hall.

20 WRO, 705:332 BA1943.

21 Poor Law and Settlement Documents of Oldswinford.

22 John Jeston, bur. 30th Sep 1727, Oldswinford.

23 Humphrey Jeston, son of John Jeston and his wife Mary, nee Henzey, bap. 5th Oct 1692, Oldswinford.

24 William Penn (1656-1731) married Mary Tristram (1672-1729), daughter of William Tristram of Oldswinford, reputedly the inventor of the glass cone (according to MSS of Dr John Tristram of Moor Hall, Belbroughton, quoted by Grazebrook, *The Heraldry of Worcestershire* (1873), pp580-3), at Broome on 16th Nov 1693. William Penn was also the grandfather of the poet and landscape artist William Shenstone of the Leasowes, Halesowen. His daughter, Ann Penn (1702-1732) married Thomas Shenstone (1686-1724) at Pedmore 8th Feb 1715 and they were the parents of William Shenstone, b. 13th Nov 1714 at the Leasowes, Halesowen; d. 11th Feb 1763.

25 WRO, 705:332 BA1943.

26 WRO, 705:332 BA1943.

27 London Gazette, 19th Nov 1734, 'Bankrupt, Humphry Jeston, of the Heath near Stourbridge, glass-maker.'

28 London Evening Post, 31st Aug 1736. 'To be lett by the year, or any term of years, Heath's New Glasshouse near Stourbridge, with all conveniences, late in the possession of Mr. Humphry Jesson [sic].'

29 Edward Russell, son of Joseph Russell of Kingswinford and his wife Sarah, nee Patchett, bap. 10th Sep 1727, Oldswinford.

30 Poor Law and Settlement Documents of Oldswinford. Examination of Parish of Settlement was a function of the archaic and chaotic Poor Laws. Until 1662 the poor were entitled to relief from Parish funds wherever they resided, and only rogues and vagabonds were removed. After an Act of 1662 any person at all likely to be a liability to a parish could be removed to their parish of settlement, unless they could give security or produce a certificate from another parish. Thus new arrivals in a parish were examined by two Justices of the Peace to establish their status. On this occasion John Brisco, a glassmaker was examined at Oldswinford and stated that he was born in 1732 and at the age of thirteen was apprenticed to Edward Russell, glassmaker of Oldswinford, for seven years. This suggests his apprenticeship as a glassmaker with Edward Russell began in 1745.

31 William Penn, d. 6th Jan 1731. His memorial is a white marble wall slab in Hagley Church.

32 WRO, 705:332 BA1943.

33 Ibid, J.A. Langford.

34 Ibid, D.R. Guttery, p111.
35 PRO, RAIL 874.1.
36 Francis Witton, b. c1725.
37 Mar. Francis Witton and Mary Russell, 5th Dec 1750, Oldswinford.
38 Mary Russell, daughter of Joseph Russell and his wife Sarah, nee Patchett, bap. 28th May 1725, Oldswinford.
39 Joseph Heely, *Letters on the Beauties of Hagley, Envil, and the Leasowes* (1778).
40 Edward Russell, d. 9th Sep 1778; bur. 15th Sep 1778, Oldswinford.
41 Birmingham Gazette, 14th Sep 1778.
42 WRO, 705:332 BA1943.
43 John Hill had married Edward Russell's niece. Mar. John Hill and Mary Russell, 27th Oct 1771, Oldswinford.
44 Francis Witton, son of Francis Witton and his wife Mary, nee Russell, bap. 25th Sep 1751, Oldswinford.
45 Richard Russell Witton, son of Francis Witton and his wife Mary, nee Russell, bap. 11th Jan 1761, Oldswinford.
46 Serjeant Witton, son of Francis Witton and Mary, nee Russell, bap. 31st Jan 1762, Oldswinford.
47 Francis Witton d. 14th Jan 1792; bur. Stourbridge Presbyterian (Unitarian) Church.
48 County Express, 10th Oct 1959.
49 Richard Serjeant, son of Humfrey Serjeant of Kings Norton, Worcestershire; b. 17th Jun 1621; Vicar of Stone, Worcestershire from 31st Oct 1656 until ejection in 1662; will, as of Hagley, 26th Apr 1693. The Nettlefolds and Chamberlains of Birmingham are descended from Richard Serjeant.
50 Supra, Henzey's Brettell Lane Glasshouse.
51 Birmingham Gazette, 1st Apr 1793.
52 Bristol Journal, 30th May 1801, 'Bankrupt, Serjeant Witton of Oldswinford, ... glass manufacturer.'
53 H.E. Palfrey, *Gentlemen at the Talbot Stourbridge*, p27.
54 Mr Serjeant Witton, bur. 10th Apr 1810, Oldswinford.
55 Francis Rufford, son of Philip and Margaret Rufford, bap. 18 Feb 1755, Worcester, All Saints. Francis married Elizabeth Biggs, 23rd Oct 1777, Oldswinford.
56 Benjamin Richardson's notebook of 1886.

57 Philip Rufford, son of Francis Rufford and his wife Elizabeth, nee Biggs, bap. 30th Jan 1783, Oldswinford.
58 Thomas Biggs, son of Thomas and Elizabeth Biggs, bap. 22nd Oct 1750, Oldswinford.
59 Pigot and Co.'s National Commercial Directory, 1828 and 1829 editions.
60 Francis Rufford, bur. 27th Jun 1831, Oldswinford.
61 PRO, PROB 11/1792 85RH-86RH, PCC will of Francis Rufford, 18th Nov 1831.
62 Sarah Rufford, daughter of Philip and Margaret Rufford, bap. 25th Nov 1756, Worcester, All Saints. Sarah married Edward Bury, 14th Oct 1784, Stanford on Teme.
63 Francis Rufford, son of Francis Rufford and his wife Elizabeth, nee Biggs, bap. 29th Jun 1779, Oldswinford. In Jun 1837, when an Act was obtained for the Stourbridge Extension Canal, Francis Rufford, clay merchant of Prescot, subscribed £3,000 and became chairman.
64 George Pierpoint Rufford, son of Francis Rufford and his wife Elizabeth, nee Biggs, bap. 29th Sep 1781, Oldswinford.
65 Francis Rufford married Emma Francis Blakiston, the daughter of the Rector, 4th Aug 1828, Belbroughton. He made a mansion out of what had previously been Yew Tree Farm. He parked the land and made artificial pools and cascades on the line of the Belbroughton river, which comes down from Walton Hill.
66 1851 Census of Stourbridge PRO HO0107/2035/083 shows Philip Rufford and his wife Margaret still living at Heath House described as a banker, farmer employing 8 labourers and glass manufacturer employing 71 people.
67 Thirteenth Report of the Commission into the Glass Excise, 1835, Appendix 7.
68 William Walker, son of James and Sarah Walker, bap. 27th Dec 1801, Dudley St. Thomas's. William Walker married Jane Floyd 2nd Apr 1831 at Oldswinford. In the marriage licence he is described as a gentleman of Oldswinford. However, when William and Jane Walker baptised their son, William, on 30th Dec 1833 at Oldswinford, he is described as a glass manufacturer of the Heath.
69 Benjamin Richardson's notebook of 1886.
70 Pigot and Co.'s National Commercial Directory of 1835.
71 Charles John Wragge, son of John and Elizabeth Wragge, bap. 22nd Apr 1799,

Oldswinford; solicitor of Red Hill House, Stourbridge; joined the bank about 1835.

72 Infra, Phoenix Glassworks, 1844.

73 E.T. MacDermot, *History of the Great Western Railway, Volume One 1833-1863* (1964), p252.

74 Benjamin Richardson's notebook of 1886.

75 Bedcote Mill was on the River Stour, 630 yards east of Stourbridge

76 James Walker, son of William Walker and his wife Jane, nee Floyd, bap. 8th Apr 1832, Oldswinford.

77 Infra, Coalbournhill, Audnam and North Street Glassworks.

78 £65.

79 Cassey's 1860 Directory of Worcestershire.

80 PRO, 1861 census.

81 The glassworks was owned by the executors of ironmaster Alexander Brodie Cochrane II JP (1813-63) who had lived at Heath House. The improvements and extension of the lease were part of their stewardship of his estate.

82 William Walker, bur. 27th Dec 1868, Oldswinford.

83 PRO, Will of William Walker, 27th Jan 1869.

84 William Walker, son of William Walker and his wife Jane, nee Floyd, bap. 30th Dec 1833, Oldswinford.

85 James Walker, son of William Walker and his wife Jane, nee Floyd, bap. 8th Apr 1832, Oldswinford.

86 Philip Walker, son of William Walker and his wife Jane, nee Floyd, bap. 21st Dec 1837, Oldswinford.

87 Benjamin Richardson's notebook of 1886.

88 James Harry Walker, son of James and Mary Walker, bap. 13th Jan 1859, Oldswinford.

89 PRO, 1881 census of Upperswinford, RG11/2888/74/35.

90 FGMM for quarter ending 25 May 1889.

91 PG, Apr 1897.

92 He subsequently retired to Curborough, College Grove, Great Malvern where he was living in 1896.

93 Infra, Albert Glassworks.

94 WRO, 705:260 BA4000 p315 s4.

95 DA, unindexed Harward & Evers papers.

CHAPTER 18

Fimbrell Glasshouse, Amblecote

Thomas Bradley junior[1] built the Fimbrell glasshouse in 1687, five years after his younger brother Edward built Jacob's Well Glasshouse. Thomas had been a glassmaker for at least ten years, probably working for either his younger brother or the Henzeys. He is described as a glassmaker of Oldswinford when he administered his father's estate in 1677[2]. He built the glasshouse on land called Fimbrell Leasow, near the corner of Brettell Lane[3], from which the glasshouse derived its name.

After only four years of operating Fimbrell Glasshouse Thomas leased it to Benjamin Batchelor[4]. Why he should choose to do so after such a short time is not clear, but he immediately started a new glasshouse at Coalbournhill. Perhaps in that short time he had gained experience and thought he could build a better glasshouse than the one he built four years earlier. The indenture, dated 9th May 1691, states that Thomas Bradley, glassmaker of Oldswinford, leased the glasshouse to Benjamin Batchelor, glassmaker of Coalbournbrook, for nine hundred and ninety-nine years at an annual rent of £30[5]. Benjamin Batchelor was the son of Thomas Batchelor[6], a glasscutter who worked for Paul Henzey. He was obviously a trusted friend, as there were two occasions when Thomas Batchelor witnessed a Henzey will.

Thomas Batchelor was evidently involved in the business with his son Benjamin and appears to take over the lease made to his son. In 1699 he was found out by the exciseman selling bottles without declaring them for duty payments and his stock of a thousand dozen bottles was seized. He petitioned the commissioners for their return, pleading both ignorance and poverty. His pretence of ignorance was audacious; as an experienced glassmaker, he must have known the risk he was taking. However, his ploy worked and the Treasury responded with a warrant to the commissioners to return his stock. This was provided that he paid the outstanding duty, the expenses of the seizers and a gratuity to them 'he being poor and ignorant and this being his first offence.'[7] As for his being poor, nothing could be further from the truth. He made his will on 22nd July 1702[8] and stated that he was a glasscutter of Amblecote who owned the leases on two glasshouses. He also owned a well-furnished fourteen-room house in Amblecote, lands and tenements in Lichfield, a leasehold house in Oldswinford and a lease on lands and tenements in Wordsley. He died the following month[9] and an inventory of his estate was prepared by Gray Jevon and Joseph Hart[10]. The inventory lists extensive personal possessions and the contents of a broad glasshouse and a bottle glasshouse. The contents of the broad glasshouse included 'Ashes Cratewood Broad & Cut glass' valued at £141 5s. Among the contents of the bottle warehouse were 'The furnace, sand, salt, clay, Ashes, fretting and some Glasswares' valued at £49 16s. 'Leases of the two Glasshouses with the buildings Lands & appurtenances thereto belonging' were valued at £335. The total value of his estate was £1,908 1s—rather a lot for someone 'poor and ignorant'. He willed 'my said two glasshouses with the stock tools and utensils thereto belonging . . . to my said three sons.' The sons being Benjamin, Humphrey[11] and Elijah[12].

The three Batchelor brothers, Benjamin, Elijah and Humphrey were all party to the 1703 Perrot cartel[13]. Benjamin died intestate in 1707. Letters of administration were proved for his estate[14] but have not survived. Elijah died in 1719[15], aged forty-five, which left Humphrey on his own.

Thomas Milward had been a friend and attorney of many local glassmakers. He died in 1724 and at his funeral on 6th August Humphrey Batchelor was among the mourners along with several other glassmakers[16].

In 1725 Humphrey Batchelor called himself a broad-glass

maker when taking a lease of 'Lord Dudley's Glasshouse clay Worke'.[17] On the occasion of his marriage in the same year he decided a different appellation would be more appropriate. He married Elizabeth Hill[18] and in their marriage licence[19] he is described as a gentleman of Oldswinford.

On 25th March 1728 Humphrey Batchelor made an agreement with Henry Barrar concerning the Fimbrell Glasshouse. The agreement made Barrar a partner for a fixed term of fourteen years and effectively established him as Batchelor's manager. The document gives a rare early insight into the products being manufactured. These included flint glass, common green glass, crown glass, bottles, drinking glasses, cruets and apothecaries' phials. There is a reference to spreading plates, these being the plates upon which the glass was flattened[20].

By this time Humphrey's nephew, Elijah junior[21], was working in the business[22]. On 1st March 1738 Humphrey Batchelor took a fresh nine hundred and ninety-nine year lease on the estate including:

> 'that messuage or tenement wherin the said Thomas Bradley did formerly dwell and all that glasshouse heretofore in the tenure of the said Thomas Bradley and also all those four closes or inclosures of arrable meadow or pasture ground conteyning by estimation five and thirty acres or thereabouts be the same more or less commonly called or known by the name of Dennis . . . and all the glasshouses at or near Coleborn Brook from Charles Fox of Chacomb, Northants at an annual rent of £50.'[23]

Charles Fox had become the owner of the Dennis estate and Coalbournhill Glassworks via their descent from the Bradley family. Thomas Bradley junior had died in 1707 and in his will[24] ownership passed to his son John[25]. John Bradley had married Mary Bysell in 1701[26], and their only issue was a daughter, Frances[27]. She married in 1732 to Charles Fox of Chacombe Priory, Northamptonshire. John Bradley died in 1739[28] and ownership of the Dennis estate passed to Charles Fox.

Humphrey Batchelor died in 1741[29], aged sixty, just three years after obtaining his new lease. His only son Thomas[30] was only fourteen years old so his widow Elizabeth ran the business until Thomas was old enough to take over. This was the period when 'sealed' wine bottles were in vogue. Mrs Batchelor supplied thousands of such bottles that found their way to the cellars of All Souls College. A thousand or so bottles such still remained there in 1969, sealed 'All: Souls College 1764' and 'All Souls Coll: C:R.'. Jeremy Haslam who examined them concludes that with a few exceptions they all came from 'Mrs. Batchelor's glasshouse at Stourbridge.' Entries in the Wine Cashbooks show a total of 920 dozen bottles purchased from Mrs Batchelor for £91 19s 1d. This suggests the price was 2s per dozen[31].

On 13th December 1749 Thomas Batchelor paid Ben Ord, the local exciseman £249 12s 2d for glass duty[32]. However, he only lived to twenty-three years of age and died in 1750[33]. Letters of administration were proved for his estate but have not survived.

Elizabeth Batchelor, the widow of Humphrey, died in 1762[34]. She had made a will, which was proved in PCC[35]. As her only son Thomas had died in 1750 she left her estate—including the Fimbrell Glasshouse—to her brothers Waldron[36] and Thomas Hill[37]. Both Hill brothers had no experience of glassmaking but had inherited two glassmaking businesses. They chose to continue glassmaking at Coalbournhill, and to close the older Fimbrell Glasshouse. The works stood empty and eventually fell into disrepair[38]. Sometime after gaining his inheritance in 1762 Thomas Hill of Coalbournbrook built a mansion on the land and called it Dennis House; this handsome Georgian house still stands today. However, when he built Dennis House, there had been no proper conveyance to him of the land upon which it stood. The Batchelor family eventually conveyed the land to him on 3rd July 1777. The deed assigned to him:

> 'all that the site of the aforesaid glass-house theretofore in the tenure of Thomas Bradley, but then fallen down and gone to decay, and also a glass-house theretofore in the holding of Jeremiah Minors and Edward Bradley, and since of John Bradley.'

When Thomas Hill of Coalbournbrook died[39] ownership of the

Dennis estate passed to his nephew, also Thomas Hill[40], the son of his brother Waldron. Thomas Hill of Dennis was by this time forty-six years old and ran a slitting mill at Wollaston. He used his inheritance wisely. His neighbour Francis Homfray[41] of Wollaston Hall ran the Hyde slitting mill at Kinver[42] and Stourton Mill. In the same year, 1782, Homfray began to invest in South Wales. His sights were set on an eighteen mile crescent of land little more than a mile wide at the head of the valleys to the south of the Black Mountains that run from Hirwain to Blaenavon. Here, millstone grit overlaid an outcrop of coal measures of unsurpassed quality for smelting purposes. Ironstone was to be found in abundance and limestone for fluxing was available nearby. His first venture was a mill for boring cannon at Cyfarthfa. He then established his sons Jeremiah[43], Samuel[44] and Thomas[45] in a new ironworks at Pennydarran. In 1789 Jeremiah started the Ebbw Vale Iron Works. News of this flourishing venture would have come freely to Thomas Hill as Thomas Homfray was a partner at Pennydarran and continued to run the Hyde with his other half-brother Jeston[46] and his brother Francis junior[47].

Thomas Hill of Dennis could see that Wales was an infinitely better location for ironmaking than the cluttered banks of the River Stour and in 1789 founded what was to become the great ironworks and town of Blaenavon. Hill, with partners Thomas Hopkins[48] of Rugeley and Benjamin Pratt[49] of Great Witley, obtained a lease on land known as Afon Lwyd from the Earl of Abergavenny in 1787. Their investment exceeded £40,000 before any return was obtained. However the ironworks went on to make an immense fortune for Thomas Hill. By 1801 the works employed 350 men[50].

Thomas Hill of Dennis had purchased one of Stourbridge's longest established banks from George Collis, which by the seventeen-nineties was known as the 'Old Bank'[51]. In 1808 he and his son Thomas of Broome[52] admitted William Robbins, a coalmaster of Hagley House[53], and Thomas Bate[54] of Oldswinford as partners. The bank traded as Hill, Bate & Robins.

Thomas Hill lived at Dennis House[55] and in 1796 became High Sheriff of Worcestershire[56]. His son Thomas Hill of Broome had long been involved with the Staffordshire businesses. He now took on responsibility for the South Wales business as well. His wife Anne, died in 1804, aged 35[57] leaving Thomas with motherless young children. In April 1816 he moved with his children Thomas, Jane, Eliza and Anne from Broome to Blaenavon to take over the management of his eighty year-old father's ironworks. He became an ironmaster in his own right when his new works at Garndyrus began producing iron in 1817.

Thomas Hill of Dennis had married Anne Melsup in 1766[58]. She died on 7th December 1810 and the following year he erected a memorial to her that exists today in the north aisle of Oldswinford church.

The old Fimbrell Glasshouse had been standing idle for over sixty years and was derelict. About 1813, it was demolished and Thomas Hill of Dennis gave the bricks to build the first school on Lye Waste[59].

Thomas Hill of Dennis died at Blaenavon on 17th September 1824, aged eighty-seven, and was buried alongside his wife at Oldswinford. His memorial also exists today in the north aisle of Oldswinford church. After his death, his grandson—Thomas Hill of Blaenavon[60]—was admitted as a partner in the family bank. In 1827 Thomas Hill of Broome died[61] and the bank was carried on by Thomas Hill of Blaenavon, Thomas Bate and William Robbins.

Thomas Hill of Blaenavon retired from the bank in 1833. His objective being to focus on the Blaenavon ironworks with Robert Wheeley[62] as his trusted right hand man. Hill and Wheeley sold out to the Kennard Group in 1836. Then, on Friday 18th May 1838 Hill sold the Dennis estate at an auction held in the Fish Inn in Coalbournbrook[63]. Thomas Hill retired to Rudhall, near Ross in Herefordshire where he eventually died in 1868.

The Fish Inn was the unofficial Town Hall of the hamlet, where all the public meetings and vestries were held. The estate was divided into forty lots of which the greater part was purchased by Robert Wheeley's brother, William Seager Wheeley who was prospering as a glassmaker in Brettell Lane. In 1839 he was the owner of Dennis House and forty-one acres of land in Dennis Park[64], and in 1841, a glass manufacturer of Dennis House[65]. Wheeley's prosperity ended when he was accused of fraud[66]. He was forced to sell the Dennis estate and it was broken up. In 1851 Dennis House was tenanted by John Grier MA, the incumbent of Amblecote[67].

1 Thomas Bradley, son of Thomas Bradley and his wife Frances, daughter of Richard Bradley, b. 21st Oct 1658; bap. 21st Nov 1658, Oldswinford.
2 WRO, Admon of Thomas Bradley, 15th Oct 1677.
3 R.L. Chambers, *Perambulation Roll of the parish of Oldswinford*, 1733, p43.
4 Benjamin Batchelor, son of Thomas Batchelor and his wife Mary, nee White.
5 WSL, 254/2/81, lease of 1738 refers to this earlier lease.
6 Thomas Batchelor, son of William Batchelor, bap. 25th Sep 1633, Wisborough Green, Sussex.
7 Ibid, D.R. Guttery, pp21, 37.
8 PRO, PROB II/466.
9 Thomas Batchelor, bur. 26th Aug 1702, Oldswinford.
10 PRO, PROB4/22230 PFW/1435, Inventory of the estate of Thomas Batchelor, appraised 22nd Sep 1702.
11 Humphrey Batchelor, son of Thomas Batchelor and his wife Mary, nee White, bap. 10th Oct 1681, Kingswinford.
12 Elijah Batchelor, son of Thomas Batchelor and his wife Mary, nee White, bap. 24th Aug 1674, Kingswinford.
13 Supra, Colemans.
14 WRO, Admon of Benjamin Batchelor, 6th Nov 1707.
15 Elijah Batchelor, bur. 26th Nov 1719, Oldswinford.
16 Oldswinford PR; ibid, D.R. Guttery, p58.
17 DA, Box 4 Bundle 1.
18 Mar. Humphrey Batchelor and Elizabeth Hill, 3rd Dec 1725, Stone, Worcestershire.
19 WRO, marriage licence dated 12th Nov 1725.
20 WRO, Palfrey Collection.
21 Elijah Batchelor, son of Elijah and Elizabeth Batchelor, bap. 4th Nov 1699, Oldswinford.
22 He is described as a glassmaker of Amblecote in an examination of parish of settlement conducted in 1728.
23 WSL, 254/2/81.

24 Infra, Coalbournhill.
25 John Bradley, son of Thomas and Alice Bradley, bap. 13th Nov 1680, Oldswinford.
26 Mar. John Bradley and Mary Bysell, 28th Feb 1701, Oldswinford.
27 Frances Bradley, daughter of John Bradley and his wife Mary, nee Bysell, b. 7th Mar 1704; bap. 15th Apr 1704, Oldswinford.
28 John Bradley, bur. 7th Feb 1739, Oldswinford.
29 Humphrey Batchelor, bur. 26th Nov 1741, Oldswinford.
30 Thomas Batchelor, son of Humphrey Batchelor and his wife Elizabeth, nee Hill, bap. 23rd Nov 1727, Oldswinford.
31 J. Haslam, *Oxford Taverns and the Cellars of All Souls in the 17th Century* (1969); J. Haslam, *Sealed Bottles from All Souls College* (1970).
32 WRO, Palfrey Collection.
33 Thomas Batchelor, bur. 10th Dec 1750, Oldswinford.
34 Elizabeth Batchelor, bur. 20th Oct 1762, Oldswinford.
35 PRO, PROB 11/881 RH17-18, PCC will of Elizabeth Batchelor, 6th Nov 1762.
36 Waldron Hill, son of John Hill, sythesmith of Oldnall and his wife Elizabeth, nee Waldron, b. 7th Mar 1706; bap. 26th Mar 1706, Oldswinford.
37 Thomas Hill, son of John Hill, sythesmith of Oldnall and his wife Elizabeth, nee Waldron, b. 26th Jun 1711; bap. 16th Jul 1711, Oldswinford.
38 SRO, Tp 1273, private collection, 1769 map of Amblecote shows no glasshouse at Dennis.
39 Thomas Hill, d. 11th Mar 1782; bur. Oldswinford.
40 Thomas Hill, son of Waldron Hill and his first wife Sarah, nee Badger, bap. 19th Oct 1736, Kingswinford.
41 Francis Homfray, son of Francis Homfray and his second wife Mary, nee Jeston; b. 9th Sep 1726; bap. 22nd Sep 1726, Oldswinford.
42 The Hyde Mill, 0.5 miles NNE of Kinver, was started by William Brindley and became the first commercially successful slitting mill in England when he was joined by his son-in-law Richard 'Fiddler' Foley in 1623.
43 Sir Jeremiah Homfray Knt. of Llandaff House, son of Francis Homfray and his second wife Catherine, nee Caswell; bap. 7th Mar 1759, Kinver; died bankrupt in France.
44 Samuel Homfray, bap. 10th Mar 1762, Oldswinford, son of Francis Homfray and his second wife Catherine, nee Caswell.

45 Thomas Homfray bap. 12th Jun 1760, son of Francis Homfray and his second wife Catherine, nee Caswell.

46 Jeston Homfray of Broadwaters, Kidderminster, son of Francis Homfray and his first wife Hannah, nee Popkin; b. 1752; married Sarah Pidcock 20th May 1776, Oldswinford; d. 1816.

47 Francis Homfray of the Hyde, son of Francis Homfray and his second wife Catherine, nee Caswell; married Mary Pidcock 2nd Mar 1778; d. 1809.

48 Thomas Hopkins was Thomas Hill's brother-in law, having married Sarah Hill, 2nd Feb 1761 at Kingswinford. Hopkins died in 1798 and was buried in Rugeley. He was succeeded in the business by his son Samuel Hopkins, bap. 24th Feb 1762 at Rugeley.

49 Benjamin Pratt; b. c1742; died unexpectedly in the dining room of the Angel Inn at Abergavenny when travelling to Blaenavon in 1794; bur. St. Cassion's, Chaddesley Corbett; memorial on the south wall of the nave of St. Woolos' Cathedral, Newport.

50 Revd. William Coxe, *An Historical Tour in Monmouthshire* (1801); A Lady (i.e. Miss Coxe, the author's sister), *A Picture of Monmouthshire or an Abridgement of Mr Coxe's Historical Tour in Monmouthshire* (1802), p99; E.J. Davies, *The Blaenavon Story* (1975).

51 Its premises were on the corner of Coventry Street and High Street, Stourbridge, opposite the town's market hall. The bank was rebuilt in 1917 and remains today although the site is now the premises of the Yorkshire Bank.

52 Thomas Hill, son of Thomas Hill and his wife Anne, nee Melsup, bap. 24th Feb 1765, Kingswinford.

53 Hagley House was situated on the corner of Stourbridge Road and Birmingham Road in Hagley.

54 Thomas Bate, son of Overs Bate, banker and mercer of Stourbridge and his wife Susannah, nee Brettell, great-great-great granddaughter of Joshua Henzey I; b. 23rd Dec 1778; bap. 31st Jan 1779, Oldswinford; Justice of the Peace of the Birches, Hagley where he died 13th Oct 1846; bur. Pedmore.

55 Holden's Triennial Directory for 1809, 1810 & 1811.

56 H.S. Grazebrook, *The Heraldry of Worcestershire* (1873).

57 Anne Hill, nee Lilley, d. 22nd Sep 1804; bur. 29th Sep 1804, Oldswinford; graceful white marble memorial in Broome Church.

58 Mar. Thomas Hill and Anne Melsup, 22nd Nov 1766, St. Andrew's, Holborn, London.

59 Notebook of the Revd. David Robertson, Vicar of Lye in the second half of the nineteenth century; ibid, George Griffith. The school had been made possible by an endowment from Thomas Hill's uncle, Thomas Hill of Coalbournbrook (1711-1782), former owner of the Dennis property. He left £130 in his will dated 11th Mar 1782 for 'educating and teaching to read twenty poor children of The Waste, the Lye and Carless Green, in the parish of Old Swinford, whose parents are not able to pay for such learning . . .' The bricks from the old glassworks were drawn to the foot of The Waste bank, which had been chosen as the site. The roads were so bad that, for the last stage of the journey, the bricks were carried in baskets, on the heads of some of the local inhabitants.

60 Thomas Hill, son of Thomas Hill and his wife Anne, nee Lilley, bap. 31st Mar Broome, Worcestershire.

61 Thomas Hill of Broome d. 29th Nov 1827; bur. Blaenavon.

62 Robert Wheeley, son of Thomas Wheeley and his wife Susanna, nee Seager, bap. 2nd May 1793, Brierley Hill. Robert Wheeley was taken to Blaenavon by Thomas Hill I and loyally served all three generations. He married a local girl, the daughter of Parson Jenkins and became a Blaenavon man, steering Hill and Wheeley as its major partner and director.

63 H. Ridley FLA, *A few notes on Amblecote*, County Express, 30th Jun 1917.

64 Tithe apportionment, 1839.

65 Bentley's 1841 Directory of Stourbridge.

66 Infra, Wheeley's Brettell Lane Glasshouses, 1841.

67 PRO, HO0107/2035/143 1851 census of Amblecote.

CHAPTER 19

Harlestones Glasshouse, Coalbournbrook

Thomas Henzey₁ built the glasshouse at Harlestones field, Coalbournbrook, about 1692. Thomas was the oldest son of Joshua Henzey II who had been running a glassworks at Woolwich and acting as a merchant for the output of the Stourbridge district glassworks. Thomas had probably been involved in these ventures with his father. He had obviously achieved financial independence by the age of thirty-six as he was Overseer of the Poor for Oldswinford in 1682. In 1692 he leased Harlestones field, west of the Stourbridge Road and south of the road to Wollaston, and built a glasshouse there. He did not work the glasshouse himself, but put his younger son John₂ in charge.

Eighteen-year-old John Henzey broke away from the family tradition of broad-glass and produced flint glass, bottles and vessels, besides broad-glass, and lived in a large house nearby. The house was later occupied for a time by Revd. Henry Oseland, the Henzeys' sales manager₃.

Harlestone House, Coalbournhill Glassworks

The venture was profitable and Thomas Henzey began to live a life typical of the merchants of his time. Information was a precious commodity to them, and many clubs were formed providing a forum for the exchange of news. These clubs also provided the opportunity to indulge in another passion of the time—carousing. Interestingly, this divertissement played a part in the development of the shape and style of drinking glasses[4]. On 31st December 1702 Thomas Henzey was admitted to the Talbot Club[5]. This was a club for the merchants and gentlemen of the district meeting at the Talbot Inn in Stourbridge. In the following year, 1703, the father and son partnership of Thomas and John Henzey was involved with the Perrot cartel[6]. It is almost inevitable that the seeds of this bold and imaginative business venture were sowed in the Talbot Inn. The Talbot Club also provided the forum for another pastime of dissolute Georgian gentlemen—gambling. The local attorney Thomas Milward kept meticulous personal accounts that include his gambling losses. Despite being married to Martha, the daughter of Dr. Simon Ford, Rector of Oldswinford, he was an inveterate gambler, one of the chief organisers of the Stourbridge races. In 1704 he wrote 'lost at Hazard at the Talbot with Mr. Chas. Lytleton[7] and Mr. John Henzey—49 Guineas, he forgave me four, again 21.'[8] Hazard was a game of dice and one can just imagine the thirty-year old John Henzey, comfortable and confident, after his favourable cartel arrangement, gambling with the other gentlemen of the district.

At the age of thirty-four John Henzey decided to settle down and married Elizabeth White[9]. Their marriage was by a licence[10] in which the bondsmen were Henry White, white-glassmaker of Oldswinford and Joshua Henzey, broad-glassmaker of Kingswinford. John Henzey's respectability was further strengthened in 1711 when, following in the tradition of his father, he became a churchwarden of Oldswinford.

Thomas Henzey died in 1712[11], aged sixty-seven. He had made a will on 9th January 1709, witnessed by Humphrey Batchelor of Fimbrell Glasshouse. It was proved on 28th November 1712 and left John Henzey still running the business.

John Henzey again appears as a winner of Thomas Milward's gambling losses[12]. Marriage for both Henzey and Milward had not dulled their appetites for this notorious vice. Milward's daybook contains many details of travels with his wife with sessions of gambling interspersed with shopping for clothes, presumably to placate her. In 1715 he recorded:

> Jan 1st
> Lost at Mr. Hickman's[13]—Mr. Arthur Dean, Mr. John Wheeler[14] & J. Henzey at Hazard   17-0-0

Jan 2
Spent with Thomas Littleton Esq. and Will Plowden Esq.,
Mr. W. Foley, John Henzey and Gregory Hickman at the
Talbot at cards and Hazard   5-7-6

Milward also records that in 1718 John Henzey sold his seat in Oldswinford church on 27th May[15]. John Henzey died in 1719[16], aged forty-five, having made his will two years earlier, in which he is described as a broadglassmaker of Haylestones, in Amblecote[17]. He died a wealthy man, owning lands in 'Castle Morton, Birch Morton, Longdon, Kingswinford and elsewhere in the counties of Worcester and Stafford'. He owned a twelve-roomed house in Amblecote, £223 of money in the house, a hundred and thirty-two ounces of plate and 'debts due' of £860. He had a stock of '50 case of broad-glass in the hands of Mr. Joshua Henzey.' However, the value of this would be questionable, as the price was severely depressed due to the public's growing preference for crown glass. A lengthy inventory of the testator's estate was prepared by his brothers-in-law, William Godwin[18] and William Pidcock, which totalled £1,390 12s 2d.

John Henzey fathered six children by his wife Elizabeth, but three died in infancy. At the time of his death his three remaining children were still very young: Frances aged ten, Mary aged eight, and John aged four. The glasshouse was therefore rented out, the tenancy being taken by Henry Barrar.

Henry Barrar obviously had some relationship with the Batchelors who were running the Fimbrell Glasshouse. On 25th March 1728 Henry Barrar became a partner in the Fimbrell Glasshouse with Humphrey Batchelor and in 1729 Barrar married Carolina[19], the daughter of Elijah Batchelor, who had been a partner at the Fimbrell Glasshouse. A letter dated 7th February 1759 from E. Milward to her father, states that Miss Batchelor had made substantial bequests to certain ladies of the Barrar family[20]. The business was as profitable for Henry Barrar as it had been for John Henzey and in 1749 Barrar became a Churchwarden of Oldswinford. In 1760 he was producing best and ordinary flint glass, and phials$_{21}$. Henry Barrar died in 1760$_{22}$ and his son Elijah$_{23}$ continued the business with the same product range.

Unfortunately, Elijah did not enjoy the same prolonged success as his father. In 1767—after only seven years of operation—he was declared bankrupt$_{24}$. This was during the uneasy period after the Seven Years War of 1756 to 1763. The dislocation of trade was substantial. Beginning in North America, conflict spread all over Europe, India and America. Trade at Holloway End Glasshouse was similarly affected; it was vacant and available to let at the time. Elijah died two years later in London on 21st May 1769$_{25}$.

When John Henzey died in 1719 he left three surviving children, but his only surviving son, John, outlived him by just three years and died in 1722, aged seven. His oldest child was a daughter, Frances, who lived to the age of seventy-five and never married, but ownership of the glasshouse passed to his second child, Mary$_{26}$. In 1737 Mary married Johnathan Dixon of Caldwell Hall, Kidderminster$_{27}$. Their marriage was by a licence$_{28}$ in which Johnathan Dixon is described as a gentleman of Kidderminster aged twenty-seven. Mary Henzey is described as a spinster, aged twenty-three years, of the parish of St. Michael in Bedwardine. Johnathan Dixon$_{29}$ was the fourth (surviving) son of Oliver Dixon$_{30}$ of Dudley and was descended from a line of eminent Dixons from Dudley. His grandfather, also Oliver Dixon$_{31}$, was Mayor of Dudley in 1690. His great-grandfather, also Oliver Dixon$_{32}$ of Dudley, was a royalist Captain during the Civil War.

When Johnathan Dixon died in 1738 ownership of the glassworks passed to his only son Oliver$_{33}$. Oliver Dixon was a barrister and Justice of the Peace who lived at Red Hill House in Oldswinford. He had no interest in the glass trade and having lost the Barrars as tenants let the glasshouse again. On 4th May 1768 he leased the Coalbournbrook works to John Pidcock, George Ensell and Richard Bradley.

John Pidcock was a nephew and legatee of Joshua Henzey III, from whom he inherited the Dial and Platts Glasshouses in 1738. He had also been involved at the Ridgrave Glasshouse in 1761. George Ensell was the brother-in-law of Richard Bradley, having married Phebe Bradley in 1765[34]. Their marriage was by a licence[35] in which George Ensell is described as a 'Glass Factor.' Ensell was the driving force behind this partnership. It was certainly his achievements as a glassmaker that came to the attention of the public. Pidcock was probably involved for his capital and experience. Bradley was primarily a source of capital. He was a typical Georgian entrepreneur, involved in many trades, including coal and iron, willing to participate in any venture that might make money. The firm operated under the title of Pidcock, Ensell and Bradley, with George Ensell acting as the manager.

The second earliest recorded reference to glass engraving in the Stourbridge district is associated with this firm. The Newcastle Chronicle of 30th December 1769 reports 'Samuel Richards, apprentice to Pidcock, Ensell and Bradley, to the glass-engraving business, near Stourbridge, absconded his master's service . . . '[36] After a few years the partnership was dissolved and by 1774 George Ensell was left in sole possession of the Harlestones glasshouse[37]. Whitworth's 1774 canal map shows both 'Messrs Ensell's & Hills Glafs Houses' south of Wollaston Road at Coalbournbrook. This has been construed to mean the two were in partnership, but it refers to two individuals and two glasshouses. In 1776 both the owner of the Harlestones glasshouse, Oliver Dixon, and his tenant, George Ensell, were among the seventy-two named proprietors in the Stourbridge Canal Act. Oliver Dixon signed the minutes of the first General Assembly of the Stourbridge Navigation Company[38].

One of many fascinating tales within the history of Stourbridge glassmaking concerns George Ensell and his invention, or discovery, of the process of sheet glass manufacture. Until this time the older Stourbridge manufacturers produced plates with an area of no more than four square feet. Ensell succeeded in producing sheets, by the Lorrainer broadglass method, of more than six square feet. He is said to have found the secret of producing such large sheets in Germany by stealth. The story is that he disguised himself as a travelling fiddler and visited the German glasshouses to observe their processes. Once, when his purpose was realised, he narrowly escaped with his life. This appears to be a story with a small element of truth in it, embellished and exaggerated over the years. It also sounds too similar to another early and better-substantiated feat of industrial espionage—performed by Richard 'Fiddler' Foley in the iron industry[39]—to be reliable. Whether he discovered, or invented the process, George Ensell certainly received the accolades for it. The Society for the encouragement of Arts, Manufactures & Commerce had been founded in 1754 and offered awards for examples of great endeavour in these areas. At a meeting on 22nd January 1778, George Ensell was awarded a £50 prize by the Society for his sheet glass:

> 'February 7 1778. Fifty Pounds being the Prem: offered for Plates of Glass equally fit for the Purpose of glazeing Prints, as those imported from Holland was adjudged to Mr George Ensell of Amblecoat near Stourbridge.'[40]

The volume also contains two covering letters from George Ensell dated 5th and 6th December 1777, with certificates from Richard Peterson, Officer of Excise and John Beazley, Surveyor of Ensell's Warehouse, confirming the glass was made by Ensell:

> 'These are to certify all those whom it shall or may concern, that I have charged his Majesty's Duty of fourteen shillings by the hundred weight, on Thirtyfour hundred weight of German sheet Glass, made by Mr Goerge [sic] Ensell of Amblecoat, near Stourbridge in the County of Worcester, and parish of Oldswinford, between the sixth Day of July 1777 and the twenty second Day of November following, witness my hand, Richard Peterson, Officer of Excise.' 'I do hereby certify that the above mentioned Mr George Ensell hath and now has in his Warehouse in the parish of Kingswinford and County of Stafford which Warehouses are in my Division. Fifty sheets of German sheet glass and that the Dementions [sic] of each and every of the said Sheets were not less than thirty six Inches in length, And Twenty six Inches in breadth, Witness my hand this fifth day of December 1777.' John Beazley, Surveyor of the said Mr Ensell Warehouses'[41]

In 1779 Oliver Dixon assigned the lease to Thomas Hill—who

already owned the Coalbournhill works next door—for £200[42]. Ensell's position was unaffected and he remained as Thomas Hill's tenant. The deed of sale refers to the works being 'now held by the said George Ensall [sic].'[43] The outline of the cone is clearly shown on Court's map of c1780[44], when the occupier was 'Mr Insale[sic]'.

George Ensell continued to pioneer new techniques. In 1780 he perfected a new tunnel-type lehr that largely replaced the old kilns[45]. Ensell's improvements were used with Josiah Wedgwood's pyrometer, invented in 1784, with which furnace temperatures could be accurately gauged[46]. Both advances were necessary to facilitate the emerging fashion for deeply cut glass. The lehr allowed glassware of greater thickness to be annealed and to withstand cutting in deep relief. Accurate control of furnace temperature enabled a consistent quality of glass to be attained. Before the invention of the pyrometer, the science of glassmaking was such a mystery, it was more akin to alchemy than it was to chemistry. Previously, temperature in the lehr was a matter of chance, dependant partly on the direction of the wind and 'measured' by observing the time taken for a wad of paper tossed into the tunnel entrance to burst into flames.

About 1780 George Ensell went into partnership with Robert Honeyborne the younger. However, this was probably an arrangement for Honeyborne to supply sufficient capital to bring Ensell's revolutionary product to a broader market. Robert Honeyborne ran Moor Lane Glassworks and was already a successful wealthy man. An announcement was made:

> 'German sheet and crown glass. Honeyborne and Ensell having established a manufactory of German Sheet & Crown glass near Stourbridge beg leave to inform the public that they may be supplied with any quantity on the shortest notice and upon the most reasonable terms[47].'

The wording of the advertisement causes some confusion for the researcher. The fact that they had 'established a manufactory' has been interpreted to mean a new glassworks was built, or at least rented, to produce the new 'German sheet and crown glass'. It could have been at the Moor Lane Bottleworks, offered to let in

1771 by Thomas Seager. It could even have been at Honeyborne's main glassworks in Moor Lane. While there is no documentary proof that the Honeyborne and Ensell partnership was based at this glassworks, it is the most likely location. The wording of the advertisement 'having established a manufactory' was probably meant to be interpreted by the public as the establishment of a new works for a new product, but was simply a new partnership at the existing works. This theory is further strengthened by the fact that Robert Honeyborne's involvement with George Ensell does not appear to have lasted long. There are no further references to their partnership after the placing of the advertisement. Three years later Ensell was the sole proprietor again$_{48}$.

Benjamin Richardson told an interesting story that the old cone became very dilapidated and full of holes. One day a nanny goat climbed up the outside to the top of the cone. It was unable to get down so the glassmakers shot the goat; the goat fell down and they cooked and ate it!$_{49}$ It was not long before dilapidation turned to ruin:

> 'the glasshouse of Mr George Ensell of Coalbournbrook fell almost entirely in ruins to the ground . . . the damage, we understand will not be so great as was at first apprehended.'$_{50}$

However, the glassworks was pulled down and the bricks re-used elsewhere$_{51}$. The collapse was not unique, the same thing happening to an Irish glasshouse$_{52}$. After the collapse of the Harlestones Glasshouse cone Ensell transferred his activities to Holly Hall Glassworks and later Wordsley.

---

1 Thomas Henzey, son of Joshua and Dorothy Henzey, bap. 6th Jul 1646, Oldswinford.
2 John Henzey, son of Thomas Henzey and his wife Frances, nee Croker, b. 1674, probably in Ireland.
3 Supra, Henzey's Brettell Lane Glasshouse.
4 For example, a style of ballustroid drinking glasses is known as Kit-Kat glasses. They take their name from a painting by Sir Godfrey Kneller of members of the Kit-Kat club, including the Duke of Newcastle, drinking one of their famous toasts. The Kit-Kat club functioned between 1688 and 1720.

5 Society of Antiquaries, Prattinton collection. v 30, p57 *Account book of Thomas Milward*. Microfilm copy in WRO.
6 Supra, Colemans.
7 of Hagley Hall.
8 Society of Antiquaries, Prattinton Collection, *Account Book of Thomas Milward*. Microfilm copy in WRO; R.L. Chambers, *Thomas Milward's Seventeenth Century Daybook*, p23.
9 Mar. John Henzey and Elizabeth White, 7th Dec 1708, Mitton, Kidderminster, Worcestershire.
10 WRO, marriage licence dated 3rd Dec 1708.
11 Thomas Henzey, bur. 3rd May 1712, Oldswinford.
12 Society of Antiquaries, Prattinton Collection v 30, *Account Book of Thomas Milward*. Microfilm copy in WRO; R.L. Chambers, *Thomas Milward's Seventeenth Century Daybook*, p24.
13 Gregory Hickman, clothier of Green Close, Stourbridge, son of Richard Hickman, clothier of Stourbridge and his wife Mary, bap. 3rd Nov 1651, Oldswinford. Gregory Hickman was of a prominent and wealthy local family and was a sleeping partner at the Henzeys' Brettell Lane Glasshouse. For genealogy see Aleyn Lyell Reade, *The Reades of Blackwood Hill* (1906), pp103-123 and M.V. Herbert, *The Hickmans of Oldswinford* (1979), p67.
14 John Wheeler junior of Wooton Lodge, owner of Lye Forge.
15 Society of Antiquaries, Prattinton collection. v 30, p57 *Account Book of Thomas Milward*. Microfilm copy in WRO.
16 John Henzey, bur. 6th Feb 1719, Oldswinford.
17 WRO, Will of John Henzey, 7th Apr 1719.
18 Mar. William Godwin of Abbot's Bromley, Staffordshire and Dorothy Henzey, b. 1670, probably in Ireland, 25th April 1698, Lichfield Cathedral.
19 Mar. Henry Barrar and Carolina Batchelor, 31st Jul 1729, Oldswinford.
20 WRO, Palfrey collection.
21 Ibid, J.A. Langford.
22 Mr Henry Barrar, bur. 4th Oct 1760, Oldswinford.
23 Elijah Barrar, son of Henry Barrar and his wife Carolina, nee Batchelor, bap. 26th Feb 1733, Oldswinford.
24 London Gazette, 29th Sep 1767 and Lloyd's Evening Post, 26th May 1767 'Bankrupt, Elijah Barrar of Amblecot, in Old Swinford, glass-maker.'
25 Lloyd's Evening Post, 26th May 1769.

26 Mary Henzey, daughter of John Henzey and his wife Elizabeth, nee White, b. 19th Apr 1711; bap. 30th Apr 1711, Oldswinford.

27 Mar. Johnathan Dixon and Mary Henzey, 7th Oct 1737, Worcester Cathedral.

28 WRO.

29 Johnathan Dixon, son of Oliver Dixon and his wife Elizabeth, nee Taylor, bap. Oct 1713, Dudley, St. Thomas's.

30 Oliver Dixon, son of Oliver Dixon and his wife Frances, nee Jellian, bap. 26th Jul 1666, Dudley St. Thomas's; churchwarden of Dudley St. Thomas's in 1695 and 1712; d. 17th Dec 1738; bur. 20th Dec 1738, Dudley.

31 Oliver Dixon, son of Oliver Dixon and his wife Margaret, nee Hill, bap. 26th Dec 1642, Halesowen; Mayor of Dudley in 1690; principal steward to Lord Dudley and Ward. The 'Coleworks' in Dudley 'Forren' were under his care in conjunction with Ferdinando Dudley; bur. 15th Mar 1725 Dudley St. Thomas's.

32 Oliver Dixon, son of Oliver Dixon, bap. 16th Jul 1599, Dudley, St. Edmund's; bur. 20th Jun 1682, Dudley.

33 Oliver Dixon, son of Johnathan Dixon and his wife Mary, nee Henzey, bap. 8th Jul 1738, Kidderminster, Worcestershire.

34 Mar. George Ensell and Phebe Bradley, 29th Sep 1765, Dudley St. Thomas's.

35 WRO, marriage licence dated 9th Sep 1765.

36 The first reference in the district was two years earlier, when Samuel Benedict of Stourbridge, an engraver of glass was declared bankrupt. London Gazette, 28th Jul 1767. The earliest newspaper reference to glasscutting in London was 1735. Between 1735 and 1751 there are a further eleven known occurrences. After 1760, references to cutting in the provinces are manifold.

37 Ibid, D.R. Guttery, p97.

38 PRO, RAIL 874.1.

39 Richard 'Fiddler' Foley, son of Richard Foley and his wife Anne, nee Robinson, b. c 1573. Richard like his father was a nailor of Dudley and their trade was prosperous. He became Mayor of Dudley in 1616. In 1630 he moved with his family from Dudley to Stourbridge in 1630 and bought The Brick House in Stourbridge High Street (now the Talbot Hotel). He was churchwarden of Oldswinford 1634-35 and sidesman 1636-7. His second wife was Alice, daughter of William Brindley of the Hyde Works Kinver. Brindley and Foley were concerned that their nail trade was under pressure from cheaper Swedish products made with slitting mills and machinery instead of hand pro-

cesses. Richard Foley gained access to the Denemara works in Sweden posing as a travelling musician. After two trips to Sweden he mastered the process and in 1629 set up the first slitting mill in England at the Hyde in Kinver, followed by others at Swindon, Prestwood and Whittington. This laid the foundations of a large fortune for his family and brought prosperity to Kinver. WRO Palfrey Collection BA3762 6-12 (3), Family Archives of the Foley Family. Op cit, H.E. Palfrey, *Foleys of Stourbridge* (1944); R.K. Dent, *Historic Staffordshire* (1896), p265.

40 MS Transactions of the Society of Arts, 1777-78.
41 MS Transactions of the Society of Arts, 1777-78.
42 Oliver Dixon had inherited the business and lease from his father. He then renewed the lease with Thomas, Lord Foley on 2nd Sep 1776.
43 Ibid, D.R. Guttery, p97.
44 DA, C621.
45 Birmingham Journal, 31st May 1851.
46 The invention had been a long time in the making. John Whitehurst FRS (1713-1788), member of the Lunar Society, clockmaker and scientist of Derby, wrote to Matthew Boulton in January 1758 with a proposal to make a pyrometer for Boulton.
47 Birmingham Gazette, 3rd Jul 1780.
48 Bailey's Western and Midlands Directory of 1783.
49 Benjamin Richardson's notebook of 1886.
50 Worcester Journal, 6th Oct 1785.
51 It is not shown on Snape's canal map of 1785.
52 The English Post No 7, Friday 25th Oct 1700. 'It is said, that a new-built Glass-house in Goodman's fields that cost near £2,000 and was never used fell down on Saturday last of it self.'

CHAPTER 20

Worcester City Glasshouse, Claines

Worcester City Glasshouse stood in the parish of Claines, on the west bank of the River Severn, about half a mile upstream from the cathedral, just beyond Pitchcroft$_1$. It is unclear who built it and it is only conjectural who ran it.

In the Topographical Collections of John Aubry 1659-70, he states (p14) 'but now are goeing up no lesse than 3 glasse-houses between Gloucester and about Worcester . . ' in the context of discussing window glass. It is not clear what Aubry meant by 'now.' A later editor has suggested 1671, but that seems doubtful since the passage was in a preface dated April 1670. Haughton records a glasshouse in Worcester in 1696 making Flint, Green and Ordinary Glass$_2$.

When an assessment for the relief of the poor of the parish of Claines was carried out in 1696 Robert Modarat was assessed the modest sum of 8d on behalf of 'Mrs Cook of ye glasshouse.'$_3$

The glasshouse then appears to come under the control of Edward Dixon$_4$, son of Oliver Dixon of Dixon's Green, Dudley, principle steward to Lord Dudley$_5$.

That there was indeed a glasshouse in the city of Worcester is proved by an obscure newspaper reference in 1736:

'The 26th February last there was taken from the River-side, out of a meadow near the Glass-house, about ½ mile above Worcester, a fishing rod &c.'$_6$

A map of 1751 graphically shows a cone and connected buildings standing alone in a meadow, close to—but not alongside—the River Severn, upstream from Barebone Brook, in free land held by

'Mr Long.'[7] A map of 1774 shows the same site labelled 'old Glafs Houfe' in land 'late belonging to the widow Long' and surrounded by land belonging to the Cook family[8].

So where does this evidence lead us? If the Worcester City Glasshouse was being built in 1670 and operational in 1696 it would be too early for Edward Dixon who would be aged 14.

Edward Dixon, was definitely a glassmaker of Worcester when he became insolvent and was jailed at the Fleet prison in 1729[9]. He presumably took over the business some time after 1703, when he reached his majority, and ran it until his bankruptcy in 1729 when it was probably abandoned. It may or may not be a co-incidence that in the same year, 1729, his brother Gilbert and nephew Gillims, glassmakers of Lynn Regis, Norfolk were also declared insolvent and imprisoned in the Fleet. Were they perhaps in partnership?

---

1 The present-day site of Worcester Racecourse.
2 J. Houghton, *A Collection for Improvement of Husbandry and Trade*, ix, no. 198, 15 May 1696.
3 WRO BA8742 42 Box 899:749 H16/4.
4 Edward Dixon, son of Oliver Dixon and his wife Frances, nee Jellian, bap. 23rd Jul 1682, Dudley St. Thomas's.
5 Infra, Dixon's Green Glasshouse.
6 Weekly Worcester Journal of 5th Mar 1736.
7 WRO BA 5403/10 S009:1, *An Exact Map of the Manor of Clains*.
8 WRO BA 5403 b009:1, parcel 20, *Plan of certain lands in the parish of Claines and near Pitchcroft, Worcester City*.
9 London Gazette, 3rd Jun 1729; 'Insolvent debtor in the Fleet Prison, London, Edward Dixon, late of Worcester, glassmaker.'

CHAPTER 21

Dial Glasshouse, Brettell Lane

The original Dial glasshouse was established about 1704 by Thomas Henzey who already operated Harlestones Glasshouse. His success there—including his involvement in the Perrot cartel—has already been described. He probably built the Dial works to increase his output of broad-glass. He obtained a ninety-nine-year lease on the Dial property in 1704 and built the glasshouse on the northeast corner of Brettell Lane at its junction with the Stourbridge to Wolverhampton road.

Henzey died in 1712[1], having made his will[2] three years earlier. He left his Dial interests equally between three of his sons, Joshua III[3], John[4], and Edward[5].

John died in 1719. Edward died in 1726[6]. In his will[7] he called himself a broad glassmaker, but also refers to the 'trade or business of a maltster which I now follow'. Having died unmarried, he made token bequests to his brothers and sisters and left much to his servant Elizabeth Westwood, his sole executrix.

Joshua Henzey III died without issue in 1738[8]. He was the last of the Stourbridge Henzeys[9] and left the residue of his real and personal estate to his nephew John Pidcock[10]. Pidcock then went into partnership with his cousin, John Godwin.

In 1745 John Pidcock married Mary[11], the daughter of Robert Honeyborne who operated the Moor Lane Glassworks. She was independently wealthy, having been the residuary legatee of her grandfather, Thomas Hamond, of Bague's Glasshouses, when he died in 1743. The marriage was by a licence[12] for St. Martin's, Birmingham, Aston or Handsworth churches. It is intriguing why these churches were chosen because they were both 'of Kingswinford'.

The partnership between John Pidcock and John Godwin was dissolved in 1747. It is not known whether John Godwin chose to retire or if John Pidcock made him an offer he could not refuse. It is clear that the partnership dissolution and the sale of the lease were merely mechanisms to release Godwin from the business:

> 'To be sold, the remainder of a lease, being a term of 56 years, of the Dyal Glass-House, near Stourbridge, now in the occupation and possession of Messrs. Godwin and Pidcock, together with all convenient outbuildings necessary for glassmaking, and in very good repair, at the yearly rent of £18 5s 0d. Also a lease for 3 lives (all now existing) of an estate called the Platts and Meadows, on which is erected a Bottle-House, with adjoining buildings &c. at the yearly rent of £38. N.B. The stock in trade, together with the utensils of the said business, will be sold to the purchaser. Enquire of Mr John Godwin or Mr John Pidcock at the said Dyal Glasshouse.'[13]

John Pidcock then became the sole proprietor of the Dial business. He is mentioned in the Worcester Journal of 8th April 1749, then follows an eleven-year gap during which nothing more is heard of Pidcock or the Dial business. More often than not these lapses of extant records reflect periods of settled times and good trade. The principle 'no news is good news' was as true then as it is now. It could certainly be so here. England had founded an empire and became the greatest trading nation in the world. The year of 1759 was known as the 'Year of Victories'[14].

In 1760 Pidcock was one of the three Stourbridge manufacturers still producing broad-glass, as well as bottles and phials[15]. The following year an advertisement repeated the range of products:

> 'Wanted in the Broad Glass and Bottle Glass Trade, several hands, viz. Workmen, Blowers, Gatherers, Founders and Teezers. Any such by applying to Mr Pidcock at the Dial Glasshouse near Stourbridge, will meet with great encouragement and constant employment.'[16]

This adherence to the Lorrainer tradition of broad-glass was peculiar to the Dial Glasshouse. Most of the other glasshouses producing window glass had converted to the production of crown glass after about 1730. Dial Glasshouses continued to produce broad-glass until about 1841.

In 1763 Mr John Pidcock of Kingswinford appeared in an examination of parish of settlement[17]; then follows another gap, this time of fourteen years, during which no more is heard of Pidcock or his business. These were times of invention, discovery and expanding trade for Britain. Josiah Wedgwood[18] produced a new kind of earthenware. Crompton[19] invented the mule. Hargreaves[20] invented the spinning jenny. Arkwright invented the spinning frame[21]. Captain Cook[22] started on his first voyage of discovery. All these events occurring in a short period were accompanied by expanding trade and markets for British manufacturers; the Industrial Revolution was in full progress.

A significant manifestation of the Industrial Revolution was 'canal mania'. Whitworth's canal survey of 1774 shows the old Dial glasshouse on the east side of the turnpike road, on the corner of Brettell Lane. Significantly, the intended route was going to position Dial Glasshouse close to the intended canal, but not on its banks. However, John Pidcock was one of the seventy-two proprietors named in the Stourbridge Canal Act and signed the minutes of the proceedings at the first General Assembly.

The canal was fully opened to traffic in December 1779 and was an immediate success. In 1783 'John Pidcock Glass manufacturer' was still at the original site on the corner of Brettell Lane[23]. The canal was by now the main route for raw materials in, and finished goods out. However, Pidcock was at a disadvantage to many of his competitors as his goods were double-handled and hauled by wagon from the canalside to and from his works. He must have contemplated a move to the canalside even before John Snape surveyed the area in 1785. Snape's plan clearly shows the Dial Glasshouse in its old location, on the corner of Brettell Lane.

The following year, in 1786, the possibility of an alternative means of transport and distribution was raised. Turnpike trusts had been established throughout Britain to improve roads and provide for their upkeep. Loans with interest were raised from interested parties on the security of the expected tolls. Such a scheme greatly improved the Stourbridge to Wolverhampton road. In 1786 Messrs Pidcock & Grazebrook along with two other 'landlocked' glassmakers, Thomas Rogers and Thomas Hill, each lent the trust £100. In their case they were so keen it was without interest$_{24}$.

Despite this attempt to improve road transport, the benefits of canal transport were clearly greater. So great, that in 1788 John Pidcock decided to relocate his works. He built a new glassworks on the opposite side of the turnpike road, in a prime position, still close to the turnpike, but right on the bank of the canal.

The old Dial glasshouse on the corner of Brettell Lane probably ceased operation shortly after the new one was constructed. The Audnam Garage occupied the site of the old works for many years, but this was demolished at the end of 1992 and the site was redeveloped$_{25}$.

---

1 Thomas Henzey, bur. 3rd May 1712, Oldswinford.

2 Will of Thomas Henzey, 28th Nov 1712.

3 Joshua Henzey, son of Thomas Henzey and his wife Frances, nee Croker, b. c1672.

4 John Henzey, son of Thomas Henzey and his wife Frances, nee Croker, b. c1674.

5 Edward Henzey, son of Thomas Henzey and his wife Frances, nee Croker, bap. 3rd Jan 1677, Kingswinford.

6 Edward Henzey, bur. 24th Dec 1726, Kingswinford.

7 PRO, PCC will of Edward Henzey, 18th Nov 1727. The will was witnessed by Henry Bradley who was running the Audnam Glassworks.

8 Joshua Henzey, bur. 8th Feb 1738, Oldswinford.

9 His older brother John died in 1719, supra, Harlestones.

10 PRO, PCC will of Joshua Henzey, 5th Apr 1738.

11 Mar. John Pidcock and Mary Honeyborne, 22nd Jul 1745, St. Martin's, Birmingham.

12 LJRO, marriage licence dated 22nd Jul 1745.

13 Weekly Worcester Journal, 9th Oct 1747.

14 The best remembered of these victories being General Wolfe's capture of Quebec, others being in Africa and against the French in Hanover. It was crowned by the battle of Quiberon Bay, one of England's finest naval victories.
15 Ibid, J.A. Langford.
16 Birmingham Gazette, 5th Jan 1761.
17 Poor Law and Settlement Documents of Oldswinford.
18 Supra, Holloway End.
19 Samuel Crompton, 1753-1827.
20 James Hargreaves, 1720-1778.
21 Sir Richard Arkwright; b. 1732, Preston, Lancashire; d. 1792.
22 James Cook, 1728-1779.
23 Bailey's 1783 Western and Midland Directory.
24 WRO, Palfrey Collection, Stourbridge Road Order Book.
25 In March 1993 the author visited the site and recovered a large quantity of glass and pot fragments.

CHAPTER 22

Platts Glassworks, Amblecote

Thomas Henzey built the Dial glasshouse in 1704 where he made broad-glass and set up his son John to make flint glass at Coalbournbrook. To complete his diversification, Thomas Henzey built a new bottle-works for his son Joshua III at Platts Leasow. This was a new site, not far from the Dial works, on meadowland between the Stourbridge Road and the River Stour, in the northwest corner of Amblecote. The date of its establishment is not known, but it must be before 1712 when Thomas Henzey died. Building a bottlehouse was a novelty for a Lorrainer—broad-glass was their forte—but the move showed great foresight. Between 1710 and 1720 the price of broad-glass fell disastrously and many local broad-glassmakers were bankrupted$_1$.

When Joshua Henzey III remarried to Bridget Thompson, he left the house next to the Brettell Lane Glasshouse he had shared with his first wife. He made his new home at the Platts, building a house just to the south of the glassworks$_2$.

Joshua Henzey III died in 1738 and from then on the ownership and history of the Platts Glassworks is virtually indistinguishable from that of Dial Glasshouses. Joshua's nephew, John Pidcock, inherited both businesses and Platts House. As already described, Pidcock went into partnership with his cousin John Godwin. When their partnership was dissolved in 1747, the notice$_3$ makes it clear they were operating both the Dial and Platts Glasshouses. Platts is specifically described as a bottle-house.

Sometime before 1769 John Pidcock built a new Platts House, replacing the original home of Joshua Henzey III. In 1769 it stood in twenty-six acres, with extensive lawns₄. This was for many years the home of John Pidcock and subsequently his son John junior. Whitworth's canal map of 1774 labels the land at Platts as 'Mr Pidcock's'. The outline of a cone is shown on the plan, but displaced one field further north than it should be.

John Pidcock died in 1791₅. His sons, Thomas, John and Robert inherited Platts and Dial Glasshouses. During their ownership there are no specific references to the Platts business, but 'Platts' is clearly marked on Sherriff's plan of 1812. After the deaths of Robert and Thomas Pidcock, the business was run in the same way as Dial Glasshouses by John Pidcock junior and his sons John Henzey and George. John Pidcock junior made Platts House his home after the death of his father₆.

The first specific extant reference to Platts occurs in the excise records of 1833. John Henzey Pidcock & Co. paid £2,637 12s excise duty for the year ending 5th January 1833₇, suggesting this was the tenth largest of the sixteen Stourbridge/Dudley glasshouses of the day. However, as there is no separate entry for Dial Glasshouses, this was probably the duty payable for the entire business covering the output of both glasshouses.

John Pidcock junior died in 1834. His son John Henzey Pidcock continued the business. One of John Henzey Pidcock's first actions was to cease production at Platts Glassworks. The only trade directory entries in 1834 and 1835 are for some spinster members of the Pidcock family at Platts House₈. Shortly after this, Pidcock sold Platts House and glassworks to Thomas Webb.

Thomas Webb dissolved his partnership at the White House with his retired partner, John Shepherd, in 1836. Then in December of that year he resigned from the Richardson and Webb partnership at the Wordsley Flint Glassworks. He moved into Platts House in 1836₉ and undertook the building of a new glassworks adjoining Platts House. The baptism of two of Thomas Webb's children confirms this change of address and his status. In July 1835 he was a glass manufacturer of Longlands Villa. Then, in November 1836 he had become a gentleman of Platts, Amblecote.

The new Platts Glassworks was completed in 1840 and Webb

transferred his business from the White House Glassworks between June and November[10]. Thomas Webb moved into Platts House and the new glassworks was used to manufacture plain and cut flint glass[11]. An indication of the cost of this venture was given by his ex-partner Benjamin Richardson of Wordsley Flint Glassworks. In 1842 Richardson commented that by paying £10,000, Thomas Webb had expended a huge sum of money, for premises no better than those he had vacated at the White House[12]. However, there is more than a hint of jealousy in this comment. After their partnership was dissolved, relations between Webb and the Richardson brothers were very strained. A certain degree of enmity developed that was probably made worse as Webb's business began to flourish in direct competition to the Richardsons'. An article in Art Union magazine of April 1846 states:

> 'Mr. Webb devotes his attention chiefly, if not exclusively, to the manufacture of flint-glass; and it is only justice to him to state that, in clearness and purity, he is confessedly unsurpassed in Europe. Hence, much of his produce goes to the creation of chandeliers, candelabras, and objects in which the quality alluded to is of the highest importance.'

In a similar way to Benjamin Richardson, Thomas Webb was astute in developing new products in keeping with the prevalent style of the day. Art Union magazine in 1847 refers to Thomas Webb making opalescent glass decorated in *Etruscan* style[13].

Thomas Wilkes Webb[14] joined the firm in 1850 as a clerk, having left school at the age of fourteen. He began an apprenticeship under the watchful eye of his father and was destined to propel the firm to even greater heights. The family lived at Platts House, next to the glassworks[15].

Thomas Webb exhibited a wide range of table and decorative glass at the 1851 Great Exhibition held in the 'Crystal Palace' in Hyde Park[16] and won a medal for cut glass.

In 1853 Thomas Webb became a founding partner of Mills, Webb & Stuart at the newly opened Albert Glassworks. He contributed £500 but was sought as a partner for his experience and his capital. He sustained his efforts at Platts Glassworks and was not involved day-to-day at the Albert Glassworks. He left the partnership after less than a year[17].

Webb had been applauded for the excellent working conditions at the Platts Glassworks[18], but after fifteen years he decided a further move was required. He purchased part of the Dennis estate and built a new glassworks at the rear of Dennis House. He left Platts in 1855 and moved to his new works at Dennis.

Platts Glassworks then had a succession of tenants. It was first leased to Samuel Bowen, originally of West Bromwich, who had failed earlier as a glass manufacturer at the Nailsea glassworks near Bristol[19]. He subsequently failed at Platts as well and became bankrupt again.

During the eighteen-sixties the Nailsea & Stourbridge Glass Company operated Platts works. A contemporary advertisement describes the firm as 'Manufacturers of Crown, Sheet, Rolled Plate, Brilliant-Cut, Painted, Enamelled, & patent Undulated Interlocking Ornamental Glass.'[20] Evidence of the glass being produced at Platts appears in a report of a traditional glassmakers procession in 1865:

> The members of the glasscutter's and glassmakers' trades, numbering about 800, met at the 'Marquis of Granby' Inn, Audnam Bank, and there formed themselves into a procession. Each member had hoisted some specimen of his branch of the trade, amongst which were richly cut decanters, goblets, wine-glasses, jugs of all colours, shapes and sizes, crinoline, birdcages, fireirons, glass hats and a variety of articles. There was also a sheet of glass manufactured at the Platts Sheet Glassworks, which was erected on a dray and drawn by a horse. The sheet of glass was 134 inches long and 39 inches wide. There was a large cylinder of glass raised above it which appeared to be nearly as long. There were also a large number of flags and banners with the following mottoes, which were very conspicuous, being displayed on coloured canvas—'Prosperity to our employers and success to the glass trade', 'United we stand, divided we fall', 'John Bright and Free Trade', 'To the memory of Cobden, Gladstone and the franchise.'[21]

Further reference to the relative novelty of plate glass in the Stourbridge district appears in a newspaper article of 1867:

> 'Of late years a new branch of the glass trade has been introduced, the Stourbridge Glass Co., now make sheet glass, rolled plate and rough plate. About 170 men and boys are employed. The labour of the men in this trade is much more severe than in flint glass; a founder remains on duty for twenty or twenty-five hours at a stretch.'[22]

Later in 1867 Messrs. J. Hartley & Co. bought the works[23] and promptly closed it[24]. J. Hartley & Co. was a major manufacturer of plate glass[25], but the purchase was an attempt to stifle competition rather than a serious intention to use the works. Hartleys operated a cartel with their former partners in Chance Brothers & Co. and the Pilkingtons of the St. Helen's Glass Co. In 1861 they purchased and closed the glassworks of Joshua Bower, at Hunslet, near Leeds[26]. Having purchased the Platts works Hartleys received two-fifths of the loss on purchase from Chance Brothers & Co. and a further two-fifths from the St. Helen's Glass Co.

Isaac Nash[27] had an interest in the Platts Glassworks and upon his death in 1887 his trustees conveyed this to John Guest of Coalbournbrook.

In 1894 Messrs Flemming and Co. occupied the Platts works[28]. The stay was a brief one, as the firm—then known as Joseph Flemming & Co.—moved to Holloway End Glasshouse in 1900[29]. Various trade directories for the year 1900 have no entry for Platts, suggesting it was not in use.

Sometime in the early part of this century, Tom Dukes started glassmaking at the Platts[30]. The firm was still there in 1910 when, on 15th June, Dukes (Stourbridge) Ltd. registered patent No 324521.

In 1920 F. Wilkinson & Co. occupied Platts works. Frank Wilkinson[31] ran a small decorating business employing four engravers, three intaglio cutters, fourteen glasscutters, and eight in an etching department. The firm carried out work for the local manufacturers, many wholesalers, and all of the brewers in the Midlands area, stamping, marking and badging their glassware, mainly continental imports. This small firm was responsible for two important developments in the English glass trade. Frank Wilkinson worked under Lionel Pearce at Thomas Webb & Sons Ltd. up to and just after the First World War when he set up on his own. He developed a new method of polishing glass with acid. He carried out this polishing for nine of the local factories for nearly twelve months, until one by one they all established their own polishing plants. His brother, R. Wilkinson introduced the practice of using carborundum wheels for cutting instead of the traditional steel wheels. From 1925 onwards, this method was taken up by the whole of the glass trade throughout the country. This was despite the protestations of the unions that the work was being performed in a quarter of the time that the old method took. Frank Wilkinson contracted pneumonia in February 1927 and died within four days. No doubt his lungs had been damaged during his two years of experimentation with acids[32].

From 1924 onwards, Harbridge Crystal Glass Co.[33] ran a small factory, slightly west of the main Platts factory. Their production ceased in 1955, but the company then leased two furnaces at Webb Corbett's Coalbournhill works. They continued to cut glass at the Platts until 1966 when the site was sold[34].

The use of the original premises by a variety of firms is illustrated by Kelly's 1928 Directory of Staffordshire. It lists the Harbridge Crystal Glass Co., and J.F. Bolton Bowater as glass manufacturers at the Platts. Furthermore, it also lists the Decorative Glass Co. and F. Wilkinson & Co., both as glass decorators at The Platts.

John Frederick Bowater[35] had previously run a small glassworks in Brettell Lane with his uncle, John Bolton, then started a small glassworks of his own in Platts Road in the early nineteen-twenties. The works made fancy glass including epergnes, flower stands and centrepieces. Bowater went into partnership with Cyril Manley and another glass dealer, Arthur Guest as the Britannic Manufacturing Co. to produce the metal fittings for this type of glassware. Within a few years, coloured fancy glass became unfashionable and J.F. Bolton Bowater closed down.

J.K. Davies and Son operated part of the original works until

1970. The Ducat Heating Co. then occupied part of it, with the rest standing empty.

Platts House had been gradually surrounded by later buildings and became known simply as number 66 Platts Crescent. It was demolished in 1967 and in 1992 the whole of the area around where the house stood was cleared for redevelopment. The chimney of Harbridge's factory was still standing in 1991, but has since been demolished.

---

1 While the glassmakers primary problem was an excess of supply over demand, any hope of recovery was quashed by the collapse of the economy in 1720. This followed the bursting of the 'South Sea Bubble', a speculative venture originally supported by the Tory ministers of Queen Anne's reign to solve the problem of public debt. It brought about a fitting conclusion to the frenzied and inflated commercialism of the 'monied interest' in the preceding years. The results were catastrophic, particularly for those who had sold substantial assets in land or other forms of property to buy at absurdly inflated prices. Those most affected were the primary source of the glassmakers' income.

2 'The Platt Leasows, which are Mr Henzey's' op cit, R.L. Chambers, *Perambulation Roll of the parish of Oldswinford* (1733).

3 Supra, Dial Glasshouse.

4 SRO, Tp 1273 Map of Amblecote 1769, Private collection.

5 Infra, Dial Glasshouses.

6 Pigot and Co.'s National Commercial Directory for 1828-9.

7 Thirteenth Report of the Commission into the Glass Excise, 1835, Appendix 7.

8 White's 1834 Directory of Staffordshire; Pigot's 1835 National Commercial Directory.

9 SRO, D 356A; D 585/159/1/1, p. 1 and HWRO(H) E 12/S, Iverley II, deed of 26th Dec 1836.

10 Ibid, H.W. Woodward, p9.

11 Pigot and Co.'s 1841 Directory of Birmingham.

12 BHGM, Letter of Benjamin Richardson to William Haden Richardson.

13 Infra, Wheeley's Brettell Lane Glasshouses 1851 and Wordsley Flint Glassworks, 1847.

14 Thomas Wilkes Webb, son of Thomas Webb and his wife Elizabeth, nee

Hemming, b. 9th Oct 1836, Stourbridge; bap. 9th Nov 1836, Oldswinford.
15 1851 census PRO HO0107/2035/046
16 *Official Descriptive and Illustrated Catalogue*, v 2, p699.
17 SRO, D648/86, Deed of dissolution of partnership as far as regards Thos. Webb, 1854.
18 Art Union, Apr 1846.
19 By 1862 the only surviving partners at the Nailsea Glassworks were Henry Lucas Bean and Isaac White. They leased the Nailsea works to Samuel Bowen a glass merchant of West Bromwich and John Powis of London. Then in 1867 Bean and White sold the property to the Hartleys. Some rolled plate glass was made in the smallest of the three Nailsea glasshouses, 'The Lily' and consigned to Crewe and other railway stations for roofing. However, Bowen overreached himself and was adjudged bankrupt in July 1869 owing about £30,000. He and Powis surrendered their lease to the new owners, the Hartleys. Brierley Hill Advertiser, 30th Nov 1872 and 5th Jun 1873; Birmingham Daily Gazette, 12th Nov 1872. Bowen was to fail for a third time in 1872.
20 Margaret Thomas, *The Nailsea Glassworks* (1987), p25.
21 Stourbridge Observer, 31st Jul 1865.
22 Brierley Hill Advertiser, 1867.
23 Littlebury's 1873 Directory.
24 C.M. Brown, *The Changing Location of the West Midlands Glass Industry during the Nineteenth Century* (1978).
25 James and John Hartley were partners with William and Lucas Chance trading as Chances & Hartleys from 1833 until their partnership was dissolved 18th Nov 1836. The Hartley brothers then left the Midlands to establish themselves at Sunderland. For a precis of their Sunderland history see *The Glass Industry of Tyne and Wear Part 1: Glassmaking on Wearside* (1979).
26 Bower, Smith & Co. established a glasshouse in Hunslet around 1814. By 1818, the two Bower brothers; John and Joshua started their own businesses. John made bottles, flint glass, wine and porter bottles, coloured sheet glass, stained and painted. A bill heading from 1832 shows three large glass cones and substantial workshops. John Bower's business closed sometime between 1849 and 1853. Joshua Bower's business concentrated on crown glass. By agreements of 31st May and 27th Dec 1861, the Hartleys, Chances and Pilkingtons took over in equal shares all of Joshua Bower's plant, stock and liabilities, undertaking to pay him £1,000 per year for fourteen years on

condition of his abstaining from the manufacture of or trade in glass in the counties with which they were concerned, op cit, J.F. Chance, *A History of the Firm of CHANCE BROTHERS & CO Glass and Alkali Manufacturers* (1919), p94. Joshua Bower (1773-1835) was an enterprising man. As well as glassmaking and coalmining interests he became one of the greatest toll 'farmers' in England and at one time is said to have possessed nearly all the tolls between Leeds and London as well as many others in other counties, op cit T.C. Barker, *The Glassmakers Pilkington: 1826-1976* (1977), p106 & pp498-499.

27 SRO, D695/4/16/29. Isaac Nash son of William Nash and his wife Phoebe, nee Rusgrove; b. 22nd Aug 1818, Kingswinford; bap. 1st Jun 1819, Stourbridge High Street Independent Chapel; wealthy edge tool manufacturer, magistrate and popular local benefactor; d. 12th Sep 1887; apprenticed to James Griffin of Dudley where he learned forging and plating; rented Newtown Forge, Belbroughton in 1840; rented Galtons Grinding Mill, Belbroughton in 1846; rented Hillpool Mill in 1854; rented Drayton Mill in 1865; purchased Weybridge Forge and expanded it in 1866; lived at Belle Vue, Belbroughton in 1871; purchased the once dominant Belbroughton sythemaking business of Thomas and William Waldron in 1873; purchased the six Somerset mills of Fussels in 1880; lived at The Laurels, Belbroughton in 1881 (PRO, 1881 census of Belbroughton, RG11/2941/124/24). This was the former Yew Tree Lodge on Branthill Farm, later to be the scene of the murder of newspaper delivery boy, Carl Bridgewater in 1978. Wollaston Mill on the River Stour, purchased in 1887, was the centre of Nash's business empire. In 1942 Isaac Nash & Sons Ltd. merged with Joseph Tyzack and Sons Ltd. of Sheffield, founded in 1837, to form Nash & Tyzack Industries Ltd. In 1951 Nash & Tyzack Industries Ltd. merged with William Hunt & Sons, Brades Steel Works of Oldbury to form Brades & Nash Tyzack Industries Ltd. In 1962 Brades & Nash Tyzack Industries Ltd. was acquired by Spear & Jackson. The U.S. company Neill Tools acquired Spear & Jackson in 1985. The Wollaston Mills site became superfluous to requirements and was acquired in the late nineteen-fifties by BSR and subsequently in the nineteen-nineties by Sunrise Medical.

28 R. Simms, *History of Glassmaking in South Staffordshire.*

29 Ibid, M.W. Greenslade, p58.

30 Ibid, D.R. Guttery, p147.

31 1897-1927.
32 R. Wilkinson, *The Hallmarks of Antique Glass* (1968).
33 Harbridge is a conjunction of Harvey and Bridges.
34 Ibid, D.R. Guttery, p147.
35 John Frederick Bolton Bowater, b. 1880, Brettell Lane, son of Henry Bowater, licensed victualler of 6 St. Johns Road, Dudley and his wife Margaret, nee Bolton, sister of John Bolton of Dial Glasshouses and Albert Glassworks.

CHAPTER 23

Waterford Glassworks

It may appear unusual to comment on an Irish glassworks in a book on Stourbridge glass. However, the Henzey family established glassworks in Ireland as well as Stourbridge and many glassmakers moved between England and Ireland. The need for this section on the Waterford Glassworks is because of the involvement of a central character in the Stourbridge story—John Hill.

Glass was made at Ballynegeragh, County Waterford as early as 1622, but despite extant meticulous accounts of this enterprise[1], we have no record of its owner. The first glassworks around the city of Waterford was probably built by John Head, on the River Suir near Gurteens, just a few miles from the town. A merchant advertised its wares in 1729:

> 'These are to give notice that The Glass-house near Waterford is now at work, where all persons may be supplied with all sorts of flint glass, double and single, also garden glasses, vials and other green glassware. Sold at reasonable rates by Joseph Harris, Merchant'[2].

Two years later John Head placed his own advertisement. He was of an old Waterford family; his predecessors had been High Sheriffs and Mayors of Waterford in the seventeenth Century:

> 'The Glass-house at Waterford belonging to John Head, Esqr. has been at work for some time, where all gentlemen and others may be supplied with bottles, with or without marks, or at the ware house in Waterford. There will also soon be made there best London crown and other glass windows, and sold at reasonable rates'[3]

Head ran the glasshouse for eight years until it closed when he died. The main Waterford Glassworks was established in 1783 by George and William Penrose, after the repeal in 1780 of Section XXI of the 1746 Finance Act that prohibited Ireland from exporting glass of any kind. The Penroses were prosperous merchants with no previous experience of the glass trade. The saw an opportunity under the Free Trade Act and chose Waterford, with its splendid quays by the River Suir for their business. Not surprisingly, they went to Stourbridge to seek expert assistance, where they hired John Hill. Having prepared their factory they placed an announcement:

> 'Waterford Glass House. George and William Penrose having established an extensive glass manufactory in this city, their friends and the public may be supplied with all kinds of plain and cut flint glass, useful and ornamental. They are now ready to receive orders and intend opening their warehouse the 1st of next month.'[4]

The business was immediately successful, particularly the Penroses' innovative designs for decanters. The style was barrel-shaped with three neck rings. The decoration included swags filled with finely cut diamonds, or simple engraving with motifs such as rose, thistle and shamrock. These decanters were not of superlative quality, but are highly prized, and priced accordingly today, because of their rarity. In 1784 the Penroses advertised:

> 'a complete flint glass manufactory', making cut and engraved glass, 'of as fine a quality as any in Europe.'[5]

In 1785 a committee was appointed to explore the commercial relations between Great Britain and Ireland. In the evidence presented, John Blades, the well-known cut-glass manufacturer of Ludgate Hill, London, stated:

> 'a Mr Hill, a great manufacturer at Stourbridge, had lately gone to Waterford, and had taken the best set of workmen he could get in the county of Worcester, and that English glass workers were constantly going backwards and forwards to Ireland, six a short time ago, and four or five quite recently.'[6]

This was John Hill of Kingswinford, the son of Waldron and Elizabeth Hill. He had been first at the Ridgrave Glasshouse and then at Wordsley Flint Glassworks before moving to the Waterford Glassworks where he started recruiting Stourbridge workmen. He had received a legacy from his wife's uncle, Edward Russell of the Heath Glassworks in 1778 that presumably left him sufficiently financially independent to execute this audacious manoeuvre. Further evidence that George and William Penrose had been recruiting Stourbridge workmen appears in a petition of 1786 to the Irish House of Commons:

> 'they had with great difficulty, and at the expense of nearly £10,000 established a complete flint glass manufactory. The works employ from fifty to seventy manufacturers, who have mostly been brought from England at heavy Expense...'[7]

About 1786 John Hill became involved in a dispute concerning William Penrose's wife, Rachel. He felt he was wrongly accused but decided to leave and go to France. During the four years of his stay in Ireland[8] he befriended another Englishman, Johnathan Gatchell of a Somerset family, a Quaker and a clerk at the works[9]. On his departure, John Hill left a letter for his friend in which he protested his innocence:

> Dr Jonothan
>
> It is impossible for me to express the feelings of my poor mind when I acq. thee that I am obliged to leave this Kingdom, my reasons I need not tell thee, but I sincerely wish I had been made acquainted with the base ingratitude of the worst of Villians sooner & probably then I might have remedied it, but now 'tis too late. For heavens sake don't reproach me but put the best construction on my conduct. I wish it was in my power to pay thee & all my Creditors but if ever Fortune should put it in my power depend upon it I will satisfy every one—My mind is so hurt I scarcely know what to write. I sincerely wish thee every sucess & am tho' the most miserable of mankind.
>
> thine very Sincerely

J. Hill[10]

Before he left, being grateful for Gatchell's kindness and pity, John Hill gave him all his recipes for compounding the glass[11]. Armed with Hill's recipes, Gatchell became more prominent in the business and eventually became its sole owner.

In 1788 the firm announced it had sent a gift—'a very curious service' of glass to the British Royal family[12]. Further publicity was obtained in November 1790 when Lady Westmoreland[13] with Lord and Lady Waterford and the Bishop of Ossory arrived in the city from Curraghmore 'to visit Penrose's glass factory.'[14]

William Penrose died in 1796. Then in 1799 Johnathan Gatchell bought out George Penrose and formed a partnership with James Ramsey and Ambrose Bancroft. Ramsey died in 1811 and Johnathan Gatchell bought out Bancroft to become the sole owner. John Hill's skill and experience had thus allowed Gatchell to rise from a lowly clerk to become proprietor of one of the premier glass works in the country. He proudly announced:

> 'Permit me to take the liberty of informing that the partnership lately subsisting under the firm of Ramsey, Gatchell and Bancroft, in the established Flint-Glass manufactory, in this city, has been dissolved on the 19th inst., the term having expired: in consequence, I have purchased the stock of my late partners, engaged the whole of the concerns, and am now carrying on the business, in the same extensive manner as heretofore, intending to use my best endeavours to give full satisfaction. May 20th 1811.'

Later, in 1823, Johnathan Gatchell formed a partnership with his brothers James and Samuel, and his nephew Joseph Walpole, the son of William Walpole, who had married Johnathan Gatchell's sister, Sarah. The firm was styled Gatchells and Walpole[15]. However, the partners all died in short succession: Johnathan Gatchell in 1823, Joseph Walpole in 1824, Samuel Gatchell in 1825 and James Gatchell in 1830.

Gatchell & Co. paid £3,002 7s 9 1/2d excise duty for the year ending 5th January 1833[16], suggesting the Waterford Glassworks was larger than many Stourbridge glassworks of the day. Steam-powered cutting wheels had enabled a tremendous output of goods. In 1832 Mrs Elizabeth Walpole, one of the partners, wrote 'if the steam engine pours out such a flood of goods so that there is no room [to store it] and that sales cannot be effected in self defence, it would seem desirable that the engine should be stopped entirely.' However, she concludes 'I am quite satisfied as to the employing of turners in this way.'

Because of the death of its partners, the original partnership was dissolved in 1835[17] and George Gatchell[18] took control under the terms of his father's will[19], having attained the age of twenty-one. He took a partner, George Sanders, although Sanders had left by 1848[20]. This left Gatchell perilously short of capital and his business began losing money. As a final fling, Gatchell exhibited at the 1851 Great Exhibition held at the 'Crystal Palace' in Hyde Park:

> 'Etagere, or ornamental centre stand for a banqueting table; consisting of forty pieces of cut glass, so fitted to each other as to require no connecting sockets or any other material. Quart and pint decanters, cut in hollow prisms. Centre vase, or bowl, on detached tripod stand. Vases with covers. Designed and executed at the Waterford Glassworks.'[21]

Sadly this exhibition of fine wares could not prevent the firm's descent into bankruptcy and the business closed in 1851, shortly before the Exhibition closed on 11th October. George Gatchell moved to England and retired to Tormoham, Devon[22], without returning to Ireland.

One hundred years after the closure, a new factory opened in 1951 as Waterford Glass Ltd. to revive the tradition of Waterford crystal. The founders were Joseph McGrath and Joseph Griffin. The chief designer based many of his designs on the patterns recorded by his predecessor, Samuel Miller, in the eighteen-twenties and thirties. The history of the glassworks to the present day is more one of high finance than one of glassmaking. In 1986 Waterford made a reverse take-over of the fine-china manufacturer Wedgwood, acting as a 'white knight' against a hostile bid from London International Group. In 1989 the perceived strength of the two brands, Wedgwood and Waterford, led Tony O'Reilly, chairman and chief executive of the food company Heinz, and Morgan Stanley the US investment bank, to pay £79m for a 29.9% stake in Waterford. They paid 37.5p per share although the returns initially were dismally poor.

By 1993 the company was suffering badly from east European competition. The workforce had already been reduced from four thousand in 1983 to one and a half thousand. To try and remain competitive management confronted the workforce and demanded swingeing pay cuts. A mass meeting of workers agreed to the deal and the future of the company was secured. In 1993 the company, valued at £155m, reported an operating profit of £0.5m, the first profits since 1986.

On 1st September 1994, Tony O'Reilly was able to announce a substantial interim profit of £5.1m for the six months to June and hinted at 'the prospects for the near-term resumption of dividend payments.'

In 1995 Waterford Crystal mounted a successful bid for Stuart Crystal and saw the group return to profit. Results for 1996 showed earnings of £29.2 million, up 24 percent and the third successive year of growth. Waterford's sales continued to grow, but in the aftermath of the terrorist attack on New York on 11th September 2001, group profits halved to £25m with crystal sales especially hard hit.

---

1 Marsh's Library, Dublin.
2 Dublin Journal, 24th May 1729.
3 Dublin Journal, 1731.
4 Dublin Evening Post, 4th Oct 1783.
5 Leinster Journal, 27th Oct 1784.
6 Appendix to the Journals of the Irish House of Commons quoted in M.S. Dudley Westropp, *Irish Glass* (1920), p71.
7 Irish House of Commons Journal 1786, Petition of George and William Penrose of Waterford, quoted in M.S. Dudley Westropp, *Irish Glass* (1920), p69.
8 1783 to 1786.
9 Phelps Warren, *Irish Glass* (1970), p38.
10 Gatchell Letters, Waterford Glassworks, No 1-78, 154-1956, v 1, document

7(a).
11 Gatchell Letters, Waterford Glassworks, No 1-78, 154-1956, v 1, document 7(d); ibid, M.S. Dudley Westropp, p69; ibid, Phelps Warren, p38 & Appendix D.
12 'a very curious service of glass has been sent over from Waterford to Milford for their Majesty's use, and by their orders forwarded to Cheltenham, where it has been much admired and does great credit to the manufacturers of this country.' Dublin Chronicle, 1788.
13 The wife of the Viceroy.
14 Hibernian magazine, Nov 1790.
15 Ibid, M.S. Dudley Westropp, p75; Phelps Warren, p39.
16 Thirteenth Report of the Commission into the Glass Excise, 1835, Appendix 7.
17 Dublin Gazette, 15th Oct 1835.
18 George Gatchell, son of Johnathan Gatchell, b. 21st Apr 1814, Ireland.
19 Will of Johnathan Gatchell, 30th Mar 1823.
20 Waterford Evening News, 22nd Dec 1848. 'The Partnership of George Gatchell and Co. (George Gatchell and George Sanders) is this day dissolved. George Gatchell will carry on the flint glass business, which has been going on for over half a century and carried on by his late father Jonathan Gatchell.'
21 *Official Descriptive and Illustrated Catalogue*, v 2, p698.
22 PRO, 1881 census of Devon, RG11/2167/32/9.

CHAPTER 24

Coalbournhill Glassworks, Amblecote

Coalbournhill Glassworks was the second glassworks built by Thomas Bradley junior. It has already been described that he built the Fimbrell Glasshouse in 1687, then leased it to Benjamin Batchelor in 1691. In the same year, 1691[1], he took a lease of land at Coalbournhill and built a glassworks on the corner of Amblecote High Street, south of the road to Wollaston. It is not known what career Thomas junior followed before opening the glassworks, but it seems that he was a Captain. On 16th December 1702 Thomas Milward recorded, 'Sold my Black Mare to Capt. Bradley for 34 gross of glass buttons.'[2] A further similar reference occurs in an 1733 examination of parish of settlement[3].

By 1703 Thomas Bradley junior was assessed to be a sufficiently wealthy landowner to qualify as a juror[4]. He died shortly after making his will on 10th August 1705[5]. The will and inventory are full of references to his trade as a glassmaker and make his intentions that the trade be carried on quite clear. He gave to his widow Alice 'one moiety or half part of all my household goods & of all the working tools potts ashes sand glasses in the warehouse & of all other stock & utensils whatsoever belonging or in any way relating to my glasshouse in Oldswinford.' In the time-honoured fashion the other half was bequeathed to two of his sons. 'I give devise & bequeath unto my two sons Joseph[6] & Edward[7] the other moiety or half part of my household goods & all the working tools potts ashes sand glasses stock & other utensils whatsoever belonging or relating to my said glasshouse to be equally shared between them part & part alike.' The first half was also to come to them after the death of his widow. A bequest to his son Thomas makes it clear that flint glasses were among his products. 'In case my son Thomas Bradley shall at any time hereafter return into this kingdom of England it is my will & I do hereby direct that my executors hereafter named do & shall give & deliver unto him within two months next after such his arrival one or more chest or chests of flint glasses of the value of ten pounds at least.' The testator willed that his apprentices and servants should continue their work 'with my said wife & two sons Joseph & Edward whom I desire to continue & carry on the said glasswork & trade . . .' He then set certain conditions for his wife and instructed that if these should not be met, her half was to go to their son John Bradley. Among the items on the detailed inventory were: 'three little barrels of red lead and a small bagg of saltpeter' in 'the mixing house', £5 worth of 'glasses in the white warehouse' and £6 worth of 'glasses in the green warehouse.' The testator's total estate was valued at £155 18s 0d.

Thomas Bradley's son, Edward, initially worked the glassworks with Jeremiah Minors as his partner. Subsequently, it came under the control of Edward's older brother, John[8]. Whether this was because their widowed mother, Alice, had not met the conditions stipulated in her husband's will, or whether she had died is not clear.

John Bradley decided to let the Coalbournhill works to the Batchelors, who were already operating the family's Fimbrell Glasshouse under a lease from his late father. So, on 9th April 1714, John Bradley, the son and heir of Thomas Bradley junior, leased Coalbournhill Glassworks to Elijah and Humphrey Batchelor for nine hundred and seventy-six years at a rent of £11 5s. In the lease[9] they are described as co-partners and broadglass makers of Amblecote. The fortunes of the Batchelor family have already been described as they pursued their trade at Fimbrell Glasshouse. It has also been described that Fimbrell and Coalbournhill Glassworks both came to be owned by Charles Fox.

The history of the two glasshouses diverges after the death of Mrs Elizabeth Batchelor, widow of Humphrey, in 1762[10]. She had made a will, which was proved in PCC on 6th November 1762[11].

Her only son, Thomas Batchelor had died in 1750[12], so she left her estate to her brothers Waldron and Thomas Hill. As already described, they ceased glassmaking at the older Fimbrell Glasshouse but continued the business at Coalbournhill. Both brothers were in their fifties and had no previous experience of glassmaking. Waldron Hill lived at the Tiled House, Pensnett, where the family had a blade-mill for making edge tools. They promptly took into partnership William Waldron—another edge-tool manufacturer—who had no glassmaking experience either. No records exist to enlighten the researcher about their products, but they suffered a misfortune, brought to the public's attention in 1771:

> 'Thomas Willetts, clerk or agent to Waldron Hill and Thomas Hill of Amblecoat, glassmakers, was robbed of £125 2s 6d money of the said W. Hill and T. Hill and also of William Waldron of Stourbridge, glass-maker and copartner with the sd. W. Hill and T. Hill.'[13]

Three years later, in 1774, Whitworth's canal map shows Hill's glasshouse at Coalbournhill. Waldron Hill's son, known at the time as Thomas Hill junior, was one the proprietors named in the Stourbridge Canal Act of 1766[14].

Clear evidence of the problems caused by the imposition of excise duty on glass appears in correspondence from William Waldron. The Georgian era was a period of growth and expanding trade, but frequently at the expense of war. The background to the first duty on glass in Georgian times began in 1743. At this time the British Government had been dragged unwillingly into the War of the Austrian Succession. British involvement began with the battle of Dettingen where George II personally led an army of British, Hanoverian and other troops[15]. The Government's problems continued with the Jacobite rising under the Young Pretender[16]. The uprising had French support and under threat of invasion by the French, the Government was in need of funds and introduced the notorious Glass Excise Act. One of its clauses imposed a tax of 9s 4d on every 100lbs of raw material used. Turning to the period now in question, in 1777 the Government was in need of more money to finance its efforts in the War of American Independence and the level of tax was doubled. The previous duty was a big enough problem for the manufacturers, but the new imposition was an appalling burden. In 1777 the attorney Thomas Milward was seeking to raise a loan and approached William Waldron. He received the following reply:

> 'I wish I could assist you with the sum you require. Give me leave truly to assure you my inclination is not wanting but you must believe me when I tell you it is out of my power to raise you any sum at present unless I shut up the Glasshouse. Since the additional Duty our payments there are enormous, a sum not less than 600 li for duty every seven weeks.'[17]

Despite the burden, the partners were still wealthy men, supported by other business interests apart from glassmaking. John Jones, an 'Apprentice to Hill & Waldron, glassmakers of Stourbridge' is recorded on 23rd May 1778 in the admission register of Oldswinford Hospital. Hill and Waldron, merchants and glass manufacturers, are listed in Bailey's Western and Midland Directory of 1783. In the same directory Hill and Waldron are additionally listed as bankers. William Waldron was also involved in the clay business; in 1784 he was mining twenty-one acres of the best clay and had pot rooms in Amblecote[18]. As with so many other glassmakers, their wealth and stability enabled them to undertake the civic responsibilities reserved for the gentry of the day. Thomas Hill was Overseer of the Poor for Oldswinford in 1778. William Waldron was a churchwarden of Oldswinford in 1779 and 1780.

Glassmaking continued despite the burden of the glass excise. In 1785 the cone was shown, but not named on Snape's canal map. However, Snape placed it on the northwest corner of the road junction, instead of the southwest, where it actually stood. About this time Waldron Hill retired or died and his son Thomas[19] took his place in the business It has already been described[20] that Thomas Hill was one of the 'landlocked' glassmakers who, in 1786, contributed to the building of the Stourbridge to Wolverhampton turnpike, without interest.

Hill & Waldron, bankers and glass manufacturers appear in

trade directories throughout the seventeen-eighties and nineties. Their combined business interests evidently generated great wealth for the partners. William Waldron became High Sheriff of Worcestershire in 1795 and Thomas Hill senior followed him in 1796[21]. It should be explained that this is the same Thomas Hill, son of Waldron Hill, who used to be styled Thomas Hill junior to distinguish him from his uncle of the same name. When his first son was born in 1765, he was also named Thomas[22]. So the same Thomas, who used to be known as junior, subsequently became known as Thomas Hill senior, to differentiate him from his son.

According to D.N. Sandilands, the business run at Coalbournhill by Hill & Waldron in 1796 consisted of two bottle-houses. His reference was taken from a list that was in Stourbridge library but can no longer be found. However, the partnership of Hill, Waldron, Littlewood & Hampton was definitely making bottles[23]. Sandilands' observation is borne out by Sherriff's plan of 1812 that graphically shows two cones on the site, labelled 'Hill and Waldron'[24].

The reference to Littlewood and Hampton is a clear indication that Thomas Hill and William Waldron were involving new partners in the business. The Littlewood mentioned here is almost certainly Benjamin Littlewood of Holloway End Glasshouse. In 1818 the firm traded as Hill, Hampton & Co.[25] Then, by 1820 the partnership changed again and traded as Hill, Hampton, Harrison and Wheeley[26]. The new partner, Wheeley, would probably be William Seager Wheeley who by 1820 was in sole charge of Wheeley's Brettell Lane Glasshouses.

Hill, Hampton, Harrison & Wheeley traded until about 1835. The firm has regular entries in trade directories during this period as manufacturers of black bottles, although sometimes the title was abbreviated to Hill, Hampton & Co. A Thomas Hill was always the senior partner, although between 1809 and 1835 there were three generations of Thomas Hills. Thomas Hill senior died on 17th September 1824, aged eighty-seven and was buried alongside his wife at Oldswinford. His memorial exists today in the north aisle of Oldswinford church. His son, Thomas Hill II, died in 1827, leaving an only son, Thomas Hill III of Blaenavon. It was Thomas Hill III who was responsible for excise payments in 1833, when he paid £1,645 14d for the year ending 5th January 1833.[27] A straight comparison of amounts of duty paid would suggest this was the fifteenth largest of the sixteen Stourbridge/Dudley glasshouses of the day. However, it should be noted that this was a bottleworks on which the rate of duty was lower.

The last reference to the firm appeared in 1835 as 'Hill, Hampton and Co. (Bottle), Coalbourn Brook.'[28] Sometime after this the glassworks was closed because of poor trade and stood empty for some time. The lack of trade must have been the fault of the firm as the years 1834 to 1837 was a period of relative prosperity; the great depression only began to develop in 1838.

In 1837 the glassworks was acquired by Joseph Stevens[29], who had been so successful at Holly Hall Glassworks that he needed larger premises. He took over Coalbournhill Glassworks and adjoining firebrick works and brought in his younger brother James Stevens[30] as his partner. They converted one of the two old bottlehouses into a works for making flint, pressed and ruby glass. Joseph Stevens built himself a house nearby. James Stevens now had shares in two factories, Coalbournhill and Moor Lane Glassworks. The wages books[31] show the co-operation between the two factories, with workers working two weeks at each factory alternately.

Robson's Birmingham and Sheffield Directory of 1839 provides some information about how the two brothers worked the Coalbournhill site. It lists Stevens Brothers & Co., Colbourn Hill, black and german amber bottle manufacturers. It also lists Joseph Stevens & Son, flint glass works, producing ruby, achromatic and flint glass—as they had at Holly Hall Glassworks. This suggests that the two glasshouse cones on the Coalbournhill site were run under the auspices of two different firms. Joseph Stevens and his brother James operated the one as Stevens Brothers & Co. Joseph Stevens and either his oldest son James[32], or his middle son William[33], operated the other as Joseph Stevens & Son.

This split responsibility did not last long. James Stevens senior retired from the business in November 1840 and Joseph Stevens brought his second son, William into the business. The firm traded as Joseph Stevens, manufacturer of ruby, achromatic, and flint glass[34]. In Bentley's 1841 directory the listing is the same but it also lists James Stephens [sic], clerk and manager, Coalbourn-hill. This James was the oldest son of Joseph Stevens[35], not James Stevens senior who had retired the previous November.

In 1841[36] Joseph Stevens senior lived in Coalbournbrook with his third son Joseph[37]. The background to this is that sometime before the date of the census James Stevens junior—previously clerk and manager—had left the family firm and moved to Holly Hall Glassworks. Joseph Stevens senior brought his third son, Joseph, into the firm to replace him. It is interesting to chart Joseph's progress after joining the firm at the age of nineteen. Joseph Stevens junior married Caroline[38], the daughter of Richard Banks, a coalmaster. Their marriage was by a licence[39] in which Joseph Stevens junior is described as a gentleman. Then, one week after his marriage, his name appears in the Coalbournhill wages book as a clerk. Obviously, as a married man he needed a source of income. He only appears in the wages book until 1842 and in the parish registers of 1844 he describes himself as a clay agent. By 1847 he described himself as a glass manufacturer and his name appears for a time in the wages books at Moor Lane Glassworks.

William Stevens lived about two hundred yards away from his father and brother at The Platts. Next door to him lived William Couch, an excise officer aged forty-five[40]. Until the glass excise was repealed in 1845, the exciseman was a hated figure in the glass industry, but this one must have been out of the ordinary as Joseph Stevens senior's daughter Eliza married him. The death of Eliza Couch on 30th November 1892, aged sixty-five, at Ashby de la Zouch, is recorded on the Stevens' family vault in Brierley Hill churchyard.

Subsequently, both William Stevens and Joseph Stevens junior ceased their interest in the firm. Joseph's last entry in the Coalbournhill wages book[41] was in 1842 after which he became a clay agent. William's last entry was in August 1842, after which he moved to Golds Green, West Bromwich and worked as a furnaceman. Joseph Stevens senior had now run out of sons to involve in the firm and so took into partnership his son-in-law Benjamin Coltman.

Benjamin Coltman[42] was the son of Michael Coltman, glass-manufacturer of Brettell Lane[43]. Benjamin had married Joseph Stevens's second daughter Fanny in 1840[44]. No record remains of what, if anything, he contributed to the firm, but he was only there for three years before he died in 1844, aged twenty-seven.

Joseph Stevens senior always wanted the support of his family as partners. So, he requested his oldest son James to return to the family firm from the Holly Hall Glassworks where he had gone in 1841. This he did, and took Benjamin Coltman's place in the partnership.

This was the period when cut flint glass was the dominant product in most of the Stourbridge glasshouses; many of them were actually called 'flint glassworks.'[45]

During a time of depressed trade Joseph Stevens senior ran into financial difficulties. Benjamin Richardson commented 'something occurred between Bate & Robbins, the bankers at Stourbridge and Joseph Stevens and the works closed'.[46] What occurred is that when Joseph Stevens took over the valuable Coalbournhill site in 1837 from Thomas Hill, a partner in what was then Hill, Bate & Robins Bank[47], he bought the business with the help of a large mortgage from the bank. From a peak of prosperity and full employment in 1837 the Black Country economy plunged into recession, 1842 being probably the worst year of the century[48]. Although the economic climate improved again by 1846, Joseph Stevens' debt problems were insurmountable[49]. On 26th December 1846 the firm closed and Joseph Stevens retired, aged sixty-three. The property was sold at the Talbot Hotel in January 1850. The sale comprised: the glassworks with tunnel leading to the canal, wharfage, and the adjacent fire brick works. It also included the stock of window glass, plain and coloured domestic ware, chandelier drops, lenses, bottles and coloured canes[50].

James Stevens moved with his family to Aston Brook House, Aston in 1847[51], and ran the Victoria Glassworks in Dartmouth

Street with his son James[52] of Copeley Hill, Ivy Bank, Aston[53] until about 1880. James senior eventually retired to Stokeinteighhead, Devon[54]. He died on 5th December 1882, aged seventy-three, and was buried at Brierley Hill.

Joseph Stevens senior died in 1852 and was buried at Brierley Hill in accordance with his wishes in his will. In the burial register two addresses are given, All Saints, Birmingham and Netherton. He was buried in the same vault as his first wife Frances, nee Hale, who predeceased him. He had made a will on 3rd October 1847[55], nine months after the firm's closure, but two years before it was sold. In the will he is described as 'late of Coalbournhill, Amblecote, Glass Manufacturer, but now of the City of Worcester, Gentleman'. He intended to leave the Coalbournhill Glassworks and adjoining brickworks to his middle son William and his nephew Samuel Pitt who appears in the wages book as a clerk, 'in recognition of his long and faithful service'. However, by the time the will was proved on 28th October 1852 the testator no longer owned it.

Joseph Webb purchased the glassworks in November 1850[56] and moved to Coalbournhill[57] from the Holloway End Glasshouse where he had been in business with his cousin Edward. He continued the tradition at the Coalbournhill works by making flint and coloured glass, but also introduced pressed glass[58]. Joseph Webb was at the forefront of designs in pressed glass. The first designs were registered in 1853 and were followed with a stream of further design registrations throughout the eighteen-fifties. This was a much finer product than the debased articles that were to appear later. Although using the laboursaving technique of pressing, the quality was excellent. Both the metal itself and the artistic designs were on a par with the hand-blown and decorated articles with which they competed.

The first successful trade union in the glass industry had been formed in 1851 and by the beginning of 1858 unionisation of labour was almost complete[59]. A minor strike broke out at the Coalbournhill Glasshouse early in 1858. Like other model unions of the time, the Glassmakers Society regarded strikes as evil and it ended in a friendly agreement. A dinner was arranged, attended by both the employer

Joseph Webb, and the men[60]. Faced with an increasing outbreak of strikes, the employers responded by holding a meeting on 1st November 1858 at the Talbot Hotel, Stourbridge, where they formed a manufacturers' organisation. Joseph Webb became a founder member of the Flint Glass Manufacturers Defence Association. Despite the conciliatory atmosphere at Coalbournhill, strikes spread throughout the district in October 1858[61] and in December the Association of Flint Glass Makers enforced a national lockout lasting for seven months. In April 1859, after the lockout, Joseph Webb claimed £58 1s from the association's defence fund. The amount implies the firm was the eighth largest of the thirteen firms in the Midlands Association.

After the strike, business gradually returned to normal, although attitudes were never the same again. Joseph Webb continued to manufacture at Coalbournhill and lived with his family at Coalbourn House[62], next to the Fish Inn at Coalbournbrook. He died at Coalbournbrook on 1st May 1869, aged fifty-six[63]. When his will was proved at Lichfield[64] it shows that he was concerned about two issues. First, his executors should complete the erection of a house then in progress at Penkridge, Staffordshire. Second, because his two sons Henry Fitzroy[65] and Joseph junior were minors, he wished the business to be continued until they attained the age of twenty-one. The business had a stock of 234,588 items of which more that 140,000 can be identified as pressed. Most of the stock was tableware from knife rests to decanters. A few hundred lamps, plus a thousand pressed miners lamps, but virtually no ornamental glass. There were 180 moulds, one stopper shop and three cutting shops with a total of fifty-six frames.

His widow Jane[66], and Jane's brother, Joseph Hammond[67] as executors, decided to continue the business. Joseph Hammond took on the management and lived at Cobden Street, Wollaston[68]. He had previously run a cutting shop at Dennis, either as a partner or tenant of his brother-in-law Richard Webb[69]. In 1872 Hammond leased the cutting shop to Thomas Webb & Co.[70] Littlebury's directory of 1873 lists 'Joseph Webb (The executors of the late) Coalbourn Hill.'

However, Joseph Hammond's management was not successful and the business absorbed much of Jane Webb's assets[71]. Hammond was forced out and on 15th January 1881 a circular announced that:

> Mr Joseph Hammond has ceased to represent the firm and is now wholly unconnected with the business which will be carried on by Mrs Jane Webb and H F Webb with assistance from Joseph Webb jun and Benjamin Robinson.

Shortly after, in early 1881 the glasshouse manager, Lewis John Murray[72], left to start in business on his own[73]. He moved from Field House, Buckpool[74] and spent ten months in Capetown as a freelance glass manufacturers' agent[75], then returned to manage John Walsh Walsh's[76] Soho and Vesta Glassworks in Birmingham[77].

Joseph Webb junior[78] had been working in the business but also decided it was time to go. He renounced all interest in his father's estate and emigrated to Philadelphia, USA in 1881 where he worked for the Phoenix Glass Company.

Jane Webb continued to live at Coalbourn House with her other children until she died in 1899[79]. The Pottery Gazette of March 1883 describes *New Gold Glass* from the executors of the late Joseph Webb as a 'Crumpled surface, coloured with gold.' An article in the June 1884 issue of the Pottery Gazette comments:

> 'On a visit to Stourbridge during the past month, we had the pleasure of seeing, in an advanced state of completion, a magnificent glass chandelier made by the Executors of the late Joseph Webb, of Coalbourn Hill Glass Works. But to adequately describe the beautiful suite of crystal glass furniture, upholstered in crimson satin, that we also saw, would be extremely difficult. The design is of a medieval kind, and what, under ordinary circumstances, would be a display of artistically carved woodwork is here represented in tastefully cut crystal glass. The harmony in the colours employed for decoration, leaves nothing to be desired, and the whole reflects the highest credit on the firm producing it, while at the same time, it is another proof of the rapid strides that are being made in the development of the glass-making indus-

try. We understand that the suite referred to is intended for an oriental court.'[80]

A further article in the Pottery Gazette of December 1884 comments:

> 'We have recently had the pleasure of inspecting a magnificent billiard table, the entire framework of which is made of richly cut crystal glass. It has been manufactured by the executors of the late Joseph Webb of Stourbridge, for a wealthy East Indian Merchant. The work is very finely executed, and the effect when lit up by brilliant light, is truly beautiful. This enterprising firm has been very successful lately in obtaining orders from India for crystal glass furniture and they have now another billiard table in hand, in addition to a suite of chairs, settees and sofas. We are pleased to see Stourbridge coming to the front of this class of work, which we believe has hitherto had its home in Birmingham, and wish the executors of the late Joseph Webb every success in the new branch of trade they have taken up. Drawings of the billiard table and other furniture may be seen at their London showrooms 30 Holborn, EC.'[81]

It is possible to observe today the elaborate ostentation of such pieces of glass furniture. Birmingham Museum and Art Gallery possesses an etagere made of cut glass with mirrors and electroplated supports, made by the Birmingham firm of F. & C. Osler about 1882[82].

A downturn in trade brought about the end of the firm in 1886[83]. The works and adjoining house were put up for sale in January 1886 but failed to attract a single bid and the firm closed. The moulds that Joseph Webb and his successors had used to produce pressed glass were sold to Edward Moore. Henry Fitzroy Webb became a commercial traveller in the glass trade.

Unable to sell the works, Jane Webb leased it to Thomas Michell for fourteen years from 14th September 1887 at £150 per annum. Kelly's 1888 Directory of Staffordshire lists the occupier as 'Thomas Michell, Coalbournhill Glass Works'. No other reference to Thomas Michell has been identified. Kelly's 1892 Post Office Directory of Staffordshire and Warwickshire shows the occupiers to be again 'Joseph Webb (executors of) Coalbourn Brook, Amblecote, Stourbridge.' It also lists Mrs Joseph Webb living at Coalbourne House, Amblecote. This could be because Jane Webb had reopened the works; or might just reflect her ownership of the works. According to Roland Wakefield[84] the executors of Joseph Webb carried on the business 'until about 1892 after which the works remained closed for a few years.'

Early in 1897, the British Lens and Glass Co. Limited occupied the works as manufacturers of lenses for ships, railways, harbours and general purposes. This enterprise was run by Sir Alfred J. Loftus who had perfected and patented a process of manufacturing glass lenses[85]. The firm also manufactured 'Loftus Patent' street lamps, in which compound curved panes were used, focused to throw a long beam of light from lamp pillars. The glasshouse was managed by Joseph Davis who also had patents registered in his name for lenses. The commercial side of the business was controlled by George Howard Cartledge and Tregarthen Douglass who rapidly became insolvent 'paying their creditors 5 shillings in the pound to those who will take it.'

Douglass died and Cartledge reformed the company under the name of the British Opal Wall and Glazing Co. This was much to the disgust of Jane Webb's solicitors, as Cartledge had induced her—seven days before her death—to authorise a new repairing lease for seven, fourteen or twenty-one years at £127 per annum. By 6th April 1897 the firm was known as the British Lens and Wall Glazing Co. Limited when it registered patent number 203,871. The significance of wall glazing is apparent in a letter from M. Fairfax Muckley, to a contemporary newspaper:

> 'I visited the new glass works at Coalbourn Hill, viz., the British Lens and Glass Company, Limited, a few days ago, and was much surprised and pleased to see the various kinds of coloured glass in sheets for windows, for covering walls, and decorating generally. All the most delicate tints are produced, and the sheets are clear and bright. I also saw a "proof" from one of the pots of metal, that I quite thought was our

best English batch metal, being of such pure crystal. This metal is made into lenses, of which they have a great variety in their showrooms. Such diversity of reflecting powers is most surprising. There is every evidence of great practical knowledge and a life's study in bringing out these lenses and lamps that will soon be placed before the public. This is the labour of Sir Alfred Loftus. The various kinds of glass that are being manufactured in these works speak for the ability of the metal makers and the excellence of their furnaces, particularly as these furnaces were very difficult to work at the commencement of their glass-making, from various causes that have been corrected . . . '[86]

Jane Webb died on 25th May 1899 and the works and adjoining house were put up for sale by auction on 4th May 1900. It is not known who bought the works for £2,125, but Coalbourn House was sold to William Arthur Holmes for £1,000 and sold again in 1902 when Holmes removed to Kinver. On 22nd December 1901, the sons and daughters of Joseph and Jane Webb presented a lectern to Amblecote church in memory of their parents. This remains today in the southeast corner of the church.

In 1914 Thomas Webb & Corbett Ltd suffered a disastrous fire at the White House works[87] and moved its operation to Coalbournhill where it remained until its closure. The firm has an entry in Kelly's 1928 Directory of Staffordshire as '(Thomas) Webb & Corbett Ltd, Coalbourn Hill, Amblecote and Ludgate Street, Tutbury.'

The firm gradually began to grow in stature in its new location. In the nineteen-twenties Webb Corbett introduced a range of coloured glass with the title *Agate Flambé*, the New English Art Glass. The range comprises vases, a ginger jar, a powder bowl and a candlestick in purple/blue and orange/red glass mottled with powdered colour and coloured chips imitating semi-precious stones. During the nineteen-thirties Herbert Webb designed various pieces for a new range, cut with horizontal wavy lines, so typical of the period. Herbert Webb was the chairman and managing director, but not much is known about the designers of the period. At the

1935 'British Art in Industry' exhibition at the Royal Academy, most of Webb Corbel's glass was designed by A.H. Hall, A.H. Andrews and Alice Hindson. As nothing is known about these three, it may be that they were outsiders brought in especially for the exhibition. In the mid nineteen-thirties Albert Oakden[88], a former teacher at Brierley Hill School of Art, joined the firm as works artist and designer. He may have been responsible for some of the later Art Deco designs.

In 1937 Thomas Webb & Corbett produced a set of loving cups, acid etched, engraved and gilt, for the coronation of King George VI and Queen Elizabeth. In 1938 Freda Colebourn, the wife of a teacher at Stourbridge School of Art, carried out some design work, but this appears to be a one-off event.

No crystal was produced at Webb Corbett between 1942 and 1945; instead the factory was commissioned by the Government to produce lamp chimneys, tubes for liquid air, glassware for scientific purposes, tumblers for service departments, and domestic utility ware (excluding stemware) for the home market[89].

Charles Walter Herbert Webb, who had been chairman, died in 1946, aged seventy-five, and his younger son, John Herbert Webb, took over[90]. After the Second World War, the firm had to readjust to the changed circumstances. The factory had been partly occupied by the Admiralty during the war and it took some time for the firm to reoccupy the site and rebuild its labour force. The firm was forward thinking and threw away all but the best of its pre-war designs and took on Miss Irene M. Stevens[91] as a designer in 1946. She introduced softer lines to both shape and cut patterns. However, she also worked with massive designs using sandblasting techniques. She was the daughter of Fred Stevens who had assisted his father William Stevens in a small glassworks at Bromsgrove[92]. Her designs brought great commercial success and positioned the firm at the forefront of design. They managed to lead the public instead of being led by them[93].

In 1952 the firm abandoned its historical connotations with the name 'Thomas Webb'. It had no real significance since the firm was founded in 1897 and the firm of Thomas Webb and Sons was now a deadly rival in the harsh commercial world of post-war Britain. The firm was renamed Webb Corbett Ltd.

Irene M. Stevens left in 1957 to become head of the department of glass design at Stourbridge School of Art, although she continued to work for the firm as a design consultant until 1963. She was replaced as chief designer by the production manager, Len Green, who had already worked with Stevens in the design studio. Green was a versatile designer who could work in any style, although his true sympathies lay with traditional cut glass.

In 1963 Webb Corbett commissioned a range of decorative cut glass from David Queensbury, professor of ceramics at the Royal College of Art and one of the leading industrial art designers of his day. The company wanted something that was 'essentially modern' but which would 'extend rather than break with tradition.' This was a difficult brief for, as Queensbury said, 'all the qualities of sparkle and intimacy expected of cut glass seem to be in opposition to the current demand for simplicity of line.' Queensbury designed four basic patterns which he called: *Random*, *Harlequin*, *Diadem* and *Mitre*. The designs were a critical success, winning in 1964 the Duke of Edinburgh's Prize for Elegant Design, organised by the Design Council. On the strength of this, Webb Corbett commissioned another cut range from Queensbury in 1965 which included the *Domino*, *Soliloquy* and *Cascade* patterns. In 1965 David Smith moved from the Tutbury factory and became chief designer for both factories.

The original glass cone had not been worked for many years and was used only for storage. By 1966 it was dangerously unstable and had to be demolished. Attempts were made by various societies to secure the preservation of the structure. A consultant to the Ministry of Public Buildings and Works, visited the site, but he concluded that the cone was collapsing and its immediate demolition was necessary. Measurements and drawings were made by Mr Jim Thompson of the Birmingham School of Architecture. However, his work was not completed before the cone was demolished, so no accurate record of its height remains[94].

In 1969 Webb Corbett Ltd. became part of Royal Doulton

Group and David Ferguson became technical director. New techniques were introduced, typical of which was the work of John Finnie who experimented with stipple engraving, carving and enamelling. Chris Smith, the son of David Smith, joined the firm in 1978.

In the mid nineteen-seventies Webb Corbett introduced a range of traditional cased crystal under the name *Kohinoor*. Articles included vases, bowls, chalices and baskets, made in ruby, cobalt blue and turquoise. David Smith had for a long time dreamed of reviving the Stourbridge cameo tradition. In 1978 he used *Kohinoor* blanks and his extensive knowledge of sandblasting techniques to create a new type of cameo glass. David Smith left Webb Corbett in 1982 and set up a studio near the bottom of Brettell Lane to continue his cameo work. When that business closed, his stock of unused blanks was purchased by the Stourbridge Cameo Glass Company, which established a decorating works in New Road, Stourbridge and produced cameo in a similar style.

Brand marketing became paramount in the highly competitive environment under Margaret Thatcher's premiership. In 1980 the firm closed the Tutbury Glassworks[95] and began to market its products as 'Royal Doulton Crystal by Webb Corbett.' By 1986 this had been reversed, so that glass was marketed as 'Webb Corbett by Royal Doulton Crystal.'

During the early nineteen-nineties trade was depressed as recession in the UK and America reduced demand for luxury products. To remain competitive the firm introduced many modern innovations, but fine quality crystal was still produced by traditional methods. An example of revised working practices was that the chairs producing traditional handmade wineglasses were reorganised into teams of seven men. Working on piecework, each chair produced about five hundred and forty three-piece wineglasses per day.

Competition from cheap European imports increased and in April 1994, the product range was rationalised. This led to the loss of twenty glassmakers' jobs[96]. Then in March 1999 glass melting ceased entirely and forty skilled glassmakers were made redundant. Decorating by forty cutters continued on imported blanks.

The works eventually closed entirely in April 2000 and the site was put up for sale. Harlestone House was taken over by Ruskin Mill, a Gloucestershire-based educational charity. It now houses students in a 'cottage industry' development promoting various crafts, including glass and pottery.

---

1 The date is extrapolated because the lease had nine hundred and seventy-six years unexpired in 1714.

2 Society of Antiquaries, Prattinton Collection, v 30, *Account Book of Thomas Milward*. Microfilm copy in WRO; R.L. Chambers, *Thomas Milward's Seventeenth Century Daybook*, p22.

3 The Poor Law and Settlement Documents of Oldswinford. A widow, Margaret Richardson, avowed that her late husband, Thomas Richardson, had been an apprentice to 'captain Bradley, glassmaker.' As the couple had married in 1713 this would date the time of his apprenticeship to the relevant period.

4 H.S. Grazebrook, *The Heraldry of Worcestershire* (1873), p737.

5 WRO, Will of Thomas Bradley, 4th Nov 1707.

6 Joseph Bradley, son of Thomas and Alice Bradley, bap. 26th Dec 1684, Oldswinford.

7 Edward Bradley, son of Thomas and Alice Bradley, bap. 18th May 1687, Oldswinford.

8 John Bradley, son of Thomas and Alice Bradley, bap. 13th Nov 1680, Oldswinford.

9 WSL, 254/2/81.

10 Elizabeth Batchelor, bur. 20th Oct 1762, Oldswinford.

11 PRO, PROB 11/881 RH17/18.

12 Thomas Batchelor, bur. 10th Dec 1750, Oldswinford.

13 London Gazette, 16th Jul 1771.

14 PRO, RAIL 874.1.

15 This battle is notable as the last time that a British King took personal command in the field.

16 The 'forty-five'.

17 WRO, Palfrey collection.

18 SRO, Tp 1273/25, rate book. 1784 pp3,5,7.

19 Thomas Hill, son of Waldron Hill and his wife Sarah, nee Badger, bap. 19th Oct 1736, Kingswinford.

20 Supra, Dial Glasshouse.

21 H.S. Grazebrook, *The Heraldry of Worcestershire* (1873), p690.

22 Thomas Hill, son of Thomas Hill and his wife Anne, nee Melsup, bap. 24th Feb 1765, Kingswinford. Thomas lived at Broome House in the village of Broome, not far from Stourbridge. His wife Anne, nee Lilley died there, 22nd Sep 1804 and has a memorial by Flaxman in Broome Church. Thomas left Broome House and went to join his father at the Blaenavon ironworks, supra Fimbrell Glasshouse.

23 Holden's Triennial Directory for 1809, 1810 & 1811.

24 Thomas Hill leased the property from Sir Edward Winnington Bart., Revd. Richard Francis Onslow, Vicar of Kidderminster and the Right Honourable Thomas Lord Foley on 15th Jun 1802, probably in their capacity of trustees of Oldswinford School. The business had been purchased from Oliver Dixon, who had inherited it along with the Haylestones property from his father, Johnathan Dixon.

25 James Pigot's 1818 Commercial Directory.

26 Lewis's Worcestershire General and Commercial Directory which also listed Hill, Hampton and Co., Fire Clay and Brickworks.

27 Thirteenth Report of the Commission into the Glass Excise, 1835, Appendix 7.

28 Pigot and Co.'s 1835 National Commercial Directory.

29 Waldron and Thomas Hill assigned the lease on the property to Joseph Stevens on 23rd and 24th Mar 1838. The following day, Joseph Stevens took out a mortgage with the bankers Thomas Bate and William Robbins.

30 James Stevens, son of William Stevens and his wife Susannah, nee Cartwright, bap. 8th Apr 1798, Brierley Hill.

31 Royal Brierley Archive.

32 James Stevens, son of Joseph Stevens and his first wife Frances, nee Hale, bap. 21st May 1809, Brierley Hill.

33 William Stevens, son of Joseph Stevens and his first wife Frances, nee Hale, bap. 13th Sep 1818, Brierley Hill.

34 Bentley's 1840 directory of Stourbridge.

35 James Stevens, son of Joseph Stevens and his first wife Frances, nee Hale, bap. 21st May 1809 Brierley Hill.

36 PRO, 1841 census of Kingswinford.

37 Joseph Stevens, son of Joseph Stevens and his first wife Frances, nee Hale,

bap. 29th Sep 1822, Brierley Hill.
38 Mar. Joseph Stevens and Caroline Banks, 20th Nov 1841, Oldswinford.
39 WRO. A letter accompanying the licence requests 'to send the licence by return of post directly to Mr Joseph Stevens, Coalburn Hill Glass Works, Stourbridge'.
40 Not necessarily his precise age. The 1841 census only quoted adult ages to the nearest five years.
41 Royal Brierley Archive.
42 Benjamin Coltman, son of Michael Coltman and his second wife Frances, nee Johnson, b. 5th May 1817; bap. 17th Jun 1817, Stourbridge High Street Independent Chapel.
43 Infra, Grafton's Brierley Glasshouse.
44 Mar. Benjamin Coltman and Fanny Stevens, 10th Dec 1840, Oldswinford.
45 Post Office Directory of the Neighbourhood of Birmingham, 1845.
46 Benjamin Richardson's notebook of 1886.
47 Supra, Fimbrell Glasshouse.
48 Infra, Audnam Glassworks.
49 Joseph Stevens had taken a further mortgage from Messrs Bate and Robbins on 4th Aug 1843.
50 WRO, Palfrey collection.
51 PRO HO/107/2061 Fol. 74 p1, 1851 census of Aston.
52 James Stevens, son of James and Elizabeth Stevens, b. 16th Dec 1835, privately bap. 10th Jan 1836; bap. 19th Jul 1838, Dudley St. Thomas's.
53 PRO, 1881 census of Aston, RG11/3047/109/8.
54 PRO, 1881 census of Devon, RG11/2170/115/7.
55 PRO, PROB 11 2160.
56 The lease was conveyed from William Robbins to Joseph Webb on 18th Dec 1850.
57 1851 census PRO HO0107/2035/020.
58 Pressed glass was introduced to the area about 1831. Infra, Wordsley Flint Glassworks.
59 FGMM quarter ending 29th May 1858.
60 FGMM quarter ending 27th Feb 1858.
61 Infra, Audnam and North Street Glassworks.
62 PRO, 1861 census RG 9/2068 ED22 Sched 6. Later sale particulars show this to be a substantial property; 'Entrance Hall and staircase, Dining Room 24'

3" x 15' 3", Drawing Room 32' x 13', Library 20' x 12', Long Front Kitchen, Cooking Kitchen, Fitted Store Room, Butlers Pantry, Laundry, Back Stairs.' On the first floor was a 'lofty well lighted Billiard Room with full size table, 6 Bedrooms, Bath with lavatory, WC, Laundry.' There were large dry cellars. Outside was a large Coalhouse, Stables and Looseboxes, Conservatory 29' 6" x 11" and vinery 33' x 14' 6". A picturesque ivy covered garden house and a tennis lawn in all amounting to 1 acre 1r 4p.

63 Joseph Webb, bur. 1869, Amblecote. An obelisk surrounded by an iron fence marks his grave.

64 PRO, Will of Joseph Webb, 23rd Jul 1869.

65 Henry Fitzroy Webb, son of Joseph Webb and his wife Jane, nee Hammond, bap. 7th Dec 1854, Amblecote.

66 Jane Hammond, daughter of Joseph Hammond, head groom to the Earl of Stamford at Enville and his wife Frances (Fanny), nee Crudgington, bap. 27th Sep 1818, Enville St. Mary's.

67 Joseph Hammond, son of Joseph Hammond, head groom to the Earl of Stamford at Enville and his wife Frances (Fanny), nee Crudgington, bap. 24th Jun 1821, Enville St. Mary's.

68 PRO, 1881 census of Wollaston, RG11/2890/110/33.

69 Richard Webb, bap. 16th May 1802, Wolverley, son of Richard Webb and his wife Mary, nee Stamford. Webb had acquired the 1,200 square yard cutting shop, complete with steam engine, formerly in the occupation of Samuel Robinson, from the trustees of the will of William King on 12th May 1854.

70 SRO, D695/4/1/7.

71 DA, unindexed Harward and Evers Papers. A later letter to the Estate Duty Office observed that 'the works carried on by the widow and Joseph Hammond proved a disastrous failure and in 1881 the real and personal estate was absorbed in [servicing] the £12,000 [trust fund].'

72 Lewis John Murray, b. c1844, Bloomsbury, Middlesex. Murray had previously worked at the Birmingham glassworks of F. & C. Osler.

73 PG, Feb 1881.

74 PRO, 1881 census of Kingswinford, RG11/2891/53/16.

75 PG, Nov 1881.

76 John Walsh Walsh, son of Samuel and Anne Walsh, b. 11th Jul 1804, Bulwell, Nottinghamshire, bap. 2nd Aug 1804, St. Mary's Independent Church,

Nottingham. For biography see, Eric Reynolds, *Glass of John Walsh Walsh 1850-1951* (1999).

77 PG, Sep 1882.

78 Joseph Webb, son of Joseph Webb and his wife Jane, nee Hammond, bap. 31st May 1852, Amblecote.

79 PRO, 1871 census, RG10 3021 ED22 Sched 5; PRO, 1881 census of Amblecote, RG11/2890/56/1.

80 PG, Jun 1884.

81 PG, Dec 1884.

82 For further information on glass furniture see the article by John Smith, *Glass Furniture in the Nineteenth and Early Twentieth Centuries*, JGA, v 4 (1992), pp18-25.

83 Supra, Heath 1882.

84 Ibid, R. Wakefield, p21.

85 PG, Jul 1897.

86 PG, Jul 1897.

87 Infra, White House Glassworks.

88 Albert Oakden, b. 1875, Brierley Hill, son of Edward Oakden, a glassworks manager and his wife Amelia; d. 1942.

89 PG, Mar 1952.

90 His older son, Thomas Fisher Wilkes Webb had died in 1942.

91 Irene M. Stevens, daughter of Frederick Stevens, b. 1917.

92 William Stevens, b. c1850 at Stourbridge began his working life at Boulton & Mills' Audnam glassworks, but was not taken on as an apprentice. So, in 1867, aged 16, he moved to work for James Harrop at his glasshouse at Worms Ash, near Bromsgrove. After a brief venture with James Harrop's nephew William at Hart's Hill Glassworks (infra), he began his own glasshouse at Bournheath, Belbroughton in 1880. He married Rosannah Brighton, 17th Nov 1872 at Birmingham St. Martin's. Frederick, their youngest son, started working in the glasshouse, but left in 1902 to work for the Birmingham Guild. He spent thirty-three years of his working life as an architectural metal fitter and erector. He briefly returned to his father's glasshouse in 1914 due to the shortage of work in his trade. Op cit, Sir Hugh Chance, *Bromsgrove Glasshouses* (1959), pp 42-51.

93 PG, Mar 1952.

94 Express and Star, 17th Jan 1966 and County Express, 9th Apr 1966.
95 One hundred and fifty employees were made redundant. Some of them banded together and purchased the factory. It reopened on Thursday 4th Mar 1982 as Tutbury Glassworks Ltd. In 1984 the name was changed to Tutbury Crystal Glass Ltd. It is still in operation today.
96 The same month in which Tudor Crystal closed.

CHAPTER 25

Audnam Glassworks

In 1716[1] Henry Bradley built his own glasshouse at Audnam, near to the Jacob's Well Glasshouse started by his father Edward. Here he lived and worked as a white glassmaker, deep in debt and faced with declining prices. Unable to make ends meet Henry was forced to sell even more of his assets. On 1st January 1719 he sold a ninety-nine year lease on copyhold land at Wordsley to his father-in-law Windsor James[2].

Henry continued in business and took an Oldswinford Hospital boy as an apprentice on 17th March 1724. By 1725 things were so bad Henry was forced to sign an indenture to regulate many mortgages and agreements concerning his glassworks. Joshua Henzey III of Dial Glasshouses, Jeremiah Rogers of Holloway End, Thomas Hamond of Brettell Lane, Windsor James of Dob Hill, all glassmakers, Joseph Finch an ironmonger, and John Gibbons a saddler, had all been concerned in agreements concerning Henry's business. A tripartite agreement was signed on 6th July 1725, between Joshua Henzey III glassmaker of Audnam on the one part, Henry Bradley, glassmaker and his wife Mary on the second part, and John Ward of Sedgley Park[3] on the third part. This stated Joshua Henzey III was then owed £479 10s 7d. Henry Bradley, the son of the founder Edward Bradley senior, was 'the real owner who can get possession from J. Ward for £500 paid in six months.'[4] These people supporting Henry Bradley's business were all his relations. Thomas Hamond was his brother-in-law. Windsor James was his father-in-law. Joseph Finch was his stepfather. John Gibbons of Stourbridge was probably related, having married Sarah Bradley of Kingswinford in 1711.

The relentless fall in the price of broad-glass finally led to the downfall of Henry Bradley's business. His bankruptcy was reported in 1727₅. Two days later, on 11th May 1727, Henry's father-in-law Windsor James added a codicil to his will. Clearly concerned for his daughter and son-in-law's predicament he willed the lease on copyhold land he purchased from Henry in 1719 to his brother-in-law Edward Osland₆ of Bewdley. However, as long as Henry was alive Osland was to pay 'the rents issues and profits' of the land to Mary Bradley or 'to whom other she shall . . . appoint to receive the same'. Although we have no record, Windsor James probably also gave immediate help to Henry Bradley to restart in business. Mary Bradley was James' only child and being aged sixty-seven James may have concluded it was only a matter of sooner or later. Windsor James eventually died 30th October 1729 and after providing for his wife willed everything between his daughter Mary and his Bradley grandchildren.

Things did not improve for Henry. His oldest son Edward₇ who presumably worked with him in the business was declared bankrupt in 1743₈. As previously noted, Joshua Henzey III was owed £479 10s 7d from his original mortgage to Henry Bradley, but he had sold these rights to John Ward of Sedgley Park in 1733₉. The notorious Glass Excise Act was passed in 1745 and it proved to be the last straw for Henry Bradley. Unable to proceed any further under the weight of debt, he finally surrendered his business in 1747 to John Ward, who had become Baron Ward in 1740₁₀.

Baron Ward immediately let the glasshouse to Michael Grazebrook I at an annual rent of £50, thus beginning an association that lasted a hundred and twelve years. Michael Grazebrook was of a wealthy and armigerous family₁₁. He was the sixteenth generation to bear the family's arms and had been Overseer of the Poor for Oldswinford in 1721.

Trade was buoyant under Michael Grazebrook's management and he soon introduced his son, Michael II₁₂, to the business. In

1753 Michael II married Sarah Worral, the only child and heiress of Thomas Worral of Stourton, Staffordshire[13]. They married by licence[14] in which he is described as of Kingswinford and she of Bilston; although her family was originally from Chaddesley Corbett, Worcestershire.

Michael Grazebrook I died in 1756[15], aged sixty-nine and his will[16] was proved the following year. In his will he is described as a glassmaker of the Heath, Oldswinford and left his estate to his widow Elizabeth, his sole executrix. His son, Michael Grazebrook II who lived at Audnam, succeeded him.

A list of glassworks in 1760 shows Grazebrook producing smooth enamel glass, best and ordinary flint glass, and phials[17]. Other writers on the subject of the Stourbridge glass industry have confessed themselves unable to find any reference to the name following Grazebrook's, that of Denham. It is possible this is not the name of a person, but a contraction, either deliberate or in ignorance, of Audenham[18], where Grazebrook's works stood. However, in contradiction to this hypothesis, Benjamin Richardson wrote that his own glassworks, Wordsley Flint Glassworks, had previously been worked by Wood and Denham[19]. A William Denham occupied land next to the Audnam glassworks in 1776[20].

Michael Grazebrook II of Audnam Brook only lived to forty-two years of age and died in 1766[21], five years before his mother. In his will[22] he is described as a master glassmaker and desired his trade be carried on by his widow, Sarah. He also directed that his stock in trade, book debts, personal estate and effects be equally divided between his only two sons, Thomas Worral Grazebrook[23] and Michael Grazebrook III[24] so they could carry on the trade. Sarah Grazebrook continued to manage her late husband's business for many years and although both her sons were involved, they developed many other interests.

Elizabeth, the widow of Michael Grazebrook I died in 1771[25]. She died intestate and letters of administration[26] were proved for her estate. She outlived her son, and her grandsons were by now wealthy men, so her daughter Sarah Littlewood and Sarah's husband, Benjamin Littlewood, administered her estate. Benjamin Littlewood was a blacksmith of Amblecote at the time, but later became a partner at Wheeley's Brettell Lane Glasshouses.

Sarah, the widow of Michael Grazebrook II, ran the business for many years. The cone is shown on Whitworth's canal map of 1774. In 1777, when the land around was enclosed, Mrs Sarah Grazebrook was the occupier of the glasshouse at Audnam owned by Lord Dudley, and the Dob Hill Glassworks, owned by Robert Honeyborne$_{27}$. She was a glass manufacturer in 1783$_{28}$ and in the same year took a further twenty-one-year lease from Lord Dudley. By the terms of the lease the glasshouse with furnaces, millhouse, warehouses and buildings was rented at £52 per annum with maintenance and repairs to be undertaken by the lessee at her own cost$_{29}$. The premises were insured on 5th May 1783 by Sarah, Thomas Worral and Michael Grazebrook. The policy shows that they were potters as well as glass manufacturers, with 'seven rooms for earthenware', housing stock valued at £20$_{30}$. Five years later, when the policy was renewed, the schedule suggests they had ceased pottery manufacture$_{31}$.

In 1785 Michael Grazebrook III married a distant cousin, Mary Anne, the oldest daughter and co-heir of Thomas Needs of London, by his wife Mary, nee Grazebrook$_{32}$. Shortly afterwards the newlyweds moved into the Grazebrook family home, Audnam House, where their family of eleven children were all born. The family tradition states he always carried a small dog whip in his pocket to keep his large family of spirited youngsters in order$_{33}$.

After his marriage Michael Grazebrook III, and to a lesser extent his brother Thomas Worral Grazebrook, took over the running of the glass business from their mother Sarah. Their wealth and influence grew as they prospered as glass, coal and iron masters. They moved in the higher echelons of society and were involved with many improvement schemes in the area. For example, turnpike trusts were established to improve the roads in the locality and provide for their upkeep. The Stourbridge to Wolverhampton road was greatly improved as a result. To fund the work, loans were raised on the security of the expected tolls. There were four glassmakers whose premises were not on the banks of the newly built canal. They were so keen to see the roads improved that they lent money to the trust without interest. In 1786 Thomas Rogers, Thomas Hill and Messrs Pidcock & Grazebrook lent the trust £100 each[34].

For many years the two brothers ran the firm with an eight-pot furnace under the trading title of T. & M. Grazebrook[35]. Their mother remained the head of the firm until she died in 1799. In 1795 it was Sarah Grazebrook, not her sons, who paid £53 rent for the Glassworks to Lord Dudley[36].

In 1796 the Grazebrooks took a lease on Lord Dudley's land at the Delph to supply clay to the Audnam Bank Glass Works. Under the terms of the lease, thirty acres were occupied at a rent of £32 per annum with the right to 'erect Engines etc to mine Glasshouse Clay at 9/–per ton Royalty, Pot Clay, 5/–per ton, Offal Clay, 2/6 per ton, Potters Clay, 2/-.'[37]

One of the many children born to Michael Grazebrook III and his wife Mary Anne was George Grazebrook[38]. He married Jane, the youngest daughter of Joseph and Elizabeth Smallman, and one of their six children was Henry Sydney Grazebrook[39]. H.S. Grazebrook became a barrister of the Inner Temple and an ardent genealogist. He wrote prolifically upon the gentry of Worcestershire and the Stourbridge glass industry. He eventually died unmarried at Chiswick on 19th June 1896 and was buried at Oldswinford.

As late as 1798 Sarah Grazebrook was still the glassworks leaseholder, holding a twenty-one-year lease from Lord Dudley at £53 3s a year[40]. Presumably this lease would have run from 1794 to 1815, but Sarah Grazebrook died in 1799[41], aged seventy-eight. Her obituary read, 'Died at Stourbridge on Friday, aged 80, Mrs Glazebrook [sic].'[42] Her will[43] divided her estate between her two sons, Michael Grazebrook III and Thomas Worral Grazebrook.

The firm continued to trade under the management of the two brothers in the face of punitive excise duties. On 17th January 1803 a meeting took place at the Stewponey Inn, Stourton to petition the Government to have the duty on flint glass based on manufactured goods instead of metal or raw materials. Michael Grazebrook III of

Thomas & Michael Grazebrook contributed £50 to the fund. The amount contributed implies it was one of the smaller firms of the district. However, glassmaking was only one of the trades the Grazebrook brothers were involved in. They were also merchants and dealers in clay and firebricks[44].

Thomas Worral Grazebrook died in 1816[45], aged sixty. His widow Elizabeth continued to live at their home, Stourton Castle, with her two children, Thomas Worral Smith Grazebrook and Elizabeth, until 1832 when they left Stourton and moved to Dallicot House near Bridgnorth in Shropshire. In June 1837 Mrs T. Grazebrook had her late husband's remains exhumed and reburied in a vault in Claverley churchyard, near to Dallicot, only to die herself on 18th June 1837, aged sixty-five, and was also buried at Claverley. Thomas Worral Smith Grazebrook became a barrister of Lincoln's Inn, but died on 1st August 1846, aged 37[46]. The accumulated family wealth and estates, derived from: Wilkes, Smith, Grosvenor and Worral passed to his sister Elizabeth Mackenzie Kettle. As he was the last male of his line, the representation of the family and its arms passed to his cousin, Michael Grazebrook IV of Audnam.

After the death of Thomas Worral Grazebrook in 1816, Michael Grazebrook III took his two oldest sons, Michael[47] and William[48] into the business. The firm continued making flint and coloured glass, trading as M. Grazebrook and Sons[49] or Grazebrook and Sons[50]. The outline of the cone and surrounding buildings are clearly shown on Fowler's 1822 map, occupied by Michael Grazebrook and owned by Lord Dudley[51].

In 1821 Michael Grazebrook IV married Elizabeth Wallace, the only child and heiress of John Phillips of the Old Square, Birmingham[52]. They met under unusual circumstances at Brighton, which was at the height of fashionable popularity in Regency times. Michael Grazebrook was seized with cramp while bathing, and when he finally struggled to shore was unconscious with exhaustion. Miss Phillips attended him and had him removed to her hotel. Not long after this they became engaged. Despite the romantic background to their meeting, and the fact that they were both over thirty years old and quite able to choose for themselves, Michael's new bride was not welcomed in the Grazebrook family circle. Elizabeth's father was a self-made man, who through his personal industry and energy had established a flourishing business in coopering and woodturning. His lack of polish displeased the more fastidious of Michael's sisters. Despite his artisan background he seemed to get on with one of them, Charlotte, as he and Charlotte both held political views of 'the crusted Tory type'. After Michael and Elizabeth's marriage they rented Kingswinford Rectory for a year, then moved to Corbyn's Hall, Pensnett[53], where their two oldest children, Michael Phillips and Elizabeth were born[54].

Early in 1826 Michael Grazebrook IV and his family moved to Belle Vue[55], at the top of Mucklow's Hill in Halesowen, where in April their second son John Phillips Grazebrook was born[56]. Two months later Michael Grazebrook III died at Audnam[57], aged sixty-eight. It has not been possible to find his will but evidently his sons Michael IV and William continued the business; Michael riding over from Halesowen when not shooting, and William attending to the business when not hunting. William Grazebrook's love of hunting is legendary. Known as 'gruff Will' he was for many years secretary to the Albrighton pack. After the death of Michael Grazebrook III, his widow Mary Anne and their unmarried children, including William, continued to live at Audnam House. The firm began to operate under the title of Michael & William Grazebrook[58].

It is indicative of the status of the Grazebrook family to note the marriage of Elizabeth[59], one of the six daughters of Michael Grazebrook III. Although her father did not live long enough to see it—having died four years earlier—on 5th October 1830 she married Lieutenant-Colonel Ferdinando Lea Smith[60] of Halesowen Grange, the senior co-heir to the ancient barony of Dudley.

Although profitable, the Audnam Glassworks was one of the smaller works in the district. Michael Grazebrook paid £2,218 5s 3d excise duty for the year ending 5th January 1833[61], suggesting this was the thirteenth largest of the sixteen Stourbridge/Dudley glasshouses. Pigot and Co.'s 1835 National Commercial Directory shows how conservative remained their range of products by listing 'Michael & Wm. Grazebrook, Audnam, manufacturers of Flint Glass, Plain and Cut'.

Besides crippling excise duty the glassmasters had to contend with a new problem—the organisation of labour. On 5th December 1837 a meeting took place at the Dudley Arms Hotel[62] where the manufacturers considered their response to the formation of the first glassmakers trade union, Michael Grazebrook IV was one of those attending:

> 'At a special meeting of the Flint Glass Manufacturers of the Midland district, convened by circular, to consider the best means of preventing injurious consequences resulting from the combination of workmen. PRESENT: Thomas Hawkes, Esq., M.P., M. Grazebrook, Esq., Thomas Badger, Esq., Thomas Webb, Esq., Messrs. S. Badger, Gammon, Green, Harris, Shakespear, Greathead, Richardson, Stevens, Davis, Wheeley, and Davis. RESOLVED: That it is the opinion of the meeting that the union formed by the workmen in 1836, will, if persevered in, operate very prejudicillly to the trade, that this meeting pledges itself individually to express to his workmen, his disapprobation of all combinations, and that he will not take into his employ any workmen who is a member of the Glass Makers' Union; also, that if any workman, who is not articled, continues a member of the union more than fourteen days after notice, which begins on the 16th instant, he shall forthwith be discharged, and that the same notice shall apply to articled servants as their articles expire. RESOLVED: That if any manufacturer shall find it necessary to discharge a workman, he shall send a circular to any house informing them of the fact, and that 500 circulars be printed and sent to the trade generally for that purpose, and that in the circular the wages such individual received be inserted.'[63]

In 1838 Michael Grazebrook IV and his family left Belle Vue, Halesowen, and moved into the family house at Audnam. The older generation of the family, including Michael Grazebrook III's widow and William Grazebrook, moved to Summerhill, Kingswinford. When he left Halesowen, the inhabitants presented Michael Grazebrook IV with a silver salver as a mark of their esteem and goodwill. He was a very popular man who maintained goodwill with the populace throughout the politically turbulent times of the eighteen-thirties. The period before and immediately after the passing of the Reform Bill in 1832 had stirred the country to its profoundest depths. Halesowen, where the Grazebrooks had ironworks at the bottom of Mucklow's Hill, had been affected by the disturbances. The nailmakers formed a large proportion of the working population there and had been stirred to high spirits by the oratory of the reformists. Terrible rioting and arson had afflicted Birmingham and a large mob gathered in Halesowen much to the consternation of the householders and shopkeepers. The situation looked ugly and the military were about to be summoned. Michael Grazebrook coolly rode into the thick of the mob and by a combination of his personal popularity and adroit handling of the rougher elements, diffused the situation and dispersed the mob. This led to a strong sense of gratitude from the law-abiding citizens of Halesowen, and their gift of the salver was a symbol of their respect.

Michael Grazebrook IV was a strong Whig in politics, the only member of his family who strayed from the Tory fold. Political debate was therefore commonplace in the Grazebrook family; particularly between Michael Grazebrook IV and his sister Charlotte or his father-in-law John Phillips, who were both virulent Tories. Many were the debates between 'church and king' and 'church and state'. In 1841 Michael Grazebrook IV lived at the family home at Audnam, described as a glassmaster. His son, Michael Phillips Grazebrook lived with him, described as an iron master[64]. The family's iron business traded as Michael & William Grazebrook, Iron & Coal Masters, Netherton Works, Woodside, Dudley[65].

The eighteen-forties were years of great depression in the Black Country; 1842 was probably the worst year of the century. The miners were on strike, Chartism was rife and there was great distress and starvation. Riots at Stourbridge and Dudley in May led to detachments of the Worcestershire Yeomanry and 3rd Dragoon

Guards being quartered in the neighbourhood. Although it is clear that in common with employers in all trades the Grazebrooks were having problems with their workforce, they survived the recession[66]. On 12th November 1845, during a period of unrest between employer and employee, the Master Flint Glass Cutters met at the Stork Hotel in Birmingham. The employers' main weapon was that they agreed not to employ any glasscutters laid off by another firm. Among employers from all over the country the firm of M. & W. Grazebrook was a signatory. Michael Grazebrook chaired the meeting and resolved:

> 'That this meeting recognises no right or authority in any body of workmen to interfere with their arrangements for carrying on their business and is determined to resist any such interference to the utmost.'[67]

In 1851 William Grazebrook headed the household—including his brother and sister—at Summerhill, Kingswinford. He was an iron master, glass master and farmer of a hundred and forty acres, employing four labourers[68]. By this time he no longer participating in the Audnam Glassworks, but continued to enjoy its profits, while he spent his days hunting. Michael Grazebrook lived with his family at Audnam, a magistrate and glass manufacturer employing a hundred people[69].

Michael Grazebrook IV died at Audnam in 1854[70], after a long and painful illness. During his distinguished life, besides his varied business interests, he had been a Justice of the Peace for Stafford, Worcester and Shropshire, and Deputy Lieutenant for Worcester.

After his death, his sons, Michael Phillips Grazebrook[71] of Holly Grove, Hagley and John Phillips Grazebrook of The Court, Hagley took over the family firm.

John Phillips Grazebrook began his education in Edgbaston, near Birmingham. He came under the influence of his grandfather, John Phillips, whose house he visited regularly, particularly after his mother died in 1833[72], when he was only seven years old. He spent many happy hours in his grandfather's woodturning factory watching and learning. While playing amid the chips and shavings, he acquired a love for machinery and woodwork that lasted throughout his life.

After completing his education, he began working for the family firm as a traveller. His father and their agent, a lively Irishman called Chamberlain introduced him to the firm's customers all over the country. Their early journeys were by gig, but as the railway network developed, the train eventually became his favourite mode of transport[73].

In 1855 John Phillips Grazebrook married his childhood sweetheart, Harriet Draffen, the youngest daughter of Thomas Francis of Edgbaston[74]. They moved to a little old cottage by the roadside at Hagley and lived a long happily married life of sixty-four years there until John Phillips Grazebrook died in 1919[75].

Serious disharmony in the glass trade between employer and workmen first began in February 1858 at E. & J. Webb's[76], but erupted at Stevens and Williams'[77] and Grazebrooks'. Grazebrooks' caused dissent by an unsuccessful action against five men who left their situations without due notice[78]. The glassmakers' union realised that control of the apprenticeship system allowed the employers to generate a surfeit of skilled labour and therefore depress wages. The union therefore attempted to wrest control of the apprenticeship system. Matters came to a head when Grazebrooks' wished to employ a man but refused to employ one sent from Edinburgh by the union[79]. A dispute took place that led Grazebrooks' to issue a circular on 16th October 1858 naming workmen discharged and requesting their fellow glass manufacturers not to employ them. On 23rd October 1858 the workmen proposed terms to their employer for re-engagement but John Grazebrook replied 'he had made his arrangement; he would have no society men, and meant to pursue a different system in future.' Faced with an outbreak of strikes, the employers responded by holding a meeting on 1st November 1858 at the Talbot Hotel, Stourbridge, where they formed a manufacturers' organisation. Many local glassmasters attended including John Phillips Grazebrook and William Webb Boulton who subsequently took over the glassworks. From October 1858 onwards the strike spread throughout the district and in December the Association of Flint Glass Makers enforced a national lockout that lasted for seven months. In 1859, after the lockout, the Grazebrook brothers decided to quit the glass trade. A hundred and twelve years of Grazebrook tradition at Audnam ended. William Webb Boulton took over the glassworks and agreed to employ only society labour.

William Webb Boulton[80] was the son of Richard Boulton, who farmed 215 acres at Sillings Farm, Feckenham[81] and his wife Jane, nee Webb. His mother was the sister of Edward Webb, for whom William Webb Boulton had worked, first at the Holloway End Glasshouse, and then at the White House Glassworks[82]. In October 1859 he was admitted to membership of the Midland Association of Flint Glass Manufacturers which had been attempting to recruit the remaining manufacturers as members after the strike of 1858-9.

William Webb Boulton invited his second cousin Frederick James Mills[83] to join him in partnership. Mills quit his partnership in Richardson, Mills & Smith at Holloway End glassworks on 13th August 1861 and they started the firm of Boulton and Mills.

In 1861 William Webb Boulton lived at Audnam with his sister[84], then in the following year he married[85] his new partner's sister, Jane[86], daughter of Richard Mills of the Albert Glassworks. Their marriage was witnessed by Jane's brother, Frederick James Mills and her mother's brother, Joseph Webb of Coalbournhill Glassworks.

Under the management of Boulton and Mills there was an almost immediate change in the style of glassware produced. Little is known about the Grazebrooks' output, but it appears to be traditional cut glass of Georgian style lingering on conservatively into the Victorian age. Boulton and Mills began to manufacture contemporary articles in the prevalent style and were particularly noted for flower stands. Designs for some ornate styles were registered in 1864 and the firm registered the first design for a flower stand with a mirror base on 25th January 1871.

In 1871 William Webb Boulton lived with his family at Audnam House, a glass manufacturer employing seventy-one men, thirty-one boys and seven girls[87]. This suggests the scale of operations at Audnam had not grown appreciably in the twelve years since William Webb Boulton took over the works. However business was prospering and he began to invest in property and fine art. On 19th

December 1872 he bought Foster House, Wordsley and the land adjoining it from William Orme Foster[88] for £1,472. It was then let at a yearly rent of £88. As profits permitted, he began to indulge his love of art and buy paintings. He eventually amassed a significant collection.

The flow of registrations for flower holders continued. In 1873 Boulton and Mills registered plateau centrepieces decorated with long leaf-shaped components, as did Philip Pargeter at the Red House glassworks. Fern leaves were a traditional feature of Venetian chandeliers and were extensively imitated by the Stourbridge manufacturers. On centrepieces the fern leaves were usually placed alternately with the flower holders or the basket supports, as in the 1873 example registered by Philip Pargeter. In Boulton and Mills' 1873 example they were arranged in a circle around a solitary central, flower holder.

The original lease William Webb Boulton took from Lord Dudley in 1859 was for twenty-five years so in 1874 it became due for renewal. William Webb Boulton of Audnam Bank House leased the Audnam Glassworks from the Earl of Dudley on 25th March 1874 for a term of fourteen years. The rent was to be four hundred pounds per year[89]. Details of the lease refer to:

> 'that piece or parcel of land with the capital messuage or tenement commonly called or known by the name of Audnam Bank House thereon erected and built and the glass house three dwelling houses stabling barns and other outbuildings and offices thereto adjoining or contiguous with the gardens and pleasure ground thereto respectively belonging situate at Audnam in the parish of Kingswinford.'
> It obliged the lessee to insure the 'buildings used as the glass manufactory' for 'three thousand pounds at the least.' The first schedule to the lease showed that the 'glass works and two smaller houses with stabling barns and other outbuildings garden and part of lawn' occupied 1 acre 3 roods 4 perches. 'House yard and part of glassworks' occupied 1 acre 1 rood 9 perches. The second schedule listed the fixtures belonging to the landlord: 'In the glass works ten pot fur-

nace and stack with pot arch and iron doors damper grate bars and stays and pipes to furnace (exclusive of fire brick pillars seige and crown). Two double lears and kiln with winding apparatus, sand caulker iron doors bars grates and stays complete clay tempering tank lined with slate slabs with hot air pipes from furnace to heat the pot. Eight pot furnace and stack with all ironwork to support the same (exclusive of fire brick pillars seige and crown). Blacksmith shop and engine house with sealing and stack boiler and twenty horse power steam engine shaft flywheel et cetera complete.'

Audnam Bank House—referred to in the lease—was the Grazebrooks' old family home, which was now William Webb Boulton's residence[90].

1877 was a significant year for the partners. They renewed their partnership agreement and Frederick James Mills prudently made a will. On 23rd June 1877 William Webb Boulton sold a spade and shovel works at Wall Heath to his friend Isaac Nash for £1,500. He used the money to buy Siden Hill Field and adjoining meadow from Michael Phillips Grazebrook for £1,700. This is the land Michael Grazebrook had bought in 1788 to build his Canalside Glassworks[91]. It was the first of several property purchases buying up the old Grazebrook holdings around the Audnam glassworks.

In 1879 William Webb Boulton continued his path of innovation with a patent for a form of *Vasa Murrhina* glass in which the body was transparent and showed imbedded pieces of coloured glass and mica flakes:

> '314. Coloured glasses or enamels, powdered or crushed, are spread on an iron slab, and the glass surface to be ornamented is rolled in this powder while in a plastic or semi-molten state, so that the coloured particles adhere and spread a little on the surface. A thin layer of flint glass may be afterwards attached to the ornamented surface. A cracked appearance may be produced on it by plunging in water. Glass so ornamented may be blown, moulded, pressed, cut, &c. as usual. Flower vases, lamp reservoirs, chandelier bod-

ies, &c. may be ornamented in this way, as well as sheets, slabs, or blocks of glass, The coloured particles may be arranged in stripes or other patterns.[92] '

In 1881 William Webb Boulton lived with his family and four servants at Audnam House, a glass manufacturer employing seventy-two men, thirty boys and ten women[93]. This represents no increase in the size of the workforce since 1871. Frederick James Mills lived at Hagley Road, Upper Swinford with his wife and two servants[94].

The partners began to restructure the business and plan for their succession. Since November 1867, the firm's commercial traveller had been Oswald James Meatyard[95] who lived with his family at Audnam Cottage, just the other side of the coachhouse from the Boulton's residence at Audnam House[96]. In 1880 the firm appointed a commission agent for France and in 1883 engaged a new traveller, Francis James Shea[97] of 12 Grove House, Hornsey, London[98]. Meatyard was now promoted. On 14th February 1881 the partners relinquished management of the works to Meatyard who was appointed manager at a generous salary of £120 per quarter, plus travel expenses and a one fifth share of the profits.

Glass in the Venetian style became very popular with the British public in the eighteen-eighties. Ever eager to meet demand, William Webb Boulton patented an invention in this style for *Improvements in Decorating Glass With Stripes* on 15th July 1885. Ever since 1881 there had been a succession of designs, building on Richardsons' patent of 1857 for air-trap decoration[99]. On 7th August 1885 William Webb Boulton patented *Nacre de Perle*. This is significant as the first patent to give a particular name to a variety of satin glass.

In 1888 the fourteen-year lease on the glassworks expired. A revised lease was drawn up that includes a detailed plan of the glassworks site[100]. The new lease should have run from Lady Day 1888, but it is written on the plan that this was not carried out. Frederick James Mills retired from active participation in the business on 19th April 1888 and moved to The Uplands, Hagley Road, Stourbridge. William Webb Boulton, still living at Audnam House, involved his sons, Harry Boulton[101] and William Boulton[102] in the business[103].

William Webb Boulton died on 21st February 1892[104], aged fifty-nine. He left the Audnam Glassworks the previous day in apparently good health and visited the Central Club, Corporation Street in Birmingham, where he fell ill and died. When his will[105] was proved, he left an estate valued at £9,367 16s 2d. However, considerable difficulty was experienced in finding disinterested trustees and so the administration of the estate commenced with no trustees. His collection of seventy-five paintings was sold in three separate auctions raising over £3,700[106]. The family home was sold at auction so his widow, Jane and her unmarried children moved to Thornleigh, Oldswinford.

However, the will did not contain any power to continue the business. To the contrary, to realise William Webb Boulton's £6,000 capital in the business, left to his wife, the business would have to be liquidated. Therefore Jane Mills was admitted as a partner in the business with her sons Richard Harry Webb Boulton and William Webb Boulton, 'formerly styled the younger' and Oswald George Meatyard on 16th August 1892. Frederick James Mills retained a financial interest.

The turn of the century represented not only the end of the Victorian era and a change in styles, but also the complete end of the founding dynasty of Boulton and Mills. In 1903 the Midland Association of Glass Manufacturers was wound up, the confrontation with trade-unionism being largely settled. Boulton and Mills, one of the last firms to join, was among the eight firms that were still members at the time of its demise[107]. Oswald George Meatyard and Jane Mills left the firm on 1st August 1903 leaving her sons in control.

Meatyard died on 4th May 1906 and was buried in the close proximity of so many other great glassmakers in Wordsley churchyard. His monument, a white granite cross, records the poignant epitaph that he had been a warden of the church for twenty-one years. Frederick James Mills died on 12th January 1908, aged seventy-three, at his home, 101 Gloucester Terrace, Hyde Park, London, and was also buried in Wordsley churchyard beneath a sandstone tomb. When his will[108] was proved, he left an estate valued at £50,985 8s 6d. He had no children, and his wife predeceased him, so he willed that his estate should be converted into money and divided among his sisters, nephews and nieces. He specifically instructed his trustees that in winding up his estate they should not put pressure upon his nephews, Richard Harry Webb Boulton and William Webb Boulton still trading as Boulton and Mills.

The brothers made a new agreement on 20th March 1911 that was to run for five years. By this time, Richard Harry Webb Boulton was living at Amblecote House, Brierley Hill and William Webb Boulton at Red House, Harvington. Their capital, including land and buildings, was valued at £6,000 each. Possibly reflecting on the fate of Mills and Walker, the agreement contained several clauses about the lunacy of a partner.

On 29th September 1920 the partners renewed their lease on the works with the trustees of the Earl of Dudley for a rent of £225 per annum. Richard Harry Webb Boulton died in 1922[109] and his son Howard Gilbert Boulton MC[110] succeeded him in the business. Howard and his uncle, William Webb Boulton formed a private limited company with capital of £10,000. William's sister, Laura Mary Boulton[111] bought £1,000 worth of preference shares.

Boulton and Mills Ltd was incorporated on 24th May 1922, but only two years later William Webb Boulton decided to leave the business. On 30th June 1924 he resigned as managing director and sold his shares. He sold 2,750 £1 ordinary shares to Howard Gilbert Boulton for £1,000, then 2,745 of these were sold the next day to Charles Herbert Thompson for the same amount[112].

Sadly, lacking the imagination of its Victorian founding partners the firm lost its direction and reputation for innovation. Finally, like so many other firms, Boulton and Mills fell victims to the great depression. The firm closed its London showroom on 9th March 1925 and ceased trading in early 1926. The works stood vacant until the summer of 1928 when it was demolished[113]. A modern ESSO petrol station now stands on the site[114]. The private houses still standing next to the garage were originally part of the glassworks complex. Howard Gilbert Boulton MC died in 1936 in a mental institution.

---

1 The letter heading later used by Boulton and Mills, Audnam Glass Works, states 'Established AD 1716'.

2 LJRO, Will and codicil of Windsor James, 10th Nov 1730.

3 John Ward, b. 6th Mar 1704, Sedgley Park, heir apparent of William Ward, fifth Baron Ward of Birmingham, tenth Baron Dudley and his wife Mary, daughter of Hon. John Grey of Enville Hall.

4 DA, Earl of Dudley's Estate Records. The reference to Edward Bradley as founder is nothing to do with this glassworks. Joshua Henzey originally lent money to Henry Bradley to mortgage his interest in Jacob's Well Glasshouse of which Edward Bradley was the founder.

5 London Gazette, 9th May 1727, 'Bankrupt, Henry Bradley, late of Audenbrooke, in the county of Stafford, Glassmaker.'

6 Edward Oseland, oldest son of Revd Henry Oseland and his wife Mary, nee Bradley; succeeded his father as Presbyterian minister at Bewdley; d. 1750.

7 Edward Bradley, son of Henry Bradley and his wife Mary, nee James, bap. 31st Dec 1713, Kingswinford.

8 London Gazette, 21st Jun 1743, 'Insolvent Debtor, Edward Bradley, late of Wordsley, in the County of Stafford, white glass maker.'

9 Ibid, D.R. Guttery, p61.

10 John, Viscount Dudley and Ward; MP for Newcastle, 1727-48; succeeded as the sixth Baron Ward, 10th May 1740; created Viscount Dudley and Ward 1763; d. 6th May 1774.

11 Michael Grazebrook, son of Joseph Grazebrook of Stourbridge and his wife Elizabeth, nee Milward, bap. 11th Feb 1687, Oldswinford. Joseph was the third son of Michael Grazebrook, originally of Middleton, Warwickshire, who settled in Stourbridge about 1640, and his wife Dorothy. Op cit Sir John Bernard Burke, *A Genealogical and Heraldic Dictionary of the Landed Gentry* (1882), p682-4; *Miscellanea Genealogica et Heraldica* v 3, Third Series, pp117, 158, 212, 246.

12 Michael Grazebrook II, son of Michael Grazebrook I and his wife Elizabeth, nee Hunt, b. 21st Jun 1723; bap. 30th Jun 1723, Oldswinford.

13 Mar. Michael Grazebrook II and Sarah Worral, 16th Jan 1753, Wolverhampton.

14 LJRO, B/C/6,7.

15 Michael Grazebrook, bur. 13th Dec 1756, Oldswinford.
16 WRO, Will of Michael Grazebrook, 25th Oct 1757.
17 Ibid, J.A. Langford.
18 Audenham was a contemporary spelling of Audnam, as seen on early maps.
19 Benjamin Richardson's notebook of 1886.
20 DA, Ashwood Hay and Wall Heath Enclosure Act, 16 Geo III, cap 33, 1776.
21 Michael Grazebrook, d. 14th May 1766; bur. Oldswinford. His grave is a large chest that was to become the family tomb.
22 PRO, PROB 11 918, PCC will of Michael Grazebrook, 27th May 1766.
23 Thomas Worral Grazebrook, son of Michael Grazebrook and his wife Sarah, nee Worral, b. 11th Aug 1756; bap. 2nd Sep 1756, Kingswinford.
24 Michael Grazebrook, son of Michael Grazebrook and his wife Sarah, nee Worral, b. 7th Mar 1758; bap. 11th Apr 1758, Kingswinford.
25 Elizabeth Grazebrook, bur. 15th Feb 1771, Oldswinford.
26 WRO, Admon of Elizabeth Grazebrook, 22nd Feb 1771.
27 DA, Ashwood Hay and Wall Heath Enclosure Act, 16 Geo III, cap 33, 1776.
28 Bailey's 1783 Western and Midlands Directory.
29 Ibid, T.J. Raybould, p133.
30 Guildhall MS v 11,936, Sun fire insurance policy registers, 313/477930.
31 Guildhall MS v 11,936, Sun fire insurance policy registers, 353/542507.
32 Mar. Michael Grazebrook III and Mary Anne Needs, 21st Dec 1785, St. Giles', London.
33 WRO, Class 899:31 BA/4380/39, MS Lucy Ellen Grazebrook, *Collections and Recollections of John Phillips Grazebrook* pp11-2.
34 Supra, Dial Glasshouse.
35 Universal British Directory, 1793.
36 DA, Lord Dudley's Rent Rolls.
37 Ibid, T.J. Raybould, p133.
38 George Grazebrook, son of Michael Grazebrook and his wife Mary Anne, nee Needs, b. 21st Jul 1796; bap. 23rd Jul 1796, Kingswinford.
39 Henry Sydney Grazebrook, son of George Grazebrook and his wife Jane, nee Smallman, b. 6th Jun 1836.
40 DA, Right Honourable William Lord Viscount Dudley and Ward's Rental Roll for 1798 and County Express, 23rd Sep 1961.
41 Mrs Sarah Grazebrook, d. 7th Jun 1799; bur. 13th Jun 1799, Oldswinford family tomb.

42 Birmingham Gazette, 10th Jun 1799.
43 LRJO, Will (and codicil) of Sarah Grazebrook, 8th Jan 1800.
44 Holden's Triennial Directory for 1809, 1810 & 1811.
45 Thomas Worral Grazebrook, d. 9th Aug 1816; bur. Oldswinford family tomb.
46 Gentleman's Magazine Sep 1846, p332; Foster, *Alumini Oxonienses*, Series II, p554.
47 Michael Grazebrook, son of Michael Grazebrook and his wife Mary Anne, nee Needs, b. 6th Jun 1788; bap. 8th Jun 1788, Kingswinford.
48 William Grazebrook, son of Michael Grazebrook and his wife Mary Anne, nee Needs, b. 31st Mar 1791; bap. 9th Apr 1791, Kingswinford.
49 James Pigot's 1818 Commercial Directory; Wrightsons' 1823 Triennial Directory of Birmingham and Wrightsons' 1825 Triennial Directory of Birmingham.
50 Lewis's 1820 Worcestershire General and Commercial Directory.
51 DA, William Fowler's 1822 *Map of the Parish of Kingswinford*. Plot 311 Audenham Bank Glass Ho – Lord Dudley & M. Gl'k
52 Mar. Michael Grazebrook IV and Elizabeth Wallace Phillips, 28th May 1821, St. Philip's, Birmingham.
53 Corbyn's Hall stood east of Kingswinford, south of Tansey Green. It remained the Corbyn family home from the reign of Edward I until the early 1800s when it was purchased by John Hodgetts who sold it to the ironmaster, John Gibbons (1712-1779) in 1747. The hall occasionally hosted Kingswinford manorial court. It was demolished in 1910 after standing for almost six hundred years, the victim of subsidence caused by the colliery that bore its name.
54 Ibid, Lucy Ellen Grazebrook, pp7-9.
55 This house was the home of ironmaster James Male J.P. until his death in 1824 and had been attacked in the Priestley riots of 1791. In more recent times it housed the offices of Midlands Electricity Board.
56 John Phillips Grazebrook, son of Michael Grazebrook and his wife Elizabeth Wallace, nee Phillips, b. 7th Apr 1826; bap. 11th Apr 1826, Halesowen.
57 Michael Grazebrook, d. 11th Jun 1826; bur. Oldswinford family tomb.
58 Pigot and Co.'s National Commercial Directory for 1828-9; Pigot and Co.'s Commercial Directory of Birmingham, 1829 and 1830 editions.
59 Elizabeth Grazebrook, daughter of Michael Grazebrook and his wife Mary Anne, nee Needs, b. 26th Mar 1801; bap. 5th Apr 1801, Kingswinford.
60 Ferdinando Lea Smith, b. 1779, oldest son of Ferdinando Lea Smith and his

wife Elizabeth, nee Lyttelton; magistrate and deputy-lieutenant for several counties; Lieutenant-Colonel of Worcester Militia with which regiment he served in Ireland during the Rebellion, and on his return was presented with the freedom of the city of Worcester; first married in 1802, Eloisa, daughter of Major-General St. George Knudson; she died in 1805.

61 Thirteenth Report of the Commission into the Glass Excise, 1835, Appendix 7.

62 The Dudley Arms Hotel was once the leading hotel in Dudley. Coaches left daily for London, Birmingham, Liverpool and Worcester. The Court Leet met there to elect its Mayor and it became the headquarters of the Town Commissioners who provided what little local government there was between 1791 and 1852. It was built in the Market Place in 1786 on the site of the earlier Rose and Crown Inn and demolished in 1968 to provide a site for a Marks and Spencer's store.

63 PG, Jul 1891.

64 PRO, 1841 Census of Kingswinford.

65 Post Office Directory of the Neighbourhood of Birmingham, 1845.

66 Pigot and Co.'s 1841 Directory of Birmingham.

67 Royal Brierley Archive.

68 PRO, 1851 Census HO 107/2036 08/145/049.

69 PRO, 1851 Census HO 107/2036 06/111/078.

70 Michael Grazebrook, d. 24th Apr 1854; bur. Oldswinford family tomb.

71 Michael Phillips Grazebrook, son of Michael Grazebrook and his wife Elizabeth Wallace, nee Phillips, b. 24th Sep 1822; bap. 29th Sep 1822, Kingswinford.

72 Elizabeth Wallace Grazebrook, d. 12th May 1833 at Belle Vue, Halesowen; bur. Oldswinford.

73 Michael Grazebrook IV had been a director of both the Great Western and the Severn Valley Railways.

74 Mar. John Phillips Grazebrook and Harriet Draffen Francis, 3rd May 1855, Edgbaston. The Francis family was a wealthy and old-established Birmingham dynasty. Francis Road in Edgbaston is named after one of the family.

75 John Phillips Grazebrook d. 2nd Mar 1919 and has a memorial in Hagley churchyard. His obituary appeared in County Express, 9th Mar 1919.

76 Supra, Coalbournhill.

77 Infra, North Street Glassworks.

78 FGMM quarter ending 27th Nov 1858.

79 Royal Commission on Trade Unions, 1867-69, 10th Report, 32 Parliamentary Paper 1867 (3952) xxxii.
80 William Webb Boulton, son of Richard Boulton and his wife, Jane, nee Webb, b. 7th Feb 1833 probably at Sillings Farm, Feckenham, Alcester; bap. 28th Dec 1833, Feckenham, Worcestershire.
81 PRO HO/107/2075 Fol. 421 p9, 1851 census of Feckenham, Alcester, Warwickshire.
82 At the time of the 1851 census William Webb Boulton was an eighteen year old glasshouse clerk, lodging at the back of Webb's Glass House. PRO HO0107/2035/013
83 Frederick James Mills, son of Richard Mills and his wife Elizabeth, nee Webb, b. Wordsley; bap. 7th Jun 1835, Kingswinford.
84 PRO, 1861 census RG 9/2069 ED2 Sched 155.
85 Mar. William Webb Boulton and Jane Mills, 23rd Jul 1862, Wordsley.
86 Jane Mills, b. 11th Oct 1842, daughter of Richard Mills and his wife Elizabeth, nee Webb.
87 PRO, 1871 census RG10 3025 ED1 Sched 102.
88 William Orme Foster MP, son of William and Charlotte Foster, bap. 12th Sep 1816, Oldswinford, nephew and heir of ironmaster James Foster; lived Apley Park, near Bridgnorth.
89 DA.
90 Kelly's 1876 Post Office Directory of Staffordshire and Warwickshire.
91 Infra, Grazebrook's Canalside Glassworks.
92 Patent number 314, 25th Jan 1879.
93 PRO, 1881 census of Kingswinford, RG11/2891/16/23.
94 PRO, 1881 census of Upper Swinford, RG11/2888/8/12.
95 Oswald George Meatyard, son of William Meatyard, upholsterer and wallpaperhanger of 78 Mount Street, Westminster b. 5th Jun 1838, Hanover Square, St. George's, London. Meatyard initially worked at a glassworks in London and according to surviving descendants was 'supposed to be an expert in stained glass.'
96 PRO, 1871 census RG10/3025/1/103 and 1881 census RG11/2891/16/23.
97 Francis James Shea, b. c 1839, Liverpool.
98 He was to receive £200 per annum plus 21 shillings per day when travelling in England and 26 shillings in Scotland and Ireland plus agreed expenses.
99 Infra, Wordsley Flint Glassworks.
100 DA, Lord Dudley's estate records.

101 Richard Harry Webb Boulton, son of William Webb Boulton and his wife Jane, nee Mills, bap. 17th Aug 1864, Kingswinford.
102 William Webb Boulton, son of William Webb Boulton and his wife Jane, nee Mills, b. c1866, Kingswinford.
103 Information on the partnership from an unidentified newspaper obituary.
104 William Webb Boulton, d. 21st Feb 1892; bur. Wordsley. His grave is a grey stone vault.
105 PRO, Will of William Webb Boulton, 5th Apr 1892.
106 The collection included two works by William Jabez Muckley: Group of Roses 20" x 16" - £19 19s and Grapes 20" x 16" - £26 5s.
107 County Express, 23rd May 1903.
108 PRO, Will of Frederick James Mills, 21st Feb 1908.
109 Richard Harry Webb Boulton d. 12th Feb 1922 without leaving a will. Letters of administration were granted in London on 27th Mar 1923 to his surviving son, Howard Gilbert Boulton of Ye Olde House, Amblecote.
110 Captain Howard Gilbert Boulton MC, son of Richard Harry Webb Boulton and his wife Marian, nee Matthews, b. c1897.
111 Laura Mary Boulton, daughter of William Webb Boulton and his wife Jane, nee Mills, b. c1863 Kingswinford.
112 Charles Herbert Thomson was a Doctor of Chemistry who lived at Battenhall Mount, Worcester. He was probably the father of Howard Gilbert Boulton's wife, Marie Beatrix, nee Thompson. He ran the firms of Bullers Ltd in Tipton and Thompson L'Hospied and Co. Ltd., in Amblecote. He owned a ceramic factory in Golfe Juan in France, conducted experiments with enamel colours on porcelain plaques at his home in Stourbridge and designed industrial furnaces (DA, Thompson family papers). About 1895 he invented *Verre sur Verre*, enamelled glass which had the background taken down by acid etching leaving a raised area in the exact shape and outline to match the final, enamelled decoration (PG, Aug 1901).
113 Ibid, R. Wakefield, pp11-12.
114 In 1995 Esso deposited a planning application for the replacement of below ground fuel tanks An archaeological condition was imposed in the form of a watching brief. Work began on 2nd August 1999 and an archaeological survey of the exposed remains was conducted. John Hemingway, *Archaeological Survey of a Glasshouse Site at the Boundary Service Station, Audnam, Stourbridge*.

CHAPTER 26

Dob Hill Glassworks, Wordsley

Dob Hill Glassworks stood in Wordsley, on the north side of the Brierley Hill Road, opposite what is now called Dock Road. It stood at the southwest foot of Dob Hill, a small hill rising above an area known as Bugpool, or later, Buckpool[1].

The first reference to a glassworks at Dob Hill is from Guttery who stated 'Windsor James was at Dob Hill in 1710'[2], although no substantiation of this is quoted. Windsor James was the son of Walter James of Powick, Worcestershire[3]. In 1713 his daughter Mary married Henry Bradley[4], who ran the Jacob's Well Glasshouse.

For some time up to 1723 James and Thomas Compson worked the glasshouse, although it has not been possible to find any genealogical background to these two people. By 1723 they were bankrupt[5], probably because of the steep fall in the price of broad-glass.

Windsor James then ran the glasshouse for six years until his death. He was a man of high social standing and was either a friend or client of the attorney Thomas Milward. When Milward died in 1724, Windsor James and several other glassmakers were among the mourners at the funeral held on 6th August.

Windsor James died in 1729[6], his position being demonstrated by the burial register entry of 'Mr. Windsor James'. His will[7] describes him as a whiteglassmaker of Wordsley and refers to his 'glasshouse and lands at Wordsley'. A codicil dated 11th May 1727 refers to the complicated agreement he had made to support the Audnam Glasshouse of his son-in-law, Henry Bradley. He left his interest in the Audnam business in trust to his brother-in-law Edward Oseland[8] of Bewdley, for the benefit of his daughter Mary

Bradley. The inventory of his goods and chattels was valued at £178 15s 2d and provides some interesting references to the contents of the glasshouse. The testator had no male heir and so after leaving legacies to his widow and Bradley grandchildren, his residual estate was left in the trust of his executors. His witnesses and executors were all connected with the Stourbridge glass trade.

After Windsor James' death a fifty-year gap follows during which no more is heard of Dob Hill Glassworks until 1776 when the land around was enclosed. In the Enclosure Act Volume[9] Mrs Sarah Grazebrook is shown as the occupier of two glasshouses. One was the Audnam works owned by Lord Dudley, the other Dob Hill now owned by Robert Honeyborne. Sarah Grazebrook was the widow of Michael Grazebrook II, who had been running the Audnam Glassworks. When Michael Grazebrook II died in 1766, his sons were too young to inherit his business. So he left a will[10] stipulating 'I desire my trade may be carried on by my loving wife'. His wishes were carried out; his widow, Sarah, ran the glassworks at Audnam and Dob Hill until she retired about 1790 when her sons took over. Further references to Sarah Grazebrook operating as the principal occurred in 1783 and 1789[11].

Presumably the Grazebrooks needed the Dob Hill Glassworks in addition to their Audnam Glassworks to make bottles. Benjamin Richardson wrote 'There used to be a very old Glass House opposite the Boat Inn and near to Dob Hill and it used to be worked by Madam Grazebrook. They used to take the material from the glasshouse at Audnam to Dob Hill glass works and vice versa.'

The exact date of cessation of Dob Hill Glassworks is not known, but Benjamin Richardson further recorded 'After the old glass house fell down they put up a new cone by the canalside . . . '[12] Dob Hill Glassworks was remote from both the turnpike and the new canal opened in December 1779. It was logical to build its replacement alongside the canal, with the improvements in transport envisaged. The location of the new glasshouse referred to by Benjamin Richardson had been a mystery until its remains were discovered in 1993 on the west side of the Stourbridge Canal[13].

Available evidence from contemporary maps does not provide

a conclusive date for the cessation of the Dob Hill Glassworks. An undated map in Dudley Archive of about 1800 names the site as Glasshouse Close and the adjoining field as Great Dob Hill. Fowler's 1822 map shows the site containing a House, Offices, Barn, Land etc, owned by Richard Ensell. The adjoining field was still called Dob Hill$_{14}$.

---

1 Buckpool is an area 1.25 miles NNW of Amblecote in Kingswinford ancient parish. The pool is said to have been used a ducking pool.
2 Ibid, D.R. Guttery, p154.
3 Windsor James, son of Mr Walter James, bap. 15th Dec 1660, Oldswinford.
4 Mar. Henry Bradley and Mary James, 14th Feb 1713, Kingswinford.
5 Ibid, D.R. Guttery, p62.
6 Windsor James, d. 30th Oct 1729; bur. Kingswinford.
7 LJRO, Will of Windsor James, 10th Nov 1730.
8 Edward Oseland, son of Revd. Henry Oseland, non-conformist minister who succeeded his father at Bewdley and his wife Mary, nee Henzey.
9 DA, Ashwood Hay and Wall Heath Enclosure Act, 16 Geo III, cap 33, 1776.
10 PRO, PROB 11 918.
11 Bailey's 1783 Western and Midlands Directory and Tunnicliffe's 1789 Survey.
12 Benjamin Richardson's notebook of 1886.
13 P. Boland & J. Ellis, *A Lost Stourbridge Glassworks Rediscovered*, JGA, v 5 (1977), pp6-25.
14 DA, William Fowler's 1822 *Map of the Parish of Kingswinford*. Plot 617.

CHAPTER 27

Moor Lane Glassworks, Brierley Hill

Moor Lane Glassworks was the first to be built at Brierley Hill and is symbolic of the expansion of the industrialised area. As has already been described, the original seat of Stourbridge's glass industry was in the valley of the River Stour. It then expanded along the route of the Stourbridge to Wolverhampton road, even before it was turnpiked, first into Amblecote, then Wordsley. As demand for land continued, and more coal was discovered, it continued eastward up the hillside towards the Pensnett Chase.

Robert Honeyborne[1] began his working life as a maltster. In 1722 he married[2] Ann[3], the only child of Thomas Hamond of Bague's Glasshouses. Their marriage was by a licence[4] that states Anne Hamond to be a spinster of about eighteen years of age. However, she was baptised in 1707 and if baptised promptly after her birth she would be fifteen years old at the time of her marriage. Their first child Mary was born in 1724[5] and their second Hamond in 1726[6], but Ann died nine months later[7]. She was in the fifth year of her marriage and aged no more than twenty years old. Robert's tragedy was further compounded when his only son Hamond died eighteen months later[8].

Robert enjoyed modest success as a maltster and on 16th November 1732 bought several pieces of land from the Bradley family 'existing at or near the place called Moor Lane' and the house there in which he lived at the time[9].

His father-in-law Thomas Hamond of Bague's Glasshouses died with no surviving children in 1743 and Robert was a beneficiary in his will proved in September 1744. It is not clear what then happened to Bague's, but with his inheritance Robert built the Moor Lane Glassworks on the land he already owned.

Little is known about his products. He probably made bottles and window glass by the Lorrainer 'broad' method.

After being widowed for eighteen years, Robert remarried to Jane Hodgetts[10]. The following month, his daughter Mary married John Pidcock[11], who operated Dial and Platts Glasshouses. This marriage united the wealth of three important glassmaking families. John Pidcock was the nephew of, and had just inherited from Joshua Henzey III. Besides the glassmaking interests of Mary's father, she was the granddaughter and heiress of Thomas Hamond of Bague's Glasshouses.

In 1760 Robert Honeyborne manufactured best and ordinary flint glass and phials[12]. He died in 1769[13], aged sixty-seven and in his will[14] describes himself as a glassmaker of Moor Lane. He was clearly a wealthy man and left a wide spread of generous legacies to his children. For his son John he stated 'I have lately purchased for him a commission in the Army which has cost me twelve hundred guineas.' He left four hundred and fifty pounds to be divided between his Pidcock grandchildren. Most of his estate was left to his eldest son from his second marriage, Robert II[15].

Whitworth's 1774 canal map shows land labelled as Mr Honeyburns [sic] in a coal-rich area, but does not show the outline of the glassworks. Whitworth's design allowed for a collateral branch of the canal to be built into the heart of the coal-mining area on the Pensnett Chase. Robert Honeyborne was a founder of the Stourbridge Navigation Company[16]. As a coalmaster as well as a glass manufacturer, the potential benefits to him of canal transport were obvious. He took up the maximum allotment of ten shares, a shrewd investment worth some £3,500 twenty years later.

Robert Honeyborne appears as a glass manufacturer in many newspapers and trade directories between 1781 and 1793. The first to specifically describe his products is the Universal British Directory of 1793, which shows him making flint glass. A list of glassworks dated 1796 shows Honeyborne at Moor Lane Glassworks with a nine-pot works[17].

Robert Honeyborne the younger died in 1802[18], aged fifty-six, and left his estate to his younger brother Thomas[19]. His will has not survived, but Thomas signed a form of receipt for £24,392 on 20th August 1803 'on account of the estate of Robt. Honeyborne of Moor Lane Glass manufacturer.'

Thomas Honeyborne took over running the firm and changed the trading title to his name. On 17th January 1803 a meeting took place at the Stewponey Inn, Stourton to petition the Government to have the duty on flint glass based on manufactured goods instead of metal or raw materials. Thomas Honeyborne contributed £50 to the fund, implying it was one of the smaller firms.

The first detailed evidence available of the output of Moor Lane Glassworks comes from a priced bill dated 1804. It identified some of the products as:

> 'Square foot ales fluted and hollows and foot cut; Gills cut and puntyed; Gills fluted and puntyed; Wines fluted; Pint and Quart Decanters cut to pattern; Round foot Goblets fluted puntyed and Shanked; Canns fingered and Cut handles; Wines fluted; Coolers fingered; Mustard Pots; Decanters slopes and fingered.'[20]

A further bill dated March 1804[21] records the purchase of glass by J. Dovey and Son from Honeyborne & Batson of Moor Lane. This would almost certainly be James Dovey and his son Richard. In 1772 James Dovey, of Wollaston Mill, advertised for a boy to learn to be a glasscutter[22]. A further note[23] states that James Dovey, who died in 1827, aged eighty, introduced cutting into the region. James Dovey and John Benson of Dudley are believed to be the first to employ steam power to turn their wheels. At a General Assembly of the Stourbridge Navigation Company held on 5th July 1790 it was minuted:

> 'that the Company's Committee be impowered to treat and agree with James Dovey of Wollaston Glass cutter for the letting of a parcel of land at the Company's Wharf at Stourbridge to erect a Steam Engine and Shops upon and to grant a leave thereof for him . . .'[24]

Before the steam engine, their source of power was a traditional water mill at their premises at Wollaston Mill. James Dovey is the only glass cutter mentioned in Stourbridge trade directories around the turn of the century. Richard Dovey is shown as a cut glass manufacturer in the Commercial Directory for 1818. In 1823 he worked at Rye Market, Stourbridge$_{25}$.

John Benson manufactured glass in Dudley from at least 1803 to 1812. In 1805 he was at the Priory, Dudley$_{26}$ and was the largest of several suppliers of glass to the silversmiths M. Fenton & Co.$_{27}$ He was probably related to James and William Benson, cut glass manufacturers at Priory Mill, Dudley from 1823 to 1841. In 1841 James and William Benson lived in Wolverhampton Street, Dudley, both described as glassmasters$_{28}$. By 1845, James Benson alone was listed in Priory Street.

Returning to the story of Moor Lane Glassworks itself, it received a great boost in December 1779, when the Stourbridge Canal was fully opened to traffic. An extant document dated August 1804$_{29}$ records the delivery of twenty tons of Lynn sand at 32s per ton, by canal to Honeyborne & Batson. The new partner was James Batson, whose provenance is unclear.

Sometime between 1803 and 1809 Thomas Honeyborne retired to Woodhead, an estate near Cheadle in north Staffordshire, where he farmed and lived the life of a country squire. He continued to own the glassworks but it was managed and worked by his older brother John$_{30}$. John continued to produce flint and stained plate glass$_{31}$. Thomas Honeyborne returned to the area occasionally on business, but mainly lived in retirement in Cheadle until he died in 1831$_{32}$. After his retirement the title of the firm remained unchanged as Honeyborne and Batson$_{33}$. James Batson is described as a glass manufacturer of Stourbridge when he made his will on 11th January 1820$_{34}$. He presumably retired about this time and died in 1825. A memorial inside Amblecote Church commemorates the fact that he left one hundred pounds for the poor of the parishes of Amblecote and Kingswinford.

The ownership and management arrangement of the glassworks is confirmed by Fowler's map of 1822. This shows John Honeyborne in possession of the glasshouse, with the proprietor being Thomas

Honeyborne. The site consisted of 'Pool piece, Moor Lane Glass House, Shops, etc.[35]'

Trade was poor in the early eighteen-twenties and in 1823 John Honeyborne was declared bankrupt. The sale of his stock took place on 29th December 1823. His stock was extensive and the existence of the sale catalogue today gives an insight into the products being made at that time. These included flint-glass—particularly drinking glasses—coloured window glass, glass canes and enamellers' cakes. This extensive range of products being made in the same glasshouse is peculiar to Moor Lane Glassworks. Most other glasshouses tended to specialise in one or two products[36]:

> 'A CATALOGUE of the valuable STOCK OF WINES, ALE, Large Stock of rich Cut and plain GLASS, Upwards of 800 unspread coloured Muff Glass, 30 Tons of Cullet, . . . belonging to Mr. John Honeyborne, of Moor Lane, In the Parish of Kingswinford, in the County of Stafford, a Bankrupt, which will be SOLD BY AUCTION BY G. ALLEN: On Monday, the 29th December, 1823, and three following Days . . .'[37]

Thomas Honeyborne still owned the property and as he had no intention of returning to the business he leased it out. On 2nd February 1824 he leased for fourteen years to 'Joseph Silvers and Joseph Stevens both of Moor Lane . . . Glassmanufacturers . . . all that glasshouse now used for manufacturing of flint glass with the Warehouses Pot Rooms Store Rooms Crate Shops Barns Hovels and other outbuildings . . situate at Moor Lane.' The annual rent was £80. Joseph Stevens[38] was the oldest son of William Stevens, a glass packer of Brierley Hill and worked as an agent for Benjamin Littlewood at Holloway End Glasshouse. Joseph Silvers[39] came from Woodside, the son of Benjamin Silvers, who owned properties and nail-shops in that area. Eighteenth century Dudley trade directories frequently show the name Silvers as glasscutters, but there is no firm evidence of descent to Joseph Silvers. When he baptised his daughter, Eliza in 1814[40], Joseph Silvers is described as an agent. He and his family lived next to the Swan Inn in Moor Lane[41] and he probably worked for the Honeybornes at Moor Lane

Glassworks. He was certainly working for Thomas Honeyborne in 1824 as a trusted servant. Thomas Honeyborne recorded in his account book that he had sent him 'on account of the colliery' £50 on 2nd January and £70 on 4th January 1824. This would be in relation to Thomas Honeyborne's firm of coalmasters, Honeyborne, Pidcock and Brettell at Brierley Hill. The two partners, Silvers and Stevens, were brothers-in-law. Joseph Silvers married Joseph Stevens' sister, Anna Maria[42] in 1805[43] when Joseph Stevens witnessed the marriage. After taking the lease on the glassworks, Joseph and Anna Maria Silvers moved into Moor Lane House[44].

Sometime after 1824 and before 1828 Joseph Silvers and Joseph Stevens were joined in partnership by James Mills[45] and the firm traded as Silvers, Mills & Stevens, making flint glass[46]. However, this arrangement was short-lived. Joseph Stevens either fell out with his partners, or more likely wanted the freedom of running his own business, so in 1828 they dissolved the partnership:

> 'Notice is hereby given, that the partnership subsisting between us the undersigned, Joseph Silvers, James Mills and Joseph Stevens, as Flint Glass-manufacturers, at Moor Lane in the Parish of Kingswinford, in the county of Stafford, is this day dissolved by mutual consent. Dated this 10th day of May 1828.'[47]

Joseph Stevens took control of Holly Hall Glassworks, just outside Dudley and his younger brother James[48] took his share in Moor Lane Glassworks. The new firm still advertised its wares as flint glass and continued to trade as Silvers, Mills and Stevens[49].

Thomas Honeyborne had been living in retirement in Cheadle for over twenty years and was still the proprietor of Moor Lane Glassworks. He died in 1831[50], aged eighty and his estate passed to his brother-in-law and agent, Joseph Atkinson[51].

Joseph Silvers & Co. paid £2,438 11s 6d excise duty for the year ending 5th January 1833[52], suggesting this was the eleventh largest of the sixteen Stourbridge/Dudley glasshouses of the day. In 1835 there was a change in the advertised products of Silvers, Mills and Stevens, now comprising flint glass, plain and cut[53].

There are some interesting references to the business in

Robson's 1839 Birmingham and Sheffield Directory. The firm is listed as Stevens & Silver (flint), Brierley Hill, suggesting that James Mills was no longer a partner. It also lists James Stevens, flint glass manufacturers, Brierley Hill and W. Silvers, Moor Lane, Wordsley, Wine Glass Manufactory. This relatively unusual mention of wine glasses in a trade directory suggests they were a speciality. Even more intriguing is the reference to W. Silvers who cannot be identified. It could be a reference to William Silvers, the son of Joseph Silvers, who had certainly been involved in the business, although he had died in 1836[54].

Bentley's 1840 Directory of Stourbridge again lists the firm as Silvers and Stevens, glass manufacturers, Brierley Hill. It also lists Joseph Silvers living in Moor Lane and James Stevens living in Brierley Hill. Fowler and Son's 1840 map shows Joseph Atkinson as the owner of the glassworks, and J. Silvers and J. Stevens as the occupiers. In 1841 Joseph Silvers lived with his wife and two of his daughters at Moor Lane House[55].

In November 1845 James Stevens represented the firm at a meeting of the Master Flint Glass Cutters at the Stork Hotel in Birmingham. He died in 1846[56], aged forty-eight. He had made a will on 27th January 1837[57], describing himself as a gentleman of Brierley Hill. As he never married, he left his estate to his many nephews and nieces. This left Joseph Silvers in sole control of the business, who—now aged sixty-seven—decided to retire. His only son William had died at the age of twenty-seven, so he handed the business to his two sons-in-law, William Stevens and Samuel Cox Williams. They leased the works for seven years from Joseph Atkinson and founded the firm of Stevens and Williams in 1847.

William Stevens[58] was the son of Joseph Stevens senior and had married his cousin Maria[59], the youngest daughter of Joseph Silvers. After working for his father at Coalbournhill Glassworks, he had worked as a furnaceman, living at Golds Green, West Bromwich. On taking over the firm, William and Maria moved to High Street, Brierley Hill. They lived there in 1851 when he was described as a glass manufacturer[60].

Samuel Cox Williams[61] was the son of Michael Williams, a

stocktaker of Horsehay. He came originally from Dawley Magna, Shropshire, where he had been involved in the local iron trade with his brother Richard. He therefore brought a useful knowledge of furnace technology with him. Samuel married Ellen, the daughter of Joseph Silvers in 1844[62]. After only five-and-a-half years of marriage, Ellen died in 1850[63], aged twenty-seven. Samuel Cox Williams then married her older sister Eliza[64]. They married in Birmingham[65] then again in Edinburgh[66], probably because under the law of the day it was illegal for a man to marry his widow's sister. However, they certainly lived together for the rest of her life, and had a child, James Williams.

Eight years after retiring, Joseph Silvers died in 1854[67], aged seventy-five. He had made a will[68] on 11th January 1848 and added a codicil on 13th December 1850, in which he is described as a Gentleman of Moor Lane, Kingswinford. He left several properties to his widow Maria and various legacies to his daughters.

Serious disharmony in the glass trade between employer and workmen first began in February 1858 at E. & J. Webb's[69], but erupted at Grazebrooks'[70] and Stevens and Williams'. Early in October 1858, Stevens and Williams proposed that one of their apprentices should be taken on as a journeyman footmaker at something less than the 14s nominal wages per week. This ignored the rules and regulations of the Association of Flint Glassmakers that only four months before had been revised and ratified at a conference in London[71]. On 12th October 1858, twenty-two men gave fourteen days notice to leave, and all left on 23rd October. Three days later, on 26th October, Stevens and Williams issued a leaflet to all the other flint glass manufacturers, listing the names of the workmen concerned and urging their fellow employers not to employ them:

> 'Dear Sir, in consequence of our refusal to submit to the dictation of the glass makers in our employ, the undermentioned have signified their intention of not recommencing work until we comply with their demands, we shall feel obliged by you not employing them, as it is in the interest of the Trade generally to support us in resisting such

tyrannical proceedings. Yours respectfully Stevens and Williams.'[72]

Faced with an outbreak of strikes, the employers responded by holding a meeting on 1st November 1858 at the Talbot Hotel, Stourbridge, where they formed a manufacturers' organisation. Predictably, Stevens and Williams became a founder member of the Flint Glass Manufacturers Defence Association. From October 1858 onwards the strike spread throughout the district and in December the Association of Flint Glassmakers enforced a national lockout that was to last for seven months. In April 1859, after the lockout, Stevens and Williams claimed £75 from the association's defence fund. The amount claimed implies the firm was the second largest of the thirteen firms in the Midlands Association.

In 1864 Samuel Cox Williams brought his oldest son, Joseph Silvers Williams,[73] into the business, having recently finished schooling in Bromsgrove. William Stevens died in 1869[74] and within a few days of his partner's death, Samuel Cox Williams circulated a message to his customers. He informed them that in future the works would be carried on by himself alone 'under the style of Stevens and Williams as before . . . hoping by promptness and usual good quality to merit continuance of their favours'. He bought out his late partner's share in the business from William Stevens' widow, Maria, but kept on their son, William Henry Stevens[75], in the pay of the company.

The old glassworks was in poor condition, exacerbated by subsidence caused by the extensive coalmining in the area. So in 1870 Samuel Cox Williams built a new factory, a quarter of a mile away, in North Street, near to Brierley Hill Church. The old Moor Lane premises were then demolished.

---

1 Robert Honeyborne, b. c 1702.

2 Mar. Robert Honeyborne and Ann Hamond, 17th Oct 1722, Lichfield Cathedral.

3 Ann Hamond, daughter of Thomas Hamond and his wife Mary, nee Bradley, bap. 13th Oct 1707, Kingswinford.

4 LJRO, marriage licence dated 1st Oct 1722.

5 Mary Honeyborne, daughter of Robert Honeyborne and his first wife Ann, nee

Hamond, bap. 6th Jan 1724, Kingswinford; d. 28th Sep 1807; bur Pidcock family vault, middle aisle Brierley Hill Church.

6 Hamond Honeyborne, son of Robert Honeyborne and his first wife Ann, nee Hamond, bap. 10th Oct 1726, Kingswinford.

7 Ann Honeyborne, bur. 27th Jul 1727, Kingswinford.

8 Hamond Honeyborne, bur. 11th Jan 1729, Kingswinford.

9 Kingswinford Court Rolls.

10 Mar. Robert Honeyborne and Jane Hodgetts, 6th Jun 1745, Kingswinford.

11 Mar. John Pidcock and Mary Honeyborne, 22nd Jul 1745, St. Martin's, Birmingham.

12 Ibid, J.A. Langford.

13 Robert Honeyborne, bur. 28th Oct 1769, Brierley Hill.

14 PRO, PROB 11/953 LH168-RH169, PCC will of Robert Honeyborne, 19th Dec 1769.

15 Robert Honeyborne, son of Robert Honeyborne and his second wife Jane, nee Hodgetts, bap. 11th Jul 1746, Kingswinford.

16 The first General Assembly of the Stourbridge Navigation Company was held at the Talbot Hotel on 1st Jun 1776 and Robert Honeyborne was among those who signed the minutes of the proceedings. PRO, RAIL 874.1.

17 D.N. Sandilands.

18 Robert Honeyborne, bur. 18th Aug 1802, Brierley Hill.

19 Thomas Honeyborne, son of Robert Honeyborne and his second wife Jane, nee Hodgetts, bap. 18th Dec 1751, Kingswinford.

20 WRO, Palfrey collection.

21 WRO, Palfrey collection.

22 Aris's Birmingham Gazette, 22nd Jun 1772.

23 WRO, Palfrey collection.

24 PRO, RAIL 874.1.

25 Wrightson's 1823 Triennial Directory of Birmingham.

26 Holden's Triennial Directory for 1805, 1806, 1807.

27 Ibid, Frederick Bradbury, pp67-8.

28 PRO, 1841 Census of Dudley.

29 WRO, Palfrey collection.

30 John Honeyborne, son of Robert Honeyborne and his second wife Jane, nee Hodgetts, bap. 7th Sep 1747, Kingswinford.

31 Holden's Triennial Directory for 1809, 1810 & 1811.

32 Thomas Honeyborne, d. 24th Jul 1831; bur. 30th Jul 1831, Brierley Hill.
33 Lewis's 1820 Worcestershire General and Commercial Directory.
34 PCC, PROB11/1694, will of James Batson, proved 15th Jan 1825.
35 DA, William Fowler's 1822 *Map of the Parish of Kingswinford.*
36 From 1798 to 1848 an Act of Parliament (51 George III c. 69) prohibited any glasshouse making flint glass from making any other kind of glass.
37 WSL, Accession no 64/61; R.J. Charleston, *A Glassmaker's Bankruptcy Sale*, JGC, v 2 (1975), pp4-16.
38 Joseph Stevens, son of William Stevens and his wife Susannah, nee Cartwright, bap. 3rd Aug 1783, Brierley Hill.
39 Joseph Silvers, son of Benjamin Silvers and his wife Hannah, nee Smith, bap. 1st Nov 1778, Dudley St. Thomas's.
40 Eliza Silvers, daughter of Joseph Silvers and his wife Maria, nee Stevens, bap. 16th Jan 1814, Brierley Hill.
41 DA, William Fowler's 1822 Plan of the Parish of Kingswinford.
42 Anna Maria Stevens, daughter of William Stevens and his wife Susannah, nee Cartwright, bap. 10th Feb 1788, Brierley Hill.
43 Mar. Joseph Silvers and Anna Maria Stevens, 4th Aug 1805, Dudley St. Thomas's.
44 Rent Rolls.
45 James Mills was possibly related to Joseph Stevens as he married Ann Stevens on 18th May 1794 at Kingswinford. However, it has not been possible to prove the descent of James Mills nor Ann Stevens.
46 Pigot and Co.'s National Commercial Directory for 1828-9.
47 London Gazette, 27th May 1828.
48 DA, 1829 Electoral Register. James Stevens, son of William Stevens and his wife Susannah, nee Cartwright, bap. 8th Apr 1798, Brierley Hill.
49 Pigot and Co.'s 1829 Commercial Directory of Birmingham.
50 Thomas Honeyborne, d. 24th Jul 1831; bur. 30th Jul 1831, Brierley Hill.
51 Joseph Atkinson of Dublin and Fairy Hall, Rathowen, Westmeath County married Anna Maria Honeyborne in 1775.
52 Thirteenth Report of the Commission into the Glass Excise, 1835, Appendix 7.
53 Pigot and Co.'s 1835 National Commercial Directory.
54 William Silvers, d. 15th Apr 1836.
55 PRO, 1841 Census of Kingswinford.

56 James Stevens, bur. 4th May 1846, Brierley Hill.
57 PRO, PROB 11/2038, Will of James Stevens, 22nd Jun 1846.
58 William Stevens, son of Joseph Stevens and his first wife Frances, nee Hale, bap. 13th Sep 1818, Brierley Hill.
59 Maria Silvers, daughter of Joseph Silvers and his wife Anna Maria, nee Stevens, bap. 13th Jan 1828, Brierley Hill.
60 PRO, 1851 Census HO 107/2036 21/417/045.
61 Samuel Cox Williams, son of Michael Williams and his wife Lucy Mary, nee Cox, bap. 23rd May 1818, Dawley Magna, Shropshire.
62 Mar. Samuel Cox Williams and Ellen Silvers, 26th Nov 1844, Brierley Hill.
63 Ellen Williams, d. 7th Jun 1850; bur. Brierley Hill.
64 Eliza Silvers, daughter of Joseph Silvers and his wife Anna Maria, nee Stevens, bap. 16th Jan 1814, Brierley Hill.
65 Mar. Samuel Cox Williams and Eliza Silvers, 6th Oct 1851, St. Peters' Dale End, Birmingham.
66 Mar. Samuel Cox Williams and Eliza Silvers, 1st Mar 1852, Edinburgh Parish Church.
67 Joseph Silvers, d. 22nd Jan 1854; bur. Brierley Hill.
68 PRO, PROB 11, Will (and codicil) of Joseph Silvers, 27th Mar 1854.
69 Supra, Coalbournhill.
70 Supra, Audnam Works.
71 FGMM quarter ending 26 Aug 1876.
72 Royal Brierley Archive.
73 Joseph Silvers Williams, son of Samuel Cox Williams and his wife Ellen, nee Silvers, b. c1849, Brierley Hill
74 William Stevens, d. May 1869, as he was living at Elderfield, he was probably buried at Kidderminster.
75 William Henry Stevens, son of William Stevens and his wife Maria, nee Silvers, bap. 22nd Nov 1840, West Bromwich All Saints.

CHAPTER 28

Springsmire Glasshouse, Dudley

The evidence for the existence of Springsmire Glasshouse is almost entirely conjectural. However, that makes it all the more important to document what little evidence there is.

Springsmire is an area on the north side of the Stourbridge Road at Scots Green, Dudley. A reservoir and pumping station was built there in 1898 on land purchased from the Earl of Dudley on the site of an old colliery[1]. Humble Ward and his wife Frances reserved the mineral rights in this area in 1648. The lease describes the land as 'Gorton's Plain' and 'Hayden's Payne', lying probably between the present Wellington Road and Scots Green[2]. Eighteenth century canal maps show the entire area north and south of Scots Green as coalbearing. The 1903 Ordnance Survey shows many 'old coal shafts' in the area.

In 1756, which is the year that he died, John Green[3] was a 'Whiteglass maker of Dudley.'[4]. He married twice and had seven children. Two of his sons became Dudley glassmasters.

John's oldest (surviving) son Joseph[5] was born in 1707. He married Elizabeth Finch[6] of the wealthy Dudley ironmaker family in 1734 when he is described as a glassman[7]. That he worked as a 'white glassmaker of Dudley' from at least 1737 to 1744 and employed Benjamin James[8] as an apprentice is clear from a Quarter Session examination of James' subsequent situation as a vagabond many years later in Upton-on-Severn[9].

Aris's Birmingham Gazette of 12th January 1778 reports the death on 6th January 1778, at an advanced age, of 'Mr Joseph Green, at Dudley, who had many years retired from the glass trade, which he carried on with the greatest reputation.' In his will[10] Joseph left £20 to John Robinson, 'my late partner', presumably in the glassmaking business.

John Green's youngest son Jonathan was born in 1725 and ran Dixon's Green Glassworks in partnership with Joseph Price[11].

So we know that John Green was a glassmaker of Dudley. We know that his son Joseph was a glassmaker of reputation and possibly succeeded him in the family business. We know that his youngest son built and ran Dixon's Green Glassworks. So if John and his son Joseph Green operated a glassworks in Dudley where was it?

The first definite evidence is in Lord Dudley's Rent Rolls. For some inexplicable reason Lord Dudley collected no rent for twenty-three years from Joseph Green[12] who, according to Guttery 'had a glass-house at Springsmire (Scots Green) where the Dudley-Kingswinford road joins that from Dudley to Brierley Hill.'[13]

Pottery Gazette reported in Trade Reminiscences c1897 'There were then six houses, if not more, who made glass in Dudley, which have now dwindled down to one. There was one at Springs Mire – was it? – kept by Joseph Green, probably the Green from whom so many glass-making Greens have sprung.'

So the evidence suggests that John Green ran Springsmire Glasshouse from at least 1734 and it was carried on by his son Joseph 'with the greatest reputation' from about 1743 until he retired around 1766.

Zachariah Parkes paid the poor rate on Springsmire in 1807, by which time there was no mention of a glasshouse.

---

1 B.J. Williams and J. Van-Leerzem, *100 Years of Springsmire Reservoir*, Blackcountryman, Spring 1998, v 31, No 2, pp19-20.

2 DA, 5/2, lease dated 20th Oct 1648.

3 John Green, son of David Green, collier of Kingswinford and his wife Elizabeth, bap. 31st May 1680, Kingswinford.

4 Kingswinford Court Rolls of 1756 'John Green of Dudley, White glassmaker.'

5 Joseph Green, son of John Green and his first wife Isabell, nee Bird, bap. 17th May 1707, Kingswinford; d. 6th Jan 1778; bur Dudley St Thomas's.

6 Elizabeth Finch, daughter of Joshua Finch, Master of Dudley Grammar School

(appointed 22nd Nov 1688) and his wife Esther, daughter of Edward Elwall, bap. 23rd Jul 1707, Dudley; bur. 17th Sep 1740, Dudley St. Thomas's.

7 WRO Marriage licence of Joseph Green and Elizabeth Finch 6th Nov 1734.

8 Benjamin James, son of Esquire [sic] James and his wife Sarah, nee Daniel, bap. 11th Aug 1723, Kingswinford.

9 WRO BA1 110:462-464 doc 27, Quarter Session papers, Examination of a vagabond 21st Feb 1776.

10 PRO PROB11/1038 will of Joseph Green proved 10th Jan 1778.

11 Infra.

12 Lord Dudley's Rent-Roll, 28th Feb 1766, 'Mr Joseph Green for the Glasshouse Croft and House for the year 1743 to this Time being 23 Years at 22. 10. 0 p. Ann. £517 10. 0.' The same roll shows that Michael Grazebrook paid his £50 regularly each year.

13 Ibid, D.R. Guttery, p103.

CHAPTER 29

Holly Hall Glassworks, Dudley

Holly Hall is about a mile southwest of Dudley town centre, and the glassworks there stood on the north side of what is now called Stourbridge Road. The earliest reference possibly linking Holly Hall and glassmaking occurred in 1754. The Birmingham Gazette reported an apprentice had run away from Thomas Griffin of Holly Hall and was thought to have gone to Bristol[1]. Bristol was another glassmaking centre, so this could refer to a glass business.

The glassworks was probably built by John Keelinge[2] who was an attorney and steward to Lord Dudley. In 1770 he was living in the centre of Dudley, trading as John Keeling Esq.[3], glass maker, Sheep Lane[4].

John Keelinge died in 1783, aged seventy, having made his will on 16th October. When his will[5] was proved he left property and land at Summerhill and Ashwood in Kingswinford. The most fascinating part of the will concerns his 'undutiful son Joseph Ffreman[6]' to whom he left:

> 'the weekly sum of six shillings . . . for the term of his natural life or until he shall marry any other woman of fortune than a daughter of Johnathan Green of the Parish of Dudley Glass Maker and upon his marriage with any other woman other than a Daughter of the said Johnathan Green I give and devise unto the said Joseph Ffreeman . . . all my said mansion house Buildings Gardens and lands.'

Johnathan Green was running Dixon's Green Glassworks, but thirteen years earlier, in 1770, he had been accused of lunacy. John Keelinge obviously disapproved of an intended match between his son and Johnathan Green's daughter. Immediately after the death of John Keelinge the glassworks was advertised as available to let:

> 'To be let and entered upon immediately, a glass-house in full work, belonging to the late John Keelinge Esq., situate at Holly Hall within a mile of Dudley, with all convenient out-houses and several houses for workmen. And to be sold all the stock in trade belonging to the said glass-house. Enquire of Joseph Nicklin, at Holly-Hall, who will shew the premises.'[7]

No suitable tenant was found, so the executors allowed the firm to operate as before, still trading as John Keelinge. The following year the firm of John Keelinge manufactured a style of decanter known as a 'Prussian Decanter', barrel-shaped in silhouette[8]. The same year, Holly Hall Glassworks advertised 'Barrel and Prussian-shaped decanters cut and plain.' This is a relatively late reference to the style; from 1770 onwards the shape of decanters had been evolving into the barrel shape. As early as 1775, Christopher Haedy, a cutter and dealer, advertised 'curious barrel-shaped decanters cut on an entire new pattern.'[9] The pattern associated with this shape is one of broad flutes on the neck or round the base or sometimes fluted from top to bottom and broken by thin horizontal cuts. The term 'Prussian' decanter properly describes the later and broader decanters with neck-rings that came to be typical of the Irish factories.

As no tenant had been found after the advertisement of 1783, the executors decided to auction the business:

> 'To be sold by auction, the whole of the very valuable manufactured stock of glass-ware, late belonging to John Keelinge Esq. deceased, at his glasshouse at Holly-Hall consisting of above 140 doz. decanters, barrel and Prussian shaped, cut and plain; 80 doz. goblets, sorted sizes, square and round feet, cut and plain; 800 doz. wines, cut and plain; 1100 doz. pint, half-pint, and quarter-pint Weight and Tale tumblers; 640 doz. punch glasses and tumblers; 40 doz. cut and plain ale glasses; 41 doz. rummers, cyders and carofts; 116 doz. castors and cruets, cut and plain; 262 doz. salts and salt

> linings, cut and plain; 154 doz. sorted smelling bottles; 206 gross white and green phials, sorted sizes; 43 gross Lavender's, Daffy's, Turlington's and Smith's Bottles; 216 doz. bird fountains and boxes; 52 street lamps. Together with a large quantity of salvers, butter-boats, trifle dishes, scollop-shells, mustards, patty-pans, candlesticks, compleat apparatus, blue basons, cream jugs and many other articles . . . Also the furnaces, moulds, machines, and all other the utensils and interiors of the said glasshouse and mill; together with a large quantity of cullet, about 140 pounds of borax, about 3 cwt. of American pearl-ashes, salt-petre, arsenic, emery, antimony, pumice stone, &c., &c.'[10]

Most of the articles are recognisable today, those that might not be so obvious are the forty-three gross of patent medicine bottles, including the famous Daffy's.

The outline of a cone is distinctly shown in a cluster of buildings including the New Inn[11] on Snape's 1785 canal map, but the works were idle at this time. Then along came a glassmaker in need of new premises. George Ensell's Coalbournbrook works had collapsed in 1785 and he took over Holly Hall works in 1786.

George Ensell became involved with the entrepreneurs of Dudley[12], but less than six months after taking on Holly Hall Glassworks he was bankrupt[13]. It is possible he was still suffering the financial consequences of the collapse of his Coalbournbrook glassworks in 1785. The glassworks was again advertised as available to let:

> 'To be let and entered upon immediately a glass-house, situate at Holly-Hall in the Parish of Dudley, together with all necessary buildings for carrying on the flint glass trade. The manufactory is now in full work by the assignee under a commission of bankruptcy against George Encell [sic].'[14]

Sometime between 1787 and 1803 the glassworks was let to Zachariah Parkes[15]. Zachariah and his brothers were typical of the Dudley entrepreneurs of the day. They were nonconformists, involved in ironfounding and coalmining, with a record of public service and altruism, the sons of Joseph Parkes, originally of Hunts

Hill, Gornal. Zachariah Parkes became Mayor of Dudley in 1796. In 1800 he donated £10 10s and James Grainger donated 5s 'to relieve the distress of the poor.'[16]

James Grainger had joined Zachariah Parkes as a partner in the glassworks and they were later joined by Parkes' brother-in-law, John Roughton[17]. The descent and significance of James Grainger and John Roughton are unclear. As both surnames could have spelling variants, a further investigation of euphonious names might prove fruitful.

On 17th January 1803, a meeting took place at the Stewponey Inn, Stourton to petition the Government to have the duty on flint glass based on manufactured goods instead of metal or raw materials. Zachariah Parkes of Roughton, Parkes & Co. contributed £50 to the fund. The amount contributed implies it was one of the smaller firms.

Zachary Parkes, iron founder & auger manufacturer, is listed in Holden's Triennial Directory for 1805, 1806 & 1807. However, there is no entry for him as a glass manufacturer, suggesting that production had temporarily ceased[18].

Holly Hall is shown on Sherriff's 1812 plan, but not labelled as a glassworks. The partnership was certainly still in existence. John Roughton's first wife, Hannah, died in 1810[19] and he married again to Mary Arnott in 1813[20]. Their marriage was by a licence[21], in which John Roughton is described as a glass manufacturer of Holly Hall.

Zachariah Parkes died two months later[22], aged sixty-four and the partnership was dissolved[23]. John Roughton moved to the Phoenix Glassworks in Dudley. A new partnership at Holly Hall was formed involving James Grainger, other members of the Parkes family and George Joseph Green[24]. George Joseph Green was certainly involved by 1815, when he baptised his first child that year he was described as a glass manufacturer of Holly Hall[25].

George Joseph Green was still a glass manufacturer of Holly Hall in March 1817, as this was how he described himself when he baptised his second child[26]. However, the partnership of Parkes, Grainger and Green was dissolved later that year:

'The partnership carried on by Zepheniah Parkes, Major Parkes, James Grainger and George Joseph Green of Holly-Hall in the Parish of Dudley, glass manufacturers, under the firm of 'Parkes, Grainger and Green' was dissolved the 19th July, 1817, so far as relates to the said G. J. Green.'[27]

George Joseph Green left Dudley to set up the Union Glassworks in Birmingham for the family firm of Bacchus and Green. He moved from Dudley, initially to Hockley in Birmingham, and later, when profits permitted to Edgbaston. Most of his sons worked in the glass trade. When the employers' organisation was renamed as The Midland Association of Flint Glass Manufacturers[28], his oldest son George Joseph Green was appointed secretary, with a salary of £120 per year.

The reconstituted firm at Holly Hall had a constantly changing set of partners. It traded in 1818 as Major Parkes and Co.[29] and as Zepheniah Parkes and Co, in 1820[30]. Then, in 1821 the partnership of Major Parkes & Co. was dissolved[31].

Major Parkes set up a new firm trading as Maj. Parkes, cut glass manufacturer[32]. Like its predecessors, this business did not survive for very long. Sometime between 1825 and 1828 Parkes had a dispute with his men and production stopped[33].

In 1828 the glassworks was bought by Joseph Stevens, who was in partnership at Moor Lane Glassworks. The new firm appears as Joseph Stevens, Holly Hall, glass manufacturers, in a succession of trade directories[34]. Joseph Stevens & Co. paid £2,938 14s 3d excise duty for the year ending 5th January 1833[35], suggesting this was the eighth largest of the sixteen Stourbridge/Dudley glasshouses of the day; larger than the Moor Lane business Joseph Stevens left five years earlier. The glassworks is clearly marked on the 1834 Ordnance Survey[36].

In 1835 Joseph Stevens advertised that his product range now included coloured glass. This is an early reference to the availability of coloured products, even the Richardsons[37] who became famous for their use of colour, were not advertising coloured products until 1839. Trade directory entries show that Joseph Stevens included among his products: ruby, achromatic, and coloured glass[38].

His trade grew, and it was probably increased sales that led him to require larger premises. In 1837 he left Holly Hall and moved his business to Coalbournhill Glassworks.

Edward Page[39] then leased the glassworks. It appears that some time after Richard Bradley Ensell failed at the Red House glassworks in 1834 he had formed a partnership with Edward Page trading as Page and Ensell[40]. A draft lease was drawn up for fourteen years at £120 per year between the executors of the late Earl of Dudley and co-partners and glass manufacturers Edward Page and Richard Bradley Ensell. It contains a plan view of the premises and a schedule of a nine-pot furnace with nine arches, lear and kiln, two pot arches, calcining calker and glory hole. However this lease was never signed and all references to Richard Bradley Ensell were replaced with Thomas Somerville of Hockham, Rowley Regis[41]. The lease was guaranteed by a bond for £340 from Thomas Somerville's father-in-law[42], Alexander Brodie Cochrane[43], ironmaster of Blowers Green, Dudley and William Page, machine keeper of Harts Hill. Edward Page and Thomas Somerville began to make flint glass at Holly Hall trading as Page & Somerville[44].

Rather confusingly, Pigot's directory also lists 'James Stevens (ruby, achromatic and coloured), Holly Hall.' However, this was not James Stevens senior who left Holly Hall and moved to Coalbournhill in 1837. It refers to James Stevens junior, the son of Joseph Stevens, who had been in partnership with his father and two brothers at Coalbournhill. In 1841 James Stevens and his family lived at Harts Hill, close to Holly Hall[45]. Having left the family firm at Coalbournhill, he either worked for Edward Page or sublet his own facilities within Holly Hall glassworks. In 1844 James Stevens was asked to rejoin his father in the family firm at Coalbournhill Glassworks. Joseph Stevens senior always wanted the support of his family as partners. After the death of his son-in-law, Benjamin Coltman, he asked his son James to rejoin him in partnership, which he did.

Edward Page carried on the business until at least 1850[46], probably closing it in 1852. On 25th April 1850 he entered into an agreement with F. & C. Osler of Birmingham to build a new flint glassworks on the branch of the old Birmingham Canal in Freeth Street, Rotton Park, Birmingham$_{47}$. This new glassworks went into production in late 1851 or early 1852 which is when Page probably left Holly Hall. He had certainly moved to a new house in Icknield Street West, Birmingham by March 1851$_{48}$.

The buildings were demolished sometime between 1870 and 1886 and the land was redeveloped for housing. The site of the glassworks in now enclosed by the modern Bushey Fields Road, Abbottsford Drive and Kingswinford Road.

---

1 Birmingham Gazette, 11th Mar 1754. Thomas Griffin's trade is not stated.

2 John Keelinge, son of Richard Keelinge of Summerhill, Kingswinford and his wife Patience, daughter of John Hodgetts of Shut End, bap. 18th Jul 1713, Kingswinford.

3 Sketchley and Adam's 1770 Universal Directory of Birmingham, Wolverhampton, Walsall and Dudley.

4 Sheep Lane ran from Hampton Lane to Horse Pool Green and is now known as Priory Street.

5 PRO, PROB 11/1110 RH185-RH188, PCC Will of John Keelinge, 25th Nov 1783.

6 John Keelinge married his cousin Ann, widow of Randolph Stevens and daughter of Revd. Thomas Hodgetts, Rector of Kingswinford. 18th Dec 1744 at Kimberton. She died childless and was buried at Kingswinford 23rd May 1766, aged 57. Joseph Freeman of Pedmore Hall was one of three children born subsequently to John Keelinge and his housekeeper Mary Dovey. She was baptised 7th Jan 1733 at Oldswinford, daughter of Henry and Rachel Dovey. It has not been possible to prove if John Keelinge and Mary Dovey ever married.

7 Birmingham Gazette, 1st Dec 1783.

8 BM, Trade card of 1784.

9 Bath Chronicle, 21st Dec 1775.

10 Birmingham Gazette, 19th Apr 1784.

11 The New Inn was a large old house, reputably the resting place of John 'Tinker' Fox's Parliamentary troopers on their retreat from the siege of Stourton Castle.

12 Infra, Dudley Flint Glassworks, 1786.

13 'Bankrupt, George Encell [sic], of the parish of Dudley, Glassmaker.' London Gazette, 10th Jun 1786. This was also reported somewhat belatedly in Gentleman's Magazine of Sep 1787, p842. 'Bankrupts; G. Enfell Dudley Worcs Glassmaker.'

14 Birmingham Gazette, 3rd Jul 1786.

15 Zachariah Parkes, son of Joseph Parkes and his wife Ann, nee Taylor, bap. 26th Jun 1751, Dudley Old Meeting House.

16 Birmingham Gazette, 19th May 1800.

17 John Roughton (1765-1837) had married Hannah Parkes. The marriage record has not been found, but the Parkes family were nonconformists, which could explain why.

18 This was a time of great commercial difficulty for Great Britain. In 1805 Nelson defeated the French and Spanish fleets off Cape Trafalgar, completely destroying the naval power of France. Napoleon then attempted to force a commercial embargo on Britain. In 1806 he issued the Berlin Decree, which declared that he would go to war with any country that traded with Britain. The British retaliated with Orders in Council, which decreed that no neutral power should trade with France or her allies.

19 Hannah Roughton, d. 11th Jun 1810; bur. Kingswinford.

20 Mar. John Roughton and Mary Arnott, 18th Jan 1813, Oldswinford.

21 WRO.

22 Zachariah Parkes, bur. 16th Mar 1813, Kingswinford.

23 London Gazette, 31st Aug 1813. 'The partnership lately subsisting between John Roughton, Zachariah Parkes the elder and James Grainger, glass manufacturers at Holly-Hall near Dudley, under the firm of 'Roughton, Parkes & Co.' was dissolved the 28th August 1813. J. Roughton to collect debts &c.'

24 George Joseph Green, son of James Green and his wife Martha, bap. 13th Jan, St. Mary Queenhithe, London. James Green was the brother of John and Joseph Green of Dixon's Green Glassworks. James probably ran the London operation of Green & Co. where the firm had premises in Upper Thames Street as early as 1776. The Greens formed a partnership, to trade as Bacchus and Green, with George Bacchus (1776-1840) about 1812 after the retirement of Bacchus' previous partner and father-in-law John Ogden (1746-1818).

25 George Joseph Green, son of George Joseph Green and his first wife Mary Ann, b. 3rd Jun 1815; bap. 30th Jun 1815, Dudley St. Thomas's.

26 Mary Ann Green, daughter of George Joseph Green and his first wife Mary Ann, bap. 16th Mar 1817, Dudley St. Thomas's.
27 London Gazette, 9th Aug 1817.
28 Meeting held in Dudley 15th Nov 1858.
29 James Pigot's 1818 Commercial Directory.
30 Lewis's 1820 Worcestershire General and Commercial Directory.
31 London Gazette, 14th Aug 1821. 'The partnership between Zepheniah Parkes, Major Parkes and James Grainger, as glass manufacturers at Holly Hall, Dudley, under the firm of 'Major Parkes & Co.' was dissolved the 1st Mar 1821.'
32 Wrightson's Triennial Directory of Birmingham, 1823 and 1825 editions.
33 Benjamin Richardson's notebook of 1886.
34 Pigot and Co.'s National Commercial Directory for 1828-9; Pigot and Co.'s Commercial Directory of Birmingham, 1829 and 1830 editions.
35 Thirteenth Report of the Commission into the Glass Excise, 1835, Appendix 7.
36 1834 Ordnance Survey, sheet 62, scale one inch to one mile,
37 Infra, Wordsley Flint Glassworks.
38 Pigot and Co.'s 1835 National Commercial Directory; Pigot & Co.'s 1836 National Directory.
39 Edward Page, son of John Page and his wife Mary, nee Smallman, bap. 30th Jul 1797, Brierley Hill.
40 Bentley's 1840 Directory of Worcestershire and Bentley's 1841 guide to Dudley.
41 DA, Earl of Dudley's Records, The trustees of the late Earl of Dudley to Messrs Page and Somerville. Lease of a glasshouse and messuages at Holly Hall, 25th Mar 1840.
42 Mar. Thomas Somerville and Mary Maria, oldest child of Alexander Brodie Cochrane I and his wife Mary, 23rd Dec 1830, Dudley St. Thomas's.
43 Alexander Brodie Cochrane I, son of Thomas Cochrane and his wife Lilias, nee Brodie, b. c 1786 Eddlestone, Peebleshire; d. 8th Dec 1853, Netherton, Dudley.
44 Pigot and Co.'s 1841 Directory of Birmingham.
45 PRO, 1841 Census of Dudley.
46 Kelly's Directory, 1845 and 1850 editions.
47 Smith, John P., *Osler's Crystal for Royalty and Rajahs* (1991), pp25-6.
48 PRO HO/107/2051 Fol. 307 P1, 1851 census of Birmingham.

CHAPTER 30

Dudley Flint Glassworks, Dudley

Dudley Flint Glass Works was built on Horse Pool Green on the corner of Stone Street and Priory Street, Dudley and for many years was synonymous with the Hawkes family. The works developed a well-deserved reputation for enamelled ornamental ware and coloured glass of a very high quality. Several craftsmen who developed their skills at the Dudley works later left and took those skills to Wordsley, contributing in no small part to the reputation of Stourbridge as a glassmaking centre. It is easily overlooked that their heritage was in Dudley.

Abiathar Hawkes[1] established the works. A trade directory dates this to 1766, but as he was only seventeen years old at the time, this is unlikely. He probably learned his trade at John Keelinge's glassworks at Holly Hall.

Hawkes' first recorded location is not at the Dudley Flint Glassworks location, but in High Street. This is where Abiathar Hawkes probably commenced business on his own account. In 1770 Geast [sic], Hawkes and Seagar were trading as glassmakers etc. in High Street, Dudley[2]. The Seager referred to here was probably Thomas Seager[3]. Abraham [sic] Hawkes, Glassmaker, High Street, Dudley is listed in trade directories of 1780 and 1781[4].

In 1774 Abiathar Hawkes married Mary Wright[5]. The marriage was by a licence[6], in which Abiathar Hawkes is described as a Gentleman of Dudley; Mary Wright was of the parish of St. Mary in Stafford. About this time Abiathar Hawkes became involved in promoting the proposed Dudley Canal. Hoping to benefit from the improved communication it was expected to provide, he became treasurer of the Dudley Company and a proprietor of the Stourbridge Company. On 18th February 1778 he bought five shares in the new Dudley Canal Navigation from Henry Seager, a chapman of Birmingham, for £400[7]. Three months later, on 22nd May 1778, he sold two of the shares to Frances Ward, Lady Viscountess Dudley and Ward for £260[8]. Assuming he bought and sold at the fair market price, they had risen in value from £80 to £130 each in three months.

The first record of the Dudley Flint Glassworks at Stone Street is also connected with the canal building scheme. The outline of the cone is shown, but not named, on Snape's canal map of 1785. This suggests Hawkes left his High Street premises and built his new cone some time between 1781 and 1785. Dudley's Poor Rate Assessment of 1787[9] proves this to be the established location. It states that Abiathar Hawkes was the owner and occupier of 'ye glasshouse' in Stoney Lane[10]. He had a house and offices in High Street, which was probably the site of his earlier business. He also owned property in other parts of Dudley, including Back Lane[11] and Wolverhampton Street. In 1788 he had a new ten-pot furnace built for him at the end of Priory Street by the local Wordsley furnace-builder, Joseph Richardson[12].

Abiathar Hawkes was probably among the 'respectable Gentlemen and Professional men in the neighbourhood' educated by Benjamin Clements at Dudley Grammar School[13]. These respectable gentlemen and professional men were the driving force behind industry and social development in Dudley. On 13th April 1786 one of the earliest building societies in England was formed to establish an hotel—The Dudley Arms—in High Street, Dudley, with a new market place at the rear[14]. The initial list of subscribers included many of the leading gentry and tradesmen of Dudley. Among them were: Abiathar Hawkes, George Ensell of Holly Hall Glassworks and William Penn of Phoenix Glassworks[15].

In 1794 a price list was issued, *Prices of Flint Glass by Tho. and Geo Hawkes, At their Manufactory, Dudley, Worcestershire 1794*. This suggests that Abiathar's two oldest sons[16], Thomas[17] and George Wright Hawkes[18] now managed the firm. The price list shows an incredible range of goods, some sold per each and some sold by weight. Apart from the expected beers, wines, tumblers and vials, there were some more interesting products: Antigulars, Bosom Bottles, Cupping Glasses, Scurvy-glass bottles and Urinals. Altogether two hundred and seven different products were advertised[19]. A list of glassworks dated 1796 shows Hawkes & Co. operating two glasshouses, with twenty pots[20].

Abiathar Hawkes died, after a long illness, in 1800[21], aged fifty. His memorial exists today on the south wall of the chancel in St. Edmund's church in Dudley. He made a lengthy will[22] on 9th January that year and added a codicil on 11th January, six days before his death. In the will he refers to 'my Glass Trade' and 'my Glass Houses.' His two oldest sons, Thomas and George Wright Hawkes took control of the business. The sons set about the modernisation of the glassworks and in 1801 Joseph Richardson was employed again to build a new eleven-pot furnace in a large cone in Stone Street[23].

On 17th January 1803, a meeting took place at the Stewponey Inn, Stourton to petition the Government to have the duty on flint glass based on manufactured goods instead of metal or raw materials. Thomas Hawkes and George Hawkes of Thomas & George Hawkes contributed £100 to the fund. The amount contributed implies it was one of the larger firms.

William Haden Richardson[24] joined the firm in 1810, aged twenty-five, and subsequently became the firm's traveller. His own notebook dated 1819[25] states that he began his glassmaking career in Bilston in 1802[26], then moved on to Grafton's Brierley Glasshouse, then to Hawkes', where he worked from 1810 to 1828. His younger brother Benjamin[27] joined the firm later and rose to become the Works Manager, a position he held for many years. The Richardson brothers were the oldest sons of Joseph Richardson, the Wordsley furnace-builder who built the new furnace for the Hawkes brothers in 1801. It is quite possible that Joseph Richardson recommended his sons to them.

About this time, a large quantity of the Hawkes brothers' output was being shipped to Russia. Their sister Sarah[28] married John Michael Molyneaux[29], a merchant who arranged the sale of their goods in Russia and other places[30].

Thomas Hawkes was an ambitious man, the dominant partner

in the business. He became the High Sheriff of Worcestershire in 1811[31] and in 1814 he secured a good match for himself by marrying[32] Alice Anna Blackburne[33]. Their marriage was by a licence[34] in which Thomas Hawkes is described as Esquire of the parish of Himley. His bride was the daughter and heir of John Blackburne, of Blackburne House, Liverpool[35] and Hawford Lodge, Worcestershire[36] who was Mayor of Liverpool in 1788.

The firm's products secured a wide export market, with a good trade to America, as well as Russia. Two price lists for *Flint Glass for Exportation* were issued, dated 12th April 1815. Both lists mention Slater & Co. as the firm's Philadelphia agents:

> One list was for druggists' furniture: Phials, measures, salt and smelling bottles, cupping glasses, funnels, rounds and stoppers etc. The Flint Glass list included: 'cans, lemonade, common or double flint; cruets, custard cups, finger cups, white, blue, green or purple; water bottles, hock glasses; mustards; muffineers; pattypans; root glasses; syllabubs; salts; sweetmeat shells'; and dessert and table services 'from 40 to 500 guineas and upwards.'[37]

When St. Thomas's church in Dudley was rebuilt in 1816 Thomas Hawkes was one of the most generous benefactors who donated £150[38]. Thomas Hawkes was not content with just a life of business and put himself forward for public service. Back in 1794 Mr Pitt carried a proposition for a levy of volunteers of Horse and Foot in every county. Their duty was not only to defend the country against foreign enemies, but also to assist in preserving peace at home. On 4th July 1794, a meeting was called by the Lord Lieutenant in Lichfield to consider the establishment of a local force to defend the country in the event of a French invasion, which was considered as inevitable and imminent. Fear of the radical antimonarchist Government of France was sweeping Britain. One of the new forces established was called the Staffordshire Regiment of Gentlemen and Yeomanry. This was a part-time cavalry unit of volunteers that was to evolve into the Queen's Own Royal Regiment, Staffordshire Yeomanry[39]. After Wellington's victory over Napoleon at Waterloo on Sunday 18th June 1815, the euphoria rapidly dissipated and great distress followed the sudden cessation of the protracted wars in Europe. The importation of foreign corn was prohibited. Prices were high and wages low; the miners were on strike. Riots became general, and a law was passed in 1819, to keep the people from rising in revolt. At a mass meeting in Manchester that August, detachments of the 15th Hussars and the Manchester Yeomanry charged the crowd, killing seven and wounding fifty or sixty people. This has been called derisively, the 'Battle of Peterloo.' The possible threat of revolution in England loomed. In the face of this threat, on 29th December 1819 Thomas Hawkes of Himley House, Himley was commissioned as Captain and raised the Himley and Enville Troop of the Staffordshire Yeomanry. Revolution never occurred, but the Himley and Enville Troop still saw action. At a time when the country was largely without a police force, the authorities began to call upon the Yeomanry as mounted riot police to maintain law and order.

The business continued to trade as Thomas Hawkes & Co.[40] and about 1821 Roger Wright Hawkes[41], the next oldest of the Hawkes brothers, joined the firm. He had been practising as a solicitor[42] and was the beneficiary of his uncle, Doctor Wright of Wolverhampton. When Doctor Wright died, he left £40,000 to Roger Wright Hawkes, much of which he invested in the business[43].

Political unrest broke out again in Dudley over the Queen Caroline affair in 1820. This concerned the attempts of the Prince of Wales, the future King George IV[44], to divorce his wife Caroline[45] and thus deprive her of her rights as Queen. This sordid affair revealed to the public that Caroline was a loose-living woman. However, the morals of the Prince Regent had been so notorious that Caroline received an enormous amount of sympathy and support that tended to crystallise along the political lines of reform versus constitutionalism. Eventually, a *Bill of Pains and Penalties* against Caroline had to be dropped and this led to a tremendous outburst of enthusiasm in the Black Country, as in the country at large. As soon as George III[46] died on 29th January 1820, Caroline returned to England to claim her position as Queen. The day of 19th July 1820 was to have been their coronation day. Loyal citizens assembled at the Dudley Arms to celebrate the King's coronation with a dinner. Opponents paraded the street opposite shouting 'the Queen, the Queen for ever!' The Himley and Enville troop of Yeomanry, who were present after carousing all day at Wolverhampton began to fight among themselves and this quickly deteriorated into a general affray. The windows of the room at the Dudley Arms where the diners sat were assailed, until scarcely a pane of glass was left. Thomas Hawkes was forced to read the Riot Act but was assailed with brickbats and was in imminent danger of his life. Tension was defused by the inspiration of commencing the planned firework display immediately[47].

George Wright Hawkes died in 1821[48], aged forty-one. His memorial exists today, next to his father's, on the south wall of the chancel of St. Edmund's church in Dudley. The following year the partnership was dissolved:

>'The partnership between Thomas Hawkes, Roger Wright Hawkes, and the executors of the late George Wright Hawkes, deceased, as glass manufacturers at Dudley, under the firm of 'Thomas Hawkes & Co.' was as regards the executors of the said G.W. Hawkes dissolved on the 1st July 1822.'[49]

A new firm was formed to trade as Thomas & R.W. Hawkes. It advertised its wares as cut glass and lustres[50]. This is an early reference to lustres and the fact they were mentioned presumably means they were among the firm's specialities.

On 5th July 1825 T. & R.W. Hawkes issued a letter accompanying their latest price list. Their frustration with the effects of the glass excise was apparent:

>'We beg leave to enclose you a new List of Glass Prices, which would have been issued before this, but that Government had it in contemplation to alter the manner of collecting the duty on glass, and we considered it advisable to wait till that alteration was decided on, before we sent out our new list . . . The new system of charging the duty operates greatly against the manufacturer . . .'[51]

Himley troopers were called out on 27th February 1826 to West

Bromwich and Wednesbury, where colliers from Dudley and Tipton were causing a disturbance. The troop was subjected to heavy stoning and several Yeomen were hurt including Thomas Hawkes who was injured in the face. The rioters were ultimately dispersed[52].

By 1827 Thomas Hawkes was so frustrated with the excise duty on glass he decided to quit the firm and handed it to two of his younger brothers[53]. Roger Wright Hawkes was joined by his younger brother, Abiathar Hawkes II[54], who had been Mayor of Dudley in 1824. The firm then traded as Roger Wright and Abiathar Hawkes[55], but after only a year they came to the same conclusion as their older brother. The excise duty made the business almost pointless so they retired, leaving Thomas Hawkes to take control again. Business activity had declined from a peak of prosperity in 1825 to the depths of depression in 1829-30. It did not recover until 1834.

> 'The partnership between Roger Wright Hawkes and Abiathar Hawkes, as glass manufacturers, under the firm of 'Roger Wright and Abiathar Hawkes' is this day dissolved by mutual consent. 24th December 1828.'[56]

Once again the firm traded as Thomas Hawkes, Stone Street, glass manufacturers[57]. In 1829 Thomas Hawkes was portrayed in a painting titled *The Smoke Room of the Dudley Arms Hotel* by W. Pringle[58]. This shows him in the company of his Tory allies, including the Badger brothers of Phoenix Glassworks.

During the eighteen-thirties William Herbert and the rest of his family became noted for their wheel-engraving, often on ruby-stained crystal at the firm of Thomas Hawkes. William Herbert[59] married Rebecca Petters Shaw[60] and in 1841 they lived with their three daughters, in High Street, Dudley, when he was described as a glass engraver[61]. He and his brother, John, were reputably good artists, and are accredited with being pioneers in the art of glass engraving. When trade in the glass industry became bad John became a beerseller. William continued to work at the Hawkes factory until its closure, after which he moved to Bristol[62]. A nostalgic article in the Pottery Gazette of January 1882 states:

> 'as early as 1830 etching on glass was rendered commercially

useful by Thos. Hawkes and Co. of Dudley, where gold enamelled plates were made and ornamented by the etched process by a Mr. Wainwright and others. In 1835 the firm produced a plateau presented to the Hon. Spring Rice, afterwards Lord Monteagle. This was engraved by William Herbert, and etched by the same artist.'

In anticipation that the town of Dudley was to have a representative in Parliament under the Reform Bill, efforts were made by both political parties to secure a preponderance of power and influence. A petition was submitted to J.C. Brettell, the Mayor of Dudley on 7th February 1831. Among seventy-four signatories were: Abiathar Hawkes, Thomas, Isaac, and Septimus Badger of Phoenix Glassworks, and Joseph and Edward Guest of Castle Foot Glassworks:

> 'We, the undersigned, request you will convene an early meeting of the principal inhabitants of this town for the purpose of petitioning for a Moderate Reform in Parliament, and at the same time praying that any reform that may be adopted may not include Vote by Ballot, Universal Suffrage or Annual Parliaments. Also to petition that our ancient privilege of returning two members to Parliament may be restored to us.'[63]

Thomas Hawkes paid £5,593 1s 6d excise duty for the year ending 5th January 1833[64], suggesting this was the second largest of the sixteen Stourbridge/Dudley glass firms of the day. However, in 1834 Benjamin Richardson of Wordsley Flint Glassworks wrote in a letter to his brother that rumours in the trade were that business was so bad, 'Hawkes' was very likely to close'[65]. The Black Country economy had been in recession since about 1827, but 1834 was the year that recovery began.

Thomas Hawkes had earned great credit among the Dudley glassmakers in the days of poor trade as their spokesman to the Commission on Glass Excise. Through their influence, and that of his other political allies, he was selected by the Dudley Tories to contest the Dudley parliamentary seat. He won it on 27th February 1834 by a majority of sixty-eight votes and became Dudley's second member of parliament, the first being a Whig, Sir John Campbell, Bart. who had been elected in 1832, after the Reform Act. This was a great personal victory for Hawkes as he and Campbell had both contested the borough of Stafford in 1830 and 1831. Whereas Campbell won on both occasions in a three candidate contest, Hawkes had finished last.

The Reform Bill was passed, after much rioting, especially in Birmingham, and disqualified fifty-six small boroughs from returning members to Parliament, and left thirty others with only one member each. These seats were then transferred to more populous towns like Manchester and counties like Yorkshire. By this Act, Dudley gained its first member of parliament of modern times. The Act gave the franchise to a £10 householder in boroughs, and extended the county franchise to copyholders, leaseholders, and tenant occupiers of premises of a certain rental value. In the 1832 election, Thomas Hawkes' brother Abiathar II had been a candidate, but retired from the field.

In the 1834 by-election when Sir John Campbell lost the Dudley seat to Thomas Hawkes serious disturbances took place. It was 'one of the most riotous elections ever known in England.'[66] Campbell had fallen out of favour with the Radicals who previously supported him, but by then he had become Attorney General and any reforming tendencies he may once have possessed had long since disappeared. It was Campbell's elevation to chief law officer of the Crown that caused the by-election[67]. The election of Thomas Hawkes, a well-known Tory, came as something of a shock, but by dedication to the people of Dudley, he gained favour that helped him defend many subsequent contests against a variety of Radical and Chartist contestants. Thomas Hawkes held the seat for a further ten years with increasing majorities. Ben Boucher, the Dudley poet[68], penned a satirical verse on the occasion of Campbell's defeat:

> Hawkes to Cape__ll gave a note,
> And for five pounds bought his vote;
> He therefore thus did change his coat
> And to the Tories gave his vote.

Hawkes had now secured the position of influence he so long desired. His glassworks is clearly shown on Treasure's plan of 1835. The firm also had premises at 13 Pancras Lane, Queen Street, London[69]. However, the glass excise remained a constant impediment to the glassmaking industry. In 1835 Thomas Hawkes MP gave evidence to the Commission of Enquiry into the Glass Excise:

> 'I was out of business for a short time, for three years; I gave it over to my brothers, and they were so disgusted with it that they retired. I renewed the business with the hope that some alteration would take place, and I carry it on for one of my younger sons, to whom I thought I was doing an act of justice.'

Thomas Hawkes and Thomas Badger of Phoenix Glassworks submitted a memorial [deposition] to the Chancellor of the Exchequer, Sir Robert Peel. It stated that the legal, licensed trade of glass manufacture was doomed to extinction in the face of the competition from illegal, unlicensed manufacturers. The commissioners accepted this view:

> 'this concurrence of evidence would certainly lead to the conclusion that if things are permitted to remain much longer in their present state, the business in question must at no distant period be universally abandoned by the established and legal manufacturers . . . '[70]

Despite the burden of excise duty the firm continued in business and in 1836 was praised for its 'Gold-enamel' wares, acid-etched[71]. About this time Thomas Hawkes brought two new employees into the firm who—like the Richardsons before them—were later to have a great influence on the trade in Wordsley. First to join was William Greathead[72], who had worked for William Gammon & Co., glassmakers of Aston, near Birmingham. His father, Francis Greathead, was an Excise Officer originally from Yorkshire. William was born in Louth, Lincolnshire while his father was posted there. The family moved many times until Francis was posted to Dudley in 1816. From there his subsequent postings were to Stourbridge, Birmingham and Bewdley[73]. William married a Midlands' girl, Anna Maria Green[74] in 1827[75]. Then in 1837 he introduced his wife's younger brother, Richard Green[76], to the firm at the age of fifteen. In 1840 Green was promoted to the position of traveller[77].

A meeting took place on 5th December 1837 at the Dudley Arms Hotel where the manufacturers considered their response to the formation of the first glassmakers' trade union. Thomas Hawkes MP attended as chairman and Messrs. Greathead and Green were also present. The resolution passed at their meeting has already been described[78].

In 1838 a square glasshouse was added next to the large cone in Stone Street, described in 1801 as having eleven pots. By this time the old cone at the end of Priory Street was 'down and nearly forgotten.'[79] The firm now traded as Thomas Hawkes & Co., flint glass manufacturers of Stone Street[80]. An article in Bentley's directory states:

> 'their articles in opal turquoy, and gold enamel, being universal allowed to stand unrivalled. The last mentioned inimitable article was first brought to perfection here in 1834, and this is still the only house who succeed in bringing it to perfection. The splendid gold enamel desert service, furnished to the Corporation of London on her Majesty's first visit to the Guildhall on the 9th November, 1837, was manufactured here.'

By 1841 William Greathead was a partner in the business, now trading as Hawkes & Greathead[81]. He lived in Priory Street, Dudley with his wife Anna Maria and his widowed mother Eleanor[82].

At the age of sixty-four, Thomas Hawkes MP resigned his commission as Captain of the Himley Troop. He was succeeded by the Hon. Humble Dudley Ward[83], commissioned on 31st January 1843[84]. Later the same year Ward married[85] Thomas Hawkes' third daughter, Eleanor Louisa. They remained married until Ward died, after which she married twice more[86].

Another trade depression, which began in 1838 and reached its depths in 1842, brought about the end of Hawkes' business and the works closed in 1843:

> 'the great distress amongst the glassworkers results from the

termination of Mr Hawkes' works, some of the largest in the Kingdom for flint glass.'[87]

William Greathead was offered a position by Hawkes' friends, the Badger brothers of Phoenix Glassworks. Thomas Hawkes was forced to resign his parliamentary seat the following year. The Daily News of 1st November 1849 carried a damning article on Dudley's parliamentary representation that states:

> 'Mr. Hawkes was an amiable man whose family had made their property in Dudley, and who had himself been engaged in the glass trade of the district. He was a man of some ambition, and had aimed for a long time at high society and a seat in Parliament, without having either the means sufficient for the one, or the ability desirable for the other. However, the Dudley Tories were disposed to gratify him, the more so as he was a man very likely to succeed at an election from his general popularity, and the more so from his residence being next door to Himley Hall (the seat of the Earls of Dudley). Mr. Hawkes probably acquired some additional influence in consequence of the marriage of one of his daughters with the brother and heir presumptive of Lord Ward. The peer himself was for a long time understood to be the lady's suitor, but the younger brother ultimately obtained her hand. Mr Hawkes might have continued, under these circumstances, to represent the town, but unfortunately the pressure of pecuniary embarrassments obliged him, in 1844, to go abroad, with a view to repair his fortunes. He accordingly relinquished his seat.'

Thomas Hawkes' wife, Alice Anna, died in 1853[88]. Her memorial exists today on the south wall of the nave in Himley parish church, the village where the Hawkes family lived for many years. Thomas Hawkes died in 1858[89], aged eighty. His memorial is alongside his wife's in Himley parish church. The Mayor of Dudley, Elliott Hollier, suggested to the townsmen of Dudley:

> 'it may be desirable that some mark of respect should be shewn towards his memory by the PARTIAL CLOSING of their respective Establishments . . .'

This was willingly observed, the Pottery Gazette reported:
> 'When his remains passed through Dudley, the borough he represented, almost every shop was closed, out of respect to his memory; and the late Earl of Dudley met the cortege at the entrance to Himley, and saw the last of an old friend, as the ground closed over him. Nor was he unrepresented by the most humble of his old neighbours, for there was a goodly muster of those who remembered his munificence, as well as his kindness to the humblest villager.'[90]

After standing empty for nearly fifty years, the old glassworks was used by a Mr Rossiter as a hide and skin market. On Monday 14th December 1886 he suffered damage to two carts and a pair of scales when part of the cone collapsed. Dudley Council agreed he should quit possession and compensated him. The glassworks was demolished in July and August 1886. The front walls, by then the only parts remaining, were pulled down with ropes by workmen helped by local tradesmen on Saturday 14th August 1886[91]. The derelict state of the works was a regular topic in the local press and articles still appeared after the demolition, as late as 1888. Obviously still a subject of interest to the inhabitants of Dudley, the 1902 Almanac of Dudley, shows a sketch of how the glassworks used to look, with an article concerning its demise[92]. Again in 1903, the Almanac of Dudley shows a picture of the 'Old Glasshouse, Stone Street, Dudley.'[93]

Today the site of the glassworks is the open, cobbled car parking area opposite the Saracen's Head public house and Dudley Museum and Art Gallery.

---

1 Abiathar Hawkes, son of Thomas Hawkes and his wife Sarah, nee Parkes, bap. 6th Feb 1749, Dudley St. Thomas's.

2 Sketchley and Adam's 1770 Universal Directory of Birmingham, Wolverhampton, Walsall and Dudley.

3 Thomas Seager, son of William Seager and his second wife Mary, nee Dixon, bap. 2nd Jun 1740, Kingswinford. Thomas Seager was a wealthy landowner of Dudley. In 1771 he was the proprietor of the bottleworks in Moor Lane, Brierley Hill. His younger sister Susanna Seager, who married Thomas Wheeley

at Kingswinford, 14th Oct 1784, was running Wheeley's Brettell Lane Glasshouses.

4 Pearson and Rollason's Directory of Birmingham, Wolverhampton, Walsall, Dudley, Bilston and Willenhall, 1780 and 1781 editions.

5 Mar. Abiathar Hawkes and Mary Wright, 27th Oct 1774, St. Mary's, Stafford.

6 LJRO, B/C/6,7.

7 BRL, 335785 DV298.

8 BRL, 335772 DV298.

9 DA.

10 Now called Stone Street.

11 Now called King Street.

12 Stuart Crystal, Joseph Richardson's notebook.

13 Supra, Dixon's Green.

14 Seymour J. Price, *Building Societies Their Origin and History* (1958), pp59-60.

15 Ibid, G. Chandler & I.C. Hannah, p138; J.S. Roper, *Dudley, the Town in the Eighteenth Century* (1968), p16.

16 Abiathar Hawkes resigned as Treasurer of the Dudley Canal Company before 1796 for health reasons.

17 Thomas Hawkes, son of Abiathar Hawkes and his wife Mary, nee Wright, bap. 3rd Jan 1779, Dudley St. Thomas's.

18 George Wright Hawkes, son of Abiathar Hawkes and his wife Mary, nee Wright, b. 15th May 1780; bap. 15th Aug 1780, Dudley St. Thomas's.

19 PG, Mar 1895.

20 D.N. Sandilands.

21 Abiathar Hawkes, d. 17th Jan 1800; bur. 27th Jan 1800, Dudley St. Thomas's.

22 PRO, PROB 11/337 F142RH to F149LH, PCC Will (and codicil) of Abiathar Hawkes, 15th Feb 1800.

23 Stuart Crystal, Joseph Richardson's notebook.

24 William Haden Richardson, son of Joseph Richardson and his wife Martha, nee Haden, bap. 27th Mar 1785, Kingswinford.

25 Stuart Crystal.

26 The Glassborough glasshouse was started at Bilston about 1761. It was carried on by John Florry of Birmingham until 1774 when the premises were sub-let to H. Loxdale & Co. Thomas Loxdale and George Elwell Jackson made flint glass as Loxdale and Jackson from at least 1802, when they installed a new

ten-pot furnace, until their partnership was dissolved 4th Dec 1810. G.T. Lawley, *History of Bilston* (1893) states that a large glasshouse was erected at Bradley (in Bilston) in 1674, which soon became disused and was taken down in 1790. Its location was commemorated for many years by the road Glass-house Row.

27 Benjamin Richardson, son of Joseph Richardson and his wife Martha, nee Haden, b. 9th Mar 1802; bap. 4th Apr 1802, Kingswinford.

28 Sarah Hawkes, daughter of Abiathar Hawkes and his wife Mary, nee Wright, bap. 12th Jun 1777, Dudley St. Thomas's.

29 Mar. John Michael Malonet and Sarah Hawkes, 26th Aug 1806, Dudley St. Thomas's.

30 Benjamin Richardson's notebook of 1886.

31 H.S. Grazebrook, *The Heraldry of Worcestershire* (1873), p690.

32 Mar. Thomas Hawkes and Alice Anna Blackburne, 11th Aug 1814, Claines, Worcestershire.

33 Alice Anna Blackburne, daughter of John Blackburne and his wife Mary, nee Blundell, bap. 14 Sep 1792, Liverpool, St. Peter's.

34 WRO, marriage licence, 10th Aug 1814.

35 Most of Blackburne House remains today in Hope Street, Liverpool. When it was built for John Blackburne in 1790 it was a mansion in open countryside. In 1874 it housed England's first grammar school for girls. After refurbishment in 1991 it now provides a conference and exhibition venue.

36 Hawford Lodge stands today, a handsome three-storey Georgian house in thirty acres at Lock Lane, King's Hawford, on the northern outskirts of the city of Worcester, operating as a private school.

37 Library of the Henry Ford Museum and Greenfield Village, Dearborn, Michigan, op cit Charles R. Hajdamach, *British Glass 1800-1914* (1991), p67.

38 Ibid, C.F.G. Clark, p327.

39 Disbanded in 1967.

40 Lewis's 1820 Worcestershire General and Commercial Directory.

41 Roger Wright Hawkes, son of Abiathar Hawkes and his wife Mary, nee Wright, b. 11th Jan 1782; bap. 5th Jul 1782, Dudley St. Thomas's.

42 Lewis's 1820 Worcestershire General and Commercial Directory.

43 Benjamin Richardson's notebook of 1886.

44 George IV, 1762-1830, regent from 1811, r1820-1830.

45 Caroline of Brunswick-Wolfenbuttell, 1768-1821.

46 George III, 1738-1820, r1760-1820.

47 G.J. Barnsby, *The Dudley Working Class Movement 1750 to 1860* (1967), pp10-11; ibid, C.F.G. Clark, p331-5, although their interpretation of events differ markedly.

48 George Wright Hawkes, d. 18th Jan 1821; bur. Dudley St. Thomas's.

49 London Gazette, 31st Aug 1822.

50 Wrightson's Triennial Directory of Birmingham, 1823 and 1825 editions.

51 DA.

52 MS Memoirs of Serjeant Robert Leigh.

53 London Gazette, 20th Mar 1827. 'The partnership between Thomas Hawkes and Roger Wright Hawkes, as glass manufacturers at Dudley, was dissolved by mutual consent on the 31st Dec 1826.'

54 Abiathar Hawkes, son of Abiathar Hawkes and his wife Mary, nee Wright, b. 13th Jul 1786; bap. 7th Sep 1786, Dudley St. Thomas's.

55 Pigot and Co.'s National Commercial Directory for 1828-9.

56 London Gazette, 6th Mar 1828.

57 Pigot and Co.'s Commercial Directory of Birmingham, 1829 and 1830 editions.

58 Dudley Art Gallery. From left to right it shows Joseph Peyton, Mr Jenkins, Isaac Badger, Lawyer Fellows, Thomas Badger (standing), Major Hawkes, Joseph Haden, Mr Jeavons, Captain Harris and Richard Dudley.

59 William Herbert, son of Samuel and Sarah Herbert, bap. 22nd Sep 1805, Brierley Hill.

60 Mar. William Herbert and Rebecca Petters Shaw, 25th May 1830, Dudley St. Thomas's.

61 PRO, 1841 Census of Dudley.

62 PG, Feb 1896.

63 Ibid, C.F.G. Clark, p26-7.

64 Thirteenth Report of the Commission into the Glass Excise, 1835, Appendix 7.

65 BHGM, Letter of Benjamin Richardson to William Haden Richardson.

66 Following a brawl between rival supporters that turned into widespread fighting and looting, the magistrates read the Riot Act and summoned military assistance from Birmingham. Two troops of the 3rd Dragoon Guards arrived within a couple of hours and soon cleared the streets without seriously injuring anyone.

67 A precedent was followed in the early eighteenth century that on appointment

to an office of profit under the Crown, the sitting MP had to seek the approval of his constituents through a by-election.
68 Ben Boucher, 'The Dudley Poet and rhymist.' b. 1769, Horsley Heath; a collier. Boucher's output of doggerel was prolific and provided much amusement for the local populace. He sold his rhymes at one penny each, but they evidently did not earn him a fortune as he died in Dudley Workhouse in 1851.
69 Pigot and Co.'s 1835 National Commercial Directory of 1835.
70 Thirteenth Report of the Commissioners of Excise Enquiry, 1835, Appendix No 28.
71 PG, 1882.
72 William Greathead, son of Francis and Eleanor Greathead, bap. 17th Aug 1799, St. James's, Louth, Lincolnshire. For genealogy see D.J. Greathead, *A Passage to the Cape of Good Hope* (1997).
73 PRO, CUST. 47/402-597.
74 Anna Maria Green, daughter of Richard and Elizabeth Green, bap. 4th Apr 1803, St. Philip's, Birmingham.
75 Mar. William Greathead and Anna Maria Green, 21st Nov 1827, St. Mary's, Handsworth.
76 Richard Green, son of Richard and Elizabeth Green, bap. 15th Sep 1830, St. Martin's, Birmingham.
77 SRO, D648/38/1.
78 Supra, Audnam Glassworks.
79 PG, Feb 1897.
80 Bentley's 1841 guide to Dudley.
81 Pigot and Co.'s 1841 Directory of Birmingham.
82 PRO, 1841 Census of Dudley.
83 Hon. Humble Dudley Ward, b. 20th Dec 1821, second son of Revd. William Humble Ward, tenth Baron Ward of Birmingham and his wife Amelia, nee Pillars; heir presumptive to the Barony.
84 P.C.C. Webster, *Records of the Queen's Own Royal Regiment, Staffordshire Yeomanry* (1870).
85 Mar. Hon. Humble Dudley Ward and Eleanor Louisa Hawkes, 17th Dec 1843.
86 Eleanor Louisa, nee Hawkes married secondly 13th Apr 1812 John Gerard Leigh, of the Hoo, Luton, Bedfordshire. Leigh died 24th Feb 1875. She then married thirdly Christian Frederic de Falbe, the Danish Ambassador in London. De Falbe died in 1886. Eleanor Louisa died 16th Dec 1899 at Luton Hoo.

87 Parliamentary Reports, Midland Mining Commission, 1853, pXXIV.
88 Alice Anna Hawkes, d. 7th Oct 1853 at Trouville Sur Mer, in France.
89 Thomas Hawkes, d. 3rd Dec 1858 in Brighton; bur. Himley.
90 PG, Jul 1888.
91 Blocksidge's Almanac of Dudley, 1902; The Blackcountryman, v 17, No 2, Spring 1984, p20-26.
92 Blocksidge's 1902 Almanac of Dudley, p35.
93 Blocksidge's 1903 Almanac of Dudley.

CHAPTER 31

Dixon's Green Glassworks, Dudley

Dixon's Green was anciently in the foreign of Dudley and takes its name from the Dixon Family. The Dixon family lived there in a mansion with extensive estates since the time of Henry VII or earlier[1]. Hall Street, which leads direct from Dudley town to Dixon's Green, was formerly known as Hall Lane and colloquially as Old Hall Street. The Dixon family has been prominent in Dudley for at least ten generations since the name appears on the first page of Dudley's Parish Registers, begun in 1540.

Buckley[2] and Wakefield[3] both credit the Dixons with being the pioneers of glassmaking in Dudley and in the case of Buckley, possibly also in Worcester. Oliver Dixon[4], principal steward to Lord Dudley, and his wife Frances, nee Jellian[5] had five (surviving) sons; Oliver, Richard, Gilbert, Hugh and Edward. The oldest, Oliver[6], was expected to inherit the family wealth and live his life as a gentleman—which he did. All four of his brothers became glassmakers—only one of them was successful.

Richard[7] was the successful one. He and his wife Elizabeth raised a family of six children in Oldswinford[8], although one of them was buried at Dudley in 1703 when Richard is described as a glassmaker[9]. Shortly after this he left the area and moved to manage the Bolsterstone Glasshouse in South Yorkshire. Some time before 1710 he moved to Whittington, Derbyshire and started his own glasshouse there[10], which his family ran successfully for four generations[11].

Edward[12] ran the Worcester City Glasshouse[13] until he was declared insolvent in 1729.

285

Gilbert's[14] career was varied. He married[15] in Kinver and worked there as a yeoman, where his first five children were born[16]. He returned to Dudley about 1708 to work as a clothier, where his next two children were born[17]. By 1715 he attempted to set up as a glassmaker in Dudley. In August 1715 the Quarter Sessions adjourned from the Guildhall in Worcester to the Talbot Inn in Stourbridge to hear the complaint of an aggrieved apprentice, Abraham Guest. The justices, John Foley, North Foley[18] and Revd. William Hallifax[19], ordered that 'Abraham Guest, apprentice to Gilbert Dixon of Dudley be at liberty to work with any other master till the said Gilbert Dixon shall exercise his trade as a glass master and imploy his apprentice pursuant to his indentures..'[20] Whether Gilbert succeeded, or even started, as a glassmaker in Dudley is not known, but he moved, presumably with five of his seven children to Norfolk[21]. In 1726 he leased one of three glasshouses in Lynn for three years[22]. In June 1729 he and his oldest son Gillims (named after his grandmother) were both imprisoned in the Fleet, London as insolvent glassmakers, late of Lynn Regis, Norfolk.

Only Hugh[23] remained in Dudley. It is clear that Hugh Dixon was a white glassmaker of Dudley. We have no evidence of where he carried on his business, but it seems probable that it was on his father's estate at Dixons Green. Hugh married Joyce Hodgetts in 1701[24] and two years later he was sufficiently prosperous to build, in Sheep Lane[25], the first known example of a brick-built house in Dudley. It is a well-designed house with channelled quoins of stone, having a heavy stringcourse and cornice, and it still stands today. The initials of Hugh and Joyce Dixon are shown with the date, 1703, in a cartouche on the tympanum.

Hugh Dixon's House, Dudley

In August 1712 Hugh apprenticed William Westwood[26] of Kingswinford for seven years to learn 'white glass making.'[27] However, fifteen months later Hugh was bankrupt[28].

This brief involvement with the Dixons and glassmaking thus comes to an end in Dudley. Only Richard, the oldest of the Dixon glassmakers succeeded at his works at Whittington, Derbyshire. What happened to Hugh, Edward and Gilbert is not known, but they appear not to have returned to Dudley[29]. One dreadful possibility is that all three may have spent the remainder of their lives in prison.

The patriarch, Oliver Dixon[30], gentleman of Dixon's Green, former Mayor of Dudley and principal Steward to Lord Dudley[31] died in 1725[32] and his will was proved 5th May 1726[33]. The witnesses were his wife's nephew, Samuel Shaw$_{34}$, glassmaker John Green and Joseph Green suggesting that a position of trust existed between Oliver Dixon and the Greens.

As the original Tudor house at Dixon's green had decayed the Dixon family left it and removed a short distance into the town of Dudley. The Dixon's Green property was first let—and afterwards sold – to John Green's son, Johnathan$_{35}$. This would be some time after 1746, when Johnathan reached his majority. Johnathan then left Springsmire Glasshouse where he had worked with his father and stepbrother Joseph and erected a glasshouse at Dixon's Green$_{36}$. He built it at the rear of Dixon's Green House and its parkland on what was then the southern extremity of Dudley. It stood in the area known as the Buffery on a long oval green through which was cut the modern Rowley road.

Johnathan Green hit the headlines in bizarre fashion in 1770 when he published notices about his wife in the Birmingham Gazette of 4th June and 2nd July as 'Johnathan Green, white glass maker, near Dudley' signed 'J. Green, Green's Own Green'. His wife Mary$_{37}$, perhaps with others, was trying to have him committed as a lunatic. He responded via his solicitor:

> 'Mr Green, who on the 14th day of this month fell into hands, which in defiance of law and reason, as he enjoys a clear exercise of his understanding and prosecutes his business with industry, have under a pretence of lunacy dragged him into an unknown confinement. Reward Offered (Signed) James Shaw.'$_{38}$

This public airing of his misfortunes and grievances did not prevent his continuance in business$_{39}$. The economic significance of the glassworks is shown by an advertisement placed the following year:

> 'To be sold immediately, A Coal Mine . . . situate near to and convenient for the sale of the coal at Dixon's Green Glass-house, at Dudley.'$_{40}$

While it is impossible to speculate after this passage of time what occurred to cause such a hiatus in Johnathan Green's life, it did not stem from a lack of education. He was probably educated at Dudley Grammar School under the headmastership of Benjamin Clements[41]. Clements later became the headmaster of Wolverhampton Grammar School and subsequently became the first minister of the newly consecrated St. John's church in Wolverhampton[42]. After Clements' death in October 1786, his widow published two volumes of his sermons[43] and the subscription list appended to them lists many prominent Dudley people. Among them are: John Finch of Horsley House[44], the surgeon Joseph Wainwright, Joseph Dixon, Abiathar Hawkes and Johnathan Green—all of whom had probably been Clements' pupils at Dudley Grammar School. Clements 'was an excellent master . . . some of the most respectable Gentlemen and Professional Men in the neighbourhood' being educated there in his time[45].

Green's problems resurfaced in 1783 concerning John Keelinge of Holly Hall Glassworks, who disapproved of an intended match between his son and Johnathan Green's daughter, possibly because of the earlier accusations of lunacy. John Keelinge attempted, and apparently succeeded, to influence events from beyond the grave. When he made his will on 16th October 1783[46], he referred to his 'undutiful son Joseph Ffreman' to whom he left 'the weekly sum of six shillings . . . for the term of his natural life or until he shall marry any other woman of fortune than a daughter of Johnathan Green of the Parish of Dudley Glass Maker and upon his marriage with any other woman other than a Daughter of the said Johnathan Green I give and devise unto the said Joseph Ffreeman . . . all my said mansion house Buildings Gardens and lands.' John Keelinge succeeded in his deathbed wishes as his son Joseph Ffreman eventually married Emette, daughter of Revd. Thomas Pettener, Rector of Duntisborne, Gloucestershire[47].

Johnathan Green did not live long enough to dwell on any possible indignation this may have caused him. He died fourteen months later in 1784. His position in society was obviously still respected, as the burial register records him as 'Mr Johnathan Green'[48]. He made a will on 18th August 1774 describing himself as a white glassmaker of Dudley. When it was proved in 1786[49] he made provision for his five children. He left most of his estate in trust with 'my good friends Joseph Wainwright of Dudley, Surgeon, Edward Dixon[50] of Dudley, his wife Mary and his son-in-law Thomas Richards, Gentleman of Dudley . . . all my messuage dwelling house or tenement, glass House closes pieces or parcels of land or grounds with the appurtenances situate at Dixon's Green in the Parish of Dudley.' This was to be until his son achieved the age of twenty-one. The will also shows that he had been in partnership with Joseph Price, about whom little is known[51].

The business was subsequently carried on[52] by his sons, John[53] and Joseph[54]. John initially lived in the original Dixon's Green House, just behind the glassworks[55]. Joseph built himself a large house opposite the glassworks, which he called Spring Field[56]. John appears to have been the controlling partner and about 1790, certainly by 1793, he demolished the original Tudor Dixon's Green House and adjoining glasshouse and built a new dwelling house and a new glasshouse[57]. John married well[58] and became a leading citizen of Dudley. In 1791 he was one of the four surviving feoffes of Dudley Grammar School.

In 1796 the firm of J. & J. Green operated a glasshouse with nine pots[59]. The trading title of the firm is confirmed by an advertisement of 1801 when J. & J. Green advertised for glass cutters. The wording suggests good workmen were in short supply:

> 'To glass cutters. Wanted several good workmen that can work over-handed. Liberal wages will be given and full employ. J. & J. Green, Dudley.'[60]

John Green died in 1802[61] leaving Joseph running the firm. On 17th January 1803 a meeting took place at the Stewponey Inn, Stourton to petition the Government to have the duty on flint glass based on manufactured goods instead of metal or raw materials. Joseph Green of Joseph Green & Co. contributed £50 to the fund. The amount contributed implies it was one of the smaller firms. In the same year, 1803, their furnace was rebuilt by the local Wordsley furnace-builder, Joseph Richardson.

He put in place a new ten-pot furnace for Joseph Green and Co.[62]

After this, the ownership and proprietorship of Dixon's Green Glassworks passes through a very muddled phase. The firm of Joseph Green & Co., glass Manufacturers, Dixon's Green, is listed in Holden's Triennial Directory for 1805, 1806 & 1807. Two individuals, Lee and Large, then had some involvement with Dixon's Green Glassworks, but exactly when or how is not clear. It seems that they were originally independent glasscutters. William Large[63] was a glasscutter who lived at various times at Woodside, Holly Hall and Digbeth, Dudley. The firm of Lee and Large was one of several suppliers of glass to the silversmiths, M. Fenton & Co. in 1804 and 1805[64].

Sometime before 1806 William Rolinson Hodgetts[65] was joined by William Large in partnership. Large & Hodgetts were suppliers of glass to M. Fenton & Co. from 1806 to 1808[66]. However, it is unclear whether this change in partnership concerned solely the independent firm of glasscutters, or if by this time Large & Hodgetts had become the proprietors of the Dixon's Green glass business.

The works are shown on a map of 1808 with one cone, but a notable lack of outbuildings[67]. Sherriff's plan of 1812 shows the glasshouse graphically, but unfortunately does not name it.

By 1820 the firm traded as Davies and Hodgetts[68]. This suggests that Thomas and William Edward Davies had joined the firm. Thomas Davies was a nail ironmonger and glass manufacturer of White House, Dudley. Nothing is known of the descent of William Edward Davies. The firm traded as Davies and Hodgetts until 1832, having regular trade directory listings during this period. The partnership was dissolved in 1832 and an announcement was made accordingly:

> 'The partnership between Thomas Davies, William Edward Davies and William Hodgetts, carrying on the business of glass manufacturers at Dixon's Green in the parish of Dudley, under the firm of 'Davies and Hodgetts,' was dissolved the 1st June last. All accounts will be settled by the present firm, William Hodgetts and William Edward Davies.'[69]

Thomas Davis & Co. paid £3,460 14d 3d excise duty for the year ending 5th January 1833[70], suggesting the firm was the seventh largest of the sixteen Stourbridge/Dudley glasshouses of the day.

In 1833 a petition was issued, signed by three hundred leading inhabitants of Dudley, complaining about their member of parliament[71]. The list of signatories, headed by Revd. Luke Booker, the Vicar of Dudley[72], included William Edward Davies, William and Samuel Herbert[73], and Edward and Joseph Guest[74]. It supported their local magistrates, some of whom were themselves Dudley glassmakers:

> 'We, the undersigned, Inhabitants of the Town and Parish of Dudley, and its vicinity, having heard with surprise and Indignation of the GROSS and UNMANLY attack made by Sir John Campbell, on the acting Magistrates of this Town and Neighbourhood, in the House of Commons, in the following Words, 'That in this town, Justice is not administered to the satisfaction of the Public, and that the most serious discontent prevails, and that the Magistrates are such, as in their absence he should not like to describe'— Take the earliest opportunity of bearing our voluntary Testimony to the upright, independent, and praiseworthy conduct of the Magistrates acting for this Town and Neighbourhood; and of asserting that they have uniformly conducted themselves to the perfect satisfaction of the Inhabitants and public in general, and we deny that 'serious discontent prevails'—To Gentlemen of high respectability and character who have sacrificed so much valuable time (each of them being extensively engaged in business) we consider ourselves deeply indebted; and we beg to tender to them our most sincere and grateful thanks for their unwearied exertions in the administration of Justice and the preservation of the public peace.'[75]

By 1834 mining subsidence had badly affected the glasshouse. It has been noted that an advertisement referred to 'A Coal Mine . . . situate near to and convenient for the sale of the coal at Dixon's

Green Glass-house.' Obviously mining had encroached too near to, and was no longer at all *convenient* for the glassworks. Because of this, William Rolinson Hodgetts and William Edward Davies abandoned Dixon's Green Glassworks and moved to Wordsley in June 1834 when they took over the lease of the Red House glassworks.

The glasshouse remained standing at Dixon's Green for several years[76]. It probably remained until 1868 when the site was levelled and sold as prime building land.

---

1 Arthur A. Rollason, *The Dixon Family of Dudley, Anciently of Dixon's Green.*

2 Francis Buckley, *The Glasshouses of Dudley and Worcester* (1927), p287.

3 Ibid, R. Wakefield, p30.

4 Oliver Dixon, son of Oliver Dixon and his wife Margaret, nee Hill, bap. 26th Dec 1642, Halesowen.

5 Frances Jellian, daughter of Gilbert Jellian and his wife Elizabeth, nee Wilmer, bap. 7th May 1643, Dudley St. Thomas's; bur. 5th May 1715, Dudley St. Thomas's.

6 Oliver Dixon, son of Oliver Dixon and his wife Frances, nee Jellian, bap. 26th Jul 1666, Dudley St. Thomas's; Mayor of Dudley in 1690; Churchwarden in 1695 and 1712; referred to as Captain; d. 17th Dec. 1738; bur. 20th Dec 1738, Dudley St. Thomas's.

7 Richard Dixon, son of Oliver Dixon and his wife Frances, nee Jellian, bap. 12th May 1667, Dudley St. Thomas's.

8 Margrett, bap.16th Nov 1689; Richard, bap. 28th Dec 1691; Henry, bap. 22nd Jan 1693; Frances, bap. 8th Feb 1698; Anne, bap. 15th Apr 1702 and an unknown male child.

9 Bur. Unreadable name, 11th Oct 1703, child of Richard Dixon, Glassmaker, Dudley St. Thomas's.

10 Frederick Bradbury, *History of Old Sheffield Plate* (1912), p67-69, states that Richard Dixon was a 'Worcester man, who had been employed [at Bolsterstone], removed in 1704 to Whittington, where he established a glass factory. Bradbury performed no original research but quoted from a Mr R.E. Leader. Francis Buckley in *The Glasshouses of Dudley and Worcester* (1927), p287, states that 'A member of this enterprising [Dixon] family founded the Whittington glasshouse near Chesterfield in 1704. D. Ashurst, in *The History of South Yorkshire Glass*, p27, suggests Richard Dixon moved to manage

Bolsterstone "in the late seventeenth century" and that he "left in 1702 to found his own works at Whittington." The author has confirmed that Ashurst based his comments on Bradbury. The facts suggest that both of Richard Dixon's moves were later than these authors believed.

11 Richard Dixon died intestate and was buried 31st Aug 1727 at Whittington. He was succeeded by his oldest son Richard, bap. 28th Dec 1691, Oldswinford. Richard lived at Thorpe Farm, Whittington and was churchwarden, constable and surveyor of Whittington. Richard died 20th Dec 1736 and by will dated 17th Dec 1736 left the glassworks and its assets to his sons William (1714-1743) and Richard (1719-1769) to carry on the trade in partnership. William died intestate 25th Feb 1743, aged 29, leaving Richard in charge. Richard died 12th Mar 1769 and by will dated 2nd Apr 1768 left the glassworks to his brother Gilbert (1715-1777) and nephew John (1742-1815), son of his brother Isaiah, to carry on the trade in partnership. Gilbert was a lawyer and attorney clerk to the Sheffield Cutlers Company and probably took no part in the business. He was buried at Whittington 26th Apr 1777, described as 'of Sheffield'. John Dixon of Key Farm, Whittington was constable, churchwarden, overseer of the poor and surveyor of the highways in Whittington. He married twice but had no issue. In his will (3rd Jul 1815 PRO PROB11/1580) he provides extensive information about his industrial activities on Glasshouse Common but no mention of the glassworks, suggesting it had closed by then. The family wealth passed to Henry Dixon alias Offerton, the grandson (by adoption) of his younger brother Henry (bap. 3rd Dec 1736, Sheffield). Henry built Whittington Hall in 1835, became Lord of the Manor and the principal landowner of the parish.

12 Edward Dixon, son of Oliver Dixon and his wife Frances, nee Jellian, bap. 23rd Jul 1682, Dudley St. Thomas's.

13 Supra.

14 Gilbert Dixon, son of Oliver Dixon and his wife Frances, nee Jellian, bap. 1st Mar 1676, Dudley St. Thomas's.

15 Mar. Gilbert Dixon and Margaret Hale, 13th Apr 1699, Kinver.

16 Margaret bap. 1700; Gillims bap. 16th Nov 1702; William 16th Nov 1702; Francis bap. 24th Dec 1704; Mary bap. 25th Apr 1707.

17 Herbut bap. 26th Dec 1709; Dianah bap. 1st May 1712.

18 North Foley, son of Robert Foley and his wife Anne, daughter of Dudley, Lord North, bap. 16th Sep 1677, Oldswinford.

19 William Hallifax DD; b. Lincolnshire; Fellow of Corpus Christi College, Oxford; Rector of Oldswinford 1699-1722; bur. St. Michael's, Salwarpe.
20 WRO BA6 class 118 folio 11b, Quarter Session Order Book.
21 Margaret married William Millard 8th May 1722, Dudley; Dianah died two months later. Francis may have initially moved with him when aged twenty-two, but is recorded as an insolvent glassmaker of Christchurch, Surrey in 1731.
22 Dr David R.M. Stuart, *Glass in Norfolk* (1997), p3.
23 Hugh Dixon, son of Oliver Dixon of Dixon's Green, principal steward to Lord Dudley and his wife Frances, nee Jellian, bap. 9th Dec 1679, Dudley St. Thomas's.
24 Mar. Hugh Dixon and Joyce Hodgetts, 2nd Nov 1701, Dudley St. Thomas's.
25 Now called Priory Street.
26 William Westwood, son of glassmaker Samuel Westwood who was buried 10th Oct 1728, Kingswinford.
27 WRO BA1 ref. 110/229 doc 23, Quarter Session Papers, Apprentice Indenture, 20th Aug 1712.
28 London Gazette, 7th Nov 1713; 'Bankrupt, Hugh Dixon, of Dudley, glassmaker.'
29 None of their names appear in the Dudley burial register.
30 Oliver Dixon, son of Oliver Dixon and his wife Elizabeth, nee Hill, bap. 26th Dec 1642, Halesowen.
31 The 'coleworks' in Dudley 'forren' were under his care in conjunction with Ferdinando Dudley.
32 Oliver Dixon bur. 15th Mar 1725, Dudley St. Thomas's.
33 WRO will made 4th Mar 1724, proved 5th May 1726.
34 Samuel Shaw, son of Oliver Shaw and his wife Alice, nee Jellians, bap. 20th Feb 1693, Dudley St. Thomas's.
35 Johnathan Green, son of John Green and his second wife Ann, nee Brooke, bap. 30th Jul 1725, Dudley.
36 WRO BA3762 899:31 folio 233, MS *Some account of the family of Dixon*. The critical words are hidden behind the glue in the original scrapbook. The author discovered them with the aid of an ultra violet lamp reading through to the reverse side of the document.
37 Mary, daughter of John Wells, a lampblower and glass toymaker of Steelhouse Lane, Birmingham, b. 1732, d. 4th Sep 1787.
38 Birmingham Gazette, 23rd Jul 1770. James Shaw is probably the great-nephew

of the above-mentioned Samuel Shaw, son of Read Shaw and his wife Mary, nee Dicks, bap. 21st Oct 1746, Oldswinford.

39 Pearson and Rollason's directory of Birmingham, Wolverhampton, Walsall, Dudley, Bilston and Willenhall, 1780 and 1781 editions.

40 Birmingham Gazette, 20th May 1782.

41 Benjamin Clements, b. 1716, Dudley, son of Samuel Clements; Univ. Coll. Ox.; BA, 1741; Headmaster Dudley Grammar School 1739-1760; of Wolverhampton Grammar School; First Vicar of St. John's Church, Wolverhampton, 1760; Preb. of Collegiate Church, Wolverhampton; Vicar of Braunton, Devon; d. 1768; bur. Dudley.

42 G.P. Mander, *The History of Wolverhampton Grammar School* (1913), pp189-190; J.S. Roper, *A History of St. John's Church Wolverhampton* (1958), p8.

43 Benjamin Clements, *Sermons on Several Occasions. In Two Volumes . . . Published from the Author's Manuscripts for the benefit of his Family* (1768).

44 Horsley House was a handsome, three-storey Georgian House that stood in two acres of ground in Wolverhampton Street, Dudley. It next became the home of the banker Edward Dixon who died there 10th Aug 1807. In its later years it was the home of the Hughes family, who provided several Mayors of the Borough. It was purchased by Dudley Corporation in 1955 and demolished three years later.

45 Nicholas Carlisle, *A Concise Description of the Endowed Grammar Schools in England and Wales* (1818), p753.

46 PRO, PROB 11/1110 RH185-RH188.

47 Their eldest son John Freeman Keelinge of Metchley Harborne, married Mary Ann, daughter of William Carlis and died 21st Nov 1824, leaving amongst other children, Edward Augustus Freeman Keelinge, b. 2nd Aug 1823, d. Mar 1892, the celebrated historian.

48 Johnathan Green, bur. 6th Dec 1784, Dudley St. Thomas's.

49 PRO, PROB 11/1138, PCC will of Johnathan Green, 10th Feb 1786.

50 Edward Dixon, son of Charles Dixon and his wife Elizabeth, nee Gilbert, bap. 29th Jun 1749, Dudley St. Thomas's was also a surgeon (of Oldswinford). This suggests that Johnathan Green was grateful for his medical attention.

51 He is possibly the same Joseph Price who was in partnership at the Castle Foot Glassworks in 1820.

52 Birmingham Gazette, 1st Apr 1793 lists John and Joseph Green among Dudley traders.

53 John Green, son of Johnathan Green and his wife Mary, nee Wells, b. 5th Dec 1752; bap. 10th Jan 1753, Dudley St. Thomas's.
54 Joseph Green, son of Johnathan Green and his wife Mary, nee Wells, b. 12th Oct 1757; bap. 19th Dec 1757, Dudley St. Thomas's.
55 Dudley Poor Rate Book of 1793; J. Treasure's 1835 *Plan of the Town of Dudley.*
56 Joseph Green leased the land at Dixon's Green for ninety-nine years from 25th Oct 1790, at the yearly rental of £3 3s and subject to 'the lessee expending a sum of £300 in erecting a messuage thereon.' The house was named Springfields, although by the nineteenth century it was known as The Woodlands. Dudley Poor Rate Book of 1787 and 1793; J. Treasure's 1835 *Plan of the Town of Dudley.* The lease became vested in the Bourne family until it ran out in 1889.
57 WRO BA3762 899:31 folio 233; Dudley Poor Rate Book of 1793 refers to a house, glasshouse and land at 10s 5d, a new glasshouse at 3s 9d and Lord's land 2s 1/2d all in the hands of John Green.
58 John Green married Elizabeth, daughter of Walter Woodcock, 26th Aug 1784. His brother Joseph married Elizabeth's sister Frances. The sisters were co-heirs to the barony of Dudley, which led to subsequent, prolonged litigation, op cit, H.S. Grazebrook, *The Barons Dudley*, in *Collections for a History of Staffordshire,* v 10, Part 2 (1888).
59 D.N. Sandilands.
60 Birmingham Gazette, 16th Feb 1801.
61 John Green d. 8th Dec 1802 at Halesowen.
62 Stuart Crystal, Joseph Richardson's notebook.
63 William Large, b. c1776.
64 Ibid, Frederick Bradbury, pp67-8.
65 William Rolinson Hodgetts, son of Charles Hodgetts and his wife Elizabeth, nee Stevens, b. 10th Jan 1784; bap. 21st Apr 1784, Dudley St. Thomas's.
66 Ibid, Frederick Bradbury, pp67-8.
67 DA, Plan of Land at Dixon's Green, 1808. Cutting activities would only take place in outbuildings, not in the cone itself.
68 Lewis's 1820 Worcestershire General and Commercial Directory.
69 London Gazette, 21st Aug 1832.
70 Thirteenth Report of the Commission into the Glass Excise, 1835, Appendix 7.

71 Believing that they had successfully reformed government at Parliamentary level, the Whigs turned their attention to local government, appointing in July 1833 a commission to enquire into the state of municipal government. On 1st August Thomas Kennedy, MP for Ayr, moved to bring in a Bill to regulate the election of magistrates. In the debate Dudley's MP, Sir John Campbell made some serious criticisms and was reported by the John Bull newspaper of 18th August as having 'put his foot in it.'

72 Luke Booker, b. 20th Oct 1762, Nottingham, son of a schoolmaster; ordained 1785; LL.D.; F.R.L.S.; Headmaster of Dudley Grammar School in 1794; Lecturer St. Peter's, Wolverhampton, 1785; Incumbent of St. Edmund's, Dudley 1789; conferred Doctor of Laws by the University of Aberdeen Dec 1791; Rector of Tedstone-de-la-mere, Herefordshire, 1805; Vicar of Dudley 1812 to death; Chaplain to King George IV; feoffe of Dudley Grammar School; supporter of Dr. Jenner, the discoverer of vaccination; d. 1835.

73 Engravers employed at Dudley Flint Glass Works.

74 Proprietors of Castle Foot Glassworks.

75 C.F.G. Clark, *The Curiosities of Dudley and the Black Country* (1881), pp62-5.

76 It is clearly marked on Treasure's plan of 1835 when it was by far the largest structure in the area, if not the whole of Dudley.

CHAPTER 32

Phoenix Glassworks, Dudley

Phoenix Glassworks stood on the east side of Hall Street in Dudley, at the back of shops nearly opposite King Street. A narrow passage at the rear is still known as Phoenix Passage. Phillips Penn built the glassworks about 1780[1]. Penn was in business with two of his sons, Bate[2] and William[3], trading as Penn and Sons, Hop Merchants and Glassmen, High Street, Dudley[4]. Bate specialised in the hop trade and William in the glass trade. The description glassmen suggests that at this stage they were decorators and merchants of glass not manufacturers; a view reinforced by a contemporary newspaper notice:

'Whereas James Horton (glass cutter) hired servant to Philips Pen [sic] of Dudley in the County of Worcestershire absconded his master's service on the 25th May 1772. At the same time went away Daniel Newton (apprentice).'[5]

The first reference to the business in Hall Street occurs in 1780. A trade directory lists Philip[sic] Penn of Hall Street, Dudley and William Penn, Glassmaker of Hall Street, Dudley[6]. This suggests the glassworks had been built by this date.

Phillips Penn died in 1781[7]. In his will[8] he left an estate shared between his widow, children and grandchildren. It includes the legacy 'I give to my son William Penn all those Mesuages Tenements Warehouses Glasshouse . . . and likewise a bond that I have of his debt due upon it one thousand pounds with all interest upon it I give it to him for ever.' The cone is shown, but not named, on Snape's 1785 canal map.

William Penn was a substantial property owner. He owned and

occupied 'ye Glasshouse' in Hall Street and had a house and offices at Waddam's Pool. He also owned seventeen houses in various parts of Dudley[9]. He was also involved with the Dudley Arms building society scheme in 1786[10].

Dudley became an important centre for Methodism and several new nonconformist churches were built about this time. In 1788 two nonconformist chapels were built in the same road, King Street. The first was a Methodist chapel. The second, only a few yards away, was acquired by a group of 'Protestant Dissenters'. The trust deed for this chapel includes many local businessmen including William Penn, glass-merchant[11].

In 1796 Penn operated two glasshouses, with twenty pots[12]. In 1798 he employed the local Wordsley furnace-builder, Joseph Richardson to build him a new thirteen-pot furnace[13].

Penn, like many other glassmasters, gave generously to noble causes. In 1798 he contributed £21 to 'the Defence of the Realm.'[14] This was the height of the war against the French under Napoleon[15]. In 1800 he donated £10 10s 'to relieve the distresses of the poor.'[16]

A contemporary reference suggests the glasshouse was a square design. In October 1800 the Manorial Court ordered Joseph Clarke to abate a nuisance in the road 'leading from the Pinfold to Mr Penn's Square Glass House.'[17] In 1810 it had a fourteen-pot furnace. Benjamin Richardson wrote 'it was the largest furnace that I ever saw.'[18]

An indenture of 4th July 1807 describes William Penn as a glass manufacturer with rights reserved to the mines of glasshouse pot clay, fire brick, and white clay, under his lands and premises at Nether Gornal[19]. It is not known how much longer after this he operated the works, but sometime between 1813 and 1818 John Roughton took over the works, having left Holly Hall Glassworks[20]. Roughton did not stay long and left few records before moving to Cheltenham[21].

By 1820 Phoenix Glassworks was occupied by Isaac[22] and Thomas[23] Badger[24], the two oldest sons of Isaac Badger senior[25], a prominent Dudley builder[26]. The Badger brothers were already significant manufacturers of nails, chains, vices, malt mills etc. at Eve Hill, Dudley. They were prominent in the political life of Dudley and held strong anti-Chartist views. They occupied the key posts of magistrates and Town Commissioners and were two of a small Tory clique that ruled the town for many years with the tacit approval of Lord Dudley. Isaac Badger was described as 'audacious but unlettered.' Isaac Badger senior built the family fortune as a builder and industrialist at a time when the Black Country was undergoing meteoric expansion. His enterprise was large scale; in 1788, as a lessee of Lord Dudley, he paid a royalty of £18 for having manufactured three hundred and sixty thousand bricks that year[27]. As well as glass manufacturers, the Badgers were coalmasters, nail factors, bankers and notorious slum landlords[28].

Before acquiring a reputation as a slum landlord, Isaac Badger's family is credited with some fine buildings such as Finch House. This superb example of an early Queen Anne style townhouse was built in 1707 in Wolverhampton Street, Dudley. It was built for John Finch[29] and his wife Mary, nee Bate, and still stands today[30].

Finch House, Dudley

Thomas and Isaac Badger involved their younger brothers, Septimus[31] and Edward[32] in the business, but Edward died the following year, aged twenty-one. His memorial at the west end of the north aisle of St. Edmund's Church, Dudley reads:

> 'Having embarked in commercial life by joining his brothers in the Phoenix Glass Works and displaying habits of business which justified his relatives and friends in forming high expectation of his future success . . . was prematurely cut off in the 21st year of his age on 20th April 1821.'

The firm continued to trade successfully as Badger Brothers & Co., cut glass manufacturers[33]. In 1829 Thomas Badger was portrayed addressing local industrialists in a painting entitled *The Smoke Room of the Dudley Arms Hotel*, painted by W. Pringle[34].

It also shows his brother Isaac and his fellow glassmaker and political ally, Thomas Hawkes.

In anticipation that the town of Dudley was to have a representative in Parliament under the Reform Bill, efforts were made by political parties to secure a preponderance of power and influence. A petition was submitted to J.C. Brettell, the Mayor of Dudley on 7th February 1831. Thomas, Isaac and Septimus Badger were among the seventy-four signatories[35].

Thomas Badger & Co. paid £4,870 7s 3d excise duty for the year ending 5th January 1833[36], suggesting this was the third largest of the sixteen Stourbridge/Dudley glasshouses of the day. The glassworks is clearly shown on Treasure's 1835 plan. Unlike the other Dudley glassworks, the plan outlines the circular glass cone. It also shows 'Badger's Square' on the west side of Eve Hill.

During the 1835 parliamentary election for the eastern division of Worcestershire tempers became frayed and on 15th January Thomas Badger was accused of an assault upon William Davis, a whitesmith. This was a serious matter for Badger who as a magistrate was a pillar of society and expected to uphold the law. He was tried for assault at Warwick on 28th March 1835 and found guilty[37]. However, a subsequent appeal reversed the judgement[38].

On 14th March 1835, along with Thomas Hawkes, Thomas Badger gave evidence to the Commission on Excise. Their evidence is a substantial criticism of the glass excise duty:

> 'Since the year 1826, upon the cut glass, we have made a handsome profit, and this has been swallowed by the loss upon the plain; I venture to say we have not made 2 per cent. upon our own capital.'[39]

As if the glass excise was not enough, manufacturers were faced with another problem—the combination of labour. A meeting took place on 5th December 1837 at the Dudley Arms Hotel where the manufacturers considered their response to the formation of the first glassmakers' trade union. Thomas and Septimus Badger were present. The resolution passed at their meeting has already been described[40].

By 1839 the firm traded as T. I. & S. Badger[41], suggesting the youngest brother, Septimus, had become a partner. Isaac and Septimus lived at Eve Hill, and Thomas lived at Hill House on what was then the outskirts of Dudley town[42].

Between 1840 and 1841 trade was poor, dissent was rife among the working classes and the Chartist movement was leading to a state of near anarchy. To safeguard life and property, in common with other parts of the country, Dudley formed a constabulary. John Roberts was appointed Commandant and Isaac Badger the Superintendent[43].

By 1841 the firm traded as Badger Brothers and Co.[44], suggesting the brothers had introduced a further partner. This was William Dixon Badger[45], the fourth oldest son of Thomas Badger. In 1841 Thomas Badger and his family still lived at Hill House, when he is described as an Iron Master. His oldest son Thomas was a Coal Master and his youngest son, William Dixon Badger a Glass Master[46].

Despite the opposition of local canal proprietors there was intense interest in bringing mainline railways into the Black Country area. Although the London-Birmingham Railway had opened in 1838, its rates of 38s to 40s per ton were double that of the canals[47]. The Grand Junction Railway from Birmingham to Liverpool and Manchester was opened on 4th July 1837, but initially made little provision for goods traffic. When the company recognised what an oversight this was, it was rapidly corrected. Freight prices from the Black Country to Liverpool and Manchester then fell from about 20s per ton in 1825 to 11s per ton in 1844[48]. Local capitalists decided to support the construction of the Grand Connection Railway from Worcester to Wolverhampton and a bill was placed before Parliament to that end in December 1836[49]. In the sad years that followed, the Black Country economy slumped into recession and the scheme had to be dropped. Glassmasters, coalmasters, ironmasters and other industrialists were all affected and mere survival became their primary concern. It was not until 1844 that money was available and the enterprise could be pursued in the form of the Oxford, Worcester & Wolverhampton Railway Company[50]. There was considerable public debate about the relative merits of the rival broad-gauge and narrow-gauge companies. A commission was to decide the outcome, and a public meeting was held in Dudley on 13th September 1844, shortly before the commission sat. The proposals of the Oxford, Worcester & Wolverhampton Railway were accepted by the majority[51]. Isaac Badger proposed 'that the town should give its . . . support to the Railroad in question.'[52]

The wealth and influence of the Badger family is apparent from the multitude of entries they have in an 1845 trade directory. Thomas, Isaac & Septimus Badger, are listed as glass manufacturers in Hall Street; Thomas and Isaac Badger are listed as coalmasters at Snow Hill, Dudley; Thomas Badger & Co., nail and chain manufacturers, was also at Snow Hill. Among the Dudley gentry are listed: Isaac Badger, Wolverhampton Street, Septimus Badger, Wolverhampton Street and Thomas Badger, Hall Street[53].

In 1846 Thomas Badger gave evidence to the Commission of Employment of Children where he stated '10 to 12 is the right age for children to begin work; 10 years is not too young if the boy be strong and healthy.' This was characteristic insensitivity from Thomas Badger. In 1852, William Lee, the Superintending Inspector of Health was to state 'as far as the duration of life is concerned Dudley is the most unhealthy place in the country.' Thomas Badger replied 'All I have to say is, that the town never was in a more healthy state than at present.' Memorials in St. Edmund's Church show just how appalling the mortality rate was, even in Thomas Badger's own family[54].

The following year, 1847, Chartism was prominent and the local townspeople were determined to elect a Member of Parliament free from Lord Dudley's influence. Thomas Badger was approached, but declined to put in a nomination, although he would almost certainly have been elected:

> 'they determined to be rid of lordly influence by electing a local man and it was decided to invite Thomas Badger, a large employer of labour in Dudley, to offer himself. Mr Badger was, however, counting the cost and recalling the past experiences of Mr Hawkes, the late MP for Dudley . . . '[55]

In 1851 Thomas Badger was a widower, aged seventy-two, a

coalmaster living at Hill House, Hall Street, Dudley. His two sons were still living with him: Thomas junior, also a coalmaster and William Dixon, a glass manufacturer[56].

An election of Guardians[57] in 1854 again demonstrates the Tory dominance of Dudley. Thomas Badger presumptuously produced a list of ten candidates. 'You are respectfully requested to Vote for the following Ten Persons, Nominated by Thomas Badger Esq.' The list included his brother Isaac Badger, Joseph Guest[58] and John Renaud[59]. The outcome of the election was described as:

> 'This disgraceful strangling of common sense and prostitution of all recognised rules of decent electioneering propriety came to a close with the following result: Ten Tories elected, nine Liberals rejected.'[60]

Thomas Badger died in 1856[61], aged seventy-five. His memorial is next to his brother Edward's, inside St. Edmund's Church, Dudley, and refers to him as a magistrate for the counties of Worcester and Stafford. The value of his estate was £40-50,000, a considerable amount at that time. Twenty-five years after his death Clark eulogised:

> 'This genial, but blunt and frank old gentleman, was one of Dudley's worthiest sons; his familiar figure daily moving in our midst, secured the esteem of all good people, and his quiet and unostentatious benevolence has gladdened the hearts of widows and orphans, when none were allowed to witness the tear of the giver. Mr. Badger (like a great many more of our Dudley worthies) began life in very humble circumstances, and rose step by step until he became Chief Magistrate of this Borough. He was for a lengthened period (along with his brother, Isaac Badger) very extensively engaged in the glass trade, the nail trade, the coal trade, and iron trades of this district, and it is not too much to say that Messrs. Badger Brothers at all times exercised the most potent influence upon the industries of Dudley and its neighbourhood. As a large employer of labour he was much respected by all his workforce, and a cordial feeling always existed between the head of the firm and the numerous

employees both in the ironworks and collieries. In religion he was a sound churchman, and in politics he belonged to the Tory party, but Mr. Badger was not a rabid politician, for he had the honour of once being requested to stand as a Candidate for the Borough of Dudley, on Independent principles but he declined the honour. He was a most shrewd and active Magistrate for many years, and as Mr. Badger lived through perilous times his decisions on the Bench were always tempered with a wonderful insight into the human character, accepting Mercy and Justice as his motto. His personal friendships created a halo of friendly feeling and generous sentiment amongst a large circle of personal friends and acquaintances, which will be long remembered in Dudley, and his death, at the ripe old age of 75 years, was universally regretted.'[62]

The sitting member of parliament for Dudley, Sir Stafford Northcote, Bart., MP resigned on 12th March 1857[63]. The political parties busied themselves with the selection of candidates. A handbill was printed with seventeen subscribers, headed by Isaac Badger, accompanied by his nephew Thomas Badger junior[64] and including John Renaud of Castle Foot Glassworks. It was issued on 23rd March 1857 and reads:

'We, the undersigned, request the Independent Electors of the Borough of Dudley to meet at the Old Town Hall, tomorrow, at One o'clock, to consider what steps can be best taken to secure the Independence of the Borough, and to enable the Electors to exercise their free and unbiased judgement in the choice of their Representative.'[65]

After the lockout[66], in 1859, Badger Brothers claimed £61 6s from the association's defence fund. The amount implies the firm was the seventh largest of the thirteen firms in the Midlands Association. Shortly after this Badger Brothers glassmaking business closed as a direct result of the protracted strike and lockout.

The glassworks was never used again for making glass. By 1886 it had been turned into an ironworks. The cone was still standing in 1903, being used as a furniture works and warehouse by

Charles Hale. It features in an advertisement with an aerial view of the premises.

---

1 Treadway Russell Nash, *Collections for the History of Worcestershire* (1781) includes an illustration by his artist Thomas Sanders of Dudley as seen from the lower slopes of Kate's Hill. The smoking cone of Phoenix Glassworks dominates the view.
2 Bate Penn, son of Phillips Penn and his wife Sarah, nee Bate.
3 William Penn, son of Phillips Penn and his wife Sarah, nee Bate, bap. 15th Feb 1748, Dudley St. Thomas's.
4 Sketchley and Adam's 1770 Universal Directory of Birmingham, Wolverhampton, Walsall and Dudley.
5 Bristol Gazette, 20th Jun 1772.
6 Pearson and Rollason's Directory of Birmingham, Wolverhampton, Walsall, Dudley, Bilston and Willenhall, 1780 and 1781 editions.
7 Phillips Penn, bur. 23rd May 1781, Dudley St. Thomas's.
8 WRO, Will of Phillips Penn, 7th Jun 1781.
9 DA, Dudley Poor Rate Assessment, 1787.
10 Supra, Dudley Flint Glassworks.
11 Trust deed, 4th Dec 1788, quoted in A.A. Rollason, *The old non-parochial registers of Dudley* (1899), p64.
12 D.N. Sandilands.
13 Stuart Crystal, Joseph Richardson's notebook.
14 Birmingham Gazette, 23rd Apr 1798.
15 Nelson defeated the French fleet at the Battle of the Nile, in Aboukir Bay, in 1798. Closer to home, partly through French intrigue, general discontent in Ireland broke out into open rebellion in 1798.
16 Birmingham Gazette, 19th May 1800.
17 Dudley Manor Rolls.
18 Benjamin Richardson's notebook of 1886.
19 DA, MS, M.C. Davies, *The Glass Industry in Dudley*.
20 James Pigot's 1818 Commercial Directory.
21 Dudley St. Thomas's M.I., 'John Roughton Esq., many years a resident of this town, died 2nd Feb 1837, aged 72/His remains rest in the catacombs of Trinity Church, Cheltenham.'
22 Isaac Badger, son of Isaac Badger and his wife Sarah, nee Henley, bap. 28th Dec 1784, Dudley St. Thomas's.

23 Thomas Badger, son of Isaac Badger and his wife Sarah, nee Henley, bap. 1st Sep 1782, Dudley St. Thomas's.
24 Lewis's Worcestershire General and Commercial Directory of 1820.
25 Isaac Badger, son of Edward Badger and his wife Elizabeth, nee Wells, bap. 10th Dec 1749, Kingswinford.
26 Ibid, Seymour J. Price, p62.
27 Ibid, T.J Raybould, p132.
28 Ibid, G.J. Barnsby, p45.
29 John Finch, son of William Finch and his wife Katrin, nee Roades, bap. 12th Dec 1670, Dudley.
30 The initials J & M Finch and the date 1707 appear in a cartouche on the tympanum of the building. John Finch had prospered in the iron trade in Dudley. William Finch of that family married Sarah, daughter of the great Dr Joseph Priestley in 1786. Priestley fled to Finch's house after the riots in Birmingham in 1791 when his house was burnt down. Other members of the Finch family founded the iron industry of Cambridge and became fabulously wealthy, first as merchants of the output of Dudley, then as manufacturers. William Finch II, nephew of John Finch left an estate with the incredible value of £150,000 when he died in 1762. The Magdalene bridge is made with their iron.
31 Septimus Badger, son of Isaac Badger and his wife Sarah, nee Henley, b. 11th Apr 1795; bap. 21st Apr 1795, Dudley St. Thomas's.
32 Edward Badger, son of Isaac Badger and his wife Sarah, nee Henley, bap. 15th Sep 1799, Dudley St. Thomas's.
33 Wrightson's Triennial Directory of Birmingham, 1823 and 1825 editions; Pigot and Co.'s National Commercial Directory for 1828-9; Pigot and Co.'s Commercial Directory of Birmingham, 1829 and 1830 editions.
34 Dudley Art Gallery. The gallery also possesses a full length portrait of Thomas Badger by John Calcott Horsley.
35 Supra, Dudley Flint Glass Works.
36 Thirteenth Report of the Commission into the Glass Excise, 1835, Appendix 7.
37 DA, A Report of the Trial of Mr Thomas Badger, a Magistrate of Dudley, for an assault upon William Davis.
38 It was not the first time that a Badger had been facing the bench, instead of sitting behind it. In 1821 Mr Badger appeared before Mr Baron Jarrow accused of knocking off a man's hat at the theatre, because he would not

remove it while the National Anthem was being played. In his zeal, Badger not only knocked the hat off, but also knocked the man - a teacher called Hilliard - off his seat. In summing up, Mr Baron Jarrow intimated that he thought he was rather to be commended than otherwise. He pictured to the jury 'the glorious sight of a whole audience in a theatre paying a just tribute of veneration to their sovereign.' The jury awarded damages of one farthing.

39 Thirteenth report of the Commissions of Excise Enquiry, 1835, Appendix 28.
40 Supra, Audnam Glassworks.
41 Robson's 1839 Birmingham and Sheffield Directory.
42 Bentley's 1841 guide to Dudley. Hill House stood at the southern end of Waddams Pool, on the road to Dixons Green.
43 Ibid, C.F.G. Clark, p214.
44 Pigot and Co.'s 1841 Directory of Birmingham.
45 William Dixon Badger, son of Thomas Badger and his wife Mary, nee Tilley, b. 10th Jun 1819; bap. 26th Aug 1819, Dudley St. Thomas's.
46 PRO, 1841 Census of Dudley.
47 Minutes of evidence taken before the Select Committee on the Oxford, Worcester and Wolverhampton Railway, 1845, p343.
48 Ibid.
49 Wolverhampton Chronicle, 7th Dec 1836.
50 Wolverhampton Chronicle, 22nd May 1844.
51 This railway company, chaired by Francis Rufford, had a disastrous history of inefficiency and incompetence. Its initials of the OWWR led to it being called the Old Worse and Worse Railway.
52 Ibid, T.J. Raybould, p82.
53 Post Office Directory of the Neighbourhood of Birmingham, 1845.
54 William Lee's visit to Dudley in 1852 was a compulsory enquiry arising from the fact that the death rate in Dudley was twenty-eight per thousand. A ten-year average from 1841-50 showed the average age at death in Dudley was sixteen years and seven months, when the average for England and Wales was twenty-nine years and four months.
55 Ibid, C.F.G. Clark, pp103-110.
56 PRO, 1851 Census of Dudley.
57 The board responsible for the implementation of the 1834 Poor Law Amendment Act.
58 Former proprietor of Castle Foot Glassworks.

59 New proprietor of Castle Foot Glassworks.
60 Ibid, C.F.G. Clark, pp180-8.
61 Thomas Badger, d. 16th Aug 1856; bur. Dudley, St. Edmund's.
62 Ibid, C.F.G. Clark, p199.
63 This was mainly because he had voted honourably on the subject of the China opium trade, but in a way that caused Lord Ward to withdraw his support and left him in an untenable position.
64 Thomas Badger, son of Thomas Badger and his wife Mary, nee Tilley, bap. 28th Jul 1814, Dudley, St. Thomas's.
65 Ibid, C.F.G. Clark, pp208-213.
66 Supra Coalbournhill, Audnam and North Street Glassworks.

CHAPTER 33

Moor Lane Bottleworks, Brierley Hill

It is unclear when Moor Lane Bottleworks was built. It was well established in 1771 under the ownership of Thomas Seager[1], the oldest son of William Seager, a gentleman of Kingswinford. It seems that either Thomas, or his father, had built the glassworks several years earlier. It stood south of the western extremity of North Street, Brierley Hill. The entire business was offered to let in 1771:

> 'To be let, a glasshouse, yard, pot-rooms, store rooms and other conveniences suitable and several dwelling houses for workmen, situated at Brierley-Hill in the Parish of Kingswinford, very near to the turnpike road leading from Stourbridge to Dudley. Note, the tenant if he chooses it, may get his own coal upon the premises making a reasonable allowance to the proprietor of the land. Enquire of Mr Thomas Seager at Brierley Hill aforesaid.'[2]

The glassworks was leased to a partnership known as Westwood & Moore. The first partner was probably the John Westwood who in 1766 witnessed the will of Robert Honeyborne of Moor Lane Glassworks. The second partner was possibly Joseph Moore senior[3]. The firm of Westwood and Moore was associated with another bottleworks located by the Paddington Basin in London, which was the forerunner of Davey and Moore, later absorbed into the United Glass Group[4].

The landlord of the glassworks, Thomas Seager, attorney of High Street, Dudley died in 1788[5], aged forty-eight. He had made a will dated 3rd March 1787 in which he charged his friends, Reverend Joseph Cartwright of Dudley and Robert Honeyborne of Moor Lane, to dispose of his estate for the benefit of his wife Hannah[6], his son and heir William[7], and his daughter Betty[8]. After his death, his executors auctioned a piece of land on the north side of Brockmoor Lane leading from Wordsley to Brierley Hill, called Furlborough's Innage. It was bought at public auction by Richard Bradley and conveyed to him in an indenture dated 9th July 1790[9]. Other authors have suggested this land was purchased with the intention of building a glassworks. However, on 4th April 1834, as part of a complicated legal wrangle concerning the Ensell legatees of Richard Bradley[10], the same parcel of land was sold again. It was conveyed by the legatees of Richard Bradley, to Francis Rufford of Prescott[11]. In the indenture the land is described comprehensively, but there is no mention of a glasshouse. The plan shows that Francis Rufford already owned the land adjoining Furlborough's Innage[12].

In 1793 a bottleworks, presumably this one, was in the hands of Edward Westwood, a victualler[13]. The Birmingham Gazette of 1st April 1793 lists Stourbridge traders including 'Edward Westwood'. The firm traded as Westwood, Price, Worral & Co., black bottle manufacturers in 1809[14]. By 1818 it traded as Westwood Price & Co., bottlemakers[15]. Then by 1820 it traded as Edward Westwood and Co., glass bottle manufacturers[16]. Fowler's 1822 map[17] shows the Moor Lane Bottleworks as 'Bottle House, Buildings, etc.' the property of Thomas Honeyborne[18], occupied by Westwood and Moore. From 1823 to 1825 the firm traded as Westwood, Price and Co.[19], and in 1828 the title changed again, to Westwood, Moore & Rider (black bottles)[20]. One of the new partners was John Rider, who lived at Moor Lane but whose provenance is unknown.

Edward Westwood & Co. paid £1,380 15s excise duty for the year ending 5th January 1833[21], suggesting this was the smallest of the sixteen Stourbridge/Dudley glasshouses. However, this is not a fair comparison as the rate of duty on bottles was lower than other types of glass.

In 1835 the firm traded as Westwood, Moore and Rider, bottlemakers[22], but by 1839 it had obviously started making pottery in addition to glass. The firm traded as Westwood & Co., Wordsley, Pottery & glass manufacturers[23] or Westwood and Moor, glassbottle &c., manufacturers[24]. Fowler and Son's 1840 map shows the occupier as Westwood, Moore and Co. The owner of the property was Joseph Atkinson, having inherited the former Honeyborne estates[25].

In 1845 Westwood and Moore manufactured nine hundred and eighty tons of bottles, potteryware and firebricks in a year when the output of flint glass for the whole district was two thousand three hundred tons. Their consumption of raw materials was three hundred and twenty tons of clay, four hundred and fifty tons of sand and three thousand five hundred tons of coal[26].

According to Richard Mountford Deeley, the chief partner in 1857 was Edward Westwood[27], who after losing a sister had a mental breakdown and was committed to an asylum, after which the works promptly closed down[28]. However, Edward Westwood wrote his will in 1878 in which he is described as a gentleman of Oldswinford, of sound mind. It furthermore describes that he had earlier sold the 'business of glass bottle and stone ware manufacture lately carried on by me' to his son Charles Westwood in partnership with Richard Alfred Windmill[29] for £8,592 17s 4d. Edward Westwood died in 1885[30] leaving an estate valued at £22,799 3s 8d[31].

Charles Westwood[32] was Edward's fourth son and by 1881 was a glass manufacturer, living with his wife and family at Norton Road, Upper Swinford[33]. Richard Alfred Windmill was of a Brierley Hill family, although with no obvious previous connections with glassmaking. In 1881 he was living with his wife and family at Stourbridge Road, Pedmore, described as a glass manufacturer[34].

Charles Westwood and Richard Alfred Windmill appear to cease glassmaking to concentrate on the manufacture of stoneware. The Ordnance Survey map of 1884 shows the property as a stone works. They were presumably still in business in 1885 for the provisions of Edward Westwood's will to have any relevance. Finally, in 1900 the old bottleworks was advertised for sale as a pottery:

'Important Sale of the Valuable Freehold and splendidly

situated Stoneware Pottery, Moor Lane (Founded by Messrs. Westwood and Moore upwards of a Century). This Genuine Concern is being Sold through other important engagements and for family reasons . . . The position of these works is unique, being in the centre of the Coal and Clay District, within 50 yards of a siding on the G.W.R. and a Wharf on the Stourbridge Canal . . . The total area is 3 acres, 3 roods, and 6 perches, or thereabouts$_{35}$.'

The 1901 Ordnance Survey$_{36}$ describes the site as 'Bottle Works (Glass & Stone). The final history of the bottleworks is not known, but the site was eventually covered by the expansion of the G.W.R marshalling yard.

---

1 Thomas Seager, son of William Seager and his second wife Mary, nee Dixon, bap. 2nd Jun 1740, Kingswinford.
2 Birmingham Gazette, 27th May 1771.
3 Infra, Grazebrook's Canalside Glassworks.
4 Ibid, C.M. Brown.
5 Thomas Seager, bur. 26th Oct 1788, Brierley Hill.
6 Thomas Seager married Hannah Gorton of Dudley, 3rd Jul 1754, Kingswinford.
7 William Seager, son of Thomas Seager and his wife Hannah, nee Gorton, bap. 7th Aug 1761, Kingswinford.
8 Betty Seager, daughter of Thomas Seager and his wife Hannah, nee Gorton, bap. 29th Jan 1769, Brierley Hill.
9 SRO, D648/5/22.
10 Infra, Red House Glassworks, 1834.
11 SRO, D648/5/22 5th Apr 1834 Release of Land.
12 Francis Rufford had many interests including coal, fireclay and brick making. He was a banker and co-partner with his brother Philip at the Heath Glassworks.
13 Universal Directory of 1793.
14 Holden's Triennial Directory for 1809, 1810 & 1811.
15 James Pigot's 1818 Commercial Directory.
16 Lewis's 1820 Worcestershire General and Commercial Directory.
17 DA, William Fowler's 1822 *Map of the Parish of Kingswinford.* Plot 432.
18 Thomas Honeyborne was running Moor Lane Glassworks and had inherited

the bottleworks on the death of his brother Robert Honeyborne II in 1802.
19 Wrightson's Triennial Directory of Birmingham, 1823 and 1825 editions.
20 Pigot and Co.'s National Commercial Directory for 1828 and 1829, Pigot and Co.'s Commercial Directory of Birmingham, 1829 and 1830 editions.
21 Thirteenth Report of the Commission into the Glass Excise, 1835, Appendix 7.
22 Pigot and Co.'s 1835 National Commercial Directory.
23 Robson's 1839 Birmingham and Sheffield Directory.
24 Bentley's 1840 Directory of Stourbridge.
25 Supra, Moor Lane Glassworks, 1831.
26 Ibid, T.J. Raybould, p135.
27 Edward Westwood, son of Edward Westwood and his wife Ann, b. 12th Dec 1811, Amblecote, bap. 25th Mar 1812, Oldswinford.
28 BRL, MS R.M. Deeley, *Reminiscences*, 663048.
29 Richard Alfred Windmill, son of Edward Windmill and his wife Lydia, nee Wood, bap. 10th Dec 1843, Brierley Hill.
30 Edward Westwood d. 20th Feb 1885, Oldswinford.
31 WRO, will and two codicils of Edward Westwood, 11 May 1885.
32 Charles Westwood, son of Edward Westwood and his wife Elizabeth, nee Pitt, bap. 13th Jun 1857, Oldswinford.
33 PRO 1881 census, RG11/2888/73/33.
34 PRO 1881 census, RG11/2941/9/10.
35 County Express, 23rd Jun 1900.
36 1901 Ordnance Survey of Staffordshire, 1:2500.

CHAPTER 34

Wordsley Flint Glassworks

The precise date of establishment of this important glassworks is still unclear. It stood on the west side of the Stourbridge to Wolverhampton road and although it was right on the banks of the Stourbridge Canal, it predates it. Whitworth's canal map of 1774 shows the cone on the northern bank of the intended canal. As there was no other glassworks existing in Wordsley at the time, Wordsley Flint Glassworks clearly decided the route of this part of the canal.

The glassworks was owned and probably built by John Hill[1] who in 1776 was one of the proprietors named in the Stourbridge Canal Act[2]. An Abstract of Title, dated 17th May 1776, refers to the Wordsley Glasshouse under the ownership of John Hill, producing white and flint glass. He also operated the Ridgrave Glasshouse at this time, although he abandoned the much older Ridgrave Glasshouse about 1777 and concentrated his efforts here. According to Benjamin Richardson, the cone was 'built by a mason named Guest who lived at Wordsley Green.'[3]

John Hill had married Mary Russell[4] in 1771[5] by licence[6] in which the bondsman was Martin Paddey, a mercer of Oldswinford, who later became his partner. His bride, Mary Russell, was the niece of Edward Russell of Heath Glassworks. When Edward Russell died in 1778, he left £1,000 in his will to his son-in-law John Hill.

In 1781 Hill employed the local Wordsley furnace-builder, Joseph Richardson to build a new ten-pot furnace[7]. The following year, in 1782, he took on John Kettley as an apprentice which suggests that the business was sound. However, Hill and his partner, Martin Paddy, ran into financial difficulties and assigned the property to Hill's father, Waldron[8]. Waldron Hill did not, or perhaps could not, provide any support for his son and sold the works to Richard Bradley on 25th August 1782[9].

Richard Bradley[10] was a wealthy local industrialist. He had already dabbled in the glass trade in 1768, having been entrepreneurially involved with his brother-in-law, George Ensell, at the Harlestones Glasshouse in Coalbournbrook. He recognised that Wordsley, at the crossroads of the canal and the main turnpike, was going to become an excellent location for industry and began to buy a large amount of land in the area. He also bought the Park House[11] from John Northall, an imposing Georgian house, conveniently located a short distance from the glassworks.

Bradley commenced trading immediately and was listed in 1783 as Richard Bradley, Glass manufacturer[12]. The cone is shown, but not named on Snape's 1785 canal map. His business expanded and in 1791 he took an Oldswinford Hospital boy as an apprentice.

Bradley's expansion plans quickly got him into trouble. In 1787 he was obliged to appear at the Manorial Court and pay the maximum fine the court could impose:

> 'We amerce Richard Bradley glassmaker in the sum of £1.19.11 for a Nuisance in having erected a Brick Wall or Building upon the Kings Highway at Wordsley.'[13]

Always at the forefront of industrial innovation, Richard Bradley installed a steam engine at the Wordsley glasshouse to power the cutting wheels, just two years after James Dovey installed the first for that purpose[14]. A meeting of the Stourbridge Canal Co. on 2nd August 1792 resolved:

> 'that Mr Richard Bradley have permission to take water out of the canal for the supply of the boiler in the Steam Engine proposed to be erected by him at Wordsley for grinding Glass returning an equal quantity of water into the canal.'[15]

Richard Bradley died on 23rd February 1796, aged fifty-one[16]. His obituary reads 'Died, Wednesday, R. Bradley Esq., an eminent glass manufacturer near Stourbridge.'[17] After his death, control passed with the Red House to his heirs in the Ensell family[18] who issued a notice that trade would continue as normal:

> '26th Feb 1796. Stourbridge: Messrs. Bradley and Ensells take this opportunity to return their thanks for all favours conferred on their late worthy relation, R. Bradley, and hope for a continuance of the same. The Glass and Coal trade &c. will be carried on with the same punctuality and dispatch as usual.'[19]

Bradley had written a will[20] on 10th December 1794 and later added an undated codicil. When they were proved, the glassworks was inherited by his sister Kitty Bradley[21], and his niece Lucy Mary Ensell[22] in trust. It was ultimately to be divided between them and his nephews, Charles Ensell[23] and Richard Bradley Ensell[24]. He directed that his nephew, Charles Ensell the younger 'be continued as Clerk in the said business so long as he shall conduct himself with propriety . . . and that he be paid the yearly salary of seventy pounds.' Also 'that Richard Bradley Ensell be likewise employed in the said business and be paid the yearly salary of thirty pounds.' He also refers to 'Charles Ensell the elder[25], Manager and workman at the Glass House', to whom he left a legacy of £50. So this will not only shows the change of ownership of the glassworks, but also clarifies the roles of the members of the Ensell family. His legatees, apart from his sister Kitty, were the children of his partner and brother-in-law George Ensell who was married to Richard Bradley's other sister Phebe[26]. Six weeks after the will was proved, Lucy Mary Ensell married John Holt of Wigan[27] and he took over Lucy Mary's responsibilities in the business.

The business carried on trading as Bradley, Ensells and Holt, the title for the firm running the Red House and White House Glassworks, as well as Wordsley Flint Glassworks. In 1801 the firm placed an advertisement. It could refer to any of the three glasshouses owned by the partnership, but most likely refers to Wordsley Flint Glassworks where the cutters would have the benefit of steam power:

> 'Wanted 3 or 4 good overhand glass-cutters. Apply to Bradley, Ensell and Holt, Wordsley near Stourbridge.'[28]

The first open-and-shut mould was invented by Charles Chubsee, a glassworker employed by Bradley, Ensell and Holt, in 1802. He could not afford to patent his invention and so it was soon widely copied. It was made from iron and comprised a fixed body section and two moveable shoulder sections that opened mechanically. This would have given Bradley, Ensell and Holt a great advantage in the production of bottles to a uniform shape. It predates the patent taken out by Henry Ricketts of Bristol for his elaborate multi-levered moulding mechanism by nineteen years. The mould also enabled the form of the vessel and elaborate, closely spaced designs in relief to be applied to the outer surface of flint-glass tableware in a few simple hand operations[29]. Chubsee is credited with being a very competent pattern and mould maker. By 1814 he managed a glassworks in Wolverhampton run by a Mr Buckle[30].

About 1810 glassmaking was discontinued at Wordsley Flint Glassworks in Richardson's disparaging description, 'by attitudes of the glass trade.' The glassworks was altered to a manufactory of 'Bilston' steel, iron being imported from Sweden for the purpose and managed by John Holt[31]. The cone is shown graphically on Sherriff's 1812 plan, but unfortunately its purpose is not noted. On Fowler's 1822 map it is described as 'Steel house + pot rooms.'[32]

Records detailing the closure of a footpath behind the Wordsley Glasshouse in 1817 show the works owned by the brothers-in-law, John Holt and Richard Bradley Ensell the elder[33].

John Holt died in 1820[34], aged sixty-two. He did not leave a proper will, but some unattested and undated papers expressed his wish that his one third share in the 'glass business' should go to his daughter and only child Mary Holt. Letters of administration for his estate were granted in 1821[35].

In 1827 Mary Holt married George William Wainwright[36], a plate glass manufacturer of East Smithfield, Wapping, Middlesex. After their marriage, he took over running Mary's share of the business.

After all these deaths and marriages the partnership formed out of necessity by the legatees of Richard Bradley and their offspring became unworkable. They decided to sell the entire business so those who wanted their money out could take it. Those who wished to continue glass manufacturing would be free to buy back a part of the business at the market price. An announcement was duly made:

> 'The trade formerly carried on by (the undersigned) Richard Bradley Ensell, senior, and by Charles Ensell deceased, and by John Holt, also deceased, at Wordsley under the firm of 'Bradley, Ensells and Holt.' and afterwards by the said R. B. Ensell, sen., and J. Holt, since by the said R. B. Ensell sen., (the undersigned) Richard Bradley Ensell, the younger and Mary Holt respectively under the same firm, and after the marriage of the said Mary Holt with (the undersigned) George William Wainwright, carried on as well in the firm of 'Bradley, Ensells & Holt,' as that of 'Ensells and Wainwright,' or 'Ensells & Co.' has been dissolved by mutual consent as and from the 11th April 1827. Jeremiah Matthews of Stourbridge was appointed under the decree of the High Court of Chancery as manager for winding up the affairs of the late partnership concerns.'[37]

Matthews divided the partnership property into six lots and put it up for auction. Lot two describes the works as the 'Steel' House or 'Old Glasshouse'. Two legal disputes over ownership took place but it was decided that lot two was to be sold to the highest bidder and the auction took place on 28th September 1827 at the Talbot Inn.

George William Wainwright bought the steelworks and returned it to the manufacture of glass. Wainwright took his brother Charles into the business and they appointed Benjamin Richardson—who was managing Thomas Hawkes' works in Dudley—as their manager. The furnace was lit in July 1828 and work commenced producing fine quality flint glass[38]. Both Wainwright brothers then left Wordsley to reside in London where they concentrated on their interests in the upholstery business. The firm traded as Wainwright Brothers, manufacturers of plain and cut glass[39].

After just a year, the Wainwright brothers decided to sell the business. They offered the lease to their manager Benjamin

Richardson and his brother William Haden Richardson. The Richardsons seized the opportunity to satisfy a long-held ambition to run their own glass manufacturing business and set about trying to raise capital. Benjamin Richardson describes that, 'Benjamin Webb[40] at Dock heard how things were and he said that his brother John's son would like to go into the glass trade and he got him to see me upon it and eventually it was arranged by him to join us.'[41] Thomas Webb joined the Richardsons in partnership and founded the firm of Webb and Richardsons on 25th December 1829. Thomas Webb introduced £3,000 of the capital and William Haden Richardson and Benjamin Richardson £1,200, although for this Webb was granted a half share of the business and the Richardson brothers a quarter share each[42]. Their move was a bold one; 1829 was the depth of a depression that began in 1826, but from then on business activity in the Black Country began to improve until prosperity was again attained by 1834.

Thomas Webb[43] was the twenty-five-year old son of John Webb[44], a Stourbridge farmer and butcher who later went into the glass business at the White House. He probably supplied the capital for his son.

William Haden Richardson was forty-four years old, the oldest of eleven children of Joseph Richardson, a master glasshouse furnace-builder of Wordsley. He was an experienced and knowledgeable glassmaker, with first-hand experience of several Midlands factories. His notebook[45] describes that he entered the trade in 1802 at Bilston[46]. He moved to Grafton's Brierley Glasshouse, then worked for the firm of Thomas Hawkes from 1810 to July 1828 where he became the firm's traveller. His notebook contains detailed records of all aspects of glassmaking, presumably written pending the day he could fulfil his ambition to own his own glassworks.

Benjamin Richardson was twenty-seven years old, the ninth child of Joseph Richardson. He had also learned the glass trade working for the Dudley firm of Thomas Hawkes where he rose to the position of manager until he moved to manage Wordsley Flint Glassworks for George William Wainwright.

Before the Richardson brothers entered the glass trade as manufacturers, the family tradition was in building and in particular furnace making. Their grandfather, John Richardson[47], describes himself in his will as a bricklayer[48]. His son Joseph Richardson[49] continued the trade of a 'master glasshouse furnace builder' at Wordsley. He was celebrated for the quality of his work in the local glasshouses, as well as those of Birmingham and London. His notebook, referred to several times in this text, demonstrates the extent of his work. In 1815 he built furnaces for the Whitefriars Glass Manufactory in Fleet Street, for Apsley Pellatt at his Blackfriars Glasshouse and for several other London flint-glass and bottlehouses. This trade was carried into a third generation by Joseph Richardson II[50], the brother of William Haden and Benjamin. He established himself as a master furnace-builder at Aston near Birmingham[51].

Webb & Richardsons soon began some pioneering work. In 1832 they introduced a machine for producing pressed glass. This was a relatively new invention, developed in America. It is fully described and illustrated with line drawings in the *Repertory of Patent Specifications, 1831*. Each machine, operated by a team of seven men, produced decorative hollowware at the same rate as ten glassblowing teams of four men each. Apparently Benjamin Richardson was the first in England to use the pressing machine for shaping and decorating flint glass with relief ornament[52].

Thomas Webb & Co. paid £5,745 6s excise duty for the year ending 5th January 1833[53], suggesting this had become the largest of the sixteen Stourbridge/Dudley glassmaking firms, only three years after the firm was founded.

In 1833 Thomas Webb, now aged twenty-nine, married Elizabeth[54], the daughter of Joseph Hemming, a printer, bookseller and stationer of High Street, Stourbridge. They lived in Stourbridge at Longlands Villa. From their offspring were to appear the proprietors of two of the most famous glass firms in Stourbridge.

The original five-year lease expired in 1834, but both lessor and lessee were satisfied with their situation. So, Messrs Webb and Richardson took a further lease of twenty-one years from George William Wainwright on 21st January 1834[55]. The firm continued to trade as Webb and Richardsons, Wordsley Glass Works, manufacturers of flint glass plain and cut[56]. In 1836 the glassworks had a rateable value of £44 25s. Benjamin Richardson lived in a house next to the glassworks[57].

Thomas Webb's father, John Webb, died in 1835[58] and Thomas inherited from him a share in the White House Glassworks situated just the other side of the canal. In the original Webb and Richardson partnership agreement it is stated to be renewable after seven years, the anniversary of which would be 25th December 1836. Thomas Webb decided to part from the Richardsons and concentrate his efforts at the White House. So, on 15th December 1836 he formally withdrew from the Webb & Richardsons partnership, receiving 'over £7,000'[59].

The remaining partners, Benjamin and William Haden Richardson, were joined in partnership by their youngest brother, Johnathan[60], who had previously been a clerk and bookkeeper[61].

The Excise Licences Act of 1825[62] required glass manufacturers to be licensed and to pay £20 per year for each glasshouse. A Glass Licence for the works was applied for on 23rd December 1837 and issued on 5th July 1838. It licensed William Haden Richardson, Benjamin Richardson and Johnathan Richardson of Wordsley to carry on the trade or business of glassmakers on receipt of £20[63].

A meeting took place on 5th December 1837 at the Dudley Arms Hotel where the manufacturers considered their response to the formation of the first glassmakers' trade union. One of the Richardsons was present, probably Benjamin. The resolution passed at their meeting has already been described[64].

Benjamin Richardson was at the forefront of experimentation with different colours for glass. In 1839 the firm was described as manufacturers of 'Plain & Rich Cut Glass of Every Colour.'[65]

In 1841 Benjamin Richardson and his family lived on the premises of the Wordsley Glassworks. Johnathan and his family lived in the next but one property[66]. The following year, in 1842, William Haden Richardson and Benjamin Richardson were formally joined in partnership by Johnathan Richardson under the firm of W.H., B. and J. Richardson[67].

During the period around 1842 William Haden Richardson lived at Dyers Buildings, Holborn, London[68] and acted as the firm's London sales manager. An exchange of letters during 1842 between Benjamin Richardson and William Haden Richardson is extremely informative about the state of the business and the life and times of the family. Benjamin Richardson continuously reported progress with their greenhouse and the garden being laid out at Wordsley. He also reported with great pride his experiments with new colours such as canary yellow and cornelian white. William Haden replied about customer complaints, problems of quality, cost of carriage and other business matters. The year of 1842 was a time of deep depression in the Black Country[69]. Some facts that emerge from this series of letters concern two travellers employed, Mr Keeling who covered the north and Mr Hawkins who travelled as far east as Norfolk. Complete accounts of Mr Hawkins' income and expenses are detailed in the correspondence. It reveals the glasshouse was consuming six hundred and sixty tons of coal per quarter and receipts were noted for the purchase of cullet from Hawkes' in Dudley. Benjamin Richardson's prime business concern was pessimism about price cutting in the trade. He wailed that 'Jackson is the curse of the Trade.'[70] 'Hawkes' is likely to close.' 'Littlewood and Berry are likely to shut up for a time.' 'Dial people pulled down their furnace, building a six pot furnace, their trade is down.' By the 12th February his tone was positively suicidal. He refers to 'the cursed foolishness of manufacturers giving the goods away . . . Webb selling at those prices will sink the new bank . . . cut, cut, cut, down, down, down' His proposed solution was 'Regular meeting and prices fixed!' Even an attempt at exporting to Montreal via Liverpool, was reported on 25th February as having been relatively unsuccessful because the market in Canada was saturated[71].

Apart from poor trade, the Stourbridge firms faced increasing competition from abroad, particularly Bohemia. A new product in the form of cased glass began to emanate from Bohemia in the eighteen-forties and was well liked by the public. Ever responsive to changes in public taste and fashion, the Richardsons began to experiment with cased glass. It required the development of new techniques, but the initial problems were overcome and the first examples begin to appear in the Richardson pattern books about 1844.

The hated glass excise duty was lifted in 1845[72] leading to an immediate surge of new designs and colours brought to market. At the end of 1845 W.H., B. and J. Richardson exhibited at the Manchester Exhibition where their products included opaline glass, layered, and painted work. Further evidence of the pioneering work with colour being performed by Benjamin Richardson was reported:

> 'We have intimated that Messrs. Richardson are directing considerable attention to the improvement of coloured glass; in this art we yet lag behind our neighbours; chemistry has at present done little for it in this country; these gentlemen have, however, already made great advance in rivaling [sic] the productions of Bohemia; and we have little doubt that, a few years hence, we shall see at least equal the best of the imported articles; their specimens of opal glass are remarkably successful; and of cutting, engraving, and polishing, they supply examples second to none that have ever been produced in this country.'[73]

The Richardsons were canny enough to inform their customers that the removal of the glass excise duty would not necessarily lead to a reduction in prices:

> 'We herewith hand you new List of Prices commencing this day on the abolition of the duty on Glass . . . It may perhaps be necessary to remove many erroneous impressions which prevail to state the late duties upon Glass removed by the government viz. on Window and German Sheet Glass 8 1/2d per lb, on Plate Glass 6 ½ per lb—on Flint Glass and Black Bottles, three farthings per lb so that the reduction of duty cannot influence the price of Flint and Cut Glass to any extent.'[74]

W.H., B. and J. Richardson registered two designs dated 6th July and 16th August 1847 for glassware with vitrified enamel decorations. These pieces are usually marked *Richardson's Vitrified Enamel Color* [sic]. Most of the articles were painted with simple but elegant designs in black, but later more sophisticated styles appeared, painted with several different colours. Decorators from the potteries in north Staffordshire were attracted to Wordsley by high wages and painted in the styles then fashionable on the more costly bone china. The term vitrified refers to the enamels used. These were metallic oxides, fused with a flux that vitrified at a lower temperature than the object being enamelled. The products were immediate prizewinners, but they did not win the ultimate accolade, the RSA large gold medal. However, 'as a stimulus to further improvement' W.H., B. and J. Richardson were awarded The Royal Society of Art's Gold Isis Medal:

> Special Prizes. Took into consideration the specimens of Enamelled and Gilded Glass sent in by Messrs Richardson & Co. of Wordsley Works Stourbridge in competition for the Society's Gold Medal.
>
> The specimens sent by Messrs Richardson are described as 'the colours and gilding being all burnt on by passing through the enamel Kilns similar to the mode made use of in printing upon china.'
>
> The Committee examined the specimens which consisted of Red, Blue, Green and Yellow Ground vitrified, and also some to shew the colour of the glass before enamelling, with the specimens of gilding &c and Resolved.
>
> That it is the opinion of this Committee that the Vases presented by Messrs Richardson (the only specimens before them) exhibit very considerable advances in the art of enamelling on glass, but they do not consider either of the productions good in form or execution to entitle either of them to the large Gold Medal. They do however recommend that the Gold Iris Medal be awarded to the Candidate for his Blue Vase with Grecian figures, as a stimulus to further improvement.
>
> Signed: Wm Newton, William Spencer, John I Crace, John F Christy[75].

In another example of responding to designs and matters of public interest W.H., B. and J. Richardson marketed white opaline versions of the Portland Vase, transfer printed with the design. About this time Benjamin Richardson tried to inspire his workmen by stating that a faithful reproduction of the vase could command a thousand pounds. The public interest in the Portland Vase followed a famous incident when the original Roman article dating from 25 BC was smashed by an 'inebriated neurotic' named Lloyd in the British Museum on 7th February 1845.

In 1848 W.H., B. and J. Richardson registered a design for a clear glass jug decorated with water lilies. The decoration closely followed the design of water plants by Richard Redgrave RA[76] for Henry Cole's 'Felix Summerley's Art Manufactures', registered in 1847. Although Redgrave's was naturalistic[77], and Richardsons' gushingly florid, the decoration on both articles is a good example of the contemporary style of suggestive ornament. Richardsons' jug and Redgrave's carafe were both to hold water at the table. Another example of Richardsons' use of suggestive ornament from the same period is a milk jug, enamelled with a scene of a cow and a milkmaid. Later that year the firm was awarded another prize by the Royal Society of Art, this time for engraved glass:

> 'To Messrs Richardson for the beauty and purity of their Glass and for the merit of their works in engraved Glass &c, The large Silver Medal.'[78]

The Richardsons' decorating department must have been a vibrant, stimulating and exciting place to work in 1848. A constant stream of new styles of decoration was flowing forth. It was to this hotbed of creativity that an aspiring young apprentice, John Northwood[79], came at the age of twelve. He began his apprenticeship in the decorating department learning the art of painting, gilding and enamelling[80]. Little did he know he would become one of the most influential designers and craftsmen in the history of the Stourbridge glass industry.

Despite the success of their products, the Richardsons began to experience financial difficulties. They were probably carried away by their own success and overreached themselves. To expand their capacity William Haden Richardson purchased the White House in 1841 for £3,400[81]. By 1848 the brothers were not acting together as harmoniously as they had been in the past:

'B. Richardson on 5 May, 1848 mortgaged all his interest in the glass trade to W.H. and J. Richardson as security of liabilities incurred by them in their bills without their knowledge and consent as alleged by Mr Johnathan Richardson.'[82]

The liabilities referred to amounted to £4,450. So, later that year the Richardsons mortgaged the White House Glassworks to William Webb junior[83] for £3,000 to raise some capital[84].

The Richardson partnership continued to produce glass of the finest quality and marketed it with the same vigour as they had for many years. In 1849 W.H., B. and J. Richardson exhibited coloured and opaline glass at the Birmingham Exhibition. In 1849 they were awarded the Royal Society of Art's Silver Isis Medal for 'their combination of cutting with Venetian ornament.'[85] W.H., B. and J. Richardson displayed a vast range of products at the 'Exhibitions of Specimens of British Manufacture' held by the RSA in 1847, 1848 and 1849. Some examples include:

490 Glass Decanter, a specimen of elaborate cutting. 507 Specimen of Ruby Coloured Glass. 514 and 515 Glass Water Jug and Goblet, engraved with the lotus or water lilly[86]. 518, 519, 520 and 521 Specimens of pure Glass Metal without cutting. 533 Glass Centre-Dish and Stand richly cut, as a specimen of a table service. 536 Salt and Stand, cut by the Lapidary, and showing the colour of crystal glass. 552 Flower Glass, with coloured and gold antique figures. 553 and 554 Two Glass Vases, with antique Grecian figures, in colours[87]. 555 Large Glass Vase, frosted, with two subjects enamelled upon it, from Flaxman, viz Thetis ordering the Nerids to descend into the sea, and 'Morning.' 556 Glass Vase, with Grecian figures, black enamel. 557 Glass Vase, in coloured enamelled figures, subject from Hamilton, the Priest and the Supplicant offering a libation to Apollo. 558 Glass Vase, with Grecian Figures, coloured enamel. 559 Jug, in Glass, ornamented with figures, from the antique, in black enamel[88].

Such was the result of the innovative and artistic style of Benjamin Richardson. He was later called 'the father of the glass trade.'[89] Clearly proud of their succession of awards, the firm placed an advertisement in 1849 as:

> 'Manufacturers of Every Description of Engraved, Cut, Frosted, Enamelled and Stained Glass comprising every variety of the Newest and Most Approved Style of English and French Patterns. Also Manufacturers and Patentees of a new Vitreous-Stained Figured Glass of the most Beautiful and Transparent Colour, with Richly Executed Designs of Fruits, Flowers, Figures, etc. in shades of the greatest delicacy, and admirably adapted for Churches, Chapels, Halls etc. Also of the Registered New Pattern Waterlilly Lamp Shade And a Variety of other Beautiful Cut Glass Shades. Druggists Glass of Every Description.'

In 1851 Benjamin Richardson lived with his children at Wordsley, employing a hundred and eighty-eight hands[90]. Johnathan also lived at Wordsley with his wife and family[91]. During that year the firm exhibited at the Great Exhibition held at the Crystal Palace in Hyde Park. The exhibits included:

> 'cut crystal; opal vases painted with enamel colours (Ulysses weeping at the song of Demodicus, the Judgement of Paris, Diomede casting his spear at Mars, the Dream of Penelope, Aesops Fables, etc.); opal glass ornamented with Pet Fawn in enamel colours; and Grecian figures in coloured enamels.'[92]

They won a Bronze Medal for the excellence of their crystal and coloured glass and secured an order from Queen Victoria. An accolade in the Birmingham Journal stated 'Messrs. Richardson of Wordsley are well entitled to precedence, the purity of their flint has no equal in the Exhibition.'[93]

Despite the universal approbation of their products, the firm of W.H. B. & J. Richardson was declared insolvent on 14th February 1852. William Haden Richardson clearly felt he was innocent in the matter. There are many pungent notes in his handwriting on the bankruptcy papers to that effect. He wrote:

> In Feb. 1852 I was made unjustly bankrupt thro' a Vilanous old Banker and Faculty Lawyer who swindled me out of Thousands. Notwithstanding this every creditor was paid in full. It cost me 84/– for every 20/– owed[94].

Fascinating notes appear in the Richardson papers about tools, materials and equipment buried by Benjamin and Johnathan Richardson, to hide their assets from the bankruptcy commissioner[95]. Because of the bankruptcy, the workforce was laid off. This led to the start of several new ventures by the former employees.

Philip Pargeter[96], a nephew of the Richardson brothers, who was serving an apprenticeship as an engraver, left and set up his own engraving shop. In 1861 he lived at Audnam with his mother, sister and brother, described as a glass engraver employing one man and two boys[97]. John Northwood went to work for his older brother William[98], a builder.

William Jabez Muckley began his career with Richardsons as a glasscutter and became their principal designer and engraver[99]. He was responsible for much of the engraving that brought the firm such praise in the Great Exhibition of 1851. A superb engraved goblet signed by Muckley exists today illustrated among Richardsons' products in the Art Journal catalogue of the Great Exhibition. He later achieved great fame as a painter and became Principal of the Manchester School of Art.

The first Muckley to arrive in the district was William Jabez's grandfather, William Muckley. Born at the Manor House, Halesowen, he was descended from a prominent Worcestershire family, although they had lost their family fortune in a series of disastrous lawsuits at the end of the eighteenth century. He was a Baptist preacher ordained in 1808 and lived in Birmingham. All of his children's births are recorded in the registers of Bond Street Baptist Chapel, Birmingham. In the historical records of Cradley Baptist Church a seat rent book is prefaced by an account of how the church there was formed. It records that Mr Pearse from Bond Street sent Mr Muckley, who preached at Cradley on alternate Sundays. He was also involved with the Baptist chapel in Meeting Lane, off Brettell Lane and started a chapel in Kinver in 1814[100]. He left the district in 1819 but his son Jabez[101] remained and married a local girl, Mary Ann Simpson in 1828. Their son, William Jabez Muckley, was born in 1829[102]. Jabez Muckley worked as a glasscutter in Wordsley and by 1861 was a glassworks manager, living at 35 Chapel Street[103].

In 1851, his son, William Jabez was an unmarried twenty-two-year old, lodging at 13 Bug Lane, Wordsley, described as a glass engraver[104]. Later that year he married Mary Pardoe. The Muckleys boast the Civil War commander, General Fairfax[105] among their ancestors; the name reappears as a forename from time to time. This, combined with his interest in art, explains the unusual names of some of Muckley's children: Angelo Fairfax Muckley, Jabez Rembrant Fairfax Muckley, Leonardo Fairfax Muckley and William Raphael Muckley.

After the Richardsons' bankruptcy, Muckley joined the Birmingham School of Art. He won one of the eight scholarships competed for by all the art schools of Great Britain. He obtained four art degrees of the highest class and went on to study in London and Paris. He was head of Burslem School of Art for five years[106] and was offered the headmastership of Wolverhampton School of Art[107]. Then, in 1862 he became Principal of Manchester School of Art[108]. He exhibited at the Royal Academy 1859-1904 and at Suffolk Street, the R.I. and Grosvenor Gallery. His pictures were mostly large, showy vases of flowers, set in sumptuous interiors[109]. Wood incorrectly stated Muckley's year of birth as 1837. This could be the cause of Wakefield's doubt about Muckley the glass engraver and Muckley the painter being the same person[110]. Hajdamach cautiously suggests they were probably the same person[111]. With the benefit of possessing family papers, the author suggests they were definitely the same person. As well as being a prolific painter Muckley published four books on painting. His first *Handbook for Painters and Art Students on the character and use of colours* was published in 1880 and had four editions. He eventually retired to White Notley Hall, Witham, Essex about 1900. He died at his home on 30th August 1906, aged seventy-six and was buried at White Notley parish church. An obituary describes him as a 'well-known artist, late principal of the Manchester School of Art . . . who had exhibited for 40 years consecutively at the Academy.'[112]

John Thomas Bott was another craftsman who left Richardsons' after their bankruptcy and after a brief interval in Birmingham he moved to Worcester Porcelain Works. It has been suggested[113] that he was responsible for many of the enamelled vases with floral decoration produced by Richardsons', although there is no documentary evidence to this effect.

When the works reopened, under the management of Benjamin Richardson, many craftsmen eventually returned: John Northwood, Thomas Bott, William Jabez Muckley and his brother; L. Locke, Philip Pargeter, E. Guest and others[114]. The firm got back to business by exhibiting at the 1853 Dublin Exhibition, but Benjamin Richardson's oldest son decided to seek fame and fortune elsewhere. In 1853 William Haden Richardson II[115], who was in business making gas tubes and fittings[116], was approached by James Couper to join the firm of James Couper & Son at the City Glassworks, Glasgow. James Couper senior[117] wished to retire and asked Richardson to manage the City Glassworks, working with his son, James junior[118]. Richardson accepted the offer and moved to Glasgow. He prospered as a glass manufacturer and iron founder[119] and by 1900 he was the sole proprietor[120].

In her book *Victorian Glass*, Ruth Webb Lee made the following interesting but unsubstantiated statement: 'The first English (etching) machine was made in 1855 in a very primitive way by one James Smith, an engineer in the employ of W.H. Richardson of Wordsley, being constructed out of an old lathe which had been used for turning gas butts.'[121] Certainly etching was a technique being developed about this time, as an acid-etching process was patented by Benjamin Richardson in 1857. This patent, dated 20th June 1857, was for producing cameo relief designs on a cased glass blank. The surface of a cased blank was coated with gutta-percha or india rubber, both of which are resistant to acids. Then, some of the resist was removed with pointed tools before dipping the article in acid to remove the portions of the outer casing not protected by the resist. The article, being composed of two or more casings of coloured glass, when finished, displayed a design of one colour in shallow relief on a ground of another hue. In 1857 Benjamin Richardson filed the earliest patent for satin glass. His invention for *An Improvement In The Manufacture Of Articles In Glass, So As To Produce Peculiar Ornamental Effects* was filed on 27th

July 1857 and granted on 26th January 1858. The method involved trapping air between two layers of glass in a symmetrical pattern. These developments were shown in 1857 when the firm exhibited at the Manchester Industrial Exhibition. The exhibits included ornamental coloured glass, cased work and painted opal vases. Opal glass stained yellow and green by uranium oxide was also produced.

Faced with an outbreak of strikes, the employers responded by holding a meeting on 1st November 1858 at the Talbot Hotel, Stourbridge, where they formed a manufacturer's organisation. Benjamin Richardson did not attend and refused to sign the document stating that he would not employ any of the strikers. However, he pledged his word he would not do so.

Benjamin Richardson must have been concerned about his succession in the business. His oldest son had departed to Scotland and then in 1859, at the age of twenty-seven, his second son Henry Gething Richardson[122] decided to start his own business as a glass decorator. He formed a partnership with his brother-in-law, Thomas Guest[123], and one of the family firm's more talented employees, John Northwood. John Northwood involved his younger brother Joseph[124] in the partnership. They found premises at the lower end of Barnet Lane, Wordsley, where it joins Lawnswood Road and commenced work in 1860. The initial partnership only lasted a year before it was dissolved. Thomas Guest left to start his own glass decorating business with his brothers, Edward[125] and Richard[126] which traded as Guest Brothers in Brettell Lane.

Henry Gething Richardson worked as a glass decorator for twenty years before taking over the family firm about 1881. In 1861 he lived at Coalbournbrook with his family, described as a manufacturer of flint glass[127]. In 1871 he lived in Collis Street with his family, described as a glass master employing six men, nine women and three boys[128].

John and Joseph Northwood carried on the Barnet Lane works as J. & J. Northwood[129]. From this small workshop came some of the greatest masterpieces of glass ever made: the Portland Vase[130], the Milton Vase[131], the Pargeter-Northwood tazze[132] and the Pegasus Vase[133]. John Northwood was eventually tempted away in 1882 to become the works manager and artistic director of Stevens and Williams[134]. The business continued in operation until 1927. After an illustrious history, the premises were sold on Tuesday 14th June 1927 and the site is now built over.

In 1859 Richardsons' obtained a patent for a method of decoration known as *Trapped Enamel*. This involved blowing the base of a shape such as a vase or a ewer, minus its neck. A design was then enamelled on the inside of the article, such as bright flowers, or cherubs and flower swags. A second gather was then blown inside the first, this time completing the neck or spout. The decoration was therefore trapped between two layers of glass. A frilly collar was then applied to mask the lip formed at the extremity of the first, smaller blowing.

Having been slow to accept the need for solidarity among the glassmaking employers, Benjamin Richardson joined the Association of Flint Glass Manufacturers in September 1859.

Like his older brother, Johnathan Richardson also lost his most promising son to an alternative business. In 1863 John Thomas Haden Richardson[135] joined the Tutbury Glass Company[136] as a managing partner. He moved to Scropton Road, Marston-upon-Dove, near the factory and by 1881 employed thirty men, twenty-seven boys and three women[137].

The Richardson brothers were now of an age when they must have been thinking of slowing down, if not retiring. Benjamin was sixty-one and Jonathan fifty-nine years old. Between them their three oldest sons had found independence elsewhere and so they turned to their nephews, Philip Pargeter and William James Hodgetts. Pargeter returned to the works where he had been an apprentice in 1852. William James Hodgetts had been operating the Red House glassworks with his mother Elizabeth. On 14th September 1863 they formed a partnership with their Richardson uncles to trade as Hodgetts, Richardson & Pargeter. William James Hodgetts' sister, Emily Jane, performed a painting of the interior of the glasshouse, now hanging in Broadfield House Glass Museum, Kingswinford[138].

Surprisingly the new partnership was not responsible for any significant designs or masterpieces of glass, but continued a steady output of commercial products. For example, 1864 was the tercentenary of the birth of William Shakespeare and a range of opal vases decorated with transfer printed ornament of Shakespeare's house and monument at Stratford-upon-Avon was produced. The partnership lasted six years and was dissolved in 1869[139]. Pargeter, who had been the manager, remained for a further two years.

In 1871 Benjamin Richardson lived at Wordsley Hall, Buckpool, Wordsley[140]. William James Hodgetts lived with his family in Stourbridge Road, Amblecote[141]. Philip Pargeter lived with his sister, nephew and niece at Glass House Yard, Wordsley[142].

Pargeter left the firm in 1871 to take over the Red House glassworks. Henry Gething Richardson was still running his decorating business and living at Hawthorne Cottage, next to his father's Wordsley Hall. Benjamin Richardson tempted him back to the family firm to form a new partnership trading as Hodgetts, Richardson & Son. In 1876 the partners were 'manufacturers of flint, ruby and venetian glass, and of cut, engraved, etched and ornamental glass of every description.'[143]

The contemporary style was very much one of elaborate ornamentation. Glass in the Venetian fashion with its elaborate filigree work was being reproduced and each of the glassworks vied with one another for new and more ostentatious styles. Threading on glass had been known since ancient times; it featured regularly on Roman glass, but applying it by hand was a difficult and time-consuming process. William James Hodgetts patented the first machine for applying threading on 6th May 1876. The availability of a machine to apply threading led to hundreds of designs using threading from this date onwards, both at Richardsons' and inevitably among their competitors.

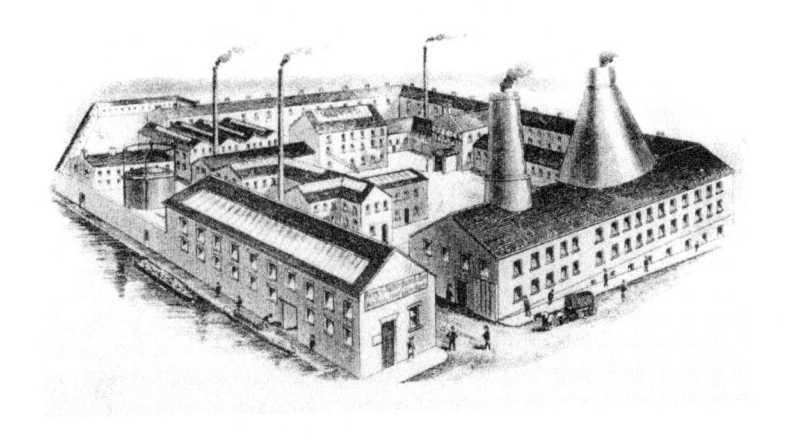

Wordsley Flint Glassworks

William Haden Richardson, the co-founder of the firm, died at Wordsley in 1876[144], aged ninety-one. He had made a will on 8th February 1866 and added a codicil on 3rd May 1870. When these were proved in 1877[145], he was described as a gentleman of Wordsley 'formerly a Glass Manufacturer but now out of business.' His will reveals that since at least 1847 he had lived with Mary Pargeter[146], the sister of Philip Pargeter, and therefore his niece. Although they had not married, they had seven children. The testator's will and codicil were mainly concerned with bequeathing property he had inherited from his late brother, Thomas Richardson[147], to his children by Mary Pargeter.

Benjamin Richardson was now seventy-five years old, but continued to drive the firm in its quest for revolutionary new colours. In 1877 he introduced blue and straw-coloured opal, quickly followed by pale green, amber, amethyst, sea-green and sky blue. In the same year, 1877, he invited Alphonse Eugene Lechevrel—a Frenchman well known as a craftsman in his own country—to Wordsley to train his workmen in the cameo technique. Lechevrel was born in Paris in 1850, where he had worked as a gem engraver and medallist, trained by Henri François, whose own work had a deep influence on him. Some of his pieces made for Richardsons' were exhibited at the 1878 Paris Exhibition. A list of six specimens issued in 1899 represents almost all of Lechevrel's known output.

All the firm's exhibits were photographed before being dispatched to Paris for the 1878 Exhibition. An album of seventy-two photographs still survives, providing a unique record of contemporary styles and designs. Prominent among the designs were examples of threaded wares, made possible by the invention of the threading machine two years earlier, such as a lustre with a tricorn shaped top and ruby threadwork$_{148}$. A second copy of the Portland Vase$_{149}$ by Joseph Locke won the firm the Gold Medal, even though it was not complete. By using a combination of carving and acids he got it to a near complete stage in less than eight months.

Joseph Locke$_{150}$ was Lechevrel's most promising and accomplished pupil. At the age of twelve he was apprenticed to the Royal Worcester china factory. When aged nineteen and still an apprentice, he won a competition$_{151}$ arranged by Guest Brothers, etchers and decorators of glass. Having won it, he went to work for them. He married into the Guest family$_{152}$ but developed a friendship with William James Hodgetts who invited him to join Hodgetts, Richardson & Co. to start an etching and decorating department. This he did—much to the displeasure of his wife's cousins, the Guest Brothers, who assumed that his family loyalty ought to be stronger. Locke later left Hodgetts, Richardson & Co. to work for Philip Pargeter. He then moved to Webb & Corbett and finally in 1882 he went to America where he joined the New England Glass Company of Cambridge, Mass. He died on 10th June 1936, aged ninety.

Another period of innovation began, this time driven by Henry Gething Richardson and supported by the many first-rate craftsmen the firm had assembled. His daughters also continued the family tradition. In 1881 Henry Gething Richardson lived at 'Hawthorns', next to Wordsley Hall, a flint glass manufacturer employing seventy-four men, twenty boys and sixteen women. His two oldest daughters, Elizabeth and Martha were described as 'artist—glass'$_{153}$.

In 1878 Hodgetts, Richardson & Son revived the applied snake decoration the firm had used mid-century to decorate the necks of decanters, stems of glasses, and bodies of vases. On 16th December 1879, Henry Gething Richardson patented *Improvements In Producing Ornaments, Designs, And Inscriptions On Or In Glass*. This was a method of enamelling on the inside of clear glass then blowing opal or another colour inside it, imprisoning the enamel between the two layers. Hodgetts, Richardson & Son registered a design in November 1881 for applied decoration in the form of a fish with an open mouth. Such zoomorphic designs were popular throughout the eighteen-eighties. Similar applied decoration was also used at Webb's and Boulton and Mills'. Fish were also a popular pattern in Rock Crystal at Webb's.

Benjamin Richardson retired from the firm sometime before 1881. He wrote his will on 18th May 1883 in which he called himself a retired glassmaker with capital still employed in the firm of Henry Gething Richardson. In 1881 he lived at White Hall, Webbs Lane, Wordsley, aged seventy-nine, with two of his daughters, described as a retired flint glass manufacturer[154].

William James Hodgetts was appointed as the Peoples' Warden of Amblecote Church in 1880[155], but retired from the business the same year because of ill-health. He wrote his will[156] on 26th October 1880 and moved from his home at the Platts to 59 Ondine Road, East Dulwich, Surrey. It was at East Dulwich that he died, four years later, on 25th August 1884. He left his entire estate, valued at £266 13s 6d, to his widow, Caroline Eunice Rosa Elizabeth.

Henry Gething Richardson now controlled the business and continued it as before. Applied decoration led to increasingly bizarre creations. A documented example of this style is the *Convolvulus Vase* made in 1885 by Henry Sutton[157], now in Broadfield House Glass Museum. The documentation describing the provenance of the vase appears in the Pottery Gazette of 1897. A style called *Tartan* glass was registered in 1886. This was an air-trap decoration with a plaid pattern resembling tartan cloth in appearance. It was part of the craze for air-trap decoration that began about 1881. Most of the manufacturers brought out their own named varieties of satin glass, all of which were developments of Richardsons' original patent of 1857.

Benjamin Richardson died in 1887[158], aged eighty-six. When his will was proved[159], it was mainly concerned with setting up a trust fund for his children, William Haden Richardson II, Henry Gething Richardson, Martha Maria Roose[160], Mary Maria Minifie[161] and Martha Haden Richardson[162]. He left an estate valued at £5,110 including lands and farms in the Transvaal, South Africa. His African properties were left to William Haden Richardson II. James Couper the younger, glassmaker of Glasgow, was one of his executors. The Daily Advertiser of 10th December 1887 carried a lengthy obituary in which the glasshouse is called the 'London Glass Works'. It is not clear how the works came to be known this way; the 1883 Ordnance Survey map labels it 'Londonhouse Works (Glass)'. However, its source can probably be found in Benjamin Richardson's own disparaging words, 'the trade was mostly a London trade not of flint quality, being made for public use.'[163] The name had disappeared on the 1903 Ordnance Survey map, which describes the works as 'Wordsley Flint Glassworks.' However, writing in 1934, Roland Wakefield states that the glassworks was known as the 'London House' at that time[164].

Benjamin Richardson's spinster daughter continued to occupy Wordsley Hall and so Henry Gething remained at his house next door, 'Hawthorne'[165].

When the chancel was added to Holy Trinity Church, Wordsley, the stained glass window in the west wall was given in remembrance of Benjamin Richardson by his daughters Martha Roose and Martha Haden Richardson. The dedication service on Friday 31st July 1891 was followed by a reception attended by the Bishop of Shrewsbury, and many distinguished visitors including: Major Webb of the White House Glassworks, Frederick Stuarts senior and junior of the Red House glassworks and Oswald George Meatyard the churchwarden and partner at Audnam Glassworks.

In 1892 the firm traded as Henry G. Richardson[166], but some time before 1897 Henry Gething introduced his sons, Benjamin[167] and William Haden Arthur[168] as partners and the firm traded as Henry G. Richardson & Sons.

In 1897 Henry G. Richardson & Sons registered a design for

miniature fir cones in opalescent glass with rustic crystal branches as a table decoration. It was followed in 1898 by the *Campanula* range with opalescent bluebell flowers arranged on straw or light amber rustic feet. This naturalistic style—involving designs resembling tree-trunks, bamboo and flowers—became increasingly popular around the turn of the century. The style is well described in a design from the Walsh-Walsh Glassworks in Birmingham, named *Rusticana*. Table-centres and flower-stands had been staple products for many of the Stourbridge glassworks from the eighteen-sixties onwards. Like most other forms of Victorian design, the styles developed to the height of florid exuberance by the late eighteen-nineties. The London firm of glass dealers, Dobson and Pearce, patented many designs in the eighteen-sixties. Twenty years later Daniel Pearce ended up at Thomas Webb's in charge of their department producing table centres[169]. Mrs Beeton's *Household Management*[170] refers to 'The important subject of table decorations ... The decoration of tables at the present time is almost universal ... Hostesses in the season vie with each other as to whose table shall be the most elegant, and are ready to spend almost, if not quite, as much upon the flowers as upon the dinner itself.'

Henry G. Richardson & Sons advertised in the Pottery Gazette Diary in 1899 'Cameo glass vases etc. in the most elaborate and in cheaper styles.' This clearly shows the era of quality cameo glass had passed. Poorer quality pieces marketed to meet the demand, especially in America, were mere shadows of the earlier magnificent pieces of craftsmanship. Experienced buyers would not purchase them, but the publicity they obtained stopped the production and the sale of genuine Cameo glass. The decline in quality continued with the advent of so-called *Mary Gregory* ware. This is a superficial technique of surface-painted white enamelled designs. Although of utterly incomparably poorer quality than cameo pieces, *Mary Gregory* ware is becoming increasingly collected and faked today.

With the turn of the century the exuberance of Victorian styles waned and the more flowing form of Art Nouveau developed. Henry

G. Richardson & Sons patented *Rominto* in September 1899 and *Ceonix* in March 1902. *Ceonix* is a series of vases with a colourful appearance caused by marbled colours in the body of the glass. The colour was given depth by a layer of clear crystal and the neck was sometimes decorated with gilding[171].

Pottery Gazette of August 1906 shows a photograph of Richardson's *Sunflower* range of flower holders. These prove the continued influence of the style of *Rusticana*. Other manufacturers were equally involved with this style. Thomas Webb's had a prodigious output of opalescent flower-holders in similar rustic style.

Henry Gething Richardson died in 1916 and the business was carried on by his sons Benjamin and William Haden Arthur. The vicissitudes of the First Great War meant that production was scaled down significantly.

On 11th June 1921 Benjamin and W.H.A. Richardson felt sufficiently confident to take a twenty-one year lease on the Wordsley Flint Glassworks and some adjoining property from the Firmstone family at an annual rent of £250[172]. The following year Henry G. Richardson & Sons exhibited at the British Industries Fair where Queen Mary was keenly interested in the firm's *Riviera* glassware[173]. However, within thirty months of taking the lease glassmaking ceased. John H. Husselbee, announced to the glassmaker's union:

> 'Fellow members, Following our last Report we unfortunately have to announce the closing of W.H. Richardson & Sons, probably the oldest Glass Works in Stourbridge, causing another 15 members becoming unemployed, 7 of whom being in arrears came under Rule XVIII, Clause 2, painfully illustrating the necessity, particularly in these uncertain times, of members paying their contributions regularly . . . '[174]

It is not clear if all trading ceased at this time, or just glassmaking. It seems likely that the firm bought in blanks from other glassworks and continued decorating. The Richardson brothers certainly continued to maintain and pay their lease and in 1928 the firm was trading as Henry G. Richardson & Sons, flint glass manufacturers[175].

In 1930 Webbs Crystal Glass Company Ltd. of Dennis Glassworks bought the firm. After almost exactly a hundred years, ownership went full-circle and reverted to the firm whose founder provided half the capital for the original partnership in 1829. Webbs Crystal Glass Company Ltd. purchased the freehold of the Wordsley Glassworks from the Firmstone family in a conveyance dated 19th December 1930 which describes the site as:

> 'ALL THAT building first used as a Glass House and called the Wordsley Glass Works but subsequently in the Steel Trade and now again used as a Glass House and called the Wordsley Glass Works situate at Wordsley . . . . and also all the other several buildings used as offices warehouses and shopping and the yard and ground thereto belonging.'[176]

Stan Eveson[177] joined Webbs' on 1st April 1929 and one of his tasks was to 'take the wages' to the newly acquired Richardson glassworks[178]. Blanks from Webbs' were finished off at the Wordsley works and marketed bearing Richardsons' Union Jack trademark. This continued until about 1934 by which time the glassworks was idle[179]. It is shown on the 1938 Ordnance Survey map, described as 'Wordsley Flint Glassworks.'

On 5th October 1945 Webbs' sold the freehold of the entire property to Ronald L. Christiansen Ltd[180]. Christiansen had been bombed out of his factory in London and used the site to manufacture centrifugal pumps. As business expanded, Christiansen decided to have the glass cone demolished. He obtained a quotation from a big demolition firm, which he accepted. Unlike the elaborate scaffolding that had just been erected on the Red House cone, they decided to put their scaffolding inside the cone. When the workmen arrived they took one look at the precarious state of the cone and immediately left the site. A local man, Bill Aston quoted £25 to demolish it with explosives. With remarkable precision, he brought the whole cone down one Sunday in 1946. German and Italian prisoners-of-war were brought in from a camp in Bromley Lane, Kingswinford, to chip all the bricks, as building materials were in short supply. However, the bricks were all hand-made and different shapes to suit the taper of the cone and so they ended up as rubble.

For many years the foundations of the cone were still visible but have now been concreted over. The entire frontage portrayed so proudly on Richardsons' letter headings has been demolished, but some of the original buildings are still quite clearly recognisable. The area where the cone stood is now a small engineering works.

---

1 John Hill, son of Waldron Hill and his second wife, Elizabeth Tyzack, widow, bap. 7th Sep 1749, Kingswinford.

2 PRO, RAIL 874.1.

3 Benjamin Richardson's notebook of 1886.

4 Mary Russell, daughter of Thomas Russell and his wife Anne, nee Haycock, bap. 17th Jun 1751, Oldswinford.

5 Mar. John Hill and Mary Russell, 27th Oct 1771, Oldswinford.

6 WRO, marriage licence, 26th Oct 1771.

7 Stuart Crystal, Joseph Richardson's notebook.

8 Waldron Hill, son of John and Elizabeth Hill, b. 7th Mar 1706; bap. 26th Mar 1706, Oldswinford. He later lived at the Tiled House, Pensnett. John was his son from his second marriage to Elizabeth Tyzack, whom he married 23rd Jun 1746, Kingswinford. His first wife was Sarah Badger, whom he married 7th Jan 1729, Kingswinford.

9 Richardson papers 27, 1827, Abstract of Title.

10 Richard Bradley, son of Peter and Mary Bradley, bap. 27th Dec 1745, Dudley St. Thomas's.

11 This house was later named Wordsley House and eventually Wordsley Manor, although there is no justification for this, as it was never formally the Manor House. It was occupied by William Foster, brother of ironmaster James Foster from the mid eighteen-thirties when it was renamed Wordsley House. William Rolinson Hodgetts, glassmaster of Red House Glassworks, owned it next. Upon his death in 1845 ownership passed to his daughter Alice Mary Hodgetts who married ironmaster, Henry Longville Firmstone in 1866. The newlyweds began married life at Springfield House - the former home of glassmaker Edward Webb - and later moved back into Wollaston Hall where Henry Firmstone had been born, leaving Alice Mary's spinster sisters occupying Wordsley House until the nineteen-thirties. Henry and Alice Firmstone had a son, George William Hodgetts Firmstone, a Captain in the Royal Munster Regiment. On marriage he lived at Wordsley House. It then passed to George's children Eldon Basil Aubrey Horatio Firmstone and Cecille

Rosemund Teresa Hope Bernadine Firmstone. Eldon, an energetic man and accomplished musician renamed the house Wordsley Manor. Eldon died in 1982, leaving the house in the hands of Cecille, now an old lady of 89 years. Cecille reached agreement with Dudley Council in 1988 to sell part of the estate on the proviso that the money be used to restore the Grade II building. Upon the death of Cecille, Eldon's son, Christopher John Eldon George Firmstone inherited the manor. As an architect, Christopher Firmstone was ideally placed to begin the restoration of the handsome building, which remains his family home today.

12 Bailey's 1783 Western and Midland Directory.
13 Kingswinford Court Rolls.
14 Supra, Moor Lane Glassworks, 1790.
15 PRO, Minutes of Committee Meetings of Proprietors 1791-1800 RAIL 874.5.
16 SRO, D648/5/22 5th Apr 1834 Release of Land.
17 Bristol Gazette, 10th Mar 1796.
18 Infra, Red House Glassworks.
19 Birmingham Gazette, 7th Mar 1796.
20 PRO, PCC will of Richard Bradley, 14th May 1796.
21 Kitty Bradley, daughter of Peter and Mary Bradley, bap. 7th Mar 1749, Dudley St. Thomas's. Although she was the co-heiress of Richard Bradley, she died before him, without issue; bur. 12th Aug 1795, Dudley St. Thomas's.
22 Lucy Mary Ensell, daughter of George Ensell and his wife Phebe, nee Bradley, bap. 29th Oct 1766, Dudley St. Thomas's.
23 Charles Ensell, son of George Ensell and his wife Phebe, nee Bradley, b. 1st Nov 1773.
24 Richard Bradley Ensell, son of George Ensell and his wife Phebe, nee Bradley, b. 14th Jun 1883; bap. 19th Jun 1783, Dudley St. Thomas's.
25 Charles Ensell, son of Edmund and Elizabeth Ensell, bap. 9th Sep 1744, Dudley St. Thomas's.
26 Mar. George Ensell and Phebe Bradley, 29th Sep 1765, Dudley St. Thomas's.
27 Mar. John Holt and Lucy Mary Ensell, 1st Jul 1796, Wigan, Lancashire.
28 Aris's Birmingham Gazette, 12th/19th Jan 1801.
29 Birmingham Journal, 31st May 1851, p7.
30 Benjamin Richardson's notebook of 1886.
31 Benjamin Richardson's notebook of 1886.
32 DA, William Fowler's *1822 Map of the Parish of Kingswinford*. Plot 267 Steel

house + pot Rms – Bradley, Ensell & Holt.
33 SRO, Sketch of Roads near Mr Holt's house at Wordsley, Dec 1817 Q/SB Epiphany 1818.
34 John Holt, d. 15th Dec 1820; bur. 20th Dec 1820, Kingswinford.
35 SRO, D648/5/22, PCC Admon of John Holt, 17th Apr 1821.
36 Mar. George William Wainwright and Mary Holt, 8th Jan 1827, Kingswinford.
37 London Gazette, 20th Jul 1827.
38 Benjamin Richardson's notebook of 1886.
39 Pigot and Co.'s Commercial Directory of Birmingham, 1829 and 1830 editions.
40 Benjamin Webb, builder of The Dock, Wordsley, son of Edward Webb, a victualler and his wife Jane, nee Westwood, bap. 27th Aug 1786, Kingswinford.
41 Benjamin Richardson's notebook of 1886.
42 SRO, D648/78/1.
43 Thomas Webb, son of John Webb, and his wife Sarah, nee Perks, b. 6th Jan 1804, Stourbridge, bap. 26th Jan 1804, Oldswinford.
44 John Webb, son of Edward Webb and his wife Jane, nee Westwood, bap. 2nd Apr 1775, Kingswinford.
45 Stuart Crystal, Notebook of William Haden Richardson, 1819.
46 Supra, Loxdale and Jackson.
47 1725-1818.
48 Will of John Richardson, 26th Dec 1813. Bricklayer was the Georgian term for a builder.
49 Joseph Richardson, son of John and Mary Richardson, bap. 23rd Dec 1759, Kingswinford.
50 Joseph Richardson, son of Joseph Richardson and his wife Martha, nee Haden, bap. 11th Dec 1796, Kingswinford.
51 In 1851 he lived with his family at 52 Woodcock Street, Aston, described as a Glass House Furnace Builder. PRO HO/107/2061 Fol. 125 P18, 1851 census of Aston.
52 Birmingham Journal, May 1851.
53 Thirteenth Report of the Commission into the Glass Excise, 1835, Appendix 7.
54 Mar. Thomas Webb and Elizabeth Hemming, 31st Aug 1833, Oldswinford.
55 Richardson Papers No 30, 1834, Lease.
56 Pigot and Co.'s National Commercial Directory of 1835.
57 SRO, Poor Rate Book 1836-7 D585/159/12.

58 John Webb, d. 8th Jan 1835; bur. Wordsley.
59 Richardson Papers No 31, 15 Dec 1836, Dissolution of Partnership.
60 Johnathan Richardson, son of Joseph Richardson and his wife Martha, nee Haden, bap. 24th Aug 1806, Kingswinford.
61 In the obituary of his son, John Thomas Haden Richardson, written in 1914, it states 'Mr. Jonathan Richardson joined his brothers as a partner in 1836, when the late Mr. Thos. Webb seceded from the firm of Webb and Richardson.'
62 6 George IV Chap 81, 5th Jul 1825, An Act to repeal several duties payable on Excise Licences in Great Britain and Ireland and to impose other duties in lieu thereof; and to amend the Laws for granting Excise Licences.
63 BHGM, Glassmakers licence 1837.
64 Supra, Audnam Glassworks.
65 Robson's 1839 Birmingham and Sheffield Directory.
66 PRO, 1841 Census of Kingswinford.
67 Richardson Papers No 37, 1842 Draft of Partnership.
68 He had leased the property from John Jones in 1827. Richardson Papers no 23, 30th Jul 1827 Lease of No 3 Dyers Court John Jones to William Haden Richardson. Dyers Buildings stood on Holborne Hill, half way between Castle Street and Fetter Lane. It is shown on John Tallis's *London Street Views 1838-1840*, Part 3 (1969), p43.
69 Supra, Audnam Glassworks.
70 Presumably Henry Jackson of Tutbury. Thomas Loxdale and George Elwell Jackson of Bilston dissolved their partnership in 1810. T. Rooker and George Elwell Jackson of Darlaston dissolved their partnership in 1807.
71 BHGM, Letter of Benjamin Richardson to William Haden Richardson.
72 Acts 8 and 9, Victoria (24 Ap, 1845), chapter 6, An Act to repeal the Duties & Laws of Excise on Glass.
73 Art-Union, Apr 1846.
74 Ibid, D.R. Guttery, p86.
75 RSA, Minutes of Committee of Manufactures, 14th May 1847.
76 Richard Redgrave, b. c1805 Pimlico, London, d. 1888.
77 Victoria & Albert Museum, 4503-1901.
78 RSA, Minutes of Committee of Fine Arts, 12th May 1848.
79 John Northwood, son of Frederick and Maria Northwood, bap. 13th Nov 1836, Kingswinford.
80 John Northwood II, *John Northwood, his Contribution to the Stourbridge*

Glass Industry (1958), p6.
81 Richardson Papers No. 34, 1841. Hill & Maurice.
82 Richardson Papers No 41, Bankruptcy notices.
83 William Webb, son of William Webb and his wife, Mary Hancox, b. Amblecote, bap. 2nd Dec 1801, Oldswinford.
84 White House papers No 2, 16 Jun 1848. Mortgage to Wm. Webb Jnr.
85 RSA, Address of the Council, p8.
86 Supra, 1848.
87 Supra, 1847.
88 RSA, MS.
89 PG, 1888.
90 PRO, 1851 Census HO 107/2036 02/045/115.
91 PRO, 1851 Census HO 107/2036 02/045/113.
92 Official Descriptive and Illustrated Catalogue, v 2, p699.
93 Birmingham Journal, 31st May 1851.
94 Richardson Papers No 41, 1851, W.H. Richardson's statement at the time of his bankruptcy.
95 Richardson Papers No 45, 1852, Tools secreted by B.R. and J.R.
96 Philip Pargeter, son of Philip Pargeter, a boatman and later a stocktaker at the firm of Messrs. John Bradley, Shutt End, and his wife Susannah, nee Richardson, a sister of the glassmaking brothers, b. 13th Feb 1826; bap. 12th Mar 1824, Kingswinford.
97 PRO, 1861 census RG 9/2069 ED2 Sched 145.
98 William Northwood, son of Frederick and Maria Northwood, bap. 28th Sep 1828, Kingswinford, d. 1st Apr 1867; bur. Wordsley.
99 Art Journal Catalogue, 1851.
100 W.T. Whitley, *Baptists in Stourbridge* (1929), p5.
101 Jabez Muckley, son of William and Elizabeth Muckley, b. 14th Jan 1803; bap. 29th Mar 1809, Bond Street Baptist Church, Birmingham.
102 William Jabez Muckley, son of Jabez Muckley and his wife Mary Ann, nee Simpson, bap. 5th Jul 1829, Wordsley. (In the parish register Jabez is spelled Javus for both father and son).
103 PRO, 1861 census RG 9/2069 ED4 Sched 103.
104 PRO, 1851 census HO 107/2036 07/121/013.
105 Thomas Fairfax (1612-1671), son of Ferdinando Fairfax; creator of the New Model Army and commander-in-chief of the Parliamentary Army.

106 Where his two oldest children were born, Beatrice in 1857 and William Raphael in 1859.
107 Where his next two children were born, Angelo Fairfax in 1860 and Jessie Fairfax in 1861.
108 Where four further children were born, Jabez Rembrant Fairfax in 1864, Wallis in 1865, Leonora Fairfax in 1867 and Jermaudo Fairfax in 1868; PRO, 1881 census of Didsbury, Lancashire, RG11/3890/45/27.
109 Christopher Wood, *The Dictionary of Victorian Painters* (1978).
110 Hugh Wakefield, *Nineteenth Century British Glass* (1961), p37.
111 Ibid, Charles R. Hajdamach, pp111-2.
112 Braintree and Bocking Advertiser, 6th Sep 1905.
113 G.W. Beard, *Nineteenth Century Cameo Glass* (1956).
114 Ibid, John Northwood II, p7.
115 William Haden Richardson, son of Benjamin Richardson and his wife Ann Eunice, nee Gething, b. 21st Oct 1825; bap. 25th Dec 1825, Kingswinford.
116 After studying metallurgy, in 1846 William Haden Richardson joined a tube manufacturing firm in Darlaston and traded as W.H. Richardson Junior & Co.
117 James Couper, b. c1798, Glasgow, Lanarkshire.
118 James Couper, son of James Couper, b. c1822, Glasgow, Lanarkshire.
119 At the time of the 1881 census he was visiting David Hulett, a gas engineer and gas apparatus manufacturer in Erith, Kent; PRO 1881 census of Erith, Kent, RG11/863/74/44.
120 William Haden Richardson II died at his home in India Street, Glasgow on 13th May 1913. He left an estate valued at £115,994.
121 PRO, 1851 Census, HO 107/2036 01/015/076 shows James Smith, a thirty-six year old glasshouse mould maker, born in Birmingham, living in Wordsley.
122 Henry Gething Richardson, son of Benjamin Richardson and his wife Ann Eunice, nee Gething, b. 11th Jan 1832; bap. 8th Apr 1832. He married Elizabeth Guest, 2nd Apr 1856, Kingswinford.
123 Thomas Guest, son of Edward Guest, cordwainer of Brettell Lane, and his wife Eliza, nee Bourne, bap. 30th Dec 1838, Kingswinford.
124 Joseph Northwood, son of Frederick and Maria Northwood, bap. 8th Sep 1839, Kingswinford.; d. 15th Nov 1915; bur. Bispham, Lancashire.
125 Edward Guest, son of Edward Guest, cordwainer of Brettell Lane and his wife Eliza, nee Bourne, b. 11th Apr 1835, Brettell Lane, bap. 17th May 1835, Kingswinford.

126 Richard Bourne Guest, son of Edward Guest, cordwainer of Brettell Lane and his wife Eliza, nee Bourne, b. 5th Feb 1837, Brettell Lane, bap. 12th Mar 1837, Kingswinford.

127 PRO, 1861 census RG 9/2068 ED21 Sched 60.

128 PRO, 1871 census RG10 3021 ED21 Sched 256.

129 Ibid, John Northwood II, p8.

130 Infra, Red House Glassworks, 1873.

131 Infra, Red House Glassworks, 1878.

132 Infra, Red House Glassworks, 1878-82.

133 Infra, Dennis Glassworks, 1880.

134 Supra, North Street Glassworks.

135 John Thomas Haden Richardson, son of Johnathan Richardson and his wife Sarah, nee Lloyd, b. 14th Jan 1835, Wordsley, bap. 26th Apr 1835, Kingswinford.

136 Infra, White House Glassworks, 1906.

137 1881 census of Marston-upon-Dove, Derbyshire, RG11/2753/71/13.

138 This painting is enigmatic. The brass plaque affixed to it dates it to 1820 and the dress worn by the glassmakers is of that period. However, in 1820 the Wordsley house was a steelworks and the Richardsons did not commence operation until 1829. Furthermore, the artist to whom it is attributed was not even born until 1835! Emily Jane Hodgetts, daughter of William Rolinson Hodgetts and his wife Elizabeth, nee Stevens, b. 6th Mar 1835; bap. 21st Sep 1846, Kingswinford.

139 Chancery Division R. No 6 filed 17th Mar 1869.

140 PRO, 1871 census, RG10 3015 ED3 Sched 145.

141 PRO, 1871 census, RG10 3021 ED21 Sched 55.

142 PRO, 1871 census, RG10 3025 ED2 Sched 100.

143 Kelly's 1876 Post Office Directory of Staffordshire and Warwickshire.

144 William Haden Richardson, d. 21st Dec 1876.

145 PRO, Will of William Haden Richardson, 23rd Jan 1877.

146 Mary Pargeter, daughter of Philip Pargeter and his wife Susannah, nee Richardson, bap. 23rd Sep 1827, Kingswinford.

147 Thomas Richardson, son of Joseph Richardson and his wife Martha, nee Haden. He was a bricklayer of Portway, Wordsley; d. 19th Jan 1866.

148 This was sold by the Stourbridge auctioneers, Giles Haywood in June 1991 and was bought for £800 by Broadfield House Glass Museum.

149 Infra, Red House Glassworks.

150 Joseph Locke, son of Edward Locke, a potter and his second wife Elizabeth, nee King, b. 21st Aug 1846; bap. 23rd Apr 1848, St. Martin's, Worcester.

151 The competition was for a fireplace design, commissioned by the Czar of Russia.

152 Mar. Joseph Locke and Louisa Drewry, 22nd Feb 1868, Stourbridge Presbyterian (Unitarian) Chapel. Louisa Drewry, daughter of Philip Drewry, builder and keeper of the Old Wheatsheaf, 12 Coventry Street, Stourbridge, and his wife Anne, nee Guest, b. 3rd Feb 1848; bap. 27th Feb 1848, Stourbridge Unitarian Chapel. Anne Guest, daughter of John Guest and his wife Phebe, nee Short, bap. Apr 1818, Dudley St. Thomas's.

153 PRO, 1881 census of Kingswinford, RG11/2891/34/17.

154 PRO, 1881 census of Kingswinford, RG11/2891/52/14.

155 Ibid, Revd. S. Pritt, pp10-11, p18.

156 PRO, Will of William James Hodgetts, 9th Feb 1885.

157 Henry Sutton, son of William and Ann Sutton, b. Wordsley, bap. 20th Mar 1842, Kingswinford; lived at Brewery Street, Wordsley

158 Benjamin Richardson, d. 30th Nov 1887; bur. Wordsley, family vault.

159 PRO, Will of Benjamin Richardson, 3rd Jan 1888.

160 Martha Maria Richardson, daughter of Benjamin Richardson and his wife Anne Eunice, nee Gething, bap. 22nd Jun 1828, Dudley St. Thomas's; married James Roose.

161 Mary Maria Richardson, daughter of Benjamin Richardson and his wife Anne Eunice, nee Gething, b. c1828, Dudley; married William Alan Minifie.

162 Martha Haden Richardson, daughter of Benjamin Richardson and his wife Anne Eunice, nee Gething, bap. 23rd Feb 1834, Kingswinford.

163 Benjamin Richardson's notebook of 1886.

164 Ibid, R. Wakefield, p14.

165 Kelly's 1888 Directory of Staffordshire.

166 Kelly's 1892 Directory of Birmingham, Staffordshire and Warwickshire.

167 Benjamin Richardson, son of Henry Gething Richardson and his wife Elizabeth, nee Guest, b. 18th Jan 1864, Coalbournbrook, bap. 25th Mar 1864, Kingswinford.

168 William Haden Arthur Richardson, son of Henry Gething Richardson and his wife Elizabeth, nee Guest, b. c1868, Amblecote.

169 Supra, Dennis Glassworks, 1884.

170 Revised edition, 1888.
171 PG, Jul 1905.
172 Abstract of Title kindly supplied by Mr John V. Sanders of Wollaston.
173 DA, *The Story of Richardsons*.
174 John H. Husselbee, General Secretary of the National Flint Glassmakers' Society of Great Britain and Ireland. *298th Report for the Quarter ending 26th January 1924*. As the 297th Report is for the quarter ending 27th Oct 1923, glassmaking must have ceased between these two dates. (Information kindly supplied by Mr John V. Sanders of Wollaston).
175 Kelly's 1928 Directory of Staffordshire.
176 Ibid, Abstract of Title.
177 Stanley R. Eveson, retired Works Director of Thomas Webb and Sons. Intra, Dennis Glassworks.
178 Stanley R. Eveson, *Reflections, Sixty years with the crystal glass industry* (1990) and as personally described to the author.
179 Ibid, R. Wakefield, p15.
180 Ibid, Abstract of Title.

CHAPTER 35

Castle Foot Glassworks, Dudley

Castle Foot Glassworks stood on the corner of Downing Street[1] and Tower Street, at the foot of Castle Hill. Two possible dates are suggested for its establishment, 1780 or 1789. Sadly, records from this period are deficient. The first reference occurs in an 1818 Dudley trade directory listing Cooke, Price & Wood as cut glass manufacturers at Castle Street. An identical listing appeared in 1820[2].

The partners in this concern were Benjamin Cooke, Joseph Price[3] and James Wood. Little is known about them, but in a deed dated 26th May 1820, James Wood, glass manufacturer, became a trustee of the Independent Chapel in King Street, Dudley[4]. The difficulty in tracing the partners' descent could be because they were nonconformists.

They dissolved the partnership in 1820 with Cooke and Price leaving the firm:

> 'The partnership between Benjamin Cooke, Joseph Price and James Wood of Dudley, glass manufacturers, was dissolved the 11th September 1820. All debts to the said firm of 'Cooke, Price and Wood,' are to be received by the said James Wood.'[5]

James Wood reconstituted the business with new partners to trade as Guest, Wood & Guest, cut glass manufacturers of Castle Street[6]. The new partners were Joseph[7] and Edward[8] Guest, sons of Edward Guest. Their family wealth came from the nailmaking industry. Edward Guest senior[9] was a member of the firm of Whitehurst, Moore and Guest and was Mayor of Dudley in 1815. The two brothers held political views as Liberals, contrary to those of the Tory Dudley glassmakers, Thomas Hawkes and the Badger brothers.

In 1825 the firm's address was still Castle Street[10] but by 1828 it was Tower Street[11]. This could suggest redevelopment of the works, but could equally be the deficient interpretation of the trade directory compilers. The trustees of Baylies' Charity School, which stood nearby, had owned the freehold of the property since 1732. In June 1831 the trustees sold 'the messuage and five cottages and glass-house' for £1,000[12].

In anticipation that the town of Dudley was to have a representative in Parliament under the Reform Bill, efforts were made by political parties to secure a preponderance of power and influence. A petition was submitted to J.C. Brettell, the Mayor of Dudley on 7th February 1831. Joseph and Edward Guest were among the signatories[13].

Joseph Guest retired from the family nailmaking business in 1832 and his brother Edward carried it on[14]. Presumably he found glassmaking more profitable than nailmaking. Joseph Guest & Co. paid £4,008 12s 9d excise duty for the year ending 5th January 1833[15], suggesting this was the fourth largest of the sixteen Stourbridge/Dudley glasshouses of the day.

In 1833 a petition was issued, signed by three hundred leading inhabitants of Dudley, complaining about their Member of Parliament[16]. Edward and Joseph Guest were among the signatories.

The glassworks is clearly shown on Treasure's 1835 plan. The firm appears in a succession of trade directories that all show Joseph Guest living in New Street and James in Wolverhampton Street[17].

The modest style of life of the Guest family and their lack of ostentation was proverbial:

> 'To give an idea of the feeling existing at the time, when a Dudley bank failed about 1842, Mr Edward Guest was met by a young sprig of a family of affluence, who said to him, 'Mr. Guest, Dixon's Bank has failed—have you any money there?' 'Yes,' he replied, 'two thousand pounds.' The questioner said, 'I will tell you what to do, Mr. Guest: go home and forget it, for you will never spend it.'[18]

The Pottery Gazette commentator goes on to explain that the great wealth the Guests were accumulating by their frugal existence was mainly to be left as charitable donations. During his life, Joseph Guest made charitable donations to the value of forty thousand pounds. Most notably, he left £20,000 in his will to endow a hospital in Dudley that subsequently became the Guest Hospital[19]. He died in 1867[20] and left his fortune to his sister. When his sister died, she left the greater part of the family wealth to the Birmingham Hospital[21].

An extant plan from 1844 gives a detailed description of the works including: one glasshouse with a mixing room, three metal rooms, two pot rooms, mould room, packing room, machine room and one room set aside specifically for excise officers. The total area covered 1,233 square yards with an annual rateable value of £140.

In 1845 the firm was still trading as Guest, Wood & Guest, glass manufacturers and cutters, Castle Glass Works, Tower Street[22], but sometime before December 1846 the glassworks was sold to Henry Homer and John Renaud[23].

Renaud was already familiar with the glass trade. When he baptised his son Edward John in 1838[24], he lived in Stourbridge and was an 'Agent in Glass Works'. Renaud made his home in Dudley at Oakham Lodge[25] and, as well as his new business, involved himself in local politics. Under the 'Health of Towns Act', Dudley was obliged to elect fifteen commissioners with powers to raise rates for improvement measures. A handbill was issued on 16th June 1853, proposing fifteen recommended persons. Among them was John Renaud, glass-master of Tower Street. He was subsequently elected on 23rd June 1853, with five hundred and four votes[26]. In 1854 there was an election for a Board of Guardians and voting as usual fell on party lines[27]. John Renaud and Joseph Guest, the former owner of the glassworks, were both elected.

Henry Homer, whose name was never prominent, ceased his interest in the business in 1856, leaving John Renaud in sole charge. In the same year John Renaud became Mayor of Dudley. An early photograph of him and other Dudley worthies was taken on the occasion of a Dudley Fete[28]. When the sitting member of parliament for Dudley, Sir Stafford Northcote, Bart., MP resigned on 12th March 1857, Renaud again involved himself in the business of electing his replacement[29].

After the lockout in 1859, Renaud's claim from the manufacturers' defence fund[30] suggests the firm was the ninth largest of the thirteen in the Midlands Association. In 1861 Renaud lived with his wife and family at Hagley Road, Upper Swinford, employing fifty-one men and twenty-five boys[31], implying he was the fourth largest employer of the six main Stourbridge area glassworks at the time.

Sometime before 1873 Renaud took his son, Edward John[32] into the partnership and the firm traded as John Renaud & Son, The Castle Glass Works, Tower Street[33]. By 1876 John Renaud had moved from Upper Swinford and lived at Dawley House, Kingswinford[34].

In 1876 Lord Dudley presented a drinking fountain to the town of Dudley. It stands twenty-seven feet tall and can still be seen in the marketplace today. The opening ceremony was an elaborate affair attended by local dignitaries, the Yeomanry and a band:

> 'He (Lord Dudley) considered that this was one of the most useful works they could be engaged in, for although he could not go so far as to advocate abstinence from intoxicating drinks of all kinds, he believed there was many a man came into the town to the markets or to his work who, if he had fresh water at hand, would not go further for wine or beer for the Purpose of slaking his thirst . . . Mr. John Renaud then presented the Countess of Dudley with a beautiful glass goblet. The goblet is made very light and of an elegant and chaste design, is made beautifully engraved with an exact representation of the Fountain, and is the production of Messrs. Renaud and Son, of the Castle Foot Works. This being filled with water from the fountain by Mr Forsyth, the sculptor, her Ladyship, after drinking a portion of the water, declared the fountain the property of the people of Dudley.'[35]

John Renaud was still active in the firm at the age of 71, when he lived at 33 Wellington Road, Dudley$_{36}$. Edward John Renaud had lost his first wife and married for the second time to Louisa Phillips in 1885$_{37}$. By this time his father had retired and Edward John was in charge of the business. John Renaud died in 1893, aged eighty-three, and has a memorial in Oldswinford churchyard.

The works closed in 1899 as a result of the glassmakers' union encouraging the men to apply for a rise in wages that could not be afforded. The workforce was dismissed and the works closed. The entire contents of the Castle Glass Works were auctioned on June 26th, 27th and 28th 1900 by the auctioneer Alfred W. Dando of Dudley. According to the auction catalogue this was because 'Messrs. John Renaud and son, are retiring from the trade.' The catalogue$_{38}$ lists the entire stock of the glassworks and all its equipment. Edward John Renaud died in 1919$_{39}$, aged eighty-one.

The glasshouse was demolished in 1902. The site where it stood is behind the Zoo office buildings and Saab dealership at the top end of Broadway, near Castle Hill. This area, at the foot of the castle walls, used to be a bustling part of the town of Dudley, with densely packed housing and industry such as the glassworks. It was annexed by Lord Dudley about the turn of the century when the Broadway was built and is now a sleepy backwater.

---

1 Now the wide, main road called the Broadway.

2 Lewis's 1820 Worcestershire General and Commercial Directory.

3 Probably Johnathan Green's ex-partner at Dixon's Green Glassworks.

4 A.A. Rollason, *The old non-parochial registers of Dudley* (1899), p36.

5 London Gazette, 19th Sep 1820.

6 Wrightson's 1823 Triennial Directory of Birmingham.

7 Joseph Guest, son of Edward and Esther Guest, b. 13th Dec 1793; bap. 15th Jan 1794, Dudley St. Thomas's.

8 Edward Guest, son of Edward and Esther Guest, b. 18th Jul 1798; bap. 22nd Sep 1799, Dudley St. Thomas's.

9 Edward Guest, b. c1766, d. at New Street, Dudley, 9th Aug 1826; bur. 13th Aug 1826, Dudley St. Edmund's. Memorial in Dudley St. Thomas's.

10 Wrightson's 1825 Triennial Directory of Birmingham.

11 Pigot and Co.'s 1828-9 National Commercial Directory; Pigot and Co's Com-

mercial Directory of Birmingham, 1829 and 1830 editions.
12 Ibid, George Griffith, pp177-181.
13 Supra, Dudley Flint Glass Works.
14 DA, LDB Guest P.
15 Thirteenth Report of the Commission into the Glass Excise, 1835, Appendix 7.
16 Supra, Dixon's Green.
17 Pigot and Co.'s 1835 National Commercial Directory; Robson's 1839 Birmingham and Sheffield Directory; Bentley's 1841 guide to Dudley; Pigot and Co.'s 1841 Directory of Birmingham.
18 PG, Feb 1895.
19 The Guest Hospital was originally built in Tipton Road, one mile from the centre of Dudley in 1860 by Lord Ward, later the Earl of Dudley. It was intended as a home for men who had lost their sight in Lord Dudley's mines, but the building was never occupied for its original purpose and lay void for several years. When Joseph Guest's executors attempted to carry out his wishes the Earl of Dudley granted the trustees the vacant building and at his own expense caused it to be altered to the requirements of the proposed hospital.
20 Joseph Guest, d. 22nd Nov 1867, at his home in New Street, Dudley.
21 PG, Feb 1895.
22 Post Office Directory of the Neighbourhood of Birmingham, 1845.
23 John Renaud, son of Edward and Ann Renaud, bap. 25th Apr 1810, St. Martin's, Birmingham.
24 Edward John Renaud, son of John and Sarah Lydia Renaud, b. Stourbridge, bap. 24th Aug 1838, Oldswinford.
25 Oakham Lodge stood southeast of Dudley at the foot of Tansley Hill.
26 Birmingham Journal.
27 Supra, Phoenix Glassworks.
28 Blocksidge's Almanac of Dudley 1902, p114b.
29 Supra, Phoenix Glassworks.
30 £57 3s.
31 PRO, 1861 census, RG 9/2066 Pg21 Fol. 77 Sch 67.
32 Edward John Renaud, son of John and Sarah Lydia Renaud, b. Stourbridge, bap. 24th Aug 1838, Oldswinford.
33 Littlebury's 1873 Directory.

34 Kelly's 1876 Post Office Directory of Staffordshire and Warwickshire.
35 Dudley Herald, 10th Oct 1876.
36 PRO, 1881 census of Dudley, RG11/2875/117/8.
37 Mar. Edward John Renaud and Louisa Phillips, 15th Sep 1885, All Saints, Clifton, Bristol.
38 DA.
39 Edward John Renaud, d. Aug 1919; bur. Oldswinford, family tomb.

CHAPTER 36

White House Glassworks, Wordsley

The land on which the White House was built belonged in 1676 to Joshua Bradley[1] who let it, for ninety-nine years, to Nicholas Hoskins. It then passed down, through his heirs, via various sales and inheritances, to Comber Raybould[2].

Whitworth's canal map of 1774 does not show the White House Glassworks but it does show Wordsley Flint Glassworks. As the canal was eventually to pass right between the two of them, it is fair to assume that the White House had not been built by 1774. Its significance to the route of the canal is such that it would have been shown if it existed at the time. Snape's canal map of nine years later clearly shows the White House cone. The Stourbridge Canal was fully opened to traffic in December 1779 so it is reasonable to assume that the White House Glassworks was built between 1779 and 1785, in a prime location on the banks of the canal and fronting the Stourbridge to Wolverhampton road.

View of Wordsley

It is not known if Comber Raybould built the glassworks or his tenant. A second smaller cone was built alongside the first sometime before 1812. This was not uncommon; two cones were built at Dial Glasshouses, the smaller one being used exclusively for bottlemaking. Sherriff's plan of 1812 clearly shows the silhouette of the original White House cone, in exactly the same location as on Snape's map, with a second smaller cone behind it, also fronting the canal.

Comber Raybould sold the White House site to the partnership of Bradley, Ensells & Holt$_3$ on 22nd January 1819. The deed refers to 'a close having two glasshouses erected thereon . . . Sold to John Holt piece or parcel of land on s. side of canal adjoining turnpike road . . . with glasshouse, pot rooms, store rooms and buildings . . . the occupation of John Holt, R. Bradley Ensell & Co . . . .'$_4$ The wording of this deed suggests Bradley, Ensells & Holt were already operating the White House.

The firm traded as Bradley, Ensells and Holt, flint glass manufacturers in 1820$_5$ but John Holt died at the end of the year, on 15th December 1820, aged sixty-two. He did not leave a proper will, only some unattested and undated papers expressing his wish that his one third share in the 'glass business' should go to his daughter and only child Mary Holt. Fowler's 1822 map shows the glasshouse occupied by Bradley, Ensell & Holt$_6$.

By 1827 the partnership formed out of necessity by the legatees of Richard Bradley and their offspring was unworkable and the partnership property was auctioned$_7$. The White House Glassworks was bought at auction by Richard Bradley Ensell the younger$_8$ for £1,695 and a further £514 for machinery (Lot 1). He also bought Lot 4, 'steam engine, forge, cutting shops etc.' for £1,095. George William Wainwright and Richard Bradley Ensell the elder conveyed the White House to Richard Bradley Ensell the younger in 1828$_9$.

Richard Bradley Ensell the younger bought the Red House Glassworks as well as the White House. He probably intended to manage the Red House works himself and to leave his uncle, Richard Bradley Ensell the elder, the last to survive of the original partnership, running the White House. However, two months later Richard Bradley Ensell the elder died[10], aged forty-four. His widow Sarah continued the business at the White House.

The firm traded as Ensells' and Co. (Plain and cut) Wordsley[11]. Sarah Ensell paid £2,254 7s 9d excise duty for the year ending 5th January 1833[12], suggesting this was the twelfth largest of the sixteen Stourbridge/Dudley glasshouses of the day.

Understandably Sarah Ensell did not wish to carry on the proprietorship of the business, although at some stage she came to own the White House property. Richard Bradley Ensell the younger was suffering under a mounting pile of debt[13], so it is possible that he sold the White House to Sarah Ensell to raise some capital. In 1833 she let the glassworks to John Webb and John Shepherd who formed a partnership to trade as Shepherd & Webb. John Webb was a successful farmer and butcher who lived at Longlands, near Stourbridge. He was probably heartened by the success of his son, Thomas Webb, who began business with the Richardson brothers, four years earlier[14]. John Shepherd previously worked for Rufford and Walker at the Heath Glassworks[15]. He had also been in business supplying sand from Kings Lynn and the Isle of Wight to the Stourbridge glasshouses[16].

In 1835 the firm traded as Shepherd & Webb, White House Glass Works, Wordsley, manufacturers of flint glass, plain and cut[17]. Then after only two years in the business, John Webb died in 1835[18], aged sixty-one. He left his share in Shepherd & Webb to Thomas Webb, his only surviving child.

Thomas Webb was already operating Wordsley Flint Glassworks in partnership with the Richardsons, but shortly after the death of his father, he withdrew from the Webb & Richardson partnership receiving 'over £7,000'. Benjamin Richardson stated that although Thomas Webb could have remained as a partner at Wordsley Flint Glassworks 'we found that he preferred to be with John Shepherd, so we agreed to part.'[19] The new partnership became known as John Shepherd and Thomas Webb.

As previously stated Sarah Ensell had at some stage come to own the White House property, although it is not known exactly when or why this occurred. The Kingswinford tithe map of 1836 shows the White House Glassworks owned by Sarah Ensell and occupied by 'John Sheppard [sic] and others'. The Poor Rate book shows one of the 'others' to be John Webb, the rateable value being £63 plus £18 for the attached flourmill[20]. The flourmill has now been incorporated into the modern offices of Stuart Crystal. Externally, the mill still looks much as it did when it was built in 1830 and the original architectural features can still be clearly identified in Stuarts' reception area. The mill was originally founded by the Richardson brothers and known as the Wordsley Steam Flour Mill. The younger members of the Richardson family worked it, but their management was inept and between 1842 and 1849 they lost about three thousand pounds. The Richardsons ceased to work it after their bankruptcy in 1851 and it was taken over by the Webbs. It housed a 28hp steam engine installed for milling operations, but also used to provide the motive power for twenty-seven glass-cutting machines. The Webb family operated the mill until 1896 when it burned down, after which it stood derelict for some time.

In May 1836 John Shepherd retired from active participation, leaving Thomas Webb in sole charge. The partnership of John Shepherd and Thomas Webb was dissolved; Thomas Webb bought John Shepherd's share in the business for £2,500, although the firm continued to trade as Shepherd & Webb. John Shepherd allowed his name to be used; and for his services and interest on his capital he received £300 per annum[21]. Thomas Webb was due to pay £250 6s 8d for excise duty on flint glass on 7th November 1836. His arrears were £253 13s 4d[22].

A meeting took place on 5th December 1837 at the Dudley Arms Hotel where the manufacturers considered their response to the formation of the first glassmakers' trade union. Thomas Webb was present. The resolution passed at their meeting has already been described[23].

Fowler & son's map of 1840 shows the White House as plot 272 still owned by Sarah Ensell and occupied by John Sheppard [sic] and others. Thomas Webb had been building a new glassworks at the Platts and the following year he transferred his business to the new glassworks, sometime between June and November of 1840[24].

Ownership of the White House may appear confusing to us today, but was equally so in 1841. A dispute over ownership was referred in 1841 and 1842 to the court of the vice-chancellor of England. The Master, Sir George Rose, decided that William Haden Richardson was allowed the purchase for the sum of £3,400[25]. It was conveyed to William Haden, Benjamin and Jonathan Richardson on 28th April 1842[26]. They built a wooden footbridge over the canal to connect their two glassworks[27].

It has been described[28] that the Richardsons ran into financial difficulty and incurred liabilities of £4,450. To raise funds, they mortgaged the White House to William Webb junior for £3,000[29]. William Webb junior was the older brother of Edward Webb and cousin of Joseph Webb who were running the Holloway End Glasshouse.

When the firm of W.H., B. & J. Richardson was declared insolvent on 14th February 1852 William Webb junior saw that he had an opportunity. He invited his brother Edward to leave the Holloway End Glasshouse and join him in partnership at the White House. This would have appealed to Edward Webb as he was becoming more interested in milling than glassmaking. At the White House he had the benefit of the two businesses side by side.

William Webb junior conveyed the Richardsons' mortgage on the White House to his brother Edward and William Blow Collis[30] and purchased the unmortgaged portion of the White House from Henry Edmunds, the assignee of the Richardsons' estate for £4,680[31]. This agreement was made the day before the property was due to be offered for sale at the Vine Inn, Wordsley on 11th January 1853[32]. The conveyance to William Webb is dated 4th March 1853[33]. Having thus ensured they each had a share in the property, Edward Webb left Holloway End and formed a partnership with his brother William.

After the lockout[34], in 1859 Edward Webb's claim from the manufacturers' defence fund[35] suggests the firm was the largest of the thirteen in the Midlands Association. However, this interpretation is dubious because in 1861—in terms of numbers employed—he was the smallest employer of the six main Stourbridge glassworks. In 1861 Edward Webb lived with his family at Wordsley, a glass master employing thirty men and five boys[36].

William Webb junior died at Wordsley in 1866[37], aged sixty-five. It is clear from his will[38] that he was no longer active in the glass trade. He ran a business as a miller with his brother Edward at Ivy House Mill, Wordsley[39] and as a maltster on his own behalf. As he never married[40], he left his estate to his brother, nephews and nieces. His nephew William Webb Boulton of Audnam Glassworks was named as one of his executors but revoked his executorship. It appears that William Webb Boulton had fallen out with William Webb and blamed him for breaking up the Holloway End partnership of Edward and Joseph Webb where he worked in 1850.

Edward Webb brought his sons, William George[41] and Edward junior[42] into the business and the firm traded as Edward Webb and Sons. They exhibited at the Wolverhampton Exhibition of 1869 and received the following accolade in the official report from Mr George Wallis of South Kensington Museum:

> 'The productions of the original seat of the glass trade in England (Stourbridge) were so thoroughly represented by Messrs. E. Webb and Sons, that it is scarcely a matter of regret no other manufacturer contributed, since this firm carried out the representation of decorated and table glass in a most effective manner. The forms of the articles were all well considered, and thoroughly adapted to the use of the vessels. The details and decorations, whether engraved, cut, or blown on, give evidence of the most perfect mastery over the material, and a distinct perception of the best art qualities, as well as when to stop in the matter of decoration, always a most difficult point to attain. Some of the specimens of 'flashed' glass were most delicate, alike in form, colour, and detail of ornamentation. it would be very difficult to particularise, were it desirable to do so where everything presented commendable features; and it is sufficient for the present purpose to say that in no previous exhibition has there been so perfect a display made by any one house. It is needless to remark on the quality of the metal or its purity of colour, since in this respect it is all that can be desired[43].'

In 1871 Edward Webb lived at White House[44], Buckpool, Wordsley, a glassmaster, miller, hop seed and corn dealer[45]. His son, William George Webb lived nearby at Ivy House, Buckpool, Wordsley[46].

Edward Webb senior died at Wordsley the following year[47]. He had made a will[48] the previous month, on 22nd October 1872 and rapidly added two codicils. He described himself as 'Edward Webb of the White House Wordsley . . . Glass Manufacturer farmer miller and seed and hop merchant carrying on business in copartnership with my two sons William George Webb and Edward Webb junior.' In the second codicil he left the White House in trust for the benefit of the children and grandchildren of his daughters.

The glassmaking business was carried on by his younger son Edward, who lived at Summerhill House[49] at the far end of Barnet Lane. His older son, William George, followed a military career and rose to become a colonel and Member of Parliament for the Kingswinford division from 1900 until his death in 1905[50]. He was also chairman of North Worcestershire Breweries.

In 1876 the business was described as 'Edward Webb, flint and coloured glass manufacturer and sole patentee of the improved process of printing on glass[51].' However, in 1881 Edward Webb described his occupation as a seed merchant, a clear indication that glassmaking was now of secondary importance to him[52].

Edward Webb's manager was Arthur John Nash[53] who lived in Wordsley and later Wollaston. He was responsible for many new designs created at the White House. In 1882 Nash patented *Vasa Murrhina* glassware[54]. This was not a new style, a similar patent having been secured by William Webb Boulton of Audnam Glassworks in 1879. In 1883 the firm of Edward Webb advertised in Pottery Gazette the use of gold or silver foil between two layers of glass called *Oroide* and *Argentine* respectively. Arthur John Nash designed both. In 1883 *Worcester Ivory Glass* was introduced, imitating Worcester porcelain and in 1885 *Dresden Cameo*, imitating Dresden porcelain.

By 1888 the Webb brothers, Edward and William George, were extremely wealthy and influential in the neighbourhood. They were both Justices of the Peace, Edward still living at Summerhill House and William George at Woodfield, Wordsley. The glass business traded as Edward Webb, flint and coloured glass manufacturers, Wordsley. Their other business interests included William & Edward Webb & Sons, seed growers, wool, hop & manure merchants, Royal Seed Establishment and William & Edward Webb, millers, Ivy Steam Flour Mills[55]. With their wealth came altruism. In 1891 Mrs Edward Webb[56] presented a magnificent reredos to Wordsley Holy Trinity Church to grace the newly built chancel[57]. William George and Edward Webb also donated a window in the south wall of the chancel in remembrance of their parents, Edward and Eliza Webb.

About 1887, Edward Webb's manager, Arthur John Nash, left to join Thomas Webb & Co. Ltd. at Dennis Glassworks, before going to the United States in 1895 to join Louis Comfort Tiffany.

Deprived of his talented manager, Edward Webb's business was never the same again. In 1897 he chose to cease glassmaking on his own behalf and leased out the glassworks[58]. His tenants were his distant cousin, Thomas Ernest Webb and George Harry Corbett[59]. They founded the firm of Thomas Webb and Corbett Ltd. and leased the White House from William George Webb and Edward Webb[60]. The trademark *Webb-Corbett* was registered the same year and examples from the new firm were approved of by Pottery Gazette in August 1897. The new firm officially commenced trading on 1st January 1898[61].

It is interesting to question why Thomas Ernest Webb, as the older son of Thomas Wilkes Webb, did not continue in the family firm of Thomas Webb & Sons, where he worked as a traveller. It could be because in 1893, two years after the death of his father, when the firm was being run by his two uncles, Charles and Walter Wilkes Webb, his salary was cut by 20 percent. Charles Walter Herbert Webb[62] decided to follow the same course as his older brother, leaving the family firm and joining Thomas Webb & Corbett in 1898. His reasons were probably the same. In 1893 he was the Australian agent for Thomas Webb & Sons and in that difficult year had seen his salary cut by 20 percent as well.

In 1898 Pottery Gazette featured the new firm's wares including: intricate cut designs, shallow rock crystal, polished bright engraving and cased glass with intaglio decoration. Enamelled decoration performed by Hugo Maisey[63] also featured prominently before and after the First World War. Typical Webb Corbett enamelling consists of fruits, flowers and foliage painted in thin translucent colours that glow intensely when light passes through. A second, less common, type of enamelled glass was etched with a stylised pattern of flowers and birds, with coloured enamel filling in the design.

In 1899 Pottery Gazette carried an advertisement for Thomas Webb & Corbett Ltd proudly describing 'New plaid effects in fancy vases etc. and new designs in Rock Crystal services and intaglio cutting.' The bulk of Webb Corbett's Rock Crystal glass was probably designed, if not executed, by William Kny[64] who was manager of the decorating shop. One of Kny's chief engravers was Jack Lloyd who worked at Webb Corbett from 1901 until 1927 when he moved to Thomas Webb's. Other Webb Corbett engravers were Valentin Weinich and W.G. Webb, who later taught engraving at Stourbridge School of Art.

Thomas Ernest Webb retired in 1903 and his younger brother Charles Walter Herbert took his place as chairman. In 1906 the firm took over a glassworks at Tutbury that made bottles for the Burton brewery trade[65]. Charles Walter Herbert Webb remained at Stourbridge, while George Harry Corbett took charge at Tutbury. Corbett remained at Tutbury until 1911, when the partnership was dissolved and he left the firm. Walter E. Guest[66] became manager at Tutbury. William Kny, who had worked for the company since at least 1898, became a director in 1910.

On Tuesday 31st March 1914 a disastrous fire broke out at the White House. Rather than renovate the damaged works, Thomas Webb & Corbett Ltd moved its operations to Coalbournhill Glassworks.

Later that year the White House was leased by the successors of the Webbs, to Stuart & Sons Limited, who were already operating the Red House Glassworks[67]. During the First World War

Stuarts' needed additional manufacturing capacity partly to satisfy the demand for light bulbs and other items for the War Ministry. So, in 1916 they purchased the White House works[68]. One of their first tasks was to renovate the hundred and thirty-year-old cone which was in a parlous state. This was carried out in 1917. The works was significantly extended in 1921. A 'New' White House was built with a ten-pot furnace between the old cone and the canal.

From 1927 onwards the trade name *Stuart Crystal* began to be used, along with the practice of etching each piece with the name *Stuart*; a useful aid to dating the firm's products.

In a drive to make production more efficient, a new large glassworks was built in 1934 in Vine Street, alongside the White House. It housed a modern recuperative furnace built by Teisen and Birlec of Birmingham. In 1936 the firm moved all its operations to the White House Glassworks and glassmaking at the Red House ceased.

Chief designer, Ludwig Kny, died the following year in 1937. His replacement was H. Reginald Pierce[69]. After an education at Liverpool School of Art, Reg Pierce joined Stoniers in 1932. He had been supplying designs to Ludwig Kny at Wordsley, some of which were immediately put into production, others of which were adapted by Kny. Reg Pierce held the position of chief designer until the outbreak of the Second World War. He now lives in Devon.

By 1939 the old White House cone had become unsafe and it was decided to dismantle it. All the underground caves and coal stores were turned into air raid shelters and the top half of the cone was dropped with the rubble left as added protection to the shelters[70].

The youngest of the Stuart brothers, Samuel Mansfield of the Woodlands, Wordsley died in 1943[71], aged seventy-two. Robert Stuart died in 1946[72], aged eighty-eight. He had dominated the partnership for many years since the death of his father, Frederick Stuart.

During the Second World War, Stuarts' worked the ten-pot furnace in the Vine Street factory producing aircraft landing lights, cathode ray tubes, valves for radar and other specialised electronic and chemical equipment. After the war the factory was managed by Frederick H. Stuart[73], the son of Frederick Stuart junior. He was assisted by his cousins, William Arthur Stuart[74] and Eric M. Stuart[75], and the fourth generation members: Geoffrey W. Stuart, William E.C. Stuart, F. Churlton Pauli[76] and Frederick G. Stuart[77]. In 1946 they were joined by Ian M. Stuart[78].

A new designer, G. John Luxton, ARCA, joined the firm in 1948. Working closely with Stuarts' directors, Frederick H. Godfrey and Derek Stuart, he was responsible for many new designs for the post-war catalogue. He remained the chief designer until his retirement in 1985.

Taking advantage of government encouragement, in 1966 Stuarts' opened another factory at Aberbargoed in South Wales. Then in 1980 Stuarts' took over the management of Strathearn Glass at Crieff in Scotland and formed a new company—Stuart Strathearn.

The remaining part of the old White House cone was capped in 1969 and in 1979 it was totally demolished. The area where it stood became the factory car park. Stuart & Sons Ltd. survived the recession of the early nineteen-nineties by an enterprising approach to production techniques, while continuing the high-class tradition of Stourbridge crystal.

However, in April 1995 the company became the target of a take-over bid from Waterford Wedgwood. Former chairman Ian Stuart and Roger Pauli were in favour and bought sufficient shares to give them a controlling 51.2 percent. Most of the other shareholders and the five hundred and thirty employees were opposed. Waterford Wedgwood wrote to Stuarts' fifty-three shareholders, proposing an offer at about £6 a share, valuing the company at £2.9 million. Stuart management, led by managing director John Temple, proposed a management buyout at £9 a share valuing it at £4.2 million.

Waterford's bid succeeded and in July 1995 purchased the company for £4.24 million. John Temple found himself in an 'untenable' position as managing director and resigned to be replaced by Greg Rogers.

In October 1999 Stuarts' announced the Jasper Conran collection, described as an 'important step in the strategy for the new millennium.' The range included champagne flutes, martini glasses, wine goblets, shot glasses and vases[79]. The firm also produced a replica range of crystal with the White Star liner logo used on the Titanic, to capitalise on the success of the blockbuster movie released that year.

Foreign competition intensified; exacerbated by a high sterling exchange rate and over a hundred employees lost their jobs during 2001. After months of rumour, management announced the closure of the works and the loss of all two hundred and twenty manufacturing jobs. Production in the glasshouse ceased on 23rd November 2001. The cutting and polishing shops closed on 15th Feb 2002. The cuts were part of fourteen hundred and forty redundancies announced by John Foley, chief executive of Waterford Wedgwood Group[80].

---

1 Another branch of the Bradley family was later to enter the glass trade at Fimbrell Glasshouse and Joshua Bradley was a grandson of Joshua Henzey I, but he appears not to have involved himself directly in glassmaking. He made his will on 18th Jan 1697 (PRO, PROB 11/466) and stated that he lived in Stourbridge, but owned a cottage in Audnam, 'near to the glasshouse of Thomas Henzey glassmaker'. His friend, Edward Henzey was one of his executors. The testator was clearly a wealthy man. His will mentions ironworks and lands in Oldswinford, Bedcote, Stourbridge, Amblecote and Wednesbury.

2 Richardson Papers No 25, 1827. Ensell & Ensell, Abstract of title.

3 This was the partnership formed in 1804 between John Holt, Charles Ensell II and Richard Bradley Ensell the elder (infra, Red House Glassworks).

4 Richardson Papers No 25, 1827. Ensell & Ensell, Abstract of title.

5 Lewis's 1820 Worcestershire and Commercial Directory.

6 DA, William Fowler's 1822 *Map of the Parish of Kingswinford.* Plot 268 Glass House and wharf, forge & shops – Bradley, Ensell & Holt.

7 Supra, Wordsley Flint Glassworks.

8 Richard Bradley Ensell, son of Charles Ensell and Betsey Gwinnett, later to become his wife, b. 21st Aug 1800; bap. 9th Apr 1802, Kingswinford.

9 Richardson papers No 26, 18 Jan 1828. Conveyance of White House from Wainwright & Ensell to Richard Bradley Ensell.
10 Richard Bradley Ensell, bur. 18th Mar 1828, Oldswinford.
11 Pigot and Co.'s 1828 National Commercial Directory for 1828-9, Pigot and Co.'s Commercial Directory of Birmingham, 1829 and 1830 editions.
12 Thirteenth Report of the Commission into the Glass Excise, 1835, Appendix 7.
13 Infra, Red House Glassworks.
14 Supra, Wordsley Flint Glassworks, 1829.
15 Ibid, H.W. Woodward, p7.
16 PG, Mar 1878.
17 Pigot and Co.'s 1835 National Commercial Directory.
18 John Webb, d. 8th Jan 1835; bur. Wordsley, family sandstone tomb. He has a memorial in Kingswinford Church.
19 Benjamin Richardson's notebook of 1886.
20 SRO, Poor Rate Book 1836-7 D585/159/12.
21 Ibid, H.W. Woodward, p8.
22 BHGM, Demand note for Excise Duty, 1836.
23 Supra, Audnam Glassworks.
24 Ibid, H.W. Woodward, p9.
25 Richardson Papers No 34, 1841. Hill & Maurice.
26 White House Papers No 1, 28 Apr 1842. Conveyance from Maurice, Ensell and others.
27 Ibid, R. Wakefield, p17.
28 Supra, Wordsley Flint Glassworks, 1848.
29 White House papers No 2, 16 Jun 1848. Mortgage to Wm. Webb Jnr.
30 William Blow Collis, solicitor of Stourbridge; acquired Wollaston Hall in 1848 for £3,500; clerk to the Magistrates and Board of Guardians; superintendent registrar of the Stourbridge Union, treasurer of the County Court; director of Stourbridge Water Company for 42 years (27 as Chairman); Churchwarden of Amblecote 1854-5; infra, Wheeley's Brettell Lane Glasshouses, 1841.
31 White House Papers No 4, 10 Jan 1853. Agreement for sale from Assignee of Richardsons to William Webb.
32 White House papers no 5, 11th Jan 1853, Particulars of Sale at Vine Inn.
33 White House papers No 6, 4th Mar 1853, Conveyance of Sale to William Webb.

34 Supra Coalbournhill, Audnam and North Street Glassworks.
35 £78 2s 6d.7
36 PRO, 1861 census RG 9/2069 ED3 Sched 46.
37 William Webb, d. 21st Aug 1866 at Wordsley.
38 PRO, Will of William Webb, 10th Dec 1866.
39 Ivy Mills occupied a plot north of Plant Street and east of Mill Street.
40 Although he was living with Leticia Hazeldine.
41 William George Webb, son of Edward Webb and his wife Eliza, nee Banks, b. 15th Dec 1842; bap. 21st Dec 1842, Wordsley.
42 Edward Webb, son of Edward Webb and his wife Eliza, nee Banks, b. 2nd May 1844; bap. 31st Aug 1844, Wordsley.
43 Ibid, J.A. Langford.
44 This should not be confused with his glassworks of the same name. It was a house that stood on the west corner of Mill Street and Brierley Hill Road in Wordsley. It was later the residence of Owen Gibbons, tile manufacturer of Brockmoor and Dr William Tweddell (b. 1897), a local doctor and golf champion. It was demolished in the 1930s for the widening of Brierley Hill Road.
45 PRO, 1871 census RG10 3025 ED3 Sch 144.
46 PRO, 1871 census RG10 3025 ED3 Sch 149.
47 Edward Webb, d. 15th Nov 1872; bur. 21st Nov 1872, Wordsley.
48 PRO, Will of Edward Webb, 21st Nov 1874.
49 This handsome Georgian mansion still stands today on the corner of Swindon Road and Summerhill, Kingswinford. After the Second World War it became the home of Sir Sidney Barratt, chairman of Albright and Wilson, chemical manufacturers of Oldbury. It was converted into Summerhill House Hotel in 1988.
50 Colonel William George Webb, d. 14th Jun 1905; bur. 19th Jun 1905, Wordsley.
51 Kelly's 1876 Post Office Directory of Staffordshire and Warwickshire.
52 PRO, 1881 census of Kingswinford, RG11/2891/156/34.
53 Arthur John Nash, b. c1850 at Shipston on Stour, Worcestershire; d. 1934.
54 Patent number 5324, 8th Nov 1882.
55 Kelly's 1888 Directory of Staffordshire.
56 Edward Webb married Margaret Jane Evers-Swindell, 17th Aug 1871, Pedmore.
57 This is probably the finest feature of the whole church. It was designed by Mr J.A. Chatwin FRIBA of Birmingham and crafted by Mr R. Bridgman of Lichfield.

58 Edward Webb retired to Heath House, Stourbridge, next to the Heath Glassworks and renamed it Studley Court. He died in Paris on 21st Jan 1913, leaving an estate valued at £947,663 12s 2d.

59 George Harry Corbett, b. c 1857 Kingswinford, son of George and Emma Corbett, who ran a confectioners and frutiers shop in Market Street, Kingswinford.

60 White House papers No 8. 20 Dec 1897, Lease to Webb & Corbett.

61 PG, Jan 1898.

62 Charles Walter Herbert Webb, son of Thomas Wilkes Webb and his wife Helen Constance, nee Carter, b. c1871, Stourbridge.

63 1882-1932.

64 William Kny, son of Frederick Englebert and Sarah Lavinia Kny, b. c1870, Amblecote; d. 1942.

65 A glassworks was established in Ludgate Street, Tutbury, Staffordshire in 1720 by the Jackson Family (who are reputably related to General Andrew 'Stonewall' Jackson, seventh President of the United States). The glassworks was rebuilt and re-equipped in 1836 by Henry Jackson who ran it until he died in 1880 when it closed.

66 Walter E. Guest, son of John and Margaret Guest, b. c 1875, Amblecote.

67 White House Papers No 11, 21st Oct 1914, Lease to Stuart & Sons Ltd.

68 White House Papers No 12, 20th Sep 1916, Conveyance to Stuart & Sons Limited.

69 H. Reginald Pierce, b. 11th Sep 1911.

70 W.E.C. Stuart, *Crystal Makers in the Village of Wordsley* (1977).

71 Samuel Mansfield Stuart, d. 31st Aug 1943; bur. Wordsley. A white stone cross marks his grave.

72 Robert Stuart, d. 4th Mar 1946; bur. Wordsley, family grey granite vault.

73 Frederick H. Stuart, son of Frederick Stuart and his wife Mary Ann, nee Harvey, b. c1884.

74 William Arthur Stuart, son of William Henry Stuart and his wife Charlotte, nee Palmer, b. c1879, Wordsley.

75 Eric M. Stuart, son of Samuel Mansfield Stuart and his wife Elizabeth Mary, nee Parsons, b. c1898.

76 F. Churlton Pauli, son of Mr Pauli and his wife Mary Margaret, nee Stuart.

77 Frederick G. Stuart, son of Frederick H. Stuart.

78 Ian M. Stuart, son of Eric M. Stuart.

79 It was later reported that Waterford Wedgwood had been over optimistic about the demand for millennium memorabilia. *The Times* business commentator estimated it would cost the firm £7.5 million. *The Times*, 8th Nov 2001.

80 Express & Star, 7th Nov 2001.

CHAPTER 37

Red House Glassworks, Wordsley

The Red House glassworks cone still stands today in the heart of Wordsley, the only complete cone left in the Stourbridge area. There has probably been more research performed on the Red House cone than on any other, and there is possibly more documentary evidence about this site than about all the others put together. Despite this, it is still impossible to define the exact year the cone was built.

Snape's canal map of 1785 shows no evidence of any buildings at the current Red House site. On 21st June 1788 John Southwell[1], a gentleman of Stafford, and Ann, his wife, and Rebecca Stokes[2], the widow of Johnathan Stokes[3], gentleman of Worcester, sold a one acre plot of land to Richard Bradley, glass manufacturer—the current Red House site[4]. The background to the ownership of this land and the families of Southwell and Stokes is covered in detail, including a contemporary family tree, in a lengthy document[5].

Richard Bradley was an enterprising businessman and industrialist. He owned coal mines at nearby Brockmoor and during the seventeen-eighties and nineties he bought several pieces of land in and around Wordsley, all close to the Stourbridge Canal. He had bought Wordsley Flint Glassworks in 1782 and was clearly planning industrial expansion in Wordsley, the industrial heart of Kingswinford.

If Richard Bradley began the construction of the Red House cone shortly after purchasing the land it stands on, then this would date it to about 1790. The cone was built by Bradley in partnership with his brother-in-law George Ensell to make window glass by the broad method. It was built 60ft in diameter and 90ft tall. Ensell was probably keen to repeat his earlier well-publicised successes with broad-glass. Having been financially affected by the collapse of his Coalbournbrook works and his bankruptcy at Holly Hall, George Ensell had to persuade his brother-in-law, Richard Bradley, to finance the new construction. They also took into partnership a Pagett; one of a family long associated with broad-glassmaking[6].

Ensell repeated the innovation he began at Coalbournbrook by installing a moving lehr[7]. This fascinating feature, the only one surviving in the world, can still be seen at the Red House. Completed glassware was introduced at the glasshouse end onto two rows of metal pans, each pan weighing about 12lbs. A hand-turned crank pulled the train of pans via chains and pulleys down the length of the lehr into the shrawer[8]. Fires were lit under the lehr at the glasshouse end and the journey down the lehr gave the glass opportunity to anneal as the temperature gradually reduced. As the pans of annealed glassware arrived in the shrawer, after about thirty-six hours, the glassware was removed and washed. The pans were unhooked and returned to the glasshouse end.

Ensell's lehr at the Red House

A list of glassworks dated 1796 names the firm as Bradley & Ensell, Wordsley$_9$. It was in this year the Red House switched from broad-glass to the production of bottles. The most plausible reason for this is that public demand for crown glass was replacing that for broad-glass. By the end of the century crown had almost completely replaced broad-glass production in Britain, Dial Glasshouses being a peculiar exception. Changing to bottle manufacturing was probably an attempt to restore or increase profitability at the Red House. An announcement was duly made:

> 'Glass Bottle Manufactory. Messrs. Bradley, Ensell, Pagett and Co. having established a Manufactory for Glass Bottles of all Kinds at Wordsley, near Stourbridge, respectfully beg leave to inform the Public in general, that they may be supplied with those Articles of as good a Quality, and upon

as reasonable Terms, as from any other Manufactory whatever.'[10]

Just before the announcement was published, Richard Bradley died, on 23rd February 1796[11]. His obituary reads 'Died, Wednesday, R. Bradley Esq., an eminent glass manufacturer near Stourbridge.'[12] The firm made a further announcement accordingly:

> '26th Feb 1796. Stourbridge: Messrs. Bradley and Ensells take this opportunity to return their thanks for all favours conferred on their late worthy relation, R. Bradley, and hope for a continuance of the same. The Glass and Coal trade &c. will be carried on with the same punctuality and dispatch as usual.'[13]

As previously explained Bradley wrote his will[14] on 10th December 1794 and later added an undated codicil. When they were proved, the Red House was inherited by his sister, Kitty Bradley[15] and his niece, Lucy Mary Ensell in trust and ultimately to be divided between them and the testator's nephews, Charles Ensell and Richard Bradley Ensell.

Six weeks after the will was proved, Lucy Mary Ensell married John Holt of Wigan[16]. Lucy Mary Holt, as she now was, became Richard Bradley's main legatee.

As the surviving legatee, Lucy Mary was formally granted ownership of the Red House property on 26th October 1797. It included land of about one acre and thirty-two perches 'with the glasshouse warehouses and other buildings thereto atchd.'[17] Her husband John took over the running of her business affairs.

On 17th January 1803 a meeting took place at the Stewponey Inn, Stourton to petition the Government to have the duty on flint glass based on manufactured goods instead of metal or raw materials. John Holt of Bradley, Ensells & Holt contributed £100 to the fund. The amount contributed implies it was one of the larger firms.

On 31st December 1804 John Holt formed a partnership with his brothers-in-law, Charles Ensell II and Richard Bradley Ensell the elder, to trade as 'Bradley, Ensells and Holt'. This was a direct result of the requirements of Richard Bradley's will. Each partner was to have a third equal share with John Holt acting as treasurer[18]. They were trading informally under that name as early as 1801.

Lucy Mary Holt died in 1805[19], aged thirty-nine, but the partnership continued unaffected[20]. The firm continued to trade as Bradley, Ensells & Holt, flint glass manufacturers, Wordsley[21].

One of the partners, Charles Ensell II, died in 1815[22], aged forty-one. He had made a will on 9th September 1809 and added a codicil on 25th February 1815 which were proved in PCC on 29th August 1815[23]. In the will he stated his claim to his inheritance, but the consequences of his will, and subsequent litigation, led to the eventual dissolution of the partnership in 1827:

> 'Whereas I am entitled under the will of my (late) uncle Richard Bradley to one third share of and in certain glasshouses, iron works and coal works now carried on in partnership with the said John Holt and Richard Bradley Ensell.'

The firm continued to trade as Bradley, Ensells & Holt, Wordsley Glass Works[24]. However, a second partner, John Holt, died in 1820[25], aged sixty-two. He did not leave a proper will, only some unattested and undated papers expressing his wish that his one third share in the 'glass business' should go to his daughter and only child, Mary Holt. Mary Holt took control of the Red House on 12th February 1821[26]. Letters of administration were granted for the estate of John Holt in PCC on 17th April 1821[27]. Mary became the owner of the land attached to the works and some of the properties, including Park House, where she lived[28]. Although Richard Bradley Ensell the elder was the only surviving member of the partnership, the firm continued to trade as Bradley, Ensells & Holt, Wordsley glass works[29].

In 1827 Mary Holt married George William Wainwright, a plate glass manufacturer of East Smithfield, Wapping, Middlesex and after their marriage he took over running his wife's share of the business[30]. The firm then operated as 'Ensells and Wainwright' or 'Ensells and Co.'

By 1827 the partnership formed out of necessity by the legatees of Richard Bradley and their offspring became unworkable and the business was put up for sale[31].

The partnership property was divided into six lots and put up for auction. Two legal disputes concerning ownership took place but the appeal found for the Wainwrights and they were admitted to the ownership of the Red House on the same day[32]. The property was auctioned as planned on Friday 28th September 1827 at the Talbot Inn.

Richard Bradley Ensell the younger bought the Red House for £3,207. A complete and very detailed inventory of the contents at the time of the sale still exists today and provides valuable information[33]. Although Richard Bradley Ensell the younger purchased the property, it did not officially come into his hands until 31st May 1828 when the Wainwrights signed a deed of covenant to surrender it to him[34].

Richard Bradley Ensell the elder, the last to survive of the original partnership, died in 1828[35], aged forty-four. The business then traded under the title of Richard Bradley Ensell senior (Executors of), Wordsley[36].

Richard Bradley Ensell the younger began a major programme of building work, erecting many structures that still stand at the Red House site today. In 1830 he radically changed the output of the glasshouse from phials and bottles to table glass. Table glass required a longer annealing time and so the lehr and shrawer were extended. Today the shrawer looks much as it did in 1830, but different brickwork clearly shows where the old shrawer ended and the extension was added.

At the time of the sale in 1827 Richard Bradley Ensell the younger bought the White House as well as the Red House glassworks and probably overreached himself. On 7th June 1830 he surrendered—but did not sell—the Red House as security to Messrs. Rufford and Co., bankers of Stourbridge and Bromsgrove, in lieu of debts to them totalling £8,000. The value of the Red House was accepted at the rather low price of £3,661 14s 5d and Ensell bound himself to repay the total sum with interest[37]. This covenant also holds the first reference to a steam engine at the Red House: 'the Steam Engine and other machinery and apparatus utensils articles and effects . . . '

Richard Bradley Ensell paid £1,758 2s 3d excise duty for the year ending 5th January 1833[38], suggesting this large glasshouse had only the fourteenth largest output of the sixteen Stourbridge/Dudley glasshouses of the day. No wonder Ensell was in trouble!

Richard Bradley Ensell the younger was unable to extricate himself from his mounting debts and so he sold the Red House to his bankers, Messrs Rufford & Co., for £2,111 on 8th May 1834. By this time he had made his new home at 3 Warwick Court, High Holborne, London[39]. He eventually died on 6th September 1862 at Inworth in Essex[40].

Rufford & Co. leased the works as quickly as possible. On 14th June 1834 they leased the Red House to William Edward Davies and William Rolinson Hodgetts for twenty-one years at an annual rent of £140[41]. Davies and Hodgetts had previously been partners at Dixon's Green Glassworks, until it was damaged by mining subsidence. On taking over the Red House, a condition of their lease was that they should build a perimeter wall at least five feet tall with a gateway wide enough for carriages. This is the wall and gateway that survive today.

The new firm traded as Davies and Hodgetts, Red House Glass Works, Wordsley and advertised its wares as flint glass, plain and cut[42]. Kingswinford Poor Rate Book of 1836 shows the Red House in the possession of Hodgetts and Davies with a rateable value of £56 1s[43].

Sometime about 1837 William Edward Davies died leaving the business controlled by William Rolinson Hodgetts[44]. Fowler & Son's map of 1840 shows the Red House as plot 363 owned by Philip Rufford and occupied by William Hodgetts. There are further references to the firm as William Hodgetts, glass manufacturer[45].

William Rolinson Hodgetts made his will on 3rd September 1845 and died soon after. The will was proved 19th March 1846[46] in which he provided for his widow, Elizabeth[47], and their son William James Hodgetts[48] to carry on the business.

In 1851 the business traded as William Hodgetts (Executors of), Wordsley[49]. Elizabeth Hodgetts lived with her children, including William James, at Townsend, close by Kingswinford church[50].

In July 1851 the bankers Messrs. Rufford and Wragge were

declared insolvent. Mr John Harward called the creditors to the Talbot Hotel to hear that the bank's debts amounted to £225,000 in respect of their Stourbridge Bank and £227,000 for the one at Bromsgrove$_{51}$. As a result, on 21st September 1852, the Red House property, still occupied by the Hodgetts, was conveyed by John Balguy, Rufford's bankruptcy commissioner, to William Webb and his brother Edward Webb for £1,750. The conveyance describes Edward Webb as a glass manufacturer and William Webb as a miller$_{52}$.

In August 1856 the new owners leased the works to Elizabeth and William James Hodgetts for a further fourteen years at an annual rent of £140$_{53}$. This lease refers to 'the cutting shops lately erected and built by . . . Hodgetts.' As the shops were not listed in 1852 they must have been built between then and August 1856. This therefore suggests an increase in cutting activity at the Red House.

Faced with an outbreak of strikes, the employers responded by holding a meeting on 1st November 1858 at the Talbot Hotel, Stourbridge, where they formed a manufacturer's organisation. Mrs Hodgetts did not attend but stated that she would not employ any strikers until she had consulted her son. She would not undertake to make undecorated goods for the two firms involved.

In 1863 William James Hodgetts cut his mother's apron strings and went into partnership with his cousin Philip Pargeter and his Richardson uncles at their Wordsley Flint Glassworks. Elizabeth Hodgetts continued to run the Red House until she retired in 1870.

On 14th July 1871—Elizabeth Hodgetts having retired – Philip Pargeter leased the Red House site for ten years. Working with Benjamin Richardson he was much involved with his pioneering work with coloured glass. However, Pargeter wanted the freedom to experiment further, and at the Red House he introduced the manufacture of coloured glass alongside cut, etched, and engraved crystal. One of Pargeter's first innovations was to install a Frisbie feeder that supplied fresh coal from the tunnel below the hearth right into the eye of the furnace. A new tunnel was built to bring coal directly from the canalside to the feeder. This enabled higher furnace temperatures, as the old method was for teazers to shovel coal onto the surface of the fire from inside the glasshouse. This had the effect of temporarily reducing the fire's temperature and releasing dense sulphurous fumes. Furthermore, the very presence of coal inside the glasshouse was a possible source of contamination of the glass.

Red House Glassworks and Canal

By 1873 Philip Pargeter felt his glassmakers had the skill to reproduce the Portland Vase[54]. He discussed the notion with John Northwood, who agreed to execute the carving. Northwood had just completed his spectacular carving of the famous Elgin Vase in flint glass—an achievement that left no doubt as to his ability to do the job. Northwood and Pargeter, when serving their apprenticeship, had seen Benjamin Richardson inspire his workmen by bringing into their midst a Wedgwood jasper copy of the Portland Vase and hear him exclaim 'There is a thousand pounds for him who can produce that in glass!'[55] On several occasions Pargeter took groups of his best workmen to the British Museum to study the original.

They undertook many experiments and experienced many failures, but eventually produced a suitable blank. Credit for blowing the blanks is given to the chair[56] headed by Daniel Hancox[57], assisted by Joseph Worrall[58], Charles Hancox[59], and Benjamin Downing[60]. The carving took three years to complete and was subject to many trials and tribulations. It was finally completed, signed and dated in 1876 when it was widely publicised and exhibited. Pargeter displayed it at the Red House works for two weeks and then took it to his London showrooms. In January 1877 it was exhibited at Stoke-on-Trent. With the Milton vase it formed the centre of attraction on Thomas Webb's stand at the Paris Exhibition in 1878. In 1905 it was back on display in Stourbridge. The vase remained the property of Philip Pargeter who estimated it had cost him over £500. It was lent to the British Museum by his descendant, Mrs E. Mary Duffy, from 1959 to 1975. When it was sold at Sotheby's (Belgravia) in 1975, it fetched the—then record—price for a piece of glass of £30,000. A private collector in the United States now owns the vase. Philip Pargeter's reputation was elevated to almost superlative levels. For example, the Reliquary wrote:

> We notice these productions the more readily, because to our minds they are the most truly artistic, the most perfectly beautiful, and the most faultlessly perfect example of the "verrier's art" that have yet come under our notice. The productions of the "Red House Works" at Stourbridge, are of the most varied character, and of the greatest possible extent, and are, as far as we have has the opportunity of seeing examples, of faultlessly excellent quality. In pure taste and artistic nature of the designs, Mr. Pargeter's glass takes foremost rank, and in manipulation is not excelled by any . . . It is manifestly impossible to enumerate even a tithe of the exquisite articles produced by Mr. Pargeter at these famed works. All we can say is, that we have seen nothing that has emanated from them that is not thoroughly good in every particular, both of form, of workmanship, of decoration, and of artistic treatment.'[61]

Philip Pargeter collaborated with John Northwood in 1878 to

produce another masterpiece of cameo glass, the Milton Vase, the subject being taken from Milton's *Paradise Lost*. Its shape was designed by Pargeter and the decoration was performed by Pargeter and Northwood, who engraved it, and signed and dated it 1878. It was made in blue glass overlaid with opaque white glass, of truncated conical shape and with two scroll handles. The decoration is a carved scene of the avenging angel, Raphael, on one side, and Adam and Eve on the other. It was lent to the British Museum from 1959 until 1975, when it was sold in London at Sotheby's (Belgravia) for £26,000. The Reliquary again praised the quality of Pargeter's work:

> 'We have on more than one occasion, in our 'Quarterly Papers on Improvements in Art Manufactures,' called attention to the beautiful works produced by and for Mr. Philip Pargeter, of the Red House Glass Works at Stourbridge, and have always done with a more than ordinary degree of pleasure, because whatever we have seen that has emmanated from him, or has been effected under his auspices, bears upon it both in design and in execution the stamp of faultless excellence and of almost unapproachable skill. We now have the gratification of directing attention to another high achievement of Art, which in skill in manipulation is equal to anything yet attempted in cameo-glass . . .'[62]

The team of Pargeter and Northwood worked together over four years to produce a group of three tazze in blue cameo glass, now known as the Pargeter-Northwood Tazze. The central portraits were Isaac Newton, John Flaxman and William Shakespeare[63]. All three were signed by Northwood and dated respectively 1878, 1880 and 1882. Their rims are decorated with wreaths of ivy, hawthorn leaves, and acorns and oak leaves respectively. The domed feet are decorated with acanthus leaves. Pargeter bore the complete cost of production and paid Northwood seventy-five guineas for the carving of each tazze[64]. They were lent to the British Museum by Mrs E. Mary Duffy from 1959 to 1975 when they were sold on 24th July at Sotheby's (Belgravia)[65].

In 1881 Philip Pargeter, flint glass trade master, employing fifty-five men, eighteen boys and five girls, lived at Rose Cottage, Coalbournbrook, unmarried. His unmarried sister, Elizabeth lived with him[66]. Pargeter gave up his glass business later in 1881 because of his frustration with union intransigence. The glassworks was taken by Frederick Stuart, who had fallen out with his partner George Mills at the Albert Glassworks. The Red House was leased to Frederick Stuart on 29th April 1881, where he had previously been employed in 1827. By this time he was sixty-five years old, but he had seven sons and the oldest ones came with him: William Henry Stuart[67], Frederick Stuart the younger[68] and Robert Stuart[69].

Frederick Stuart finally parted from George Mills at the Albert Glassworks in October 1882. In 1883 he made a partnership agreement between himself, William Henry Stuart, Frederick Stuart the younger, Robert Stuart, Arthur Stuart[70] and George Stuart[71]. Allowance was made for Walter Mansfield Stuart[72] to become a partner in due course. The indenture states that on 9th September 1882 an agreement had been made between Philip Pargeter and Frederick Stuart, whereby Frederick Stuart acquired the leasehold of the glassworks and premises known as the Red House Glasshouse in Wordsley and the various showrooms and premises in London. The agreement describes Frederick Stuart as the senior partner and the others as junior partners[73].

On 13th December 1885, William George Webb and Edward Webb renewed the lease to Frederick Stuart and others trading under the name 'Stuart and Sons', for twenty-one years at £195 per year[74]. A new cutting shop was opened in 1885 and the old one became an etching shop[75].

The firm traded as Stuart & Sons, flint glass manufacturers, Red House Glass Works[76]. Frederick Stuart lived at The Mount, Wordsley; Frederick Stuart junior lived at Field House, Wordsley and William Henry Stuart lived at Bank House, Wordsley.

Frederick Stuart senior was eventually persuaded to retire from the partnership in 1897, aged eighty-one. He was paid 10 percent interest per annum upon the balance showing to his credit, the balance being £5,468 11s 10d. A new partnership was formed to run from 1st March 1897 for fourteen years. The partners were William Henry Stuart, Frederick Stuart junior, Robert Stuart, Walter

Mansfield Stuart and Samuel Mansfield Stuart. Provision was made for William Henry's son, Charles[77] to be admitted to the partnership in due course. By this time Arthur Stuart[78] and George Stuart[79] had died. Robert Stuart had been educated at King Edward School, Stourbridge and articled in London to his uncle, a solicitor. On joining the family firm he quickly became a driving force. He was a strict disciplinarian, who neither smoked nor drank.

The patriarch of the family business, Frederick Stuart senior, died in 1900[80], aged eighty-three. He had made a will on 11th February 1897[81] and added three codicils. When proved at Lichfield, his estate was valued at £44,637 18s 7d. In his will he described himself as a glassmaster, but made little reference to his business. He made several legacies and his residual estate was shared between his five surviving sons: William Henry, Frederick, Robert, Walter Mansfield and Samuel Mansfield. Robert Stuart had been living at The Mount with his father, then after his father's death, he moved to Ashfield, Wordsley. William Henry Stuart and his wife Charlotte then moved to The Mount from their previous home at Bank House. Unlike his father, William Henry Stuart played an active part in the local community. He was a Justice of the Peace and a prominent member of the Conservative Party.

The furnace at the Red House was rebuilt in 1901. H.J. Ingram was paid £21 4s to dismantle the old one and £64 12s to build the new one. The total cost, including materials, was £324 18s.

Frederick Stuart junior and his wife Mary Ann[82] had been living at Field House, New Street, Wordsley, then in 1901 they moved to Green Bank. This is a regency period house above the war memorial at Wordsley that still stands today. At the time it was set in two acres, with entrances from Plant Street and Brewery Street. Frederick was known for an eccentricity of walking from the back gate of Green Bank to the Red House in the middle of the road.

The fifty-year long battle with trade unions was largely over and on 23rd May 1903 the County Express reported the winding up of the Midland Association of Glass Manufacturers. Stuart and Sons were one of the eight firms who were still members at the time of its demise.

The business was incorporated as a limited company in 1911.

However, before any great advances could be made, the outbreak of the First World War brought a long period of disruption to the entire trade of Great Britain. During the war years Stuart and Sons built a new furnace for making electric light bulbs and by 1923 were turning out about 40,000 bulbs per week[83].

After the war, great efforts were made to return to normality and of course profit. Ludwig Kny[84] was appointed chief designer in 1918, a position he held until his death in 1937[85]. He was the oldest son of the celebrated engraver Frederick Englebert Kny. Ludwig Kny was an innovative designer who did much to encourage the transition of designs from the Victorian tradition of heavy cutting to the freer and lighter designs of the new century. Artistic development was under the direction of Robert Stuart and later Geoffrey Stuart and both worked closely with Ludwig Kny producing many new designs and techniques. He particularly used intaglio cutting in his many designs. As tastes progressed with time, he progressed from stylised leaf and floral designs to abstract Art Deco designs.

Geoffrey Stuart, a grandson of the founder, joined the firm in the late nineteen-twenties and immediately started to promote a modern image for the company's products. His first collection of designs appeared in 1933.

Stuart & Sons purchased the Red House from the successors to William Webb and Edward Webb on 3rd September 1920. The successors were William Harcourt Webb[86], Charles Webb[87] and others[88]. William Harcourt Webb was the son of Colonel William George Webb MP and had been in partnership with his father and brother as a seed merchant. He was an extraordinarily wealthy man, having been the main beneficiary in his father's will[89] valued at £559,984 1s 5d.

A range of new designs was registered in 1921, one version of which was later known as *Stratford*. It featured moulded rings between bowl and stem. The ringed designs became the foundation of the range of enamelled ware developed by Ludwig Kny from 1928 onwards.

William Henry Stuart JP died in 1927[90], aged seventy-seven.

His widow, Charlotte, moved from the family home, The Mount, to a smaller house at Red Hill, south of Stourbridge. The Mount was sold and the land was used for housing. Robert Stuart then became chairman of the firm. He lived a comfortable bachelor life until 1934 when he married to Emma Brooks at the age of 77.

In 1932 Thomas Atland Fennymore of E. Brain & Co. Ltd, Foley China Works, Fenton, had the idea of inviting outside designers to contribute fresh ideas to ceramic design—both glass and pottery. His project was supported by designers Milna Gray and Graham Sutherland who assisted him in involving twenty-eight of the finest artists of the day. The first exhibition of their designs was held at Dorland Hall, London in 1933. Stuarts' was commissioned to contribute to the scheme in 1934 and in October of that year exhibited products at Harrods 'Modern Art for the Table' exhibition. Because of the short timescale, many of Stuarts' pieces were not ready in time and only appeared at the follow-up Royal Academy exhibition in 1935.

Harrods exhibition showed pieces from Stuarts, Foley China and Royal Staffordshire Pottery, designed by artists Eric Ravilious[91], Ernest[92] and Dod Proctor[93], Paul Nash[94], Dame Laura Knight, Graham Sutherland[95], Gordon[96] and Moira Forsythe and Vanessa Bell[97].

Working at a distance, the artists never really understood the medium for which they were designing. Laura Knight was probably the only one who ever visited the factory. The venture, which followed Keith Murray's arrival at Stevens and Williams, was not commercially successful. None of the three companies involved took on any of the designers. However, it inspired Geoffrey Stuart to some remarkable designs in the Art Deco style using a combination of straight cuts and curved intaglio lines.

The furnace at the Red House was finally put out in 1936 and production was transferred to a new factory on the old White House site. For many years the old cone was used for storage but gradually it began to deteriorate. In 1966 the Red House became a grade two listed building. Stuart & Sons decided to make the cone sound and began a process of gradual renovation of the whole site.

The site is now run as a museum. During 2001 Dudley Metropolitan Borough Council undertook a comprehensive renovation of the 208 year-old site backed by grants from Advantage West Midlands (£350,000), the Heritage Lottery Fund (£375,000), the European Development Fund (£570,000), English Heritage (£109,000) and the last owners of the site, Stuart Crystal (£11,500). The premises opened to the public as a tourist attraction in the spring of 2002. An admirable feat of heritage preservation, for which all concerned locally deserve the greatest of praise. However, coinciding as it does with the closure of Stuart Crystal, and the transfer of production offshore, what a condemnation of contemporary government's ineptitude and disdain for the entrepreneurial and manufacturing skills that once made the Red House a powerhouse of the Industrial Revolution.

---

1 A John Southell was Master of Stafford Grammar School in 1738.

2 Ann Southwell and Rebecca Stokes were sisters, nee Allen.

3 Johnathan and Rebecca Stokes were the parents of Johnathan Stokes MD, pioneering botanist and member of the Lunar Society. After a substantial European tour, Johnathan Stokes returned to London in May 1783 when he attended the Royal Society as Priestley's guest. He then settled down as a physician in Stourbridge. Linnaeus's Correspondence V14, Archives of the Linnean Society of London.

4 Red House Papers No 1, 21 Jun 1788. Surrender and Admission of Land.

5 SRO, D695/4/16/4-5, Abstract of the Title of Messrs Hunt and Kell as surviving trustees under a deed of family arrangement dated 14th Mar 1840 to certain copyhold estates situate in the manor and parish of Kingswinford in the County of Stafford being lot one at the sale by Auction on 29th August 1859.

6 Supra, Colemans.

7 A lehr is a glassmaker's annealing facility. Previously, this was a small furnace, independent of the main glassmaking furnace. It was filled with the finished glass, heated up to high temperature, then allowed to cool, in much the same way as a potter's kiln. Ensell's main improvement was that it allowed continuous production. It also provided a more precise control of the reducing temperature.

8 The shrawer is the room into which the lehr discharges.

9 D.N. Sandilands.
10 Birmingham Gazette, 29th Feb 1796.
11 SRO, D648/5/22 5th Apr 1834 Release of Land.
12 Bristol Gazette, 10th Mar 1796.
13 Birmingham Gazette, 7th Mar 1796.
14 PRO, PCC will (and codicil) of Richard Bradley, 14th May 1796.
15 Kitty Bradley died four months before Richard Bradley, but he had not altered his will accordingly. She was buried 12th Aug 1795, Dudley St. Thomas's.
16 Mar. John Holt and Lucy Mary Ensell, 1st Jul 1796, Wigan, Lancashire.
17 Red House Papers No 2 1797, Admission Lucy Mary Holt under the Will of Richard Bradley.
18 Red House Papers No. 5, Masters Report, 1827.
19 Lucy Mary Holt, d. 23rd Dec 1805; bur. 2nd Jan 1806, Dudley St. Thomas's.
20 SRO, D648/5/22 1834 Release of Land.
21 Holden's Triennial Directory for 1809, 1810 & 1811.
22 Charles Ensell, d. 6th Mar 1815; bur. 13th Mar 1815, Dudley St. Thomas's.
23 SRO, D648/5/22 1834 Release of Land.
24 James Pigot's 1818 Commercial Directory and Lewis's 1820 Worcestershire and Commercial Directory.
25 John Holt, d. 15th Dec 1820; bur. 20th Dec 1820, Kingswinford.
26 Red House Papers no 3 1821 Admission of Miss Mary Holt.
27 SRO, D648/5/22.
28 DA, William Fowler's 1822 *Map of the Parish of Kingswinford*.
29 Wrightsons' Triennial Directory of Birmingham, 1823 and 1825 editions.
30 Red House Papers No 3, Admission of Miss Mary Holt, 1821.
31 Supra, White House Glassworks.
32 Red House papers No 4, 2 Jul 1827. Copyhold Recovery.
33 Red House Papers No 5, 1827.
34 Red House Papers No 6, Deeds of Covenant, 1828.
35 Richard Bradley Ensell, bur. 18th Mar 1828, Oldswinford.
36 Pigot and Co.'s National Commercial Directory for 1828-9; Pigot and Co.'s 1829 Commercial Directory of Birmingham.
37 Red House Papers No 7, 1830 Covenant.
38 Thirteenth Report of the Commission into the Glass Excise, 1835, Appendix 7.
39 SRO, D648/5/22, Release of land, 5 Apr 1834. Warwick Court stood off High

Holborne, almost opposite Chancery Lane. It is shown on John Tallis's *London Street Views 1838-1840*, Part 8 (1969), p53.

40 Information supplied by Mr F. Ensell.

41 Red House Papers No 9, 14 Jun 1834. Lease to Davies and Hodgetts.

42 Pigot and Co.'s 1835 National Commercial Directory.

43 SRO, Poor Rate Book 1836-7 D585/159/12.

44 Robson's 1839 Birmingham and Sheffield Directory.

45 Bentley's 1840 Directory of Stourbridge; Pigot and Co.'s 1841 Directory of Birmingham.

46 PCC PROB11/2032 360/363, will of William Hodgetts, proved 19th Mar 1846.

47 Elizabeth, nee Stevens, b. c1799 Dudley, married William Rollason Hodgetts, 28th Feb 1827, Birmingham, St. Philip's.

48 William James Hodgetts, son of William Rolinson Hodgetts and his wife Elizabeth, nee Stevens, b. 4th Mar 1828, privately bap. in Dudley, confirmed by the Bishop of Lichfield, 5th Aug 1846.

49 William White's 1851 History Gazetteer and Directory of Staffordshire.

50 PRO, 1851 Census HO 107/2036 08/147/061.

51 H.E. Palfrey, *Gentlemen at the Talbot Stourbridge*, p20.

52 Red House Papers No 10, 21 Sep 1852 Conveyance.

53 Red House Papers No 11, 1856 Lease.

54 A more cynical view of this is that Pargeter had probably been experimenting on the techniques during his partnership of Hodgetts, Richardson and Pargeter. Certainly Benjamin Richardson was obsessed with the reproduction of the Portland Vase. Having solved the problems of blowing the blank, Pargeter probably left the partnership and set up his own firm where he could concentrate on the project, but more importantly, take the sole credit for it.

55 E. Mary Duffy, *Philip Pargeter and John Northwood : cameo glass pioneers*, AM, Dec 1962, pp639-41; ibid, John Northwood II, p7.

56 PG, Jun 1960.

57 Daniel Hancox, son of John and Elizabeth Hancox, bap. 15th Jul 1821, Brierley Hill; d. 20th Mar 1879; bur. Wordsley.

58 Joseph Worral, son of John and Ann Worral, b. 20th Jan 1840, Wordsley, acted as servitor. At various times he kept the Queens Head and Acorn public houses in Brettell Lane; d. 1909.

59 Charles Hancox, son of Daniel and Ann Hancox, bap. 25th Mar 1849, Kingswinford was the footmaker.

60 Benjamin Downing, son of James and Ann Downing, b. c1859 Wollaston was the other footmaker; d. 2nd Jul 1950; bur. Wordsley.
61 Mr. Pargeter's Art Productions in Glass, RM v 19 (1877), pp 57-58.
62 RM v 19 (1878-9), p243.
63 Symbolic of science, art and literature respectively.
64 Ibid, E. Mary Duffy.
65 Dr and Mrs L.S. Rakow of the USA bought the three tazze and the Portland vase.
66 PRO, 1881 Census of Kingswinford, RG11/2890/29/12.
67 William Henry Stuart, son of Frederick Stuart and his wife Lucy Mansfield, nee Bill, bap. 11th Jul 1849, Kingswinford.
68 Frederick Stuart, son of Frederick Stuart and his wife Lucy Mansfield, nee Bill, b. c1851, Wollaston.
69 Robert Stuart, son of Frederick Stuart and his wife Lucy Mansfield, nee Bill, b. c1857, Kingswinford.
70 Arthur Stuart, son of Frederick Stuart and his wife Lucy Mansfield, nee Bill, b. c1853.
71 George Stuart, son of Frederick Stuart and his wife Lucy Mansfield, nee Bill, b. c1855, Wollaston.
72 Walter Mansfield Stuart, son of Frederick Stuart and his wife Lucy Mansfield, nee Bill, b. c1864, Kingswinford.
73 Ibid, W.E.C. Stuart.
74 Red House Papers No 12, 1885 Lease.
75 Ibid, Referred to in an indenture dated 31 May 1890 on the back of the 1885 lease.
76 Kelly's 1888 Directory of Staffordshire.
77 Charles Frederick Stuart, son of William Henry Stuart and his wife Charlotte, nee Palmer, b. c1876, Wordsley.
78 Arthur Stuart, d. c1896.
79 George Stuart, d. c1895.
80 Frederick Stuart, d. 21st Apr 1900; bur. Wordsley, granite vault.
81 PRO, will of Frederick Stuart, 14th Jun 1900.
82 Mary Ann, nee Harvey, 1849-1924. She was known as Polly.
83 Harry J. Powell, *Glass-making in England* (1923), p171.
84 Ludwig Kny, son of Frederick Englebert Kny and his wife Sarah Lavinia, b. c1869, Amblecote.

85 Ludwig Kny bur. Stourbridge Cemetery.
86 William Harcourt Webb, son of William George Webb and his wife Ada Blanche, nee Broughton Pryce, b. 27th Oct 1875; bap. 14th Feb 1876, Wordsley.
87 Charles Webb, son of Edward Webb and his wife Margaret Jane, nee Evers-Swindell, bap. 26th Sep 1878, Wordsley.
88 Red House Papers No 13, 3rd Sep 1920, Conveyance.
89 PRO, Will of William George Webb, 28th Oct 1905.
90 William Henry Stuart, d. 15th Feb 1927; bur. Wordsley. A white stone cross marks his grave.
91 Eric Ravilious (1903-1942) appears to have been one of the more accommodating artists. His correspondence with Geoffrey Stuart shows a deference to Stuart's better understanding of the medium.
92 Ernest Proctor produced some whimsical figurative designs.
93 Dod Proctor worked with Geoffrey Stuart to recommend new shapes as well as designs, whereas the designs for ceramics had to utilise existing blanks.
94 Paul Nash carried over his eathernware and bone china designs into the medium of glass. Correspondence in the Stuart archives suggests he was the most difficult of the designers for Geoffrey Stuart to work with.
95 Graham Sutherland produced some very bold dramatic designs.
96 Gordon Forsyth was director of one of Stoke-on-Trent's art schools. He was the only designer to use applied decoration, such as green trailing, which he did in abundance.
97 Vanessa Bell's designs are the least prolific. Only one sheet of her designs exists in the Stuart archives.

CHAPTER 38

Dial Glasshouses, Audnam

When the Stourbridge Canal was built it left the old Dial Glasshouse on the corner of Brettell Lane close to the canal, but not on its banks. The canal was fully opened to traffic in December 1779 and was an immediate success. The canal became the main route for raw materials in, and finished goods out. However, John Pidcock was at a disadvantage to many of his competitors as his goods were double-handled and hauled by wagon from the canalside to and from his works. So, in 1788 he built a new glassworks on the opposite side of the turnpike road, in a prime position, still close to the turnpike, but right on the bank of the canal. Messrs. Pickford & Co brought raw materials to the works[1]. The new cone was built 70ft in diameter, although the height to which it was built is not known. Its construction is dated fairly safely to 1788 as a large datestone in the brickwork survives today. Two cones were built, one for bottle glass and the other smaller cone for making broadglass. The larger cone originally had a sundial with the motto *Ut Vitrune, sic Vita*[2], although no trace of this remains. Both cones are graphically shown on Sherriff's plan of 1812.

John Pidcock could be proud of his achievements. He had developed a thriving trade and built a new glassworks with the latest means of distribution. He lived in style at Platts House and was a Justice of the Peace for Worcestershire; but he was ageing. Sometime before 1790, by which time he was seventy-three years old, he took his sons, Thomas[3], John junior[4] and Robert[5] into partnership. The firm then traded as John Pidcock and Sons.

John Pidcock died in 1791[6], aged seventy-four. His obituaries

397

were extensive, even by contemporary standards[7]. His will[8] contains several minor legacies, but he left all his real and personal estate to his sons Thomas, John, and Robert.

The partnership continued to trade as John Pidcock & Sons for a few years after John Pidcock's death[9]. Dial Glasshouses had a prolific output of bottles and although there was competition from London glasshouses the firm had its own bottle warehouse in London at Lambeth Hill, Thames Street[10]. By 1793 the Pidcock brothers were using a different trading title. The Birmingham Gazette of 1st April 1793 carries a report of 'Merchants of Stourbridge using local banknotes:—T. J. & R. Pidcock.' In 1798 another London bottle warehouse is listed; 'T. J. & R. Pidcock, Bottle Warehouse, 11 Bush Lane, Cannon Street.'[11]

Robert Pidcock was the youngest of the three brothers in the partnership. His home was at Lydney in Gloucestershire. He never married and made his career in the army, where he served as a Captain. He died in 1799[12], aged thirty-eight. In his will[13] he left money to his brother Thomas and various legacies to his sisters. He did not mention involvement in glass manufacturing. The most singular aspect of his will is that it reveals he had a son and a daughter by two different women, neither of who had he married.

The two surviving brothers traded as Thomas & John Pidcock, glass and glass-bottle manufacturers[14]. They were also proprietors of the Stourbridge clay-mines and fire brick manufacturers. John Pidcock II managed the business and introduced his two sons, John Henzey Pidcock[15] and George Pidcock[16], to the partnership.

Thomas Pidcock, the oldest of the three brothers was the next to die. Like his brother, he never married and similarly followed a military career as a Major in the 17th Light Dragoons. He died in 1813[17], aged sixty-three. The partnership was revised and an announcement was made, although the wording is misleading as Thomas Pidcock had died:

> 'The partnership between John Pidcock, John Henzey Pidcock, George Pidcock and Thomas Pidcock trading as John Pidcock and Co. was dissolved 18 Oct 1814, Thomas

Pidcock having retired, trade being continued by remaining partners.'[18]

After the dissolution of the family partnership, John Henzey Pidcock of Belle Vue, Stourbridge, became the senior member of the firm. His father John Pidcock was by then aged sixty and had most likely retired. His younger brother George was only aged twenty-seven, but had moved to the island of Guernsey and sunnier climes[19]. This left John Henzey Pidcock in charge. He decided to wind down operations at the Platts Glassworks and to take on new partners at Dial Glasshouses.

William Henry Cope[20] left his active role in Mountford, Biddle & Cope at the Wrockwardine Glassworks in Shropshire on 20th December 1814[21] and moved to Coalbournhill House[22] to become a partner. He later moved to Holbeche House, which stands today about a mile north of Kingswinford. Holbeche House is situated about a mile from Kingswinford, on the Wolverhampton road, close to the junction of Holbeach Lane. It is a fine Jacobean where the gunpowder plotters, Robert Catesby, Thomas Percy, Jack and Kit Wright were killed and Thomas Wintour, Ambrose Rockwood and John Grant taken prisoner[23].

Holbeche House

The other partner was Richard Mountford[24], glassmaster of Shifnal. Mountford remained a partner in the Wrockwardine Glassworks, various ironworks, and copper mines in Cornwall. This was a return to his roots for Richard Mountford as he had previously been an undermanager at the Dial Glassworks until he left shortly after the death of John Pidcock in 1791 to run the Wrockwardine Glassworks[25].

His great-nephew Richard Mountford Deeley drew an amusing comparison between the physical characteristics of these two partners when he was asked to weigh them on the glasshouse scales. John Henzey Pidcock was a slim figure weighing eight stones and Richard Mountford was double his weight at sixteen stones. Richard Mountford arranged for his nephew, Edwin Deeley, to become an apprentice at the Dial Glasshouses. Edwin[26] was the son of Edward Deeley, Richard Mountford's brother-in-law, an engineer and millwright by trade. He eventually became the manager of Dial Glasshouses[27]. The firm then began to trade as Pidcock, Cope & Co. There are entries for Dial Glasshouses in a succession of trade directories between 1820 and 1841, usually as manufacturers of broad-glass and bottles. The outline of the cones and surrounding buildings is clearly shown on Fowler's 1822 map, labelled as Dial Glasshouses[28].

Richard Mountford prospered with his income from many profitable businesses. In 1824 he invited John Biddle and William Henry Cope to join him in the venture of re-establishing the Old Bank at 4, Market Place, Shifnal that had belonged to the Botfields family of Decker Hill. They invited their fellow glassmaking partner, John Pidcock to join them. In 1835 the partnership amalgamated with Reynolds, Charlton & Co. of Newport and Darby & Co. of Coalbrookdale to form the Shropshire Banking Co[29]. Mountford was appointed chairman with the famous ironmaster Abraham Darby III[30] as one of his directors. Mountford built himself a fine new home, Park House in Park Street, Shifnal[31] that stands today functioning as a hotel.

In 1834 Benjamin Richardson commented that the 'Dial people' had pulled down their furnace and were replacing it with a six-pot furnace[32]. He added, despondently, that their trade was down[33].

John Pidcock junior served in public office as his father had before him. After the death of his father, he made his home at Platts House and became a Justice of the Peace and Deputy Lieutenant of Worcestershire. He died on 2nd August 1834, aged seventy-eight[34]. A window in remembrance of him and a memorial on the north wall of the chancel exist today in Wordsley Church. It would appear from subsequent references that his son, John Henzey Pidcock, was his principal beneficiary. John Henzey's interests certainly extended beyond his involvement in Dial Glasshouses. In 1839 he was also involved in the clay business with William Henry Cope on the northwest boundary of Amblecote[35].

New Dial Glassworks from the Canal

While Edwin Deeley was the glassworks manager, his wife Margaret gave birth to their first son at their house on the glassworks premises. He was born on the 10th October 1825 and was christened Richard Mountford Deeley. He left school in 1841 and started work in the offices at Dial Glasshouses, where he learned bookkeeping. One of his tasks was to deal with the endless demands of the exciseman. It was obvious he was being groomed for more than a clerk's position when he was introduced to the hunt meeting at the Stewponey Inn[36] by William Henry Cope and Edwin Deeley. He recorded, 'There were many gentlemen I knew who followed the hounds, George Grazebrook, Michael Grazebrook[37], James Evers-Swindell[38], Charles Evers-Swindell[39], Richard Webb etc.'[40] It appears from this statement that glassmasters were prominent in the local Hunt. It forms an interesting contrast to the lot of the average working man. 1842 was probably the worst year of the century with great distress, starvation and rioting in the Black Country[41].

Edwin Deeley managed the glassworks for some time. Then, after the death of his uncle, Richard Mountford, in 1842[42], he became a partner with William Henry Cope[43]. There were other sleeping partners such as John Biddle, former partner at Wrockwardine Glassworks, who did not play an active part. About this time John Henzey Pidcock retired from business and passed the remainder of his life as a gentleman. He removed to Hastings and kept a house at No 22 Orsett Terrace, Gloucester Gardens, Middlesex. He lived until 1861 and upon his death, on 7th February, he left an estate worth £7,000, but his will[44] does not mention glassmaking at all. This dates the final stage of the remnants of Lorrainer family descendants in the Stourbridge glassmaking industry.

The firm's traveller was Samuel Marshall Parrish[45], of Brettell Lane, son of glassmaker and cutter, Thomas Parrish[46]. Samuel is described as a 'very fine handsome man of good address who drove a gig.'[47] In 1842 he became a partner with Edwin Deeley and William Henry Cope and put £1,000 into the business. Sadly for him, ill health forced him to relinquish his position[48] after a year or two and his share in the partnership was taken by his younger brother Joseph[49]. The firm then operated as 'Cope, Deeley & Parrish', selling 'bottles, crown & coloured glass[50].'

Joseph left the partnership after an accident when he was travelling, in which his horse bolted and collided with a bridge. Edwin Deeley therefore offered the position of traveller for the firm to his nineteen-year old son Richard Mountford Deeley, who was serving his apprenticeship in the glassworks offices. He accepted the offer and acted as the firm's traveller for six years. Deeley travelled widely, driving a horse and dogcart, spending about forty weeks each year on the road. The firm had a warehouse in Canon Street, London, which he visited by rail four times per year. He also travelled occasionally by rail and steamer to Dublin via Liverpool.

In 1846 trade was very lean and William Henry Cope decided

to retire from the glass business. He retained his interests as a banker, iron master and magistrate[51]. Edwin Deeley carried on the business and took his son Richard Mountford Deeley, the firm's traveller, into partnership. Richard Mountford Deeley used a legacy of £2,000 from his uncle to buy out William Henry Cope's share in 1849, for which he paid £2,048 10s. The property of Dial Glasshouses was made over to Cope, and the Deeleys rented it from him. The firm then traded as Edwin Deeley & Son[52]. Their products included bottles for Schweppes, patent medicine bottles including those to contain the famous Daffy's Elixir[53], carbuoys for vitriol manufacturers, sauce bottles for Lea & Perrins of Worcester, and wine and stout bottles for various merchants.

In 1850 the price of coal in the district doubled, partly due to the demands of the local iron trade. This put the Stourbridge glasshouses at a disadvantage to those in competing glassmaking districts. As a way of reducing costs, Richard Mountford Deeley and his father took out patents for 'Inclined bars' for use in the grates of glass furnaces. His invention allowed slack to be burned, costing about 4s 6d per ton instead of 'Brazil' coal at 9s 6d per ton[54]. Other firms such as Richardsons'[55] tried the same plan. However, the workforce, having recently joined the newly formed trade union, refused to work with the new furnace and was laid off. Labour was imported from wherever it could be found, including Yorkshire and Bristol. It was soon found that the new men were not capable of making the bottles required, mainly soda water bottles for Schweppes, and as a result the firm's trade was ruined[56].

Richard Mountford Deeley credits Dial Glasshouses as the birthplace of the first oval form of Schweppes bottle, sufficiently strong to withstand the pressure required for soda-water[57]. While improvements in bottle design for Schweppes may well have occurred there, no documentary evidence remains. The history of soda-water bottle development is well documented[58] and neither Dial Glasshouses nor its proprietors are credited with specific significance. The two most significant developments were the egg-shaped 'Hamilton' bottle in 1809 and the marble-stoppered 'Codd' bottle in 1870.

The firm never really recovered from the problems with its

workforce and in 1850 traded at a loss. In 1851 the firm employed fifty-seven people[59], but in 1853, the partners decided to wind up the firm. The firm's bankers, the Shropshire Banking Co., found the firm had a modest deficiency of £500. The workmen could not understand why the old established firm was being closed and nor could relatives and friends in the district. At this fateful time Richard Mountford Deeley was offered a contract to supply black wine bottles to the established firm of Betts & Co., brandy distillers of 7, Smithfield Bars, London[60]. Betts offered to buy up the entire output of Dial Glasshouses to provide the bottles for his thriving trade to India and elsewhere. Somewhat reluctantly Richard Mountford Deeley took £100 capital each from John Round of Audnam, George While of Ebbw Vale and James Williams of Whittington, and reopened the works. However, his misgivings were well founded, for in September 1853 Turkey declared war on Russia and their Black Sea Fleet was destroyed in November; the Crimean War had begun. Betts' trade to India was disrupted and Richard Mountford Deeley found himself totally ruined. All his savings had been expended in the reopening of the glassworks and he was left almost penniless. He left the district and took a small house in Birmingham[61]. He lived for a while in Beeston, Nottinghamshire[62] then eventually moved to Derby and died at his son's house in Osmaston Road, Derby, on 21st January 1909, aged eighty-four[63].

In 1853 the glassworks was advertised for sale as a flint glasshouse and a six-pot bottle house occupied by E. Deeley & Son[64]. It was purchased in November 1853[65] by George Robinson[66].

It presumably stood unoccupied for seven years until it was let on 30th March 1860 to Davis, Greathead and Green for twenty-one years at an annual rent of £200[67]. Davis, Greathead and Green had been running a successful business at Brettell Lane Glasshouses.

John Davis was the principal partner, as he had been at Brettell Lane. In 1861 he employed sixty-nine men, sixteen boys and nine women[68], making him the second largest employer of the six main Stourbridge glassworks. William Greathead and his wife lived at Dennis Park[69]. Richard Green left the partnership on 1st June 1865[70] to manufacture glass in Manchester.

William Greathead, still living at Dennis Park, made his will[71] on 21st February 1867 and died five days later[72], aged sixty-seven. He left his estate to his widow, Anna Maria, nee Green. One of his executors was his brother-in-law and former partner, Richard Green, glass manufacturer of Manchester. On 12th March 1869 Richard Green assigned the lease on Dial Glasshouses 'with the steam engine therin' to John Davis[73]. Davis now had sole responsibility for the business and the £200 per year lease payments.

In 1871 John Davis lived close to the Fish Inn in Amblecote[74]. On 7th August 1875 he introduced members of his family to the partnership, including his son-in-law, John Bolton[75] although the firm had traded as John Davis & Co. since 1873[76]. John Davis died in 1878[77], aged seventy-five. His will[78] was witnessed by his glassworks manager, John Venables[79] of Dial Lane when the testator's estate was valued at less than £4,000. He appointed two of his sons, William Solomon Davis[80] and John Davis[81] as his executors, along with his son-in-law John Bolton the younger of Hawbush Cottage, Brettell Lane. The will makes it clear the testator operated the business in partnership with the three of them, and gave them the opportunity to continue the business. However, John Davis left the business in April 1879 and went to join his father-in-law Josiah Muckley[82], a glass decorator and merchant of Ivy Lane, Audnam. The business continued as Davis and Bolton, paying a lease of £205 per year to the Robinson family.

In 1888, when living at Hawbush House, Brettell Lane, John Bolton is listed among the private residents in Kelly's Directory of Staffordshire. In August 1888 he dissolved the partnership without taking out any capital and after paying £1,400 to the bank. This left William Solomon Davis alone at Dial Glasshouses but in this time of trade depression[83] he was unable to survive. A creditor applied for a winding-up order on 26th April 1889. In May 1889 John Davis & Co. of Dial Glasshouses was declared insolvent[84].

The firm may have recovered temporarily as John Davis & Co., Dial Flint Glass Works, Amblecote, Stourbridge is listed in Kelly's 1892 Post Office Directory of Staffordshire and Warwickshire. The directory also shows John Davis living at

Coalbourne Hill House. In the same year, 1892, the firm of Webb, Shaw & Co. moved to the Dial works from its previous premises in Kinver Street. The glasshouse produced gas and electric lampshades as well as cut and table glass[85].

On 4th October 1901 Webb, Shaw & Co. Ltd. took out a patent[86], suggesting it was in a healthy state, but in 1902 the firm became involved in a union dispute. It refused to stop supplying goods to Thomas Webb & Co., which had locked out its workforce[87]. When the Midland Association of Glass Manufacturers was wound up in 1903 Webb, Shaw and Co. was one of eight firms that were still members at its demise[88].

The glassworks was briefly occupied, about 1910, by a firm called Mallen, Pratt and Green making fancy tableware[89]. Sometime before 1919 the glassworks was vacated, probably because of the labour shortage and trade disruption during the First World War[90].

In 1922 Mr and Mrs Plowden and Mr Thompson started the firm of Plowden & Thompson Ltd. The partnership only lasted about eighteen months when Mrs Plowden was joined by Richard Evelyn Threlfall[91] who introduced much-needed capital. At that time the firm had about eighty to a hundred employees. Mrs Plowden introduced her middle son to the firm but he died young. The partnership remained a family concern until the nineteen-fifties. Threlfall died in 1977[92]. The present managing director, Richard Biedman, joined the firm in 1979[93].

The firm has always been renowned for speciality high-technology glass such as *Chemical* glassware[94]. Various patents have been registered under the tradename of *KODIAL* glass.

By 1935 the old glasshouse was in a dangerous condition and so the top of the cone was taken down and capped with a self-supporting steel structure. The cone base, with its datestone, remains in use today. The original air-tunnels under the cone, including the one down to the canal, are still in existence. The second cone had been turned into a foundry some time before 1886[95].

Plowden & Thompson, truncated Dial cone.

The firm's speciality of hand-drawn tubing and rods[96] was in great demand during the Second World War[97]. Precision tubing was supplied for the detonator mechanism of sea-mines and a special composition glass was developed for valve envelopes. To achieve this critical output:

> 'A skilled tube-drawer cannot be trained in the course of a given war, a thing which Government Departments did not easily realise. He has to work, roughly speaking, to a millimetre in diameter (all by eye), to maintain a set and even wall, to draw the glass straight, to avoid steps and bulges (this alone calls for most delicate footwork) and he must have lungs capable of blowing the guts out of a trombone. He must be able to work continuously in heat, to

control his gang and not get rattled. He should in fact have the temperament of a good n.c.o., and skill at least equivalent to that of the first violin of a Philharmonic Orchestra, and such men are rare.'[98]

After the war, the firm laid plans to introduce mechanical techniques for the production of tubing[99]. However, after careful consideration the directors decided to continue with hand-drawn products. Increasingly, the firm's market was eroded by foreign competitors using mechanical techniques until in 1969 glassmaking ceased entirely. The firm's customers were amazed and initially thought it was a ploy to increase prices. The Ministry of Defence was seriously concerned because many speciality products they required could only be produced by Plowden & Thompson. However the decision was made and the workforce was laid off. Most of the craftsmen found work at Thomas Webb's and other local firms.

Although the furnaces were put out, Plowden & Thompson still mixed their batch and sent it to Thomas Webb's to be melted and drawn. The firm began to research techniques for even greater precision in the production of fine-bore glass tubing. This research was successful, enabling tubing to be produced with a bore of fifty microns.

Demand for this unique product increased so in 1980 the firm built two new furnaces and began to manufacture its own glass again. Coloured tubing was supplied to fluorescent lighting manufacturers and precision tubing to thermometer manufacturers. Tubing is now produced with the incredible bore size of five microns. Customers include Rolls Royce and commercial aircraft manufacturers.

In March 2000 Plowden & Thompson Ltd. bought the rights to use the Tudor Crystal brand from the receivers of Dennis Hall Co-operative Crystal Ltd. Crystal glass is now being produced in the old Dial cone. A shop was opened in October 2001 and managing director, Richard Biedman is looking forward to providing the same excellent service to the crystal trade as he long has to the tubing trade.

Plowden & Thompson Ltd. continues in business today employing forty-three staff, making glass rod and tubing to fine tolerances and crystal glass. The use of traditional methods in the Dial glasshouse, long forgotten elsewhere, is an incredible sight to observe.

---

1 Benjamin Richardson's notebook of 1886.
2 Loosely translated this reads *as glass, so is life*. Like Maynard's epigram it was probably intended as a metaphor referring to the fragility (or possibly transparency) of glass - and life.
3 Thomas Pidcock, son of John Pidcock and his wife Mary, nee Honeyborne, b. 11th May 1749; bap. 3rd Jun 1749, Kingswinford.
4 John Pidcock, son of John Pidcock and his wife Mary, nee Honeyborne, b. 1st Mar 1756; bap. 2nd Apr 1756, Kingswinford.
5 Robert Pidcock, son of John Pidcock and his wife Mary, nee Honeyborne, b. 9th Mar 1762; bap. 5th Sep 1762, Kingswinford.
6 John Pidcock, d. 8th Nov 1791; bur. family vault, middle aisle of Brierley Hill Church.
7 Birmingham Gazette, 7th Nov 1791, 'Died on Tuesday morning at the Platts near Stourbridge, John Pidcock Esq., one of the magistrates of the County of Worcester; Gentleman's Magazine, Nov 1791, 'At the Platts, near Stourbridge, John Pidcock Esq., in the commission of the peace for the county of Worcester'; European Magazine and London Review, Nov 1791, p399 contains a briefer version.
8 PRO, PCC will of John Pidcock, 21st Nov 1791.
9 Universal British Directory of 1793.
10 Lowndes' 1792 London Directory.
11 Kent's 1798 London Directory.
12 Robert Pidcock, d. 21st Dec 1799; bur family vault, middle aisle of Brierley Hill Church.
13 PRO PROB 11/1344, PCC will of Robert Pidcock, 14th Jun 1800.
14 Holden's Triennial Directory for 1809, 1810 & 1811.
15 John Henzey Pidcock, son of John Pidcock and his wife Elizabeth, nee Barker, b. 30th Sep 1787; bap. 14th Oct 1787, Oldswinford.
16 George Pidcock, son of John Pidcock and his wife Elizabeth, nee Barker, b. 9th Nov 1788; bap. 2nd Dec 1788, Oldswinford.

17 Thomas Pidcock, d. 21st Oct 1813; bur. family vault, middle aisle of Brierley Hill Church.
18 London Gazette, 5th Nov 1814.
19 George Pidcock married Giacomina Giosephina Manerin at the British Embassy in Paris on 3rd May 1832.
20 William Henry Cope, son of William and Mary Cope, bap. 15th May 1787 St. John, Deritend and Bordesley, Warwickshire. His move to Coalbournbrook can be dated to 1814. On 22nd Oct 1813, he baptised a son, William, in Wrockwardine. Then, on 29th May 1815 his daughter Elizabeth was baptised at Oldswinford, when he was described as a glass manufacturer of Coalbourn Brook. William became a barrister and married the daughter of a baronet. Elizabeth married Henry Hodgetts Deacon, Proctor of Doctors Commons, London, 15th Mar 1836, Kingswinford.
21 London Gazette, 20th Aug 1816.
22 Coalbournhill House stood just to the rear of the Fish Inn.
23 The original Holbeche House of 1605 was badly damaged by an explosion of gunpowder during the plotters desperate final stand. As the captors were taken away by Sir Richard Walsh, the High Sheriff of Worcestershire, the house was left roofless and burning. The Bendy family later rebuilt the house in its original style. Antonia Fraser, *The Gunpowder Plot Terror & Faith in 1605,* pp183-7; Treadway Russell Nash, *Collections for the History of Worcestershire* (2nd ed. 1799), pp31-33; U.A. Beddall, *An Historical Sketch of the Parish of Kingswinford* (1885), pp7-9; K.C. Hodgson, *Out of the Mahogany Desk* (1971), p18; R.K. Dent, *Historic Staffordshire* (1896), pp218-222.
24 Richard Mountford, son of Richard Mountford and his wife, Ann, nee Collins, b. 6th Sep 1771 at Lye, bap. 13th Oct 1771, Oldswinford.
25 Wrockwardine Wood Glassworks opened on 6th Aug 1792. It was founded by ironmasters William and Joseph Reynolds of Ketley Bank, who commenced partnership 14th Jul 1792 and employed William Phillips of Donnington Wood as their manager (SRO, Box 10, Bundle 10, No. 218, Lilleshall Company). Phillips resigned in January 1797 and was probably replaced by John Biddle, a chemist who was involved in a sulphuric acid works at nearby Wombridge. Richard Mountford joined the partnership about 1798. After first supplying window glass for the Reynolds brothers' house-building projects, production turned to bottle glass and the novelties for which the

Wrockwardine works is famed. William Henry Cope is first mentioned as being in partnership with Mountford and leasing land at Wrockwardine Wood in 1802. After the death of William Reynolds on 3rd Jun 1803 the glassworks was run by a partnership of Richard Mountford, his brother-in-law William Henry Cope and John Biddle. The glassworks ran on a modest scale until it closed temporarily in 1816 suffering from the depression following the cessation of Napoleonic hostilities. Mountford rescued the business but reduced his involvement and in 1822 it traded as Biddle & Cope. The landlord issued notice to quit on 27th Sep 1841 and business ceased.

26 Edwin Deeley, son of Edward Deeley and his wife Sarah, nee Mountford, b. Lye, bap. 8th Nov 1801, Oldswinford.

27 BRL, MS R.M. Deeley, *Reminiscences*, 663048.

28 DA, William Fowler's 1822 *Map of the Parish of Kingswinford*. Plot 291-2, Pidcock, Cope & Co. – Dial Glasshouses.

29 Shropshire Records and Research Centre, 6001/6823.

30 Abraham Darby III (1750-1791), son of Abraham Darby II (1711-1763). Although the Darbys' fame is associated with Coalbrookdale and Ironbridge Gorge, Abraham Darby I was born, the son of a Quaker farmer, nailer and locksmith, John Darby and his wife Ann, nee Bayliss, at Wrens Nest, Dudley 14th Apr 1678 (although then in the parish of Sedgley); apprenticed to Jonathan Freeth, maltmill maker of Birmingham; completed apprenticeship in 1699, moved to Bristol and opened a brass foundry; moved to Coalbrookdale, Shropshire in 1708 where his work became world famous; d. 5th May 1717.

31 Shropshire Records and Research Centre, Shifnal Rate Book 1837, 1335/6/7.

32 This six-pot furnace was referred to as a bottlehouse when the glassworks was advertised for sale in 1853.

33 BHGM, Letter of Benjamin Richardson to William Haden Richardson.

34 John Pidcock, bur. 9th Aug 1834, Wordsley.

35 SRO, D. 356A, nos 62-3; D. 585/159/1/1, p5.

36 The Stewponey Inn is an old tavern standing at the junction of the Wolverhampton to Kidderminster and Stourbridge to Bridgnorth roads in Stourton on the east side of the River Stour. The current inn dates from the early eighteenth century, but it replaced taverns that date back to the middle ages. It has an extensive history including being the subject of Revd. Sabine Baring Gould's novel, *Bladys of the Stewponey* (1897).

37 Infra, Audnam Glassworks.

38 James Evers, son of Samuel Evers and his wife Leticia, bap. 6th Apr 1817, Oldswinford; mar. Anne Jane Rose Swindell 8th June 1841, Halesowen; adopted name James Evers-Swindell on death of his father-in-law; d. 1910; bur Oldswinford.

39 Charles Evers, b. 28th Mar 1819, Oldswinford; mar. Rose Swindell in 1843; adopted name Charles Evers-Swindell on death of his father-in-law; d. 9th Jun 1891; bur. Pedmore.

40 BRL, MS R.M. Deeley, *Reminiscences*, 663048.

41 Infra, Coalbournhill.

42 Richard Mountford died of bronchitis, 23rd Jan 1842 at his home, Park House, Shifnal, with William Cope 'present at the death.' Shrewsbury Chronicle of 4th Feb 1842 records; 'at Shifnal on Saturday the 29th Jan the remains of our respected Magistrate and Townsman Richard Mountford Esquire were conveyed to the tomb. The shops in the town were closed all day and many of the tradesmen joined the procession to testify their regard and love for so kind a friend and neighbour.' His memorial stands inside St. Andrew's Church, Shifnal.

43 BRL, MS R.M. Deeley, *Reminiscences*, 663048.

44 PRO.

45 Samuel Marshall Parrish, son of Thomas Parrish and his wife Sarah, nee Holloway, b. 20th Apr 1802; bap. 26th Oct 1810, Brierley Hill.

46 Thomas Parrish and his brother James had been glassmakers at Holloway End Glassworks until they became bankrupt in 1803.

47 Due to the parlous state of the roads, previous travellers had carried their wares by packhorse.

48 Although he must have retained some interest in the business. At the time of the 1851 census he lived at Coalbournhill and was still described as a Glass Manufacturer. PRO HO0107/2035/019.

49 Joseph Parrish, son of Thomas Parrish and his wife, Sarah, nee Holloway, b. 23rd Sep 1806; bap. 26th Oct 1810, Brierley Hill.

50 Post Office Directory of 1845.

51 PRO, 1851 census HO 107/2036 08/158/143.

52 Ibid, R.M. Deeley and William White's 1851 History, Gazetteer and Directory of Staffordshire.

53 For information on Daffy's Elixir and other quack remedies see John Stockton, *Victorian Bottles* (1981), pp69-70.

54 The patents are numbered No. 13,711, 1851 for Glass Furnaces etc and No. 142, 1853 for Grates of Furnaces used for the Manufacture of Glass.
55 Supra, Wordsley Flint Glassworks.
56 BRL, MS R.M. Deeley, *Reminiscences*, 663048.
57 R.M. Deeley, *The Genealogy of Deeley and Montford-sur-Risle* (1941).
58 Olive Talbot, *The Evolution of Glass Bottles for Carbonated Drinks*, JPMA, v 8 (1974), pp29-62; Douglas A. Simmons, *Schweppes the First 200 Years* (1983).
59 1851 census of Stourbridge shows Edwin Deeley living at Park House, employing 36 men, 18 boys and 3 women. PRO HO/0107/2035/066.
60 Betts's Patent Brandy Establishment is pictured in John Tallis's *London Street Views 1838-1840* (1969), p110.
61 Ibid, R.M. Deeley, *Reminiscences*.
62 PRO, 1881 census of Beeston, RG11/3331/97/24.
63 PG, Feb 1909.
64 WRO, Palfrey collection.
65 DA, Harward & Evers papers, box 65, Conveyance by Wm Henry Cope to George Robinson, 28th Nov 1853.
66 George Robinson b. c1811, Rowley, Staffordshire; wealthy ironmaster with works in Brettell Lane; lived at Park Field House, Coalbournbrook, PRO 1851 census of Stourbridge, HO0107/2035/093; Churchwarden of Amblecote in 1851 and 1853; later built Parkfield Glassworks.
67 SRO, D648/38/2. The agreement includes a detailed plan and schedule of the glassworks. Special mention is made of its steam engine, which is described in detail.
68 PRO, 1861 census.
69 PRO, 1861 census RG 9/2068 ED21 Sched 140.
70 SRO D648/38/3.
71 PRO, G29/92-8-1109, Will of William Greathead proved 28th Feb 1867.
72 William Greathead, d. 26th Feb 1867; bur. Amblecote. A stone slab in Amblecote churchyard marks his grave.
73 SRO D648/38/3.
74 PRO, 1871 census, RG10 3022 ED22 Sched 9.
75 John Bolton son of John Bolton and his wife Sarah, nee Plant, b. c1848, Brettell Lane; married Esther Jane, the daughter of John and Esther Davis, b. Brettell Lane, bap. 25th Apr 1843, Kingswinford.

76 Littlebury's 1873 Directory.
77 John Davis, d. 27th Jun 1878; bur. 2nd Jul 1878, Wordsley, family sandstone tomb.
78 PRO, Will of John Davis, proved at Lichfield, 12th Oct 1878.
79 John Venables, b. c1844 Hordley, Shropshire.
80 William Solomon Davis, son of John and Esther Davis, b. c1850, Kingswinford.
81 John Davis, son of John and Esther Davis.
82 Josiah Muckley, son of Jabez Muckley and his wife Mary Ann, nee Simpson, bap. 26th Dec 1832 Kingswinford.
83 Supra, Heath Glassworks, 1882. Infra, Coalbournhill 1886.
84 FGMM for quarter ending 15 May 1889.
85 Kelly's 1892 Directory of Birmingham, Staffordshire and Warwickshire.
86 Patent Number 241076.
87 Supra, Dennis Glassworks.
88 County Express, 23rd May 1903.
89 Ibid, R. Wakefield, p9.
90 The Ordnance Survey map of 1919 labels it disused.
91 Richard Evelyn Threlfall, b. 1891, son of scientist, Sir Richard Threlfall, KBE, FRS; Professor of Physics in the University of Sydney; who died in 1932. Richard Evelyn Threlfall became a director of Chance Brothers & Co. Ltd. c1912. He was wounded on active service in the First World War, but returned to the Spon Lane works after convalescing.
92 Richard Evelyn Threlfall d. 1977; bur. Pedmore.
93 His wife, Barbara Biedman, joined as Sales and Marketing Director in 1994.
94 Kelly's 1928 Directory of Staffordshire.
95 Benjamin Richardson's notebook of 1886. When the foundry was demolished, the lane called Stewkins was developed as the main entrance to Dial Glasshouses. Previously the entrance was from Dial Lane.
96 According to Richard E. Threlfall the art of pulling glass tubes by hand was passed to the local glassmakers by Belgian refugees in the course of the First World War.
97 One of their craftsmen who enlisted in the RAF was summoned back to the glassworks as the Ministry of Defence thought he could make a greater contribution there.
98 Richard E. Threlfall, *Glass Tubing* (1946), p16.
99 The firm still has these plans for two furnaces and two mechanical lines.

CHAPTER 39

Grazebrook's Canalside Glassworks, Audnam

The Grazebrook family had their main glassworks at Audnam and also ran a second glasshouse at Dob Hill until it fell down sometime around 1800. In his notebook of 1886 Benjamin Richardson records, 'After the old glass house fell down they put up a new cone by the canalside . . .' The Dob Hill Glassworks was remote from both the turnpike and the newly cut Stourbridge Canal and it was logical to build its replacement alongside the canal with the improvements in transport envisaged. The location of this new glasshouse had been a mystery until its remains were discovered in 1993[1] on the west side of the Stourbridge Canal during redevelopment of land between the canal and the River Stour.

Evidence for the date of building this canalside works is still being sought, but its location suggests a date after the building of the Stourbridge Canal. Whitworth's canal map of 1774 shows no indication of any buildings on the area between the intended Stourbridge Canal and the River Stour. The land was divided into fields suggesting agricultural use. Snape's map of 1785 shows a small cluster of buildings near the glasshouse site that could include the glasshouse. However, the plan shows the buildings closer to the Stour than it does the canal, suggesting it was probably a mill and not the glassworks. The Act for the Stourbridge Canal was passed on 2nd April 1776 and it was fully opened to traffic by December 1779.

When the need arose to replace the Dob Hill Glassworks, the Grazebrooks would logically have chosen a site on the canal, but as close as possible to their main Audnam works. John Pidcock built his new Dial Glasshouse in 1788 on the land directly opposite the Audnam Glassworks, so Michael Grazebrook bought all the land around it. This comprised fields called Siden Hill to the north of Dial Glasshouse, Stewkins to the south and Sawkins meadow to the west, on the far side of the canal. It was in Sawkins meadow that the Grazebrooks built the glassworks. The evidence therefore suggests a date for the erection of the Canalside Glassworks between 1788 and 1816.

Benjamin Richardson refers to the Grazebrooks exchanging material between their main Audnam Glassworks and their glassworks at Dob Hill and vice versa. After the new cone was built by the canalside, material travelled 'from the Audnam Glass works across the top of the Siden field to the new cone near the bridge at the canal.' Siden Hill, or Siden piece was the field that ran from the turnpike, opposite the Audnam Glassworks, to Chubb's Bridge across the canal and had been purchased by Michael Grazebrook to provide access$_2$. By the time of the 1834 ordnance survey, this route was identified as a road, and in the 1866 Kingswinford Parish Survey$_3$ it was called the Occupation Road to Chubb's Bridge. This description coincides precisely with the location of remains discovered in February 1993 when contractors clearing the land, Konrad Construction, revealed the foundations of the cone. Peter Boland, the Archaeologist for Dudley Metropolitan Borough was given three days in which to survey the site during which details were recorded. The site has now been developed for housing.

Primrose Rostron$_4$ mentioned the glassworks in a brief article in the Blackcountryman magazine, without being aware of where it stood, stating it was put up by Michael Grazebrook soon after settling at Audnam, which occurred in 1785. This therefore reinforces the hypothesis in relation to the canal maps, suggesting that the glasshouse was built post 1785. The glasshouse was built on land owned by a Mr Thomas, including land called the 'Stewkins', the name still in use today for the lane running down to the canal alongside the Dial Glasshouse property. Mr Thomas was paid £10 10s for the use of the land and £5 6s 8d moiety of the joint land. The Audnam business paid Mr Thomas £52 10s annual rent for his eight cottages and buildings.

The Grazebrooks presumably built this glasshouse to continue making bottles$_5$. However, by 1822 it had been leased to John Swift. The outline of the cone and adjoining buildings is clearly shown on Fowler's map of 1822$_6$. The property is described as glasshouse and shops, owned by Michael Grazebrook and occupied by John Swift. A small piece of land adjoining, comprising house and garden was also owned by Michael Grazebrook and occupied by Joseph Moore, who was probably the glasshouse manager$_7$.

Extensive research into the genealogy of John Swift suggests this was the John Swift who married Ann Alen at Kingswinford on 24th April 1803. They had six children and when the eldest, Mary, was baptised at Oldswinford on 28th April 1816, John Swift was described as a bottlemaker$_8$.

Fowler & son's 1840 map describes the property as a glasshouse still owned by Michael Grazebrook still occupied by John Swift.

Evidently the glasshouse was converted into a foundry, as the glasshouse is shown on the 1883 ordnance survey map$_9$, described as Audnam Foundry (Iron & Brass). There was a cluster of buildings surrounding a circular structure, the typical size of a glass cone. In 1886 Benjamin Richardson gave a contemporary view 'There is a glass house cone by the Stourbridge Canal that Thomas & Michael Grazebrook built and worked for a short time then turned into an iron foundry and is now carried on by Cookson & Sons.' He drew a sketch of the works that matches in all aspects the plan views seen on ordnance survey maps.

The glasshouse is shown on the 1903 ordnance survey map$_{10}$, described as Audnam Foundry (Disused), the outline of the buildings unchanged since the map of 1883. By 1919 the site was called the Audnam Works (Anchor & Shackles), with no trace of the original cone structure remaining$_{11}$. Finally, by 1938 the site was considerably developed although still called the Audnam Works (Anchor & Shackles)$_{12}$.

1 P. Boland & J. Ellis, *A Lost Stourbridge Glassworks Rediscovered*, JGA, v 5 (1977), pp6-25
2 DA, William Fowler's *1822 Map of the Parish of Kingswinford.*
3 DA, 58A.
4 *Nom du plume* used by a descendent of the Grazebrook family.
5 The 1745 Excise Act enforced the division of the glass industry into five distinct and closely regulated parts. Each was permitted to manufacture only the type of glass for which it was licensed, no overlapping was permitted. This is why so many manufacturers operated more than one glasshouse or built a second cone on the same site.
6 DA, William Fowler's 1822 *Map of the Parish of Kingswinford.*
7 Joseph Moore, glassmaker of Brookmoor Green, Kingswinford who died 4th Feb 1813 sired an extensive family that included fifteen glassmakers over five generations. The oldest sons were all named Joseph, and all were glassmakers: Joseph Moore, oldest son of the aforementioned Joseph Moore and his wife Sobieskey, nee Silvers (aunt of Joseph Silvers of North Street Glassworks), bap. 4th Nov 1770 at Brierley Hill. He married Maria Chebsey 29th Jul 1792 at Kingswinford (Chebsey was a glassmaking family). Their oldest son was Joseph Moore bap. 9th Jun 1793 at Brierley Hill. He married Jane Edwards of Kinver on 22nd Sep 1822 at Oldswinford. Their oldest son was Joseph Moore bap. 12th Jan 1823. The glasshouse manager was most likely Joseph Moore II, bap. 1770. He was a glassmaker most of his life although he ended his days as a weaver in Coleshill, Warwickshire, dying 25th Apr 1844.
8 This research was doubly difficult because of the coevality in Wordsley of a far more famous John Swift; a substantial ironmaster of Wordsley Green, then Stourbridge. Originally from Lambeth, London, he also married a Kingswinford girl, Sarah Matilda Hobson on 4th Jan 1816. They had four children, all baptised at Kingswinford, then they separated. His ironworks stood on the Stourbridge Canal Arm. In 1835 he formed a company with five other partners to build Stourbridge's first gasworks. Op Cit Bentley's 1841 Directory of Stourbridge. This John Swift died 23rd Jan 1841 and has an impressive monument in Wordsley Churchyard. The opportunity for confusion is exacerbated because in his will, proved 16th Mar 1841, he made William Grazebrook, ironmaster of Kingswinford his joint executor and joint guardian of his children.

9 Ordnance Survey map 1883, 25in to a mile.
10 Ordnance Survey map 1903, 25in to a mile.
11 Ordnance Survey map 1919, 25in to a mile.
12 Ordnance Survey map 1938, 25in to a mile.

CHAPTER 40

Wheeley's Brettell Lane Glasshouses

Thomas Wheeley's first Brettell Lane glasshouse was built some time before 1796. His partner, Benjamin Littlewood, probably provided the capital. The glassworks stood a little way back from Brettell Lane on its south side, on the northeast side of the Stourbridge Canal. The glassworks is not shown on Whitworth's canal map of 1775, nor Snape's of 1785, so the date of construction can reasonably be defined as after 1785 and before 1796, when the first reference is found.

Thomas Wheeley was born in 1749_1. In 1784 he married$_2$ Susanna Seager$_3$. Their marriage was by a licence$_4$ that describes Wheeley as a glass house clerk.

Benjamin Littlewood$_5$ was the third son of Thomas Littlewood. Father and son worked together as blacksmiths, having a smithy in Amblecote, near the Fish Inn, almost opposite the road to Wollaston$_6$. After being widowed, Benjamin remarried in 1766 to Sarah$_7$, the daughter of Michael Grazebrook I of Audnam Glassworks. Their marriage was by a licence$_8$ that describes Benjamin Littlewood as a widowed blacksmith of Oldswinford. Five years later in 1771, Benjamin Littlewood was again described as a blacksmith of Amblecote. He could have prospered as a blacksmith, but more likely he benefited from the estate of his late father-in-law when he administered the estate of Elizabeth Grazebrook in 1771_9. By 1786 he had gained the financial independence to become a Churchwarden of Oldswinford.

The first extant reference to Wheeley and Littlewood's business is not the ubiquitous trade directory entry describing their products, but a more unusual newspaper report:

> 'The accounting house of Thomas Wheeley and Benjamin Littlewood of Brettell Lane, near Stourbridge, was opened by thieves[10].'

Benjamin Richardson credited Thomas Wheeley with having built two cones 'near the long canal bridge in Brettell Lane and on the north side of the Stourbridge Canal[11].' A list of glasshouses in 1796 shows Wheeley and Littlewood, Brettell Lane, with one glasshouse having ten pots[12]. This suggests that only one cone had been built by this time, the other being added sometime between 1812 and 1822.

It is significant that Richardson's reference was only to Thomas Wheeley and not equally to Benjamin Littlewood. It seems that Littlewood was not actively involved at Brettell Lane Glasshouses. Although clearly a partner, he was probably providing capital and not actually involved in the trade. When his son Benjamin II married Esther Badger[13] in 1800, their marriage licence[14] described Benjamin junior as a gentleman of Oldswinford. If the son could warrant that sobriquet, surely the father could.

On 17th January 1803 a meeting took place at the Stewponey Inn, Stourton to petition the Government to have the duty on flint glass based on manufactured goods instead of metal or raw materials. Benjamin Littlewood of Wheeley and Littlewood contributed £100 to the fund. The amount contributed implies it was one of the larger firms.

Thomas Wheeley the elder died in 1803[15], aged fifty-four and his will was proved 8th May 1804. His widow, Susanna, and their two oldest sons, Thomas[16] and William Seager[17] carried on the business. They traded initially under the original firm of Wheeley and Littlewood and subsequently in their own name.

Sometime before 1809 Benjamin Littlewood took over the Holloway End Glasshouse, probably wishing to start his own firm. The last reference to the firm of Wheeley & Littlewood occurred in 1809[18]. Sherriff's 1812 plan graphically shows one cone on the Wheeley site. In 1816 Susanna Wheeley ceased her interest in the firm and a notice was issued accordingly:

'The partnership under the firm of T. & W. Wheeley, glass manufacturers of Stourbridge, and carried on by Susannah Wheeley (one of the executrixes of Thomas Wheeley deceased) and Thomas Wheeley and William Seager Wheeley, so far as respects the said Susannah Wheeley was dissolved the 26th March 1816. T. & W.S. Wheeley to carry on the business[19].'

She retired, aged 59, to a house with gardens on the north side of Brettell Lane directly opposite the old Toll House[20]. Her two sons carried on the business for three years trading as T. and W.S. Wheeley[21], until the death of Thomas Wheeley the younger in 1819[22], aged thirty-three. His will was proved in PCC on 27th March 1820. This left William Seager Wheeley in sole charge of the glass and coal business.

He traded in his own name as W.S. Wheeley, flint glass manufacturer and coal master[23] and the business flourished. By 1822 he had built a second cone and manufactured his own red lead in premises on the opposite side of the canal to the glasshouse. He owned three pairs of coal pits, land on the south side of Brettell Lane and a large house in its own grounds on the edge of Dennis Park[24]. In 1824 he made developments to the design of the glass furnace, producing a glass of 'purity and crystalline appearance.'[25] By 1833 he was running the fifth largest of the sixteen Stourbridge/Dudley glasshouses[26]. He undertook his share of civic duties. Upon the formation of the Worcester Yeomanry Cavalry (The Queen's Own) on 24th May 1831, he was gazetted as Lieutenant of the Stourbridge Troop[27].

By 1834 William Seager Wheeley had taken on partners and the firm began to trade as Wheeley and Davis[28]. One partner was his younger brother, John Wheeley[29]. The other was John Davis[30] who lived near the works in Brettell Lane. The following year the products of the firm were 'flint glass, plain & cut[31]', suggesting the capital introduced by the partners had facilitated a venture into glasscutting. By 1839 Wheeley had amassed significant wealth from his endeavours in the glass and coal business. He was the owner of Dennis Hall—the handsome house built by Thomas Hill—and forty-one acres of land in Dennis Park[32].

His younger brother John Wheeley was an inspirational employer$_{33}$ who ran an iron works in Brettell Lane$_{34}$ and the Bromley Colliery$_{35}$ at Pensnett as well as his partnership in the glassworks.

Successive trade directories show Wheeley and Davis as glass manufacturers, listed among the nobility and gentry; but as in all too many cases hubris begot nemesis. The firm conducted a prosperous export business in glass and at the time there was a stiff excise on glass, but a rebate of ten pence per pound on glass for export$_{36}$. Excise officers discovered the Wheeleys were packing firebricks in with glass in their export crates! They were accused of fraud and this led to the failure of their business.

William Seager Wheeley and his brother, both bachelors, were substantial landowners owning much land on both sides of Brettell Lane. On the northeastern side their holding extended from Hawbush, across Nagersfields to the lower end of Buckpool, Wordsley$_{37}$. On the southwest, it ran from Silver End to the top of Collis Street, and included all the land as far as the Corbett Hospital. They owned and lived at Dennis Hall and farmed the land at the rear of the Hall, the original Dennis Park. Because of their business failure, sometime between 1841 and 1845, they were forced to sell their lands on the south side of Brettell Lane. William Blow Collis and William King, lawyers of Stourbridge, purchased the Dennis part of their estate. They commenced the development of Dennis Park, making two roads named after themselves, Collis Street and King William Street$_{38}$. John Davis escaped from the scandal, probably unaware of the fraud being perpetrated by his partners, although he was left with considerable debt. The Wheeleys eventually sold their Hawbush estate, on the north side of Brettell Lane at an auction held at the Talbot Hotel on Monday 16th November 1857.

On 24th June 1846 John Davis leased the glassworks from William Seager Wheeley for twenty-one years$_{39}$. In 1850 Davis formed a partnership with William Greathead and Richard Green. Greathead had worked for William Gammon, glass manufacturer of Aston, near Birmingham, then from 1836 to 1843 at Hawkes' Dudley Flint Glassworks, the last two years as a partner. After the failure of

Hawkes' business he then spent a further seven years at Badgers' Phoenix Glassworks. Richard Green was also very experienced, having been involved in the glass trade since joining Hawkes' in 1837 at the age of fifteen. On 12th September 1850 they formed the partnership of Davis, Greathead and Green. William Greathead contributed £1,500 for two shares in the business. John Davis was granted two shares in the new firm for his existing capital. Richard Green contributed £500 and was granted one share until he contributed a further £1,000$_{40}$.

John Davis dominated the partnership$_{41}$. He lived with his wife and family in Brettell Lane$_{42}$. William Greathead lived with his wife (they had no children) at Field House, Audnam. Richard Green, his partner and brother-in-law, was a guest in his house on the night of the 1851 census. Green is described as a glass manufacturer, twenty-eight years old, born in Birmingham$_{43}$.

The Great Exhibition of 1851, held in the Crystal Palace in Hyde Park, gave the newly formed firm of Davis, Greathead and Green an excellent opportunity to display its wares. The official catalogue shows examples of their painted glass imitations of Greek pottery. These were thought sufficiently noteworthy to figure among the very few illustrations of glassware in the official descriptive and illustrated catalogue. Their exhibits included:

> 'A great variety of vases, jars and scent-jars for holding flowers, &c. in the Egyptian, Etruscan and Grecian styles; many of them cut, coated, gilt, painted in enamel colours, after the antique, with figures, ornaments, flowers, landscapes, and marine views, of the following colours, viz., ruby, oriental blue, chrysoprase, turquoise, black, rose colour, opal-coated blue, cornelian, opal frosted, pearl opal, mazareen blue, &c., Topaz, flints &c.$_{44}$'

Despite this varied output, as their glass was not marked, it is not possible to identify their products conclusively today. However, in May 1991 a pair of vases were identified and purchased at Newark Antique Fair by Charles Hajdamach for Broadfield House Glass Museum directly matching a contemporary drawing from the 1851 Exhibition Catalogue. They are tall vases in white opaque glass decorated in the Etruscan style. As much as we may revere these products today for their historical importance, they did not necessarily impress contemporary commentators. For example, in a review of the glass exhibited at the Great Exhibition, the Birmingham Journal reports:

> 'We may here be allowed to remark that the attempts by Messrs. Davis and Co., to imitate in glass the productions of Etruria, ancient and modern, is not, nor is it likely to be, successful. The dead colour of the clay harmonised excellently well with the hieroglyphic like figures which adorned their surface. Masses of black when introduced in the same manner on glass, even though roughed, will not compete with those exhumed from the ancient tombs, or which were produced with so much success by Wedgwood. As a general feature, we may remark that the crysophias, blues, &c., approach mediocrity; but their ruby has a tendency towards brown, a defect, however not confined to that of these contributors, but more or less observable in all.'[45]

Following the lockout, in 1859[46], Davis, Greathead and Green's claim from the manufacturers' defence fund[47] suggests the firm was the third largest of the thirteen in the Midlands Association.

In 1860 Davis, Greathead and Green vacated Brettell Lane glassworks and moved to Dial Glasshouses. It is not clear what caused this move. When the Wolverhampton and Worcester railway was built in 1852, it passed right by the rear of their premises and provided them with access to a goods yard south of Brettell Lane. The railway line dissected their road route to the coalfields to the east, Lower Lane,[48] but they still had excellent wharfage on the canal.

The glassworks was then altered and used for a time as an ironworks; the glasshouse being known as 'the old shell'. By 1882, probably much earlier, it became unsafe and was demolished. In 1934 Samuel Taylor and Son's Chain and Anchor Works covered the original site[49].

---

1 Thomas Wheeley, son of John Wheeley and his wife Elizabeth, nee Hughes,

bap. 9th Apr 1749, Kingswinford.
2 Mar. Thomas Wheeley and Susanna Seager, 14th Oct 1784, Kingswinford. Susanna's oldest brother, Thomas Seager, was the proprietor of the Moor Lane Bottleworks in 1771.
3 Susanna Seager, daughter of William Seager, gentleman of Kingswinford and his second wife Mary, nee Dixon, bap. 3rd Apr 1757, Kingswinford.
4 LJRO, marriage licence, issued at Kinver, 8th Oct 1784.
5 Benjamin Littlewood, son of Thomas Littlewood and his wife Mary, nee Higgs, bap. 14th Jul 1743, Oldswinford.
6 Benjamin Richardson's notebook of 1886.
7 Mar. Benjamin Littlewood, widow and Sarah Grazebrook, 10th Sep 1766, Oldswinford.
8 WRO.
9 Supra, Audnam Glassworks.
10 Birmingham Gazette, 21st Nov 1796.
11 Benjamin Richardson's notebook of 1886.
12 Ibid, R. Wakefield, p22.
13 Mar. Benjamin Littlewood and Esther Badger, 19th Oct 1800, Oldswinford.
14 WRO.
15 Thomas Wheeley, d. 11th Oct 1803; bur. 17th Oct 1803, Kingswinford. A tomb with a plinth, which became the family tomb, marks his grave.
16 Thomas Wheeley, son of Thomas Wheeley and his wife Susanna, nee Seager, bap. 22nd Aug 1785, Oldswinford.
17 William Seager Wheeley, son of Thomas Wheeley and his wife Susanna, nee Seager, bap. 12th Feb 1788, Oldswinford.
18 Holden's Triennial Directory for 1809, 1810 & 1811.
19 London Gazette, 11th May 1816.
20 DA, William Fowler's 1822 *Map of the Parish of Kingswinford*. Plot 358 House & Garden – Susannah Wheeley.
21 James Pigot's 1818 Commercial Directory.
22 Thomas Wheeley, d. 26th May 1819; bur. 2nd Jun 1819, Kingswinford, in the same tomb as his father.
23 Lewis's 1822 Worcestershire General and Commercial Directory.
24 DA, William Fowler's 1822 *Map of the Parish of Kingswinford*. Plot 1025 House & Gardens – Wm Wheeley. Plot 1026 Brettell Lane Glass House Owner – Wm Wheeley. Plot 1028 House and gardens including Peter Plant –

Timber Yard; William Edge Pottery works; Wheeley, Smith & Morris – Red Lead Manufacturers. Plot 1029 Brickkiln Piece; 3 pairs of coalpits and land – Wm Wheeley. Plot 1030 House & Premises – Wm Wheeley.

25 G. Bernard Hughes, *English Glass for the Collector* (1958), p26.

26 Thirteenth Report of the Commission into the Glass Excise, 1835, Appendix 7 shows William Seager Wheeley paying £3,667 8s 6d excise duty for the year ending 5th Jan 1833.

27 Anon, *The Worcester Yeomanry Cavalry (The Queen's Own)* (1843), p1; Q.L., *The Yeomanry Cavalry of Worcestershire 1794-1913* (1914), p38.

28 White's 1834 Staffordshire Directory.

29 John Wheeley, son of Thomas Wheeley and his wife Susanna, nee Seager, bap. 30th Aug 1790, Oldswinford.

30 John Davis, son of Solomon Davis, a glasshouse overlooker and his wife Sarah, bap. 21st Nov 1802, Kingswinford.

31 Pigot and Co.'s 1835 National Commercial Directory.

32 1839 Tithe apportionment.

33 A memorial in Wordsley churchyard describes 'Thomas Wellings who died 10 Nov 1873 was for 35 years a servant to John Wheeley of Brettell Lane.'

34 In 1840 William and John Wheeley ran the Brockmoor Iron Works previously run by Emus, Saunders & Haywood in 1822.

35 Robson's 1839 Birmingham and Sheffield Directory.

36 In 1833 duty on crown glass was £3 13s 6d per cwt and the drawback was £4 18s per cwt. This was to compensate for the fact that crowns were cut into panes before packing for export and wastage was high. The drawback was gradually reduced because some manufacturers, especially sheet glass manufacturers whose wastage was much lower, were accused by the excise commissioners of manufacturing glass for export just for the bounty. The drawback was reduced to £4 4s per cwt in 1836 and reduced again to £4 per cwt in 1838.

37 Thomas Wheeley, glass manufacturer of Brettell Lane, purchased the Hawbush Estate on 2nd November 1797 from Richard Brettell, gentleman of Stourbridge and Thomas Worral Grazebrook and Michael Grazebrook, glass manufacturers of Kingswinford. Original indenture of sale in author's collection.

38 BHGM, MS *Memoirs of Benjamin Richardson J.P. of Wordsley Hall*, 29th Sep 1947; ibid, M.W. Greenslade, p51.

39 SRO, D648/38/1.

40 SRO, D648/38/1-3.
41 William White's 1851 History, Gazetteer and Directory of Staffordshire. Despite their legal title of Davis, Greathead and Green the firm was described as John Davis and Co., Brettell Lane.
42 PRO, 1851 Census, 107/2036 12/229/018.
43 PRO, 1851 Census, 107/2036 06/110/075.
44 *Official Descriptive and Illustrated Catalogue*, v 2, p699.
45 Birmingham Journal, 31st May 1851, p6.
46 See Coalbournhill, Audnam and North Street Glassworks.
47 £74 17s.
48 Later known as Meeting Lane.
49 Ibid, R. Wakefield, pp22,3.

CHAPTER 41

Grafton's Brierley Glasshouse, Brettell Lane

Brierley Glasshouse was a large cone that stood on the north side of Brettell Lane, south of the Stourbridge Canal, opposite Brierley Bridge. It is not clear when it was built, nor whom by, but it was run by William Grafton[1] and his brother-in-law Michael Coltman[2]. Both families were non-conformist.

Coltman & Grafton are shown on a list of Stourbridge traders in 1793, although their trade is not stated[3]. A list of glassworks dated 1796 shows Coltman and Grafton at the Brierley Glasshouse with a nine-pot furnace[4]. The glassworks is clearly shown, adjacent to the canal, on a map of 1803[5].

William Grafton's youngest brother Edward[6] was presumably employed in the business but left in 1801 to join John Davenport[7] and Thomas Kinnersley in a new venture into glassmaking at Longport, Staffordshire. Davenport was extending his business interests from the pottery for which the firm became famous to manufacture tableglass, plain, cut and engraved, and ordinary glass, trading as Davenport, Kinnersley and Grafton.

Thomas Kinnersley's father was Thomas Kinnersley[8] of Loxley Hall, who ran the bank at Newcastle-under-Lyme, where John Davenport had been apprenticed. His mother was Penelope, nee Wheeler who had inherited and subsequently sold Ridgrave Glasshouse[9].

Davenport provided the premises, Kinnersley the capital and Grafton the glassmaking experience. The partnership lasted until 1807[10] when Edward Grafton presumably returned to Brettell Lane.

On 17th January 1803 a meeting took place at the Stewponey

Inn, Stourton to petition the Government to have the duty on flint glass based on manufactured goods instead of metal or raw materials. Michael Coltman of Coltman & Grafton contributed £50 to the fund. The amount contributed implies it was one of the smaller firms.

Coltman & Grafton traded as flint glass manufacturers in 1809[11] and William Haden Richardson joined the firm some time between 1802 and 1810[12]. The partnership included William Bacon of Wolverhampton about whom nothing is known. However, in 1811 he left the partnership:

> 'The partnership between Michael Coltman of Wordsley, William Grafton of Brittle [sic] Lane and William Bacon of Wolverhampton, glass manufacturers and trading under the firm of 'Coltman and Grafton' this day expires and is dissolved as far as relates to the said W. Bacon 30th Dec 1811.'[13]

The wording of the announcement suggests that only Bacon retired, leaving Coltman and Grafton in business. If this was so, it was not for many more years. In 1822 the site was occupied by William Bailey and Company's Iron Foundry[14]. Benjamin Richardson confirms that the glassworks was turned into an iron foundry run by the firm of Bayley & Pegg[15]. The Brierley Foundry of Bailey, Pegg and Co. became prominent in the local iron industry and famous as a manufacturer of cannonballs. The equally important Brierley Ironworks of John Bradley and Co. stood on the opposite bank of the canal.

William Grafton's son, John Henry[16] continued to work as a glassmaker. He married Louisa Jones[17], sister of ironmaster John Jones, but judging by the diverse locations of their nine children's baptisms he was forced to move around to find work.

In October 1895 John Shelton Hatton[18], a Stourbridge glass engraver, leased the old foundry from Lord Dudley at £30 per year[19] and renovated it to make fancy glassware. He was one of the first, if not the first, art masters at Stourbridge School of Art and combined his evening employment at the Art School with his manufacturing business[20]. However, his venture was not successful and by September 1897 he owed £45 of back rent. Unable to pay, he quit the premises and surrendered his lease to Lord Dudley on 17th November 1897.

Writing in 1934, Roland Wakefield remembered the remaining glasshouse having an 'immense and unusual bell-shaped dome which was a landmark for the locality.'[21] Guttery confirmed this; writing in 1956, he states 'within living memory the shell of a huge glasshouse cone still towered there.'[22] By 1947 the site had been redeveloped and council housing was built upon it[23].

---

1 William Grafton, oldest son of William Grafton and his wife Margaret, nee Alport, bap. 11th Apr 1764, Stourbridge; mar. Mary Coltman, 25th May 1789, St Mary's, Hinckley, Leicestershire.

2 Michael Coltman, son of John Coltman, bap. 24th Jun 1751, Lutterworth Independent Chapel, Leicestershire.

3 Birmingham Gazette, 1st Apr 1793.

4 Ibid, R. Wakefield, p23.

5 DA, C488.

6 Edward Grafton, son of William Grafton and his wife Margaret, nee Alport, bap. 12th Jan 1773, Stourbridge.

7 John Davenport, son of Jonathan and Ellin Davenport, b. 1st Sep 1765, Derby Street. Leek; bap. 11th Nov 1765, Leek; elected MP for Stoke-on-Trent 1832; magistrate and deputy lieutenant for Staffordshire; mar. Diana Smart Ward 8th Dec 1795, Burslem; d. 12th Dec 1848 at Westwood, Leek; bur. Leek parish church.

8 Thomas Kynnersley, son of Henry Kynnersley, bap. 24th May 1713, Uttoxeter, Staffordshire.

9 Thomas Kinnersley, son of Thomas Kynnersley and his wife Penelope, nee Wheeler, bap. 3rd Jun 1750, Uttoxeter, Staffordshire.

10 London Gazette, 1807, p1289; Roland B. Brown, *The Davenports and their glass 1801-1887*, JGA, v 1 (1985), pp30-40; T.A. Lockett & G.A. Godden, *Davenport China, Earthenware & Glass 1794-1887* (1989).

11 Holden's Triennial Directory for 1809, 1810 & 1811.

12 Stuart Crystal, William Haden Richardson's notebook, 1819.

13 London Gazette, 31st Dec 1811.

14 DA, William Fowler's *1822 Map of the Parish of Kingswinford*.

15 Benjamin Richardson's notebook of 1886.

16 John Henry Grafton, son of William Grafton and his wife Mary, nee Coltman, b. 5th Nov 1806, Kingswinford, bap. 6th December 1808, Stourbridge High Street Independent Chapel.
17 John Henry Grafton married first Sophia Smythe 20th Dec 1818, Dudley St. Thomas's and second Louisa Jones, 18th Sep. 1835, Dawley Magna, Shropshire.
18 PRO 1881 census RG11/2886/66/3 shows John S. Hatton, b. c1858, Stourbridge, living at 9 Mount Street, Stourbridge.
19 DA Earl of Dudley's Records, Lease of glassworks and premises at Brettell Lane from the Rt. Hon. Wm Humble Earl of Dudley to Mr John Shelton Hatton dated 11th Oct. 1895.
20 MS *Stourbridge Glass*, based upon hand-written manuscripts written by J.B. Hatton, now in the possession of Prof. R. and Mrs S.M. Davies of Alvechurch, Worcestershire.
21 Ibid, R. Wakefield, p23.
22 Ibid, D.R. Guttery, p20.
23 Ibid, R. Wakefield, pp23,4.

CHAPTER 42

Novelty Glassworks, Wollaston

The Novelty Glassworks is unique in having its location in Wollaston. Most of its history is associated with one family by the name of Edwards.

The first reference to the Edwards family as glassmakers occurs in 1839 when Samuel Edwards[1] of High Street, Stourbridge is listed as a fancy glass manufacturer and register office for servants[2]. Five years earlier, Samuel had married Anne, the daughter of John Evers[3], who was coachman to Thomas Hill of Dennis Hall. As the Edwards family had no prior experience of glassmaking it is conceivable that it was pressure from his father-in-law – seeing the wealth that Thomas Hill had generated through glassmaking – that led young Samuel to enter the trade. By 1840 Samuel was listed as a glass manufacturer of High Street, Stourbridge[4].

Samuel had a son, Edward Edwards born in 1840[5]. His birth certificate describes his father Samuel as a glassmaker. Samuel is further shown as a glass manufacturer of High Street, Stourbridge in 1841[6]. By 1842 he was a china and glass dealer and glass manufacturer, still in High Street, Stourbridge[7]. By 1845 he was a glass manufacturer of Upper High Street, Stourbridge[8] and still there in 1851[9].

A traditional glassmakers' fete in 1859 started from the Toll Gate at Wordsley and visitors were:

> 'initiated into the mysteries of glass making by Mr. S. Edwards of Stourbridge, who manufactured all kind of fancy ornaments or anything that was required by the visitor, by

means of the lamp and pipe, with surprising facility and evident skill.'[10]

Edward Edwards married in 1864 and is described on his marriage certificate[11] as a glassmaker. His daughter Grace Annie Edwards[12] married in 1899. Her marriage certificate[13] describes Edward Edwards as a glass manufacturer. In 1881 Edward Edwards lived at 299 Bridle Road[14], Wollaston, a master glassmaker employing two men and one boy[15]. Despite the grandiose title of Master Glassmaker, his business was a family affair. His two men were probably his brothers, Samuel[16] and James[17], his boy, probably his stepson John Green[18].

Edward Edwards purchased the premises in 1888 from a Mr Grainger. Two years later the premises were sold again at an auction held in the nearby Gate Hangs Well public house. The purchaser was James Marshall[19], who in 1892 set up a limited company to develop and extend the Novelty Glassworks[20]. However, the company struggled to survive and was wound up at the Talbot Hotel on 20th March 1893. The last reference to the business occurs in 1900 when Edwards & Co. is listed in a trade directory. According to Manley, this was the year in which the glass cone was demolished[21], although anecdotal evidence suggests that it was only trimmed at this time for safety reasons and the remainder was demolished at a later date.

A cottage now stands on the site. There is anecdotal evidence of ruby red and blue glass fragments being found on the site by a member of the family who lived there in the first half of the twentieth century. According to her brother, who lives in South Africa, the furnace flues remain under the existing garages. It is hoped that the site will be archeologically excavated when the existing cottage is demolished.

---

1 Samuel Edwards, son of John Edwards, nailer of Stourbridge and his wife Susannah, nee Beddow, b. Amblecote, bap. 22 Jun 1815, Oldswinford.

2 Robson's 1839 Birmingham and Sheffield Directory.

3 Anne Evers, daughter of John Evers, coachman to Thomas Hill of Dennis Hall

and his wife Hannah, nee Waldron of the Belbroughton sythesmith family, bap. 10th Oct 1816, Oldswinford.
4 Bentley's 1840 Directory of Stourbridge.
5 Edward Edwards, son of Samuel Edwards and his wife Anne, nee Evers, b. 20th Feb 1840, Stourbridge, bap. 15th Mar 1840, Oldswinford.
6 Bentley's 1841 Directory of Stourbridge; Pigot and Co.'s 1841 Directory of Birmingham.
7 Pigot & Co.'s 1842 Worcester Directory.
8 Post Office Directory of the Neighbourhood of Birmingham, 1845.
9 PRO 1851 census of Stourbridge HO 107/2035/59
10 Dudley MBC, Glasshouses.
11 Mar. Edward Edwards and Frances Nisbett, 17th Jul 1864, Cookley, Worcestershire.
12 Grace Annie Edwards, daughter of Edward Edwards and his wife Frances, nee Nisbett, b. c1874, Wollaston.
13 Mar. John Christopher Davies and Grace Annie Edwards, 3rd Mar 1899, Hitchin, Hertfordshire.
14 Later called Gladstone Road.
15 PRO, 1881 census of Wollaston, RG11/2890/120/53.
16 Samuel Edwards, son of Samuel Edwards and his wife Ann, nee Evers, b. c1846 Stourbridge; lived at Hanbury Hill, Stourbridge.
17 James Edwards, son of Samuel Edwards and his wife Ann, nee Evers, b. c1850 Stourbridge; lived at Belle Vue, Kingswinford.
18 John Green, b. c1867, Stourbridge, son of an unknown Mr Green and his wife Jane who remarried to Samuel Edwards.
19 James Marshall, son of an unknown Mr Marshall and his wife Julia, nee Hipwood, b. c1858 St. Marylebone, Middlesex. PRO 1881 census RG11/2890/116/46 shows James Marshall as a glass flowerstand fitter living with his widowed mother in the house of his maiden aunt, Jane Hipwood at Bridgnorth Road, Wollaston.
20 Information provided by Peter Skidmore of History of Wollaston Group.
21 Ibid, C. Manley, p26.

CHAPTER 43

Parkfield Glassworks, Amblecote

Parkfield Glassworks stood on the south side of King William Street, Amblecote at its eastern end. The cone has long since gone, but the facade fronting King William Street remains today. It covered two thousand, one hundred and forty-four square yards and was established sometime in the eighteen-fifties by George Robinson[1] and was managed for him by Joseph Stevens[2]. As George Robinson lived at Park Field House, Amblecote, this may explain the name of the glassworks.

Sometime before 1868, a venture known as the Stourbridge Co-operative Flint Glass Manufacturers started business at the Parkfield Glassworks[3]. However, by 1873 Parkfield Glassworks was occupied by George Robinson's son, Frederick[4], suggesting the co-operative venture had failed. Frederick similarly made little profit and gave up the trade.

Sometime before 1881 Parkfield Glassworks was taken over by two cousins, James[5] and Alfred Davies[6]. They took a lease from George Robinson at £185 per year. In 1881 James was a glass manufacturer employing fifty-three people, living in King William Street[7]. Alfred was a glass manufacturer, living at Coalbournbrook[8]. The firm traded as Alfred & James Davies, Dennis Park, Amblecote[9].

James still lived at The Limes, King William Street in 1891[10], but died four years later[11]. He left no will and so letters of administration[12] were granted that describe him as a 'Glass Manufacturer, of the Limes and of Parkfield Glass Works.' Probate was granted to his widow Hannah Maria Davies[13] when his estate was valued at £5,338 10s 9d.

The firm continued to trade as A. and J. Davies and in 1902 it became involved in a union dispute. A. and J. Davies refused to stop supplying goods to Thomas Webb & Co, which had locked out its workforce[14]. The battle with the trade union was fought and won. The County Express of 23rd May 1903 reported the winding up of the Midland Association of Glass Manufacturers. A. and J. Davies were one of the eight firms that were still members at the time of its demise.

Alfred Davies died at his home, Park Field House, in 1910[15]. His will[16] describes him as a glass manufacturer and valued his estate at £4,679 8s 9d. His oldest son Harry[17] was successfully employed assisting the Woodalls at Thomas Webbs'. So, the testator's business was left to his second son Alfred Edward Davies[18], glass manufacturer of Park Field House, his joint administrator:

> 'I devise and bequeath my freehold Glass Works known as Parkfield Glass Works situate at Dennis Park Amblecote with the land outbuildings and appurtanences thereto belonging and now in my occupation and my business of a Glass Manufacturer which I carry on there and the stock in trade credits and effects belonging thereto and cash in hand and at the Bank unto my son Alfred Edward Davies.'

Records of the British Flint Glass Manufacturers Association for 1920 list A. & J. Davies with sixty-three employees, made up of forty-one men, fourteen women and eight boys. However, the firm went into a steep decline during the great depression. The year 1926 is the last recorded occasion of a subscription paid by A. & J. Davies to the British Flint Glass Manufacturers Association. The firm was still trading as A. & J. Davies Ltd in 1928[19]. However, by 1930 the workforce was reduced to a mere twelve employees[20]. The firm was unable to survive the recession and closed about 1932.

In recent years R.H.M. Bakeries (Midlands) Ltd. used the site as a *Mothers Pride* transport depot. The cone has long been demolished and concreted over, but the main facade fronting King William Street still stands today and has been renovated.

---

1 Robinson was a wealthy ironmaster who purchased Dial Glasshouses in 1853, but leased it to Davis, Greathead and Green.
2 Benjamin Richardson's Notebook of 1886.
3 Kelly's 1868 Post Office Directory.
4 Littlebury's 1873 Directory; Frederick Robinson, son of George and Ann Robinson, b. c1849, Amblecote; Frederick subsequently lived the life of a gentleman at Bardley Court, Stottesdon, Shropshire, while running a glass merchant business at 6 Clifton Terrace, Woodpecker Road, New Cross, Kent.
5 James Davies, son of Joseph Davies, glassmaker of Audnam Bank and his wife Lydia, b. 18th Jul 1834, Wordsley, bap. 3rd Jul 1836, Kingswinford.
6 Alfred Davies, son of Edward Davies, glassmaker of Audnam and his wife Mary Ann, b. Wollaston, bap. 7th Oct 1838, Kingswinford.
7 PRO, 1881 Census, RG11/2890.
8 PRO 1881 census of Amblecote, RG11/2890/28/10
9 Kelly's 1888 Directory of Staffordshire; Kelly's 1892 Directory of Birmingham, Staffordshire and Warwickshire.
10 PRO, 1891 census RG12/2305.
11 James Davies, d. 6th Apr 1895; bur. Wordsley.
12 PRO, Admon of James Davies, 6th May 1895.
13 Hannah Maria (1836-97) was his second wife. His first wife Mary died 17th Nov 1879 and was buried at Wordsley.
14 Supra, Dennis Glassworks.
15 Alfred Davies, d. 14th Jan 1910.
16 PRO, Will of Alfred Davies, 7th Feb 1911.
17 Harry Davies, son of Alfred Davies and his wife Emma, b. c1862, Wollaston.
18 Alfred Edward Davies, son of Alfred Davies and his wife, Emma, b. c1879, Amblecote.
19 Kelly's 1928 Directory of Staffordshire.
20 Records of the British Flint Glass Manufacturers Association.

CHAPTER 44

Albert Glassworks, Wordsley

Richard Mills, Edward Webb, Frederick Stuart and Thomas Webb formed the firm of Mills, Webb & Stuart in 1853. Richard Mills and Edward Webb each contributed £1,000, Frederick Stuart and Thomas Webb £500 each to the partnership, the agreement being for a term of twenty-one years. Richard Mills purchased the Wordsley Iron Foundry, behind the Red House glassworks for £1,000 and changed its name to the Albert Glassworks, presumably named after the Prince Consort. The cone they built was the last of the traditional type to be built in the Stourbridge district. Richard Mills agreed that his son George[1] should devote the whole of his time to the business[2].

Richard Mills[3] married Elizabeth Webb[4] in 1834[5] and had a varied and entrepreneurial career. He kept the Vine Inn, Wordsley from at least 1841[6] until his death in 1860. He was also assistant clerk to the magistrates and Registrar of births, deaths and marriages for Kingswinford and Oldswinford from 1840 until at least 1851[7]. His signature is on the 1841 census for the whole of Kingswinford parish.

This Edward Webb has long been assumed by researchers to be the same Edward Webb who ran the Holloway End Glasshouse and subsequently White House Glassworks. Recent research shows this Edward of Springfield House, Wordsley to be his cousin[8] of the same name making his first foray into the glass business[9].

Frederick Stuart was the son of Samuel Stuart of Codsall[10]. He was orphaned when aged about eleven and went to live with

Robert Bill, a farmer in Wollaston. He began work as an office boy with Richard Bradley Ensell at the Red House in 1827 and then worked for many years as a traveller for John Parish & Co. Richard Mills lent him the £500 for his partnership share on 17th October 1853 at five per cent per annum.

Thomas Webb, cousin of Edward, was successfully running Platts Glassworks. He was presumably invited to join the partnership for reasons of his capital and experience. Thomas Webb remained a partner for less than a year before he left in 1854[11] to build Dennis Glassworks.

The partners needed to raise more capital and so on 1st July 1855 they took out a mortgage secured on the premises from the trustees of the estate of William King, who were Edward Westwood, William King Perrens and George King Harrison[12]. Richard Mills, Edward Webb and Frederick Stuart agreed new articles of partnership on 24th December 1856 for a term of fourteen years. However, the partnership is deemed to have started on 25th August 1854 – the date when Thomas Webb left.

The first successful trade union in the glass industry had been formed in 1851 and by the beginning of 1858 unionisation of labour was almost complete[13]. Faced with an outbreak of strikes, the employers responded by holding a meeting on 1st November 1858 at the Talbot Hotel, Stourbridge, where they formed a manufacturer's organisation. Frederick Stuart, of Mills, Webb and Stuart, became a founder member of the Flint Glass Manufacturers Defence Association. Strikes began in October 1858 and spread throughout the district. In December 1858 Idas Ogle, a glasscutter at the Mills, Webb & Stewart factory, claimed for £3 under the Master and Servant Acts. This was because, although no strike had been declared, he and his colleagues had been discharged on 28th November. On that day he was told 'there was no more work for him in consequence of the glass-blowers having ceased to work.'[14] The Association of Flint Glass Makers enforced a national lockout in December 1858 that was to last for seven months. In April 1859, after the lockout, Mills, Webb and Stuart claimed £73

11s from the association's defence fund. The amount implies this relatively new firm was the fourth largest of the thirteen firms in the Midlands Association.

Richard Mills died in 1860[15], aged forty-eight, at the Vine Inn, Wordsley. In his will[16], he is described as 'Innkeeper and Glass manufacturer of the Vine Inn at Wordsley.' It states 'I am at present engaged in carrying on in copartnership with Edward Webb and Frederick Stuart the trade or business of a Glassmanufacturer.' The testator left his estate to his wife Elizabeth in trust for his children. Elizabeth inherited his partnership in Mills, Webb and Stuart but renounced it as she was permitted to do under the terms of the will. Instead, their son George Mills[17] became a partner.

Edward Webb died later the same year, aged 39[18]. As he had never married he left all his real and personal estate to his father Joseph[19] and his interests under trust or mortgage to his brother-in-law, Henry Smith[20] of Harts Hill[21].

In 1861 Frederick Stuart lived with his family at Audnam, a flint glass manufacturer employing fifty men, thirteen boys and nine women[22]. This suggests the firm was the fifth largest employer of the six main Stourbridge glassworks in 1861.

In 1871 Frederick Stuart lived with his large family at The Cliff, Buckpool, Wordsley, a glass manufacturer employing sixty-nine men, forty-two boys and twenty-one women[23]. George Mills lived with his family at Stourbridge Road, Amblecote[24].

On 25th August 1868 the fourteen year term of the partnership expired and the partnership was dissolved. The value of the business was assessed at £10,996 11s. Elizabeth Mills and her co-executor Isaac Nash[25] were entitled to £3,548 6s 9d. Henry Smith, now of California, Summerhill, Kingswinford, the brother-in-law and sole executor of Edward Webb was due £3,792 9s 7d. Frederick Stuart was due £3,652 14s 8d.

Frederick Stuart and George Mills wished to carry on the business, but it had to be refinanced for George Mills to take a fifty percent stake in the business. The stock in trade was sold to Frederick Stuart and George Mills and the sum realised, plus the cash in hand, was divided equally between the executors of Richard Mills and

Edward Webb. Elizabeth Mills and Isaac Nash agreed to sell their remaining interest in the business to George Mills. Henry Smith agreed to sell the late Edward Webb's interest equally between Frederick Stuart and George Mills. This established the new partnership of Stuart & Mills in an agreement dated 19th September 1868. The new partnership assumed the debts and mortgage of the previous one. To raise further capital Frederick Stuart and George Mills took out a mortgage secured on the Albert Glassworks for £3,792 9s 7d at 7½% with Henry Smith. Then, on 3rd December 1869 Frederick Stuart repaid his original £500 partnership stake to the executors of Richard Mills.

A trade directory entry of 1876 shows the large range of products manufactured—'Stuart & Mills (late Mills, Webb & Stuart), manufacturers of cut glass chandeliers, lustres, wall lights, hall lamps, moons &c & cut, engraved, etched & ornamental glass ware, Wordsley.'[26]

Frederick Stuart lived at the Stuart family home, The Mount, High Street, Wordsley, a large Georgian house that stood close to the Red House glassworks on the site now occupied by the Conservative Club. Profits were buoyant[27] and in March 1877, George Mills moved from Park Field House, Brettell Lane to The Hill, the large mansion in Amblecote owned earlier by the Rogers family[28].

In 1876 Stuart and Mills supplied a large order for the steamship, the *Great Eastern* and subsequently became major contractors to the shipping trade. However, in 1875 contention developed between the partners concerning the style of glass they should make. George Mills preferred making chandeliers and lighting ware while Frederick Stuart and his sons were fascinated by Philip Pargeter's virtuoso glassmaking next door at the Red House. Frederick Stuart's oldest son William Henry showed his preference when he registered a patent in 1880[29]. This was a method of applying decorative glass threads to glass articles. It involved rolling the plastic parison in pulverised glass or enamel before threading the bulb. Reheating caused the finely pulverised glass or enamel to melt and run, while the glass threads remained intact and in place on the bulb.

George Mills resented Frederick Stuart's dominance of the firm and the presence of two of his sons in the business. Their relationship became so bad that they would not even speak to each other and only communicated by written messages. George Mills consulted his solicitor, John Bullas Shepherd$_{30}$ of Harwood, Shepherd and Mills$_{31}$. On 3rd April 1875 Mr. Shepherd noted that he had spoken to Mr Stuart who said that his sons would remain at the works as long as he himself remained whether Mr Mills consented or not and that he would not make any special arrangements with his sons. Frederick Stuart responded via his London based solicitor brother William$_{32}$ on 29th May 1875. The response suggests that the first area of contention was George Mills' chandelier department 'his creation – his speciality – now that difficulties are experienced in it and it is admitted to be a comparative failure.' The second area of contention was George Mills' insistence that he would not continue the partnership without an alteration of its terms and his insistence on the dismissal of Frederick Stuart's two sons.

Somehow, the business continued, although profits continued to decline, but Frederick Stuart was thoroughly sick of working with George Mills. As the end of the fourteen-year partnership term approached, Frederick Stuart made plans for a new business. Although he was sixty-five years old, he had seven sons he wanted to set up in business. On 2nd April 1880 the two partners had capital amounting to £8,460 9s 2 1/2d each. They took a share of the accumulated profits of £1,851 4s 3 1/2d each in addition to drawings of £1,468 15s 2d each. On 29th April 1881 Frederick Stuart took over the lease of the Red House Glassworks and presumably announced his intention to quit the partnership when it expired on 25th August 1882.

George Mills immediately sought a new partner familiar with chandelier manufacturing. On 11th May 1882 he agreed with Philip Walker to buy the assets and goodwill of William Walker & Sons at the Heath Glassworks and to form a partnership with his nephew James Harry Walker as Mills & Walker. The Heath Glassworks was famous for its prowess with chandeliers and twenty-three year old James Harry Walker was an experienced glassmaker and designer, unlike his accountant uncle Philip. The deal was agreed. James Harry borrowed £2,000 from his father James Walker and formed the partnership of Mills, Walker & Co.

At about the same time George Mills offered £8,277 10s to Frederick Stuart for his share of the business. However, this did not include goodwill and a half share was subsequently valued at £5,222. On 13th May 1882 George Mills concluded an agreement in the name of Mills, Walker & Co to buy Frederick Stuart's share for £13,500.

On 1st September 1882 James Walker agreed to loan his son a further £2,000 and George Mills contributed £8,000 to bring the capital up to £12,000. James Walker was to provide some initial assistance to get the business started, especially representing it in London.

On 29th September George Mills agreed to pay Frederick Stuart a further £10,120 in three equal six-monthly instalments for certain real and personal property giving him complete ownership of the Albert business. The London showrooms at Hatton Garden were transferred to Mills & Walker as part of the deal. Frederick Stuart finally parted company in October 1882[33] and moved to the adjoining Red House glassworks, which he had leased the previous year.

George Mills proudly announced his situation:

> Dear Sirs,
>
> I beg to inform you that I have bought the freehold Glass Works and premises lately belonging to Mr Stuart and me, at Wordsley near Stourbridge, and the assets and goodwill of the business of Glass and Chandelier Manufacturers carried on by Mr Stuart and me under the style or firm of Stuart & Mills, at the above works, and that I have also bought the Leasehold Glasshouse, Works and Premises, lately belonging to Messrs W. Walker & Son, at the Heath, near Stourbridge, and the assets and goodwill of the business of Glass Manufacturers carried on by them at the above works. I have taken into partnership with me Mr JH Walker, son of Mr Jas Walker and grandson of the late Mr Wm Walker; we intend to carry on both the above businesses as heretofore, but with greatly improved management, under the style or firm of Mills, Walker & Co.
>
> Requesting your attention to our signatures as at foot
> I am dear Sirs

Yours Truly

George Mills

George Mills was entrusted with the financial management of the company but as early as February 1884 his mental health began to deteriorate. Trade began to decline, stock increased and the company's bankers demanded a reduction of their account. On 19th March 1884 the partners took out a mortgage with the Birmingham and Midland Bank for £3,628 2s 6d and James Walker agreed to postpone repayment of his loan capital of £2,000 due on 1st September 1887. By May 1884 Mills' health deteriorated further and so did the business. Mills was urged to seek rest and recuperation and to cede management of the business to James Walker. He agreed to pass management of the business to Walker but, instead of rest, Mills took a short holiday then began to travel around the country collecting orders and conducting the country business of the firm. From a desperate situation, James Walker rescued the business; customers and workmen were reconciled and finances restored. However George Mills suffered from frequent relapses and continued to cause problems. He quarrelled with his partners, was unreasonable with customers and was violent towards the workmen. Through his solicitor, John Bullas Shepherd, James Walker sought to oust George Mills from his control of the business and reduce his share of its profits[34]. A meeting was held on 12th September 1884 and it was agreed that the partnership should be dissolved. However, the fraught relationship deteriorated further. On Sunday 19th July 1885 George Mills' wife wrote urgently to their solicitor J.B. Shepherd:

> 'On Saturday might Mr J H Walker made a most violent and mad attack on Mr Mills completely disabling his left knee and he will be confined to bed for some days to come. Will you kindly telegraph if you can get here tomorrow night in time to be of service. Please bring the agreements with you and see Mr Harry Mills first.'

Three days later George Mills wrote to J.B. Shepherd instructing him to issue a writ for the dissolution of the partnership and the appointment of a receiver. However, the Walkers delayed their response and Mills again wrote an angry letter to J.B. Shepherd dated 1st September 1885. The letter explains George Mills' opinion of the Walkers and the state of the business, but its tone is one of paranoia. In the same way he resented the presence of Frederick Stuart's sons in the business, he now resented that of the Walkers. On 4th September he wrote again to J.B. Shepherd:

> 'Please telegraph to Mr James Walker for appointment and follow him to London at once. Do not on any pretence submit to further procrastination but insist upon an immediate understanding
>
> There is no reason whatever for his absence they are or have been trifling with you and so long as they can go on drawing money and bleeding me to death all 3 of them will, neither have any of them *ever* had any intention of leaving here. When they have it out, will you come to reasonable terms or will you not.
>
> Almost anything is better than the present state of things. Mind that I have told you the real character of these people again and again.
>
> Yours truly
>
> Geo Mills.'

The company's situation worsened and on 26th September George Mills' brother Frederick James Mills$_{35}$ guaranteed the wages bill of £160. By 7th November the partnership had still not been dissolved and the company had completely run out of cash. These problems were dramatically addressed when George Mills shot himself on 13th November 1885 at Five Ways, Iverley$_{36}$.

George Mills had made a will on 16th May 1873 and it was proved on 25th January 1886$_{37}$ by his widow Mary Kate$_{38}$. After specific bequests, including £500 to his wife, he gave all his real and personal estate to his wife and his two brothers upon trust for sale, conversion and investment for the benefit of his wife and children. The problem was that he was in debt to the value of £11,344 12s 6d. The Hill, the huge mansion that he had lived in for the last ten years, was unsaleable. On 8th June 1886 the valuer, Mr King, reported that the house was very much in need of repair. The vineries and greenhouses were in a state of 'great dilapidation' and the property needed at least £1,000 spending on it to bring it up to standard. He put the saleable value at £5,500 but added there was no demand for this class of residence, which is 'old, large, inconvenient and expensive to keep up and is likely to stand void for many years.'[39] The contents were auctioned on 8th March 1886 and raised £1,118 17s.

Mr King was even gloomier about the business than he had been about The Hill'. 'The depression has caused a great depreciation in freeholds . . . In the last two years at auction I have failed to get more than a nominal bid . . . glassworks are very unsaleable, three standing void in the district at present . . . stock and tools are likely to incur a 50 to 70% loss on valuation after sale and advertising expenses etc.' He valued Mrs Mills' share of the business at £2,280.

Clearly, liquidation would not raise sufficient money to clear George Mills' liabilities, some of which were to members of the family, so a decision was taken to attempt to trade out of difficulty. However, Mills' will contained no powers to enable the executors to carry on the business and no partnership agreements had been formally entered into. Therefore, counsel's opinion was sought from Mr C.S. Medd on the legality of continued trading. The solicitor's brief for counsel said, 'it may be opined that the business is a valuable one but if the works are closed and the business compulsorily wound up at once, there being a forced sale of the stock then the estate will not produce enough to pay the expenses and the creditors in full. But if further capital is found to carry on the business it is confidently believed that in, say, three or four years the present debts and liabilities will be paid off out of net profits after allowing something for the partners in the meantime.'

A plan was agreed. On 17th March 1886 George Mills' widow conveyed her interest in the Albert Glassworks to James Harry Walker for £100 in return for which he undertook to repay the £3,471 14s 2d owing to the bank and the £2,000 owing to James Walker. The business was saved and continued to trade as Mills, Walker & Co. Although managed by James Harry Walker, the agreement still recognised that capital due to the estate of George Mills remained in the business.

In 1886 the firm introduced *Corolene* decorated glass called *Verre de Neige* or snowflake glass that looked like coral. It was described in Pottery Gazette and appears in the Silber & Flemming catalogue of 1889. In 1888 *Carrara* ware was introduced, in imitation of marble. A trade directory of 1888 shows the firm to still have an interest in lighting ware—'Mills, Walker & Co., Glass chandelier & lamp manufacturers, Wordsley.'[40]

A further deed of arrangement and partnership was concluded on 26th February 1889. The various interested parties in the Mills and Walker families gave their agreement for James Harry Walker to enter into partnership with John Bolton in the firm of Mills, Walker & Co. for a term of twenty-one years. John Bolton had been a partner in John Davis & Co at Dial Glasshouses but dissolved that partnership in August 1888.

Trading in the first half of 1890 was profitable but the second half showed losses. This was followed by unsatisfactory audit results for January and February 1891[41]. The company's insolvency and interminable legal manoeuvrings were presumably an unbearable burden for the fifty-nine year old James Walker. He shot himself on 2nd March 1891. The coroner recorded a 'state of temporary insanity' at an inquest held on 4th March. The Albert Glassworks had claimed its second death by suicide.

On 18th April 1891, the business being insolvent, the creditors elected to try and salvage their money by supporting Mills & Walker as a going concern and forming it into a limited liability company. The creditors took preferred shares of £10 each in proportion to the money they were owed. The bank loan was converted to a debenture. Mary Kate Mills still held influence as the amount due to the estate of George Mills was still in the business. She agreed to take nine hundred shares in the business on the condition that Philip Pargeter became chairman and John Bolton and Benjamin Robinson would be appointed managing directors[42].

The business was therefore saved but continued to incur losses. The fifteen months to 30th June 1892 showed a trading loss of £461

7s and a small loss of £27 7s 4d was recorded for the following year. The loss for the year to 30th June 1894 was £499 13s 9d. The bank decided to intervene and insisted on the appointment of a new manager. On 26th November 1894 John Alexander Service[43] was appointed co-managing director with John Bolton[44]. Service had previously been connected with Coalport China to whom he gave notice before joining Mills & Walker.

The following year Mills, Walker & Company Limited called an Extraordinary General Meeting on 8th October 1895 to reconstitute the board of directors. The new board comprised Harry Mills[45], solicitor of The Elms, Stourbridge as chairman. George Simkins, lithographer of Newton Street, Birmingham, became vice-chairman[46]. John Alexander Service, glass manufacturer of Carlton Villa, Wollaston, became general managing director. The other directors were John Bolton the younger, glass manufacturer of Wordsley and Benjamin Robinson, glass manufacturer of 19 Charterhouse Street, London E.C.[47]

Service instituted changes such as an agreement with Edward Locke of Worcester[48] to manufacture china for Mills & Walker. After six months in the job he made a written report to the board of directors. This gives a fascinating insight of the strengths and weaknesses of the business. The chandelier business, which had been George Mills' 'speciality', he considered to be a 'perfect farce' and were it not for the large stock of finished goods and materials he would have recommended its immediate closure. As to management, Service observed that Benjamin Robinson was leaving at Christmas and 'I will not comment on the past beyond remarking that Mr R does not appear to have shown much energy and that Mr Bolton has rendered him but little assistance.'

However, the bank gave their appointee little time to turn the business around and applied for a winding-up order when he had been in his post for just over a year. A receiver was appointed on 21st August 1896 and he put the business up for sale as a going concern. The business comprised a twelve-pot furnace, two kilns, two winding lehrs, shrawer room, three glory holes, pot room and pot arch.

Levi$_{49}$, Silas$_{50}$ and George Silas$_{51}$ Hingley purchased the business for £4,500. On 13th October 1896 they bought the glassworks as a going concern, purchasing the premises, business and stock in trade$_{52}$. They retained the entire workforce and immediately set about remodelling and refitting the works$_{53}$. The new owners told Pottery Gazette's reporter that they were getting the business of the old firm 'which had been allowed to fall away' into good order again and were making efforts to bring back the chandelier business.

John Bolton set up a small glass manufacturing business in Brettell Lane, with his nephew John Frederick Bolton Bowater. It traded as Bolton (John) & Bowater$_{54}$.

The Hingley brothers were sons of Thomas Hingley, a nailer of Holly Hall$_{55}$. Levi was the oldest son and began his working life as a potter's works clerk. After he married$_{56}$ in 1852 he moved from Brettell Lane to King William Street, Amblecote. Behind his house, which still stands today, he set up a glass decorating workshop and made his entry to the glass trade. Silas was two years younger and after an education at Oldswinford Hospital, was apprenticed at the age of thirteen to John Herbert, a Dudley glass engraver$_{57}$. Silas married$_{58}$ in 1862 and moved from Collis Street to set up his family home at Chesnut House in Villa Street, Amblecote. He and his younger brother, Jabez$_{59}$, worked with Levi, as decorators and merchants of glass in Brettell Lane$_{60}$. Many of their children worked in the glass trade in various guises, such as dealers, clerks, or engravers$_{61}$.

Levi's two elder sons George and Alfred$_{62}$ joined the business, as did all three of Silas' sons: William$_{63}$, Charles$_{64}$ and Harold$_{65}$. Alfred Hingley was a talented artist and produced many designs for glass cutting. His cousins did not fit in so well and following a family disagreement Silas' sons were paid out. When Levi's youngest son John Oswald$_{66}$ became of age he began a glass and china business called Clay Brothers with his older brother Thomas$_{67}$. They both acted as travellers and, with the aid of a third traveller called Will Egan, covered the whole of Great Britain. They rented a warehouse at the Platts from A.H. Guest.

In 1902 L. & S. Hingley advertised threaded glassware and fancy epergnes with threaded decoration in the Pottery Gazette Diary, but during that year they became involved in a union dispute. They refused to stop supplying goods to Thomas Webb & Co., which had locked out its workforce[68].

Levi Hingley died in 1905[69], aged seventy-seven. Silas sold his interest to Alfred Hingley for £250 on 9th September 1911 and died in 1918[70], aged eighty-seven. The firm continued under the management of their sons, trading as L. & S. Hingley & Sons[71]. George Hingley then introduced his three sons to the business. The oldest, Clement[72], attained an MA and was a master at Preston, Leatherhead. Poor mental health led to many sojourns in Stafford Asylum. He joined L. & S. Hingley & Sons as a traveller where he travelled extensively, including America, but ended his days in the asylum. George's second son, Norman[73], worked before the Great War for a London clothing firm called Boyd's. He joined the Artists' Rifles in 1915 and became an officer in the 13th Middlesex Regiment, achieving the rank of Lt. Colonel. He joined the family firm after the Great War. George's youngest son Noel[74] worked in the firm's London showroom managed by a Mr Service.

In common with so many other businesses, L. & S. Hingley struggled through the depression years and the period of the Second World War. The firm survived until 1948 when the glassworks was advertised for sale. A buyer was promptly found in the firm of W.H. Swingewood & Co. Ltd. that had operated in a small way in Dial Lane for the previous twelve months. The two directors were Mr H.A. Marler and Mr A.E. Marler, both of whom were local publicans. H.A. Marler ran the Bulls Head in Wollaston and A.E. Marler ran the Vine Inn in Blackheath. The old twelve-pot furnace had not been used since the time of the First World War and as part of a modernisation programme the cone and furnace were demolished on 28th January 1949. A new glasshouse was built and part of the old premises was adapted as decorating shops[75]. It is not known how long W.H. Swingewood & Co. Ltd. was in business, but some of the original buildings are still standing today.

1 George Mills, son of Richard Mills and his wife Elizabeth, nee Webb, b. Wordsley, bap. 17th Dec 1837, Kingswinford.
2 Stuart Papers No 1, Partnership agreement.
3 Richard Mills, son of Thomas Mills, chairmaker of Stourbridge and his wife Sarah, nee Howells, b. Stourbridge, bap. 27th Dec 1812, Oldswinford.
4 Elizabeth Webb, daughter of Richard Webb, a glass packer, and his wife Mary, nee Stamford, b. Wordsley, bap. 30th Apr 1815, Kingswinford.
5 Mar. Richard Mills and Elizabeth Webb, 5th Aug 1834, West Bromwich.
6 PRO, 1841, census of Kingswinford.
7 PRO, 1851 census HO 107/2036 06/102/013.
8 Edward Webb, only son of Joseph Webb, boat builder and landed proprietor of Springfield House, Wordsley and his wife Ann, nee Harper, bap. 3rd Mar 1820, Kingswinford.
9 The author is indebted to Mr Geoffrey Kernan, who in a lengthy exchange of research was the first to suggest this.
10 Frederick Stuart, son of Samuel Stuart and his wife Ann, nee Fowler, b. 6th Jun 1816, Codsall, near Wolverhampton.
11 SRO, D648/86, Deed of dissolution of partnership as far as regards Thos. Webb, 1854.
12 George King Harrison, b. c1827 Liverpool, was a colliery owner and Justice of the Peace for Stafford who lived at Hagley.
13 FGMM quarter ending 29 May 1858.
14 Brierley Hill Advertiser, 24th Dec 1858.
15 Richard Mills, d. 4th Feb 1860; bur. Wordsley, family grey stone vault.
16 PRO, Will of Richard Mills, 2nd Apr 1860.
17 George Mills, son of Richard Mills and his wife Elizabeth, nee Webb, b. Wordsley, bap. 17th Dec 1837, Kingswinford.
18 Edward Webb, d. 2nd Nov 1860; bur. Wordsley. The memorial to him on the sandstone family tomb in Wordsley churchyard is no longer readable.
19 Will of Edward Webb proven 16th Sep 1861. LJRO v 12, Fol. 145.
20 Henry Smith, b. c1824 at Pedmore was a wealthy ironmaster who married Mary Ann Webb, sister of Edward, in 1852 at Worcester.
21 Harts Hill was at this time a hamlet in the northeast corner of Brierley Hill parish, south of Woodside and north of where now stands the Merry Hill shopping centre.
22 PRO, 1861 census RG 9/2069 ED2 Sched 187.

23 PRO, 1871 census RG10 3025 ED3 Sched 64.

24 PRO, 1871 census RG10 3021 ED21 Sched 54.

25 Supra, Platts Glassworks.

26 Kelly's 1876 Post Office Directory of Staffordshire and Warwickshire.

27 Profits for 1876 were £5,686 7s 8d. SRO D695/3/34.

28 After the death of Thomas Rogers The Hill was conveyed to Henry Rogers in trust. It was sold to ironmaster Thomas Homfray in 1799. He leased it in 1811 to Joseph Lea who was succeeded by his son Joseph who died in 1821. The widow of Joseph junior married John Addenbrooke and they lived at The Hill until 1836 when the estate was sold to the Stourbridge tanner Joseph Pitman. He died in March 1871 and in Oct 1872 the house was rented to James Brock Fisher, coal and clay master. George Mills acquired the house from Pitman's trustees on 25th Mar 1877.

29 Patent Number 3675, 10th Sep 1880.

30 John Bullas Shepherd, son of glass manufacturer John Shepherd and his wife Mary, bap. 17th Nov 1828, Oldswinford.

31 George Mills' brother Harry (1848-1897) of Beech Tree House, Stourbridge was a partner in the old established legal firm that became Harward, Shepherd and Mills and after Harry's death, Harward and Evers. Harry did not act for his brother, leaving this to his partner, presumably for reasons of legal propriety. Harry's oldest son by his wife Jane Elizabeth, nee Nash was Gerald Rusgrove Mills (1877-1928) the founder of the famous publishers, Mills and Boon.

32 William Stuart, son of Samuel Stuart and his wife Ann, nee Fowler, bap. 5th Oct 1814, St. Peter or Collegiate, Wolverhampton.

33 PG, Apr 1897.

34 SRO D695/4/1/7.

35 Frederick James Mills was a partner in Boulton & Mills at Audnam Glassworks.

36 In his portmanteau, Mills was carrying a letter addressed 'To any brother in humanity.' The letter was read to the jury of the inquest held on 16th Nov at Five Ways Inn, Iverley. It read 'Gone mad. I cannot bear this depression any longer. God only knows my sufferings.' On the back was written 'I walked all day to try and throw this off. Useless, broken completely G.M.' The jury decided that he took his own life while in a state of temporary insanity. Brierley Hill Advertiser 14th and 21st Nov 1885. Five Ways is where the

minor road from Cookley to Churchill, crosses the Stourbridge to Kidderminster road.
37 PRO, will of George Mills 25th Jan 1886.
38 Mary Kate, nee Pocock, b. c1849, Bristol.
39 Mr King was probably correct in his assessment. Mary Kate Mills, George's widow eventually sold it to John Corbett MP, the 'Salt King' of Droitwich in Dec 1891. Corbett, promptly announced that he would convert the mansion into a hospital and endow it to serve the district. It opened on 31st Jul 1893 as the Corbett Hospital. The alterations included a new house built on the corner of the estate, also called The Hill, for Hyacinth d'Arcy Ellis a surgeon friend. After the Second World War the old house was almost completely demolished and the newer 'Hill' became a nurses' home.
40 Kelly's 1888 Directory of Staffordshire.
41 The company's auditors were Messrs. Baker Gibson & les Afes of Birmingham.
42 SRO, D695/3/57
43 John Alexander Service, glass and china manufacturer originally of 29 Lordship Lane, Wood Green, London, moved to Carlton Villa, Wollaston.
44 SRO, D695/1/22/2, His salary was be £350 per annum and a share of any profits above £750 per annum.
45 Harry Mills, son of Richard Mills and his wife Elizabeth, nee Webb, bap. 18th Apr 1848, Wordsley; d. 12th Feb 1897, Stourbridge. As the younger brother of the original partner George Mills, he would be representing the Mills family's interests.
46 George Simkins was probably involved in the printing business with Henry Mills, Harry Mills' uncle. In 1851, Henry Mills and George Simkins both lived in Upper Gough Street, Birmingham when George Simkins was an apprentice in Henry Mills' printing business.
47 SRO, D695/1/22/2. 19 Charterhouse Street was the London address of Mills & Walker.
48 Edward Locke of Locke & Co. Ltd., manufacturers of porcelain from 1895 to 1904 at Shrub Hill Works, Worcester and descended from the same family as glass engraver Joseph Locke.
49 Levi Hingley, son of Thomas Hingley and his wife Eleanor, nee Greenfield, bap. 29th Mar 1829, Dudley, St. Thomas's.
50 Silas Hingley, son of Thomas Hingley and his wife Eleanor, nee Greenfield,

bap. 3rd Jul 1831, Dudley St. Thomas's.
51 George Silas Hingley, son of Levi Hingley and his wife Mary Ann, nee Hill, b. Brettell Lane, bap. 14th Jul 1853, Kingswinford.
52 PG, Apr 1897.
53 PG, Nov 1897.
54 Kelly's 1904 Directory of Staffordshire.
55 He later became a grocer with a shop at 57 Pedmore Road, Woodside, Dudley. He died there 4th Mar 1871.
56 Mar. Levi Hingley and Mary Ann Hill, 1852, Kingswinford.
57 His apprenticeship began on 17th June 1845. See Herbert family, Dudley Flint Glassworks.
58 Mar. Silas Hingley and Elizabeth Amelia Hill, 27th May 1862, Oldswinford. Elizabeth Amelia Hill and Mary Ann Hill were daughters of John and Lucy Hill, so two Hill sister married two Hingley brothers.
59 Jabez Hingley, son of Thomas Hingley and his wife Eleanor, nee Greenfield, bap. 20th Mar 1842, Dudley St. Thomas's.
60 PRO, 1881 census of Kingswinford; Kelly's 1888 Directory of Staffordshire.
61 PRO, 1891 Census, RG12/2305.
62 Alfred J. Hingley, son of Levi Hingley and his wife Mary Ann, nee Hill, b c1859, Dennis Park.
63 William Hingley, son of Silas Hingley and his wife Elizabeth Amelia, nee Hill, bap. 6th Jul 1864, Amblecote.
64 Charles Edward Hingley, son of Silas Hingley and his wife Elizabeth Amelia, nee Hill, bap. 1st Dec 1869, Amblecote.
65 Albert Harold Hingley, son of Silas Hingley and his wife Elizabeth Amelia, nee Hill, b c1868, Amblecote.
66 John Oswald Hingley, son of Levi Hingley and his wife Mary Ann, nee Hill, b c1871, Dennis Park.
67 Thomas Hingley, son of Levi Hingley and his wife Mary Ann, nee Hill, b. 12th Apr 1861, Dennis Park.
68 Supra, Dennis Glassworks.
69 Levi Hingley, d. 23rd Aug 1905; bur. Amblecote. His grave has a small headstone with a gothic top.
70 Silas Hingley, d. 17th Jul 1918; bur. Amblecote. His grave is marked with a Celtic cross.
71 Kelly's 1928 Directory of Staffordshire.

72 George Clement Hingley, son of George Silas Hingley and his wife Annie Elizabeth, nee Harries, b c1888, Amblecote.
73 Alfred Norman Hingley, son of George Silas Hingley and his wife Annie Elizabeth, nee Harries, b c1890, Amblecote.
74 James Noel Hingley, son of George Silas Hingley and his wife Annie Elizabeth, nee Harries, bap. 26th Mar 1891, Amblecote.
75 County Express, 5th Feb 1949.

CHAPTER 45

Dennis Glassworks, Amblecote

Thomas Webb resigned from Mills, Webb & Stuart in 1854. He bought about five acres of the old Dennis estate and began the construction of a new glassworks at the rear of Dennis House in Amblecote. He moved his business from Platts Glassworks in 1854 and gave the new works the same name he used at the Platts—Thomas Webb Glass Works. The choice of the Dennis site is interesting, unlike the earlier glassworks it was not on the banks of a canal. However, as Stourbridge Railway Station opened in 1852, Thomas Webb probably seized the opportunity to exploit this new means of distribution. In January 1854 Webb was granted a patent for a circular lehr. He probably experimented with it in his new works at Dennis, then under construction. The lehr is described in the patent as an *improved apparatus applicable to the annealing of glass and the firing of pottery*. This circular lehr had the advantage of saving workspace and was comparatively simple in design. The main part consisted of two large circles, made of cast iron plates, which revolved horizontally, one within the other acting as conveyors. These were easily operated by two handles attached to gearwheels engaging with teeth underneath the circles. The apparatus was low geared and articles stood on the circles for annealing could be moved slowly, resting on wheels fixed to spindles. Half the lehr was in the glasshouse and the other half in the shrawer. Near the centre of the lehr, on the glasshouse side was a coal-fired box. The glass passed through a hole in the wall then along a tunnel to be taken off the conveyor at the shrawer end$_1$.

The furnace was first lit in August 1855, although the timing was not good for Thomas Webb. The eighteen-fifties had been a period of full employment, but considerable distress occurred in the summer of 1855 because of the Crimean War. There was a modest recovery after the cessation of hostilities and although the glass trade returned to full employment, the economy of the Black Country was only described as dull to steady throughout 1856 and 1857. Then, in 1858 the glassmakers national strike and lockout took place[2]. After the lockout, in 1859, Thomas Webb's claim from the manufacturers' defence fund[3] suggests the firm was the smallest of the thirteen in the Midlands Association.

Thomas Webb owned and occupied just over four acres at Dennis. This included the house, manufactory, lands and gardens, with over an acre of coppice and land, for which rent due to the Rector was £4 8s 3d per annum[4].

Thomas Wilkes Webb[5], Thomas Webb's son, had been working in his father's business since 1850, when he joined as a clerk. In 1859 he became a partner and the name of the firm was changed to Thomas Webb & Sons, Dennis Glass Works. The family lived together at Dennis House[6].

After two years Thomas Webb was content with his son's management of the business and so in 1863 he retired and moved to Cradley, Herefordshire where he acquired farms. He made his will there on 11th December 1869, when he was sixty-five years old. Thomas Wilkes Webb was joined by his younger brother Charles[7] as a partner. After leaving school Charles worked for Copeland's, the well-known china manufacturers. Alderman Copeland[8] had been a great friend of Thomas Webb for many years. Charles first learned the trade by working in Copeland's shop in Bond Street, where Webbs' glass was sold in addition to Copeland's china. Then, for about ten years he worked as a traveller for his father's firm.

Having set the foundations of a strong business, Thomas Webb watched proudly as the firm flourished under the leadership of his sons. Thomas Wilkes Webb was forward thinking and endeavoured to secure the services of the finest craftsmen. He was particularly successful in encouraging a succession of Bohemian engravers to join the firm. Their designs and products were to have a marked influence on the standing and prosperity of the firm and led to the creation of many masterpieces that are revered today. One of the first Bohemians to arrive at Dennis was William Fritsche. Born at Meistersdorf in 1853 he started work at Dennis in 1868 and spent his working life there. He worked on small pieces of cameo, but is best known as one of the finest Stourbridge engravers, credited with the introduction of 'Rock Crystal' engraving. His engraving with the copper wheel was of a superlative quality[9]. He lodged at the Red Lion Inn in Brettell Lane[10].

A succession of design registrations and patents began to flow from the Dennis factory. In 1867 a design was registered for ribbed handles and 'shell' components. This style of handle became very popular and featured on many products in years to come. Despite the design registration it was widely copied by other firms and ribbed handles appeared on hundreds of different articles until the end of the century. In 1869 Thomas Webb & Sons registered a design for a two-handled celery jug in crystal patterned with ferns, which used the ribbed handles patented in 1867.

Thomas Webb JP died at Fern Hill, Cradley, Herefordshire, in 1869[11]. When his will was proved[12], he left the Dennis Glassworks to three of his sons: Charles, Thomas Wilkes and Walter Wilkes[13]. Charles and Thomas Wilkes were already partners in the firm; Walter Wilkes joined them as the third partner. His other sons, Joseph William[14] and Henry Arthur[15], inherited his Brettell Hall Ironworks.

In 1871 Thomas Wilkes Webb lived in King William Street, Amblecote with his family, described as a glass manufacturer[16]. His brother Charles lived at the next house with his wife, also described as a glass manufacturer[17].

Another great craftsman, Thomas Woodall[18], joined Webb's about 1874. His brother, George[19] joined shortly after, working first as a draughtsman. George Woodall became a glass engraver, and started cameo carving about six years later, becoming probably the most brilliant of the cameo sculptors. George had begun his career at John Northwood's etching shop in about 1862, and while there attended Stourbridge School of Art, passing exams in model and freehand drawing. George and Thomas were sons of Thomas Woodall, a nailer and his wife Emma, nee Bott. She was a sister of John Thomas Bott[20] who had worked for the Richardsons[21] and at Worcester Porcelain Works.

Two of Webb's engravers, Frederick Englebert Kny and William Fritsche, were awarded bronze medals at the Alexandra Palace Exhibition of 1876. Kny was born at Neuforstaulde Kemnitz, in Bohemia in 1839[22] and moved to Amblecote about 1860 where he lived in Collis Street. This was after he had spent a short time at the Whitefriars Glassworks of James Powell[23]. His exquisite work is among the finest ever produced in the Stourbridge district. He worked in charge of a shop at Webb's where he produced some of his best pieces.

In 1876 Philip Pargeter of the Red House glassworks rediscovered the 'Holy Grail' of glassmaking by his successful reproduction of the Portland vase[24]. Thomas Wilkes Webb was determined that his firm should not be eclipsed by this achievement and so the same year he commissioned John Northwood to produce another masterpiece of cameo glass. It took until 1880 to complete and was known as the Pegasus or Dennis vase. Webb's eventually sold it to Tiffany of New York and it is now in the Corning Museum in the United States.

There followed a phase of design resulting from the Victorian fascination with antiquity. Thomas Wilkes Webb patented *Sidonian* or *Allasantes* glass on 9th June 1876, imitating the style of ancient glass[25]. In such wares, coloured threads of glass were attached to glass articles and expansion caused by heat developed the threads into curious but pleasing designs. The following year Webbs' introduced *Bronze* glass. *Bronze* was a form of iridescent finish developed to compete with prevalent Bohemian products. The style was an attempt to replicate the appearance of Roman and other ancient glass, with its natural iridescence, being excavated by the archaeologists of the day. *Bronze* glass was approved by Queen Victoria and was a great success at the 1878 Paris Exhibition[26]. The patent was applied for on 29th August 1877 and granted on 27th February 1878. It states:

'the glass articles are exposed, while in the nearly molten state after blowing, and before annealing, to the fumes generated by placing chloride of tin, alone or mixed with the nitrates of barium and strontium, upon a hot plate or spoon. During this process the articles are placed in a muffle or chamber into which the fumes are introduced.'

Even decoration on crystal followed the same theme of reproducing antiquity. The Elgin Claret Jug, wheel-engraved crystal by Frederick Englebert Kny was shown at the Paris Exhibition of 1878 in an unfinished state[27]. This is a magnificent crystal claret decanter, now in the Victoria and Albert Museum[28]. Its decoration is an encircling frieze in relief depicting a group of horsemen in an adaptation of a section of the Elgin Marbles. The intaglio cutting is in contrast to John Northwood's vase of comparable design cut in cameo in 1873. At the 1878 Paris Exhibition it was stated 'Messrs Thomas Webb & Co. are the best makers of Crystal Glass in England and therefore the whole world' and the firm won the only Grand Prix for glass. Thomas Wilkes Webb was awarded the *Legion d'Honneur* by the French Government.

A style of deep engraving and carving in glass began to develop, shortly before 1878 that became known as 'Rock Crystal', because of its resemblance to naturally occurring rock crystal. Once established, it became the only significant type of engraving practised in the Stourbridge district until almost the First World War. Although the style was subsequently adopted at Stevens and Williams'[29] and later at Webb-Corbett's[30], it began at Webbs'. The term 'Rock Crystal' is first found in the Webb pattern books with the date 6th July 1878. The patterns in question are numbers 10091, 10092 and 10093, bearing the note 'Engraved as Rock Crystal (Kny)' and the date. The first two patterns are tankards, the third a jug. Their design is naturalistic, the tankards being engraved with fish among rushes, the jug with an owl. The engraving was done by or under Frederick Englebert Kny[31].

Thomas Wilkes Webb's policy of employing the finest craftsmen available achieved remarkable fame for the firm; honour was heaped upon honour. Webbs' won the Gold Medal at the Sydney

Exhibition of 1879 and 1880, then two medals at Melbourne in 1880 and two more in 1881[32].

In 1879 Jules Barbe[33], a French gilder, was persuaded to set up a workshop on the premises and remained there until 1901, after which he worked on his own accord until 1925. He came to England after the death of his wife during the siege of Paris in the Franco-Prussian War[34]. His work ranks alongside that of the Beilbys[35] as some of the finest examples of gilding on glass.

In 1881 Charles Webb lived at Dennis House with his wife Maria Louisa[36] and three servants, a glass manufacturer, employing a hundred and forty men, forty boys, and ten women. Thomas Woodall lived at Rose Cottage, New Street, Kingswinford, described as a glass sculptor. George Woodall lived at Luton House, Market Street, Kingswinford, described as a glass sculptor[37].

The early eighteen-eighties were the greatest years of Webbs' inventiveness and fame. In 1883 *Ivory* glass was produced, decorated with raised gold, silver or enamel by Jules Barbe, imitating the appearance of porcelain. The same year Webbs' introduced a colour for opaque glass called *Sanguis Draconis* or dragons' blood, a rich maroon red. In 1884 the firm exhibited at the International Health Exhibition in London where Thomas Woodall was awarded a Bronze Medal for glass vases and bowls[38]. In the same year Thomas Wilkes Webb went on a trade mission to Australia; his glass was famous the world over.

Daniel Pearce[39] took over Webbs' department concerned with the design and production of epergnes and flower stands in 1884. Daniel Pearce and his son Lionel[40] traded as Messrs Dobson and Pearce at St. James Street and from 1862 as Phillips and Pearce of Bond Street and then under his own name at North End, Hammersmith. At the time of the 1867 Paris Exhibition Daniel Pearce was working for W.P. & G. Phillips and had shown a large chandelier that included an arrangement of hanging baskets. A commentator in Art Journal wrote 'Mr Pearce is unrivalled in England as a designer of works in glass'. In 1881 Daniel lived in North End Road, Fulham with his family, including Lionel, described as an Ornamental Artist Manufacturer (Of Glass Specialities) employing 26 persons[41]. The father and son team gave up their own business interests and in 1884 joined Webbs' where they designed and crafted cameo work, including snuff bottles. Daniel Pearce had obviously worked in the Stourbridge area previously. In 1871 he lodged at the house of Frederick Englebert Kny in Collis Street, when he is described as a chandelier manufacturer[42].

Peach glass was introduced in 1885. It was described as 'a new art glass—a delicate blend of colour, shaded so as to resemble a peach.'[43] It was a cased ware shading from yellow to cherry-red in the upper portion. Stevens and Williams' *Peach Bloom* was very much the same in appearance. On 11th September 1886 Thomas Webb and Sons Ltd acquired the sole right to the patent of *Burmese* glass in England. This beautiful coloured glass shades gradually from cream to pink. The main colouring agent is uranium oxide and the parts reheated by exposure at the furnace mouth changed from cream to pink. A large range of articles decorated in this fashion was produced, including small vases in many shapes, fairylights and table centrepieces.

In November 1886 the firm became a public company. A prospectus was issued on the 18th of the month and the subscription list closed five days later[44]. Walter Wilkes Webb and his brother Charles Webb became joint managing directors, with Clement F. Wedgwood also on the board. Charles Webb leased Dennis Hall from the company. Thomas Wilkes Webb was only aged fifty but his health was failing. He made his will on 2nd May 1885 and after the restructuring of the business he retired.

Sometime before 1887 Edward Webb's manager, Arthur John Nash, was tempted away from his position at the White House Glassworks to Dennis Glassworks, where he worked with the Woodall team. A patent for *Old Ivory* was taken out on 30th November 1887. It was cameo glass carved in Chinese and Japanese styles to simulate old carved ivory. Thomas and George Woodall used oriental and East Indian *objets d'art* as models and other members of the Woodall team: Jules Barbe, Jacob Facer[45] and Arthur John Nash all produced designs. Their first productions met with royal favour and were purchased by Queen Victoria. This inevitably led to an ever-increasing demand from the public.

In 1888 a design called *Old Roman* was introduced. This led to a complaint from James Couper & Son of Glasgow, alleging deliberate copying and infringement of their copyright of *Clutha* glass[46]. While the two designs are similar, *Clutha*[47] glass is distinguishable by speckles of aventurine in the metal.

In 1888 Webbs' exhibited at the Melbourne Exhibition in Australia and won a Gold Medal[48]. Zoomorphic enamelled glass decorated by Jules Barbe was exhibited at the Australian Centennial Exhibition. These were designs based upon animal shapes. They were described as 'a collection of vases painted in enamels, includes some extraordinary shapes.'[49] The pattern books[50] of the period show many designs in this style, involving animals such as turtles and frogs.

The final polishing of cut glass with acid began in the eighteen-eighties. At Webbs' the first documented example is pattern number 17723 of 1889 alongside which a note is written 'first large piece polished by acid.'[51] In 1889 the firm took out a patent for making satin glass with cameo designs. Acid was used to produce the cameo effect, but great care was required to avoid revealing the air traps in the satin glass beneath.

In 1889 Webbs' won the Grand Prix at the Paris Exhibition. This was for a magnificent chandelier rearranged to carry ninety candlelights based on the one that won the Grand Prix in 1878[52]. They also exhibited cameo and cut glass. The Prince of Wales, later to become King Edward VII, took a keen interest in the glass exhibits and the cameo work shown by Webbs'. He spoke several times to Thomas and George Woodall about the intricacies of their work. The Woodalls were principally assisted by John Thomas Fereday[53], William Hill[54], Tom Farmer[55], Harry Davies[56], William Mullett[57], G. Round, J. Reynolds and Mr Beddard. At the peak, seventy craftsmen worked in Webbs' cameo department.

Thomas Wilkes Webb died at his home, The Mount, on 21st January 1891, aged fifty-four, after many years of illness[58]. When his will was proved[59], his estate was valued at £4,715. This is not a vast amount by contemporary standards, considering the pre-eminence of the firm.

In 1891 Charles Webb lived at Dennis Hall, described as the

'Managing Director of glass manufactory.' The only other inhabitants of the large mansion were his wife Maria Louisa, and three servants. It is interesting that the house had changed its appellation from Dennis House in 1881 to Dennis Hall by 1891[60]. Walter Wilkes Webb lived at 5 Clifton Street, Stourbridge[61].

At the Chicago Exhibition of 1893 Thomas Webb and Sons Ltd displayed prestige cameo work, predominantly by Thomas and George Woodall. It was effective in attracting American attention, which has remained high to this day. There is probably more cameo glass in museums and private collections in the USA than remains in England.

In 1895 Arthur John Nash left Stourbridge and went to the United States. He was a great loss to the district, having been crucial to the success of Edward Webb at the White House Glassworks, before joining Webbs. He began experimental work in Boston then later joined Louis Comfort Tiffany at his Corona Glassworks. His sons, Arthur Douglas Nash and Leslie Nash, joined him there. His technical skill accounted for much of Tiffany's success.

In 1896 Pottery Gazette complimented Webbs' 'Engraved Rock Crystal.' 'Rock Crystal' was produced throughout the eighteen-eighties and nineties by Frederick Englebert Kny and William Fritsche.

In 1897 Thomas Wilkes Webb's oldest son, Thomas Ernest Webb[62], left the family firm of Thomas Webb & Sons, to found the firm of Thomas Webb and Corbett at the White House Glassworks. His younger brother, Charles Walter Herbert Webb[63] followed him shortly afterwards.

Walter Wilkes Webb retired from his position of joint managing director in 1899 due to ill health, although he was to live for another twenty years. Charles Webb retired as joint managing director in 1900 and Congreve William Jackson became the managing director. Jackson had been in charge of the firm's London office, but went to Stourbridge when a vitalising force was needed to take charge of their manufacturing affairs. This was at the suggestion of Cecil Wedgwood, who had a financial interest in the firm at the time[64].

In March 1902 Thomas Webb & Co. served notice on all union members it employed. This was the consequence of a dispute over the replacement of a servitor who had left the firm by a footmaker of the firm's own choice, instead of the man put forward by the union[65]. Webbs' then advertised for non-union labour and, with its help, reopened within a fortnight[66]. The dispute spread to three other firms who refused to stop making goods for Webbs': Webb, Shaw & Co. of Dial Glasshouses, L. & S. Hingley & Co. of Albert Glassworks and A. & J. Davies of Parkfield Glassworks. The lockout at Webbs' continued for many months. At the end of 1902 the union arranged for the emigration to America of some of the workers still affected. Thirteen left for America during the following year, of whom three returned by December 1903[67]. Initially there were a hundred and twenty men on strike or locked out, and there were still forty-six out in July 1903[68]. Fifteen remained out of employment in December 1904[69]. Despite the longevity of the dispute, the Times commented on the lack of animosity between employer and employed. It pointed out that the quarrel was between Webbs' and the union, rather than between the firm and its workmen[70].

Glassmaking trade unionism started in the eighteen-thirties and peaked with a rash of strikes at the end of the eighteen-fifties. From then on relationships between employers and employed matured and stabilised so that by 1903 the employers no longer required their mutual defence organisation. On 23rd May 1903 the County Express reported the winding up of the Midland Association of Glass Manufacturers. Thomas Webb and Sons was one of the eight firms that were still members at the time of its demise.

In 1907 Thomas Webb and Sons Ltd. supplied lead crystal glassware for use on the great battleship, *HMS Dreadnaught*. The navy previously used less expensive soda-lime glass, but when a salvo was fired, the shock was so great that the glass shattered:

'Before undergoing her gun-firing trials H.M.S. Dreadnaught was fitted out exclusively with Glass supplied by Thos. Webb & Sons Ltd. Those trials were exceptionally severe, the concussion being so great as to make the huge vessel heel over, and to drive it sideways several yards through the water. Yet, on her return it was found that no glass whatsoever had been broken during the time she had been at sea—a remarkable testimony to the strength of handmade glass, and its power of resisting shocks of no ordinary severity.'[71]

In 1908 Thomas Webb & Sons staged a spectacular show at the Franco-British Exhibition held at White City, in the form of an operational glasshouse. A hundred and fifty thousand people, including Queen Alexandra visited it. Pieces were exhibited by George Woodall, Jules Barbe and William Fritsche[72]. The company won a Grand Prix for table and ornamental glass.

In 1911 Pottery Gazette reported on Webbs' products at the Turin Exhibition. Their commentator praised the cameo vases and plaques of George Woodall and stated:

> 'A notable feature is the collection of cut-glass electrical fittings, some richly gilt. These must have a truly dazzling effect when lit up. Several of them represent birds—owls or parrots—swinging on golden hoops.'

The Victorian era had passed, although some aspects of Victorian style stubbornly persisted through the reign of King Edward VII. The Queen had died in 1901 and a whole generation of the Webbs and the craftsmen who brought the firm so much fame began to retire and pass away in her wake. Daniel Pearce was one of the first. He retired in 1902 and died on 7th February 1907 at his home in Amblecote[73]. Charles Webb had left Dennis Hall—where he lived for most of his life—and moved to Claremont, Kingswinford in 1904. He died there in 1908[74], aged seventy-two. In his will[75] he was described as a gentleman of Claremont, Kingswinford. Like his brother, he left a modest estate valued at £436 2s 6d and did not mention his business activities. George Woodall retired at the end of 1911. He continued to work in a workshop at the rear of his house until shortly before his death in 1925[76]. Some say the pieces of cameo glass he produced there were among his finest. He was also a photographer and his studio was shared between carving and photography. Because of this, many of Woodall's own photographs of his cameo work still exist today. Walter Wilkes Webb died on 8th July 1919, aged seventy-five. In his will[77] he was described as a gentleman of High Green, Cannock. Like both of his brothers he left a modest estate, valued at £2,673 2s 8d, and did not mention his business activities.

With the ending of the First World War trade gradually began to recover. A private limited company, Thos. Webb and Sons Limited, was formed on 25th June 1920. Thos. Webb and Sons Limited then merged with The Edinburgh & Leith Flint Glass Co. and became part of a new company, Webb's Crystal Glass Co. Ltd., based in London. Congreve William Jackson retired as managing director and set about creating his own business. The reorganisation resulting from the change of ownership at Webb's upset many members of staff. In 1922 several department managers: the designer, the accountant, and several skilled craftsmen left and joined Jackson's Stourbridge Glass Co.,[78] where they commenced manufacture of crystal glassware in competition.

Because of the decline in the cameo trade[79], John Thomas Fereday turned his attention to engraved glass and introduced the *Dynasty* crystal range. This used Egyptian motifs and such a set was chosen for a wedding gift in 1922 to HRH The Princess Royal. Fereday signed the sets. Fereday worked at Webb's for over forty years until he retired in 1922. He was an executor of George Woodall's will when it was proved on 22nd May 1925. Fereday did a fair amount of work on the borders and detail of the Woodall plaques and executed much of the geometric work. His favourite colour for cameo was yellow.

During the First World War the Ministry of Munitions requested Thomas Webb and Sons to specialise in electric lamp bulbs, glass tubing and rod. By 1923 the firm produced 400,000 bulbs per month besides six to eight tons of tubing and glass rod. Certain lines of chemical ware, such as funnels, test glasses and gas bottles were also produced. Unlike several local firms, output of table glass was maintained[80].

The nineteen-twenties were marked by the deaths of the younger generation of Webb's craftsmen. William Fritsche, of Collis

Street, Amblecote, died on 24th March 1924[81]. Before this, from 1886 to 1892, he owned the Red Lion public house in Brettell Lane[82]. Jules Barbe left Stourbridge in 1925 and subsequently died in Switzerland in 1929[83]. George Woodall died on 25th March 1925[84]. Little quality cameo glass was produced after this date. Woodall's house in Stream Road, Kingswinford was used for many years as a dental surgery and is now occupied by a branch of the TSB bank. His brother Thomas Woodall died in 1926[85], aged seventy-six.

In 1930 Webb's acquired the business of Henry G. Richardson and Sons[86]. After almost exactly a hundred years, the ownership went full circle and reverted to the firm whose founder provided half the capital for the original partnership in 1829. Webb's continued to produce Richardson patterns until the death of Ben Richardson in 1956.

Carl Gottwald Sven Harald Fogelberg was appointed General Manager of Webb's in 1932. Fogelberg had been managing director of the Swedish Kosta Glassworks and he transformed the works and particularly the firm's designs. His wife Anna worked as a designer and produced her own version of the then popular cactus design, in typically Scandinavian style, on a clear glass vase with a black foot. One of Fogelberg's first modernisations was to convert the furnaces from coal to oil firing in 1933[87]. Fogelberg was appointed managing director in 1955, a post he held until he retired in 1963. He eventually died at his Hagley home on 10th May 1971[88].

David Hammond[89] was appointed chief designer in 1951. Like John Luxton[90] he had trained first at Stourbridge College of Art followed by the Royal College of Art. He specialised in designs that subtly combined shallow intaglio cutting with engraving. He designed the *Bodiam* and *Frensham* ranges.

A further change of ownership took place in July 1964 when Webb's Crystal Glass Co. Ltd. was acquired by Crown House Ltd. Roy S. Uffindell became the chief executive. Under Uffindell's leadership another phase of modernisation took place. In 1966 a new cutting shop and warehouse were built and the factory was reorganised onto one floor on a flow line basis[91]. In 1971 Webb's Crystal Glass Co. Ltd. merged with Dema Glass Ltd., the principal table-glassware subsidiary of Crown House Ltd.

In 1978 Webb's won the Supreme Award at the International Spring Fair held at the National Exhibition Centre. It was received by managing director, Eric A. Stott, exactly a hundred years after Thomas Wilkes Webb won the *Legion d'Honneur* at the 1878 Paris exhibition.

The nineteen-seventies and eighties were not marked by any significant awards, but were years of modest and steady progress. Stanley R. Eveson retired as technical director in 1978 and both Roy S. Uffindell and Eric Stott retired in June 1984.

Then, in 1987 there was a change of ownership that was to have fatal consequences for the once proud firm. The conglomerate Coloroll Group Plc took control of Thomas Webb and Edinburgh Crystal. During the nineteen-eighties large companies were struck by two separate, but related phenomenon; the power of brand marketing and—in the retail arena—design co-ordination. Grand Metropolitan Plc set a trend for powerful brand marketing by placing a valuation on its brand names in the company's balance sheet. Companies such as Laura Ashley earned great profits by marketing collections of co-ordinated fabrics for curtains, carpets and furniture coverings. Coloroll, led by John K. Ashcroft, brought these two principles together and went on the acquisition trail, buying fabric manufacturers, wallpaper manufacturers, carpet manufacturers, pottery firms and eventually Webb's glass business. Nigel Woodlands became the new managing director. One of their first actions was to dispose of the superb collection of Webb's finest pieces assembled after great effort by Stanley R. Eveson[92]. This brought universal opprobrium on Coloroll and the threat of court action as twenty-three out of three hundred and eighty-nine pieces were disposed of overseas without the requisite export licences. Customs and Excise officers promised an investigation but before any successful outcome could be obtained, Coloroll Group Plc collapsed into receivership in 1990. The receivers of Coloroll Tableware Ltd. attempted to find a buyer for the works, but could not. In November 1990 the company was bought by its management. Production ceased at Dennis Glassworks and was moved to Edinburgh Crystal. On Thursday 24th January 1991, the equipment was auctioned in the cutting shop by Nottingham auctioneers, Walker, Walton and Hanson. The auction catalogue lists five hundred and forty-nine lots consisting of: furnaces, glasshouse pots, acid polishing equipment, annealing lehrs, glassmakers' tools, pot changing equipment, glass cutting lathes, and roughing and smoothing wheels. Much of the better equipment and moulds had been removed to Edinburgh Crystal. A group of ex-Webb's workmen bought equipment and cutting lathes and formed a new company, Dennis Hall Co-operative Crystal Ltd. Dennis works stood empty, the unsold furnaces dismantled and the entire five-acre site, with Dennis Hall at its centre was advertised for sale.

The last remnants of this famous business are about to disappear. Hassall Homes bought the site in 1992 and have built houses on the site. Dennis Hall was advertised separately, suitable for a fine corporate headquarters[93]. However, no purchaser appeared and sadly this once fine mansion is falling to rack and ruin.

---

1 H.W. Woodward, *"Art Feat and Mystery" The story of Thomas Webb & Sons, Glassmakers* (1978), p15.

2 Infra, Coalbournhill, Audnam and North Street Glassworks.

3 £17 5s.

4 Tithe apportionment, 1856.

5 Thomas Wilkes Webb, son of Thomas Webb and his wife Elizabeth, nee Hemming, b. 9th Oct 1836, Stourbridge, bap. 9th Nov 1836, Oldswinford.

6 PRO, 1861 census RG 9/2068 ED21 Sched 223 shows Thomas Webb as glass and iron manufacturer.

7 Charles Webb, son of Thomas Webb and his wife Elizabeth, nee Hemming, b. 5th Jun 1835; bap. 2nd Jul 1835, Oldswinford.

8 William Taylor Copeland, b. 24th Mar 1797, Stoke, only son of William Copeland; Manufacturer of porcelain at Stoke from 1833; Sheriff of London and Middlesex, 1828-29; Alderman of Bishopsgate Ward, 1829 to death; Lord Mayor, 1835-36; MP for Coleraine, 1833-37; Stoke, 1837-52, and 1857 - 6th Jul 1865; d. 12th Apr 1868, Russell Farm, Watford, Hertfordshire.

9 Stanislav Urban, *A Parable of Lithophanies*, Glass Review 7. (1971), pp 200-205, describes the Fritsche family, without quoting detailed sources.

10 PRO 1881 census of Kingswinford, RG11/2891/12/16.

11 Thomas Webb, d. 14th Dec 1869; bur. Wordsley, family sandstone tomb.

12 PRO, Will of Thomas Webb, 26th Feb 1870.

13 Walter Wilkes Webb, son of Thomas Webb and his wife Elizabeth, nee Hemming, bap. 24th Jan 1844, Amblecote.

14 Joseph William Webb, son of Thomas Webb and his wife Elizabeth, nee Hemming, bap. 17th Jul 1848, Amblecote. Joseph William married Fanny Yapp. In 1889 with their ten children they emigrated to Victoria B.C., Canada, where Joseph William worked for a new park that was being built. He died in 1922.

15 Henry Arthur Webb, son of Thomas Webb and his wife Elizabeth, nee Hemming, bap. 5th Sep 1842, Amblecote.

16 PRO, 1871 census, RG10 3021 ED21 Sched 94.

17 PRO, 1871 census, RG10 3021 ED21 Sched 95.

18 Thomas Woodall, son of Thomas Woodall and his wife Emma, nee Bott, b. 25th Jun 1849, Wordsley.

19 George Woodall, son of Thomas Woodall and his wife Emma, nee Bott, b. 15th Aug 1850; bap. 6th Oct 1850, Wordsley.

20 1829-1870.

21 Infra, Wordsley Flint Glassworks, 1853.

22 PRO, 1871 census, RG10 3021 ED21 Sched 173; PRO, 1881 census RG11 2890/48/49.

23 Ibid, G.W. Beard.

24 Supra, Red House Glassworks.

25 PG, Feb 1877.

26 C. Manley, *Decorative Victorian Glass* (1981), p96.

27 Art Journal, 1878 p19.

28 Victoria & Albert Museum, C.32&A-1960, Neg. HE397.

29 Infra, North Street Glassworks.

30 Infra, Coalbournhill.

31 I. Wolfenden, *English 'Rock Crystal' Glass 1878-1925* (1976).

32 Ibid, Stanley R. Eveson.

33 PRO, 1881 census of Amblecote RG11//2890/80/11 shows Jules Barbe, b. 1847 in France, as an Artiste Ceramiste, lodging in Main Road, Amblecote.

34 Anon, *The Black Country and its Industries* (1903).

35 William and Mary Beilby were famous eighteenth-century enamel painters. William (1740-1819) and Mary (1750-1797) were children of William Beilby senior, silversmith of Durham, and his wife Mary, nee Bainbridge. Op cit

James Rush, *The Ingenious Beilbys* (1973) and James Rush, *A Beilby Odyssey* (1987).

36 Charles Webb married Maria Louisa Hick of Bath in 1865. Their family bible recently came to light under tragic circumstances. On 23rd June 1978, a terrorist gang went to the Elim Pentecostal Mission near Umtali, Rhodesia, and murdered thirteen British nationals including a three-week-old baby and five children under six years old. During the follow-up operation a large bible was found, discarded in the bush. It is inscribed 'Charles Webb and Maria Louisa Hick, married at St. Michael's, Bath - Apr 25 1865'. The bible is now in the possession of Mr S.R. Simpson of Benoni, South Africa.

37 PRO, 1881 census of Kingswinford, RG11/2891/142/6.

38 Ibid, G.W. Beard.

39 1817-1907.

40 Lionel Harvey Pearce, son of Daniel and Anne Elizabeth Pearce, b. c1852 Islington; d. 1926.

41 PRO, 1881 census of London, RG11/0065/62/25.

42 PRO, 1871 census RG10 3021 ED21 Sched 173.

43 PG, 1885, p229.

44 PG, 1886.

45 PRO, 1891 census of Amblecote, RG12/2305 shows that Jacob (or Jabez) Facer was b. c1845 at Fairfield, Worcestershire and lived in Collis Street, Amblecote.

46 PG, 1888 p1115.

47 The Gaelic name for the River Clyde.

48 Ibid, G.W. Beard.

49 PG, 1st Dec 1888.

50 DA, Thomas Webb pattern books.

51 DA, Thomas Webb pattern books.

52 Ibid, D.R. Guttery, Plate 48.

53 John Thomas Fereday, son of Joseph Fereday, who ran a grocery shop in Church Street, Kingswinford and his wife Sarah; b. 18th Mar 1854, Kingswinford; PRO 1881 census of Kingswinford RG11/2893/6/6; d. 28th Feb 1942 at Llandudno.

54 William Hill, son of Thomas Hill and his wife Mary Ann, b. Wordsley, bap. 9 Apr 1849, Kingswinford.

55 1851-1933.

56 Harry Davies (1862-1937) was the oldest son of Alfred Davies (1838-1910) who was later to run Parkfield Glassworks.
57 1851-1933.
58 PG, Feb 1891.
59 PRO, Will of Thomas Wilkes Webb, 18th Mar 1891.
60 PRO, 1891 Census of Amblecote, RG12/2305.
61 Kelly's 1892 Directory of Worcestershire.
62 Thomas Ernest Webb, son of Thomas Wilkes Webb and his wife Helen Constance, nee Carter, b. c1869, Stourbridge.
63 Charles Walter Herbert Webb, son of Thomas Wilkes Webb and his wife Helen Constance, nee Carter, b. c1871, Stourbridge.
64 PG, Jul 1962.
65 Stourbridge Advertiser, 29th Mar 1902. It seems incredible that precisely the same circumstances caused the great strike and lockout forty-four years earlier. Supra, Audnam Glassworks.
66 Stourbridge Advertiser, 19th Apr 1902.
67 Stourbridge Advertiser, 25th Oct 1902 and 26th Dec 1903.
68 Stourbridge Advertiser, 13th Jun and 25th Jul 1903.
69 Stourbridge Advertiser, 3rd Dec 1904.
70 The Times, 17th Jan 1903.
71 PG, Jun 1907.
72 Ibid, H.W. Woodward, pp22-3.
73 PG, Mar 1907.
74 Charles Webb, d. 5th May 1908; bur. Wordsley, family vault.
75 PRO, Will of Charles Webb, 11th Jun 1908.
76 George Woodall, d. 27th Feb 1925; bur. Kingswinford; County Express, obituary, 7th Mar 1925.
77 PRO, Will of Walter Wilkes Webb, 20th Sep 1919.
78 Infra, Stour Glassworks.
79 Infra, Wordsley Flint Glassworks, 1899.
80 Ibid, Harry J. Powell, p171.
81 He was buried in Amblecote churchyard where his tomb is marked by a marble cross.
82 Stourbridge County Advertiser, Obituary, 29th Mar 1924.
83 Ibid, C. Manley, p44.
84 PG Apr 1925.

85 Thomas Woodall, d. 2nd Jun 1926; bur. Wordsley. A white stone memorial marks his grave.
86 Infra, Wordsley Flint Glassworks.
87 Ibid, H.W. Woodward, p25.
88 Ibid, H.W. Woodward, p25.
89 David Hammond (1931-2002) began as an apprentice glass designer at Webbs' in 1947 working under Tom Pitchford.
90 Infra, White House Glassworks.
91 PG, Oct 1966.
92 Dudley Evening Mail, 6th Oct 1987; Daily Telegraph, 8th Nov 1987; Express and Star 24th Nov 1987.
93 Express and Star, 28th Oct 1992.

CHAPTER 46

North Street Glassworks, Brierley Hill

Samuel Cox Williams and his oldest son, Joseph Silvers Williams[1] had gained control of the business they had been running in Moor Lane, but the old glassworks was in poor condition, exacerbated by subsidence caused by the extensive coalmining in the area. So in 1870 Samuel Cox Williams built a new factory, a quarter of a mile from the original Moor Lane Glassworks, on the site it occupied until recent times in North Street, near to Brierley Hill Church.

Building commenced on 20th January 1870 and was complete by August. The new works contained a twelve pot Frisbie furnace and an eight pot teaze hole furnace[2]. It is interesting that the new site was further away from the canal that served the old site, but next to the railway line. Clearly, the means of distribution were changing. The new furnace was fired and during heating several pots cracked, but the delay was not serious for on 31st August some glassmaking 'commenced at the new glass works with one chair and two others.' On 2nd September they 'filled nine large and two small pots with metal and commenced at the new place altogether.' Then, on 7th September they 'let out the old furnace.' As a celebration, the hundred or so employees were treated to a day's outing to the Clent Hills, a popular beauty spot a few miles away[3].

Samuel Cox Williams was concerned to ensure that his products competed with the finest in the district. In 1877 he recorded in his diary 'Drove to Wordsley to see John Northwood's Portland Vase . . . a great work of art.'[4] The same year his son, Joseph Silvers Williams, married Lucy Annette Thomas[5]. Their marriage certificate reveals that Samuel Cox Williams lived at Beech Tree

House, on Red Hill, Oldswinford. The newlyweds moved into Elmsley House, High Street, Amblecote, a few yards from Coalbournhill Glassworks. Joseph Silvers Williams was to spend his working life in the family business at North Street and helped expand the business to become one of the finest in the country.

Stevens and Williams had a prodigious output of glass, but had not yet developed the same reputation for innovation and design as some of their competitors, such as the Webbs or the Richardsons. For example, Stevens and Williams introduced the style of *Rock Crystal* in 1879, six months after Thomas Webb's. The first record of the term appears in Stevens and Williams' pattern books on 1st December 1879. The engravers included Frederick Kretschmann[6], Joseph Keller[7] and John Vernon Orchard[8]. Orchard's name first appears in the design books on 30th October 1883. Shortly afterwards he became the chief designer for Stevens and Williams.

William Henry Stevens, it has been noted, remained employed by the firm after the death of his father and former partner of the firm, William Stevens. On 8th December 1878 he patented a threading machine to mechanically apply narrow trails of glass, usually coloured, as a means of decoration. However, this was again following, rather than leading, fashion as it was two years after Hodgetts, Richardson and Sons[9] patented the first such machine. Despite this useful patented invention William Henry Stevens became a liability. Samuel Cox Williams recorded in his diary that he was continually lending money to William Henry Stevens and so finally, on 31st July 1880, he gave him a month's notice to quit. With his family, he followed his brother, Joseph Silvers Stevens, to Strathroy in Canada, but he died shortly after arriving. Samuel Cox Williams paid to bring his widow and children back to England[10]. Samuel Cox Williams was now sixty-two years old and it was possibly this traumatic event that led him to the conclusion that it was time to retire. He handed over control of the business to his son Joseph Silvers Williams who became chairman of the company, and moved from his house in Amblecote and retired to Parkfield, Stourbridge. Joseph Silvers Williams remained at Elmsley House, High Street, Amblecote[11].

Joseph Silvers Williams began to develop the business with a vigour equal to that shown by his father in his earlier years. In 1880 he employed Frederick C. Carder[12] on the recommendation of John Northwood. Carder's interest in art and design began at Leys pottery at Brockmoor run by his grandfather[13] and later his father[14] and uncles. He studied chemistry, electricity and metallurgy at Dudley Mechanics Institute and also attended Stourbridge School of Art. When aged sixteen, he paid a visit to John Northwood's decorating shop where he saw among other things the Portland Vase. He was 'struck with the possibilities of glass' and 'determined, if possible, to get into the business.'[15] Carder joined Stevens and Williams, aged seventeen, as a draughtsman and designer of shapes and applied decoration. Carder's first accepted designs were in the then fashionable cut crystal, which he considered 'the quintessence of vulgarity.' He soon set about replacing them with designs for coloured glass.

Then, in 1882 John Northwood was offered the position of works manager and artistic director by Joseph Silvers Williams, at the suggestion of Frederick Carder, clearly returning a favour. John Northwood had long been a business friend of Samuel Cox Williams and his son Joseph Silvers Williams[16]. He joined the firm about 24th April 1882 as 'artist Manager etc.'[17]. He moved from Elm Tree House, Back Lane, Kingswinford[18] to a house built specially for him on the works site. Because of Northwood's amazing inventiveness, this date is important as it heralds a change in design and the increased use of colour, first at Stevens and Williams, but subsequently throughout the Stourbridge district. With both Carder and Northwood working at Stevens and Williams, the whole direction of the firm changed. To the surprise of Joseph Silvers Williams their new designs met with almost instant success. Previously a follower, the firm became a leader in the field of design. From 1884 onwards there was an explosion of innovation from the firm.

In February 1884 John Northwood obtained a patent for a crimping machine[19]. This was for crimping or scalloping the top edge of an article while still hot. It was the fashion at the time for glass to be finished with such a wavy top. *Mat-su-no-ke* design by John

Northwood was registered in October 1884[20]. The decoration was Japanese inspired; *Mat-su-no-ke* translates as 'The Spirit of the Pine Tree'. Designs consisted of twisted, rustic tree-like stems, trailing around a glass body. Superimposed daisy-shaped flowers or rosettes, one overlapping the other, were applied in small clusters along the stem or branch. Joseph Keller—the main resident engraver of *Rock Crystal*—exhibited a notable example at the Wolverhampton Exhibition of 1884. Keller designed, and sometimes engraved, for Stevens and Williams from about 1880 to 1925. There are several *Rock Crystal* designs—usually described as 'polished bright'—in the Keller pattern book[21]. A *Rock Crystal* bowl designed by John Northwood and carried out by Frank Scheibner[22] was shown at the International Health Exhibition in London in 1884. The engraving on the bowl is in the Chinese taste and it was acquired directly by The Victoria and Albert Museum. The museum records[23] state that the bowl was executed by John Northwood and Frank Scheibner[24]. It was illustrated by J.M. O'Fallon in the Art Journal of 1885[25].

After the amazing flourish of 1884, there was still a continued flow of design registrations and patents. In February 1885 John Northwood obtained a patent for a 'pull-up machine.'[26] Its purpose is described to be for *ornamenting glass articles in the process of manufacture with threaded designs*. It is a year later before pull-up designs appear in Stevens and Williams' pattern books, suggesting there was some initial problem with the process. Northwood also patented, in that year, apparatus for shaping flowers. These flowers featured extensively on their applied work, such as *Mat-su-no-ke*. In 1885 Stevens and Williams patented *Damascened* glass with a deposit of silver on the surface, subsequently engraved; copper was also used. The patterns were oriental, consisting of formal arabesques, the work of Oscar Pierre Erard. In 1886 Stevens and Williams entered 'a choice collection of Table and decorative art glass in cut, engraved, crystal, cameo etc.' at the International Exhibition of Industry, Science and Art in Edinburgh. This earned them the Gold Medal Diploma. The official list of Jurors Awards makes it clear that the award was for Art Cameo Glass[27]. A design registration was taken out in 1886 for *Jewell Glass,* also described in the pattern books as *Sea Shell*[28]. This was a pattern for ornamentation using threading completely from top to pontil over dip moulding that was then cased in crystal. It featured vertical columns of small air blobs on a ribbed body. Also in 1886, pearl satin glass called *Verre de Soie*[29] was developed by Carder. This was an article made entirely of spiral shaped air pillars with the surface afterwards acidised to a satin finish[30]. It was part of the craze for air-trap decoration that developed from 1881 onwards. Most of the manufacturers brought out their own named varieties, all of which were developments of Richardsons' original patent of 1857[31]. In this case Stevens and Williams were a year behind Boulton and Mills' patent of 1885[32]. A style called *Tapestry* was patented in October 1886, designed by Oscar Pierre Erard. It featured a finely threaded surface with painted decoration in Persian, Indian or other Oriental styles that gave the effect of the horizontal ribs of a woven tapestry. This gave a design of great beauty, possibly one of the most dramatic designs in Victorian coloured glass. In February 1887 the pattern books had dozens of pull-up designs, suggesting the earlier problems with Northwood's invention had been overcome. The range was marketed under the name *Osiris*. A revolutionary design called *Moss-Agate* was developed in 1888 by John Northwood with help from the glasshouse manager, Will Bridges[33]. It was appreciated by Pottery Gazette in October 1888, whose commentator said 'It looks very well.' *Moss-Agate* glass has a deliberately crackled or crazed surface on semi-transparent alabaster; the alabaster being off-white to honey in colour and cloudy in appearance. *Moss-Agate* articles were usually enhanced with some discreet wheel decoration.

Samuel Cox Williams died at Oldswinford in 1889[34], aged seventy-one. When his will[35] was proved at Worcester, he left an estate valued at £6,012 1s 11d bequeathed in trust to his children and grandchildren.

Under the management of Joseph Silvers Williams and the inspirational guidance of Frederick Carder and John Northwood the firm continued to produce an endless succession of new designs.

Carder's earliest sketch book, dating from 1888 shows how he studied artefacts in South Kensington Museum such as Chinese porcelain and 17th century majolica as influence for products that subsequently appear in the pattern books. His third sketchbook picks up Persian designs from prayer carpets and marquetry inlaid in furniture. This found its way into the pattern books of 1887/9 as a design called *Intarsia*, the Italian word for inlaid marquetry. His fourth sketch book, which gives his address as Ivy Dean, John Street, Wordsley, includes his photographic permit for the Louvre and a pass for the Cluny Museum. It includes designs by Raphael, and many Persian designs.

On 9th May 1889 Oscar Pierre Erard and Benjamin John Round patented a method of electro-depositing silver designs on glass that was used to great effect by Stevens and Williams. *Moresque* oriental designs were prominent in the pattern books in 1889. This was another development of the technique of threading. A glass spiral was threaded on to shapes blown into dip moulds, carved on the inside with ogee-shaped arches and other Moresque patterns.

In 1898 a school of art was built in Wordsley[36]. The venture was typical of the late Victorian concern for library and school building. It was intended, and indeed did, provide an opportunity for aspiring youngsters to learn skills in art under the tutelage of the great masters of the day, including Frederick Carder who became its master. Frederick was commissioned to design two terra cotta panels for the facade and a frieze around the doorway. When the extension was added in 1907, his brother George[37] added two more matching panels with relief figures. The panels depicted classical female figures, one holding a Portland Vase. After many successful years as an art school, the building was later used as a community centre. Then in recent years it fell foul of planning blight. By 1991 it had fallen into a dangerous and dilapidated state and a plan was being discussed to remove the facade, including the panels, and to rebuild it on the Red House museum site. However, during 1992 the panels themselves were stolen, having been neatly removed from their niches in the building stonework[38]. No culprit for the crime has ever been identified, but as Frederick Carder's name is held in great reverence in America they were probably stolen to order. Certainly if they were ever to turn up in England their provenance would soon be recognised.

During the mid to late eighteen-nineties the final phase of Victorian engraving was exemplified by Stevens and Williams' exquisite intaglio work. Joshua Hodgetts[39] was in charge of a team producing some of the most elegant and sophisticated designs ever produced in the Stourbridge district.

A brief strike took place in 1896 over the offer of wages at less than standard union rate. The strike was soon over but its effect marks the decline of trade union power in the glass industry. Forty-two of the men complained they had been called out against their will and criticised the Central Secretary for calling the strike at all. Eight of those who had been called out returned to work before the final settlement, and continued to work with non-union labour[40].

The family dynasty was continued in 1897 when Joseph Silvers Williams was joined in the firm by his seventeen-year old son, Hubert[41].

John Northwood II[42] continued the pioneering work of his father and in 1900 he developed *Silveria*. This was a highly colourful, but abstract and florid design. *Silveria* articles have silver foil sandwiched between two layers of clear or coloured glass, with trails of coloured glass, often transparent green. Pieces are usually marked 'S & W', with the word 'ENGLAND' or a small fleur-de-lis. The technique was far from new; in fact it is as old as glassblowing itself, dating from Roman times. Both Edward Webb[43] and Joseph Webb[44] had produced varieties in 1883. *Silveria* differed from its competition because the silver foil remained intact rather than breaking into fragments.

Northwood's health began to fail and in 1901 Frederick Carder was appointed chief designer. This marks the end of what is known as Stevens & Williams' 'fancy' period. In glass and other decorative arts, the turn of the century marked a change in style away from the Victorian tradition towards the style known as Art Nouveau. In 1902 Stevens and Williams took out a patent[45], in which the firm is described as 'decorative art-glass manufacturers'; an interesting reference to the prevalent style.

Northwood died at Wall Heath on Thursday 13th February 1902, aged sixty-five. The County Express published a lengthy obituary in which he is called the 'grand old man' of the glass trade. It reports he had undergone an operation for eye cataracts in May 1901. The surgery was successful, but his general health was never again the same. In the biography written by his son, he describes that after the operation John Northwood remained as active as possible in the affairs of Stevens and Williams:

> 'although very ill he persisted in coming to the works and eventually had a seat made for him to sit by the furnace in the glass house on a Monday, when the glass house was not occupied by the glass makers . . . . Whilst sitting there he would receive reports and enquiries and give advice. At last he became too weak to leave his bed and there, sinking into a coma, he passed quietly away.'[46]

Northwood's funeral took place on Monday 17th February 1902 and as would be expected, many of those attending came from the glass industry. One newspaper account refers to a 'bitterly cold' day on which 'many hundreds' assembled to pay their last respects. Another lists many of Stevens and Williams' employees including Frederick Carder[47]. Northwood was buried in the family tomb at Wordsley which is mounted by a stone effigy of the Portland Vase, his most important work. It could be tempting fate to suggest it is amazing it has survived! He had made a will[48] in 1898 and when proved at Lichfield, it valued his estate at £5,622 14s 4d.

Later in 1902 Graham Balfour, director of education for South Staffordshire County Council asked Frederick Carder, now a Fellow of the Royal Society of Arts, to visit Germany and Austria and report on their glassmaking techniques. Carder fully expected to be promoted to art director after Northwood's death, but instead the position was offered to Northwood's son, John Northwood II. Carder was not happy, but his sponsors at South Staffordshire County Council were so pleased with his published report on Germany and Austria that they asked him to perform a similar mission in America. He left on 25th February 1903 and although he did not find his journeys enjoyable, found pleasurable company in somebody he later found to be Mark Twain. As part of his mission he met T.G. Hawkes, president of T.G. Hawkes and Co. who asked him to start a factory with him at Corning. Carder completed his tour and returned to England, but was so aggrieved he had been passed over as art director that he left England in July 1903 for new opportunities at Corning in New York State. He received 'a damned fine dressing down' from Graham Balfour of South Staffordshire County Council who had financed his trip. Stevens and Williams offered to triple his wages if he stayed. But at the age of forty he had achieved his ambition—a glass factory he could call his own. He became manager and a minority shareholder of the Steuben Glass Works, founded 9th March 1903[49]. Carder achieved enormous fame in America and today American collectors hold his name in total reverence. He eventually retired in 1959 and died on 10th December 1963, aged a hundred years old.

In 1903 Joseph Silvers Williams adopted the name Joseph Silvers Williams-Thomas[50]. This was at the request his father-in-law, Thomas Davies Thomas, who died without a son at his Denbighshire home, Parc Postyn, on 27th September 1902. Thomas Davies Thomas[51] had prospered as a draper in Bromsgrove. In 1858 he was appointed as a director of the Stourbridge and Kidderminster Banking Co. and became General Manager in 1867. During his involvement the bank developed strongly and steadily and in 1879 amalgamated with the Birmingham Banking Co. Thomas was allowed to live at the Bank House in High Street, Stourbridge for life and served on the board of the United Bank. His son Frank Davies Thomas LLM was Private Secretary to Lord Randolph Churchill from 1882 to 1890[52].

The heyday of Victorian design was over. The new century did not bring with it any new styles, only watered-down and cheaper versions of the previous century's. A mass market developed as the lot of the average working man began to improve, so now the emphasis was on quantity and not on quality. Stevens and Williams introduced *Crystal Cameo* in 1906. As the name implies, the glass was crystal and the decoration was carved in relief in the manner of a cameo. This new application of the cameo cutter's art was suitable for a variety of subjects, and it possessed some of the beauty, without the unavoidably high cost, of cameo glass[53].

The First World War brought great disruption to all trades and recovery was very slow after it ended. Shortly after it was over, in 1919, the firm was awarded the Royal Warrant by King George V[54]. Referring to their effort in the war years, Stevens and Williams wrote:

> 'While supplying very large quantities of table ware for the Army and Navy, we added the manufacture of chemical and medical glass ware in considerable variety, miners' lamp glasses, electric bulbs and lighting glassware. These developments and the serious depletion of our staff necessitated the abandonment of the production of decorative glass. For producing the various kinds of chemical, laboratory and lighting glass ware, a glass was used of a special formula.'[55]

The Duke and Duchess of York, later to become King George VI and Queen Elizabeth visited the works in June 1925. To capitalise on their Royal patronage, Stevens and Williams took out a patent in 1926 for 'Brierley Royal Crystal'. This has been the brand name of Stevens and Williams ever since.

Chief designer Joseph Keller retired in 1926 due to ill health[56]. The great craftsman Joshua Hodgetts retired in 1930, but despite being aged seventy-three, it was contrary to his wishes. During the depression, Stevens and Williams suffered like many other firms and had to cut costs. He was granted a pension of £1 per week on condition that he did not engage in his trade to the detriment of the company. Subsequently, he was informed that Stevens and Williams could no longer afford to pay him his pension and for the last three years of his life he worked freelance producing many prize pieces. He died on 12th May 1933, aged seventy-five[57].

During the late nineteen-twenties and early nineteen-thirties the Stourbridge firms attempted to incorporate the emerging Art Deco style into their products. However, the smooth style of Art Deco was so different to the previous tradition that few firms could create suitable products with their existing designers. At most of the Stourbridge firms outsiders were brought in. Stevens and Williams started the trend in 1932 with the appointment of Keith Day Pierce Murray[58]. Murray was a New Zealander trained as an architect but was unable to find much work in his profession during the depression. He therefore turned to the design of glass and later pottery. He began with Whitefriars at Wealdstone, Middlesex, then in 1932 agreed to work for up to three months of the year exclusively for Stevens and Williams. He worked with Stevens and Williams for seven years producing about a hundred and fifty designs each year. Some of his designs were large vases and dishes in heavy metal decorated with facet-cutting reminiscent of early Georgian work. He also designed in the contemporary genre, still usually in thick-walled glass. The British Museum has an example of his work, in the form of a vase, reminiscent by its decoration of a cactus$_{59}$.

Joseph Silvers Williams-Thomas OBE, JP died on 11th October 1933 and control of the business passed to his son Hubert Silvers Williams-Thomas$_{60}$. John Northwood II retired in 1946$_{61}$.

During the Second World War, production was mainly for military purposes such as radar tubes. After the disruption of the war, the family began to get back to business. Reginald Silvers William-Thomas$_{62}$ returned in 1946, having commanded an artillery battery during the war and risen to the rank of Lieutenant-Colonel in the Joint Allied SHAEF headquarters in Brussels. He had started at the works in 1931 and worked his way through all the departments before the outbreak of the war. He began to rebuild and reorganise the factory and it was completely remodelled and streamlined in 1949. The two old furnaces and their cones were demolished and replaced by modern furnaces in far more spacious buildings.

By 1956 Hubert Silvers Williams-Thomas FRS was chairman and his son, Colonel Reginald Silvers Williams-Thomas DSO, TD, JP was managing director$_{63}$. The remainder of the board of directors was Colonel Taylor, Howard Fletcher, John Northwood II, and Percy Scriven. Harry Whitcroft, foreman of the engraving shop became Works Manager. Tom Jones became the chief designer that year. His designs, particularly decanters and glasses, are acclaimed for their subtlety, achieving both balance and proportion. He was responsible for the development of Deanne Meanley, whose work reflected the grace and simple form found in his own work.

The tradition of Royal patronage continued with visits from

Her Majesty the Queen and HRH Prince Philip on St. George's Day 1957, The Princess Margaret and The Earl of Snowdon on 1st November 1966 and The Princess of Wales on 23rd May 1985. Joe Bridges, the glasshouse manager was frequently called upon to be the tour guide.

Hubert Silvers Williams-Thomas FRS died in 1973 and control of the business passed to his son Reginald. Lt. Col. Reginald Silvers Williams-Thomas DSO, TD, DL retired from the business in 1985 and died five years later on 4th November 1990, aged seventy-six.

The company continued in business making mainly traditional cut crystal glass. In common with many other British businesses output was reduced and staff were laid off during the recession of early 1991.

The firm was clearly struggling and chairman David Williams-Thomas announced the sale of the Royal Brierley museum collection housed in Honeyborne House. Sotheby's auctioned the collection of 289 pieces on Tuesday 3rd March 1998. The sale raised £311,443, which was expected to be used to build a new visitor centre and to be invested in training.

The business was purchased by Epsom Enterprises in 1999, who announced plans to relocate to a new site at Merry Hill with a visitor centre attached to the factory. However, this did not occur and the business was put up for sale in May 2000. Several investors expressed an interest, but none of the schemes came to fruition and the firm closed and called in receivers in October with the loss of 230 jobs. The remaining business was purchased at the end of 2000 by a consortium led by Tim Westbrook, of Royal Worcester Porcelain. In January 2002 Royal Brierley Crystal re-opened, with a £650,000 investment at Tipton Road, Dudley, on a site adjacent to the Black Country Living Museum. Head glass-blower Walter Pinchers celebrated by blowing the first gather.

---

1 Joseph Silvers Williams, son of Samuel Cox Williams and his wife Ellen, nee Silvers, b. c1849, Brierley Hill

2 Royal Brierley Archive, Diary of Samuel Cox Williams.

3 Ibid.
4 Ibid.
5 Mar. Joseph Silvers Williams and Lucy Annette Thomas, May 1877, Clent.
6 PRO, 1881 census, RG11/2890 shows that Frederick (originally Fridoline) Kretschmann was born c 1849 in Bohemia and lived with his wife and daughter in Collis Street, Amblecote.
7 Joseph Keller, b. c1850 Meistersdorf, Bohemia. He attended art school in Steinschonau, was apprenticed at twelve as an engraver and became a journeyman at sixteen, when in 1866, he immigrated to Scotland. After working in Glasgow, Warrington and Edinburgh, he joined Stevens and Williams in 1870.
8 John Vernon Orchard, b. c1854, Birmingham; lived in Rectory Street, Kingswinford; PRO 1881 census of Kingswinford, RG11/2891/110/27.
9 Supra, Wordsley Flint Glassworks, 1876.
10 Royal Brierley Archive, Diary of Samuel Cox Williams.
11 PRO 1881 census of Amblecote RG11/2890/56/1.
12 Frederick C. Carder, son of Caleb Carder and his wife Annie, nee Weidlein, b. 18th Sep 1863 at Brockmoor, bap. 18th Sep 1864, Wordsley.
13 George Carder, b. c1796, Kingswinford; d. 1878.
14 Caleb Carder, son of George and Caroline Carder, bap. 26th Mar 1837, Brierley Hill.
15 Carder's own words.
16 Ibid, John Northwood II, p67.
17 Royal Brierley Archive, Diary of Samuel Cox Williams.
18 PRO, 1881 census of Kingswinford, RG11/2892/53/33.
19 Patent number 2508, 1st Feb 1884.
20 Design Registration 15353, 18th Oct 1884. *Mat-su-no-ke* articles usually have the number Rd 15353 etched or engraved somewhere on the body.
21 Ibid, I. Wolfenden.
22 PRO, 1891 census of Amblecote, RG12/2305 show that Frank Scheibner was born in Bohemia c1853. In 1888 he lived in Queen Street, Wordsley. In 1891 he lived in Villa Street, Amblecote.
23 Victoria & Albert Museum, 92-1885.
24 Stourbridge Almanac and Directory for 1888 and 1889.
25 Art Journal, 1885, p313.
26 Patent Number 2310, 20th Feb 1885.
27 Ibid, G.W. Beard.

28 Design registration number 55693, 6th Sep 1886. Most Jewell pieces are engraved Rd. 55693.
29 Glass of silk.
30 Ibid, John Northwood II, p105.
31 Supra, Wordsley Flint Glassworks.
32 Supra, Audnam Glassworks.
33 R.S. Williams-Thomas, *The Crystal Years* (1983), p18.
34 Samuel Cox Williams, d. 2nd Dec 1889; bur. Brierley Hill, family vault.
35 PRO, Will of Samuel Cox Williams, 7th Feb 1890.
36 County Express, 2nd Jul 1898 and 11th Feb 1899.
37 George John Carder, son of Caleb Carder and his wife Annie, nee Weidlein, b. c1869, Brockmoor. He succeeded his brother Frederick as master of Wordsley School of Art when Frederick left for America in 1903.
38 This audacious crime took place in broad daylight over a period of about two weeks. The author spoke to the shopkeeper opposite, who watched the men at work each day, on a fully scaffolded platform, assuming they were from Dudley Council.
39 Joshua Hodgetts, b. c1858, Kingswinford; d. 1933.
40 FGMM quarter ending 3 Oct 1896; Stourbridge Advertiser 3rd Oct 1896 and 2nd Apr 1898; County Express 28th Jan 1901.
41 County Express, 4th May 1957. Hubert Silvers Williams, son of Joseph Silvers Williams and his wife Lucy Annette, nee Thomas, b. 12th Aug 1880, Amblecote.
42 Heacock, Measell and Wiggins, *Harry Northwood, The Wheeling Years 1901-1925* (1991), p13 states that John Northwood II, b. 7 May 1870, Kingswinford, was a child fathered by John Northwood with Margaret Lawley, an office employee at Stevens and Williams. He was certainly living with Margaret Lawley, a glass etcher, described as her son in 1881, PRO 1881 census of Kingswinford, RG11/2891/101/9.
43 Infra, White House Glassworks, 1883.
44 Supra, Coalbournhill, 1883.
45 Patent number 247,653, 21st Jul 1902.
46 Ibid, John Northwood II.
47 Advertiser, 22nd Feb 1902.
48 PRO, Will of John Northwood, 15th Mar 1902.
49 Corning Evening Leader, 11th Mar 1903.

50 Ibid, R.S. Williams-Thomas, p5.
51 Thomas Davies Thomas, b. c1813 Builth Wells, Brecknockshire, Wales.
52 H.J. Haden, *The Glassmaking Stevenses*, The Glass Cone, Nos 34 & 35; C. Fonteyn, *A History of Banking in Stourbridge (Part 2)*, The Blackcountryman, Spring 1996, v 29, No 2, pp20-24.
53 Supra, Wordsley Flint Glassworks, 1899.
54 Ibid, R.S. Williams-Thomas, p56.
55 Ibid, Harry J. Powell, p171.
56 After the death of his wife Anne, nee Bate in 1901, Keller had lived with his second daughter Louisa Blanch Cartwright and her husband. It was at their home, 64 Talbot Street, Brierley Hill that he died in 1934.
57 Stourbridge County Express, Obituary, 20th May 1933.
58 1892-1981.
59 His work is featured in the Jun 1933 edition of Design for Today magazine.
60 Hubert Silvers Williams-Thomas lived at Broome House, in the village of Broome a few miles south of Stourbridge. This charming old house had been the home of Thomas Hill from 1780 to 1820.
61 Ibid, Heacock, Measell and Wiggins, p13.
62 Reginald Silvers Williams-Thomas, son of Hubert Silvers Williams-Thomas and his wife Eleanor, nee Walker, b. c1914.
63 L.M. Angus-Butterworth, *British Table and Ornamental Glass* (1956), p34.

CHAPTER 47

Kinver Street Glassworks, Wordsley

Kinver Street Glassworks operated in Wordsley from about eighteen-eighty, but very little is known about it. It stood on the south side of Kinver Street, near its junction with High Street. The factory did not have a cone like the eighteenth century glassworks.

During the eighteen-nineties it was occupied by Webb, Shaw & Co., before they moved to Dial Glasshouses in 1892. It is shown on the 1901 Ordnance Survey as disused$_1$.

---

1 1901 Ordnance Survey of Staffordshire, 1:2500.

CHAPTER 48

Eve Hill Glassworks, Dudley

Josiah Lane built Eve Hill Glassworks about 1888. It stood in Parkway Road, close to the traffic roundabout at St. James's Church.

Josiah's father, Thomas Lane[1] started a glassworks at Hampton Street in Birmingham in 1865. He had been involved in the glass industry for some time. In 1837 he was a 'Labourer in the admixture for glass'. In 1851 and 1861 he lived in Aston, working as a glass mixer[2]. He married a Birmingham girl in 1836[3] and their son Josiah[4] was born in 1837. Josiah worked with his father and younger brother William[5] in the Hampton Street glassworks and eventually took over running the business. Josiah married a glassblower's daughter in 1855[6]. In 1871 he and his family lived at 128 Hampton Street, Birmingham when he worked as a glassblower[7]. Thomas Lane died on 11th July 1877, by which time he was retired from the business. His will refers to him as 'Formerly of Little Hampton Street, Birmingham, glass manufacturer and publican, but late of Witton Road, Aston Juxta.' By 1881 Josiah and his family had moved to the pleasant suburb of Handsworth. He managed the glassworks while his son Thomas[8] was a clerk in the glassworks[9].

About 1888 Josiah Lane built the Eve Hill glassworks in Dudley, probably because of the cheapness of coal there and brought his son Josiah junior[10] into the Dudley business. His will shows he did not abandon the earlier works in Birmingham at this time, but ran both for a while.

The County Express of 23rd May 1903 reports the winding up of the Midland Association of Glass Manufacturers. Josiah Lane and Sons was one of the eight firms that were still members at the time of its demise. In 1905 the firm employed sixty-five people.

Josiah Lane senior died in 1906[11] at his home at 16 Aston Lane, Perry Barr, near Birmingham. He had made a will on 16th June 1900 with a codicil dated 10th October 1904[12]. The will describes him as a glass manufacturer in which he appointed his son, Josiah the younger, glass manufacturer of Park Villa, Grange Road, Dudley, as one of his executors. He left to him half of the shares and half of all debentures in his business, Josiah Lane and Sons Limited. The other half went into a trust for the benefit of the children of his late son Thomas[13]. He left instructions to 'sell and convert into money my leasehold manufactory and premises situate at Hampton Street Birmingham and my freehold manufactory and premises called Eve Hill Glass Works.' The codicil intended to provide adequately for the maintenance, education and home of his younger children during their minority. The net value of the testator's estate was £8,694 15s 7d.

Josiah junior continued the firm, trading as Josiah Lane & Sons. An advertisement placed in 1912 shows a wide range of colour and decoration on lampshades, including satin finish, opalescent patterns and cutting[14].

By 1923 the firm was running at a loss. Josiah junior, by then a Councillor for Dudley, informed his workforce that the audited accounts for 1922 and 1923 showed an average loss of £25 per week[15]. The firm managed to stay in business until 1932, when it closed in December: the last of the Dudley glassworks to survive. The closure was obviously not intended as the firm had a predated entry in the Dudley Almanac of 1933 as 'J. Lane & Sons, Park Road, glass manufacturers.'[16]

---

1 Thomas Lane, son of Joseph and Mary Lane, bap. 20th Sep 1812, Oldswinford.
2 PRO HO/107/2061 163/10 1851 census of Aston; PRO, 1861 census of Aston.
3 Mar. Thomas Lane and Alice Eliza , daughter of Benjamin Elwell, 29th May 1836, St. Mary's, Handsworth.
4 Josiah Lane, son of Thomas Lane and his wife Alice Eliza, nee Elwell, b. 11th Feb 1837; bap. 5th Mar 1837, St. Peter & St. Paul's, Aston.

5 William Lane, son of Thomas Lane and his wife Alice Eliza, nee Elwell, bap. 12th Feb 1850, Birmingham.

6 Mar. Josiah Lane and Mary Ann, daughter of Timothy Nicklin, 25th Feb 1855, Aston Juxta. Mary Ann lived with her parents at Great Lister Street. Aston, although she and her parents were born in Dudley. PRO HO/107/2061 Fol. 260 p17, 1851 census of Aston.

7 PRO, 1871 census, RG10/3119 Sched 140/Dist 7/pg 181.

8 Thomas Lane, son of Josiah Lane and his first wife Mary Ann, nee Nicklin, b. 10th Mar 1865, Branston Street, All Saints, Birmingham.

9 PRO, 1881 census of Handsworth, RG11/2836/31/9.

10 Josiah Lane, son of Josiah Lane and his first wife Mary Ann, nee Nicklin, b. c1861, Birmingham.

11 Josiah Lane, d. 5th Oct 1906.

12 PRO, Will of Josiah Lane, 31st Dec 1906.

13 Thomas Lane, son of Josiah Lane and his first wife Mary Ann, nee Nicklin, b. c1865, Birmingham.

14 Dudley Chamber of Commerce Handbook.

15 Ibid, Charles R. Hajdamach, p76.

16 Blocksidge's 1933 Almanac of Dudley, p124.

CHAPTER 49

Delph Bottleworks, Brierley Hill

James Wright[1] ran Delph Bottleworks in the area originally known as the Delph, now known as Silver End. It stood on the north bank of the Stourbridge Canal, 140 yards west of Sevendwellings bridge and traded as James Wright & Co. from about 1870 to 1900. The bottleworks was obviously built specifically on the canalside, as its only road access was a lane that ran south from Lower Delph to Sevendwellings bridge.

Wright's wife Sarah Ann was born at Greasbrough, Rotherham, so it seems possible that Wright met her while learning his trade at one of the bottleworks in South Yorkshire. In 1881 Wright employed thirty-three men, twenty boys and four girls[2]. Benjamin Richardson confirms that in 1886 Mr Wright was carrying it on.

On 30th November 1893, in a terrible accident, two men, Arthur Ryder[3] and Enoch Oliver[4] were overwhelmed by molten glass and killed. They had gone underneath the large Siemens tank to investigate a small leak of glass when one of the fireclay slabs forming the base of the tank collapsed into the tunnel.

Wright and Co. was in receivership by 1900[5]. The glassworks was closed and demolished shortly afterwards. The 1901 Ordnance Survey describes the site as 'Bottle Works (glass disused).'

---

1 James Wright, son of James and Susannah Wright, bap. 3rd Dec 1837, Brierley Hill.
2 PRO 1881 census of Kingswinford, RG11/2893/145/5.
3 Arthur Ryder, son of James Henry and Ruth Ryder, b. c1868, Wordsley

4 Enoch Oliver, son of Charles and Harriet Oliver, b. c1866, Brockmoor.
5 Kelly's Directory 1900 and Mark and Moody's Stourbridge Almanac and Directory for 1900 and 1901.

CHAPTER 50

Harts Hill Glassworks, Brierley Hill

William Harrop[1] started Harts Hill Glassworks with William Stevens[2] about 1875. It stood at the far end of Vine Street[3], on the eastern side of the Dudley Road, conveniently next to Woodside Colliery.

William Harrop honed his glassmaking skills working for his uncle, James Harrop, at his Bromsgrove glasshouse[4] probably since its opening in 1867. Prior to that is seems probable that he would have worked in the glass trade, as his father was a Brettell Lane glassblower. William Stevens had also been working for James Harrop since arriving in Bromsgrove as a sixteen-year old, having failed to be taken on as an apprentice by Boulton and Mills. Their partnership did not last long, as Bill Harrop wanted Stevens to do most of the work. Stevens returned for a short while to James Harrop's Bromsgrove glasshouse until he was able to start his own at Bournheath, Belbroughton in 1880.

In 1881 William Harrop lived with his family at Hope Cottage, 41 Stourbridge Road, Dudley, a Glass Master, employing sixteen men and seventeen boys[5]. The first reference to the firm is a trade directory listing 'William Harrop, Vine Street, Harts Hill, Glass Cutters and Manufacturers'[6]. The firm's output included vases, predominantly green. They also specialised in epergnes[7].

William Harrop and his wife Anna Jane baptised two children on 15th July 1882 at Brierley Hill when he was described as a glass manufacturer of Harts Hill. In 1885 the glassworks was offered for sale[8], although it appears not to have changed hands. In 1888 the firm traded as William Harrop & Co.[9] Although their operation was not on the same scale as many of the main Stourbridge firms, their premises obviously impressed a Pottery Gazette commentator who wrote:

> 'Messrs Harrop & Co, Brierley Hill. Their extensive premises are constructed and equipped to suit all the requirements for the manufacture of fancy, flint and coloured glass.'[10]

By 1892 another firm, Pearson & Insull, traded at Hart's Hill, Brierley Hill[11]. Simms suggests the Insull partner was a Mr T. Insull[12]. However, nothing is known about this venture. William Harrop still traded at Hart's Hill in 1904 as W. Harrop & Co., glass manufacturers[13].

Sometime around 1910 George Carder[14], brother of Frederick Carder[15], was appointed manager and created a style of glass called *Flambeau*, a copy of *Burmese*[16]. Harrop's business closed in 1916[17], but the glassworks appears to have continued in production under the ownership of James Round. In 1923 Round joined Lewis Lowe from Sheffield and the Dudley Drop Forging Company was established at the old glassworks premises[18].

---

1 William Harrop, son of Joseph and Sarah Harrop, bap. 25th Oct 1845, Kingswinford. PRO 1851 census of Stourbridge HO0107/2035/117 shows that Joseph Harrop was a glassblower living in Brettell Lane when William was aged five.

2 Supra, Coalbournhill Glassworks.

3 Known at that time as New Street.

4 James Harrop, b. c1817, Longport, Staffordshire was a glassmaker of Holloway End in 1851. In 1867 he paid £100 to purchase an old nail-shop and cottage at Alfred's Well, Worms Ash, near Bromsgrove and created his own glasshouse crib. Husselbee from Stourbridge was his head glassmaker. James Harrop ran the works until he died under peculiar circumstances, aged 69 and was buried in Bromsgrove Cemetery 8th Aug 1884. The evidence suggests that he was under mounting financial pressure and one version of his demise is that he committed suicide in his own glass furnace.

5 PRO 1881 census of Dudley, RG11/2878/115/49.

6 Stevens' Directory of Wolverhampton etc, 1879-80.

7 Ibid, C. Manley, p26.
8 Brierley Hill Advertiser, 18th Jul 1885.
9 Kelly's 1888 Directory of Staffordshire.
10 PG, Nov 1890.
11 Kelly's 1892 Directory of Birmingham, Staffordshire and Warwickshire.
12 Ibid, R. Simms.
13 Kelly's 1904 Directory of Staffordshire.
14 George John Carder, son of Caleb Carder and his wife Annie, nee Weidlein, b. c1869, Brockmoor.
15 Supra, North Street Glassworks.
16 Ibid, C. Manley, p26.
17 Ibid, C. Manley, p26.
18 Birmingham Post (Supplement) 25th Oct 1978.

CHAPTER 51

Wallows Street Glassworks, Brierley Hill

Very little is known about Wallows Street Glassworks, not even its proprietors. It was a late Victorian glassworks that stood on the west side of the Dudley Road in Brierley Hill, where a footbridge crossed the OWWR railway line.

The premises appear on the Ordnance Survey map of 1884. An extant catalogue, dating from sometime in the eighteen-eighties, shows many flower stands, engraved and etched vases. Other vases in ruby glass were decorated with applied acanthus leaves in crystal. A further pattern book dating from around the turn of the century shows mainly ruby glass.

Manufacturing must have ceased before 1901 as the premises are shown as disused on the Ordnance Survey map of that year[1]. The glassworks was demolished in the early nineteen-fifties.

---

1 1901 Ordnance Survey, scale 1:2500.

CHAPTER 52

Round Oak Glassworks, Brierley Hill

Round Oak Glassworks was another late-Victorian works. It stood on the east side of the Dudley Road, just north of Round Oak Station and backing onto the OWRR railway line and Round Oak Steelworks. In 1901 it had its own railway siding that probably brought coal from the nearby Himley Colliery pit No. 10[1].

The first reference to the works is one of strife. A dispute over the employment of additional men in 1886 led to a lockout of the men by the employers[2]. The firm traded as Smart Brothers, Round Oak Glass Works[3] and in 1890 advertised:

> 'Smart Brothers, Round Oak Glass Works, near Brierley Hill.
> Manufacturers of every description of Fancy glassware, cut, etched, and engraved Table Glass.'[4]

Their reference to table glass was repeated in 1892[5], suggesting this was the staple product.

The firm underwent a change of ownership and was operated about 1894 by Arthur Pearson[6]. Harry Pearson subsequently ran the firm which in 1928 traded as 'H. Pearson & Co., Round Oak, Brierley Hill (Flint)'[7].

The cone was still standing in 1959, a short way back from the main Brierley Hill to Dudley road[8].

---

1 1901 Ordnance Survey, scale 1:2500.
2 FGMM for quarters ending 27th Nov 1886 and 26th Nov 1887.
3 Kelly's 1888 Directory of Staffordshire.
4 PG, Apr 1890.
5 Kelly's 1892 Directory of Birmingham, Staffordshire and Warwickshire.

6 Ibid, R. Simms.
7 Kelly's 1928 Directory of Staffordshire.
8 Ibid, Sir Hugh Chance.

CHAPTER 53

Premier Glassworks, Brettell Lane

The Premier Glassworks is associated with the Haden family although it was commenced sometime before 1886 by a man called Evans, until he gave up and Thomas Haden$_1$ took over. The works stood on the south side of Brettell Lane, at its eastern end.

After the death of Thomas Haden, his widow Zipporah and her sons Zachariah$_2$ and James$_3$ continued the business$_4$. In 1888 the proprietor was Mrs Thomas Haden$_5$ and in 1892 Zachariah Haden$_6$. Zachariah Haden died in 1907$_7$ and his widow Sarah Elizabeth continued the business.

By 1913 Haden's products included ruby vases, flower stands, creams, sugars and butter dishes$_8$. The last reference to the firm is a trade directory of 1928 listing Mrs Z. Haden, Oak View, Brettell Lane, Glass Manufacturer$_9$.

---

1 Thomas Haden, son of Daniel and Hannah Haden, bap. 20th Jun 1830, Kingswinford. The 1881 census PRO RG11/2890/67/23 shows Thomas Haden, living in Brettell Lane, already described as a glass manufacturer.

2 Zachariah Haden, son of Thomas and Zipporah Haden, b. 27th Jan 1860, Kingswinford.

3 James Haden, son of Thomas and Zipporah Haden, b. c1867, Brierley Hill

4 Benjamin Richardson's notebook of 1886.

5 Kelly's 1888 Directory of Staffordshire.

6 Kelly's 1892 Directory of Birmingham, Staffordshire and Warwickshire.

7 Zachariah Haden, d. 6th Apr 1907; bur. Wordsley.

8 Ibid, Sir Hugh Chance.

9 Kelly's 1928 Directory of Staffordshire.

CHAPTER 54

Brewery Street Glassworks, Wordsley

The Parrish family were cutting glass on the site of the Brewery Street Glassworks as early as 1822 when it contained a house, glasscutting shop, corn mill, steam engine and garden[1]. It is not known when glass manufacture commenced on the site, although this is probably when the glassworks gained its name. It stood on the north side of Brewery Street[2], Wordsley, halfway between Rectory Fields and High Street.

Some time before 1881 Frank Passey[3] purchased the business, but continued to trade as J. Parrish & Co. Passey got into difficulty in early 1889 and attempted to sell the business. The name, goodwill and patterns were bought by Stevens and Williams in May 1889[4]. The firm's assets were auctioned and it was wound up in September 1889. Pottery Gazette reported the situation as:

> Total realised £1,777 9s 3d. The estate realised badly due to 1) wretched condition of the stock, which was overvalued by the debtor, it being badly kept and a large portion practically unsaleable. It required large expenditure to finish before it could be put on the market. 2) It was impossible to get rid of the place for over 6 months. 3) Many allowances had to be made for book debts.[5]

Samuel Elcock[6] purchased the glassworks in October 1889[7]. He had previously been a glasscutter living at the Crown Inn, High Street, Wordsley[8]. Little is know about Elcock's glassmaking activities, but he was one of the committee responsible for the building of the Wordsley School of Art and donated 10s to the subscription. The glassworks is clearly noted on the 1901 Ordnance Survey[9] and Elcock continued in charge[10] until 1910.

In 1910 Stuart & Sons bought the entire business when it had an eight-pot furnace and cutting shops on site. Stuart family reminiscences describe the difficulty of transporting glass by horse and cart from Brewery Street, over the canal bridge, to be acid-polished at the Red House. The business closed temporarily in 1931 due to the recession. The glasshouse closed permanently in August 1934, although the cutting shop continued to work until the beginning of 1942.

Stuarts' sold the site although the cone remained standing until 1946 when it was felled. The site was used by Fry's Diecasting and then by Cooksons. It is now covered by private housing.

---

1 DA, William Fowler's 1822 *Map of the Parish of Kingswinford*. Plot 643 shows the site owned and occupied by Mary Parrish.

2 Today this road is called Brierley Hill Road. However, before being named Brewery Street it was known as Bug Pool Road. The first change of name followed Samuel Oakes' development of the Wordsley Brewery in the eighteen-sixties. The business closed in Jun 1907 and the second name change followed some time after this.

3 The 1881 census PRO RG11/2890/56/1 shows Francis Passey, b. c1844, Worcester, glass manufacturer living at Coalbournbrook with his wife Mary and two servants.

4 PG, Jun 1889.

5 PG, Oct 1889.

6 Samuel Elcock, son of William and Maria Elcock, b. Wordsley, bap. 11th Aug 1854, Kingswinford.

7 PG, Nov 1889.

8 PRO, 1881 census of Wordsley, RG11/2891/73/12.

9 1901 Ordnance Survey of Staffordshire, 1:2500.

10 Mark & Moody's 1900 Almanac and Directory for Stourbridge & District.

CHAPTER 55

Stour Glassworks, Audnam

A plan for a new firm of glass manufacturers was conceived around July 1920 when Congreve Jackson announced his resignation from the position of managing director of Thomas Webb & Sons, Dennis Glassworks. He commissioned John Guest & Son, a local firm of builders, to build a one-floor factory at Wordsley on the banks of the Stourbridge Canal. The factory was to be known as The Stour Glassworks and the company was to be entitled Congreve Jackson Ltd. The glassworks was subsequently completed, the furnaces installed and by early 1921 the glassworks was ready for production. However, Jackson had a dispute with his builders and withdrew from the project leaving the property and the entire investment in the hands of the builder, Horace Guest. He therefore approached certain senior members of the firm of Thomas Webb and Sons about forming their own company to operate the new factory. Many of the staff were disgruntled with the changes taking place at Webb's Crystal Glass Co. Ltd. and left the Dennis firm to set up their own business. These included the accountant, several department managers, many skilled craftsmen and later the designer. Mr W.H. Aston$_1$ was appointed managing director. Mr A. Horton$_2$ became director and secretary. Mr W.A. Price$_3$ also became a director. The builder, Mr Horace Guest was appointed chairman. The other director was Mr H. Wilkinson, formerly the glasshouse manager for Webb's. With an initial seventy employees they formed the Stourbridge Glass Co. About half of them were experienced craftsmen from Thomas Webb & Sons, and the remainder from Stevens and Williams, Stuarts, and Webb Corbett$_4$.

The firm was registered under the name of Stourbridge Glass Co. Ltd. in October 1921. Production commenced in May 1922, specialising in full lead$_5$ crystal tableware. Their glass was hand blown and decorated in the Stourbridge tradition of cutting. The firm was immediately successful, taking orders from the retail trade ahead of production and in some cases even receiving payment for them. Mr J.H. Cuneen, formerly designer for Webb's joined the firm in 1923. By 1925 Horace Guest had achieved his objective of rescuing his investment and left the board of directors. Although some short-time working was being worked in several local firms, full employment was maintained until 1926.

Mr A.D. Price became a director in 1935 and Mr J.H. Cuneen became a director in 1936. The glassworks is shown on the 1938 Ordnance Survey map as 'Audnam Glass Works'. By the time of the outbreak of the Second World War the firm had prospered and risen to two hundred and fifty employees, probably the height of its prosperity. During the war years numbers employed fell back to about eighty and production was limited to soda lime utility ware and lamp casings.

After the end of the war, production of lead crystal was resumed in 1946. The range of goods produced was increased to include wine glasses, tumblers, vases, bowls, jugs and decanters. Almost all the glassware was decorated by cutting, intaglio or engraving. Extensive modernisation was carried out between 1947 and 1952. Mr R.H. Price became a director in 1947 and Mrs K. Wilkinson became a director in 1949.

A slump in trade with Australia and New Zealand was experienced in 1952: business that was never fully recovered. In 1957 Mr T.C. Edwards, well known in the refractories industry, became a director.

Mr W.H. Aston who had been the first managing director retired in 1960. His son Mr William H. Aston was appointed to the board as sales director. Mr T.C. Edwards took on the position of chairman. In 1962 the firm was employing a hundred and twenty people and operating two ten-pot gas fired furnaces. The bulk of the business was traditional shapes and decorations, cutting, intaglio and engraving.

The firm changed its name to Tudor Crystal (Stourbridge) Limited in 1972. However, business continued to decline and on Wednesday 11th September 1985 Tudor Crystal called in receivers. The entire business was bought for £285,000 by United Ceramic$_6$. By 1986 the firm was running with about seventy employees still producing top quality lead crystal ware.

Stour Glassworks (Tudor Crystal)

The late nineteen-eighties and early nineties were years of severely reduced trade. The firm went through a time of financial uncertainty but continued manufacturing and decorating top quality crystal ware in the finest Stourbridge tradition. In August 1992, faced with the cost of refurbishing its furnaces, the firm decided to cease production and concentrate on decoration only. The workforce was reduced to sixty.

Competition from cheap European imports intensified and the firm experienced a slump in sales. The workforce was gradually reduced until finally, on 23rd April 1994, the firm closed and the remaining ten craftsmen were made redundant. Managing director Philip Battin said 'We have a large factory site with overheads which are too great . . . It is the end of an era . . . Crystal glass is a luxury item which has suffered like other luxury products.'[7] The recession of the nineteen-nineties claimed another victim in the once prosperous Stourbridge crystal business. The moulds, patterns and outstanding order book were sold to Dennis Hall Co-operative Crystal Ltd.

---

1 Northern representative

2 Cashier and accountant.

3 Foreman of the cutting shop.

4 PG, Jul 1962.

5 Thirty percent red lead.

6 Express and Star, 6th Nov 1985.

7 Birmingham Evening Mail, Apr 1994.

CHAPTER 56

Dennis Hall Co-operative Crystal, Brockmoor

After the bankruptcy of Coloroll that led to the closure of Thomas Webb's in 1990, many skilled glassmakers were thrown out of work. Fourteen of them, led by John Kimberley and Gordon Noble, decided to pool their redundancy pay and start a new glass company of their own. In 1991 they secured premises on the Cookley Wharf Industrial Estate at Leys Road, Brockmoor, Brierley Hill and formed the firm of Dennis Hall Co-operative Crystal Ltd. On Thursday 24th January 1991, when the remaining assets of Thomas Webb's were auctioned, the fourteen directors purchased sufficient equipment to equip their works, except a furnace.

A single-pot gas fired furnace was constructed by Sismey and Linforth of Birmingham and the first melt took place on 14th August 1991. Arrangements were made with Plowden & Thompson of Dial Glasshouse to mix their batch for traditional Stourbridge full lead crystal. The day was a momentous one for the firm. None of the glassmakers had practised making glass for a year and on their opening day they were filmed by a BBC television crew who featured the firm in a series of programs called *Second Chance*.

By 1993 the works was melting two pots per week and burning £310 of gas per week. Most of the tasks of manufacture and decoration were undertaken on the premises, except acid polishing. A convenient deal was struck with four local firms of decorators by which blanks were supplied to them in return for acid polishing services. A range of patterns was created and the firm established a thriving trade.

The skills of the original fourteen co-directors were divided into nine glassmakers and five cutters. One of the fourteen retired and two left, leaving eight glassmakers and three cutters.

When Tudor Crystal closed on 23rd April 1994 the directors of Dennis Hall Co-operative Crystal Ltd. purchased the assets. This included the moulds, pattern books and the outstanding order book. This led to an immediate upsurge in the amount of work for the small team of craftsmen to produce.

The telephone line was transferred from Tudor Crystal and customers who had waited for up to two and a half months for their orders had to be satisfied. As none of the original Tudor Crystal staff had been employed, the Dennis Hall craftsmen had to learn the new patterns and complete an enormous workload. By working very long hours the small team of craftsmen not only kept its own customers happy, but also satisfied the backlog of Tudor Crystal orders and shipped a large order of ex-Thomas Webb pattern glass to Edinburgh Crystal.

Sadly, the company ran into difficulties and in March 2000 went into receivership. The Tudor Crystal brand was purchased by Plowden & Thompson Ltd of Dial Glassworks.

CHAPTER 57

Chronology of Styles

Dates	Monarch	Period	Style
1558-1603	Elizabeth I	Elizabethan	Gothic
1603-1625	James I	Jacobean	
1625-1649	Charles I	Carolean	Baroque (c1620-1700)
1649-1660	Commonwealth	Cromwellian	
1660-1685	Charles II	Restoration	
1685-1689	James II		
1689-1694	William & Mary	William & Mary	
1694-1702	William III	William III	Rococo (c1695-1760)
1702-1713	Anne	Queen Anne	
1714-1727	George I	Early Georgian	
1727-1760	George II	Georgian	
1760-1811	George III	Late Georgian	Neo-classical (c1755-1805) Empire (c1799-1815)
1812-1820	George III	Regency	Regency (c1812-1830)
1820-1830	George IV		
1830-1837	William IV	William IV	Eclectic (c1830-1880) Arts & Crafts (1880-1900)
1837-1901	Victoria	Victorian	
1901-1910	Edward VII	Edwardian	Art Nouveau (c1900-1920) Art Deco (c1920-1936)
1910-1936	George V		
1936	Edward VIII		
1936-1952	George VI		
1952-	Elizabeth II		

513

A

A. & J. Davies Ltd 438
Abbots Bromley, Staffordshire, Glass Manufacture 46
Aberbargoed, Wales, Glass Manufacture 371
Acid etching 181, 208, 276, 333, 336, 369, 370, 384, 388, 443, 501, 502
Act of Uniformity (1662) 89, 99, 138
Addenbrooke, Dorcas 70
Addenbrooke, Henry 62
Addenbrooke, John 70, 454
Albert Glassworks 440
Alen, Ann 418
Alexandra Palace, Exhibition of 1876 461
Alfold, Surrey 33, 34, 35, 37, 44
Alfred & James Davies 437
Allan, Rebecca 392
Allen, Ann 392
Alling, John 134
Alport, Margaret 432
Amblecote Glass Co. Ltd. 86
Amblecote Hall, Staffordshire 24, 68
America, emigration to 72, 204, 338, 467
America, exports to 78, 270
America, Glass Manufacture 204, 338, 368, 466, 484
Andrews, A.H. 208
Arnold, James 35
Arnott, Mary 261, 265
Art Deco 208, 390, 391, 486
Art Nouveau 341, 483
Ashcroft, John K. 471
Association of Glass Manufacturers 86, 141, 203, 227, 228, 232, 250, 251, 262, 335, 389, 407, 438, 441, 467, 493
Astley, Mary 70
Aston, W.H. 507, 508
Aston, William H. 508
Athersich, Samuel 135
Atkinson, Joseph 248, 249, 253, 314
Audnam Bank House 229, 230
Audnam Foundry 418
Audnam Glassworks 217, 241, 417
Audnam House 220, 223, 228, 231

B

Bacchus and Green 262, 265
Bacchus, George 265
Bacon, William 431
Badger Brothers & Co. 302
Badger, Edward 309
Badger, Esther 422, 427
Badger, Isaac 282, 300, 301, 302, 303, 304, 305, 306, 307, 308, 309
Badger, Sarah 155, 211, 344
Badger, Septimus 274, 303, 305, 309
Badger, Thomas 224, 276, 282, 300, 302, 303, 304, 305, 306, 307, 309, 310, 311
Badger, William Dixon 304, 310
Bagot, Sir Richard 46, 51
Bagot, Sir Walter 47, 51
Bagots Park, Staffordshire, Glass Manufacture 46, 47, 66
Bague, Elizabeth 109, 116, 117
Bague, George 108, 109, 113, 116,

117
Bague, Jeremiah 107, 108, 109, 112, 113, 115, 116, 117
Bague, Jeremy 106, 107
Bague, John 108, 112, 117
Bague, Mary 108
Bague, Millesenta 106
Bague, Nehemiah 109, 116
Bague, Susanna 116
Bagues Glasshouses 106, 244
Bainbridge, Mary 473
Balfour, Graham 484
Balguy, John 384
Ballynegeragh, County Waterford, Glass Manufacture 187
Bancroft, Ambrose 190
Banks, Caroline 200, 213
Banks, Eliza 374
Banks, Richard 200
Banks, Sir Joseph 80
Barbe, Jules 463, 464, 465, 468, 470, 473
Barclay, Lucy 93
Barker, Elizabeth 410
Barlow, Margaret 45
Barlow, William, Bishop of Chichester 45
Barnet Lane, Wordsley 334
Barrar, Carolina 167
Barrar, Elijah 167
Barrar, Henry 150, 161, 167
Batchelor, Benjamin 121, 148, 154, 194
Batchelor, Carolina 161, 167
Batchelor, Elijah 121, 154, 161
Batchelor, Elizabeth 151, 154, 155, 195, 211
Batchelor, Humphry 121, 149, 150, 154, 155, 160, 161, 195
Batchelor, Mary 100
Batchelor, Thomas 100, 104, 125, 131, 148, 151, 154, 155, 196, 211
Bate & Robbins 201
Bate, Anne 491
Bate, Benjamin 137
Bate, Mary 301
Bate, Sarah 308
Bate, Thomas 152, 153, 212
Batson, James 246, 253
Battin, Philip 510
Bayley & Pegg 431
Bayliss, Ann 412
Bean, Henry Lucas 184
Beare, Elizabeth 64
Beare, Leonard 73
Beazley, John 164
Becku, Anthony 32, 33, 35, 38, 49
Beddow, Susannah 435
Beilby, Mary 473
Beilby, William 473
Bell, Vanessa 391
Belle Vue, Belbroughton, Worcestershire 185
Belle Vue, Halesowen 223, 224, 237
Belle Vue, Stourbridge 399
Belrupt Glasshouse 31
Benedict, Samuel 168
Benjamin Littlewood and Son 83
Benson, James 246
Benson, John 245, 246
Benson, William 246
Bentley, Thomas 93
Berne, Jean 42
Berry, John 84
Berry, William 83
Betts & Co., Brandy distillers 405
Bewdley, Port of, Worcestershire 74, 100
Biddle & Cope 412
Biddle, John 401, 403, 411, 412
Biedman, Barbara 415
Biedman, Richard 407

Biggs, Elizabeth 145, 146
Biggs, Thomas 139, 146
Bigoe, Abraham 59, 61, 63, 64, 119, 120, 122, 126
Bigoe, Catherine 124, 126
Bigoe, Cicely 120, 122
Bigoe, Hester 64
Bigoe, Philip 124, 126
Bill, Lucy Mansfield 395
Bill, Robert 441
Bilston, Staffordshire, Glass Manufacture 269, 280, 322, 347
Bird, Isabell 256
Birmingham Banking Co. 485
Birmingham, Exhibition of 1849 329
Birmingham, Glass Manufacture 201, 204, 205, 214, 262, 263, 276, 341, 424, 493
Birmingham, Hospital 91, 92, 93, 355
Birmingham, School of Art 332
Birr Glasshouse, Kings County, Ireland 126
Bishops Wood, Eccleshall, Staffordshire 44, 45, 46, 56
Bisson, Arnoul 42
Blackburne, Alice Anna 270, 281
Blackburne, John 270, 281
Blackburne, Mary 281
Blackfriars Glasshouse 323
Blades, John 188
Blaenavon, Monmouthshire 152, 153, 212
Blagden, Sir Charles 80
Blair, Captain Alexander 82
Blakiston, Emma Francis 146
Blithfield, Staffordshire 51
Blizzard, Johannes 106
Bloomfield Mill, Tipton, Staffordshire 82

Blore Park, Shropshire, Glass Manufacture 44
Blundell, Mary 281
Bohemia 28, 325, 326, 489
Boland, Peter 417
Bolsterstone Glasshouse, South Yorkshire 285
Bolton (John) & Bowater 451
Bolton, John 182, 186, 406, 414, 449, 450, 451
Bolton, Margaret 186
Bolton, Sarah 414
Bolton, Thomas 74
Booker, Luke 292, 298
Bott, Emma 461, 473
Bott, John Thomas 332, 461
Boucher, Ben 275, 283
Boulton and Mills 228
Boulton and Mills Ltd 233
Boulton, Harry 232
Boulton, Howard Gilbert 233, 239
Boulton, Jane 228, 238
Boulton, Laura Mary 233, 239
Boulton, Matthew 79, 81, 91, 92
Boulton, Richard 228, 238
Boulton, Richard Harry Webb 232, 233, 239
Boulton, William Webb 86, 227, 228, 229, 230, 231, 232, 233, 238, 239, 366, 367
Bourne, Eliza 349, 350
Bowater, Henry 186
Bowater, John Frederick 182
Bowater, John Frederick Bolton 186, 451
Bowater, Margaret 186
Bowen, Samuel 180, 184
Bower, John 184
Bower, Joshua 181, 184, 185
Bower, Smith & Co. 184
Bowes, Sir Jerome 53
Bradley, Alice 155, 211

Bradley and Ensells 319, 380
Bradley, Anne 117, 131
Bradley, Edward 73, 117, 125, 130, 131, 148, 151, 211, 217, 234
Bradley, Elinor 133
Bradley, Ensell & Holt 319, 320, 346, 362, 372
Bradley, Ensell, Pagett and Co. 379
Bradley, Ensells & Holt 84, 319, 321, 362, 380, 381
Bradley, Frances 131, 150, 154, 155
Bradley, Henry 118, 125, 131, 132, 175, 217, 218, 234, 240, 242
Bradley, John 74, 88, 150, 151, 155, 195, 211, 431
Bradley Joseph 211
Bradley, Joseph 74
Bradley, Joshua 360
Bradley, Kitty 319, 345, 380, 393
Bradley, Mary 103, 112, 113, 117, 218, 234, 241, 251, 344, 345
Bradley, Nicholas 99, 103
Bradley, Peter 344, 345
Bradley, Phebe 163, 168, 345
Bradley, Richard 131, 154, 162, 313, 318, 320, 344, 345, 362, 377, 380, 381, 393
Bradley, Sarah 218
Bradley, Thomas 131, 148, 150, 151, 154, 194, 195, 211
Brettell, Elizabeth 116
Brettell, Isabell 108, 116
Brettell, J.C. 274, 303, 354
Brettell, Joan 66, 69, 102, 103, 126
Brettell Lane Glasshouses 405
Brettell, Richard 116, 428
Brewery Street Glassworks 505
Bridges, Joe 488

Brierley Bridge 430
Brierley Foundry 431
Brierley Hill School of Art 208
Brierley Ironworks 431
Briet, Peter 35
Briggs, Humphrey 122
Brighton, Rosannah 215
Brindley, Alice 64, 168
Brindley, William 155, 168
Brisco, John 144
Bristol, Glass Manufacture 258, 320, 404
Bristol, Port of 121
Bristowe, Francis 107
Britannic Manufacturing Co. 182
British Industries Fair of 1922 342
British Lens and Glass Co. Ltd. 206
British Lens and Wall Glazing Co. Ltd. 206
British Museum 328, 385, 387, 487
British Opal Wall and Glazing Co. 206
Broadfield House Glass Museum 335, 339, 425
Brodie, Lilias 266
Bromsgrove Glasshouse, Worcestershire 208, 215, 498, 499
Brooke, Ann 295
Brooks, Emma 391
Broome House, Broome, Worcestershire 212, 491
Broome, John 23
Broughton Pryce, Ada Blanche 396
Browne, Anne 104
Buckholt Glasshouse, Hampshire 42, 45
Buckle, Mr 320
Buckpool, Wordsley 240, 424
Bullers Ltd 239
Bungar, Daniel 58

Bungar, Isaac 37, 47, 51
Bungar, John 34, 35
Bungar, Mary 62
Bungar, Peter 35, 37
Buré, Jean 42
Burghley, Lord 40, 41, 44, 48
Buriton Glasshouse, Hampshire 46
Burslem School of Art 332
Bury, Edward 146
Bysell, Mary 150, 155

C

Caldwell Hall, Kidderminster, Worcestershire 162
Campbell, Sir John, Bart. 275, 292, 298
Canada, exports to 325
Canal, Birmingham 264
Canal, Dudley 25, 267, 280
Canal, Stourbridge 25, 68, 81, 106, 114, 137, 163, 174, 196, 241, 246, 315, 317, 318, 360, 377, 397, 416, 418, 419, 421, 422, 430, 496, 507
Canal, Stourbridge Extension 146
Carder, Caleb 489, 490, 500
Carder, Frederick C. 479, 481, 482, 483, 484, 489, 499
Carder, George 489, 499
Carder, George John 482, 490, 500
Carlis, Mary Ann 296
Carlis, William 296
Carré, Jean 32, 33, 34, 35, 36, 38, 40, 42, 45
Cartel 101, 135, 149, 160, 172, 181
Carter, Helen Constance 375, 475
Cartledge, George Howard 206
Cartwright, Louisa Blanch 491
Cartwright, Revd. Joseph 313
Cartwright, Susannah 212, 253

Carver, Mary 118
Castle Foot Glassworks 298, 307, 353
Castle Street, Dudley 353
Castrey & Gee 86
Castrey, George 86, 97
Caswell, Catherine 90, 155, 156
Cecil, Sir William 36, 48
Chacombe Priory, Northamptonshire 150
Chance Brothers & Co. 181, 415
Chance, Lucas 184
Chance, William 184
Chances and Hartleys 184
Charnock, Thomas 33
Chebsey, Maria 419
Chelwood Glasshouse, Somerset 61
Chevalier, John 34, 35, 36, 38
Chicago, Exhibition of 1893 466
Chichester, Bishop of 41
Christchurch, Surrey, glass manufacture 295
Christy, John F. 327
Chubsee, Charles 320
City Glassworks, Glasgow 333
Clarke, Daniel 23
Clarke, Joseph 300
Clarke, Mary 23
Clavell, Sir William 63
Clay Brothers 451
Clay, for glasshouse pots 46, 55, 56, 82, 83, 149, 150, 197, 200, 221, 222, 300, 401
Clements, Benjamin 268, 289, 296
Clements, Samuel 296
Cliff, The, Wordsley 442
Clonbrone Glasshouse, Ireland 126
Coal 25, 52, 54, 55, 56, 61, 63, 82, 120, 152, 220, 243, 288, 292, 325, 377, 381, 404, 423, 470, 493
Coalbournhill Glassworks 194,

195, 199, 202, 249, 263, 478
Cochrane, Alexander Brodie 263, 266
Cochrane, Mary 266
Cochrane, Mary Maria 266
Cochrane, Thomas 266
Cole, Henry 328
Colebourn, Freda 208
Colemans Glasshouse 58, 60, 62
Collins, Ann 411
Collis, George 152
Collis, William Blow 365, 373, 424
Coloroll Group Plc 471
Coloroll Tableware Ltd 471
Coltman, Benjamin 201, 213, 263
Coltman, John 432
Coltman, Mary 432, 433
Coltman, Michael 201, 213, 430, 431, 432
Commission of Employment of Children (1846) 305
Commission of Enquiry into the Glass Excise 274, 303
Compson, Burlton 125
Compson, James 240
Compson, Thomas 240
Conckclaine, Ananias 63
Conckclaine, Bennett 57
Conckclaine, Francis 58, 62
Conckclaine, George 57
Conckclaine, Jacob 51
Conckclaine, John 47, 51, 62, 63
Conckclaine, Judith 57
Conckclaine, Suhanna 62
Congreve Jackson Ltd 507
Convolvulus Vase, The 339
Cooke, Benjamin 353
Cooke, Price & Wood 353
Cookson & Sons 418
Cope, Deeley & Parrish 403
Cope, Elizabeth 411
Cope, Mary 411

Cope, William 411
Cope, William Henry 399, 401, 402, 403, 404, 412
Copeland, William 472
Copeland, William Taylor 472
Corbett, Emma 375
Corbett, George 375
Corbett, George Harry 368, 369, 375
Corbett Hospital, Wordsley 76, 455
Corbett, John 455
Corbyns Hall, Pensnett 223, 236
Corning, New York State, USA 461, 485
Corona Glassworks, USA 466
Couch, Eliza 200
Couch, William 200
Couper, James 333, 340, 349
Court, Harry 23
Cox, Lucy Mary 254
Crace, John I. 327
Cradley Forge 55
Cranwell, Elizabeth 101, 104
Croker, Frances 104, 166, 175
Crown House Ltd. 470
Crudgington, Frances 214
Crutched Friars Glassworks, London 34
Cullet 74, 247, 260, 325
Cuneen, J.H. 508

D

Daffys elixir 260, 404, 413
Dalton, Thomas 134, 135, 143
Dando, Alfred W. 357
Daniel, Sarah 257
Darby & Co 401
Darby, Abraham 401, 412
Darby, John 412
Darlaston, Staffordshire, Glass Manufacture 347

Darwin, Dr. Erasmus 80, 92
Davenport, Ellin 432
Davenport, John 430, 432
Davenport, Jonathan 432
Davenport, Kinnersley and Grafton 430
Davey and Moore 312
Davies, Alfred 437, 438, 439, 475
Davies, Alfred Edward 438, 439
Davies and Hodgetts 291, 383, 394
Davies, Edward 439
Davies, Emma 439
Davies, Hannah Maria 438
Davies, Harry 439, 465, 475
Davies, James 439
Davies, John Christopher 436
Davies, Joseph 439
Davies, Mary 439
Davies, Thomas 291, 485
Davies, William Edward 291, 292, 293, 383
Davis and Bolton 406
Davis, Esther 414, 415
Davis, Esther Jane 414
Davis, Greathead and Green 405, 425, 426, 429, 439
Davis, John 405, 406, 414, 415, 423, 424, 425, 428
Davis, Joseph 206
Davis, Sarah 428
Davis, Solomon 428
Davis, William 303, 309
Davis, William Solomon 406, 415
de Falbe, Christian Frederic 283
de Hennezel, Anthoinette 38
de Hennezel, Balthazar 34, 36, 38, 42, 43
de Hennezel, Charles 31
de Hennezel, Georges 31, 69
de Hennezel, Louis 42
de Hennezel, Nicolas 38, 49, 69
de Hennezel, Peregrin 69
de Hennezel, Thomas 38
de Hennezell, Charles 69
de Hennezell, Edward 69
de Hennezell, Israëlle 69
de Massey, Moingeon 69
Deacon, Henry Hodgetts 411
Dean, Arthur 160
Dean, Forest of, Glass Manufacture 48
Dean, Forest of, Iron Manufacture 70
Decorative Glass Co., The 182
Deeley, Edward 401, 412
Deeley, Edwin 400, 402, 403, 404, 412, 414
Deeley, Margaret 146, 402
Deeley, Richard Mountford 400, 402, 403, 404, 405
Delph Bottleworks 496
Dema Glass Ltd. 470
Denham, William 219
Dennis Glassworks, Amblecote 458
Dennis Hall 423, 424, 464, 465, 468, 472
Dennis Hall Co-operative Crystal 472, 510, 511
Dennis Park 153, 423, 424
Dial Glasshouse, Audnam 397
Dial Glasshouse, Brettell Lane 172
Dicks, Mary 296
Dixon alias Offerton, Henry 294
Dixon, Anne 293
Dixon, Charles 296
Dixon, Dianah 294, 295
Dixon, Edward 170, 171, 285, 290, 296
Dixon, Frances 293
Dixon, Francis 294, 295
Dixon, Gilbert 171, 286, 294
Dixon, Gillims 171, 294

Dixon, Henry 293, 294
Dixon, Herbut 294
Dixon, Hugh 286, 295
Dixon, Isaiah 294
Dixon, John 294
Dixon, Johnathan 162, 168, 212
Dixon, Joseph 289
Dixon, Margaret 294, 295
Dixon, Margrett 293
Dixon, Mary 279, 315, 427
Dixon, Oliver 112, 162, 163, 164, 168, 169, 170, 171, 212, 285, 287, 288, 293, 294, 295
Dixon, Richard 285, 293, 294
Dixon, William 294
Dixons Bank 354
Dixons Green Glassworks 258, 285, 383
Dixons Green House, Dudley 290
Dob Hill, Buckpool, Wordsley 240, 241
Dob Hill Glassworks 109, 131, 220, 240, 416, 417
Dobson and Pearce 341, 463
Douglass, Tregarthen 206
Dovey, Henry 264
Dovey, James 245, 246, 318
Dovey, Mary 264
Dovey, Rachel 264
Dovey, Richard 246
Downing, Ann 395
Downing, Benjamin 386, 395
Downing, James 395
Downing, John 70
Downing, Zachary 70
Drayton Mill, Belbroughton, Worcestershire 185
Drewry, Louisa 351
Drewry, Philip 351
du Houx, Guilliaume 31
du Houx, Isaac 45, 59, 63
du Houx, Jacob 73

du Houx, John 59
du Houx, Pierre 42, 48
du Tisac, Jean 42
Dublin, Exhibition of 1853 333
Dudley, Arms Hotel 224, 273, 277, 302, 303, 324, 364
Dudley, Dud 54, 55, 57
Dudley Flint Glassworks 267, 268, 424
Dudley, Grammar School 256, 268, 289, 290, 296, 298
Dudley, Lord 54, 57, 125, 220, 221, 222, 229, 233, 241, 256, 279, 301, 305, 356, 357
Dudley, Mayor of 162, 261, 273, 274, 278, 303, 353, 354, 355
Dudley, Richard 282
Duffy, Mrs E. Mary 386, 387
Dukes (Stourbridge) Ltd. 181
Dukes, Tom 181

E

E. & J. Webb 84, 85, 227, 250
E. Deeley & Son 405
Ebbw Vale Iron Works 152
Eccleshall, Staffordshire, Glass Manufacture 44, 45, 46, 66
Edge, Samuel 83, 114
Edinburgh & Leith Flint Glass Co. 469
Edinburgh Crystal 471, 512
Edinburgh, International Exhibition of Industry, Science and Art (1886)
ence and Art (1886) 480
Edmunds, Henry 365
Edward Webb and Sons 366
Edward Westwood & Co. 313
Edwards & Co. 435
Edwards, Edward 434, 435, 436
Edwards, Grace Annie 435, 436

Edwards, James 435, 436
Edwards, Jane 419
Edwards, John 435
Edwards, Samuel 434, 435, 436
Edwards, T.C. 508
Edwin Deeley & Son 404
Egan, Will 451
Egerton, Mary 67, 70
Egerton, Peter 70
Elcock, Samuel 505
Elgin Vase, the 385
Ellis, Hyacinth dArcy 455
Elwall, Edward 257
Elwall, Esther 257
Elwell, Alice Eliza 494, 495
Elwell, Benjamin 494
Emus, Saunders & Haywood 428
Ensell, Charles 83, 319, 345, 372, 380, 381, 393
Ensell, George 162, 163, 164, 165, 166, 168, 260, 268, 318, 319, 345, 377
Ensell, Henry Causer 83
Ensell, Lucy Mary 319, 345, 380, 393
Ensell, Phebe 345
Ensell, Richard Bradley 263, 319, 320, 345, 362, 363, 372, 373, 380, 381, 382, 383, 393
Ensells & Co. 321
Ensells and Wainwright 321, 381
Erard, Oscar Pierre 480, 482
Eve Hill Glassworks 493
Evers, Anne 434, 435, 436
Evers, Charles 402, 413
Evers, James 413
Evers, John 434, 435
Evers, Samuel 413
Evers-Swindell, Charles 402, 413
Evers-Swindell, James 402, 413
Evers-Swindell, Jane 396
Evers-Swindell, Margaret Jane 374

Eveson, Stanley R. 471
Ewhurst, Surrey 62
Excise Duty 68, 83, 84, 95, 111, 125, 140, 178, 190, 196, 218, 223, 224, 248, 262, 273, 274, 276, 292, 303, 313, 323, 326, 354, 363, 364, 382, 419, 428

F

F. & C. Osler, Birmingham 205, 214, 263
F. Smith & Sons 114
F. Wilkinson & Co. 181, 182
Facer, Jacob 464
Farmer, John 82
Farmer, Mary 93
Farmer, Tom 465
Felix Summerleys Art Manufactures 328
Fennymore, Thomas Atland 391
Fereday, John Thomas 465, 469, 474
Fereday, Joseph 474
Ferguson, David 210
Ffreeman, Joseph 258, 289
Fimbrell Glasshouse, Amblecote 148
Finch, Edward 125
Finch, Elizabeth 255, 257
Finch House, Dudley 301
Finch, John 289, 301, 309
Finch, Joseph 113, 117, 125, 131, 217
Finch, Joshua 256
Finch, Katrin 309
Finch, Mary 301
Finch, William 309
Finnie, John 210
Firmstone, family 342, 343, 344
Fish Inn, Coalbournbrook,

Amblecote 153, 203, 406, 421
Fisher, James Brock 454
Fletcher, Howard 487
Flint Glass Manufacturers Defence Association 203, 251, 441
Florry, John 280
Floyd, Jane 146, 147
Fogelberg, Carl Gottwald Sven Harald 470
Foley China 391
Foley, John 75, 286, 372
Foley, North 286
Foley, Philip 67, 70, 100, 104
Foley, Revd. Samuel 23
Foley, Richard 168
Foley, Richard Fiddler 107, 164
Foley, Richard 'Fiddler' 64, 143, 155, 168, 169
Foley, Robert 61, 64, 65, 294
Foley, Thomas 104, 120
Foley, Thomas, Lord 169, 212
Ford, Dr. Simon 160
Ford, Martha 160
Forsyth, Mr 356
Forsythe, Gordon 391
Forsythe, Moira 391
Fosbrooke, Robert 52
Foster, James 238, 344
Foster, William 238, 344
Foster, William Orme 229, 238
Fowler, Ann 453
Fox, Charles 150, 195
Fox, John Tinker 142
Foxall, John 68
Francis, Harriet Draffen 227, 237
Francis Rufford & Co. 139
Francis Smith & Sons 114, 117
Francis, Thomas 227
François, Henri 338
Franklin, Benjamin 89, 91
Freeman, Joseph 264, 289
Freeth, Jonathan 412
Frisbie feeder 384, 477
Fritsche, William 460, 461, 466, 468, 469

G

Galton, Francis 92
Galton, Mary Anne 92
Galton, Samuel 80, 93
Galton, Samuel Tertius 93
Galtons Grinding Mill, Belbroughton, Worcestershire 185
Gammon, William 424
Gatchell & Co. 190
Gatchell, George 191, 193
Gatchell, James 190
Gatchell, Johnathan 189, 190, 193
Gatchell, Samuel 190
Gatchells and Walpole 190
Gerrard, Sir Gilbert 116, 142
Gething, Ann Eunice 349
Gibbons, John 217, 236
Gibbons, Joseph 93
Gibbons, Owen 374
Gilbert, Elizabeth 296
Glasgow, Glass Manufacture 333, 465
Glass, Achromatic 199, 200, 262, 263
Glass, Agate Flambé 207
Glass, Air-trap decoration 231, 339, 481
Glass, Allasantes 461
Glass, Argentine 367
Glass, Bodiam 470
Glass, Bottle 61, 74, 75, 78, 120, 121, 135, 136, 148, 149, 150, 158, 173, 187, 198, 199, 201, 241, 244, 260, 269, 270, 313, 320, 362,

369, 379, 382, 397, 398,
    401, 403, 404, 405, 418, 496
Glass, Bottle, Brandy 405
Glass, Bottle, Codd 404
Glass, Bottle, Hamilton 404
Glass, Bottle, Wine 151, 404
Glass, Broad 56, 61, 74, 75, 78,
    88, 98, 102, 109, 111, 121,
    131, 135, 149, 158, 161,
    172, 173, 174, 177, 218,
    240, 244, 259, 377, 379,
    397, 401
Glass, Bronze 461
Glass, Burmese 464, 499
Glass, Cameo 210, 333, 337, 341,
    387, 460, 461, 462, 464,
    465, 466, 468, 469, 470,
    480, 485
Glass, Campanula 341
Glass, Carrara 449
Glass, Cascade pattern 209
Glass, Cased 210, 325, 333, 369,
    464, 481
Glass, Ceonix 342
Glass, Chemical 407
Glass, Clutha 465
Glass, Coloured 184, 230, 329,
    409
Glass, Corolene 449
Glass, Crimping 479
Glass, Crimping machine 479
Glass, Crown 28, 34, 37, 74, 75,
    102, 150, 161, 165, 174,
    184, 379, 428
Glass, Crystal Cameo 485
Glass, Crystallo 34
Glass, Cutting 82, 165, 168, 182,
    191, 245, 246, 259, 297,
    299, 318, 326, 329, 362,
    384, 388, 390, 451, 470,
    485, 494, 505, 506, 508
Glass, Damascened 480

Glass, Decanters 180, 188, 191,
    245, 259, 329, 339, 462, 508
Glass, Diadem 209
Glass, Domino pattern 209
Glass, Dresden Cameo 367
Glass, Dynasty 469
Glass, Engraved 163, 188, 208,
    210, 273, 274, 326, 328,
    329, 330, 331, 336, 356,
    366, 369, 384, 443, 460,
    462, 466, 469, 470, 480,
    483, 490, 501, 502, 508
Glass, Etruscan style 179, 426
Glass, Excise Act 164, 196, 218,
    419
Glass, Flambeau 499
Glass, Flint 78, 81, 83, 84, 86,
    137, 140, 150, 158, 161,
    177, 179, 181, 184, 187,
    188, 189, 193, 195, 199,
    200, 201, 219, 221, 230,
    244, 245, 247, 248, 249,
    250, 253, 260, 261, 263,
    269, 277, 278, 280, 290,
    317, 321, 324, 334, 338,
    339, 342, 362, 363, 380,
    381, 383, 405, 422, 423, 431
Glass, Frensham 470
Glass, Furniture 204, 205, 215
Glass, Harlequin 209
Glass, Intaglio cutting 369, 390,
    391, 462, 470, 483, 508
Glass, Intarsia 482
Glass, Ivory 463
Glass, Jewell 481, 490
Glass, Kit-Kat 166
Glass, Kodial 407
Glass, Kohinoor 210
Glass, Lamp chimneys 208
Glass, Lustres 272, 443
Glass, Mary Gregory 341
Glass, Mat-su-no-ke 479, 480, 489

Glass, Mitre 209
Glass, Moresque 482
Glass, Moss-Agate 481
Glass, Nacre de Perle 231
Glass, New Gold 204
Glass, Old Ivory 464
Glass, Old Roman 465
Glass, Oroide 367
Glass, Osiris 481
Glass, Peach Bloom 464
Glass, Pressed 199, 202, 205, 230, 323
Glass, Price of 61, 62, 73, 74, 88, 102, 104, 109, 121, 151, 218
Glass, Pull-up 480
Glass, Random 209
Glass, Riviera 342
Glass, Rock Crystal 339, 369, 460, 462, 466, 478, 480
Glass, Rominto 342
Glass, Ruby 199, 200, 210, 262, 263, 336, 338, 425, 426, 501, 504
Glass, Rusticana 341, 342
Glass, Satin 231, 333, 339, 465, 481, 494
Glass, Scientific 208
Glass, Sidonian 461
Glass, Silveria 483
Glass, Soliloquy pattern 209
Glass, Stratford 390
Glass, Sunflower 342
Glass, Tapestry 481
Glass, Tartan 339
Glass, Threading 336, 338, 443, 478, 481, 482
Glass, Threading machine 338, 478
Glass, Trapped Enamel 335
Glass, Tubing 408, 409, 410, 469
Glass, Vasa Murrhina 230, 367
Glass, Venetian style 34, 231
Glass, Verre de Neige 449

Glass, Verre de Soie 481
Glass, Verre sur Verre 239
Glass, Vitrified 326
Glass, White 78, 135, 217, 234, 240, 255, 287, 289, 317
Glass, Window 28, 29, 37, 40, 46, 59, 61, 62, 102, 115, 120, 174, 201, 244, 247, 377, 411
Glass, Wine glasses 137, 180, 210, 245, 247, 249, 259, 268, 508
Glass, Worcester Ivory 367
Glass, Zoomorphic designs 339, 465
Godwin, John 172, 173, 177
Godwin, William 161, 167
Gorton, Hannah 315
Gothersley Mill, Kinver, Staffordshire 64
Grafton, Edward 430, 432
Grafton, John Henry 431, 433
Grafton, William 430, 431, 432, 433
Graftons Brierley Glasshouse 269, 322, 430
Grainger, James 261, 262, 265, 266
Grandmont Glasshouse 38
Gray, Milna 391
Grazebrook, Charlotte 225
Grazebrook, Elizabeth 219, 223, 235, 236, 421
Grazebrook, Elizabeth Wallace 236, 237
Grazebrook, George 221, 235, 402
Grazebrook, Henry Sydney 221, 235
Grazebrook, John Phillips 223, 226, 227, 236, 237
Grazebrook, Joseph 234
Grazebrook, Mary Anne 235
Grazebrook, Michael 218, 219, 220, 221, 222, 223, 224,

225, 226, 234, 235, 236,
    237, 241, 402, 417, 418,
    421, 428
Grazebrook, Michael Phillips 223,
    225, 226, 230, 237
Grazebrook, Sarah 95, 219, 220,
    221, 235, 236, 241, 421, 427
Grazebrook, Thomas Worral 219,
    220, 221, 222, 235, 236
Grazebrook, Thomas Worral Smith
    222
Grazebrook, Thomas Worrall 428
Grazebrook, William 223, 225,
    226, 236, 419
Grazebrooks Canalside Glassworks
    230, 416
Great Barr Hall, Staffordshire 93
Great Eastern, The 443
Great Exhibition of 1851 179,
    191, 330, 331, 425, 426
Greathead, Anna Maria 406
Greathead, Eleanor 283
Greathead, Francis 276, 283
Greathead, William 276, 277, 278,
    283, 405, 406, 414, 424, 425
Green, Anna Maria 276, 283
Green, David 256
Green, Elizabeth 256, 283
Green, George Joseph 261, 262,
    265, 266
Green, Isabell 256
Green, James 265
Green, Jane 436
Green, John 255, 256, 265, 288,
    290, 295, 296, 297, 435, 436
Green, Johnathan 256, 258, 288,
    289, 295, 296, 297
Green, Joseph 255, 256, 257, 265,
    288, 290, 296, 297
Green, Len 209
Green, Martha 265
Green, Mary 297

Green, Mary Ann 266
Green, Richard 277, 283, 405,
    406, 424, 425
Greenfield, Eleanor 455, 456
Greensforge, Swindon, Staffordshire
    54, 55
Greenwich Glassworks, London
    107
Grey, Ambrose 122
Grey, Henry 119
Grey, John Hon. 234
Grey, Lady Jane 122
Grey, Mary 234
Grier, John 154
Griffin, Joseph 191
Griffin, Thomas 258, 264
Grove, Daniel 89
Grove, John 76, 89, 112, 113
Grove, Thomas 128
Guest, A.H. 451
Guest, Abraham 286
Guest, Anne 351
Guest, Arthur 182
Guest Brothers 334, 338
Guest, Edward 274, 292, 334,
    349, 350, 353, 354, 357
Guest, Elizabeth 349, 351
Guest, Esther 357
Guest, Horace 507, 508
Guest, John 181, 351
Guest, Joseph 292, 306, 354, 355,
    357, 358
Guest, Richard 334
Guest, Thomas 334, 349
Guest, Wood & Guest 353, 355
Gunpowder Plot of 1605 411
Gwinnett, Betsey 372

H

H. Loxdale & Co. 280
H. Pearson & Co. 502

Haden, Daniel 504
Haden, Hannah 504
Haden, James 504
Haden, Joseph 282
Haden, Martha 280, 281, 346, 347, 350
Haden, Sarah Elizabeth 504
Haden, Thomas 335, 350, 504
Haden, Zachariah 504
Haden, Zipporah 504
Hagley Glasshouse 128
Hajdamach, Charles 332, 425
Hale, Charles 308
Hale, Frances 202, 212, 254
Hale, Margaret 294
Halifax, Sir Thomas 77
Hall, A.H. 208
Hallen, Edward 135
Hallifax, Revd. William 286
Hammond, David 470
Hammond, Jane 96, 214, 215
Hammond, Joseph 203, 214
Hamond, Ann 243, 251, 252
Hamond, Mary 251
Hamond, Thomas 112, 113, 117, 172, 217, 243, 244, 251
Hancox, Ann 394
Hancox, Charles 386, 394
Hancox, Daniel 386, 394
Hancox, Elizabeth 394
Hancox, John 394
Hancox, Mary 96, 348
Hanson, Thomas 23
Harbridge Crystal Glass Co. 182
Hardwick Hall, Derbyshire 40
Hardwick, Thomas 82
Harington, Theodosia 54, 57
Harlestones Glasshouse 158, 172, 318
Harries, Annie Elizabeth 457
Harris, Joseph 187
Harris, Mary 89

Harris, Rice H. 83
Harris, Samuel 89
Harrison, George King 441, 453
Harrods 391
Harrop, Anna Jane 498
Harrop, James 215, 498, 499
Harrop, Joseph 499
Harrop, Sarah 499
Harrop, William 215, 498, 499
Hart, Joseph 149
Hartley & Co. 181
Hartley, James 184
Hartley, John 184
Harts Hill Glassworks 498
Harve, Thomas 51
Harvey, Mary Ann 375, 395
Harward, John 384
Haselwood, Mary 73, 87, 88
Hatton, John Shelton 431, 433
Haughton Green Glasshouse, Lancashire 45, 63, 115
Hawbush Glasshouse 124
Hawkes & Co. 269, 271, 272, 277
Hawkes & Greathead 277
Hawkes, Abiathar 25, 267, 268, 269, 273, 274, 279, 280, 281, 282, 289
Hawkes, Alice Anna 284
Hawkes, Eleanor Louisa 277, 283
Hawkes, George Wright 268, 269, 272, 280, 282
Hawkes, Mary 267, 280, 281
Hawkes, Roger Wright 271, 272, 273, 281, 282
Hawkes, Sarah 281
Hawkes, Thomas 224, 269, 270, 271, 272, 273, 274, 275, 276, 277, 278, 279, 280, 281, 282, 284, 303, 321, 322, 354
Hawkins, Mr 325
Haycock, Anne 71, 344

Hazeldine, Leticia 374
Head, John 187
Heath Forge 55
Heath Glassworks 133, 363, 444
Heath House, Stourbridge 139, 140, 141, 146, 375
Heaton, Eleanor 57
Heaton, Francis 57
Hemming, Elizabeth 184, 323, 346, 472, 473
Hemming, Joseph 323
Henley, Sarah 308, 309
Henry, Eleanor 89
Henry G. Richardson & Sons 340, 341, 342
Henry, Revd. Philip 89
Henzey, Abraham 52
Henzey, Ambrose 46, 47, 49, 52
Henzey, Ananias 69, 98, 99, 100, 101, 102, 103, 104, 105, 109, 110, 112, 121, 124, 125, 126
Henzey, Anne 104
Henzey, Bigoe 124, 125, 126
Henzey, Bridget 101, 177
Henzey, Catherine 124
Henzey, Dorothy 104, 126, 166, 167
Henzey, Edward 46, 47, 49, 51, 52, 66, 69, 100, 101, 102, 104, 105, 121, 124, 126, 172, 175
Henzey, Elizabeth 89, 101, 104
Henzey, Fowler 56
Henzey, Frances 104, 166, 175
Henzey, George 46, 49, 50, 51, 52
Henzey, Izhac 47
Henzey, Jacob 48, 52, 56, 63
Henzey, Jeanne 51
Henzey, Jehuditha 51
Henzey, Joan 69, 98, 99, 102, 103, 104, 126
Henzey, Joane 100, 104
Henzey, John 98, 102, 121, 158, 160, 161, 162, 166, 167, 168, 172, 175, 178, 398, 399, 400, 401
Henzey, Joseph 100, 102, 105
Henzey, Joshua 61, 62, 66, 69, 72, 73, 87, 98, 99, 101, 102, 103, 104, 106, 112, 119, 121, 122, 126, 131, 133, 136, 158, 160, 161, 162, 172, 175, 177, 217, 218, 234, 244
Henzey, Marguerite 51
Henzey, Mary 99, 103, 133, 143, 144, 162, 168, 242
Henzey, Nicholas 52, 109, 116, 125
Henzey, Paul 52, 56, 60, 61, 89, 98, 99, 100, 101, 102, 104, 105, 109, 110, 119, 124, 125, 143, 148
Henzey, Peregrine 44, 50, 51, 52, 66
Henzey, Sarah 104
Henzey, Suzanna 106, 115
Henzey, Thomas 51, 104, 121, 131, 158, 159, 160, 166, 167, 172, 175, 177
Henzey, Zacharias 56
Henzeys Brettell Lane Glasshouse 98, 106
Herbert, John 208, 273, 451
Herbert, Samuel 282, 292
Herbert, Sarah 282
Herbert, William 273, 274, 282, 292
Hick, Maria Louisa 474
Hickman, Gregory 161, 167
Hickman, Richard 167
Hickman, Rose 126
Hickman, William 143

Higgs, Mary 427
Hill & Waldron 197, 198
Hill, Anne 156
Hill, Bate & Robins Bank 152, 201
Hill, Elizabeth 150, 154, 155, 189, 295, 344
Hill, Elizabeth Amelia 456
Hill, Hampton & Co. 198, 199, 212
Hill, Hampton, Harrison & Wheeley 198
Hill, Henry Thomas 24
Hill House, Hall Street, Dudley 304, 306, 310
Hill, John 68, 71, 138, 145, 155, 187, 188, 189, 190, 317, 344
Hill, Lucy 456
Hill, Margaret 168
Hill, Mary 138
Hill, Mary Ann 456
Hill, Sarah 156
Hill, The, Amblecote 76, 77, 78, 79, 443, 447, 448, 454, 455
Hill, Thomas 24, 90, 151, 152, 153, 155, 156, 157, 164, 175, 196, 197, 198, 201, 211, 212, 221, 423, 474, 491
Hill, Waldron 71, 151, 155, 196, 197, 198, 211, 212, 318, 344
Hill, Waldron, Littlewood & Hampton 198
Hill, William 465, 474
Hindson, Alice 208
Hingley, Albert Harold 456
Hingley, Alfred J. 456
Hingley, Alfred Norman 457
Hingley, Charles Edward 456
Hingley, George Clement 457
Hingley, George Silas 456, 457
Hingley, Jabez 456
Hingley, James Noel 457
Hingley, John Oswald 456

Hingley, Levi 452, 455, 456
Hingley, Silas 455, 456
Hingley, Thomas 451, 455, 456
Hingley, William 456
Hipwood, Jane 436
Hipwood, Julia 436
Hobson, Sarah Matilda 419
Hodgetts, Alice Mary 344
Hodgetts, Caroline Eunice Rosa Elizabeth 339
Hodgetts, Charles 297
Hodgetts, Elizabeth 383, 384
Hodgetts, Emily Jane 350
Hodgetts, Jane 244, 252
Hodgetts, John 236, 264
Hodgetts, Joshua 483, 486, 490
Hodgetts, Joyce 286
Hodgetts, Patience 264
Hodgetts, Richardson & Co. 338
Hodgetts, Richardson & Pargeter 335
Hodgetts, Richardson & Son 336, 339
Hodgetts, Richardson & Sons 478
Hodgetts, Thomas 264
Hodgetts, William 291, 394
Hodgetts, William James 335, 336, 338, 339, 351, 383, 384, 394
Hodgetts, William Rolinson 291, 293, 297, 344, 350, 383, 394
Holbeche House, Kingswinford 64, 399
Hollier, Elliott 278
Holliman, John 76
Holloway End Glasshouse 72, 181, 202, 365, 422
Holloway, Sarah 413
Holly Hall Glassworks 166, 199, 200, 201, 248, 258, 289, 300
Holmes, William Arthur 207
Holt, John 319, 320, 345, 346, 362, 372, 380, 381, 393

Holt, Lucy Mary 319, 380, 381, 393
Holt, Mary 320, 321, 346, 362, 381, 393
Homer, Henry 355
Homfray, Francis 90, 152, 155, 156
Homfray, Jeston 156
Homfray, Samuel 155
Homfray, Sir Jeremiah, Knt. 155
Homfray, Thomas 78, 90, 152, 156, 454
Honeyborne & Batson 245, 246
Honeyborne, Ann 252
Honeyborne, Anna Maria 253
Honeyborne, Hamond 252
Honeyborne, John 246, 247, 252
Honeyborne, Mary 113, 172, 175, 251, 252, 410
Honeyborne, Robert 113, 165, 166, 172, 220, 241, 243, 244, 245, 251, 252, 312, 313, 316
Honeyborne, Thomas 245, 246, 247, 248, 252, 253, 313, 315
Hopkins, Samuel 156
Hopkins, Thomas 152, 156
Horsley House, Wolverhampton Street, Dudley 289
Horton, A. 507
Horton, James 299
Hoskins, Nicholas 360
Houdrichapelle Glasshouse 31, 69
Houghton, Edward 135
Houghton, John 61
Howard, Diana 117
Howard, Lord 53
Howells, Sarah 453
Hughes, Elizabeth 426
Huguenot 29, 42, 43, 106, 115
Hunslet Glassworks, Leeds, Yorkshire 181, 184

Hunt, Elizabeth 234
Hunt, Joanna 92, 94
Hunter, John 80
Husselbee, John H. 342, 352
Hyde Slitting Mill, Kinver, Staffordshire 64, 90, 152, 155, 169

I

India, export trade to 405
Ingram, H.J. 389
Insull, T. 499
International Spring Fair of 1978 471
Ireland, Glass Manufacture 98, 124, 126, 187
Isle of Purbeck Glasshouse, Dorset 63, 126
Ivy House Mill, Wordsley 366
Ivy Steam Flour Mills, Wordsley 368

J

J. & J. Green 290
J. & J. Northwood 334
J. Hartley & Co. 181
J. Parrish & Co. 505
J.F. Bolton Bowater 182
J.K. Davies and Son 182
Jackson, Anne 74
Jackson, Congreve William 466, 469
Jackson, Edward 74, 88
Jackson, George Elwell 280, 347
Jackson, Henry 347, 375
Jacobs Well Glasshouse, Audnam 130
Jamaica, exports to 121
James, Benjamin 257
James Couper & Son, City Glassworks, Glasgow 333, 465
James, Esquire 257

James Evers 402
James, Mary 131, 132, 234, 242
James, Walter 240, 242
James, Windsor 125, 131, 132, 217, 218, 234, 240, 241, 242
James Wright & Co. 496
Jellian, Frances 168, 171, 285, 293, 294, 295
Jellian, Gilbert 293
Jellians, Alice 295
Jeston, Edward 126, 143
Jeston, Elizabeth 100, 104, 105, 126
Jeston, Humphry 133, 134, 136, 142, 143, 144
Jeston, John 112, 117, 133, 134, 135, 136, 143, 144
Jeston, Mary 136, 142, 155
Jeston, Rose 100, 124, 126
Jeston, Thomas 134, 143
Jeston, William 133, 134, 143
Jevon, Ann 87, 88
Jevon, Gray 73, 149
John Davis & Co. 406, 429
John Guest & Son 507
John Henzey Pidcock & Co. 178
John Pidcock & Sons 398
John Renaud & Son 356
Johnson, Frances 213
Jones, John 197, 347, 431
Jones, Louisa 431, 433
Jones, Tom 487
Joseph Flemming & Co. 181
Joseph Green & Co. 290, 291
Joseph Guest & Co. 354
Joseph Silvers & Co. 248
Joseph Stevens & Co. 262
Joseph Stevens & Son 199
Josiah Lane and Sons 494

K

Keelinge, Edward Augustus, Freeman 296
Keelinge, John 258, 259, 264, 289
Keelinge, John Freeman 296
Keelinge, Richard 264
Keir, James 78, 80, 81, 82, 90, 91
Keller, Joseph 478, 480, 486, 489
Kendall, Edward 67
Kettle, Elizabeth Mackenzie 222
Kettley, John 317
Kimberley, John 511
King, Elizabeth 351
King, William 24, 214, 424, 441
Kinnersley, Penelope 71, 430
Kinnersley, Thomas 71, 430, 432
Kinver Street Glassworks, Wordsley 492
Knight, Dame Laura 391
Knight, Martha 76, 88, 89
Knight, Richard 76, 88
Knight, Sir Richard Payne 88
Knight, Thomas Andrew 88
Kny, Frederick Englebert 375, 390, 395, 461, 462, 464, 466
Kny, Ludwig 370, 390, 395, 396
Kny, Sarah Lavinia 375, 395
Kny, William 369, 375
Kosta Glassworks, Sweden 470
Kretschmann, Frederick 478, 489
Kynnersley, Henry 432
Kynnersley, Penelope 68, 71, 432
Kynnersley, Thomas 68, 71, 432

L

L. & S. Hingley & Co. 467
Lane, Joseph 494
Lane, Josiah 493, 494, 495
Lane, Mary 494
Lane, Thomas 493, 494, 495

Lane, William 495
Large & Hodgetts 291
Large, William 291, 297
Lawley, Margaret 490
Lea & Perrins 404
Lea, Joseph 454
Lea Smith, Ferdinando 223, 236
Leasowes, The, Halesowen, Worcestershire 87, 144
Lechevrel, Alphonse Eugene 337
Lee and Large 291
Lee, William 305, 310
Leech, John 133
Legré, James 58, 62
Leigh, Elizabeth 103
Leigh, John Gerard 283
Lichecourt Glasshouse 36, 38
Lilley, Anne 156, 157, 212
Littleton, Thomas 161
Littlewood & Berry 84
Littlewood, Benjamin 83, 84, 95, 198, 220, 247, 421, 422, 427
Littlewood, King and Co. 83
Littlewood, Sarah 219
Littlewood, Thomas 83, 84, 421, 427
Liverpool, Mayor of 270
Liverpool, Port of 325, 403
Lloyd, Jack 369
Lloyd, Sarah 350
Locke & Co. Ltd. 455
Locke, Edward 351, 455
Locke, Joseph 338, 351, 455
Loftus, Sir Alfred J. 206, 207
London, Glass Manufacture 34, 98, 107, 158, 188, 238, 312
London House Glassworks 340
London International Group 191
London International Health Exhibition (1884) 463, 480
Longe, George 44
Longport, Staffordshire, Glass Manufacture 430
Lorraine 29, 31, 36, 106
Lowe, Lewis 499
Lowe, Patrick 84
Loxdale and Jackson 280, 347
Loxdale, Thomas 280, 347
Loxley Hall, Uttoxeter, Staffordshire 68, 71, 430
Lunar Society 79, 80, 81, 93, 169, 392
Luton Hoo, Bedfordshire 283
Luxton, G. John 371
Lyddiat, Hugh 64
Lyddiat, John 60, 61, 64
Lyddiat, Joyce 60, 64, 65
Lye Forge, Worcestershire 67, 70, 167
Lynn Regis, Norfolk, Glass Manufacture 171, 286
Lyttelton, Elizabeth 237
Lyttelton, Stephen 64
Lyttleton, Gilbert 57

M

M. Fenton & Co. 246, 291
Maisey, Hugo 369
Major Parkes & Co. 262, 266
Male, James 236
Mallen, Pratt and Green 407
Manchester, Exhibition of 1845 326
Manchester, Glass Manufacture 405
Manchester, Industrial Exhibition of 1857 334
Manchester, School of Art 331, 332
Manerin, Giacomina Giosephina 411
Manley, Cyril 182
Mansell, Lady 59
Mansell, Sir Edward 53
Mansell, Sir Robert 45, 47, 51, 52,

53, 54, 59, 63, 107
Marler, A.E. 452
Marler, H.A. 452
Marshall, James 435, 436
Matthews, Jeremiah 321
Matthews, Marian 239
McGrath, Joseph 191
Meanley, Deanne 487
Meatyard, Oswald George 232, 238, 340
Meatyard, Oswald James 231
Meatyard, William 238
Melbourne, Exhibitions 465
Melsup, Anne 153, 156, 212
Michell, Thomas 205
Midland Association of Glass Manufacturers 141, 228, 232, 262, 389, 407, 438, 467, 493
Millard, William 295
Miller, Samuel 191
Mills, Elizabeth 440, 442, 443, 453
Mills, Frederick James 85, 86, 228, 230, 231, 232, 238, 239, 447
Mills, George 141, 142, 388, 442, 443, 444, 445, 446, 447, 448, 453, 454, 455
Mills, Gerald Rusgrove 454
Mills, Harry 450, 454, 455
Mills, Henry 455
Mills, James 248, 249, 253
Mills, Jane 228, 232, 238, 239
Mills, Mary Kate 447, 449, 455
Mills, Richard 85, 238, 440, 441, 442, 453, 455
Mills, Thomas 453
Mills, Walker & Co. 444, 445, 448, 449
Mills, Webb & Stuart 179, 440, 443, 458
Milton Vase, The 334, 387
Milward, Elizabeth 234

Milward, Thomas 121, 143, 149, 160, 194, 197, 240
Minifie, Mary Maria 340
Minifie, William Alan 351
Minors, Jeremiah 151, 195
Modarat, Robert 170
Molyneaux, John Michael 269, 281
Monteagle, Lord 274
Moor Hall, Belbroughton, Worcestershire 144
Moor Lane Bottleworks 312, 427
Moor Lane Glassworks 243, 262, 315
Moore, Edward 205
Moore, Joseph 312, 418, 419
Moose, John 59
Mount, The, High Street, Wordsley 388, 389, 391, 443
Mountford, Biddle & Cope 399
Mountford, Richard 400, 401, 403, 411, 412, 413
Mountford, Sarah 412
Muckley, Angelo Fairfax 332, 349
Muckley, Beatrice 349
Muckley, Elizabeth 348
Muckley, Jabez 331, 348, 415
Muckley, Jabez Rembrant Fairfax 332, 349
Muckley, Jermaudo Fairfax 349
Muckley, Jessie Fairfax 349
Muckley, Josiah 406
Muckley, Leonardo Fairfax 332
Muckley, Leonora Fairfax 349
Muckley, M. Fairfax 206
Muckley, Mary 332
Muckley, Mary Ann 331
Muckley, Wallis 349
Muckley, William 331
Muckley, William Jabez 239, 331, 333, 348
Muckley, William Raphael 332, 349

Mullett, William 465
Murray, Keith Day Pierce 391, 486

N

Nailsea & Stourbridge Glass Company 180
Nailsea Glassworks, Somerset 180, 184
Nash, Arthur Douglas 466
Nash, Arthur John 367, 368, 374, 464, 466
Nash, Isaac 181, 185, 230, 442, 443
Nash, Jane Elizabeth 454
Nash, Leslie 466
Nash, Marjorie 98
Nash, Paul 391
Nash, Richard 98
Nash, William 185
Needs, Mary Anne 220, 235, 236
Needs, Thomas 220
New England Glass Co., Cambridge, Mass., USA 338
Newborough, John 76, 125
Newton, Daniel 299
Newton, William 327
Newtown Forge, Belbroughton, Worcestershire 185
Nicklin, Joseph 259
Nicklin, Mary Ann 495
Nicklin, Timothy 495
Nisbett, Frances 436
Noble, Gordon 511
Normandy 28, 29, 34, 37
North, Anne 294
North, Dudley, Lord 294
North Street Glassworks, Brierley Hill 477
Northall, John 318
Northcote, Sir Stafford, Bart., MP 307, 356
Northwood, Frederick 347, 348
Northwood, John 328, 331, 333, 334, 335, 347, 385, 386, 460, 461, 462, 477, 479, 480, 481, 483, 484, 487, 490
Northwood, Joseph 334, 349
Northwood, Maria 347, 348, 349
Northwood, William 331, 348
Novelty Glassworks, Wollaston 434

O

Oakden, Albert 208, 215
Oakden, Edward 215
Oakham Lodge, Dudley 355
OFallon, J.M. 480
Ogden, John 265
Ogle, Idas 441
Oliver, Charles 497
Oliver, Enoch 496, 497
Oliver, Harriet 497
Oliver, John 102
Onslow, Revd. Richard Francis 212
Orchard, John Vernon 478, 489
Ord, Ben 151
OReilly, Tony 191, 192
Oseland, Edward 103, 240, 242
Oseland, Revd. Edward 218, 234
Oseland, Revd. Henry 87, 99, 103, 119, 122, 138, 158, 234, 242
Overton, William, Bishop of Lichfield 45, 46, 50

P

Paddey, Martin 68, 71, 317
Page and Ensell 263
Page, Edward 263, 266
Page, John 266
Page, William 263
Paget, Anne 129
Paget, John 128
Paget, Robert 128

Paget, Sarah 144, 145
Palmer, Charlotte 375, 395
Palmer, Edward 23
Pardoe, Mary 332
Pargeter, Mary 337, 350
Pargeter, Philip 229, 331, 333, 335, 336, 337, 338, 348, 350, 384, 385, 386, 387, 388, 449, 461
Pargeter-Northwood tazze 334
Paris, Exhibitions 338, 386, 461, 462, 463, 465
Park Field House, Amblecote 414, 437, 438, 443
Park House, Shifnal, Shropshire 401, 413
Park House, Wordsley 318, 381, 414
Parkes, Grainger and Green 261, 262
Parkes, Hannah 265
Parkes, Joseph 260, 265
Parkes, Major 262, 266
Parkes, Sarah 279
Parkes, Zachariah 256, 260, 261, 265
Parkes, Zepheniah 262, 266
Parkfield Glassworks, Amblecote 437
Parnell, John 100, 104
Parrish, James 95, 413
Parrish, Joanna 95
Parrish, John 82
Parrish, Joseph 403, 413
Parrish, Mary 506
Parrish, Samuel Marshall 403, 413
Parrish, Thomas 82, 95, 403, 413
Parsons, Elizabeth Mary 375
Partridge, Elizabeth 109, 116, 117
Passey, Francis 505
Paston, Nicholas 108
Pauli, F. Churlton 371, 375

Pauli, Roger 371
Payne, Andrew 88
Payne, Elizabeth 88
Pearce, Anne Elizabeth 474
Pearce, Daniel 341, 463, 468
Pearce, Lionel 182
Pearce, Lionel Harvey 474
Pearse, Mr 331
Pearson & Insull 499
Pearson, Arthur 502
Pearson, Harry 502
Peel, Sir Robert 276
Pegasus Vase, The 335
Pellatt, Apsley 323
Penn and Sons 299
Penn, Ann 144
Penn, Bate 299, 308
Penn, Phillips 299, 308
Penn, William 73, 136, 144, 268, 299, 300, 308
Penrose, George 188, 189, 190, 192
Penrose, Rachel 189
Penrose, William 188, 189, 190, 192
Pepys, Samuel 65
Percival, Edward 59
Perks, Sarah 346
Perrens, William King 441
Perrot, Benjamin 121
Peterson, Richard 164
Pettener, Emette 289
Pettener, Revd. Thomas 289
Peyton, Joseph 282
Phillips and Pearce 463
Phillips, Elizabeth Wallace 222, 236, 237
Phillips, John 222, 225, 226
Phillips, Louisa 357, 359
Phillips, William 411
Phoenix Glass Company, USA. 204
Phoenix Glassworks, Dudley 261,

299
Pidcock, Cope & Co. 401
Pidcock, Ensell and Bradley 163
Pidcock, George 398, 410, 411
Pidcock, John 68, 162, 172, 173, 174, 175, 177, 178, 244, 252, 397, 398, 399, 401, 410, 412, 417
Pidcock, John Henzey 178, 398, 399, 400, 401, 403, 410
Pidcock, Mary 156
Pidcock, Robert 398, 410
Pidcock, Sarah 156
Pidcock, Thomas 178, 398, 410, 411
Pidcock, William 161
Piers, Christiana 92
Pillars, Amelia 283
Pinchers, Walter 488
Pitman, Joseph 454
Pitt, Elizabeth 316
Pitt, Samuel 202
Plant, Sarah 414
Platts, Glassworks 177
Platts House, Amblecote 177, 178, 179, 183, 397, 401
Playfer, Thomas 46, 47, 51
Plowden & Thompson Ltd. 407, 409, 410, 511, 512
Plowden, William 161
Pocock, Mary Kate 455
Politics, Chartist 225, 275, 304, 305
Politics, Liberal 290, 306, 353
Politics, Tory 76, 77, 223, 225, 273, 275, 301, 306, 307
Politics, Whig 77, 88, 225, 275, 298
Popkin, Hannah 156
Portarlington Glasshouse, Queens County, Ireland 124
Portland Vase, The 327, 334, 338, 385, 394, 477, 479, 482, 484
Potier, Claude 42
Pottery 114, 220, 313, 425, 451, 471, 487
Powell, James 461
Powis, John 184
Pratt, Benjamin 152, 156
Premier Glassworks, Brettell Lane 504
Prestwood House, Stourton, Staffordshire 104
Price, A.D. 508
Price, Joseph 290, 353
Price, R.H. 508
Price, Richard 89
Price, W.A. 507
Priestley, Revd. Dr Joseph 89, 309
Priestley, Sarah 309
Pringle, W. 273, 302
Proctor, Dod 391
Proctor, Ernest 391
Pyrometer 165, 169

Q

Queensbury, David 209

R

Rachetti, Caesar 61, 65
Radford, Daniel 77, 89, 90
Radford, Mary 77, 89, 90
Radford, Samuel 89
Railway, Grand Connection 304
Railway, Grand Junction 304
Railway, Great Western 237
Railway, London-Birmingham 304
Railway, Oxford, Worcester & Wolverhampton 140, 304, 310
Railway, Severn Valley 237
Rainsford, Dorothy 100
Rainsford, Thomas 104

Ramsey, Gatchell and Bancroft 190
Ramsey, James 190
Ravilious, Eric 391
Raybould, Comber 360, 362
Raybould, Thomas 68
Rea, William 70
Red House Glassworks 293, 319, 335, 336, 362, 369, 377
Red Lion, Brettell Lane 470
Redgrave, Richard 328, 347
Reform Act of 1832 225, 274, 275, 303, 354
Renaud, Ann 358
Renaud, Edward 358
Renaud, Edward John 357, 358, 359
Renaud, John 306, 307, 355, 356, 357, 358
Renaud, Sarah Lydia 358
Reynolds, Charlton & Co 401
Reynolds, J. 465
Reynolds, Joseph 411
Reynolds, William 411, 412
Rice, Honourable Spring 274
Richards, Samuel 163
Richards, Thomas 290, 337
Richardson & Co. 327
Richardson & Smith 86
Richardson and Webb 178
Richardson, Benjamin 83, 85, 95, 140, 179, 274, 281, 282, 321, 322, 323, 324, 325, 326, 328, 329, 330, 333, 334, 335, 336, 337, 339, 340, 347, 349, 351, 384, 385, 394, 401, 412
Richardson, Eleanor 96
Richardson, Henry Gething 334, 336, 338, 339, 340, 342, 349, 351
Richardson, John 323, 346
Richardson, John Thomas Haden 347
Richardson, Johnathan 324, 329, 330, 335, 347, 350
Richardson, Joseph 82, 268, 269, 280, 281, 290, 300, 317, 322, 323, 346, 347, 350
Richardson, Margaret 211
Richardson, Martha 346, 347
Richardson, Martha Haden 340, 351
Richardson, Martha Maria 351
Richardson, Mary 346
Richardson, Mary Maria 351
Richardson, Mills & Smith 86, 228
Richardson, Susannah 348, 350
Richardson, Thomas 211, 337, 350
Richardson, William 85, 86, 96
Richardson, William Haden 95, 269, 280, 282, 322, 324, 325, 328, 330, 333, 337, 340, 347, 349, 350, 365, 412, 431
Richardson, William Haden Arthur 351
Ricketts, Henry 320
Rider, John 313
Ridgrave Glasshouse, Hungary Hill 66
River, Severn 20, 25, 74, 121
River, Stour 17, 20, 57, 64, 70, 147, 152, 177, 185, 243, 412, 416
River, Suir 187, 188
Roades, Katrin 309
Robbins, William 152, 153, 212
Roberts, John 304
Robinson, Ann 439
Robinson, Anne 168
Robinson, Benjamin 449, 450
Robinson, Frederick 437, 439
Robinson, George 405, 414, 437, 439

Robinson, John 256
Robinson, Samuel 214
Rogers, Anne 88
Rogers, Daniel 90
Rogers, Greg 371
Rogers, Henry 454
Rogers, Jeremiah 217
Rogers, Martha 89
Rogers, Paul 73, 76, 87, 88
Rogers, Samuel 89, 90
Rogers, Thomas 73, 74, 75, 76, 77, 78, 87, 88, 89, 90, 131, 175, 221, 454
Rooker, T. 347
Roose, James 351
Roose, Martha Maria 340
Rose, Sir George 365
Roughton, Hannah 265
Roughton, John 261, 265, 300, 308
Roughton, Parkes & Co. 261, 265
Round, Benjamin John 482
Round, G. 465
Round, James 499
Round, John 405, 482
Round Oak Glassworks 502
Round Oak Steelworks 502
Royal Academy 208, 332
Royal College of Art 209, 470
Royal Doulton 209
Royal Society of Arts 80, 81, 89, 91, 94, 327, 328, 329, 484
Royal Staffordshire Pottery 391
Rudyard, Jane 64
Rufford & Co. 383
Rufford and Walker 140, 363
Rufford and Wragge 383
Rufford, Francis 139, 140, 145, 146, 310, 313, 315
Rufford, George Pierpoint 146
Rufford, Margaret 145, 146
Rufford, Philip 139, 140, 146, 383

Rufford, Sarah 146
Rusgrove, Phoebe 185
Russell, Edward 71, 78, 136, 138, 144, 145, 189, 317
Russell, Joseph 144, 145
Russell, Mary 68, 71, 145, 317, 344
Russell, Thomas 71, 344
Russia, exports to 269
Ryder, Arthur 496
Ryder, James Henry 496
Rye, Sussex 50, 246

S

Samuel Taylor and Son 426
Sandblasting 208, 210
Sanders, George 191, 193
Sanders, Henry 74
Sanders, Sarah 74
Sawkins, Audnam 417
Scheibner, Frank 480, 489
Schimmelpenninck, Lambert 93
Schimmelpenninck, Mary Anne 80
Schweppes & Co. 404
Scott, Joanna 94
Scott, John 94
Scott, Jones & Co. 82
Scott, Keir, Jones & Co. 82
Scott, Sarah 92
Scott, Sir Joseph, Bart. 93
Scott, William 81, 92, 94
Scriven, Percy 487
Seager, Betty 315
Seager, Hannah 315
Seager, Henry 268
Seager, Susanna 279, 421, 427, 428
Seager, Thomas 166, 267, 279, 312, 315, 427
Seager, William 113, 279, 312, 315, 422

Senades Glasshouse 50
Serjeant, Humfry 145
Serjeant, Richard 138, 145
Service, John Alexander 450, 455
Shaw, James 288, 295
Shaw, Oliver 295
Shaw, Read 296
Shaw, Rebecca Petters 273, 282
Shaw, Samuel 288, 295, 296
Shea, Francis James 231
Shenstone, Thomas 144
Shenstone, William 87, 144
Shepherd & Webb 363, 364
Shepherd, John 178, 363, 364, 454
Shepherd, John Bullas 444, 446, 447, 454
Short, Phebe 351
Shropshire Banking Co. 401, 405
Shropshire, Glass Manufacture 44, 120, 399, 400, 411
Siden Hill, Audnam 230, 417
Silber & Flemming 449
Silver End, Brierley Hill 424, 496
Silvers, Anna Maria 248
Silvers, Benjamin 247, 253
Silvers, Eliza 253, 254
Silvers, Ellen 254, 488
Silvers, Joseph 247, 248, 249, 250, 253, 254, 419
Silvers, Maria 248, 254
Silvers, Sobieskey 419
Silvers, William 249, 253
Silversmiths 246, 291
Simkins, George 450, 455
Simpson, Mary Ann 331, 348, 415
Sismey and Linforth 511
Skey, Samuel 78, 92, 94
Skey, Sarah 92
Skey, Thomas 92
Skrimshire, Mary 64
Slater & Co. 270

Small, Dr. William 78, 91
Smallman, Elizabeth 221
Smallman, Jane 221, 235
Smallman, Joseph 221
Smallman, Mary 266
Smart Brothers 502
Smith, Chris 210
Smith, David 209, 210
Smith, Elijah 85, 86, 96
Smith, Francis 114
Smith, George 96
Smith, Hannah 253
Smith, Henry 442, 443, 453
Smith, James 333, 349
Smith, Nancy 96
Smiths Pottery, Brettell Lane 114
Smythe, Sophia 433
Snedshill Glassworks, Shifnal, Shropshire 120
Society for the Encouragement of Arts, Manufacture and Commerce
nd Commerce 164
Soho and Vesta Glassworks, Birmingham 204
Soho House, Handsworth, Staffordshire 92
Soho Manufactory, Handsworth, Staffordshire 81, 91, 92
Somerset, Lady Jane 56
Somerville, Thomas 263, 266
South Kensington Museum 366, 482
Southwell, Ann 392
Southwell, John 377
Spencer, William 327
Spon Lane Glassworks, Smethwick, Staffordshire 415
Spratt, Gertrude 62
Spring Field, Dudley 290
Spring Grove, Bewdley, Worcestershire 92

Springfield House, Wordsley 344, 440, 453
Springsmire Glasshouse, Dudley 255
Squire, John 52, 59, 63
St. George Knudson, Eloisa 237
St. Helens Glass Co. 181
Staffordshire Yeomanry 270
Stamford, Earl of 214
Stamford, Mary 96, 214, 453
Steel House 320, 346
Steel manufacture 320, 321
Stevens and Williams Ltd. 227, 249, 250, 251, 335, 464, 478, 479, 480, 482, 483, 484, 485, 486, 489, 505
Stevens, Ann 253, 264
Stevens, Anna Maria 253, 254
Stevens Brothers & Co. 199
Stevens, Elizabeth 213, 297, 394
Stevens, Fanny 213
Stevens, Frederick 208, 215
Stevens, Irene M. 208, 209, 215
Stevens, James 199, 200, 201, 212, 213, 249, 253, 254, 263
Stevens, Joseph 85, 199, 200, 201, 202, 212, 213, 247, 248, 249, 253, 254, 262, 263, 437
Stevens, Joseph Silvers 478
Stevens, Maria 253, 254
Stevens, Randolph 264
Stevens, William 200, 208, 212, 215, 247, 249, 251, 253, 254, 478, 498
Stevens, William Henry 251, 254, 478
Stewkins, Audnam 415, 417
Stewponey Inn, Stourton, Staffordshire 221, 245, 261, 269, 290, 380, 402, 422, 431
Stokes, Johnathan 377, 392
Stokes, Rebecca 377, 392

Stott, Eric A. 471
Stour Glassworks, Audnam 507
Stourbridge and Kidderminster Banking Co. 485
Stourbridge Co-operative Flint Glass Manufacturers 437
Stourbridge Glass Co. Ltd. 181, 469, 507, 508
Stourbridge, Navigation Company 25, 163, 244, 245, 252
Stourbridge, School of Art 208, 209, 369, 431, 460, 479
Stourton Castle, Staffordshire 142, 222
Stourton Mill, Staffordshire 152
Strafford, Earl of 115
Strathearn Glass, Scotland 371
Stringer, Mary 93
Stuart & Mills 443, 445
Stuart and Sons 388, 389, 390
Stuart, Arthur 388, 389, 395
Stuart, Charles 389
Stuart, Charles Frederick 395
Stuart, Derek 371
Stuart, Eric M. 371, 375
Stuart, Frederick 142, 340, 370, 371, 375, 388, 389, 395, 440, 441, 442, 443, 444, 445, 453
Stuart, Frederick G. 371, 375
Stuart, Frederick H. 371, 375
Stuart, Geoffrey 390, 391
Stuart, Geoffrey W. 371
Stuart, George 388, 389, 395
Stuart, Ian M. 371, 375
Stuart, Mary Margaret 375
Stuart, Robert 370, 375, 388, 389, 390, 391, 395
Stuart, Samuel 440, 453
Stuart, Samuel Mansfield 375, 389
Stuart Strathearn 371
Stuart, Walter Mansfield 388, 389,

395
Stuart, William 444
Stuart, William Arthur 371, 375
Stuart, William E.C. 371
Stuart, William Henry 375, 388, 389, 390, 395, 396
Studley Court, Stourbridge 142, 375
Summerhill, Kingswinford 225, 226, 258, 264, 367, 368, 442
Sutherland, Graham 391
Sutton, Ann 351
Sutton, Edward, Earl of Dudley 54, 57
Sutton, Henry 339, 351
Sutton, William 351
Sweden, iron imports from 169, 320
Swift, John 418, 419
Swin Forge 55
Swindell, Anne Jane Rose 413
Swindell, Rose 413
Sydney, Exhibitions 463

T

T.G. Hawkes and Co. 484
Talbot Hotel, Stourbridge 17, 18, 25, 86, 139, 141, 143, 160, 168, 201, 203, 227, 251, 252, 321, 334, 382, 384, 424, 435, 441
Taylor, Ann 265
Taylor, Elizabeth 168
Taylor, John 78, 91
Taynton, Robert 102
Temple, John 371
Tetrye, Sara 47, 51
Thomas Badger & Co. 303, 305
Thomas Davis & Co. 292
Thomas, Frank Davies 485
Thomas Hawkes & Co. 271, 272,

277
Thomas, Lucy Annette 477, 489, 490
Thomas, Thomas Davies 485, 491
Thomas Webb & Co. 203, 323, 368, 407, 452, 462, 467
Thomas Webb & Sons 142, 459, 460
Thomas Webb and Corbett 207, 208, 368, 369, 466
Thomas Webb and Sons Ltd 208, 464, 466, 467, 468, 469, 507
Thompson, Bridget 101, 177
Thompson, Charles Herbert 233, 239
Thompson, Jim 209
Thompson L'Hospied and Co. Ltd 239
Thompson, Marie Beatrix 239
Threlfall, Richard Evelyn 407, 415
Threlfall, Sir Richard 415
Tiffany, Louis Comfort 368, 466
Tiled House, Pensnett 196, 344
Tilley, Mary 310, 311
Tittery, Anne 74, 87, 117, 130, 131
Tittery, Daniel 72, 87, 130
Tittery, Joshua 87
Tittery, Paul 131
Tomlinson, Elizabeth 54, 57
Tompson alias Beare, Anne 87
Trade Unions 84, 202, 224, 238, 277, 303, 324, 364, 389, 404, 438, 441, 467, 483
Tristram, Dr John 144
Tristram, Mary 144
Tristram, Richard 73
Tristram, William 144
Tudor Crystal (Stourbridge) Ltd. 509, 512
Turin, Exhibition of 1911 468
Turnpike Trusts 19, 174, 197, 220

Tutbury Crystal Glass Ltd. 216
Tutbury Glass Company 335
Tutbury Glassworks, Staffordshire 209, 210, 347, 369, 375
Tyzack, Abraham 48
Tyzack, Anne 89, 104
Tyzack, Benjamin 128
Tyzack, Bridgit 56, 64, 122
Tyzack, Christophe 38
Tyzack, Edward 88, 120, 121, 123
Tyzack, Elizabeth 71, 123, 344
Tyzack, John 56, 58, 62, 87, 99, 119, 122, 128, 129
Tyzack, Joyce 65
Tyzack, Judith 62
Tyzack, Meriall 61, 65
Tyzack, Nicole 38
Tyzack, Paul 54, 56, 58, 59, 60, 61, 62, 64, 65, 100, 119, 128, 129
Tyzack, Samuel 120, 121, 122, 123
Tyzack, William 120, 121, 123, 128
Tyzack, Zachariah 58, 61, 62, 64, 119, 120, 121, 123

U

Uffindell, Roy S. 470, 471
Union Glassworks, Birmingham 262
United Ceramic 509
United Glass Group 312

V

Vaillant, Pierre 42
Venables, John 406, 415
Victoria Glassworks, Aston 201
Vine Inn, Wordsley 365, 440, 442
Vitrarius, Laurence 32

W

W.H., B. & J. Richardson 85, 365
W.H. Richardson Junior & Co. 349
W.H. Swingewood & Co. Ltd. 452
Wainwright Brothers 321
Wainwright, Charles 321
Wainwright, George William 320, 321, 322, 323, 346, 362, 381
Wainwright, Joseph 289, 290
Waldron, Elizabeth 155
Waldron, Hannah 436
Waldron, Thomas 185
Waldron, William 185, 196, 197, 198
Walker, Eleanor 491
Walker, James 142, 146, 147, 444, 446, 448, 449
Walker, James Harry 141, 142, 147, 444, 448, 449
Walker, Jane 146
Walker, Philip 141, 142, 147, 444
Walker, Sarah 146
Walker, William 140, 141, 146, 147
Wallows Street Glassworks 501
Walpole, Elizabeth 191
Walpole, Joseph 190
Walpole, William 190
Walsh-Walsh Glassworks, Birmingham 341
War, Crimean 405, 459
War, English Civil 60, 64, 107, 108, 133, 162
War, First World 342, 369, 390, 407, 469
War, of American Independence 196
War, of the Austrian Succession 196
War, Second World 208, 370, 408, 487
War, Seven Years 162

Ward, Anthony 136
Ward, Diana Smart 432
Ward, Elizabeth 136
Ward, Frances, Lady Viscountess 268
Ward, Hon. Humble Dudley 277, 283
Ward, John, sixth Baron Ward, first Viscount Dudley and Ward and Ward 117, 217, 218, 234
Ward, Revd. William Humble, tenth Baron Ward 283
Ward, William, Baron Ward 117, 234
Wassell Grove, Hagley, Worcestershire 77
Waterford Glassworks 187
Waterford, Lady 190
Waterford, Lord 190
Watt, James 78, 80, 91
Weald, The 32, 33, 35, 44, 66
Webb & Richardson 84, 323, 324, 363
Webb, Benjamin 322, 346
Webb, Charles 390, 396, 459, 463, 464, 465, 466, 468, 472, 474, 475
Webb, Charles Walter Herbert 208, 368, 369, 375, 466, 475
Webb Corbett 182, 207, 208, 209
Webb, Edward 84, 85, 96, 142, 228, 346, 365, 366, 367, 368, 374, 375, 384, 388, 396, 440, 442, 453, 466, 483
Webb, Elizabeth 238, 440, 453, 455
Webb, Henry Arthur 473
Webb, Henry Fitzroy 203, 214
Webb, Herbert 207
Webb, Jane 204, 206, 207, 214, 215, 228, 238, 346
Webb, John 322, 324, 346, 347, 363, 364, 373
Webb, John Herbert 208
Webb, Joseph 84, 85, 96, 202, 203, 204, 205, 206, 214, 215, 228, 365, 366, 483
Webb, Joseph William 473
Webb, Mary 348
Webb, Mary Ann 453
Webb, Richard 96, 203, 214, 402, 453
Webb, Sarah 346
Webb, Shaw & Co. 407, 467, 492
Webb, Thomas 178, 179, 183, 224, 322, 323, 346, 363, 364, 440, 441, 458, 459, 460, 472, 473
Webb, Thomas Ernest 368, 369, 466, 475
Webb, Thomas Fisher Wilkes 215
Webb, Thomas Wilkes 179, 183, 368, 375, 459, 460, 461, 462, 463, 464, 465, 466, 471, 472, 475
Webb, W.G. 369
Webb, Walter Wilkes 368, 464, 466, 468, 469, 473, 475
Webb, William 96, 329, 348, 365, 366, 374, 384
Webb, William George 366, 367, 368, 374, 388, 390, 396
Webb, William Harcourt 390, 396
Webbs Crystal Glass Co. Ltd. 469, 470, 507
Wedgwood, Cecil 466
Wedgwood, Clement, F. 464
Wedgwood, Josiah 80, 81, 93, 165, 174
Wedgwood, Richard 93
Wedgwood, Sarah 93
Wedgwood, Thomas 93
Weidlein, Annie 489, 490, 500
Weinich, Valentin 369

Welch & Rogers, bankers of Cornhill 77
Welch, George 77
Welch, Thomas 77
Wellings, Thomas 428
Wells, Elizabeth 309
Wells, John 295
Wells, Mary 295, 297
Wentworth Glasshouse, South Yorkshire 115
Westbrook, Tim 488
Westwood & Co. 314
Westwood & Moore 312
Westwood, Ann 316
Westwood, Charles 314, 316
Westwood, Edward 313, 314, 316, 441
Westwood, Elizabeth 172
Westwood, Jane 346
Westwood, John 312
Westwood, Moore & Rider 313
Westwood, Price and Co. 313
Westwood, Price, Worral & Co. 313
Westwood, Samuel 295
Westwood, William 295
Wheeler, Edward 67, 70, 71
Wheeler, John 67, 68, 69, 70, 71, 135, 160, 167
Wheeler, Mary 71
Wheeler, Penelope 68, 71, 430, 432
Wheeler, Richard 67, 70, 71
Wheeley, John 423, 424, 426, 428
Wheeley, Robert 153
Wheeley, Susanna 422
Wheeley, Thomas 83, 279, 421, 422, 423, 426, 427, 428
Wheeley, William Seager 83, 153, 198, 423, 424, 427, 428
Wheeleys Brettell Lane Glasshouses 198, 220, 421
Wheeley's Brettell Lane Glasshouses 280
While, George 405
Whitcroft, Harry 487
White, Elizabeth 160, 167, 168
White Hall, Webbs Lane, Wordsley 339
White, Henry 160
White House Glassworks 360, 466
White, Isaac 184
White, Mary 154
White, Paul 112
Whitefriars Glassworks 323, 461, 487
Whitehurst, John 169
Whitehurst, Moore and Guest 353
Whitworth, Robert 25
Wilcox, Henry 102
Wildsmith, Robert 133
Wilkinson, Frank 181, 182
Wilkinson, H. 507
Wilkinson, Mrs K. 508
Wilkinson, R. 182
Willetts, Thomas 196
William & Edward Webb & Sons 368
William Bailey and Company 431
William Gammon & Co. 276
William Harrop & Co. 498
William Walker & Son 444
Williams, Ellen 254
Williams, Hubert Silvers 487, 488, 490, 491
Williams, James 250, 405
Williams, Joseph Silvers 251, 254, 477, 478, 479, 481, 483, 485, 487, 488, 489, 490
Williams, Michael 249, 254
Williams, Samuel Cox 249, 251, 254, 477, 478, 479, 481, 488, 490
Williams-Thomas, Hubert Silvers 487, 488, 490, 491
Williams-Thomas, Joseph Silvers

251, 254, 477, 478, 479,
481, 483, 485, 487, 488,
489, 490
Williams-Thomas, Reginald Silvers 487, 488, 491
Willoughby, Sir Percival 52, 63
Wilmer, Elizabeth 293
Windmill, Edward 316
Windmill, Richard Alfred 314
Winnington, Sir Edward 212
Winshurestand, George 135, 136
Wisborough Green, Sussex 36, 37, 38, 43, 44, 47, 51, 52, 66
Withymoor Glasshouse 62, 99, 119, 128
Witley Court, Worcestershire 104
Witton, Francis 137, 138, 145
Witton, John 138
Witton, Richard Russell 138, 145
Witton, Serjeant 138, 139, 145
Wollaston Hall, Worcestershire 60, 64, 67, 152
Wollaton Glasshouse, Nottinghamshire 48, 52, 63
Wolverhampton, Exhibitions 366, 480
Wolverhampton, Glass Manufacture 320
Wolverhampton, Grammar School 289, 296
Wolverhampton, School of Art 332
Wombridge Ironworks, Shropshire 120
Wood, James 353
Wood, Lydia 316
Woodall, George 460, 463, 464, 465, 466, 468, 469, 470, 473
Woodall, Thomas 460, 463, 464, 466, 470, 473, 476
Woodcock, Elizabeth 297
Woodcock, Frances 297
Woodcock, Walter 297

Woodfield, Wordsley 368
Woodlands, Nigel 471
Woodlands, The, Dudley 297
Woodlands, The, Wordsley 370
Woolwich, Glass Manufacture 98, 158
Wooton Lodge, Ellastone, Staffordshire 67, 70
Worcester City Glasshouse, Claines 170
Worcester, Porcelain Works 332, 461
Wordsley Flint Glassworks 317
Wordsley Hall, Buckpool, Wordsley 336, 338, 340
Wordsley House 344
Wordsley Iron Foundry 440
Wordsley Manor 344
Wordsley, School of Art 490
Wordsley Steam Flour Mill 364
Worral, Ann 394
Worral, John 394
Worral, Joseph 386, 394
Worral, Sarah 219, 234, 235
Worral, Thomas 219
Wragge, Charles John 146
Wragge, Elizabeth 146
Wragge, John 146
Wright & Co. 496
Wright, Doctor 271
Wright, James 496
Wright, Mary 267, 280, 281, 282
Wright, Sarah 269
Wright, Susannah 496
Wrockwardine Glassworks, Shropshire 399, 400, 411
Wyatt, Samuel 23

Y

Yapp, Fanny 473
Yorkshire, Glass Manufacture 115,

181, 184, 285, 404, 496

Z

Zepheniah Parkes and Co. 262
Zouche, Sir Edward 58

Abbreviations

ACC	Antique Collectors Club
ADCG	Antique Dealer & Collector's Guide
ANT	The Antiquary
AM	Antiques Magazine
BM	British Museum
BMSGH	Birmingham and Midland Society for Genealogy and Heraldry
BHGM	Broadfield House Glass Museum
BRL	Birmingham Reference Library
CL	Country Life Magazine
CM	Connoisseur Magazine
DA	Dudley Archive
GMF	Glass Manufacturers Federation
JBSGP	Journal of British Society of Glass Painters
JGA	Journal of the Glass Association
JGC	Journal of the Glass Circle
JGS	Journal of Glass Studies
JPMA	Journal of Post Medieval Archaeology
LJRO	Lichfield Joint Record Office
PCC	Prerogative Court of Canterbury
PG	Pottery Gazette & Glass Trade Review
PRO	Public Record Office
RM	Reliquary Magazine
SAC	Surrey Archaeological Collections
SPCK	Society for Promoting Christian Knowledge
SRO	Stafford Record Office
TNS	Transactions of the Newcomen Society
TNSFC	Transactions of North Staffordshire Field Club
TWAS	Transactions of Worcester Archaeological Society
TSGT	Transactions of the Society of Glass Technology
WSL	William Salt Library, Stafford
WRO	Worcester Record Office

BIBLIOGRAPHY

Author	Title	Date	Publisher
Agricola, Georgius	De Re Metallica, quibus officia instrumenta, machinae . . .	1566	Basle. Trans. and ed. H.C. Hoover and L.H. Hoover, Dover Publications Inc., New York 1950.
Aitken, William Costen	Glass Manufacturers of Birmingham & Stourbridge	1851	J F Feeney, Birmingham
Allen, George Cyril	The Industrial Development of Birmingham and the Black Country 1860-1927	1929	G. Allen & Unwin, London
Allwood, John	The Great Exhibitions	1977	Studio Vista
Angus-Butterworth, Lionel Milner	British Table And Ornamental Glass	1956	Leonard Hill Ltd, London
Angus-Butterworth, Lionel Milner	The Manufacture of Glass	1948	Sir Isaac Pitman & Sons, London
Anon	Art-Journal Illustrated Catalogue of The Industry of all Nations	1851	
Anon	Crown Glass - Its History and Manufacture	1849	Practical Mechanic's Journal (Glasgow)
Anon	English Drinking Glasses in the Ashmolean Museum	1977	Ashmolean Museum, Oxford

Anon	Making Pottery and Glassware in Britain	1954	Scott Greenwood & Son Ltd, London
Anon	Mr Pargeter's Milton Vase	1878	RM 19 p243
Anon	Mr Pargeter's Art Productions in Glass	1877	RM 19 pp57-58
Anon	Official Descriptive Catalogue of the Great Exhibition	1851	Spicer Brothers, London
Anon	Recipes for Flint Glass Making	1900	Scott Greenwood and Co, London
Anon	Stourbridge, the Manufacture of Glass	1846	Art Union, p102-7
Anon	The Black Country and its Industries No 1	1903	Mark and Moody, Stourbridge
Armitage, Edward Liddall	Stained Glass History, Technology and Practice	1959	Leonard Hill
Art-Journal	Art-Journal Illustrated Catalogue of the International Exhibition 1862	1862	James S Virtue, London
Arwas, Victor	Glass, Art Nouveau to Art Deco	1987	Academy Editions, London
Ash, Douglas	How to Identify English Drinking Glasses and Decanters	1962	G. Bell and Sons Ltd, London

Ash, Douglas	Dictionary of British Antique Glass	1975	Pelham Books, London
Ashdown, Charles Henry and Tippets	History of the Worshipful Company of Glaziers of the City of London	1919	Blades, East & Blades, London
Ashton, Thomas Southcliffe	The Industrial Revolution 1760-1830	1948	London
Ashurst, Denis	The History of South Yorkshire Glass		Alden Press, Oxford
Bacon, John Maunsell	Bottle-decanters and Bottles	1939	Apollo, xxx
Bacon, John Maunsell	Decanters, 1677-1750 and 1745-1800		JGC v41 & 42
Bacon, John Maunsell	English Glass Collecting for Beginners	1942	Reed, Penrith
Baker, John and Lammer, Alfred	English Stained Glass of the Medieval Period	1978	Thames & Hudson
Balderson, Marion (ed)	James Claypoole's Letter Book, London and Philadelphia 1681-1684	1967	Huntingdon Library, San Marino, California
Bangert, Albrecht	Glass Art Nouveau & Art Deco	1979	Studio Vista/Christies
Bardrof, Frank E.	Frederick Carder: Artist in Glass	1939	Glass Industry v20 No 1 April

Barker, Theodore Cardwell	The Glassmakers Pilkington: the rise of an international company 1826-1976	1977	Weidenfeld and Nicolson, London
Barnsby, George John	Social Conditions in the Black Country 1800-1900	1969	Integrated Publishing Services, Wolverhampton
Barnsby, George John	The Dudley working class movement from 1750 to 1860	1986	Dudley Leisure Services
Barraud, Ronald	John Davenport, a Nineteenth-Century Glass Decorator	1970	CM, Mar
Barrelet, James	La Verrerie en France de l'époque gallo-romaine à nos jours	1953	Librairie Larousse, Paris
Bate, Percy	English Table Glass	1905	Charles Scribner's Sons New York
Battie, David and Cottle, Simon (editors)	Sotheby's Concise Encyclopedia of Glass	1991	Conran Octopus
Beard, Geoffrey William	Nineteenth Century Cameo Glass	1956	Ceramic Book Company, Newport, Monmouth
Beard, Geoffrey William	The Documentation and Variety of Stourbridge Glass	1964	JGC v135
Beard, Geoffrey William	English makers of cameo glass	1954	AM, p472-4

Beaupre, Jean Nicolas	Les Gentilshommes Verriers ou Recherches sur l'industrie verrière et les privilèges des verriers de l'ancienne Lorraine.	1846	Nancy
Beck, Doreen	The Book of Bottle Collecting	1977	Hamlyn
Beddall, U.A.	An Historical Sketch of the Parish of Kingswinford	1885	U. Beddall, Brierley Hill
Bedford, John	Bristol and Other Coloured Glass	1964	Cassell & Co Ltd, London
Bedford, John	English Crystal Glass	1966	Cassell & Company Ltd
Bennett, Raymond	Collecting for Pleasure	1969	Bodley Head
Bentley, R.	Thomas Bentley, 1730-1780, of Liverpool, Etruria, and London	1927	Billing & Sons, Guildford
Bickerton, Leonard Marshall	English Drinking Glasses	1984	Shire Publications Ltd
Bickerton, Leonard Marshall	Eighteenth Century English Drinking Glasses	1971	Barrie & Jenkins, London
Biser, Benjamin Franklin	Elements of Glass and Glassmaking	1899	Glass & Pottery Publishing Co. Pittsburg
Bishop, Morchard (Ed)	Recollections of the Table-Talk of Samuel Rogers	1952	The Richards Press Ltd, London

Bisset, James	A Poetic Survey round Birmingham	1800	Printed for the author, Birmingham
Haudicquer de Blancourt, François	The Art of Glass	1699	London
Bles, Joseph	Rare English Glasses of XVII & XVIII Centuries	1925	Geoffrey Bles
Bloch, Marc	Feudal Society, 2 vols (original French edition 1940)	1965	Routledge Paperbacks, London
Boland, Peter and Ellis, Jason	A Lost Stourbridge Glassworks Rediscovered	1997	JGA, v5, pp6-25
Bolas, Thomas FCS, FIC	Glass Blowing and Working	1898	Dawbarn & Ward Ltd, London
Bontemps, Georges	Guide du Verrier	1868	Paris
Bowles, William Henry	History of the Vauxhall and Ratcliff Glass Houses.	1926	Privately printed
Boydell, Mary	Irish Glass	1976	Eason & Son, Dublin
Bradbury, Frederick	History of Old Sheffield Plate	1912	Macmillan & Co. Ltd
Bray, Charles	Dictionary of Glass Materials and Techniques	1995	A & C Black (Publishers) Limited, London
Bridgewater, N.P.	Glasshouse Farm, St. Weonards: A small Glassworking site.	1963	Transacs of Woolhope Field Club v 37 pp300-315

Briggs, Dennis Brook	Practical Glass Manipulation	1926	Crosby, Lockwood and Son, London
Brooks, John	Glass Tumblers 1700-1900	1987	John A. Brooks, Leicester
Brooks, John	Stourbridge Collection of 19th Century Glass	1974	
Brooks, John	The Arthur Negus Guide to British Glass	1981	Hamlyn Publishing Group Ltd
Brooks, John A.	Glass 100 masterpieces of crystal and colour	1975	Camden House Books
Brown, C.M.	The Changing Location of the West Midlands Glass Industry	1978	West Midlands Studies, Winter 78 v11 W'ton Poly.
Buckley, Francis	Notes on the Glasshouses of Stourbridge 1700-1830	1927	TSGT 11 pp106-7
Buckley, Francis	A History of Old English Glass	1925	Ernest Benn Ltd, London
Buckley, Francis	Monographs on Glass	1925	TSGT
Buckley, Francis	The Birmingham Glass Trade 1740-1833	1927	TSGT, 11, 374-86
Buckley, Francis	The Glasshouses of Dudley and Worcester	1927	Richard Clay & Son Ltd, Bungay, Suffolk
Buckley, Francis	Old London Glasshouses	1915	Stevens & Sons London

Buckley, Francis	The Glass Trade in England in the Seventeenth Century	1914	Stevens & Sons, Privately published
Buckley, Francis	The Taxation of English Glass in the Seventeenth Century	1914	London, privately printed
Buckley, Francis	English Baluster - stemmed Glasses of the 17th & 18th Centuries	1912	Ballantyne Press, Edinburgh
Buckley, Francis	Old London Drinking Glasses	1913	Ballantyne Press, Edinburgh
Buckley, Wilfred	The Art Of Glass	1939	The Phaidon Press
Buckley, Wilfred	European Glass	1926	E. Benn, London
Buckley, Wilfred	Diamond Engraved glasses of the Sixteenth Century	1929	E. Benn Ltd, London
Buechner, Thomas S.	The Glass of Frederick Carder	1961	The Connoisseur Handbook, pp39-43
Bungard, G.D.	'MEN OF GLASS' A Personal View of the De Bongar Family in the 16th and 17th Centuries	1979	JGC v3
Bund, John William Willis.	The Civil War in Worcestershire 1642-1646; and the Scotch Invasion of 1651	1905	Midland Educational Co., Birmingham

Bunt, Cyril G.E.	Wonderful Waterford – Ireland's debt to English craftsmen	1959	ADCG, Oct
Burke, John	A Genealogical and Heraldic History of the Commoners of Great Britain and Ireland (4 vols)	1838	Henry Colburn, London
Burke, Sir John Bernard	A Genealogical and Heraldic Dictionary of the Landed Gentry of Great Britain and Ireland for 1850 (2 vols)	1882	Harrison, London
Burn, John Southerden	The History of French, Walloon, Dutch and other Protestant Refugees	1846	Longman & Co., London
Burritt, Elihu	Walks in The Black Country	1868	Sampson Low, Son and Martson
Burton, John	Glass - Philosophy and Method	1967	Sir Isaac Pitman & Sons Ltd, London
Bury, Shirley	Felix Summerlys' Art Manufactures	1967	Apollo
Byrne, D. and J.	Webb Corbett and Royal Doulton English Full Lead Crystal	1978	Royal Doulton Tableware Ltd
Campbell, Alister	Early English Glass-makers	1954	ADCG, Mar
Campbell, Alister	How Glass came to England	1954	ADCG, Feb

Challands, Christine	A Lifetime of Change, Kingswinford Parish 1775-1850	1974	Dudley Teachers Centre
Chambers, R.L.	Oldswinford, Bedcote and Stourbridge Manors & Boundaries	1978	Dudley Teachers Centre
Chambers, R.L.	Thomas Milward's Seventeenth Century Daybook	1978	
Chance, Henry MA	On the Manufacture of Crown and Sheet Glass	1856	J. Franklin Institute
Chance, James Frederick	A History of the Firm of CHANCE BROTHERS & CO.	1919	Spottiswoode, Ballantyne & Co Ltd.London
Chance, Sir Hugh	Records and the Nailsea Glassworks	1967	CM
Chance, Sir Hugh	The Bromsgrove Glasshouses	1959	TWAS v 36, pp42-51
Chandler, George and Campbell	Dudley, as it was and as it is today	1949	Batsford
Charleston, Robert Jesse	English Eighteenth - Century Opaque - White Glass	1954	AM (Oct-Dec 1954) 294-7, 487-91
Charleston, Robert Jesse	A Glassmaker's Bankruptcy Sale	1975	JGC v2

Charleston, Robert Jesse	Glass Furnaces Through the Ages	1978	JGS, v20 pp9-33
Charleston, Robert Jesse	Masterpieces of Glass, A World History from the Corning Museum of Glass	1990	Harry N. Abrams, New York
Charleston, Robert Jesse	English Glass and the glass used in England c400-1940	1984	George Allen and Unwin (Publishers) Ltd
Churchill, Arthur Ltd	History In Glass. A Coronation Exhibition of Royal, Historical, Political and Social Glasses commemorating 18th and 19th century events in English History	1937	Arthur Churchill Ltd, London
Clark, Charles Francis George	The Curiosities of Dudley and the Black Country	1881	Buckler Brothers, Birmingham
Clark, E. Graham	Glass-making in Lorraine	1931	TSGT v 15
Clark, George T.	Some Account of Sir Robert Mansell Kt	1883	Dowlais, Privately Printed
Clayden, Peter William	The Early Life of Samuel Rogers	1887	Smith, Elder & Co, London
Clements, Revd. Benjamin	Sermons On Several Occasions	1768	G. Smart, Wolverhampton
Clepham, J.	The Manufacture of Glass in England - Rise of the Art on the Tyne	1880	Archealogia Aeliana, New Series, v VIII p123

Cook, W.E.	The Art and Craft of Glassmaking	1934	Stuart & Sons Ltd, Stourbridge
Cooke, Frederick	Glass, Twentieth-Century Design	1986	E.P. Dutton, New York
Cooper, Stephen	Chiddingfold Glass Manufacturers	1886	Notes and Queries ser.7 v 2 10 Apr 1886
Cooper, William	Crown Glass Cutter & Glaziers Manual	1835	Oliver & Boyd, Edinburgh
Coppen-Gardner, Sylvia	A Background for Glass Collectors	1975	Pelham Books
Court, William Henry Bassano	The Rise of the Midland Industries 1600-1838	1938	Oxford University Press
Cousins, Mark	Twentieth Century Glass	1989	Chartwell
Crellin, John Keith and Scott, J.R.	Glass and British Pharmacy 1600-1900	1972	Wellcome Institute of the History of Medicine
Crompton, Sydney	English Glass	1967	Ward Lock & Co Ltd, London and Sydney
Crossley, David W.	Glassmaking in Bagot's Park, Staffordshire, in the 16th Century	1967	JPMA v 1, 44-83
Crossley, David W.	The Performance of the Glass Industry in Sixteeth-Century England	1972	Economic History Review, xxv No.3 pp421-433

Crossley, David W. and Aberg, F.A.	Sixteeth-Century Glass-Making in Yorkshire: Excavations at Furnaces at Hutton and Rosedale, North Riding	1972	JPMA v 6 pp 107-59
Crossley, David W.	Sir William Clavell's Glasshouse at Kimmeridge, Dorset: The Excavations of 1980-81	1987	Archeological Journal v 144 pp340-382
Cunningham, William	Alien Immigrants to England	1897	Swann Sonnenschein & Co, London
Curtis, Tony	Antiques and Their Values - Glass	1976	Apollo Press, Worthing
Curzon, William D.	The Manufacturing Industries of Worcestershire	1883	W.D. Curzon, Birmingham
Daniel, Dorothy	Cut and Engraved Glass, 1171-1905	1950	M. Barrows and Company, New York
Daniels, J. Stuart	The Woodchester Glasshouse	1950	John Bellows Ltd
Davidson, David M'Bride Johnstone	Glass and Glazing	1946	Crosby Lockwood & Son Ltd., London
Davidson, Ruth	English Cameo Glass	1963	AM, p694
Davies, Edward John	The Blaenavon Story	1975	Torfaen Borough Council

Davies, V.L. and Hyde, H.	Dudley and The Black Country 1760-1860	1970	County Borough of Dudley
Davis, Derek Cecil and Middlemas, Robert Keith	Coloured Glass	1968	Herbert Jenkins, London
Davis, Derek Cecil	English and Irish Antique Glass	1965	Arthur Barker Limited, London
Davis, Derek Cecil	Glass for Collectors	1971	Hamlyn, London
Davis, Derek Cecil	English Bottles & Decanters 1650-1900	1972	Charles Letts and Company, London
Davis, Derek Cecil	The Walter Hale Collection at Grocer's Hall	1970	Grocer's Company
Davis, Frank Cecil	Early Eighteenth Century English Glass	1971	Country Life Books, Hamelyn
Davis, Frank	Antique Glass and Glass collecting	1973	Hamlyn
Davis, Frank	Continental Glass from Roman to Modern Times	1972	Arthur Barker
Dawson, Charles	Old Sussex glass, Its Origin and Decline	1905	ANT v 41, p8-11
Debette, L.P.	The Manufacture of Glass in Bohemia	1844	J. Franklin Inst
Delomosne & Son Ltd	Gilding the Lilly - Rare forms of decoration on English Glass of the later 18th century	1978	Delomosne & Son Ltd., London

Dent, Robert, Kirkup	The Making of Birmingham	1894	J.L. Allday, Birmingham
Dent, Robert, Kirkup and Hill, Joseph.	Historic Staffordshire	1896	The Midland Educational Co, Birmingham
Deville, Achille	Histoire de L'Art de la Verrerie dans l'Antiquite	1873	A. Morel at Cie, Paris
Dexel, W.	Glass	1950	Revensburg, Otto Maier
Diamond, Freda	The Story of Glass	1953	Harcourt, Brace and Co., New York
Dickson, John Home	Glass. A Handbook for Students & Technicians	1951	Hutchinsons, London
Diderot, Denis	Encyclopédie, ou Dictionaire raisonné des sciences, des arts et des métiers, par une sociéte de gens de lettres.	1751	Paris
Dillon, Edward MA	Glass	1907	Methuen, London
Dodd, George	Days at the Factories The book of English Trades	1821	1975 E P Publishing
Dodsworth, Roger	Glass and Glassmaking	1982	Shire Publications
Dodsworth, Roger	British Glass Between The Wars	1987	Dudley Leisure Services
Douglas, Jane	Collectable Glass	1961	Longacre Press

Douglas, Ronald Walter and Frank Susan	A History of Glassmaking	1972	G T Foulis and Company, Henley on Thames
Downey, Alan	The Story of Waterford Glass	1952	Carthage Press, Waterford
Drabble, Phil	Black Country	1952	William Clowes & Sons Ltd, London
Drahotová, Olga	European Glass	1983	Peerage Books, London
Dresser, Christopher	Principles of Decorative Design	1873	London
Dudley, Dud	Mettallum Martis	1665	London
Duffy, E. Mary	Philip Pargeter and John Northwood I, cameo glass pioneers	1962	AM, Dec
Dumbrell, Roger	Understanding Antique Wine Bottles	1983	ACC
Duncan, George Sang MA	Bibliography of Glass from the earliest records to 1940	1960	Dawsons of Pall Mall, for the SGT
Duthie, Arthur Louis	Decorative Glass Processes	1908	Archibald Constable & Co. Ltd., London
Dyer, Walter A.	The Earliest Recorded Glassmaker in England	1960	TSGT v1 No 4 Aug 1960 p137
Eastlake, Charles Lock	Hints on Household Taste	1868	London

Ebbott, Rex	British Glass of the seventeenth and eighteenth centuries	1971	Oxford University Press, Melbourn
Edwards, Bill	The Standard Encyclopedia of Carnival Glass	1982	Collectors Books, Paducah, KY USA
Edwards, M.H.	Stourbridge Fireclays, and the Manufacture of Glasshouse pots	1927	TSGT v 11 pp400-406
Eisen, Gustavus A.	Glass, Its Origin, History . . .	1928	William Edwin Rudge, New York
Elliott, Patricia Marguerite and Smythe, Sidney George Lyle	Modern Industries – Glass	1965	Wheaton, Exeter
Elville, Ernest Michael	The Collector's Dictionary of Glass	1961	Country Life
Elville, Ernest Michael	English and Irish Cut Glass 1750-1950	1953	Country Life
Elville, Ernest Michael	English Tableglass	1951	Country Life
Engle, Anita	Readings In Glass History (Four Vols)	1973	Phoenix Publications, Jerusalem
Epstein, Sam and Beryl	The First Book of Glass	1955	Ward
Ericson, Eric E.	A Guide to Coloured Steuben Glass, 1903-1933		Lithographic Press, Loveland, Colorado

Evans, Wendy; Ross, Catherine and Werner, Alex	Whitefriars Glass James Powell & Sons of London	1995	Museum of London
Evans, Wendy and Weeden, Cyril	Making Glass	1968	GMF, London
Evans, Wendy	Glass History	1968	GMF, London
Eveson, Stanley R.	Reflections: Sixty years with the crystal glass industry	1990	SGT. Reprinted from Glass Technology V 31
Fisher, Leonard	The Glassmakers	1964	Watts, USA
Fitzjohn, G.J. Monson	Drinking Vessels of Bygone Days	1927	Herbert Jenkins Ltd, London
Fleming, John Arnold	Scottish and Jacobite Glass	1938	Jackson Son & co Glasgow
Fossing, Paul	Glass Vessels before Glass-blowing	1940	E. Munksgard, Copenhagen
Foster, Kate	Scent Bottles	1966	Connoisseur and M. Joseph
Fox, C.S.	Notes on Glass Manufacture	1923	Bulletins of Ind & Lan no29, Calcutta
Fox, Russell & Lewis, Elizabeth	William Overton & Glassmaking in Buriton	1982	Petersfield Historical Society
Francis, Grant Richardson	Old English Drinking Glasses, Their Chronology & Sequence	1926	Herbert Jenkins, London

Frank, Susan	Glass and Archaeology	1982	Academic Press, London
Frantz, Susanne K.	Contemporary Glass, A World Survey from the Corning Museum	1989	Harry N. Abrams, New York
Freeman, Larry	Iridescent Glass	1964	Century House, Watkins Glen, New York
Gabriel, Ronald	English Drinking Glasses	1974	Charles Letts and Company Limited
Gandy, Walter	The Romance of Glass-Making	1898	S.W. Partridge & Co, London
Gardner, Paul Vickers	Frederick Carder: Portrait of a Glassmaker	1985	The Corning Museum of Glass, New York
Gardner, Paul Vickers	The Glass of Frederick Carder	1971	Crown Publishers Inc, New York
George, Raymond	Lichecourt, Les Feux de la Voge	1993	
Gibbs-Smith, C.H.	The Great Exhibition of 1851	1981	HMSO
Gillinder, William	Treatise on the Art of Glass Making	1851	S Russell, Birmingham
Glass Sellers Company	Essays on The Glass Trade in England	1883	London
Glickman, Jay L.	Yellow-Green Vaseline! A guide to the Magic Glass	1991	Antique Publications, Marietta Ohio

Godden, Geoffrey Arthur	Makers Marks on 19th Century Glass	1962	CL v 131
Godfrey, Eleanor Smith	The Development of English Glassmaking 1560-1640	1975	Clarendon Press
Goldstein, Sidney M.; Rackow, Leonard S. & Rackow, Juliette K.	Cameo Glass, Masterpieces from 2000 Years of Glassmaking	1982	Corning Museum of Glass
Goodyear, G.H.	Stourbridge, Old and New	1908	Mark & Moody Ltd, Stourbridge
Gordon, Alexander, M.A.	Freedom After Ejection. A review (1690-1692) of Presbyterian and Congregational Nonconformity in England and Wales	1917	Manchester University Press
Graham, F.	Thoughts on Early British Glass	1948	Apollo Annual, pp 79-82
Gray, John Miller	James and William Tassie	1894	W.G. Patterson, Edinburgh
Grazebrook, Henry Sydney	Collections for a Genealogy of the Noble Families of Henzey, Tyzack and Tittery	1877	Stourbridge
Grazebrook, Henry Sydney	The Heraldry of Worcestershire	1873	John Russell Smith, London
Greathead, D.J	A Passage to the Cape of Good Hope. A History of the Greatheads	1997	Published by the author

Greenslade, Michael Washington	A History of Amblecote	1984	Staffordshire Libraries
Griffith, George	The Free Schools of Worcestershire and their Fulfilment	1852	Charles Gilpin, London
Grehan, Ida	Waterford: An Irish Art	1981	Portfolio Press, Huntington, N.Y.
Gros-Galliner, Gabriella	Glass, A guide for collectors	1970	Muller
Grover, Ray and Lee	English Cameo Glass	1980	Crown Publishers Inc., New York
Grover, Ray and Lee	European Art Glass	1975	Tuttle, Rutland Vermont, US
Grover, Ray and Lee	Art Glass Nouveau	1967	Charles E. Tuttle Vermont, US
Guttery, David Reginald	From Broad-glass to Cut Crystal	1956	Leonard Hill (Books) Ltd, London
Guttery, David Reginald	These are Glassmakers	1956	TSGT (news and reviews) 1956 p21-32
Hackwood, Frederick W.	Inns, Ales and Drinking Customs of Old England	1909	T. Fisher Unwin. London
Haden, Harry Jack	Notes on the Stourbridge Glass Trade	1949	Brierley Hill Libraries & Arts Committee
Haden, Harry Jack	The Stourbridge Glass Industry in the 19c	1971	Black Country Society

Haden, Harry Jack	The Richardson Bequest of Stourbridge Glass	1953	Glass Notes 13 (Dec 1953)
Haden, Harry Jack	Artists in Cameo Glass incorporating Thomas Woodall's Memoirs	1993	Black Country Society
Hadfield, Charles	The Canals of the West Midlands	1966	David & Charles, Newton Abbot
Hajdamach, Charles R.	British Glass 1800-1914	1991	ACC
Halahan, Brenda C.	Chiddingfold Glass and its Makers in the Middle Ages	1925	TNS, Apr, p77-85
Hallam, Angela	Carnival Glass	1981	Wise Books
Hallen, Arthur Washington Cornelius	French 'Gentlemen Glass-makers' their work in England and Scotland	1893	T & A Constable, Edinburgh
Hancock, E. Campbell	The Amateur Pottery & Glass Painter	1879	Chapman & Hall
Harden, Donald Benjamin; Painter, Kenneth Scott; Wilson, Ralph Hutchinson Pinder and Tait, Hugh	Masterpieces of Glass	1968	BM
Harding, Walter	Collection of Old Irish Glass, Including Old English	1923	Liverpool Printing & Stationery Co Ltd.

Harrison, Kenneth	The Windows of King's College Chapel, Cambridge	1952	Cambridge University Press
Harrison, William	The Description of England	1968	Cornell University Press, NY
Harrington, Jean Carl	Glassmaking at Jamestown, Va. 1608	1952	The Dietz Press Inc.
Hartshorne, Albert	Old English Glasses	1897	Edward Arnold, London
Hartshorne, Albert	Antique Drinking Glasses	1968	Brussel & Brussel
Haslam, Jeremy	Oxford Taverns and the Cellars of All Souls in the 17th Century	1969	Oxoniensia XXXIV
Haslam, Jeremy	Sealed Bottles from All Souls College	1970	Oxoniensia XXXV
Hasluck, Paul N.	Glass Working By Heat and By Abrasion	1899	Cassell & Co London
Hayes, John	The Garton Collection of English Table Glass	1965	London Museum
Haynes, Denys Eyre Lankester	The Portland Vase	1964	BM
Haynes, Edward Barrington	Glass Through The Ages	1948	Penguin, London
Heacock, William; Measell, James and Wiggins Berry	Harry Northwood, The Early Years 1881-1900	1991	Antique Publications, Ohio, USA

Heacock, William; Measell, James and Wiggins Berry	Harry Northwood, The Wheeling Years, 1901-1925	1991	Antique Publications, Ohio, USA
Heely, Joseph	Letters of the Beauties of Hagley, Envil, and the Leasowes	1777	London
Heller, David	In search of VOC Glass	1951	Maskein Millar Ltd, Capetown
Herbert, Michael Vaughan	The Hickmans of Oldswinford	1979	The Research Publishing Co, London
Hobbes, Robert George	Reminiscences of Seventy Years Life, Travel & Adventure	1893	Elliot Stock, London
Hodgson, K.C.	Out of the Mahogany Desk	1971	The Research Publishing Co., London
Hodkin, Frederick William and Cousen, Arnold	A Text-book of Glass Technology	1925	New York
Hollingsworth, Jane	Collecting Decanters	1980	Studio Vista
Honey, William Bowyer	Glass, A Handbook for the Study of Glass Vessels of all Periods and Countries	1946	Victoria & Albert Museum, London
Honey, William Bowyer	English Glass	1946	Collins, London
Hopkins, Eric	An Anatomy of Strikes in the Stourbridge Glass Industry	1973	Midland History v II No I

Horridge, W. Captain	The Lorraine Glassmakers in North Staffordshire	1946	JGC v72
Houghton, John	A Collection of Letters for the Improvement of Husbandry and Trade	1696	London, two vols, 1681-1683 and 1692-1703
Howell, James	Epistolae Ho Elianea . . . Familiar Letters domestic and forren	1645	Moseley, London
Hughes, George Bernard	English Glass for the Collector 1660-1860	1958	Lutterworth, London
Hughes, George Bernard	English, Scottish and Irish Table Glass From the Sixteenth Century to 1820	1956	B.T. Batsford Ltd., London
Hughes, George Bernard	After the Regency, a guide to late Georgian & early Victorian Glass	1952	Butterworth
Hughes, Therle	Decanters and Glasses	1982	Country Life
Hughes, Therle	Sweetmeat & Jelly Glasses	1982	Lutterworth Antique Collectors
Hughes, Therle	Glass	1965	Homes & Gardens Collectors Guide
Hulme, Edward Wyndham	English Glass-making in the Sixteenth and Seventeenth Centuries	1895	ANT v 30 & 31 July-Dec 1895
Hulme, Edward Wyndham	On the Invention of English Flint Glass	1925	TNS, v I pp75-84.

Hulme, Edward Wyndham	The French glass-makers in England in 1567	1898	ANT v 34 p 142-5
Hulme, Edward Wyndham	The Early History of the English Patent System	1909	Little, Brown & Co, Boston
Hurst, D. Gillian	Post Medieval Britain in 1966 – Glass	1967	JPMA v 1 p118-9
Hurst, Joseph	The Rosedale Glass Furnace and the Elizabethan Glassworkers	1970	Ryedale Folk Museum
Hutton, William	An History of Birmingham	1783	Pearson and Rollason
Jenkins, J.G.	The Staffordshire Glass Industry	1967	Staffordshire Libraries
Jokelson, Paul	Sulphides - The Art of Cameo Incrustation	1968	Thomas A. Nelson, New York
Jones, Dorothy Lee	The Glass of Thomas Webb and Son	1962	Bul. Nat. Early American Glass Club Mar p5-11
Jones, Gwyn Owain	Glass	1956	Methuen & Co., London
Kampfer, Fritz and Beyer, Klaus G.	Glass: A World History, The story of 4000 years of fine Glass-Making	1966	Studio Vista Ltd. London
Kell, E.	On the Discovery of a Glass Factory at Buckholt	1861	Jnl British Arch. Assoc. v XVII pp55-58
Kelsall, Keith	Glass in 18th Century England, The Footed Salver	1989	Sheffield Academic Press Ltd

Kempe, Sir Alfred John	The Loseley Manuscripts	1836	John Murray, London
Kenyon, George Hugh	A Sussex yeoman family as glassmakers	1951	TSGT (News & Reviews) 1951 p6-8
Kenyon, George Hugh	Some comments on the medieval glass industry in France and England	1959	TSGT (News & Reviews) 1959 p17-20
Kenyon, George Hugh	Some Notes On The Glass Industry In England Prior to 1567	1956	JBSGP, p103-7
Kenyon, George Hugh	Some Notes on Wealden Glass	1951	TSGT (News & Reviews) pp9-11
Kenyon, George Hugh	The Glass Industry of the Weald	1967	Leicester University Press
Keyes, Homer Eaton	Cameo Glass	1936	AM, Sep
Kiddle, A.J.B	Advertisements in the seventeenth and eighteenth century		JGC v76 & 77
Kirk, R.E.G & Kirk, E.F. (eds.)	Returns of Aliens Dwelling in the City and Suburbs of London	1900	Publications of the Huguenot Society
Klamkin, Marian	The Collector's Guide to Carnival Glass	1976	Hawthorn, USA
Klein, Dan	Glass. A contemporary Art	1989	Collins

Klein, Dan and Lloyd, Ward	The History of Glass	1984	Orbis Publishing Ltd, London
Klesse, Brigitte and Mayr	European Glass from 1500-1800	1987	Vienna - Kremayr & Scheriau
Knowles, John Alder	The History of Copper Ruby Glass	1925	TNS, v I, 66-74
Kulasiewicz, Frank	Glassblowing	1974	Watson-Guptill Publications, New York
Lagerberg, Theodore C. and Viola V.	Collectible Glass - Book 4 British Glass	1963	New Port Richey, Florida
Langford, John Alfred, Mackintosh, C.S. and Tildesley, James Carpenter	Staffordshire and Warwickshire, past and present	1874	William Mackenzie, London
Lattimore, Colin R.	English 19th Century Press Moulded Glass	1979	Barrie and Jenkins
Launert, Edmund	Scent and Scent Bottles	1974	Barrie & Jenkins
Lawrence, Sarah	The Descendants of Philip Henry, M.A.	1844	Simpkin, Marshall and Co., London.
Lazarus, Peter	Cinzano Glass Collection	1974	Cinzano
Lee, Lawrence; Seddon, George and Stephens, Francis	Stained Glass	1982	Artists House, London

Lee, Ruth Webb	Victorian Glass. Specialities of the nineteenth century	1944	Lee Publications, Massachusetts
Lewis, J. Sydney	Old Glass and how to collect it	1916	T. Werner Laurie Ltd, London
Lennard, T. Barrett	Glass-making at Knole, Kent	1905	ANT, v 41, pp127-9
Lillich, Meredith Parsons	Rainbow like an Emerald Stained Glass in Lorraine in the Thirteenth and Early Fourteenth Centuries	1991	Pennsylvania State University Press
Lipson, Ephraim	The Economic History of England. v II & III The Age of Mercantilism	1931	A. & C. Black, London
Litherland, Gordon	Antique Glass Bottles	1976	Midlands Antique Bottle Publishing, Burton-on-Trent
Littleton, Harvey Kline	Glassblowing - A Search for Form	1971	Van Nostrand Reinhold Co., New York
Lloyd, Ward	Investing In Georgian Glass	1969	Barrie & Rockcliff at the Cresset Press
Lockett, Terence Anthony and Godden, Geoffrey Arthur	Davenport, China, Earthenware, Glass 1794-1887	1989	Barrie & Jenkins
Loftie, Mrs M.J.	The Dining-Room	1878	Macmillan and Co.

Logan, H. (ed)	How much do you know about glass?	1951	Dodd, Mead & Co., New York
Luter, Paul Andrew	The History of Broad & Bottle Glass Production in East Shropshire	2000	
MacDermot, Edward Terence	History of the Great Western Railway Volume One 1833-1863	1964	Ian Allan Ltd, Shepperton, Surrey
MacMullen Major General H.	Waterford Glass	1946	Country Life
Maddison, John	Magic of Glass	1946	Pilot Press, London
Maloney, F.J. Terence	Glass in the Modern World	1968	Aldus Books Ltd., London
Mander, Gerald Poynton	The History Of Wolverhampton Grammar School	1913	Steens Limited
Mankowitz, Wolf	The Portland Vase and the Wedgwood Copies	1952	Deutsch
Manley, Cyril	Decorative Victorian Glass	1981	Ward Lock Ltd. London
Mariacher, Giovanni	Glass from Antiquity to the Renaissance	1970	Hamlyn
Marshall, Jo	Glass Source Book	1990	Collins & Brown Ltd, London

Marson, Percival	Glass and Glass Manufacture	1918	Pitman, London
Matcham, Jonathan and Dreiser, Peter	The Techniques of Glass Engraving	1982	B.T. Batsford Ltd, London
Matthews, Arnold Gwynne	Calamy Revised being a Revision of Edmund Calamy's Account of the Ministers and others Ejected and silenced, 1660-2	1934	Clarendon Press, Oxford
Matsumura, Takoa	The Labour Aristocracy Revisited	1983	Manchester University Press
McGrath, Raymond; Frost A.C. and Beckett, H.E.	Glass in Architecture and Decoration	1937	Architectural Press
Mehlman, Felice	Phaidon Guide to Glass	1982	Phaidon Press Ltd, Oxford
Meigh, Edward	The Story of the Glass Bottle	1972	C.E. Ramsden & Co Ltd., Stoke-on-Trent
Middlemas, Keith	Antique Coloured Glass	1971	Barrie & Jenkins
Miller, George	The Parishes of the Diocese of Worcester (two vols)	1889	Griffith & Farran, London
Miller, Muriel M.	Popular Collectables Glass	1990	Guinness Publishing Ltd
Moilliet, Amelia Mrs	Sketch of the life of James Keir Esq FRS	1868	Privately printed by Robert Edmund Taylor

Moore, N. Hudson	Old Glass - European & American	1924	Tudor Publishing Co, New York
Morgan, Roy	Sealed Bottles, Their History and Evolution (1630-1930)	1980	Southern Collectors Publications
Morris, Barbara	Victorian Table Glass and Ornaments	1978	Barrie & Jenkins, London
Mortimer, Martin C.F.	Dating an early glass chandelier	1970	CM, v 174 No 701 July
Mountford-Deeley, R.	A Genealogical history of Montford-sur-Risle and Deeley	1941	
Nash, Margaret, E.	Stourbridge Glass Industry 1845-1900	1964	DA, MSS
Nash, Treadway Russell	Collections for the History of Worcestershire	1781	Payne, London
Nef, John Ulric	The Rise of the British Coal Industry	1932	George Routledge and Sons, London
Nef, John Ulric	Industry and Government in France and England (1540-1640)	1940	The American Philosophical Society, Philadelphia
Neri, Antonio	L'arte Vetraria	1612	Translated by Christopher Merret, London 1662
Nesbitt, Alexander	Glass	1888	Chapman and Hall

Nesbitt, A.	Notes on the history of glass-making	1869	Privately printed
Neuberg, Frederic	Ancient Glass	1962	Barrie & Rockliff
Neuburg, Frederic	Glass in Antiquity	1949	Art Trade Press
Newman, Harold	An Illustrated Dictionary of Glass	1977	Thames and Hudson, London
Newton, R.G.	Metallic Gold and Ruby Glass	1970	JGS, v 13
Norman, Barbera	Engraving and Decorating Glass	1972	David & Charles
Northwood, John II	The Reproduction of the Portland Vase	1924	TSGT, v 8
Northwood, John II	Stourbridge Cameo Glass	1949	TSGT, v 33 pp106-113
Northwood, John II	John Northwood, His contribution to the Stourbridge Glass Industry	1958	Mark & Moody, Stourbridge
O'Looney, Betty	Victorian Glass	1972	Victoria and Albert Museum (HMSO)
Over, Naomi L.	Ruby Glass of the 20th Century	1990	Antique Publications, Marietta, Ohio
Palfrey, Harry Evers and Guttery, David Reginald	Gentlemen at the Talbot, Stourbridge	1952	Mark & Moody, Stourbridge

Palfrey, Harry Evers	A Short Account of the Talbot Hotel in the High Street of Stourbridge	1927	Mark & Moody, Stourbridge
Palfrey, Harry Evers	Early Stourbridge Industries	1928	Paper read at the Talbot 21st Jun 1928
Palfrey, Harry Evers	Notes on Early Stourbridge History	1920	Dudley Teachers Centre
Palfrey, Harry Evers	The Civil War Round About Stourbridge	1943	County Express
Palfrey, Harry Evers	A Worcestershire Library	1943	TWAS v 20, pp1-14
Palfrey, Harry Evers	Foleys of Stourbridge	1944	TWAS v 21, pp1-15
Pape, T.	Early Glass-Workers in North Staffordshire	1929	JBSGP, v3 169-72 and v4 17-22
Pape, T.	Medieval Glassworkers in North Staffordshire	1934	TNSFC, v 68
Pape, T.	The Glass Industry in the Burnt Woods	1930	TNSFC
Pape, T.	The Lorraine Glassmakers In North Staffordshire	1947	TNSFC v 82
Pape, T.	An ancient glass-furnace at Eccleshall, Staffordshire	1934	Antiquaries Journal v14 1934 p141-2
Pape, T.	An Elizabethan glass furnace (at Bishop's Wood)	1933	CM Jul-Dec, p172 175-7

Parnell, Edward Andrew (ed)	Applied Chemistry; in Manufactures, Arts, and Domestic Economy	1844	Taylor and Walton, London
Parnell, Edward Andrew	The Manufacture of Glass. The Useful Arts and Manufactures of Great Brtitain	1845	SPCK
Parry, Stephen	Dwarf Ale Glasses and their Victorian Successors	1978	Polyproton
Parry, Stephen	Rummers and Goblets	1987	Polyptoton
Payton, Mary and Geoffrey	The Observer's Book of Glass	1976	Penguin Books
Peace, David	Engraved Glass - Lettering & Heraldry	1980	Privately published
Peace, David	Glass Engraving - Lettering & Design	1985	Batsford
Peddle, Cyril James	Defects in Glass	1927	Glass Publications, London
Pellatt, Apsley	Curiosities of Glass Making	1849	David Bogue, London
Pellatt, Apsley	Memoir on the Origin, Progress, and Improvement of Glass Manufactures: Including an Account of the Patent Crystallo Ceramie or, Glass Incrustations	1821	B.J. Holdsworth, London

Percival, MacIver	The Glass Collector, A guide to Old English Glass	1918	Herbert Jenkins Ltd., London
Perkins, M.	Dudley Tradesmen's Tokens Part 1	1905	E. Blocksidge, Dudley
Perret, J.B.	The 18th-century Chandeliers at Bath	1938	CM
Pesatove, Zuzana	Bohemian Engraved Glass	1968	Hamlyn
Petrova, Sylva and Olivié, Jean-Luc	Bohemian Glass	1990	Flammarion
Phillippe, Joseph	Glass: History and Art	1982	Liege
Phillips, C.J. and Duffin, D.J.	Get Acquainted with glass	1950	Pitman Publishing Corp., New York
Phillips, Charles John.	Glass, the Miracle Maker	1941	Pitman, New York
Phillips, Charles John	Glass, its Industrial Applications	1960	Chapman & Hall Ltd
Phillips, Phoebe (editor)	The Encyclopedia of Glass	1981	Heinemann
Philpot, Cecily and Gerry	Creations by Carder of Steuben: His American Art Glass	1963	Fieldstone Porch, Glenbrook, Conneticutt
Pilkington Brothers Limited	"Now Thus - Now Thus" 1826-1926	1926	Pilkington Brothers

Pitt, William	A Topographical History of Staffordshire . . .	1817	J. Smith, Newcastle-under-Lyme
Plot, Robert LLD	The Natural History of Stafford-shire	1686	Oxford
Pocoke, Richard	The Travels through England of Dr R Pococke (two vols)	1888	Camden Society, London
Polak, Ada	Glass - Its makers and its public	1975	Weidenfeld and Nicholson, London
Porter, George Robinson	Treatise on the Origin . . . Of the manufacture of Porcelain and Glass	1832	Longmans & Co, London
Powell, Arthur Cecil	Glass-making in Bristol	1925	Trans Bristol and Gloucs Arch Soc XLVII pp238-40
Powell, Harry James	The Principles of Glass-making	1883	Geo. Bell & Sons, London
Powell, Harry James	Glass-making in England	1923	Cambridge University Press
Powell, Harry James	The development of coloured glass in England	1922	TSGT 1922 p249-55
Price, Seymour James	Building Societies: their origin and history	1958	Franey & Co., London
Price, William Hyde	The English Patents of Monopoly	1906	A. Constable & Co., London

Pritt, Revd. Stephen	Holy Trinity Church Amblecote 1842-1942 A brief outline of its history	1942	
Pullin, Anne Geffken	Glass Signatures Trademarks and Trade Names from the Seventeenth to the Twentieth Century	1986	Wallace-Homestead Book Company, Pennsylvania
Rackham, Bernard	A Key to Pottery and Glass	1940	Blackie & Son Ltd, London
Rakow, L.S. and J.K.	Franz Paul Zach, Nineteenth-Century Bohemian Engraver	1983	JGS, v 25
Ramsey, William	The Worshipful Company of Glass Sellers of London	1898	For private circulation
Raybould, Trevor John	The Economic Emergence of the Black Country	1973	David & Charles, Newton Abbot
Reade, Aleyn Lyell	The Reades of Blackwood Hill	1906	Privately printed by Spottiswoode & Co. Ltd, London
Revi, Albert Christian	Nineteenth Century Glass - Its Genesis and Development	1967	Schiffer Publishing Ltd, Pennsylvania
Revi, Albert Christian	Victorian Glass. . . From the Victoria and Albert Museum	1971	Corning
Reynolds, Eric	The Glass of John Walsh Walsh 1850-1951	1999	Richard Dennis, Shepton Beauch, Somerset

Reyntiens, Patrick	The Technique of Stained Glass	1977	Batsford, London
Richardson, William Eric	William Fowler's Kingswinford the man, his maps and the people and places of 1822 and 1840	1999	Black Country Society
Robertson, Robert Alexander	Chats on Old Glass	1954	Ernest Benn Ltd
Robertson, Robert Alexander	Early English Glass Making, Foreign Craftsmen Revived	1956	Ant. Deal. & Col. Guide Mar 1956 p17-9
Roche, Serge	Mirrors in Famous Galleries and Collections	1957	Gerald Duckworth & Co
Rogers, Frances and Beard, Alice	5000 Years of Glass	1937	Frederick A. Stokes Co., New York
Rohan, Thomas	Old Glass Beautiful, English and Irish	1930	Mills & Boon, London
Rollason, Arthur Adolphus	The old Non-parochial Registers of Dudley	1899	Society of Friends, Independents, Methodists
Rollason, Arthur A.	Early Glass-workers at Eccleshall	1922	TNSFC
Rollason, Arthur Adolphus	The Dixon Family of Dudley, Anciently of Dixon's Green		
Roper, John Stephen	A History of St. John's Church Wolverhampton	1958	Wolverhampton
Roper, John Stephen	Dudley: the seventeenth century town its history to 1660	1965	County Borough of Dudley

Roper, John Stephen	Dudley: The town in the eighteenth century	1968	County Borough of Dudley
Roper, John Stephen	The Dudley Churchwarden's Book 1618-1725	1980	BMSGH
Rose-Villequey, Germaine	Verre et Verriers de Lorraine au début des Temps Morernes de la fin du XV au debut du XVII siècle	1971	Presses Universitaires de France, Paris
Rosenhain, Walter	Glass Manufacture	1908	Archibald Constable, London
Ross, Catherine	The Excise Tax and Cut Glass In England and Ireland	1982	JGS, v 24
Rothenberg, Polly	The Complete Book of Creative Glass Art	1974	George Allen & Unwin Ltd
Ruggles-Brise, Lady Sheelah Maud Emily	Sealed Bottles	1949	Country Life
Runyan, Bill & Irma	George Woodall and the Art of English Cameo Glass		
Rush, James	The Ingenious Beilbys	1973	Barrie and Jenkins
Rush, James	A Beilby Odyssey	1987	Nelson & Saunders
Ruskin, John	Handbook of Art Culture	1877	John Wiley & Sons, New York

Ruskin, John	The Stones of Venice	1851	London
Salzman, Louis Francis	Sussex Glass. In v 2 Victoria County History of Sussex	1907	Constable, London
Sanders, Revd Henry	The History and Antiquities of Shenstone	1794	John Nichols
Sanders, Victor	Stourbridge and its Glass Industry	1986	Dulston Press
Sandilands, D.N.	The Early History of Glassmaking in the Stourbridge District	1931	TSGT v 15 pp219-27
Sandilands, D.N.	The Last Fifty Years of the Excise Duty on Glass	1931	TSGT v 15, pp 231-245
Sandilands, D.N.	Chapters in the history of Midlands glass industry	1931	TSGT v 15
Sandilands, D.N.	History of the Midland Glass Industry	1927	Thesis, University of Birmingham Library
Sauzay, Alexandre	The Marvels of Glassmaking in All Ages	1870	Sampson, Low & Marston, London
Savage, George	Glass, Pleasures & Treasures	1965	George Weidenfeld and Nicholson Ltd
Savage, George	Glass and Glassware	1973	Octopus Books Ltd, London
Schrijver, Elka	Glass and Crystal (two vols)	1963	Merlin Press, London

Schofield, Robert Edwin	Josiah Wedgwood and the Technology of Glass Manufacturing	1962	
Schofield, Robert Edwin	The Lunar Society of Birmingham	1963	Clarendon Press, Oxford
Scott, William	Stourbridge and its Vicinity	1832	J. Heming, Stourbridge
Scoville, Warren Candler	Capitalism and French Glassmaking 1640-1789	1950	University of California Press
Seddon, Geoffrey, B.	The Jacobites and their Drinking Glasses	1995	ACC
Serge, Roche	Mirrors	1957	Gerald Duckworth & Co, London
Sheppard, Christopher R.S. and Smith, John P.	A Collection of Fine Glass from the Restoration to the Regency	1990	Mallett and Sheppard and Cooper Ltd, London
Silber & Fleming	The Silber & Fleming Glass & China Book	1990	Wordsworth Editions
Simms, Rupert	Contributions towards a History of Glass Making and Glassmakers in Staffordshire	1894	Whitehead Brothers, Wolverhampton
Simms, Rupert	History of Glassmaking in South Staffordshire some notes		
Simms, Rupert	Bibliotheca Staffordiensis	1894	A. C. Lomax, the "Johnson's Head", Lichfield

Smith, David and Chris	Cameo Glass	1982	Broadfield House Glass Museum
Smith, John P.	Osler's Crystal for Royalty and Rajahs	1991	Mallett
Smith, R.S.	Glass-Making at Wollaton in the Early Seventeenth Century	1962	Transactions of Thoroton Society of Nottingham v 66 pp24-34
Slack, Raymond	English Pressed Glass 1830-1900	1987	Barrie & Jenkins
Spillman, Jane Shadel	American and European Pressed Glass in the Corning Museum	1981	Corning Museum of Glass
Spillman, Jane Shadel	The American Cut Glass Industry T.G. Hawkes and his Competitors	1996	ACC
Spillman, Jane Shaden, Hermanos, Susan S. & Kuharic, Gregory A.	The Elegant Epergne From the Bunny and Charles Koppelman Collection	1995	Harry N. Abrams, Inc. New York.
Stankard, Paul	Flora in Glass	1981	Spink & Son Ltd, London
Stannus, Mrs Graydon	Old Irish Glass	1921	Connoisseur Series, London
Stratton, Deborah	Mugs and Tankards	1975	Souvenir Press, London
Stockton, John	Victorian Bottles A Collector's Guide to Yesterday's Empties	1981	David & Charles, Newton Abbot

Stuart, David R.M.	Glass in Norfolk A history of glassmaking and decoration in Norfolk	1997	Dr David R.M. Stuart
Stuart, W.E.C.	Crystal Makers in the Village of Wordsley	1977	TSGT v 18 No 2 April 1977
Tait, Hugh	Five Thousand Years of Glass	1991	BM
Talbot, Olive	The Evolution of Glass Bottles for Carbonated Drinks	1974	JPMA v 8, pp29-62
Tallis, John	London Street views, 1838-1840	1969	Reprinted by London Topographical Society
Tallis, John	Tallis's History and Description of the Crystal Palace	1852	T. Tallis & Co London
Tawney, R.H. and Power, Eileen	Tudor Economic Documents (3 vols)	1924	Longmans Green and Co
Taylor, M.V. (Miss)	Stourbridge Glass. In v 2 of Victoria County History of Worcestershire	1906	Archibald Constable & Co Ltd, London
Temple, David Crichton	Dudley Grammar School: a chronicle of four centuries 1562-1962	1962	Dudley Grammar School
Thomas, Margaret	The Nailsea Glassworks	1987	University of Bristol
Thompson, Jenny	The Identification Of English Pressed Glass 1842-1908	1990	Privately Printed by the Author

Thompson, Robert D.	Rock	1981	Kenneth Tomkinson, Kidderminster
Thorpe, William Arnold	History of English and Irish Glass (two vols)	1929	Medici Society, London
Thorpe, William Arnold	The Collections of Glass at the Brierley Hill Public Library	1949	Brierley Hill Libraries & Arts Committee
Thorpe, William Arnold	The Glass Sellers' Bills at Woburn Abbey	1938	TSGT v 22, pp165-205
Thorpe, William Arnold	English Glass	1935	Adam & Charles Black, London
Thorpe, William Arnold	English and Irish Glass	1927	Medici Society, London & Boston
Threlfall, Richard E.	Glass Tubing	1946	The British Association of Chemists, London
Timbs, John	The Year-Book of Facts in the Great Exhibition	1851	London
Timmins, S. (Editor)	The Resources, Products and Industrial History of Birmingham and the Midland Hardware District	1866	Robert Hardwicke, London
Tolman, Ruel P.	The Portland Vase	1937	AM, Nov
Tomson, afterwards Marriott Watson, Rosamund	The Art of the House	1897	G. Bell & Sons, London

Truman, Charles	English Glassware to 1900	1984	Victoria & Albert Museum, HMSO
Turberville, T.C.	Worcestershire in the Nineteenth Century	1852	London (Printed in Birmingham)
Turnbull, George A. and Herron, Anthony G.	The Price Guide to English 18th Century Drinking Glasses	1970	ACC
Turner, William Ernest Stephen	Studies in Ancient Glasses and Glassmaking Processes	1956	TSGT, v 40
Turner, William Ernest Stephen	A notable British Seventeenth-Century Contribution to . . .	1962	TSGT, v 3
Turner, William Ernest Stephen	Twenty-one Years, a Professor looks out on the glass industry	1938	TSGT
Tyzack, Don	Glass, Tools & Tyzacks	1995	Don Tyzack
Uhlic, E.C.	Useful Arts & Manufactures of Great Britain The manufacture of Glass	1845	SPCK
Urban, Stanislav	A Parable of Lithophanies	1971	Glass Review v 7, pp200-5
Urešová, Libuše Dr	Bohemian Glass (Catalogue of Exhibition)	1965	Victoria and Albert Museum, HMSO
le Vaillant de la Fieffe, O.	Les Verreries de la Normandie, les Gentilhommes et Artistes Verriers Normands	1873	C. Lanctin, Rouen

Vavra, Jaroslav. R.	Five Thousand Years of Glassmaking: The History of Glass	1954	Artia, Prague
Vince, Alan G.	Newent Glasshouse	1977	Committee for Rescue Archaeology in Avon, Gloucestershire and Somerset
Vincent, Keith	Nailsea Glass	1975	David & Charles, Newton Abbot
Vose, Ruth Hurst	Glass	1980	Collins Archaeology
Vose, Ruth Hurst	Glass, The Antique Collectors Guides	1975	Ebury Press, London
Vose, Ruth Hurst	Excavations at the 17th-century glasshouse at Haughton Green, Denton, near Manchester	1994	JPMA 28 pp1-71
Wakefield, Hugh	Nineteenth Century British Glass	1961	Faber, London
Wakefield, Hugh	Richardson Glass	1967	AM, May
Wakefield, Hugh	Victorian Flower Stands	1970	AM, Aug
Wakefield, Hugh	Early Victorian Styles in Glassware	1968	Studies in Glass History and Design pp50-4
Wakefield, Roland	The Old Glasshouses of Stourbridge and Dudley	1934	Stour Press, Stourbridge

Waring, John Burley	Masterpieces of Industrial Art and Sculpture at the International Exhibition 1862	1863	Day & Son, London (Three Vols, Glass is in v 1)
Warren, Phelps	Irish Glass, Waterford, Cork, Belfast in the age of Exuberance	1970	Faber, London
Waugh, S.	The Art of Glassmaking	1939	Dodd, Mead & Co., New York
Webber, Norman W.	Collecting Glass	1972	David & Charles, Newton Abbot
Webster, Peter Charles G.	The Records of the Queen's Own Royal Regiment of Staffordshire Yeomanry	1870	Lichfield
Weiss, Gustav	The Book of Glass	1971	Barrie and Jenkins, London
West, Mark (Consultant)	Miller's Glass Antiques Checklist	1994	Millers, London
Westropp, Michel Seymour Dudley	Irish Glass. A history of Glass-Making in Ireland from the Sixteenth Century	1920	Herbert Jenkins Ltd. London
Whitley, William Thomas	Baptists in Stourbridge	1929	Mark & Moody, Stourbridge
Wilkinson, O.N.	Old Glass, Manufacture, Styles, Uses	1968	Ernest Benn, London

Wilkinson, R.	The Hallmarks of Antique Glass	1968	Richard Madley Ltd, London
Williams, Nigel	The Breaking and Remaking of the Portland Vase	1989	BM
Williams-Thomas, Reginald Silvers	The Crystal Years	1983	Mark & Moody Ltd, Stourbridge
Wills, Geoffrey	English and Irish Glass	1968	Guinness Signatures
Wills, Geoffrey	The Country Life Collector's Pocket Book of Glass	1966	Country Life
Wills, Geoffrey	Victorian Glass	1976	G. Bell & Sons Ltd
Wills, Geoffrey	Antique Glass for Pleasure and Investment	1971	John Gifford, London
Wills, Geoffrey	English Glass Bottles 1650-1950	1974	Bartholomew
Wills, Geoffrey	English Looking-Glasses. A Study of the Glass, Frames and Makers (1670-1820)	1965	Country Life
Wills, Geoffrey	Bottles from 1720	1968	Guinness Signatures
Wills, Geoffrey	Glass	1981	Galley
Wills, Geoffrey	The Bottle Collector's Guide	1977	John Bartholomew & Son Ltd., Edinburgh

Wilmer, Daisy	Early English Glass of the 16th, 17th and 18th centuries	1910	L. Upcott Gill, London
Winbolt, Samuel Edward MA	Wealden Glass The Surrey-Sussex Glass Industry	1933	Combridges, Hove
Winbolt, Samuel Edward MA	Jean Carre's Glass Furnaces	1936	TSGT v 20 pp16-18
Witt, Cleo	Bristol Glass	1984	Redcliffe Press
Wolfenden, Ian	English 'Rock Crystal' Glass 1878-1925 (Catalogue of Exhibition 14th Aug - 18th Sep 1976)	1976	Redington & Co.
Wood, Christopher	The Dictionary of Victorian Painters	1978	Antique Collectors' Club
Wood, Eric S.	A Medieval Glasshouse at Blunden's Wood, Hambledon, Surrey	1965	SAC v 62 pp54-79
Wood, Eric S.	A 16th Century Glasshouse at Knightons, Alfold, Surrey	1982	SAC, v 73, pp3-47
Woodforde, Christopher	English Stained and Painted Glass	1951	Clarendon Press, Oxford
Woodward, Herbert W.	Stourbridge Glass, Aspects of making & decorating	1976	JGC

Woodward, Herbert W.	"Art, Feat and Mystery" The story of Thomas Webb & Sons, Glassmakers	1978	Mark & Moody Ltd, Stourbridge
Woodward, Herbert W.	The Story of Edinburgh Crystal	1984	Dema Glass Ltd
Woodward, Herbert W.	The Glass Industry of The Stourbridge District	1976	West Midland Studies v 8 p36-42
Woodward, Herbert W.	The Story of Crystal Glass	1973	Monthly Bulletin for the Glass Industry
Woodward, Herbert W.	One Hundred Years of Royal Brierley Crystal	1970	Tableware International Mag. Sep70 p74
Wyatt, Victor	From sand-core to automation		Glass Manufacturers' Federation, London
Wynn-Jones, B.	Mineral Water Bottles	1978	Southern Collectors Publications, Southampton
Young, Sidney	The History of The Worshipful Company of Glass Sellers of London	1913	Geo. Barber, The Furnival Press, London
Yoxall, Sir James H.	Collecting Old Glass English and Irish	1916	William Heinemann, London
Zerwick, Chloe	A Short history of glass	1990	Harry N. Abrams, New York.

Printed in Great Britain
by Amazon